VIOLENCE AGAINST WOMEN UNDER INTERNATIONAL HUMAN RIGHTS LAW

Since the mid-1990s increasing international attention has been paid to the issue of violence against women; however, there is still no explicit international human rights treaty prohibition on violence against women and the issue remains poorly defined and understood under international human rights law.

Drawing on feminist theories of international law and human rights, this critical examination of the United Nations' legal approaches to violence against women analyses the merits of strategies which incorporate women's concerns of violence within existing human rights norms such as equality norms, the right to life, and the prohibition against torture. Although feminist strategies of inclusion have been necessary as well as symbolically powerful for women, the book argues that they also carry their own problems and limitations, prevent a more radical transformation of the human rights system, and ultimately reinforce the unequal position of women under international law.

ALICE EDWARDS is Chief of law and policy at the United Nations High Commissioner for Refugees in Geneva. She has previously taught on the law faculties of the universities of Oxford and Nottingham, and has also worked with Amnesty International.

VIOLENCE AGAINST WOMEN UNDER INTERNATIONAL HUMAN RIGHTS LAW

ALICE EDWARDS

CAMBRIDGE
UNIVERSITY PRESS

CAMBRIDGE
UNIVERSITY PRESS

University Printing House, Cambridge CB2 8BS, United Kingdom

Published in the United States of America by Cambridge University Press, New York

Cambridge University Press is part of the University of Cambridge.

It furthers the University's mission by disseminating knowledge in the pursuit of education, learning and research at the highest international levels of excellence.

www.cambridge.org
Information on this title: www.cambridge.org/9781107617445

© Alice Edwards 2011

First published 2011
First paperback edition 2013

A catalogue record for this publication is available from the British Library

Library of Congress Cataloguing in Publication data
Edwards, Alice.
Violence against women under international human rights law / Alice Edwards.
p. cm.
Includes bibliographical references and index.
ISBN 978-0-521-76713-2 (hardback)
1. Women (International law) 2. Women–Crimes against.
3. Feminist jurisprudence. I. Title.
K644.E39 2010
342.08′78–dc22
2010035575

ISBN 978-0-521-76713-2 Hardback
ISBN 978-1-107-61744-5 Paperback

CONTENTS

Preface   *page* ix
Acknowledgements   xv
Table of cases and advisory opinions   xvii
Table of treaties and other international instruments   xxiii
Abbreviations and acronyms   xxxi

1 **Introduction**   1

A Violence against women under international law:
   progress to date   7

B Terms and terminology   12

C Employing feminist methods   27

D Structure and content   32

2 **Feminist theories on international law and
   human rights**   36

A Introduction   36

B Four stages in feminist theorising and activism on human
   rights   38

C Four feminist critiques of international law and
   human rights   43

D Conclusion   86

3 **The international human rights treaty system:
   practice and procedure**   88

A Introduction   88

B Mandates   88

C Membership and expertise of the treaty bodies   92

v

D State party reports   108

E General comments and women   115

F Interstate communications and women   117

G Individual communications and women   118

H Inquiry or fact-finding procedures and women   134

I Conclusion   136

4 **Equality and non-discrimination on the basis of sex**   140

A Introduction   140

B Equality and non-discrimination: general
  concepts and feminist critiques   141

C Equality and non-discrimination on the basis of sex in
  international law   149

D Violence against women as sex discrimination
  (VAW = SD): evaluating a feminist strategy   179

E Conclusion   196

5 **Torture and other cruel, inhuman, or degrading
  treatment or punishment**   198

A Introduction   198

B Torture and other cruel, inhuman, or degrading treatment
  or punishment under international law   199

C Violence against women as torture: emerging
  interpretations   216

D The feminist record on VAW = T   257

E Conclusion   261

6 **The right to life**   263

A Introduction   263

B The right to life under international law   264

C Violence against women as a breach of the
  right to life   290

D Conclusion   301

7 Conundrums, paradoxes, and continuing inequality: revisiting feminist narratives   304

   A Introduction   304

   B Feminist narratives on international law and human rights revisited   307

   C Conclusion   318

8 Strategising next steps: treaty body reform and towards humanising women   321

   A Introduction   321

   B Procedural reforms   322

   C Structural reforms   326

   D Contextualising interpretation: humanising women   335

   E Substantive reforms: a proposal for a protocol on violence against women   338

   F Conclusion   343

   Bibliography   344
   Index   365

PREFACE

In the 1990s I began working for the United Nations High Commissioner for Refugees (UNHCR). My first assignment was in Sarajevo, Bosnia and Herzegovina, at the end of the violent conflict there. It was at a time when feminist scholarship was becoming particularly interested in women's rights under international humanitarian law in the context of war. This was my first encounter of working with women who had survived the horrors of armed conflict during which the worst traits of humanity are exhibited, and as later conflicts continue to show, violence against civilians occurs with increasing regularity. Part of my job was to find protection solutions for the Kosovo Albanian and Roma refugees who had sought asylum in Bosnia, in particular the many victims of rape and sexual violence. These solutions included finding resettlement places for them and their families in third countries. Most of the women and girls I met had been subjected to rape and other forms of physical and sexual assault, often multiple times, held as sex slaves, and deprived of their liberty.

In order to provide protection to these women and to offer them durable solutions in the form of resettlement, we first had to establish that they were 'refugees' and that they had been 'persecuted' according to the definition of a 'refugee' under Article 1A(2) of the Convention relating to the Status of Refugees 1951.[1] We began framing their cases as incidents of torture, an approach that was later supported by feminist writings around that time. It was not yet accepted practice to proceed directly from the violence they had suffered to a finding of 'persecution'; rather one had to travel indirectly via an explicit human rights provision. This was because rape and sexual violence committed against women in times of war was still seen as an unfortunate consequence of war, or as personal rather than political and, consequently, not within the boundaries of international law. With this political background in mind, we relied

---

[1] Convention relating to the Status of Refugees 1951, GA res. 429 (V), 14 December 1950, 189 UNTS 150; entered into force 22 April 1954.

primarily on expanded interpretations of the torture prohibition to apply to various acts of violence perpetrated on women, but we also referred to the right to liberty and security of person, to privacy, and to the prohibition on slavery. In other words, in order for women's experiences of the war to be recognised as being of international concern and for these women to be viewed as 'refugees', we needed to construct our interventions in the language of the state, and as human rights violations. This was necessary because we could not point to a particular line in any human rights text that directly applied; meanwhile, the accepted understanding under international law of 'persecution' remained mostly confined to instances of torture and inhuman treatment carried out against political dissidents by public authorities in state custody, and not to victims of rape that took place in their homes, in hotels turned into rape camps, or on military bases.

Our strategy proved effective, largely owing to the fact that enough sympathy and guilt had been generated by the Bosnian and Kosovan conflicts, and the inability of the West and the United Nations to halt the war, that resettlement countries were prepared to accept my submissions without question. I found myself asking, though, why there was no international prohibition on violence against women, when clearly it was one of the most horrific violations committed in wartime. This also led to further questions about violence against women in peacetime, when international humanitarian law does not normally apply.[2] This book is very much inspired by my questions at that time, and seeks in some ways to provide answers to them.

Although the International Criminal Tribunals for the former Yugoslavia and Rwanda began developing jurisprudence on these questions, the drafters of the Statute of the International Criminal Court realised that express provisions on rape, sexual slavery, enforced pregnancy, enforced prostitution, or other sexual acts of comparable gravity were needed, at least as a way of removing any remaining doubt that such acts can constitute war crimes or crimes against humanity.[3] In contrast,

---

[2] Although crimes against humanity may be committed in peacetime, it is rarely invoked and there has never been an international decision on the same.

[3] See, Articles 7(1)(g) and 8(2)(b)(xxii), Rome Statute of the International Criminal Court 1998, UN Doc. A/CONF.183/9, 17 July 1998, 2187 UNTS 90; entered into force 1 July 2002. The inclusion of these crimes within the Rome Statute has not, of course, resolved the issue of a lack of implementation and other problems associated with attaining justice for women who are victims of such acts. See, e.g., *Prosecutor* v. *Lubanga*, ICC, Case No. ICC-01/04–01/06, Appeals judgment, 7 December 2009, on legal characterisation of the facts (case arising out of the failure to indict Lubanga for crimes of sexual slavery and

neither international human rights law nor international refugee law have followed this approach of treaty amendment, although new human rights treaties have been developed at the regional level. These areas of law are thus out of touch with other international legal developments. The institutions supervising international human rights law are, therefore, still forced to adopt various strategies of inclusion via interpretation, with mixed success. The strategies of these institutions are very much like my arguments used for refugee resettlement purposes in Sarajevo in the 1990s, and they form the focus of this book.

Drawing on feminist theories of international law, this book critically examines how women's lives, particularly the violence they face, have been understood and responded to in international human rights jurisprudence. Essentially international human rights bodies have adopted two main pragmatic strategies to include violence against women within the existing human rights framework: the first, to conceptualise violence against women as a form of sex discrimination and second, to creatively reinterpret existing human rights provisions so that they apply to the experiences of women. In this book I centre my discussion of the latter strategy on the rights to life and to be free from torture and other cruel, inhuman, or degrading treatment or punishment. Just as we used the tools at our disposal in Sarajevo, international human rights bodies have been developing similar strategies owing to the fact that there remains no universally agreed binding treaty norm explicitly prohibiting violence against women. The UN's 'gender mainstreaming' agenda has also made interpretative inclusion rather than textual amendments the preferred practice.

'Around the world at least one woman in every three has been beaten, coerced into sex, or otherwise abused in her lifetime. Most often the abuser is a member of her own family.'[4] The statistics are staggering and indicate that the phenomenon of violence against women is universal in scope. One of the manifestations of women's inequality is violence. Whether we ought to label that violence as sex discrimination or some

cruel/inhuman treatment committed against women within the context of the conflict in the Democratic Republic of Congo. Victims' rights advocates criticised the failure to do so and a legal challenge was made to change the nature of the crimes on the indictment, which ultimately failed on appeal due to the fact that no details on the elements of the offences to be considered were included, nor was there any analysis on how such elements might be covered by the facts described in the charges.)

[4] L. Heise, M. Ellsberg and M. Gottemoeller, *Ending Violence against Women* (John Hopkins School of Public Health and the Center for Health and Gender Equality, 2000), Editor's Summary, available at: www.infoforhealth.org/pr/l11edsum.shtml.

other prohibited conduct rather than violence per se is a central question this book confronts. So, too, I query whether calling certain forms of violence against women 'torture' is an appropriate, even adequate, label or response to this issue. This book investigates the jurisprudential practices of the United Nations human rights treaty bodies in particular, as well as other international and regional human rights courts as far as they have adopted complementary practices.

The starting (and ending) point of this work is the recognition of the value of international human rights law as a common language reflecting universal values, and as a shared legal system that articulates basic standards of a life with dignity. This is despite the many contradictions and concerns of human rights law, notably those highlighted by feminist theory and discourse, which I discuss in Chapter 2. In the past I have written on the possibilities and merits of reinterpreting statutes and treaties in order to include the particular harms and risks women face.[5] In most of this work I was challenged as a lawyer to articulate new arguments for women's inclusion. I have spent many hours revisiting statutes and arguing that they are broader or narrower than how they first appear. I still find this approach analytically exciting, as well as crucial to the recognition of the abuses committed daily against women. I continue to believe that women and their advocates should be free to pursue any strategy available to them in order to have their rights recognised and their concerns raised on the international agenda. However, this book is about more than that, and it is broader than my usual work. It is about the merits of these strategies in the long term. I take a step away from being the 'black letter' lawyer, and towards being a critical legal theorist. I am interested here in what these strategic choices actually mean for women – conceptually, structurally, and procedurally. The study is confronted, time and again, by the ultimate paradox of international human rights law and these so-called inclusion or 'gender mainstreaming' strategies for women: that the more that women work within the structures of existing law and institutions, the more the power and sexual inequalities inherent in the system can be reinforced.

As pragmatic responses to gender gaps in the law, I acknowledge that these feminist strategies have been both conceptually and substantively powerful for the advancement of women's rights, including putting

---

[5] See, e.g., A. Edwards, 'Age and Gender Dimensions in International Refugee Law', in E. Feller, V. Türk and F. Nicholson (eds.), *Refugee Protection in International Law: UNHCR's Global Consultations on International Protection* (Cambridge University Press, 2003), 46.

violence against women on the international human rights agenda. However, I also note that rereading existing provisions to apply them to the specific circumstances of women has had mixed results, carries its own problems and limitations, and, ultimately, and most strikingly, serves to continue to treat women unequally under international law. A common thread of the treatment of the three rights studied in this book is that women's experiences are seen as an exception to the main or general understandings of those particular provisions. That is, women are seen as a deviation from that standard and as an exception to the rule.

This observation is not merely theoretical. The practical effect of holding women to the same standards as men *de jure* is to impose additional burdens on women de facto. This is because in order to be heard, women need to convince international decision-making bodies that what has been done to them is worthy of international attention, by *either* (a) equating it to harm normally perpetrated against men and incorporating their experiences into provisions designed with those of men in mind, *or* (b) justifying why their experiences 'deserve' the establishment of an exception to the rule. The first strategy reinforces sexual hierarchies, while the second exceptionalises and 'essentialises' the experiences of women, with its attendant negative consequences for women's agency. I argue that the effect of these processes is, therefore, to treat women unequally under international law; and in turn to support the gender bias in the system and to prevent any deeper transformation. International human rights law has shifted from a period of excluding women from mainstream human rights, an exclusion that characterised its first fifty years, to a stage of rhetorical inclusion, albeit one of continuing inequality.

Yet despite this paradox, I conclude, too, that women must continue to fight for women's rights within the mainstream. Unfortunately, I do not find a suitable path out of this dichotomy, only some incremental improvements to the system as a whole. Women must therefore continue to play by men's rules, all the time slowly chipping away at the walls of the house around them and questioning the system from within. No other strategy has succeeded for any other minority group. The grace of the powerful few is a necessary, albeit unfair, prerequisite to recognition within their system. Nonetheless, while women continue this fight inside the system – including here within both the mainstream and women-specific institutions – they must also be cognisant of the broader picture, and the limitations of their strategies, in the hope of being able to elaborate, in time, better strategies for the future. The benefits of international law are there. It has been sufficiently flexible to accommodate the claims of many diverse groups – women, children, racial minorities, indigenous groups, persons with disabilities – although its work is not yet done. This book hopes to highlight that there is scope for improving the human rights house, while acknowledging the conundrums of the many rooms within the system around which women must navigate as less than equal participants; or to put it another way, as visitors to rather than owners of the house.

ACKNOWLEDGEMENTS

This book is a revised version of my doctoral thesis, which was submitted for examination through The Australian National University in 2008 and was supported by an Australian Postgraduate Award. It has benefited from the guidance, support, and patience of many persons, especially my principal supervisor, Professor Hilary Charlesworth, who is one of the greatest feminist international legal scholars around and a wonderful human being. I am also indebted to the other members of my supervisory panel, Adjunct Professor Peter Bailey and Professor Pene Mathew, for their lively discussions on various aspects of the thesis. The text of this book has also been improved thanks to the thoughtful and thought-provoking comments of my thesis examiners: Professors Andrew Byrnes, Rebecca Cook, and Dianne Otto.

There have been so many wonderful people who have inspired the writings in this book, have contributed to its content in varying ways, or who have supported my career and research, and to whom I wish to say thank you. They include Michelle Alfaro, Stephen Bailey, Azra and Matthias Behnke, Amber and Brooke Bristow, the late Rosamund Carr, Walpurga Englbrecht, Erika Feller, Carla Ferstman, the late Bettina Goislard, Guy Goodwin-Gill, Barbara Harrell-Bond, David Harris, Susan Harris Rimmer, James Hathaway, Joanne Lee, Eve Lester, Robert McCorquodale, Clare McGlynn, Daniel Moeckli, Vanessa Munro, Thérèse Murphy, Usha Natarajan, Pia Oberoi, Michael O'Flaherty, Ildi Revi, Kate Sheil, and José Sluijs-Doyle. In particular, I would like to thank Dr Volker Türk for believing in me enough to offer me my first position at the United Nations High Commissioner for Refugees, which set me on a lifelong path of human rights and refugee advocacy, scholarship, and learning.

I would also like to extend my gratitude to the Felix Topolski Estate for agreeing to allow me to reprint as the cover of this book a sketch by the chronicler of one of the early sessions of the United Nations Commission on the Status of Women in 1950.

Finally, thank you to my parents and sisters, my paternal grandmother, and my wonderful husband, Des, whose love, support, and belief in me have been ever present, even when I have been miles away geographically or mentally (being buried deeply in this book).

Parts of this book were previously published as A. Edwards, 'The "Feminizing" of Torture under International Human Rights Law' (2006) 19 *Leiden J. Int'l L.* 349–391; A. Edwards, 'Violence against Women as Sex Discrimination: Judging the Jurisprudence of the United Nations Human Rights Treaty Bodies' (2008) 18 *Texas J. Women & L.*1–59, which was awarded the Audre Rapoport Prize for Scholarship in the Human Rights of Women from the University of Texas in 2008; and A. Edwards, 'Everyday Rape: International Human Rights Law and Violence against Women in Peacetime', in C. McGlynn and V. Munro (eds.), *Rethinking Rape Law: International and Comparative Perspectives* (Routledge-Cavendish, 2010) 92–108.

CASES AND ADVISORY OPINIONS

Abad v. *Spain*, CAT 59/1996 (14 May 1998)   *page* 223n128

Abdulaziz, Cabales and Balkandali v. *United Kingdom* (1985) 7 EHRR 471,   232–33

Abu v. *Canada*, HRC 654/1995 (18 July 1997)   231–332n157

Acosta v. *Immigration and Naturalization Service*, 1985 BIA LEXIS 2, 19 I & N Dec. 211 (1985)   106n100, 239n185

Acosta v. *Uruguay*, HRC 162/1983 (25 October 1988)   209n55

A. D. v. *The Netherlands*, CAT 96/1997 (12 November 1999)   208n54

Ajaz and Jamil v. *Republic of Korea*, HRC 644/1995 (19 March 1997)   221n121

Andres v. *Law Society of British Colombia*, 1 S.C.R. 143 (1989)   145n33

A. R. v. *The Netherlands*, CAT 203/2002 (14 November 2003)   208n54

Arredondo v. *Peru*, HRC 688/1996 (27 July 2000)   213n78

A. S. v. *Sweden*, CAT 149/1999 (24 November 2000)   223–24

A. T. v. *Hungary*, CEDAW 2/2003 (26 January 2005)   121n184, 133n249, 167n147, 190, 243–44, 261n256, 293n158

Attia v. *Sweden*, CAT 199/2002 (17 November 2003)   208n53

Attorney-General of Canada v. *Lavell, Isaac* v. *Bedard*, SCC, SCR 1349 (1973)   170n155

Aumeeruddy-Cziffra et al. v. *Mauritius* (the *Mauritian Women's case*), HRC 35/1978 (9 April 1981)   80n234, 129n232, 159n109

Avellanal v. *Peru*, HRC 172/1984 (28 October 1988)   159n109

Aydin v. *Turkey* (1997) 25 EHRR 251   10n42, 132n247, 227, 254, 336

Baboeram et al. v. *Suriname*, HRC 146, 148–154/1983 (4 April 1985)   271n36, 277n69

Ballantyne, Davidson and McIntyre v. *Canada*, HRC 359/1989, 385/1989 (31 March 1993)   160n111

Banderenko (submitted by Natalia Schedkov) v. *Belarus*, HRC 886/1999 (3 April 2003)   228n144

Barbato v. *Uruguay*, HRC 84/1981 (12 October 1982)   130n234

Barcaiztegui v. *Spain*, HRC 1019/2001 (30 March 2004)   171n159

Beldjoudi v. *France* (1992) 14 EHRR 801   208n53

Belgian Linguistics Cases, ECtHR, Applic. Nos. 1474/62; 1677/62; 1691/62; 1769/63; 1994/63; 2126/64 (23 July 1968)   162

Berrehab v. *The Netherlands* (1988) 11 EHRR 322   208n53

Bevacqua and S. v. *Bulgaria*, ECtHR, Applic. No. 71127/01 (12 June 2008)   295

B. J. v. *Germany*, CEDAW 1/2003 (14 July 2004)   133n249

B. L. v. *Australia*, HRC 659/1995 (8 November 1996)   232n158

Blanco v. *Nicaragua*, HRC 328/1988 (20 July 1994)   233, 300

Bleier v. *Uruguay*, HRC 30/1978 (29 March 1982)   134n250

de Bouton v. *Uruguay*, HRC 37/1978 (27 March 1981)   213n78

Broeks v. *The Netherlands*, HRC 172/1984 (9 April 1987)   159n109

Brüggemann and Scheuten v. *Federal Republic of Germany*, ECtHR, Applic. No.
    6959/75 (1981) 3 EHRR 244   287n132

B. S. S. v. *Canada*, CAT 183/2001 (12 May 2004)   208n53

Bulus v. *Sweden*, ECmHR, Applic. No. 9330/81 (8 December 1984)   203n26

Burgos (submitted by Delia Saldias de Lopez) v. *Uruguay*, HRC 52/1979 (29 July
    1981)   209n55, 213n78

C v. *Australia*, HRC 900/1999 (28 October 2002)   228n144

Canada (Attorney-General) v. *Ward*, SCC, Can. S.C.R. LEXIS 35, 2 Can. S.C.R. 689
    (1983)   106n100, 239n185

Cariboni v. *Uruguay*, HRC 159/1983 (27 October 1987)   209n55

Miguel Castro-Castro Prison v. *Peru*, I-ACtHR (Merits, Reparations and Costs), Ser.
    C, No. 160 (25 November 2006)   10n45, 220–21

*Certain Legal Questions Concerning the Lists of Candidates submitted with a View to
    the Election of Judges to the European Court of Human Rights* (Advisory Opinion),
    ECtHR (12 February 2008)   323n9

Chahal v. *United Kingdom* (1996) 23 EHRR 413   215n84

Colamarco v. *Panama*, HRC 437/1990 (21 October 1994)   130n233

Commission Nationale des Droits de l'Homme et des Libertés v. *Chad* (Merits),
    ACmHPR, Comm. No. 74/92 (October 1995)   257n244

C. T. and K. M. v. *Sweden*, CAT 279/2005 (17 November 2006)   10n42, 224–25

Cyprus v. *Turkey* (1976) 4 EHRR 482   256

Dimitrijevic v. *Serbia and Montenegro*, CAT 207/2002 (24 November 2004)   248,
    259n249

Douglas, Gentles and Kerr v. *Jamaica*, HRC 352/1989 (19 October 1993)   130n234

Dzemajl et al. v. *Yugoslavia*, CAT 161/2000 (21 November 2002)   248, 259n249

East African Asians v. *United Kingdom* (1973) 3 EHRR 76   232n159

Egan v. *Canada*, SCC, [1995] 2 S.C.R. 513   175n174

Elmi v. *Australia*, CAT 120/1998 (14 May 1999)   247

Estrella v. *Uruguay*, HRC 74/1980 (29 March 1983)   209n55, 230n151

Exceptions to Exhaustion of Domestic Remedies (Advisory Opinion), I-ACtHR, Ser. A,
    No. 11 (10 August 1990)   130n234

Gedumbe v. *Democratic Republic of Congo*, HRC 641/1995 (10 July 1997)   221–22

Mohammed Hassan Gelle v. *Denmark*, CERD 34/2004 (15 March 2006)   173n170

Godina-Cruz v. *Honduras*, I-ACtHR, Ser. C, No. 5 (20 January 1989)   238n179

Goecke v. *Austria*, CEDAW 5/2005 (6 August 2007)   130n237, 167, 190n240

González et al ('Cotton Field') v. *Mexico*, I-ACtHR, Preliminary Objection, Merits,
    Reparations and Costs, Ser. C No. 205 (16 November 2009)   220–21, 243, 283n99,
    310n14

Grant v. *Southwest Trains*, ECJ, Case C-249/96, [1998] ECR 1–621   163

G. R. B. v. *Sweden*, CAT 83/1997 (15 May 1998)   208n53, 245–46

Guerra v. *Italy*, Applic. No. 14967/89 (1998) 26 EHRR 357   275n57

Henry v. *Jamaica*, HRC 230/1988 (1 November 1991)   130n234

Higgins v. *Jamaica*, HRC No. 792/1998 (28 March 2002)   206n42

H. M. H. I. v. *Australia*, CAT 177/2000 (1 May 2002)   247–48

Hoyos v. *Spain*, HRC 1008/2001 (30 March 2004)   171n159

Hungary v. *Slovakia* (*Case Concerning the Gabčikovo-Nagymaros Project*) (*Danube Dam Care*) ICJ, 1997, 7 ICJ 92 (25 September 1997)   275

Ireland v. *United Kingdom* (1978) 2 EHRR 25   208n52, 235n171, 252

Jabari v. *Turkey*, ECtHR, Applic. No. 40035/98 (11 July 2000)   224n133

Valle Jaramillo et al. v. *Colombia*, I-ACtHR, Merits, Reparations and Costs, Ser. C. No. 192   243n195

Jensen v. *Australia*, HRC 762/1997 (22 March 2001)   228n144

J. L. v. *Australia*, HRC 491/1992 (28 July 1992)   133n249

Juridical Condition and Human Rights of the Child (Advisory Opinion), I-ACtHR, OC-17/02 (18 August 2002)   274

Kayhan v. *Turkey*, CEDAW 8/2005 (27 January 2006)   130n236, 133n249

Keenan v. *United Kingdom* (2001) 33 EHRR 903   275n57

Kilic v. *Turkey*, ECtHR, Applic. No. 22492/93 (28 March 2000)   242n193

Kindler v. *Canada*, HRC 470/1991 (30 July 1991)   252

Kisoki v. *Sweden*, CAT 41/1996 (8 May 1996)   223

K. L. v. *Peru*, HRC 1153/2003 (24 October 2005)   130n238, 286–87

K. L. B.-W. v. *Australia*, HRC 499/1992 (30 March 1993)   221n121, 230n151

Kontrova v. *Slovakia* (2007) 4 EHRR 482 293–294   303

Lantsova v. *Russia*, HRC 763/1997 (26 March 2002)   279n82

Laureano v. *Peru*, HRC 540/1993 (25 March 1996)   213n78

L. C. B. v. *United Kingdom* (1998) 27 EHRR 212   275n57

Loayza-Tamayo v. *Peru*, I-ACmHR, Applic. No. 11154 (6 May 1993)   219n112, 226

Loayza-Tamayo v. *Peru*, I-ACtHR, Ser. C, No. 33 (17 September 1997)   219n112, 226

Lovelace v. *Canada*, HRC 24/1977 (30 July 1981)   80n234, 133n249, 169

Lyashkevich v. *Belarus*, HRC 887/1999 (3 April 2003)   228n144

Massera et al. (*including Moriana Hernandez Valentini de Bazzano*) v. *Uruguay*, HRC 5/1977 (15 August 1979)   213n78

M. C. v. *Bulgaria* (2003) 40 EHRR 20   167n144, 241, 261n255

Mejia v. *Peru*, I-ACmHR, Case No. 10.970, Res. No. 5/96 (1 March 1996)   10n42, 219

Meritor Savings Bank v. *Vinson*, 477 US 57 (1986)   184n202

Report on Mexico produced by the Committee on the Elimination of Discrimination against Women, and Reply from the Government of Mexico, CEDAW, UN Doc. CEDAW/C/2005/OP.8/MEXICO (27 January 2005)   256, 282n98

Minority Schools in Albania (Advisory Opinion), PCIJ, Ser. A/B, No. 64 (6 April 1935)   144n24, 156

M. O. v. *Denmark*, CAT 209/2002 (12 November 2003)   208n53

Khadija Mohammed v. *Attorney-General*, US, 400 F.3d 785 (10 March 2005)   133n249

Darwinia R. Mónaco (Ximena Vicario) v. *Argentina*, HRC 400/1990 (3 April 1995)   254

Morales de Sierra v. *Guatemala, I-ACtHR, Case 11.625 (2001)*   313n24

M. P. S. v. *Australia*, CAT 138/1999 (30 April 2002)   245n206

Motta v. *Uruguay*, HRC 11/1977 (29 July 1980)   209n55, 221n121

Moustaquim v. *Belgium* (1991) 13 EHRR 802   208n53

Muñoz-Vargas y Sainz de Vicuña v. *Spain*, CEDAW 7/2005 (9 August 2007)   170–71

M. V. v. *The Netherlands*, CAT 201/2002 (2 May 2003)   208n53

N v. *United Kingdom*, ECtHR, Applic. No. 26565/05 (27 May 2008)   208n53

Nguyen v. *The Netherlands*, CEDAW 3/2004 (14 August 2006)   161–62

N. S. F. v. *United Kingdom*, CEDAW 10/2005 (30 May 2007)   130n236

Öneryildiz v. *Turkey* (2005) 41 EHRR 325   275n57

Open Door and Dublin Well Woman v. *Ireland* (1992) 15 EHRR 244   288

Opuz v. *Turkey*, ECtHR, Applic. No. 33401/02 (9 June 2009)   242, 294–95, 303

Dianne Ortíz v. *Guatemala*, Case, I-ACmHR, Case No. 10.526, Res. No. 31/96, (16 October 1996)   226–27

Osman v. *The United Kingdom*, Applic. No. 87/1997/871/1083 (28 October 1998)   242

Oulajin and Kaiss v. *The Netherlands*, HRC 406 and 426/1990 (23 October 1992)   160n112

Pauger v. *Austria*, HRC 716/1996 (9 July 1997)   159n109

Peñarrieta v. *Bolivia*, HRC 176/1984 (2 November 1987)   209n55

P. O. E. M and F. A. S. M. v. *Denmark*, CERD 22/2002 (19 March 2003)   173n170

Proposed Amendments to the Naturalization Provisions of the Constitution of Costa Rica (Advisory Opinion), I-ACtHR, Ser. A, No. 4 (19 January 1984)   164

Prosecutor v. *Jean-Paul Akayesu*, ICTR, Case No. ICTR-96–4-T (2 September 1998)   7n21, 105n94, 219

Prosecutor v. *Jean-Paul Akayesu* (Appeal), ICTR, Case No. ICTR-96–4-A (1 June 2001)   7n21, 219, 260n251

Prosecutor v. *Jean-Pierre Bemba Gombo*, ICC, Case No. ICC-01/05–01/08 (15 June 2009)   321n7

Prosecutor v. *Delalic, Mucic, Delic and Landzo (Celebici)*, ICTY, Case No. IT-96–21-I (21 March 1996)   105n93, 231

Prosecutor v. *Anto Furundzija*, ICTY, Case No. IT-95–17/1-T (10 December 1998)   7n21, 105n93

Prosecutor v. *Kunarac, Kovac and Vukovic*, ICTY, Case No. IT-96–23-T and IT-96–23/1-T (22 February 2001)   7n21, 105n93, 191, 260n251

Prosecutor v. *Kunarac, Kovac and Vukovic*, ICTY, Case No. IT-96–23 and IT-96–23/1 (12 June 2002)   7n21, 105n93, 191, 260n251

Prosecutor v. *Krnojelac*, ICTY, Case No. IT-97–25-T (15 March 2002)   260n251

Prosecutor v. *Lubanga*, ICC, Case No. ICC-01/04–01/06, Appeals judgment, 7 December 2009   xn3

Prosecutor v. *Milan Lukic*, ICTY, Case No. IT-98–31/1 (20 July 2009)   321n7

Prosecutor v. *Rutaganda* (Judgment and Sentence), ICTR, Case No. ICTR-96–3-T (6 December 1999)   266n9

Prosecutor v. *Servashago* (Sentence), ICTR, Case No. ICTR-98–39–5 (2 February 1999)   266n9

Case of Pueblo Bello Massacre v. *Colombia*, I-ACtHR, Merits, Reparations and Costs, Ser. C No. 140 (31 January 2006)   242–43

Quereshi v. *Denmark*, CERD 33/2003 (10 March 2004)   173n170

Quinteros v. *Uruguay*, HRC 107/1981 (23 July 1983)   228

R. v. *Immigration Appeal Tribunal and another, ex parte Shah; Islam and others* v. *Secretary of the State for the Home Department*, UKHL, [1999] 2 AC 629, [1999] 2 All ER 545   192n247

R. v. *Turpin*, 1 S.C.R. 1296 (1989)   145n33

Ramzy v. *The Netherlands*, ECtHR, Applic. No. 25424/05 (Admissibility decision 27 May 2008)   215n84

Rantsev v. *Cyprus and Russia*, ECtHR, Applic. No. 25965/04 (7 January 2010)   124n199

Refah Partisi [Welfare Party] and Others v. *Turkey* (2003) 37 EHRR 1   80n234

Reference Re. Workers' Compensation Act 1983 (Nfld), 1 S.C.R. 992 (1989)   145n33

Rights of Nationals of the USA in Morocco (France v. *USA)*, ICJ, 1952 ICJ Rep. 176 (27 August 1952)   156n93

Velásquez Rodriguez v. *Honduras*, I-ACtHR, Ser. C, No. 4 (29 July 1988)   166n145, 237–39, 250

Rodriguez v. *Uruguay*, HRC 322/1988 (19 July 1994)   221n121

Rubio v. *Colombia*, HRC 161/1983 (2 November 1987)   271n36

Saadi v. *Italy*, ECtHR, Applic. No. 37201/06 (28 February 2008)   215n84

Sahin v. *Turkey* (2005) 41 EHRR 8   80n234

Sarma v. *Sri Lanka*, HRC 950/2000 (16 July 2003)   228n144

Case of Sawhoyamaxa Indigenous Community v. *Paraguay*, I-ACtHR, Merits, Reparations and Costs, Ser. C No. 146 (29 March 2006)   243n195

Sendic v. *Uruguay*, HRC 63/1979 (28 October 1981)   209n55

Soering v. *United Kingdom* (1989) 11 EHRR 439   203n26

South West Africa Cases (Liberia v. *South Africa; Ethiopia* v. *South Africa)* 1962 ICJ Rep. 319; 1966 ICJ Rep. 4, 303   141n3, 156–57, 159–60

Sprenger v. *The Netherlands*, HRC 395/1990 (22 March 1991)   160n112

State v. *Emery*, 224 N.C. 581, 31 S.E. 2d. 858, 868 (1944) (United States)   57–58n90

Suárez de Guerrero v. *Colombia*, HRC 45/1979 (31 March 1982)   277n69

S. V. et al. v. *Canada*, CAT 49/1996 (15 May 2001)   246–47

Szijarto v. *Hungary*, CEDAW 4/2004 (14 August 2006)   133n249, 174

Tomasic v. *Croatia*, ECtHR, Applic. No. 46598/06 (15 January 2009)   294n161, 303

Toonen v. *Australia*, HRC 488/1992 (30 March 1994)   18

Tshishimbi v. *Zaire*, HRC 542/1993 (25 March 1996)   228n144

Tysiac v. *Poland* (2007) 45 EHRR 42   296n166

V. E. M. v. *Spain*, HRC 467/1991 (16 July 1991)   222

Viana v. *Uruguay*, HRC 110/1981 (29 March 1984)   230n151

Villagrán-Morales et al. v. *Guatemala* (the '*Street Children*' case), I-ACtHR, Ser. C.,
    No. 63 (19 September 1999)   274n53

Vincente et al. v. *Colombia*, HRC 612/1995 (14 March 1996)   130n234

V. L. v. *Switzerland*, CAT 262/2005 (20 November 2006)   225, 253

Vo v. *France* (2005) 40 EHRR 12   288, 290, 300

Vos v. *The Netherlands*, HRC 786/1997 (29 March 1989)   159–60, 175n175

Vuolanne v. *Finland*, HRC 265/1987 (7 April 1989)   252, 336

Webb v. *EMO Cargo (UK) Ltd*, ECJ, Case C-32/93, [1994] ECH1–3567   163n131

Weissmann and Perdomo (including Ann Maria Garcia Lanza de Netto) v. *Uruguay*,
    HRC 8/1977 (3 April 1980)   213n78

Weisz v. *Uruguay*, HRC 28/1978 (29 October 1980)   230n151

White and Potter v. *United States of America* (the '*Baby Boy*' Case), I-ACmHR, Case
    No. 2141, Res. No. 23/81 (6 March 1981)   289–90

Wilson v. *The Philippines*, HRC 868/1999 (30 October 2003)   240

X v. *Belgium*, ECmHR, Applic. No. 984/61 (29 May 1961)   203n26

X v. *Switzerland*, ECmHR, Applic. No. 9012/80 (1980)   203n26

X and Y v. *The Netherlands* (1985) 8 EHRR 235   188n235, 241n192

Yanomami v. *Brazil*, I-ACmHR, Case No. 7615, Res. No. 12/85 (5 March
    1985)   273n52

Yildirim v. *Austria*, CEDAW 6/2005 (6 August 2007)   167n147 and 148, 190

Yilmaz-Dogan v. *The Netherlands*, CERD 1/1994 (10 August 1988)   173

Zwaan de Vries v. *The Netherlands*, HRC 182/1984 (9 April 1987)   159n109

TREATIES AND OTHER
INTERNATIONAL INSTRUMENTS

1899   Convention Respecting the Laws and Customs of War on Land (Hague
        Convention II), 29 July 1899   72n184
1904   International Agreement for the Suppression of the White Slave Traffic 1904, 18
        May 1904, 35 Stat. 426, 1 LNTS 83; entered into force 18 July 1905   72n183
1907   Convention Respecting the Laws and Customs of War on Land (Hague
        Convention IV), 18 October 1907, 36 Stat 2277, 1 Bevans 631   72n182
1919   International Labour Organization, Convention Concerning Night Work
        for Women Employed in Industry 1919 (ILO Convention No. 4)   72n182
1919   International Labour Organization, Maternity Protection Convention 1919
        (ILO Convention No. 3)   72n182
1921   International Convention on the Suppression of the Traffic in Women and
        Children 1921, 30 September 1921, 9 LNTS 415; entered into force 15 June
        1922   72n183
1933   International Convention for the Suppression of the Traffic in Women of
        Full Age 1933, 11 October 1933, 53 UNTS 13; entered into force 24 August
        1934   72n182
1935   International Labour Organization, Convention Concerning the
        Employment of Women on Underground Work in Mines of All Kinds
        1935 (ILO Convention No. 45)   72n182
1945   Charter of the United Nations, 26 June 1945, 1 UNTS XVI; entered into
        force 24 October 1945   96, 149, 308
        Preambular para. 1   148n51
        Preambular para. 2   149n52
        Article 1(3)   149n52
        Article 8   96n50, 149n52, 308n11
        Article 55(c)   149n52
1948   Universal Declaration of Human Rights 1948, GA res. 217 A (III), 10
        December 1948 (UDHR)   39, 149–50, 199, 264
        Article 1   148n51, 149
        Article 2   149
        Article 3   264
        Article 5   199
        Article 7   149

Article 10   149n56

Article 16   149n57

Article 21   149n58

Article 23   150n59

Article 25   150n60

1948   Convention on the Prevention and Punishment of the Crime of Genocide
1948, GA res. 260 A (III), 9 December 1948, 78 UNTS 277; entered into
force 12 January 1951   89n2, 150n64, 265–66

Article II   266n8

1948   American Declaration of the Rights and Duties of Man 1948, OAS res.
XXX, adopted by the Ninth International Conference of American States
(1948), OEA/Ser.L.V/II.82 doc.6 rev.1 at 17 (1992)   155, 289

Article 2   155n89

1949   Convention for the Suppression of the Traffic in Persons and of the
Exploitation of the Prostitution of Others 1949, GA res. 317 (IV), 2
December 1949, 96 UNTS 271; entered into force 25 July 1951   89n2

1949   Geneva Convention (I) for the Amelioration of the Condition of the
Wounded and Sick in Armed Forces in the Field, adopted 12 August 1949,
75 UNTS 31; entered into force 21 October 1950   280n86

Article 12(4)   280n86

1949   Geneva Convention (II) for the Amelioration of the Condition of Wounded,
Sick and Shipwrecked Members of Armed Forces at Sea adopted 12
August 1949, 75 UNTS 85; entered into force 21 October 1950   280n86

Article 12(4)   280n86

1949   Geneva Convention (III) relative to the Treatment of Prisoners of War 1949,
adopted 12 August 1949, 75 UNTS 135; entered into force 21 October
1950 (Third Geneva Convention)   280n86

1949   Geneva Convention (IV) relative to the Protection of Civilian Persons in
Time of War, adopted 12 August 1949, 75 UNTS 287; entered into force 21
October 1950 (Fourth Geneva Convention)

Articles 3(1)(a) and (c)   204n30

Article 14   280n86

Article 16   280n86

Article 23   280n86

Articles 27   204n30, 266n10

Articles 29   204n30

Articles 31   204n30

Article 38(5)   204n86

Article 50(5)   208n86

Article 89(5)   280n86

Article 132(2)   208n86

Article 138   208n86

Article 147   204n30

1950   European Convention on the Protection of Human Rights and
        Fundamental Freedoms 1950, 4 November 1950, 213 UNTS 222; entered
        into force 3 September 1953, as amended (ECHR)   270, 275, 287–88,
        293–95
        Article 2   268n25, 287–88, 295
        Article 3   204n29, 294–95
        Article 14   155n89, 295
1951   Convention relating to the Status of Refugees 1951, GA res. 429 (V), 14
        December 1950, 189 UNTS 150; entered into force 22 April 1954   ixn1,
        260n252
        Article 3   152n76
1965   International Convention on the Elimination of All Forms of Racial
        Discrimination 1965, GA res. 2106 (XX), 21 December 1965, 660 UNTS
        195; entered into force 4 January 1969 (ICERD)   88–139, 150n64, 205
        Article 1(1)   153–54
        Article 2(1) (1)   160
        Article 4   183n200
        Article 4(a)   205n38
        Article 5   22n91
        Article 5(b)   194n253
1966   International Covenant on Economic, Social and Cultural Rights 1966, GA
        res. 2200A (XXI), 16 December 1966, 993 UNTS 3; entered into force 3
        January 1976 (ICESCR)   88–139, 205
        Article 2   150
        Article 2(1)   151
        Article 2(2)   151
        Article 3   150
        Article 4(3)   160n113
        Article 10(2)   55n76
        Article 10(3)   267n16
        Article 11   267n14
        Article 15   81
        Article 15(1)(a)   76n208, 267n15
1966   International Covenant on Civil and Political Rights 1966, GA res. 2200A
        (XXI), 16 December 1966, 999 UNTS 171; entered into force 23 March
        1976 (ICCPR)
        Article 2(1)   150, 230, 270
        Article 2(2)   270
        Article 2(3)   230, 246n211
        Article 3   165
        Article 4   151
        Article 4(2)   199, 265n6
        Article 6   157n100, ch. 6

Article 7 153, 199, ch. 7

Article 8 222, 258n246

Article 9 258n246

Article 10(1) 68n163, 209, 230

Article 10(3) 158n10

Article 12 314n26

Article 13 153

Article 17 314n26

Article 18 222, 287

Article 19 314n26

Article 23(1) 68n162, 152, 222

Article 24 153, 254

Article 25 152, 158n100

Article 26 150, 153

Article 27 76n208, 169

1966   Optional Protocol to the ICCPR, GA res. 2200A (XXI), 16 December 1966, 999 UNTS 302; entered into force 23 March 1976 (OP-ICCPR) 88–139

1967   Protocol relating to the Status of Refugees 1967, GA res. 2198(XXI), 16 December 1966, 606 UNTS 267; entered into force 4 October 1967 260n253

1969   American Convention on Human Rights 1969, 22 November 1969, OAS Treaty Series No. 36, 1144 UNTS 123; entered into force 18 July 1978 (ACHR) 220–21, 274, 289

Article 1 155n89

Article 4(1) 268n25, 274, 289

Article 5(2) 204n29, 220

Article 24 155n89

1973   International Convention on the Suppression and Punishment of the Crime of Apartheid 1973, GA res. 3068 (XXVIII), 30 November 1973, 1015 UNTS 243; entered into force 18 July 1976 150n64

1975   United Nations Declaration on the Protection of All Persons from Being Subjected to Torture and Other Cruel, Inhuman or Degrading Treatment or Punishment 1975, GA res. 3452 (XXX), 9 December 1975 (UN Declaration on Torture) 88–139 199–200 Ch.5

Article 2 200n6

1977   Protocol I Additional to the Geneva Conventions of 12 August 1949 relating to the Protection of Civilians of International Armed Conflict 1977, adopted 8 June 1977, 1125 UNTS 3; entered into force 7 December 1978 (Protocol I Additional to the Geneva Conventions 1977)

Article 49 266n10

Article 75 266n10

Article 76(3) 280n86

1977   Protocol II Additional to the Geneva Conventions of 12 August 1949 relating to the Protection of the Victims of Non-International Armed

Conflicts 1977, adopted 8 June 1977, 1125 UNTS 609; entered into force 7 December 1978 (Protocol II Additional to the Geneva Conventions 1977)

Article 6(4)   280n86

Article 14   266n10

1979   United Nations Convention on the Elimination of All Forms of Discrimination against Women 1979, GA res. 34/180, 18 December 1979, 1249 UNTS 13; entered into force 3 September 1981 (CEDAW)

Article 1   143, 154

Article 2   154

Article 2(a)   189

Article 2(b)   189

Article 2(e)   68n163, 131n241, 166n140, 168, 189

Article 2(f)   80n233, 154

Article 3   283n106, 317n33

Article 4   154n83

Article 5(a)   76n206, 80n233, 82, 154, 168–69, 313n24

Article 6   186

Article 11   281

Article 12   55n76, 281

Article 14   281

Article 16   281

Article 16(e)   297n170

Article 29(1)   118n169

1981   African Charter on Human and Peoples' Rights 1981, 27 June 1981, OAU Doc. CAB/LEG/67/3 rev. 5, 21 ILM 58; entered into force 21 October 1986 (ACHPR)   288–289

Article 2   155n89

Article 3   155n89

Article 4   268n25, 289

Article 5   204n29

Article 19   155n89

Article 22   155n89

Article 28   155n89

1981   UN Declaration on the Elimination of All Forms of Intolerance and of Discrimination Based on Religion or Belief 1981, GA res. 36/55, 25 November 1981, 21 ILM 205   155n88

1984   United Nations Convention against Torture and Other Cruel, Inhumane or Degrading Treatment or Punishment 1984, GA res. 39/46, 10 December 1984, 1465 UNTS 85; entered into force 26 June 1987 (UNCAT)   88–139, 198–262

Preambular para. 5   200n9

Article 1   200–01

Article 2   251n224

Article 2(1)   202n12

Article 2(2)   203
Article 2(3)   203
Article 3   202n20
Articles 4–9   202n13
Article 10   202n14, 251n224
Article 11   202n15
Article 12   202n16, 251n224
Article 13   202n17
Article 14   202n18
Article 15   202n19
Article 16   200–01
Article 16(1)Article 16(2)

1985   Inter-American Convention to Prevent and to Punish Torture 1985,
adopted at the Fifteenth Regular Session of the OAS General Assembly at
Cartagena De Indias, Colombia, 9 December 1985, OAS Treaty Series No.
67; entered into force 28 February 1987
Article 2   200n10

1989   Second Optional Protocol to the ICCPR, aiming at the abolition of the death
penalty 1989, GA res. 44/128, 15 December 1989; entered into force 11
July 1991   265

1989   United Nations Convention on the Rights of the Child 1989, GA res. 44/25,
20 November 1989, 1577 UNTS 3; entered into force 2 September 1990
(CRC)   62, 88–139, 151–52, 267–68
Article 2(1) and (2)   151, 267
Article 3   267
Article 6   267, 276
Article 12   267
Article 23   267n21
Article 29(d)   267n20
Article 37   203n27, 267
Article 39   203n27

1990   International Convention on the Protection of the Rights of All Migrant
Workers and Members of Their Families 1990, GA res. 45/148,
18 December 1990, 2220 UNTS 93; entered into force 1 July 2003
(IMWC)   12n113, 88–139, 205, 311n18
Article 7   152
Article 9   268n24

1993   Statute of the International Tribunal for the Prosecution of Persons
Responsible for Serious Violations of International Humanitarian Law
Committed in the Territory of the Former Yugoslavia since 1991, SC res.
S/RES/827, 25 May 1993
Articles 2(b) and (c)   204n31
Article 4   266n11

Articles 5(f) and (i)   204n31

1993   United Nations Declaration on the Elimination of Violence against Women, GA res. A/RES/48/104, 20 December 1993   9, 20–22, 25, 319, 339

1994   Statute of the International Criminal Tribunal for the Prosecution of Persons Responsible for Genocide and Other Serious Violations of International Humanitarian Law Committed in the Territory of Rwanda and Rwandan Citizens Responsible for Genocide and Other Such Violations Committed in the Territory of Neighbouring States, between 1 January 1994 and 31 December 1994, SC res. S/RES/955, 8 November 1994, 33 ILM 1598, 1600 (1994)

Article 2   266n11

Articles 3(f) and (i)   204n31

Articles 4(a) and (e)   204n31

1994   Inter-American Convention on the Prevention, Punishment and Eradication of Violence against Women 1994, 33 ILM 1534, 6 September 1994; entered into force 3 May 1995 (IA-VAW)   3n11, 11, 220, 309n12, 341n75

1998   Protocol to the ACHPR for the Establishment of an African Court on Human and Peoples' Rights 1998, adopted on 9 June 1998, OAU Doc. OAU/LEG/EXP/AFCHPR/PROT (III); entered into force 1 January 2004   127n219

1998   Protocol No. 6 to the ECHR concerning the Abolition of the Death Penalty, ETS No. 155, 1 November 1998   268n25

1998   Statute of the International Criminal Court, UN Doc. A/CONF.183/9, 17 July 1998, 2187 UNTS 90; entered into force 1 July 2002 (Rome Statute of the ICC)   x, 7, 137, 222

Article 6   266n11

Article 7(1)(c)   7n21

Article 7(1)(e)   200n10

Article 7(1)(f)   204n32

Article 7(1)(g)   x, 7n21

Article 7(1)(h)   7n21

Article 8(2)(a)(ii)   204n32

Article 8(2)(b)(xxi)   204n32

Article 8(2)(b)(xxii)   x

Article 8(2)(c)   204n32

Article 36(8)   138n275

2000   Optional Protocol to the CEDAW 1999, GA res. 54/5, UN Doc. A/54/49 (Vol. I) (2000); entered into force 22 December 2000 (OP-CEDAW)   48–49, 88–139

2000   Protocol to the African Charter on Human and People's Rights on the Human Rights of Women 2000, adopted by the 2nd Ordinary Session of the Assembly of the African Union, AU Doc. CAB/LEG/66.6, 13

September 2000; entered into force 25 November 2005 (PRWA)   12, 23–25, 155–56, 309n12

Article 1(j)   21n86

Article 4(1)   268n25

Article 14(2)(c)   288n136

2000   Protocol to Prevent, Suppress and Punish Trafficking in Persons Especially Women and Children, Supplementing the United Nations Convention against Transnational Organized Crime 2000, GA res. A/RES/55/25, 15 November 2000, 40 ILM 335; entered into force 25 December 2003 (Palermo Protocol)   39n11

2002   Optional Protocol to the Convention against Torture and Other Cruel, Inhuman or Degrading Treatment or Punishment 2002, GA res. A/RES/57/199, 18 December 2002, 42 ILM 26 (2003); entered into force 22 June 2006 (OP-CAT)   90–91, 134, 203–05

2005   European Convention on Action against Trafficking in Human Beings 2005, ETS No. 197, 16 May 2005; entered into force 1 February 2008   12n54

2006   United Nations Convention on the Rights of Persons with Disabilities 2006, GA res. 61/106, 13 December 2006; entered into force 3 May 2008 (ICRPD)   90, 151–52, 268

Article 2   155

Article 4   152

Article 5   152, 155n84

Article 6   155n85

Article 6(b)   155n87

Article 8(1)   268n23

Article 8(6)   155n87

Article 10   268

Article 15   204n28

Article 26   268n23

Article 29   268n23

Article 30   268n23

2006   Optional Protocol to the ICRPD, GA res. 61/106, 13 December 2006, UN Doc. A/61/49 (2006); entered into force 3 May 2008   88–139

2006   International Convention for the Protection of All Persons from Enforced Disappearances 2006, GA res. 61/177, 20 December 2006, opened for signature 6 February 2007 (ICED)   90, 301, 310

Article 2   186, 301

2007   United Nations Declaration on the Rights of Indigenous Peoples 2007, GA res. 61/295, 13 September 2007   269

Article 7   269

2008   Optional Protocol to ICESCR 2008, GA res. A/RES/63/117, 10 December 2008 (OP-ICESCR)   134

ABBREVIATIONS AND ACRONYMS

ACHPR or African Charter	African Charter on Human and Peoples' Rights 1981
ACHR	American Convention on Human Rights 1969
ACmHPR	African Commission on Human and Peoples' Rights
CAT	Committee against Torture
CEDAW	UN Convention on the Elimination of All Forms of Discrimination against Women 1979
CERD	UN Committee on the Elimination of Racial Discrimination
CESCR	UN Committee on Economic, Social and Cultural Rights
Children's Committee	UN Committee on the Rights of the Child
CHR	UN Commission on Human Rights
CRC	UN Convention on the Rights of the Child 1989
CRPD	UN Committee on the Rights of Persons with Disabilities
CSW	UN Commission on the Status of Women
DEVAW	UN Declaration on the Elimination of Violence against Women 1993
DRC	Democratic Republic of Congo
ECHR	European Convention on the Protection of Human Rights and Fundamental Freedoms 1950
ECJ	European Court of Justice
ECmHR	European Commission on Human Rights
ECOSOC	UN Economic and Social Council
ECtHR	European Court of Human Rights
FGM	Female genital mutilation
HRC	UN Human Rights Committee
I-ACmHR	Inter-American Commission of Human Rights
I-ACtHR	Inter-American Court of Human Rights
IA-VAW	Inter-American Convention on the Prevention, Punishment and Eradication of Violence against Women 1994
ICC	International Criminal Court
ICCPR	International Covenant on Civil and Political Rights 1966

ICED	International Convention for the Protection of All Persons from Enforced Disappearances 2006
ICERD	International Convention on the Elimination of All Forms of Racial Discrimination 1965
ICESCR	International Covenant on Economic, Social and Cultural Rights 1966
ICJ	International Court of Justice
ICRPD	UN Convention on the Rights of Persons with Disabilities 2006
ICTR	International Criminal Tribunal for Rwanda
ICTY	International Criminal Tribunal for the former Yugoslavia
IMWC	International Convention on the Protection of the Rights of All Migrant Workers and Members of their Families 1990
ILO	International Labour Organization
LTTE	Liberation Tigers of Tamil Eelam
MWC	UN Committee on the Rights of Migrant Workers and Members of their Families
NGO	Non-governmental organisation
OHCHR	Office of the United Nations High Commissioner for Human Rights
OP-CAT	Optional Protocol to the UNCAT
OP-CEDAW	Optional Protocol to the CEDAW
OP-ICCPR	Optional Protocol to the ICCPR
OP-ICESCR	Optional Protocol to the ICESCR
PCIJ	Permanent Court of International Justice
PRWA or Protocol on the Rights of Women in Africa	Protocol to the African Charter on Human and Peoples' Rights on the Rights of Women 2000
Rome Statute of the ICC	Statute of the International Criminal Court
SCC	Supreme Court of Canada
SPT	Sub-Committee on the Prevention of Torture
SR-VAW	Special Rapporteur on Violence against Women, Its Causes and Consequences
UDHR	Universal Declaration of Human Rights 1948
UKHL	United Kingdom House of Lords
UNCAT	UN Convention against Torture and Other Cruel, Inhuman or Degrading Treatment or Punishment 1984
UN	United Nations
UN Declaration on Torture 1975	United Nations Declaration on the Protection of All Persons from Being Subjected to Torture and Other Cruel, Inhuman or Degrading Treatment or Punishment 1975

UNHCR	United Nations High Commissioner for Refugees
UNHRC	United Nations Human Rights Council
UNIFEM	United Nations Development Fund for Women
UPR	Universal Periodic Review
WEOG	Western Europe and Other States Group
Women's Committee	UN Committee on the Elimination of Discrimination against Women
WIGJ	Women's Initiatives for Gender Justice

1

Introduction

On the concluding day of the Fourth World Conference on Women in Beijing in 1995, the then Secretary-General of the United Nations declared: 'The movement for gender equality the world over has been one of the defining developments of our time.'[1] He added that, despite progress having been made, 'much, much more remains to be done'.[2] This book explores how the international human rights legal system has been affected by the campaign for women's equality; and conversely, what this campaign means for women's human rights. Specifically, it assesses the legal responses of the international human rights system to violence against women.

Its principal focus is on the work of the United Nations human rights treaty bodies owing to their role as the main monitoring mechanisms that oversee the implementation of international human rights treaties by states parties.[3] However, it also considers the most important jurisprudence of various other international and regional human rights and criminal law tribunals, commissions, and courts due to their influence on the work of the international treaty body system as well as international law more broadly. My focus is on the way these international human rights institutions have responded to the issue of violence against women in light of the absence of any explicit human rights prohibition at the level of international human rights law. For the purposes of this book, 'violence against women' is understood as encompassing, but is not limited to, any act, omission, or threat to life or of physical, sexual, or psychological harm or suffering perpetrated against women, as well as their structural and economic manifestations.[4]

---

[1] Statement of the UN Secretary-General, Boutros Boutros-Ghali, on the concluding day of the Fourth World Conference on Women, Beijing, 15 September 1995, 'Introduction' to *Platform for Action and the Beijing Declaration*, UN Dept. of Public Information, 1996, 2.

[2] *Ibid.*

[3] The treaty bodies and their mandates are explained in Chapter 3.

[4] This definition is explained further in section B2 below.

In order to understand how international human rights law responds to the issue of violence against women, I draw on four feminist critiques of international law and human rights. Even though these critiques have different theoretical roots and are sometimes in tension with each other, they remain important sources of analysis. These critiques are discussed in Chapter 2. My aim is to connect feminist *theories* to the *jurisprudence* of various international decision-making bodies. I do so by critically examining the two main strategies employed by the human rights treaty bodies (and many other human rights institutions) to incorporate violence against women within their mandates and 'jurisprudence'[5]: the first strategy conceptualises violence against women as a form of sex discrimination, while the second relies on creative reinterpretations of existing human rights so that the experiences of women are included. Discussion of the latter strategy centres on the right to life and the right to be free from torture and other cruel, inhuman, and degrading treatment or punishment. This type of analysis has been undertaken elsewhere primarily in relation to sexual violence perpetrated against women in armed conflict,[6] and rape in domestic criminal law.[7]

Over the past twenty years there has been extensive feminist analysis of international law. By feminism or feminist theory, I mean the body of literature, ideas, and concepts that emerged in the mid to late 1980s and which attempted to explain women's exclusion from human rights mechanisms and doctrine. This body of literature has more recently become known as 'feminist international legal scholarship'.[8] The central issue of much of this scholarship concerns why the international legal system has not done more to address the inequality and oppression of women.[9] International feminist legal scholarship is explicitly concerned with and engaged in the ways in which women have been 'excluded, marginalised, silenced, misrepresented, patronised, or victimised by [international]

---

[5] Throughout this book, when I refer to 'jurisprudence' of the human rights treaty bodies, I mean the authoritative (quasi-judicial) statements of the treaty bodies, including their concluding observations on state party reports, General Comments or General Recommendations, and 'views' (decisions) on individual communications. See Chapter 3.

[6] See, e.g., R. C. Carpenter, '*Innocent Women and Children*': *Gender, Norms and the Protection of Civilians* (London: Ashgate, 2006) and N. N. R. Quénivet, *Sexual Offenses in Armed Conflict and International Law* (Ardsley, NY: Transnational Publishers, 2005).

[7] Although see, C. McGlynn and V. Munro (eds.), *Rethinking Rape Law: International and Comparative Perspectives* (London: Routledge-Cavendish, 2010).

[8] For a discussion about whether a subdiscipline of the same name has emerged in international discourse, see D. Buss and A. Manji, 'Introduction', in D. Buss and A. Manji (eds.), *International Law: Modern Feminist Approaches* (Oxford: Hart Publishing, 2005) 1.

[9] *Ibid.*, 2.

institutions that reflect and represent the perspectives of their fore-*fathers* and their male progeny'.[10] Scholars have examined a number of areas of the international legal system, from the use of force and collective security to environmental law, self-determination, trade law, humanitarian law, refugee law, and human rights law. A common thread in these analyses is that international law privileges the realities of men's lives, while ignoring or marginalising those of women.

I find these feminist concepts, methods, and theories extremely useful for illuminating the processes at play in the context of international human rights law. They can help uncover the dynamics in a given situation. Applying feminist methods and theories to examine the work of international human rights bodies is, however, complex because these bodies may not directly or consciously apply feminist concepts or methods, and in general they offer very few signals as to how they arrive at their conclusions (see Chapter 3). For example, the terms of sex or gender are rarely explicitly mentioned in the documentation of the human rights treaty bodies; if they are referred to, they are often used interchangeably and without explanation.

The two strategies employed by the human rights treaty bodies outlined above in respect of violence against women correspond to the broader UN strategy of 'gender mainstreaming', which is explained further below. This is because there remains no universally agreed binding treaty norm explicitly prohibiting violence against women.[11] Calls have therefore been made by feminist scholars and human rights activists to reinterpret existing laws so they include women's experiences generally and of violence in particular. Underlying these strategies is an intention to benefit from the symbolic labels of such peremptory norms as the prohibition against torture and the right to life (dealt with in Chapters 5 and 6 respectively), as well as to address underlying causes of such violence by recourse to outlawing discrimination on the basis of sex and inequality between men and women (Chapter 4).

This book is interested in whether the so-called 'defining development of our time'[12] of gender equality has resulted in any real progress

---

[10] V. Munro, *Law and Politics at the Perimeter: Re-Evaluating Key Feminist Debates in Feminist Theory* (Oxford: Hart Publishing, 2007), 12 (emphasis in original).

[11] Note that there are some binding treaty rights at the regional level: see, in particular, Inter-American Convention on the Prevention, Punishment and Eradication of Violence against Women 1994, 33 ILM 1534, 6 September 1994; entered into force 3 May 1995 (IA-VAW). Also note that many women's rights activists and NGOs have promoted the agreement of separate instruments, at the same time as working within the framework that is available.

[12] Statement of the UN Secretary-General, 'Introduction' to *Platform for Action and the Beijing Declaration*.

in the practical application of international human rights law to women, especially in the area of violence against women. Has the widely pursued strategy of rereading existing human rights norms to cover some of the experiences of women produced any real results for women, or has it bolstered the myriad feminist critiques of the international system? What are the costs, if any, of these strategies of inclusion? Are women in a better position under international human rights law today than at its inception?

This book finds that the responses of international human rights institutions to women's lives in the context of violence against women have been mixed and, at times, arbitrary, superficial, and inconsistent. Although there has been a dramatic increase in the number of references to both 'women' and 'violence against women' in international jurisprudence, the analysis of women's lives has been largely 'rhetorical'[13] rather than structural. For example, women's representation on international decision-making bodies has not improved lineally, and further they are still primarily found in the specialist treaty bodies on women and children. Despite some attempts to dismantle the public/private dichotomy (discussed in Chapter 2), major hurdles to women gaining access to human rights mechanisms remain. Many norms continue to be constructed and understood around the life cycle of men, with occasional 'add on' references to women and girls. Moreover, the process of 'gender mainstreaming' as it has been pursued by the treaty bodies, women's rights activists, and some feminist theorists and reflected in international law has reinforced the feminist paradox, namely that the more that women's *specific* concerns of violence are raised in human rights institutions, the more women become reduced to essences and are marginalised. In this way, international human rights law and 'gender mainstreaming' strategies can play into the way in which women are stereotyped as victims or rendered as mothers or the 'Exotic Other Female'.[14] At the same time, harm perpetrated against men is viewed as an exclusively male preserve and, thus, similar or identical treatment faced by women is not registered as an issue of international priority.

As pragmatic responses to gaps in the law, it must be acknowledged that these strategies have been both conceptually and substantively powerful for the advancement of women's rights, not least because they

---

[13] See, also, C. Chinkin, S. Wright and H. Charlesworth, 'Feminist Approaches to International Law: Reflections from Another Century', in D. Buss and A. Manji (eds.), *International Law: Modern Feminist Approaches* (Oxford: Hart Publishing, 2005) 23.

[14] K. Engle, 'Female Subjects of Public International Law: Human Rights and the Exotic Other Female' (1992) 26 *New England L. Rev.* 1509.

put the rights of women onto the international human rights agenda.[15] However, rereading existing provisions so they can also, or equally, apply to the specific circumstances of women has had mixed results, carries its own problems and limitations, and ultimately serves to continue to treat women unequally under international law, albeit unintentionally. A common thread of the treatment of the three rights studied in this book is that women's experiences are seen as an exception to the main or general understandings of those particular provisions. That is, women are seen as a deviation from that standard and as an exception to the rule, rather than as equal beneficiaries of the human rights protection system. The practical effect of holding women to the same standards as men *de jure* is to impose additional burdens on women de facto. At issue is the fact that women need to convince international bodies that what has been done to them is *worthy* of international attention. Women are thus not yet equal under international law.

In order to obtain the protection of international human rights law, the strategies referred to in this book require women *either* (a) to equate their experiences to harm normally perpetrated against men, *or* (b) to justify why their experiences 'deserve' the establishment of an exception to the rule. The first route reinforces the sexual hierarchies of the existing system, while the second route exceptionalises the experiences of women and thereby 'essentialises' her (discussed further in Chapter 2). Although the system of international human rights law may no longer exclude women entirely, it is set up to continue to treat them unequally. By doing so, the gender bias in the system is supported and any deeper transformation is prevented. For women, this can only be described as the 'conundrum'[16] of international human rights law. These strategies reinforce many of the feminist critiques of the international system (outlined in Chapter 2), rather than respond to them, even though they arose out of feminist activism and the desire to give women an equal voice and place within the existing system.

---

[15] For background on developments in international law and violence against women, see section A below.

[16] Otto observes that her 'conundrum' is that she is uncertain that it is possible to imagine 'women's full inclusion in universal representations of humanity ... so long as the universal subject (the "standard") continues to rely for its universality on its contrast with feminized particularities (the "other")', see: D. Otto, 'Lost in Translation: Re-Scripting the Sexed Subjects of International Human Rights Law', in A. Orford (ed.), *International Law and Its Others* (Cambridge University Press, 2006) 318, at 321. My 'conundrum' is that in arguing that the international human rights system continues to treat women

The paradox is that the more that we work within the system, the more the inequalities in the system are reinforced. So what do we do, faced with this dilemma? As a pragmatist and practitioner at heart, I do not advocate a complete overhaul of the existing legal framework. The language of human rights can still be a powerful force for change, representing as it does a (relatively) universal language in which to frame grievances. Moreover, the ethos of 'gender mainstreaming', despite the many criticisms it has faced in relation to implementation rather than in its conceptualisation,[17] is now a well-established policy of the United Nations, has made some important breakthroughs (although this needs to be furthered), and any change of direction could be counter-productive. In the specific context of domestic violence, Bonita Meyersfeld has also argued, for example, that international law can improve the way we understand and respond to such violence in two main ways: by its 'expressive value' and by its 'implementing capability'. In relation to its expressive value, she refers to the processes of naming harms within existing normative arrangements, facilitating the creation of new norms, and expanding the legal categories of objectionable conduct. In relation to implementing capability, she refers in particular to the alignment of national laws with international standards.[18] However, I do make a number of recommendations for reform relating to the structures, procedures, and concepts of the existing system, including calling for the agreement of a protocol on violence against women. These are dealt with in Chapter 8.

A final word in this Introduction is that this book is focused on law. It is nonetheless cognisant of the many complementary and important non-law-based or quasi-legal approaches to violence against women, such as policy discourse, monitoring, and advocacy, and local non-legal remedies and improvements in women's education, health, and socio-economic development; and political empowerment.[19] These non-law-based or quasi-legal approaches are not, however, considered in this book.

unequally, I am partially rejecting the very system that is available to bring about other forms of equality, even if it is arguably only formal or partial equality.

[17] See, below, section B3.

[18] B. Meyersfeld, *Domestic Violence and International Law* (Oxford and Portland, OR: Hart Publishing, 2010), 266.

[19] See, e.g., J. Fitzpatrick, 'The Use of International Human Rights Norms to Combat Violence Against Women', in R. J. Cook (ed.), *Human Rights of Women: National and International Perspectives* (Philadelphia: University Pennsylvania Press, 1994) 532, who questioned the utility of a human rights approach at all, and whether the issue of violence against women may not be better dealt with through criminalisation or social policy. See, also, S. Engle Merry, *Human Rights and Gender Violence: Translating International Law into Local Justice* (University of Chicago Press, 2006).

A Violence against women under international law: progress to date

Despite women's entitlement to equality before the law and equal protection of the law being recognised as a right in all the major human rights treaties since 1945,[20] it was not until the 1990s that violence against women featured seriously on the agenda of the international community. The mid-1990s was arguably the watershed for attention to be paid to the serious violations of women's rights at the level of international law, especially in relation to violence committed against women within the context of armed conflict. The conflicts in the former Yugoslavia and Rwanda, in particular, in which women were routinely raped, sexually assaulted, incarcerated, and forcibly impregnated as part of deliberate military and political strategies to debase and humiliate them and others (including their husbands, sons, and brothers sharing the same ethnicity), attracted international condemnation and outrage, albeit belatedly. These assaults also gave rise to a number of significant judicial decisions, in which rape and sexual violence were first characterised as forms of genocide, torture, and other serious war crimes.[21]

Prior to the 1990s, however, violence against women was not seen as a major issue; and if it was recognised as an issue at all, it was considered an issue for national governments (and criminal law) rather than international law. Early international instruments relating to violence against women focused on trafficking of white women for the purposes of sexual enslavement. These date from as early as 1905, but have been heavily criticised in terms of their protective rather than empowering character, and for their racist undertones. Post-Second World War international instruments on humanitarian law took a similar approach.[22] Even during the 1975 and 1980 global women's conferences, violence against women was at most a peripheral issue.[23] Nonetheless a number of acts of violence

---

[20] See, further, Chapter 4.

[21] See, e.g., *Prosecutor v. Jean-Paul Akayesu*, Case No. ICTR-96–4-T (Judgment, 2 September 1998); Case No. ICTR-96–4-T (Appeal Court) (Judgment, 1 June 2001); *Prosecutor v. Kunarac, Kovac and Vukovic*, ICTY Case No. IT-96–23-T and IT-96–23/1-T, 22 February 2001; upheld on appeal, Case No. IT-96–23 and IT-96–23/1, 12 June 2002; *Prosecutor v. Anto Furundzija*, Case No. IT-95–17/1-T, 10 December 1998; SC res. 1325 (2000) and 1820 (2008); Articles 7(1)(g), (c) and (h) and 8(1)(b)(xxii), Rome Statute of the International Criminal Court, UN Doc. A/CONF.183/9, 17 July 1998, 2187 UNTS 90; entered into force 1 July 2002.

[22] Discussed further below.

[23] Engle Merry, *Human Rights and Gender Violence*, 21.

were identified specifically as human rights violations as early as 1975, including rape, prostitution, physical assault, mental cruelty, child marriage, forced marriage, and marriage as a commercial transaction.[24] A decision at the 1980 global conference on 'battered women and violence in the family' recognised domestic violence as 'an intolerable offence to the dignity of human beings'.[25] An explicit provision outlawing violence against women was not, however, included in the UN Convention on the Elimination of All Forms of Discrimination against Women (CEDAW), the principal women's rights treaty, adopted in 1979.[26] This glaring omission was arguably the impetus behind the committee responsible for supervising the treaty's implementation to issue two general recommendations on violence against women. In 1989, and then again in 1992, the committee declared that violence against women is a form of sex discrimination and, therefore, rightly within its mandate over issues of women's equality. This strategy is examined in Chapter 4.

Prior to this subsumption of violence against women under equality law, however, the 1985 Nairobi Forward-looking Strategies, arising out of the 1985 global women's conference and concluding the UN's Decade on Women 1975–1985, identified violence against women as interconnected with the achievement of peace. The conference did not, however, deal with the same in relation to equality or development, the other themes of the 1985 global women's conference.[27]

It has been asserted that violence against women was central to deliberations at the 1993 World Conference on Human Rights,[28] in which women's rights were recognised as human rights.[29] Both public and private forms of violence were included, as well as gender bias in the administration of justice. The Vienna Declaration on Human Rights that arose

---

[24] World Conference on Women, Declaration of Mexico on the Equality of Women and their Contribution to Development and Peace, Mexico, 1975, para. 28, UN Doc. E/CONF.66/34, 2 July 1975.

[25] World Conference on Women, Equality, Development and Peace, Copenhagen, 1980 UN Doc. A/CONF.94/35, 19 September 1980, 67.

[26] Convention on the Elimination of All Forms of Discrimination against Women 1979, GA res. 34/180, 18 December 1979, 1249 UNTS 13; entered into force 3 September 1981 (CEDAW).

[27] World Conference on Women, Report and Nairobi Forward-looking Strategies for the Advancement of Women, UN Doc. A/CONF.116/28/Rev.1, 1985.

[28] E. Friedman, 'Women's Human Rights: The Emergence of a Movement', in J. Peters and A. Wolper (eds.), Women's Rights, Human Rights: International Feminist Perspectives (New York: Routledge, 1995) 18, at 27–31.

[29] World Conference on Human Rights, Vienna Declaration and Programme of Action, UN Doc. A/CONF.157/23, 12 July 1993, Pt 1, para. 18.

out of the conference specifically called for the drafting of a declaration on violence against women and the appointment of a special rapporteur on the same subject.[30]

In 1993 the UN Declaration on the Elimination of Violence against Women (DEVAW) was adopted[31] and the first Special Rapporteur on Violence against Women appointed.[32]

Unlike the human rights treaty bodies, the mandate of the Special Rapporteur is not circumscribed by ratifications to international treaties or periodic reporting cycles and she, therefore, has a wider mandate to engage in these issues.[33] On the other hand, there is no obligation on the part of states to cooperate with the Special Rapporteur as an extra-treaty measure, and hence her reports and statements fall into the territory of 'soft' law instruments, but they are nonetheless influential. The UN Special Rapporteur on Violence against Women has issued a number of reports on various themes, including violence in the family, trafficking in persons, reproductive rights and violence against women, and the impact of economic and social policies on violence against women.[34]

Still, in 1994 the International Conference on Population and Development, held in Cairo, acknowledged the inter-linkages between women's empowerment and autonomy and protection from gender-based violence.[35]

The following year the Beijing World Conference placed violence against women squarely on the women's rights agenda, identifying it as one of twelve priority areas of concern.[36] Beijing highlighted particular

[30] *Ibid.*, Pt II, para. 38.

[31] UN Declaration on the Elimination of Violence against Women 1993 (DEVAW), GA res. A/RES/48/104, 20 December 1993.

[32] UN Commission on Human Rights (now UN Human Rights Council), Special Rapporteur on Violence against Women, Its Causes and Consequences (SR-VAW), UN Doc. E/CN.4/RES/1994/45, 4 March 1994.

[33] SR-VAW, 15 Years of the United Nations Special Rapporteur on Violence against Women, Its Causes and Consequences: A Critical Appraisal 1994–2009, no UN Doc., 8, available at: www.ohchr.org.

[34] See, e.g., SR-VAW, Ms. Radhika Coomaraswamy, *Cultural Practices in the Family that are Violent towards Women*, UN Doc. E/CN.4/2002/83, 31 January 2002; *A Framework for Model Legislation on Domestic Violence*, UN Doc. E/CN.4/1996/53/Add.2, 2 February 1996; *Trafficking in Women, Women's Migration and Violence against Women*, UN Doc. E/CN.4/2000/68, 29 February 2000; *Economic and Social Policy and Its Impact on Violence against Women*, UN Doc. E/CN.4/2000/68/Add.5, 24 February 2000.

[35] International Conference on Population and Development, Cairo Programme of Action, 5–13 September 1994 (no UN Doc.), Ch. IV.

[36] World Conference on Women, Beijing Declaration and Platform for Action, UN Doc. A/CONF.177/20 (1995) and A/CONF.177/20/Add.1 (1995), Pt. D.

harms not specifically mentioned in the DEVAW, including systematic rape and forced pregnancy during armed conflict (not, however, during peacetime), sexual slavery, forced sterilisation and forced abortion, female infanticide, and pre-natal sex selection.[37] As follow-up to DEVAW and Beijing, the UN General Assembly called upon the UN Development Fund for Women (UNIFEM) to strengthen its role in eliminating violence against women.[38] The Beijing +5 review further called for the criminalisation of all forms of violence against women[39] and recognised links between gender-related violence and prejudice, racism and racial discrimination, xenophobia, pornography, ethnic cleansing, armed conflict, foreign occupation, religious and anti-religious extremism, and terrorism.[40] Neither the Beijing Conference nor the follow-up meetings have been without constraints, not least disagreements over contentious issues such as abortion.[41]

By the late 1990s, and following developments already mentioned above in international criminal law, rape perpetrated by state officials for the purposes of interrogation or to force a confession from women within state custody had been recognised as a form of torture under international and regional human rights instruments.[42]

In 2000 two other human rights treaty bodies – the Human Rights Committee (HRC) and the Committee on the Elimination of Racial Discrimination (CERD) – issued general comments on the gender-related dimensions of human rights violations, recognising in particular that rape is a form of torture.[43] In 2005 the Committee on Economic, Social

---

[37] *Ibid.*, paras. 114–115.

[38] GA res. A/RES/50/166, 16 February 1999, UN Development Fund for Women to Strengthen Its Role in Eliminating Violence against Women, para. 2.

[39] Beijing +5, Further Actions and Initiatives to Implement the Beijing Declaration and Programme for Action, UN Doc. A/RES/S-23/3 (2000), para. 69(c).

[40] SR-VAW, 15 Years of the United Nations Special Rapporteur on Violence against Women, 5.

[41] For more on the world conferences and follow-up to Beijing, see the website of the Commission on the Status of Women (CSW), at: www.un.org/womenwatch/daw/csw/critical.htm.

[42] See, e.g., *Meija v Peru* I-A Comm. HR, Report No. 5/96, Case 10.970, 1996 OAS Doc. OEA/Ser.L/V/II.91; *Aydin v. Turkey* (1997) 25 EHRR 251; *Miguel Castro-Castro Prison v. Peru*, I-ACtHR, Judgement of 25 November 2006 (Merits, Reparations and Costs); *C. T. and K. M. v. Sweden*, CAT 279/2005, decided 17 November 2006.

[43] Human Rights Committee (HRC), General Comment No. 28: Equality of Rights Between Men and Women (Article 3) (2000), UN Doc. CCPR/C/21/Rev.1/Add.10, para. 11; Committee on Elimination of Racial Discrimination (CERD), General Recommendation No. XXV: Gender-Related Dimensions of Racial Discrimination (2000), UN Doc. HRI/GEN/1/Rev.7.

and Cultural Rights (CESCR) followed suit by specifically highlighting that obligations upon states to protect the family include taking measures against domestic and other gender-related violence in the home.[44]

Building on this momentum, the UN Secretary-General issued his first comprehensive report on violence against women in 2006[45] and the UN General Assembly adopted a resolution calling for the intensification of efforts to eliminate all forms of violence against women, thus reaffirming international focus on violence against women.[46] Several campaigns around violence against women have been mounted by UN agencies and non-governmental organisations (NGOs).[47] Most of these efforts have focused on violations of women's rights within the context of armed conflict, forms of violence that have attracted more high profile coverage than the insipid violence perpetrated against women in the everyday.[48] Moreover, since 2008 the Security Council has issued several resolutions on violence against women in armed conflict, describing such violence as a threat to international peace and security.[49] Despite all these efforts, there are still gaps in the human rights legal architecture. In 2009 the Special Rapporteur, for example, acknowledged that there are no internationally agreed benchmarks or indicators to assess progress on preventing violence against women.[50]

At the regional level, the Organization of American States agreed the text of the Inter-American Convention on the Prevention, Punishment and Eradication of Violence against Women[51] in 1994 and it entered into force in 1995. It remains the only human rights instrument covering violence

---

[44] Committee on Economic, Social and Cultural Rights (CESCR), General Comment No. 16: The Equal Right of Men and Women to the Enjoyment of All Economic, Social and Cultural Rights (Article 3) (2004), UN Doc. E/C.12/2005/3, para. 27.

[45] Report of the UN Secretary-General, *In-Depth Study on All Forms of Violence against Women*, UN Doc. A/61/122/Add.1, 6 July 2006.

[46] GA res. A/RES/61/143, 19 December 2006, on Intensification of Efforts to Eliminate All Forms of Violence against Women.

[47] See, e.g., the United Nations' UNiTE To End Violence Against Women campaign, at www.un.org/en/women/endviolence/ and Amnesty International's Stop Violence against Women campaign, at: www.amnesty.org/en/campaigns/stop-violence-against-women.

[48] A. Edwards, 'Everyday Rape: International Human Rights Law and Violence against Women in Peacetime', in C. McGlynn and V. Munro (eds.), *Rethinking Rape Law: International and Comparative Perspectives* (London: Routledge-Cavendish, 2010) 92.

[49] See, e.g., SC res. 1325 (2000), 1612 (2005) (children and armed conflict, with mention of sexual exploitation and abuse of children), 1674 (2006) (protection of civilians in armed conflict), 1820 (2008), 1888 (2009), and 1889 (2009).

[50] SR-VAW, *Indicators on Violence against Women and State Response*, UN Doc. A/HRC/7/6, 29 January 2008, para. 21.

[51] IA-VAW.

against women as its central theme. Meanwhile the Protocol to the African Charter on Human and Peoples' Rights on the Human Rights of Women[52] (PRWA) was agreed in 2003 and entered into force in 2005. Among other provisions, PRWA contains a number of specific rights relating to violence against women (discussed below). The Council of Europe is in the process of drafting its own convention on combating and preventing violence against women.[53] Meanwhile it has already agreed a convention on human trafficking.[54] Neither Asia nor the Middle East has adopted binding texts to combat violence against women.

The above brief catalogue of developments is testament to an international human rights legal system in transition.[55] The first observation of these developments is that there has been a significant shift from a system that excluded entirely the issues of violence against women from the international human rights agenda, or which dealt with them within a protective framework, to one that now recognises the elimination of violence against women as a necessary precondition to the enjoyment of other human rights for women. Second, there has been some attempt to address the structural causes of such violence by highlighting the interconnections between women's inequality and the associated risk of violence. Third, the role of the state in fostering directly and indirectly women's subordinate position in society has been acknowledged. This book is interested in how the rhetoric of this system plays out in the practice of human rights decision-making, and what all these developments mean for women's human rights.

B   Terms and terminology

There is a large amount of contested terminology in this area that needs some unpacking, including sex, gender, women, violence against women

---

[52] Protocol to the African Convention on Human and Peoples' Rights on the Human Rights of Women 2000, adopted by the 2nd Ordinary Session of the Assembly of the African Union, AU Doc. CAB/LEG/66.6, 13 September 2000; entered into force 25 November 2005 (PRWA).

[53] For documentation on the draft treaty, see: http://www.coe.int/t/dghl/standardsetting/violence/documents_en.asp.

[54] European Convention on Action against Trafficking in Human Beings 2005, ETS No. 197, 16 May 2005; entered into force 1 February 2008.

[55] For further background on the UN and violence against women, see J. Joachim, 'Shaping the Human Rights Agenda: The Case for Violence against Women', in M. K. Meyer and E. Prügl (eds.), *Gender Politics in Global Governance* (Lanham, BO: Rowman & Littlefield Publishers, 1999) 142 and Engle Merry, *Human Rights & Gender Violence*.

versus gender-based violence, and gender mainstreaming. These are discussed below.

1 Sex, gender, women

The terms of sex, gender, and women are often applied interchangeably or are misunderstood in international discourse. This book uses the categories of sex and gender in its analysis of international law, but it is primarily interested in and focused upon international responses to the lives of women. I prefer the usage of the term 'women', as it avoids the many conceptual difficulties associated with the first two terms that international decision-makers have in applying them consistently and with authority. However, it is not possible to ignore the other terms altogether and hence they are discussed here, including their conceptual difficulties, and applied throughout this book.

Many feminist scholars adopt 'gender' as a category of analysis, as do many UN human rights policies and programmes. So what is the difference between 'sex' and 'gender'? 'Gender' is generally understood as a concept that is socially constructed. Its construction is complex and influenced by culture, the roles women and men are expected to play, the relationship between those roles, and the value that society places on those roles, which then determines social standing and status. The concept of 'gender' can vary within and among cultures, and over time. That is, '[gender] draws attention to social relations that are culturally contingent and without foundation in biological necessity'.[56] Power relations are often considered to be at the root of 'gender relations'. That is, 'gender' is not about women specifically; rather it is about socially and culturally constructed roles, identities, statuses, and responsibilities that are attributed to men and women respectively on the basis of unequal power. Its usage in UN discourse applying to women has led to gender being synonymous with women, but this is not technically correct. In comparison, sex is typically used to refer to biological differences between women and men.[57]

According to the Committee on the Elimination of Discrimination against Women (the Women's Committee), 'gender' is defined as:

> the social meanings given to biological sex differences. It is an ideological and cultural construct, but is also reproduced within the realm of material

[56] H. Charlesworth and C. Chinkin, *The Boundaries of International Law: A Feminist Analysis* (Manchester University Press, 2000), 3.
[57] *Ibid.*

practices; in turn it influences the outcomes of such practices. It affects the distribution of resources, wealth, work, decision-making and political power, and enjoyment of rights and entitlements within the family as well as public life. Despite variations across cultures and over time, gender relations throughout the world entail asymmetry of power between men and women as a pervasive trait. Thus, gender is a social stratifier, and in this sense it is similar to other stratifiers such as race, class, ethnicity, sexuality, and age. It helps us understand the social construction of gender identities and the unequal structure of power that underlies the relationship between the sexes.[58]

The CESCR has also offered a definition of 'gender', providing:

> Gender refers to cultural expectations and assumptions about the behaviour, attitudes, personality traits, and physical and intellectual capacities of men and women, based solely on their identity as men or women. Gender-based assumptions and expectations generally place women at a disadvantage with respect to substantive enjoyment of rights, such as freedom to act and to be recognized as autonomous, fully capable adults, to participate fully in economic, social and political development, and to make decisions concerning their circumstances and conditions. Gender-based assumptions about economic, social and cultural roles preclude the sharing of responsibility between men and women in all spheres that is necessary to equality.[59]

The CESCR reiterated its position on 'gender' in a later General Comment issued in 2009, noting that 'the notion of the prohibited ground "sex" has evolved considerably to cover not only physiological characteristics but also the social construction of gender stereotypes, prejudices and expected roles, which have created obstacles to the equal fulfilment of economic, social and cultural rights.'[60] The CESCR does not, however, explain what it means by 'gender' in this phrase, apart from a brief reference to 'social construction'. Disappointingly, too, the examples given for how such discrimination may play out are reminiscent of traditional liberal concerns:

---

[58] UN, *World Survey on the Role of Women in Development* (New York: United Nations, 1999), ix, referred to in CEDAW, General Recommendation No. 25: Temporary Special Measures (2008) (no UN Doc.), n. 2. For the varying approaches of other UN bodies, see V. Oosterveld, 'The Definition of "Gender" in the Rome Statute of the International Criminal Court: A Step Forward or Back for International Criminal Justice?' (2005) 18 *Harv. Hum. Rts J.* 55.

[59] CESCR, General Comment No. 16: The Equal Right of Men and Women to the Enjoyment of All Economic, Social and Cultural Rights, para. 14.

[60] CESCR, General Comment No. 20: Non-Discrimination in Economic, Social and Cultural Rights (Article 2, para. 2) (2009), UN Doc. E/C.12/GC/20, para. 20.

Thus, the refusal to hire a woman, on the ground that she might become pregnant, or the allocation of low-level or part-time jobs to women based on the stereotypical assumption that, for example, they are unwilling to commit as much time to their work as men, constitutes discrimination. Refusal to grant paternity leave may also amount to discrimination against men.[61]

None of the other committees has specifically defined 'gender' or 'sex' for their purposes.[62]

Inherent in the range of definitions available is an understanding that those who fall outside the accepted construction of 'gender' may suffer varying degrees of 'ostracism or other penalties' in the societies in which they live.[63] The concept of 'gender' is similarly understood for the purposes of this book, as far as it emphasises, along the same lines as the Women's Committee's definition, that what frames understandings of 'gender' in a particular society includes historically unequal power relations between men and women (in other words, patriarchy).

Applying these terms is not always straightforward, and frequently 'gender' is used or coopted in international discourse to mean and to refer to sex and/or women. All the committees, for example, regularly request states parties to furnish them with 'gender disaggregated statistics'.[64] But what are these? 'Gender disaggregated statistics' are an anomaly, as there are only ranges of responses based on gender, rather than neat categories. What the committees really want to know is how many *women* are involved in particular activities (that is, statistics disaggregated by biological sex).[65] At times, gender is used also to apply to men when they do not conform to accepted gender-based roles and responsibilities. While not technically inaccurate, the latter can obscure and downplay the *equality* side of *gender equality*. In some instances, the *gender equality* purpose of gender mainstreaming strategies is lost altogether (see below).

---

[61] *Ibid.*

[62] See, e.g., the CERD has a specific general recommendation on gender-related dimensions of racial discrimination, in which it employs the term 'gender' twelve times, but it is not defined: CERD, General Recommendation No. XXV, Gender-Related Dimensions of Racial Discrimination. See, also, HRC, General Comment No. 28, Equality of Rights Between Men and Women.

[63] Oosterveld, 'The Definition of "Gender" in the Rome Statute of the International Criminal Court', 67.

[64] See, e.g., HRC, General Comment No. 28, Equality of Rights Between Men and Women, para. 10.

[65] *Ibid.*, para. 8.

In the early 1980s some feminists began to find problems with the sex/
gender distinction. Some argued that gender is socialised, that is, it is
behaviour learned from childhood, and that it is *individually* constructed,
reinforced and perpetuated. This approach has now been widely rejected
because it disregards the significance of power in gender relations, as well
as structural and institutional factors, and is predicated on women being
'passive subjects'.[66] But the individual component of gender relations is
not entirely obsolete. The alternative view is that gender is seen as a social
institution in and of itself. As Lorber states:

> I see gender as an institution that establishes patterns of expectations for
> individuals, orders the social processes of everyday life, [and] is built into
> the major social organizations of society, such as the economy, ideology,
> the family, and politics.[67]

Ultimately, Lorber acknowledges that both individual and structural
aspects determine gender relations, that is, women and men reinforce
individually the social spaces in which they live, work, and operate.

A further problem with gender as a concept is that the other prohibited grounds of discrimination, such as race and ethnicity, do not have
an alternative version to refer to the sociological factors attributed to
biology. Why, therefore, are there two terms in the context of discrimination against women compared with other areas of discrimination law?
Are these two terms detrimental to the overall goal of sexual equality by
obscuring it in imprecise language? 'Gender' does not necessarily mean
only the negative aspects of culture and social relations that restrict wom-
en's freedom; it simply describes and explains those gender relations. Are
we referring to discrimination, prejudice, or exclusion when we use the
language of 'gender', or simply the relations between women and men,
including the negative as well as the positive traits, attitudes, roles, statuses, and responsibilities of women and men? In contrast, race discrimination, for example, is about prejudicial attitudes attributed to persons
of particular races hidden in biological criteria but which are essentially
economic and social in nature:

> the basic causes of racialism are economic and social. However, those who
> show racial discrimination justify their attitude by ideas and illustrations

---

[66] For an excellent overview of the sex/gender distinction and its evolution see,
S. Tamale, *When Hens Begin to Crow: Gender and Parliamentary Politics in Uganda*
(Kampala: Fountain Publishers, 1999), 28–31.

[67] J. Lorber, *Paradoxes of Gender* (New Haven, CT: Yale University Press, 1994), 1.

taken from biology: on the one hand, the belief that there are innate value differences between human groups; on the other, the representation of the hereditary characteristics of members of these groups in the form of stereotypes.[68]

If we transposed sex for race in the above quote, it would also represent how sexism or sexual inequality (rather than the gender relations between women and men) affects women. The negative consequence of the emergence of the terminology of 'gender' within human rights discourse is that it can obscure the real causes of sex discrimination, which are cultural, economic, social, and political in nature, and are ultimately about maintaining and preserving power by one group vis-à-vis another. Its cooption to apply outside the context of discrimination and to apply to relations between women and men, regardless of discrimination, renders it a complex human rights tool. 'Gender' also has the added hazard that it does not always translate well into other languages.[69]

In addition to the difficulties of conceptualising gender, some feminist scholars have begun to ask whether even the biological differences between women and men are as unchangeable as assumed. Jaggar argues that changing social practices led to changes in the body. For example, a cultural preference for smaller women in some societies may have resulted in the selection of such women for procreation, or as physical fitness has become more socially acceptable for women, women's external physique has strengthened.[70] It has been further argued that sexual differences between women and men are not static, and that accepting them as distinctions between women and men does not take into account differences *between* women (or *between* men).

By the late 1980s and early 1990s a growing body of literature had begun to question the usefulness of the sex/gender distinction. Increasingly, as noted above, the terms are regularly used interchangeably, including by

---

[68] J. Heirnaux, 'Biological Aspects of the Racial Question', in UNESCO, *Four Statements on the Racial Question* (UNESCO, COM.69/II.27/A, 1969), 9.

[69] For example, in French, the word 'gender' is translated as 'genre', which also means 'class' or 'group'. It does not have an equivalent meaning in many other languages.

[70] A. Jaggar, *Feminist Politics and Human Nature* (Brighton: Harvester Press, 1983), 106–113, as cited in L. Nicholson, 'Gender', in A. M. Jaggar and I. M. Young (eds.), *A Companion to Feminist Philosophy* (London: Blackwell Publishers, 1998) 289, at 290. See, also, J. Butler, *Gender Trouble: Feminism and the Subversion of Identity* (London: Routledge, 1990). Of course the reference to the 'strengthening' of women's bodies in this way is very much a Western twentieth and twenty-first century construction of women's physical transformation, whereas women have been physically active and as strong as men in some societies for over 8,000 years, especially in hunter-gatherer societies.

some feminist scholars.[71] Relying on the work of Simone de Beauvoir, who wrote that 'one is not born a woman but rather becomes one',[72] Otto, for example, uses the terms interchangeably in order to 'disavow the idea that either of these categories might be natural and thus immutable'.[73] Instead, she argues that the law creates its own subjects, including by '(re) produc[ing] and naturaliz[ing] dominant social norms and practices'.[74] For these reasons, and others, some feminist scholars have called for a reimagination of the meaning of gender and gender relations, as fluid, variable, and multiple, rather than unchangeable, static, and singular.[75] The risk associated with such a liberal understanding, however, may erase the very female subject it seeks to embrace.[76] This concern over the 'essential' characteristics of being male or female is dealt with further in Chapter 2.

So where does the term 'woman' fit within the sex/gender distinction? Commonly, the term 'woman' has been used as a synonym for 'sex' and/or 'gender'. For example, sex discrimination and gender discrimination are used interchangeably to refer to discrimination against women. Similarly gender-based violence has been interpreted as applying to violence perpetrated solely or disproportionately against women. For the purposes of this book I am particularly interested in the experiences of women and less interested in whether one traces the discrimination and violence they face to biological or social/cultural factors or to social and cultural prejudice based on biological difference (gender). I see the main issue to be one of prejudice, domination, exclusion, and oppression, rather than about sex differences, and, at times, regret the elaboration of gender as a category of analysis. Moreover, sex and gender should not be confused with sexuality, which is another characteristic or status. While sexuality can be viewed through a gender lens (for example, lesbian women can be seen as failing to conform to appropriate behaviour for their sex dictated by social and cultural rules), it should be avoided as the two are not the same, nor are they interchangeable, despite the influence one may have over the other.[77] In addition, social mores relating to sexuality apply also to men

---

[71] See, further, D. Otto, 'Disconcerting "Masculinities": Reinventing the Gendered Subject(s) of International Human Rights Law', in D. Buss and A. Manji (eds.), *International Law: Modern Feminist Approaches* (Oxford: Hart Publishing, 2005), 105.

[72] S. de Beauvoir, *The Second Sex* (ed. and trans. H. M. Parshley, New York, 1974), 295, referred to in Otto, 'Lost in Translation', 319.

[73] *Ibid.*   [74] *Ibid.*, 320.

[75] Otto, 'Disconcerting "Masculinities"'.   [76] *Ibid.*

[77] The HRC has applied the 'sex' category to also include 'sexuality', but I believe it would have been preferable if the Committee had included 'sexuality' as a prohibited ground of

and this can therefore confuse the value of sex or gender as a category of discrimination.

In fact, the difficulties many international decision-making bodies have in tracing particular acts to sexual or gendered prejudice can render the distinctions unhelpful. In most circumstances the discrimination relates to social or cultural prejudice relating to the value and worth of women (gender). It is the social meaning (gender) given to sexual difference (sex) that creates discrimination for women. In other words, the two terms collide in discussions of women.

An understanding of gender and gender relations is therefore important to the extent that it can be used as a feminist method of analysis to excavate the landscape of discrimination against women. However, on its own it can be intangible, culturally contingent, and vague. Therefore, simplifying the focus onto the *reality* of *women's lives* may be more effective in the long term. This would involve viewing women *within their particular cultural-social-political-economic context,* including in particular their exclusion or marginalisation from sources of power. This may have been the intention of the category of gender, but it has been widely misunderstood and misapplied so that a degree of simplification is called for. It would also require taking into account a woman's membership in other marginalised or minority groups or her other identifying characteristics, such as race, ethnicity, family, clan, sexuality, age, and so on, alongside her own personalities, traits, and aspirations, which may transcend gender and/or any of these categories. This is because women face both sex-based and gender-based prejudice and discrimination, as well as other forms of discrimination. Some forms of discrimination are rooted in biological differences between women and men (for example pregnancy and childbirth) which, as shown above, are contested, and other discrimination is related to social and cultural understandings of the value and worth of women. The latter of course is generally influenced by, or in fact rooted in, the former, but not always. Focusing on *women's lives in their own context* allows us to consider the concerns and needs of women in both their individual and social and cultural context and to transcend stereotypes about women that keep them in their place. This is the approach adopted in this book, and is elaborated upon in more detail in Chapter 8.

discrimination under the 'other status' category in Article 2 of the International Covenant on Civil and Political Rights 1966 (ICCPR), GA res. 2200A (XXI), 16 December 1966, 999 UNTS 171; entered into force 23 March 1976: see, *Toonen* v. *Australia*, HRC 488/1992 (30 March 1994).

2   Violence against women

'Violence against women' has been variously defined in international law, and it too has been used interchangeably with 'gender-based' or 'gender-related' violence.[78] None of the treaty bodies has adopted definitions of 'violence against women' or 'gender-based violence' but rather rely on those elaborated in related human rights instruments. Interestingly the preference in these instruments has been the terminology of 'violence against women', whereas 'gender-based violence' has tended to be more readily applied in the jurisprudence, guidelines, and policy statements of the broader UN.

The DEVAW adopts the language of 'violence against women', which it defines in turn by reference to 'gender-based violence', as:

> any act of gender-based violence that results in, or is likely to result in, physical, sexual or psychological harm or suffering to women, including threats of such acts, coercion or arbitrary deprivation of liberty, whether occurring in public or in private life.[79]

The DEVAW further provides that:

> Violence against women shall be understood to encompass, but not be limited to, the following:
>
> (a) Physical, sexual and psychological violence occurring in the family, including battering, sexual abuse of female children in the household, dowry-related violence, marital rape, female genital mutilation and other traditional practices harmful to women, non-spousal violence and violence related to exploitation;
> (b) Physical, sexual and psychological violence occurring within the general community, including rape, sexual abuse, sexual harassment

---

[78] A range of terms are also utilised at the domestic level from 'family violence', 'domestic violence', 'spousal abuse', 'battered women', 'sexualised violence', 'intimate partner violence' and 'wife abuse', with various problems associated with them: see, L. Heise, M. Ellsberg and M. Gottemoeller, *Ending Violence against Women* (John Hopkins School of Public Health and the Center for Health and Gender Equality, 2000), available at: www. infoforhealth.org/pr/l11edsum.shtml.

[79] Article 1, DEVAW. The draft Council of Europe Convention on Preventing and Combating Violence against Women and Domestic Violence, CAHVIO (2009) 32 prov., 15 Oct. 2009, adopts a similar definition but explicitly states, too, that violence against women is a form of discrimination and a violation of human rights (Article 2(a)). The definition further includes 'economic violence', although this remains undefined.

and intimidation at work, in educational institutions and elsewhere, trafficking in women and forced prostitution;

(c) Physical, sexual and psychological violence perpetrated or condoned by the State, wherever it occurs.[80]

Appearing also in the Beijing Platform for Action[81] and most recently reconfirmed by the UN General Assembly in their 2006 resolution on violence against women,[82] this is the leading definition relied upon in international discourse.

Broadly construed and non-exhaustive, it has been praised for 'being very different from the decontextualised, feigned neutrality of traditional human rights instruments'.[83] Otto argues that, 'By introducing the notion of power into human rights discourse, the [DEVAW] takes the definition of human rights into new and transformative territory. It recognises that inequalities in power are the fundamental problem ...'.[84] Inequalities in this sense move away from the relations of power between the state and the individual as understood under traditional canons of civil liberties, and towards relations between women and men. Simply incorporating a declaration into the catalogue of international instruments, albeit non-binding, suggests 'liberation' rather than the 'status quo'.[85]

The DEVAW definition nonetheless has a number of limitations. First, it defines violence against women by reference to gender-related violence, but does not provide an explanation of 'gender'. That is, the definition is circular, and is concerned only with violence against women that contains an element of sex discrimination. This focus arguably limits the experiences of women worldwide by potentially ignoring the many violations women suffer in public, and for which gender may not be the main or even a contributing factor. Second, the definition refers to physical, sexual, or psychological harm or suffering, or acts likely to cause such harm or suffering. It does not mention structural or economic violence. This is to be compared with the PRWA, discussed below, in which 'economic violence' is expressly identified.[86]

---

[80] Article 2, DEVAW.

[81] World Conference on Women, Beijing Declaration and Platform for Action, para. 113.

[82] GA res. A/RES/61/143, 19 December 2006, on Intensification of Efforts to Eliminate All Forms of Violence against Women, para. 3.

[83] D. Otto, 'Violence against Women: Something Other than a Human Rights Violation?' (1993) 1 *Aust. Fem. L. J.* 159, at 161.

[84] *Ibid.*   [85] *Ibid.*   [86] Article 1(j), PRWA.

A third potential concern is that the DEVAW definition appears to create a hierarchy of harms, with the primary focus on family violence, followed by violence within the general community, and finally violence perpetrated or condoned by the state. The ordering of this provision is presumably intended to reverse the general presumption of international law that it applies exclusively to state-sponsored violence. However, such attempts to dismantle the public/private dichotomy contribute to simultaneously reaffirming stereotypes about women by downplaying the violence they suffer and the roles they play in the public realm, and overemphasising the woman as mother and her confinement in the home.

A fourth concern is that culture, religion, and tradition as oft-cited reasons for such violence are not strongly rejected, with the use of only recommendatory language.[87]

The final, and most significant, concern is that the DEVAW does not recognise violence against women as a violation of human rights directly. This arose out of states' concerns that 'to do so would water down their universality'.[88] 'Instead, violence-against-women is understood as a "barrier" to women's enjoyment of human rights ... [and] leaves DEVAW's subjects still marginalized in the discourse of universality, needing special measures for their protection rather than human rights.'[89] This is to be contrasted to the International Convention on the Elimination of All Forms of Racial Discrimination 1965 (ICERD),[90] which contains an express prohibition on race-based violence.[91]

The IA-VAW adopts a similar approach to the DEVAW, although in contradistinction it grants a free-standing right to be free from violence: 'Every woman has the right to be free from violence in both the public and private spheres.'[92] Article 1 provides that violence against women 'shall be understood as any act or conduct, based on gender, which causes death or physical, sexual or psychological harm or suffering to women, whether in the public or the private sphere.' Like the DEVAW, Article 2 identifies the site, rather than the nature, of the violence; and it is likewise concerned with violence perpetrated against women attributed to

---

[87] Otto, 'Violence against Women', 162, referring to Article 4 which provides that states 'should not' invoke such justifications to avoid their obligations.

[88] *Ibid.*, 161–162.   [89] Otto, 'Lost in Translation', 346.

[90] International Convention on the Elimination of All Forms of Racial Discrimination 1965, GA res. 2106 (XX), 21 December 1965, 660 UNTS 195; entered into force 4 January 1969 (ICERD).

[91] Article 5, ICERD.   [92] Article 3, IA-VAW.

their gender.[93] Many of the criticisms outlined above can also be levelled against this treaty. However, the IA-VAW has also been criticised because it does not include acts that are 'likely to cause harm' and so, if interpreted literally, only applies to any act that has actually caused harm.[94]

The PRWA, although a women's rights treaty rather than a 'violence against women' treaty, nonetheless contains a definitional clause which defines 'violence against women' as:

> all acts perpetrated against women which cause or could cause them physical, sexual, psychological, and economic harm, including the threat to take such acts; or to undertake the imposition of arbitrary restrictions on or deprivation of fundamental freedoms in private or public life in peace time and during situations of armed conflicts or of war.[95]

The PRWA definition is distinct from those contained in the DEVAW or the IA-VAW in four key ways. First, it makes clear that it covers both actual violence and acts that could lead to violence. That is, unlike the IA-VAW, it specifically covers threats of violence. Second, it encompasses acts that are not usually viewed as violence per se, but which could lead to physical, sexual, psychological, or economic harm, such as restrictions on freedom of movement, unequal rights in marriage, media campaigns that portray women in negative images, polygamy, or customary, traditional, or religious practices that view women as inferior or second-class citizens.[96]

Third, the definition is not limited to gender-related violence but applies to violence against women in a global sense. The definition is thus broader in scope than its counterparts, and covers violence that is related to gender as well as violence that is not. The logical follow-up question is, what does this

---

[93] Article 2, IA-VAW provides: 'Violence against women shall be understood to include physical, sexual and psychological violence:
   (a) that occurs within the family or domestic unit or within any other interpersonal relationship, whether or not the perpetrator shares or has shared the same residence with the woman, including, among others, rape, battery and sexual abuse;
   (b) that occurs in the community and is perpetrated by any person, including, among others, rape, sexual abuse, torture, trafficking in persons, forced prostitution, kidnapping and sexual harassment in the workplace, as well as in educational institutions, health facilities or any other place; and
   (c) that is perpetrated or condoned by the state or its agents regardless of where it occurs.'

[94] A. P. Ewing, 'Establishing State Responsibility for Private Acts of Violence against Women under the American Convention on Human Rights' *Colum. Hum. Rts. L. Rev.* 751.

[95] Article 1(j), PRWA.

[96] C. A. Odinkalu, 'Africa's Regional Human Rights System: Recent Developments and Jurisprudence' (2002) 2 *Hum. Rts L. Rev.*, 99.

add? One benefit is that it means that women are protected from violence during armed conflict in which the acts in question may be more easily described as random, generalised, or indiscriminate in nature and less easily linked to discrimination on the grounds of gender, even though statistically women as civilians are more at risk than combatants in civil conflict.[97]

Fourth, it is the only definition to include explicitly economic harm as a form of violence against women. While it neither provides a definition of 'economic violence', nor uses the language of systemic or structural violence, the inclusion here of economic harm complements that approach. Unfortunately limited discussion was held at the drafting conference on its meaning. In another setting it has been considered as 'including denial of employment and other opportunities related to income generation, denial of income-related resources and violence related to work and employment situations.'[98] It has similarly been defined as: 'property grabbing by male relatives of a deceased man, forced dependency, or neglect of a wife's material needs' in times of economic crisis and difficulty.[99] The Special Rapporteur on the Rights of Women in Africa has included within her mandate 'abuse intended to deprive women of their economic powers and to prevent them from benefiting from the products of their own efforts'.[100] It is thus normally treated within the African context as violence connected to economic activities – either caused by economic situations or exacerbated by them, whether in the specific context of employment (such as sexual harassment) or the wider context of economic exploitation

---

[97] A. Fetherston and C. Nordstrom, *Overcoming Conceptual Habitus in Conflict Management: UN Peacekeeping and Warzone Ethnography* (Canberra: Peace Research Centre, Australian National University, 1994, Working Paper No. 147), cited in Charlesworth and Chinkin, *The Boundaries of International Law*, 251. See, also, Amnesty International, *Under Fire: The Impact of Guns on Women's Lives*, AI Index: ACT 30/001/2005, available at: www.amnesty.org/en/library/asset/ACT30/001/2005/en/9751740d-d53a-11dd-8a23-d58a49c0d652/act300012005en.html (effect of small arms on injuries to civilians, in particular women and children).

[98] United Nations Economic and Social Commission for Asia and the Pacific, Gender Equality and Empowerment Section, *Violence against Women: Harmful Traditional and Cultural Practices*, 26–27 April 2007, Bangkok, Thailand, 14, available at: www.unescap.org/ESID/GAD/Publication/Others/Publication_EGM-VAW.pdf.

[99] W. Tichagwa and P. Maramba (eds.), *Beyond Inequalities: Women in Zimbabwe* (Harare: Southern African Research and Documentation Centre, 1998), cited in M. J. Osirim, 'Crisis in the State and the Family: Violence against Women in Zimbabwe' (2003) 7 *Afr. Studies Qtly* (no page no.).

[100] African Commission Special Rapporteur on the Rights of Women in Africa, Angela Melo, *Intersession Activity Report*, 41st Ordinary Session, African Commission on Human and Peoples' Rights, Accra, Ghana, 16–30 May 2007, 15, available at: www.achpr.org/english/_info/index_women_en.html.

(which could include trafficking in women for forced sexual slavery or labour, displacement caused by large-scale development projects, disenfranchisement of women in difficult economic times, lack of credit or loans, or domestic violence related to food insecurity, and so on). Some of this may be more aptly described as discrimination rather than violence, but the preference in Africa has been to couch it in the language of violence. This is an important breakthrough in international discourse on this subject and revisits earlier global women's conferences that failed to link violence against women with issues of equality and development (discussed above).

It can thus be seen that where 'violence against women' has been defined under international law, it tends to be treated as a synonym for 'gender-based' or 'gender-related' violence. The argument for this is that had these instruments incorporated all forms of violence against women, regardless of gender, it would have unfairly advantaged women vis-à-vis men who do not benefit from a specific treaty protection either. It also reflects an understanding that women are subjected to violence because of patriarchal oppression or gendered understandings of the value and worth of women. My main objection to this general conflation is that it portrays only one side of the story of women's lives: that is, women as subordinate victims. This is played out in the international system by, for example, the fact that the most of the 'mainstream' human rights provisions were transcribed into the CEDAW, yet the rights to life, to liberty and security of person, or to be free from torture were lost on the way; these 'public' rights were not readily perceived as relevant to women's lives.[101]

For the purposes of this book, therefore, violence against women is understood as encompassing, but not limited to, any act, omission, or threat to life or of physical, sexual, or psychological harm or suffering perpetrated against women, or its structural and economic manifestations. This definition is based on Article 1 of the DEVAW, although it is not restricted to violence that is gender-based or gender-related, preferring instead the all-inclusive approach of PRWA. It also incorporates 'structural' violence under which economic violence may be included, but it further covers social, cultural, and traditional practices that are of their very nature violent, or which contribute to violence against women.

---

[101] See, further, Chapter 2.

3   Gender mainstreaming

'Gender mainstreaming' is defined by the United Nations as:

> the process of assessing the implications for women and men of any planned action, including legislation, policies or programmes, in all areas and at all levels. It is a strategy for making women's as well as men's concerns and experiences an integral dimension of the design, implementation, monitoring and evaluation of policies and programmes in all political, economic and societal spheres so that women and men benefit equally and inequality is not perpetuated. The ultimate goal is achieve gender equality.[102]

As intimated above in the discussion on sex and gender, there are various levels of concern with the articulation of the 'gender mainstreaming' policy, as well as its implementation. There is concern that the 'gender mainstreaming' strategy has led at best to rhetorical change, by merely requiring international civil servants, humanitarian field workers, and other decision-makers to 'add women and stir'. There has also been disappointment that the policy has been coopted by men to give heightened consideration to their rights and needs, and that the equality goal of the strategy is often lost or missing in international discourse, policy formulation, and practical implementation. This is due in part to the watered-down language used in its design, which focuses on both men and women, rather than more directly on sexual equality, or on women. Kouvo points out that the shift from a focus on 'women' to a focus on 'women and men', which was meant to give the strategy its 'critical edge' and to be inclusive of woman rather than keeping her on the sidelines.[103] Instead it has been criticised as a 'deceptively simple concept that is likely to be extremely difficult to operationalize', as well as 'an extraordinarily demanding concept' and 'fuzzy'.[104]

I have always found it disappointing that it was not properly termed 'gender equality mainstreaming', the result being that an emphasis on inequality, disadvantage, and exclusion experienced by women has been

---

[102] See, UN Doc. A/52/3/Rev.1, Agreed Conclusions, 1997/2, I.A., p. 24, as explained further in Report of the Secretary-General to ECOSOC, Mainstreaming the Gender Perspective into All Policies and Programmes in the United Nations System, UN Doc. E/1997/66, 12 June 1997.

[103] S. Kouvo, *Making Just Rights? Mainstreaming Women's Human Rights and a Gender Perspective* (Uppsala: Iustus Förlag, 2004), 172.

[104] F. Beveridge and S. Nott, 'Mainstreaming: A Case for Optimism and Cynicism' (2002) 10 *Fem. Legal Stud.* 299 at 308, referring to S. Mazey, 'Introduction: Integrating

somewhat reduced in significance as a result.[105] Its inclusion of both men and women positions it in some ways within the traditional equality paradigm of identical treatment, discussed further in Chapter 2. Many others, however, criticise the fact that gender mainstreaming is still used primarily to refer to women, and that it has not gone far enough to include men. Arguably, the strategy of 'gender mainstreaming' has been tasked with too much – namely, to address and respond to gender inequality, at the same time advancing women's rights, all the while recognising that men's lives may also be confined by gender-prescribed roles, responsibilities, and behaviour. While I acknowledge that the latter is also the case and that a deconstruction of entire societies is needed to advance women's rights, the 'gender mainstreaming' strategy has achieved neither a focus on the disadvantaged group (women) nor the adequate inclusion of 'mainstream' or other men.

C   Employing feminist methods

This book is positioned within feminist international legal studies and feminist legal theory. It employs a number of feminist methods of inquiry, either expressly or implicitly. Feminist methods tend to emphasise conversations and dialogue rather than the production of 'a single, triumphant truth'.[106] They seek to expose and question the claim of international law to objectivity and impartiality and, in the human rights context, universality. This is done through using 'gender' or gender relations, discussed above, as a category of analysis.[107] In this way feminist methods build on aspects of critical legal thinking.[108] According to Christine Littleton:

> [A] feminist method starts with the very radical act of taking women seriously, believing that what we say about ourselves and our experience is

Gender – Intellectual and "Real" World Mainstreaming' (2000) 7 *J. Eur. Pub. Pol'y* 333, at 343 and E. Hafner-Burton and M. Pollack, 'Mainstreaming Gender in Global Governance', European University Institute Working Paper RSC No. 2001/46 (Florence: Robert Schuman Centre for Advanced Studies, EUI, 2002), 424, respectively.

[105] See, also, H. Charlesworth, 'Not Waving but Drowning: Gender Mainstreaming and Human Rights in the United Nations' (2005) 18 *Harv. Hum. Rts. J.* 1.

[106] H. Charlesworth, 'Feminist Methods in International Law' (1999) 93 *Amer. J. Int'l L.* 379, 379, referring to J. A. Tickner, 'You Just Don't Understand: Troubled Engagements between Feminists and IR Theorists' (1997) 41 *Int'l Stud. Q.* 611, at 628.

[107] Charlesworth, 'Feminist Methods in International Law', 379.

[108] H. Charlesworth, C. Chinkin and S. Wright, 'Feminist Approaches to International Law' (1991) 85 *Amer. J. Int'l L.* 613, at 613. See, further, R. West, 'Jurisprudence and Gender' (1988) 55 *U. Chi. Law Rev.* 1; R. West, 'Feminism, Critical Social Theory and Law' (1989) *U. Chi. Legal F.* 59.

important and valid, even when (or perhaps especially when) it has little
or no relationship to what has been or is being said *about* us.[109]

There are a range of feminist techniques, each with contributions to make
at each stage of the process of analysis.[110] In essence, 'feminism is a mode
of analysis, a method of approaching life and politics, a way of asking
questions and searching for answers, rather than a set of political conclusions about the oppression of women'.[111] Likening feminist theories and
methods to an archaeological dig,[112] Hilary Charlesworth points out several layers in any feminist analysis of international law:

> An obvious sign of power differentials between women and men is the
> absence of international legal institutions. Beneath this is the vocabulary
> of international law, which generally makes women invisible. Digging
> further down, the apparently neutral principles and rules of international
> law can be seen as operating differently with respect to women and men.
> Another, deeper, layer of the excavation reveals the gendered and sexed
> nature of the basic concepts of international law.[113]

I undertake a similar excavation of the layers of the 'jurisprudence' of
international human rights institutions. I use the range of feminist techniques that have been developed, but I primarily find three methodologies
particularly helpful: an adapted 'asking the woman question' alongside
'feminist practical reasoning' and 'world travelling'.

The first technique I apply in this book is Katharine Bartlett's 'asking
the woman question'. This technique is concerned with identifying and

---

[109] C. Littleton, 'Feminist Jurisprudence: The Difference Method Makes' (Book Review) 41 *Stan. L. Rev.* 751, at 764, emphasis in original.

[110] E.g. Sandra Harding has identified three categories of feminist analysis: empiricism, standpoint theories, and postmodernism: S. Harding, *The Science Question in Feminism* (Ithaca, NY: Cornell University Press, 1986), 24–29; Katharine Bartlett refers to 'ask-ing the woman question', feminist practical reasoning, and consciousness-raising: K. T. Bartlett, 'Feminist Legal Methods' (1990) 103 *Harv. L. Rev.* 829; Isabel Gunning refers to 'world travelling': I. Gunning, 'Arrogant Perception, World Travelling and Multicultural Feminism: The Case of Female Genital Surgeries' (1991–92) 23 *Colum. Hum. Rts. L. Rev.* 189; Hilary Charlesworth has added a technique called 'searching for silences': Charlesworth, 'Feminist Methods in International Law'; Marysia Zalewski asks questions such as 'What work is gender doing?' and 'What about women?': M. Zalewski, 'Well, What is the Feminist Perspective on Bosnia?' (1995) 71 *Int'l Aff.* 339.

[111] N. Hartsock, 'Feminist Theory and the Development of Revolutionary Strategy', in Z. R. Eisenstein (ed.), *Capitalist Patriarchy and the Case for Socialist Feminism* (New York: Monthly Review Press, 1979) 56, at 58.

[112] The language of an 'archaeological dig' can be traced earlier to: N. Naffine, *Law and the Sexes: Explorations in Feminist Jurisprudence* (London: Allen & Unwin, 1990), 2.

[113] Charlesworth, 'Feminist Methods in International Law', 381.

challenging those elements of existing legal doctrine that exclude or disadvantage women.[114] Bartlett writes:

> In law, asking the woman question remains examining how the law fails
> to take into account the experiences and values that seem more typical
> of women than of men, for whatever reason, or how existing legal stand-
> ards and concepts might disadvantage women. The question assumes
> that some features of the law may be not only nonneutral [sic] in a gen-
> eral sense, but also 'male' in a specific sense. The purpose of the woman
> question is to expose those features and how they operate, and to suggest
> how they might be corrected.[115]

It is much more than asking 'where are the women?' in a statistical
sense. Rather, it is about asking why women are missing from mainstream human rights law and institutions. The woman question asks
about the negative or oppressive gender implications of a social practice
or legal rules. It explores why and how social standards silence or distort
the concerns that are more typical of women than of men. Questions that
will be posed throughout this book include: Have women been left out of
consideration of international human rights law? If so, in what way? How
might that omission be corrected?[116]

A more modern rephrasing of 'the woman question' is Marysia
Zalewski's interrelated questions in relation to her work on women in
Bosnia and Herzegovina: 'What work is gender doing?' and 'What about
women?'[117] Mostly, though, she is asking the woman question in her specific field of inquiry. In this context, she is asking about the role of social

---

[114] Bartlett, 'Feminist Legal Methods', 831.

[115] *Ibid.*, 837.

[116] *Ibid.*, 837. Bartlett draws upon the work of Heather Wishik who also suggests a series
of questions that could be framed within the 'woman question' concept: (1) What have
been and what are now all women's experiences of the 'Life Situation' addressed by the
doctrine, process, or area of law under examination? (2) What assumptions, descrip-
tions, assertions and/or definitions of experience – male, female, or ostensibly gender
neutral – does the law make in this area? (3) What is the area of mismatch, distortion, or
denial created by the differences between women's life experiences and the law's assumptions or imposed structures? (4) What patriarchal interests are served by the mismatch?
(5) What reforms have been proposed in this area of the law or women's life situation?
How will these reform proposals, if adopted, affect women both practically and ideo-
logically? (6) In an ideal world, what would this woman's life situation look like, and
what relationship, if any, would the law have to this future life situation?; and (7) How do
we get there from here?: H. Wishik, 'To Question Everything: The Inquiries of Feminist
Jurisprudence' (1985) 1 *Berkeley Women's L. J.* 64, at 72–77.

[117] Zalewski, 'Well, What is the Feminist Perspective on Bosnia?', 341.

and cultural constructions of gender or the gender gaps in the legal systems at play, and how they affect women. Charlesworth's approach of 'searching for the silences' in international law performs a similar function. Searching for silences questions the objectivity of the law by detecting its silences, partly through paying attention to the various dichotomies used in international law – male/female, public/private, legal/political, protector/protected, and so on.[118] Likewise, Rhonda Copelon speaks of 'surfacing gender'.[119]

Asking the woman question is uniquely geared towards finding the underlying causes of women's exclusion and offers new insights into apparently gender-neutral social, cultural, and legal structures. Asking it can identify silences or gaps in international law. While the focus of this method is on women in particular, it is acknowledged that the approach may have significance for all disempowered persons.[120] It has also been asserted that the approach may benefit men as well as women.[121]

In contrast to its virtues, the technique has also been criticised for the underlying assumptions that it makes about women. It assumes that it is possible to speak about women uniformly and with a single voice. In spite of the validity of some of the concerns of the anti-essentialist feminist movement, which are discussed further in Chapter 2, the woman question remains an effective technique and needs updating only slightly by contextualising it to the political, social, cultural, and economic context at hand (in other words, 'asking the gender question'). Although many feminist scholars may disagree on solutions to these issues, very few disagree that starting from the experiences of real women is essential.[122]

---

[118] Charlesworth, Chinkin and Wright, 'Feminist Approaches to International Law', 615; Charlesworth, 'Feminist Methods in International Law', 381–383.

[119] R. Copelon, 'Gendered War Crimes: Reconceptualizing Rape in Time of War', in J. Peters and A. Wolper (eds.), *Women's Rights, Human Rights: International Feminist Perspectives* (New York: Routledge, 1995) 197, at 199.

[120] G. Binion, 'Human Rights: A Feminist Perspective' (1995) 17 *HRQ* 509, at 512.

[121] *Ibid.*, 514.

[122] Cf. Nussbaum who argues that deprivation and intimidation can corrupt or distort experience, making it a very incomplete guide as to what ought to be done. See, M. Nussbaum, *Sex and Social Justice* (Oxford University Press, 1999), 55–80; M. Nussbaum, *Women and Human Development: The Capabilities Approach* (Cambridge University Press, 2000); M. Nussbaum, 'Capabilities and Human Rights', *Fordham L. Rev.* 273. See, also, S. Mullally, *Gender, Culture and Human Rights: Reclaiming Universalism* (Oxford: Hart Publishing, 2006), 65, for her discussion of Nussbaum.

The second technique that I use throughout this book, also drawn from Bartlett, is what Bartlett terms 'feminist practical reasoning'. This technique expands traditional notions of legal relevance to make legal decision-making more sensitive to the features of a case not already reflected in legal doctrine.[123] It is particularly relevant to the subject matter of this book because 'it builds upon the "practical" in its focus on the specific, real-life dilemmas posed by human conflict – dilemmas that more abstract forms of legal reasoning often tend to gloss over'.[124] Practical reasoning approaches problems, not as dichotomies, but as having multiple perspectives, contradictions, and inconsistencies. New facts and new situations present opportunities for improved understandings.[125] In other words, it is a contextualised analysis: what is essential is that women's experiences are included *as relevant*.[126] This method is particularly helpful in this book as I apply and interpret three fundamental human rights principles to a specific practical context of violence against women. Both these first two outlined techniques take into account or make more facts/issues relevant than would non-feminist legal analyses.[127]

The third method employed, albeit to a lesser extent, to excavate the landscape in this book is Isabel Gunning's method of 'world travelling'.[128] This technique is based on an understanding that women are not a monolithic group and other techniques that engage in multicultural dialogue are useful, especially in so far as they highlight social and cultural differences in the construction of gender.[129] It attempts to rid feminist methods of the 'arrogant perception' of 'us'/Western feminists versus 'them'/non-Western women or 'me' versus 'the other', as the arrogant perceiver falsifies and oversimplifies the 'distance' and difference between the two groups.[130] '"Travelling" is the shift from being one person in one world

---

[123] Bartlett, 'Feminist Legal Methods', 836.

[124] *Ibid.*, 850.   [125] *Ibid.*, 851.

[126] Contextual analysis has been endorsed by some domestic courts, such as the Canadian Supreme Court in its deliberations on the meaning of equality: K. E. Mahoney, 'Canadian Approaches to Equality Rights and Gender Equity in the Courts', in R. J. Cook (ed.), *Human Rights of Women: National and International Perspectives* (Philadelphia: University of Pennsylvania Press, 1994) 437.

[127] Bartlett, 'Feminist Legal Methods', 856.

[128] Gunning develops her 'world travelling' from the work of M. Lugones, 'Playfulness, World-Traveling and Loving Perception' (1987) 2 *Hypatia* 3, in Gunning, 'Arrogant Perception, World Travelling and Multicultural Feminism', 202, n. 55.

[129] See, Gunning, 'Arrogant Perception, World Travelling and Multicultural Feminism', 191. See, further, R. Braidotti, 'The Exile, the Nomad, and the Migrant: Reflections on International Feminism' (1992) 15 *Women's Stud. Int'l F.* 7, at 9.

[130] Gunning, 'Arrogant Perception, World Travelling and Multicultural Feminism', 199.

to a different person in another world.'[131] It is a two-way dialogue in which one is required not just to speak the language of the 'other' but to understand how one is constructed by the 'other'. This is, in part, to avoid the label of cultural imperialism or colonialism. It calls for cross-cultural understanding and the recognition of both independence and interconnectedness.[132]

Gunning identifies three components of how to achieve 'world travelling':

1. To understand oneself and be clear about one's own cultural influences and pressures that are inextricably involved in one's own sense of self;
2. To understand one's historical relationship to the 'other' and to approach that understanding from the 'other's' perspective; and
3. To see the 'other' in the cultural context in which she sees herself.[133]

Gunning does not reject human rights law or norms; rather, she is interested in the process of how to transfer those human rights norms to 'other' communities without 'us' imposing these norms on 'others'. This technique could be seen as associated with ideas of intersectionality, which is discussed further in Chapter 2, or the process of considering the multiple dimensions of women's lives (what I later term 'humanising women' in Chapter 8). That is, it asks us to reflect upon how we construct 'others' within our own communities, as well as in 'other' countries.

D   Structure and content

Following this introductory chapter, Chapter 2 provides an analysis of four of the main feminist critiques of international law and human rights. These critiques are that women and women's voices are absent from mainstream institutions; that the formulation, interpretation, and application of human rights norms reflect the experiences of men while ignoring or marginalising those of women; that women's issues are relegated to the 'private' sphere and thereby outside of politics, law, and international relations; and that, throughout this process, women are stereotyped into 'gendered' roles. Chapter 2 forms the theoretical framework for the remainder of the book. It is against these four critiques that the responses

---

[131] *Ibid.*, 203.   [132] *Ibid.*, 204.   [133] *Ibid.*, 204–205.

of international human rights law to violence against women are examined in subsequent chapters.

Chapter 3 offers an overview of the United Nations' human rights treaty body system, outlining its mandates, working methods, procedural rules, and composition. It is provided as background material, although in addition I find that these structural issues also inform the treatment of the norms studied in this book. I explore women's (lack of) participation in the processes of the treaty bodies and enquire into the explanations for this persistent trend. In doing so, I find that there are few institutional safeguards or incentives to women's participation and that without them the default position of the UN system is towards gender inequality. Some of the material presented in this chapter is informed by the opinions and experiences of present and former treaty body members, as well as officials of non-governmental and international organisations working with the treaty bodies, who were interviewed for this study.[134] Questions relating to treaty body reform are dealt with in Chapter 8.

In Chapters 4, 5, and 6 I examine the interpretation and application of three human rights norms to the issue of violence against women. These norms are the right to equality and the related right to freedom from discrimination on the basis of sex (Chapter 4), the prohibition against torture and other cruel, inhuman, or degrading treatment or punishment (Chapter 5), and the right to life (Chapter 6). A separate chapter is devoted to each provision, and an account is provided of how each has developed under international human rights law and how women have fared in the respective jurisprudence.

These norms have been selected for a number of reasons. First, two of the norms chosen – the prohibition against torture and the right to life – are individually considered to be rights either of fundamental importance within the international legal system or upon which universal consensus exists. In other words, they are higher-order rights. This is in spite of the basic principle of international law that human rights are universal, indivisible, and non-hierarchical.[135] The principles

---

[134] Information in relation to Decision on Human Ethics Protocol 2006/136 (ethics approval for this project) is on file with the author and is available from The Australian National University Ethics Committee.

[135] See, e.g., statement at Vienna Declaration and Programme of Action, para. 5: 'All human rights are universal, indivisible and interdependent and interrelated. The international community must treat human rights globally in a fair and equal manner, on the same footing, and with the same emphasis.' On the hierarchy of rights idea, see e.g., K. Vasak, *The International Dimensions of Human Rights* (Paris: UNESCO Press, 1982); K. Vasak, 'Pour une Troisième Génération des Droits de l'Homme', in C. Swinarski (ed.), *Etudes et*

of non-discrimination on the basis of sex and equality between women and men are also both fundamental rights, as well as the *raison d'être* of the feminist movement.[136] These rights have in common their non-derogable status under international law; and arguably their status as norms of customary international law, if not *jus cogens* (discussed further in Chapter 4). At a minimum, they cannot be derogated from even in times of a state of emergency.[137] Thus their examination here in the context of violence against women is particularly pertinent as they can each act as a barometer to women's standing within the international system.

Second, feminist scholars have highlighted norms such as the prohibition against torture and the right to sexual equality and their early interpretation and application by international bodies as reinforcing a system that excludes women. These same norms have been later harnessed as part of feminist strategies of inclusion because of their symbolism as international crimes of abhorrence. Moreover, international institutions have attempted to extend these broad rights to cover the varying situations of women, even if their situations are not strictly covered by the terms in which the rights are expressed.

Other human rights norms could have been analysed in this book in its treatment of violence against women, such as the right to liberty and security of the person, provisions relating to slavery, freedom of movement, privacy, and health, and rights pertaining to marriage and the family. Although these rights have also been considered by the treaty bodies within the context of violence against women, they have not been as extensively considered as those studied here,[138] although where they are relevant, they will be mentioned within the context of the foregoing rights. Furthermore, where they have been applied, they have not readily

Essais sur le Droit International Humanitaire et sur les Principes de la Croix-Rouge (The Hague: Martinus Nijhoff, 1984), 837; T. van Boven, 'Distinguishing Criteria of Human Rights', in K. Vasak and P. Alston (eds.), *The International Dimensions of Human Rights* (Westport, CT: Greenwood Press, 1982), 43.

[136] F. Banda, *Women, Law and Human Rights: An African Perspective* (Oxford: Hart Publishing, 2005), 2.

[137] See, Chapters 4, 5, and 6.

[138] See, e.g., HRC, General Comment No. 28, Equality of Rights Between Men and Women (referring to a range of rights that impact on the issue of violence against women, namely Article 16 (the right to be recognised by everyone as a person before the law and therefore not to be treated as objects (para. 19)); Article 17 (the right to privacy is implicated when 'the sexual life of a woman is taken into consideration in deciding the extent of her legal rights and protections, including protection against rape' (para. 20)); Article 19 (dissemination of obscene or pornographic material which portrays women as objects

been identified as *forms* of violence against women (cf. torture or sex discrimination), but rather as rights that are nullified or impaired because
of violence against women (for example, health, privacy, freedom of
movement).

Chapter 7 revisits the many feminist narratives on international human
rights law discussed in Chapter 2, and draws out some overall conclusions
on what this system means for women, for feminist theory, and for the
four main feminist critiques of the international system. Chapter 8, in
contrast, strategises the next steps in the process of developing and articulating women's human rights by identifying needed practical reforms of a
procedural, structural, interpretative, and substantive nature.

of violence or degrading or inhuman treatment is likely to promote these kinds of treatment (para. 22)); Article 23 (right to marry without coercion and with consent or forcing
victims of rape to marry their attacker (para. 24)). See, also, HRC, General Comment
No. 19: Protection of the Family, the Right to Marriage and Equality of Spouses (1990).

2

Feminist theories on international law and human rights

A   Introduction

Animating feminist theories of the international legal system is the exclusion of women from mainstream[1] human rights norms, processes, and institutions. While there is general agreement among feminist scholars that the international human rights legal system could do more to address the particular concerns of women, there is far less agreement as to the reasons for women's exclusion, how the system may be reformed to be more inclusive, or whether it is capable of being transformed. In this chapter I explore four of the principal feminist critiques/themes of international law and international human rights law, setting out also some of the main internal contradictions and disagreements surrounding these themes within feminism. This chapter forms the theoretical framework for the remainder of the book, which is concerned with how international human rights law has responded to women's concerns in the particular context of violence against women.

In this book I adopt Janet Halley's three-tiered definition of feminism. First, to qualify as a feminist argument, a distinction must be made between men/male/masculine (which she refers to as 'm') and women/female/feminine (which she refers to as 'f'). Second, feminism must posit some kind of subordination between m and f, in which f is the disadvantaged or subordinated element. Third, in opposing this subordination and in attempting to eradicate it, 'feminism carries a brief for f.[2] I also agree with Nancy Levit and Robert Verchick's identification of two shared features of all feminist theories: the first is *an observation* – the world has been shaped by men, particularly white men, who for this reason possess larger shares of power and privilege; the second is *an aspiration* – all

---

[1] 'Mainstream' is used in this book to refer to non-women-specific human rights instruments or processes.

[2] J. Halley, *Split Decisions: How and Why to Take a Break from Feminism* (Princeton University Press, 2006), 17–18.

feminists believe that women and men should have political, social, and economic equality.[3] But while feminists agree on the goal of equality, they disagree about its meaning and on how to achieve it.

The first feminist critique outlined in this chapter is the absence of women and women's voices from most international law-making processes, including in the human rights field. This is not a new critique, yet it remains an important one as the exclusion of women from human rights discourse usually results in the omission of women's rights from international regulatory mechanisms. The second critique explores how international human rights law privileges the realities of men's lives and correspondingly ignores or marginalises the concerns of women. The third critique addresses the effect on women of the line drawn between public and private spheres of everyday life for the purposes of international legal rules. The public/private dichotomy privileges the public/male over the private/female and is manifest in the theory of state responsibility for human rights abuses. Although logically a subset of the second critique, owing to its significance within feminist discourse and its particular conceptualisation around the state-based system of international law, I examine it separately. The fourth critique details how the international human rights system has tended to treat women as a collective group with a single gender identity, with the effect that they are reduced to a single 'essence' or a monodimensional character. While I refer to this critique as a critique of international human rights law, it is also a criticism of some feminist approaches to international law. The critiques outlined in this chapter have been selected as being overarching themes of feminist inquiry, although it is acknowledged that there are other critiques than those detailed in this study.

There are many strands or schools of feminist legal thought – liberal/ equality, cultural/difference, radical/structural bias, and post-modern/ anti-essentialist.[4] In this book I am interested in identifying some

---

[3] N. Levit and R. R. M. Verchick, *Feminist Legal Theory: A Primer* (New York University Press, 2006), 15–16.

[4] See, e.g., Karen Engle, who has identified three stages in feminist theory: (1) Liberal Inclusion (1985–1990), Structural Bias (1987–1995), and Third World Feminist Critiques (since 1992). In many ways both her liberal inclusion and structural bias categories fall within my first deconstructionist phase (see below in the text), as both criticise international law for failing women – liberal inclusion for ignoring women and marginalising their participation; for structural bias feminists for failing to take account of women's experiences and structural reasons for that failing. Engle's third stage is also subsumed within my first stage as part of the internal critique of particular feminist ideas or perspectives: K. Engle, 'International Human Rights and Feminisms: When Discourses Keep

fundamental feminist theories as they relate to international human rights law and am less concerned with whether these theories fall into particular feminist 'camps' or 'schools'. I find such labels become increasingly unhelpful as many international feminist legal scholars do not fit neatly into a single school or category, or they may have started in one and moved into another over time.

Even though I am concerned with key feminist themes rather than schools of thought from which they derive or belong, the four themes reviewed in this chapter could also be classified broadly as: liberal/equality feminism (i.e., the under-representation of women – women are the same as men); cultural/difference feminism (i.e., human rights do not reflect or satisfy women's concerns – women are different to men); radical/structural bias feminism (i.e., the public/private dichotomy – public and structural power is exercised by men over women); and post-modern/anti-essentialist feminism (i.e., rejection of notions of single truths and assertions that truths are multiple, provisional, and thus linked to individuals' lived experiences).[5] By identifying points of commonality from the range of feminist views, rather than the schools to which they belong, I am able to engage in a deeper analysis of specific rights and contexts. As I am particularly interested in how women have fared in international human rights jurisprudence, I use, rather than endorse, some of the critiques outlined in this chapter as helpful tools to excavate the landscape and to dig deep into the layers of international human rights law.[6]

B   Four stages in feminist theorising and activism on human rights

Before proceeding to the feminist critiques outlined below, I situate these critiques within four developmental stages of feminist theories and

---

Meeting', in D. Buss and A. Manji (eds.), *International Law: Modern Feminist Approaches* (Oxford: Hart Publishing, 2005) 47. Other writers have classified feminist scholarship according to feminist identities drawn from other feminisms more broadly – such as Nicola Lacey's division into Liberal Feminism, Radical Feminism, Marxist and Socialist Feminism, and Difference Feminism: see, N. Lacey, 'Feminist Legal Theory and the Rights of Women', in K. Knop (ed.), *Gender and Human Rights* (Oxford University Press, 2004) 13, at 19–26. Charlesworth and Chinkin divide feminist theories of law into five categories: Liberal, Cultural, Radical, Post-Modern, and Third World: see, H. Charlesworth and C. Chinkin, *The Boundaries of International Law: A Feminist Analysis* (Manchester University Press, 2000), Chapter 2.

[5] See, Levit and Verchick, *Feminist Legal Theory: A Primer*, 8–12. They add lesbian legal theory, pragmatic legal feminism, and eco-feminism to their list of feminisms.

[6] See, Chapter 1.

activism on international law. It should be noted, however, that these stages are rather arbitrary in design with much overlap between them and that they are only sequential to a point as both deconstruction and reconstruction continue to occur all the time.

Stage 1: Formal equality 1948–1970s

The first stage is primarily one of activism around women's rights to equality in the fields of politics, marriage, and the economy. It corresponds to the immediate post-Second World War period. At this time, women were active participants in the drafting sessions of the Universal Declaration of Human Rights 1948[7] (UDHR), not least via the Commission on the Status of Women (CSW), but also due to Eleanor Roosevelt's involvement as chair of the Commission on Human Rights (CHR). In formulating their interventions, the CSW worked closely with women's non-governmental organisations. Driven by domestic liberal feminist agendas, particularly in the United States and Britain, their advocacy centred on the rights to equality and non-discrimination on the basis of sex in a formal sense.

At the first session of the CSW, members agreed that their goal was to 'elevate the equal rights and human rights status of women, irrespective of nationality, race, language, or religion, in order to achieve equality with men in all fields of human enterprise'.[8] This is reflected in the UDHR by the guarantees to sexual equality and non-discrimination on the basis of sex[9] and importantly the non-discrimination approach endorsed in the Convention on the Elimination of All Forms of Discrimination against Women of 1979.[10] These instruments formed the political framework of the UN's work on women's rights, and importantly moved beyond the protective orientation of earlier instruments of the League of Nations.[11] But it is the next three stages that are of greater relevance today and to the themes of this book.

---

[7] Universal Declaration of Human Rights 1948, GA res. 217 A (III), 10 December 1948 (UDHR).

[8] M. E. Galey, 'Promoting Nondiscrimination against Women: The UN Commission on the Status of Women' (1979) 23 *Int'l Stud. Qtly* 273, referred to in D. Otto, 'Lost in Translation: Re-Scripting the Sexed Subjects of International Human Rights Law', in A. Orford (ed.), *International Law and Its Others* (Cambridge University Press, 2006) 318, at 330.

[9] Articles 1, 2, and 7, UDHR.

[10] Convention on the Elimination of All Forms of Discrimination against Women 1979, GA res. 34/180, 18 December 1979, 1249 UNTS 13; entered into force 3 September 1981 (CEDAW).

[11] The 'protective' approach has not, however, disappeared altogether; see in particular Protocol to Prevent, Suppress and Punish Trafficking in Persons Especially Women

Stage 2: Deconstruction of law 1980s–present

The second stage of feminist scholarship on international law could be described as a period of deconstruction, which began in the mid to late 1980s and continued through to the early to mid-1990s. During this stage, feminist scholars were engaged in deconstructing or critiquing international human rights norms (and other aspects of international law) in order to identify gaps or mischiefs in the law. The four feminist critiques of international law identified in this chapter fall into this stage but are also used as platforms for the rethinking of international human rights law under the next stage. The deconstructionist stage utilises a range of feminist methods of inquiry, as set out in Chapter 1 of this book, to identify the reasons for the persistence of patriarchy (or the dominance of men over women) in the international human rights regime. These early deconstructionist approaches, however, rarely offered concrete proposals through which international human rights law could be developed or utilised to encompass the experiences of women. Nonetheless, they laid the foundations for that subsequent theorising. Only later did some of these same theorists and scholars, and new ones, alongside women's rights activists, seek to embrace aspects of international law as an avenue for the pursuit of women's rights. Although the bulk of the critical engagement with international law occurred during the 1990s, it is an ongoing process and continues today.

Stage 3: Reconstruction, reconceptualisation and reinterpretation 1990s–present

In parallel to, as well as building upon and learning from, the deconstructionist stage, a third stage can be identified during which proposals for women's inclusion within human rights doctrine were and continue to be put forward. From the mid-1990s, many feminist scholars and women's rights activists began advocating for women's inclusion within human rights norms and institutions. This period is very much shaped by the events in the former Yugoslavia in the early to mid-1990s and the widespread acknowledgement that the parties to the conflict had used rape and sexual violence as deliberate military strategies of psychological warfare. The 1990s witnessed a renewed push for women's issues to be put on

and Children, Supplementing the UN Convention against Transnational Organized Crime 2000, GA res. A/RES/55/25, 15 November 2000, 40 ILM 335; entered into force 25 December 2003. For more on this, see Otto, 'Lost in Translation'.

the human rights agenda, in particular that sexual violence perpetrated against women in armed conflict be recognised as violations of the laws of war. This was also the approach of the Vienna World Conference on Human Rights in 1993, in which it was stated that 'women's rights are human rights',[12] and which was later reiterated in the Beijing Platform for Action in 1995.[13] Feminist advocacy during this stage attempted not only to improve the system to the benefit of women, but frequently simply to engage it.

This third stage focuses less on criticising the system of international human rights law, and rejecting it, in part or in its entirety, as being irrelevant to women's lives, and more on reflecting upon the potential scope of human rights norms to be interpreted and applied in favour of women. It is a period of *reconstruction, reconceptualisation* and *reinterpretation*. It parallels the strategies of many women's rights activists and human rights advocates seeking to work within existing parameters of international law and to challenge the system from within;[14] and very much plays to the 'women's-rights-are-human-rights' agenda of the Vienna World Conference, or the 'gender mainstreaming' agenda that followed later (discussed further below). Much of this feminist scholarship argues for doctrinal inclusion and institutional expansion and has been tied to liberal feminism.[15] However, this stage has also seen calls for internal structural reform, and fits, therefore, with the views of some structural bias feminists. For example, in the absence of an explicit international treaty right protecting women from violence, women's rights activists and feminist academics alike began to argue that some existing provisions could and should be revisited to better incorporate women's experiences of violence.[16] The issue for many feminist theorists writing

---

[12] World Conference on Human Rights, Vienna Declaration and Programme of Action, UN Doc. A/CONF.157/23, 12 July 1993, para. 18. The precise wording is as follows: 'The human rights of women and of the girl-child are an inalienable, integral and indivisible part of universal human rights. The full and equal participation of women in political, civil, economic, social and cultural life, at the national, regional and international levels, and the eradication of all forms of discrimination on grounds of sex are priority objectives of the international community.'

[13] Fourth World Conference on Women, Beijing Declaration and Platform for Action, UN Doc. A/CONF.177/20 and UN Doc. A/CONF.177/20/Add.1, 15 September 1995, para. 14 (Declaration): 'are convinced that: Women's rights are human rights'.

[14] See, e.g., Amnesty International, *Human Rights are Women's Rights*, AI Index: 77/01/95, 1995.

[15] See, Engle, 'International Human Rights and Feminisms', 52.

[16] See, e.g., R. J. Cook, 'State Responsibility for Violations of Women's Human Rights' (1994) 7 *Harv. Hum. Rts. J.* 125; A. P. Ewing, 'Establishing State Responsibility for Private

in the later stages of this period has been a lack of enforcement rather than a lack of law.[17]

Feminists writing during this third stage could also be called integrationist, as they attempt to work and support women's rights *within* existing or mainstream institutions. Both stages have contributed to the UN policy and practice of 'gender mainstreaming' in so far as they seek to better understand and/or respond to the interplay between the lives of women and international law. The UN's gender mainstreaming policy is arguably one of the UN's responses to the inclusion or integration agenda. The UN human rights treaty bodies have each endorsed the 'gender-mainstreaming' agenda, adopting a set of six recommendations in 1995 which sought to integrate gender perspectives into their working methods.[18]

Acts of Violence against Women under the American Convention on Human Rights' (1995) 26 *Colum. Hum. Rts. L. Rev.* 751; D. Q. Thomas and M. E. Beasley, 'Symposium on Reconceptualizing Violence Against Women by Intimate Partners: Critical Issues: Domestic Violence as a Human Rights Issue' (1995) 58 *Alb. L. Rev.* 1119; J. D. Wilets, 'Conceptualizing Violence: Present and Future Developments in International Law: Panel III: Sex and Sexuality: Violence and Culture in the New International Order: Conceptualizing Private Violence against Sexual Minorities as Gendered Violence: An International and Comparative Perspective' (1997) 60 *Alb. L. Rev.* 989; B. C. Alexander, 'Convention Against Torture: A Viable Alternative Legal Remedy for Domestic Violence Victims' (2000) 15 *Amer. U. Int'l L. Rev.* 895; A. N. Wood, 'A Cultural Rite of Passage or a Form of Torture: Female Genital Mutilation from an International Law Perspective' (2001) 12 *Hastings Women's L. J.* 347; R. Lord, 'The Liability of Non-State Actors for Torture in Violation of International Humanitarian Law: An Assessment of the Jurisprudence of the International Criminal Tribunal for the former Yugoslavia' (2003) 4 *Melb. J. Int'l L.* 112; H. Pearce, 'An Examination of the International Understanding of Rape and the Significance of Labeling it Torture' (2002) 14 *Int'l J. Ref. L.* 534.

[17] Engle, 'International Human Rights and Feminisms', 52.
[18] UN, *Human Rights Questions: Implementation of Human Rights Instruments*, UN Doc. A/50/505, 4 October 1995, paras. 34(a)–(f), which provide: '(a) The treaty bodies shall fully integrate gender perspectives into their presessional and sessional working methods, including identification of issues and preparation of questions for country reviews, general comments, general recommendations, and concluding observations. In particular, the treaty bodies should consider the gender implications of each issue discussed under each of the articles of the respective instruments; (b) Guidelines for the preparation of reports by States parties should be amended to reflect the necessity of providing specific information on the human rights of women for consideration by the respective committees; (c) In undertaking investigative procedures, the treaty bodies should make special efforts to elicit information about the situation of women in the area of inquiry; (d) Treaty bodies should consistently request gender-disaggregated data from States parties and from United Nations specialized agencies and use the data in reviewing country reports; (e) The treaty bodies should make every effort to exchange information on progress, developments and situations concerning the human rights of women; (f) In preparing reports of the treaty body sessions, attention should be paid to the use of gender-inclusive language wherever possible.'

Not all feminist writers have gone on to embrace the integration stage fully, concluding instead that the existing system of international law is irreparable and unable to offer needed transformative outcomes to women, while others have raised concern that the system simply reinforces sexual differences (see further below under C4 Essentialised women). Regrettably, few of these feminist scholars explain what they mean by transformation or sketch what the reimagined system would look like.[19]

Stage 4: Reflection, re-evaluation, and reassessment
2000–present

From 2000 arguably a fourth stage of feminist analysis has emerged, with a handful of feminist scholars assessing the progress made and taking stock of the achievements of the feminist project and implementation strategies to date.[20] These feminist scholars are in many ways testing the integration approach of the third stage and asking questions about whether issues of gender have been mainstreamed within international law and the extent to which international law has responded to women's lives. The distinction with the previous stages of deconstruction and reconstruction (which naturally involve reflection and re-evaluation) is that this stage involves more empirical analysis. It is centred on the realities on the ground, rather than in grand theorising. Drawing on the critiques of the deconstructionist stage to assess the strategies of inclusion of the reconstructionist phase, this book is situated within the fourth stage of reflection, evaluation, and reassessment of the feminist project.

C   Four feminist critiques of international law and human rights

1   Absence of women and women's voices

1.1   Not enough women

The first feminist critique of relevance to international human rights law is the under-representation of women in international decision-making

---

[19] Cf. scholars such as Martha Nussbaum who question the usefulness of the existing international human rights system, but set about to reimagine it: M. Nussbaum, *Sex and Social Justice* (Oxford University Press, 1999) and M. Nussbaum, *Women and Human Development: The Capabilities Approach* (Cambridge University Press, 2000).

[20] See, e.g., S. Kouvo, *Making Just Rights? Mainstreaming Women's Human Rights and a Gender Perspective* (Uppsala: Iustus Förlag, 2004); M-B. Dembour, *Who Believes in*

bodies. Although this critique has fallen into disfavour with many Western domestic legal feminists for its emphasis on formal equality, the state of the international legal system as a site of over-representation of men makes this critique still important for international legal feminists. Women are still numerically under-represented in most international bodies and at all levels. At the level of law very few human rights treaties, for example, contain express provisions that require states to ensure equal or balanced representation on the basis of sex, compared with extensive provisions relating to equitable geographic representation.[21] In fact, those few provisions that exist are couched in discretionary language, and as Chapter 2 demonstrates, have done little to change the status quo.

According to feminist scholarship, the absence of female voices is a direct consequence of '[m]ale hegemony over public life and institutions'.[22] Two of the reasons for reversing this trend are because women's participation in human rights processes and institutions is considered to directly affect the relevance of laws to women[23] and because women are simply entitled to participate equally in all aspects of economic, social, cultural, civil, and political life.[24] Feminism argues that the extent to which women were (and continue to be) excluded from any meaningful participation in negotiating, developing, articulating, drafting, monitoring, implementing, and enforcing human rights norms has resulted in a rights-based system that fails to reflect fully, or ignores entirely, the rights, interests, concerns, needs, and desires of women.[25] Yet, women did participate in

Human Rights? Reflections on the European Convention (Cambridge University Press, 2006), Chapter 7; R. L. Johnstone, 'Feminist Influences on the United Nations Human Rights Treaty Bodies' (2006) 26 *HRQ* 148.

[21] See, Chapter 3.

[22] K. Mahoney, 'Theoretical Perspectives on Women's Human Rights and Strategies for their Implementation' (1996) 12 *Brook. J. Int'l L.* 799, at 810; U. A. O'Hare, 'Realizing Human Rights for Women' (1999) 21 *HRQ* 364, at 365–366. See, also, C. A. MacKinnon, 'Feminism, Marxism, Method, and the State: Toward Feminist Jurisprudence' (1983) 8 *Signs* 635, at 638.

[23] A. Byrnes, 'Using International Human Rights Law and Procedures to Advance Women's Rights', in K. D. Askin and D. M. Koenig (eds.), *Women and International Human Rights Law* (Ardsley, NY: Transnational Publishers, 2000) 79, at 96; M. Eberts, 'Feminist Perspectives on the Canadian Charter of Rights and Freedoms', in P. Alston (ed.), *Promoting Human Rights Through Bills of Rights: Comparative Perspectives* (New York: Oxford University Press, 1999, reprinted 2003), 241.

[24] H. Charlesworth, 'The Gender of International Institutions' (1995) 89 *ASIL Proceedings* 84, who identifies two reasons for calling for greater participation and representation of women in international organisations: 1. It is a question of equality and human rights; 2. Women offer different forms of decision-making.

[25] See, H. Charlesworth, C. Chinkin and S. Wright, 'Feminist Approaches to International Law' (1991) 85 *Amer. J. Int'l L.* 613; H. Charlesworth, 'The Public/Private Distinction

the drafting of the early human rights instruments, as outlined above. Rather, the problem is that they were working from a fixed set of ideas about women and were operating within a particular socio-political-historical context, not least limited by a liberal feminist agenda of formal equality.

In the contexts of violence against women and sex discrimination, Hilary Charlesworth, Christine Chinkin, and Shelley Wright have stated:

> Because men generally are not the victims of sex discrimination, domestic violence, and sexual degradation and violence, for example, these matters can be consigned to a separate sphere and tend to be ignored. The orthodox face of international law and politics would change dramatically if their institutions were truly human in composition.[26]

There is now some evidence to suggest that the inclusion of women as decision-makers in domestic as well as international tribunals and courts has had an effect on the reasoning and outcome of cases, although it provides no guarantees.[27] Research relating to female political participation has found that, although female politicians develop different styles of political engagement, they are also wary of speaking for women.[28] Other research highlights that there may be a 'numbers threshold' at which women acquire the confidence to speak for their sex.[29] Below this threshold, they refrain from asserting any sexual difference. Limited

---

and the Right to Development in International Law' (1992) 12 *Aust. YB Int'l L.* 190; A. Gallagher, 'Ending the Marginalization: Strategies for Incorporating Women into the United Nations Human Rights System' (1997) 19 *HRQ* 283; B. E. Hernández-Truyol, 'Human Rights through a Gendered Lens: Emergence, Evolution, Revolution', in Askin and Koenig (eds.), *Women and International Human Rights Law*, Vol. 1, 3, at 3 and 29; C. Romany, 'State Responsibility Goes Private: A Feminist Critique of the Public/Private Distinction in International Human Rights Law', in R. J. Cook (ed.), *Human Rights of Women: National and International Perspectives* (Philadelphia: University Pennsylvania Press, 1994), 85; D. Sullivan, 'The Public/Private Distinction in International Human Rights Law', in J. Peters and A. Wolper (eds.), *Women's Rights, Human Rights: International Feminist Perspectives* (New York: Routledge, 1995) 126; B. E. Hernández-Truyol, 'Women's Rights as Human Rights – Rules, Realities and the Role of Culture: A Formula for Reform' (1996) XXI *Brook. J. Int'l L.* 605.

[26] Charlesworth, Chinkin and Wright, 'Feminist Approaches to International Law', 622.

[27] See, further, Chapter 3.

[28] See, A. Phillips, *Engendering Democracy* (London: Polity Press, 1991, 1993, and 1997), 70.

[29] See, G. Hedlund, 'Women's Interests in Local Politics', in K. B. Jones and A. G. Jonasdottir (eds.), *The Political Interests of Gender* (London: Sage, 1988), as referred to in Phillips, *Engendering Democracy*, 70.

similar research has been conducted of the female members of the treaty bodies, although it has been argued that having only one female member renders her voice numerically insignificant and thus she is unable to have the same impact as would be achieved by the addition of even just a second female voice, which is discussed further in Chapter 3.

Catharine MacKinnon asserts that '[w]hen men sit in rooms, being states, they are largely being men'.[30] Because of this, she would argue, men do not, and cannot, represent women's interests. Put another way, Natalie Hevener Kaufman and Stefanie Lindquist claim that, when the interpretation of laws is undertaken by men (which, they note, it often is) or by women who have been socialised to accept the male elite's norms and interests as their own, women's lives within the law are constructed from a male-centred perspective.[31] They argue that there is no such thing as an 'objective' application of law or, for that matter, 'gender-neutral' norms, as law-making is a 'socially constructed enterprise'.[32] Concepts such as 'reasonableness' and 'objectivity', for example, as they are applied in law, are coopted by men, consciously or otherwise, to apply to their experiences rather than to those of women.[33] As a result, the search for equal rights may result in 'distorted (from a woman's perspective), yet logically consistent, case outcomes'.[34]

However, men do not act for the advancement of male power and to the disadvantage of women at all times. It is important that we reject such overgeneralisations that men cannot represent, understand, or empathise with the position or concerns of women. To accept this is to endorse old arguments that men, like women, are bound by their sex-determined (or socially constructed) fate. This has been a political view posited by men through the ages to keep women 'in their place', and must be rejected on that basis alone. In fact, there are a number of well-known male feminists whose work is referred to throughout this book.[35] Socio-legal theorists,

---

[30] C. A. MacKinnon, 'Rape, Genocide, and Women's Human Rights' (1994) 17 *Harv. Women's L. J.* 5, at 15.

[31] N. H. Kaufman and S. A. Lindquist, 'Critiquing Gender-Neutral Treaty Language: The Convention on the Elimination of All Forms of Discrimination Against Women', in Peters and Wolper (eds.), *Women's Rights, Human Rights: International Feminist Perspectives*, 116.

[32] *Ibid.*

[33] C. A. MacKinnon, 'Sex and Violence: A Perspective', in E. Hackett and S. Haslanger (eds.), *Theorizing Feminisms: A Reader* (Oxford University Press, 2006) 266, at 267. For further discussion on reasonableness, see Chapter 4.

[34] Kaufman and Lindquist, 'Critiquing Gender-Neutral Treaty Language', 117.

[35] See, e.g., the work of Andrew Byrnes (see Bibliography).

such as Vanessa Munro, note that men are not incapable of adopting the perspectives of women, or at least of striving to understand them better. 'It's just that, for the most part, they have not done so [or been encouraged or socialised to do so].'[36]

Even though goals of formal equality have been generally replaced by those of substantive equality in feminist literature, the former remains an important and continuing objective for women in most areas of daily life. This is not least because to de-emphasise it is to play into the hands of those who advocate against the necessity or benefits of equal membership of women and men on public bodies, which contradicts equal rights protections between men and women guaranteed under international law.[37] But in addition to the formal equal inclusion of women within international institutions, we need to look beyond it to substantive equality. Formal inclusion, while necessary, is not sufficient.

1.2   Inadequate gender expertise

Another relevant factor to ensuring equality within international human rights institutions is the inclusion of delegates and decision-makers who are qualified in or who have previous experience in women's human rights or feminist theory, whether they are women or men. This issue is taken up in Chapter 3. While the formal inclusion of women within mainstream human rights mechanisms has been shown from time to time to have a positive effect on the views expressed by such bodies, much more internalisation of women's rights and gender issues is needed. This is because, while female decision-makers may be able to use their own experiences to identify with and empathise with the situation of other women, this assumes that they share the same or similar experiences, or that women by virtue of their sex 'naturally' have an interest in women's human rights. Neither of these assumptions bears out in reality. A single focus on improving the representation of women on decision-making bodies can also lead to the situation where one of the (or the only) female members of a judicial body is unofficially expected to be responsible for women's issues, and thereby women's rights are sidelined. Instead, women's issues must become the concern of each of the decision-makers. Training, briefings, and procedural guarantees are among a range of methods used to improve judicial decision-making in respect of women's claims, and to

---

[36] V. Munro, *Law and Politics at the Perimeter: Re-Evaluating Key Feminist Debates in Feminist Theory* (Oxford: Hart Publishing, 2007), 12.

[37] Rights to equality and non-discrimination on the basis of sex are discussed further in Chapter 4.

systematise what is currently an ad hoc approach to gender in judicial decision-making, although, as Chapter 3 reveals, even formal procedural measures can be inadequate without constant pressure and monitoring by women's rights organisations.

1.3   Mainstream versus women-specific or sidestream debates

A further variation on this first feminist critique is that, if women's voices are heard, they are heard loudly within women-specific forums, but only as muffled voices within the mainstream. This critique is linked to strategic debates about whether women are better protected by inclusion in mainstream mechanisms or by special procedures. It remains an important debate not least in light of initiatives to reform the UN human rights treaty body system, which is discussed in Chapter 8, but also reform of the 'gender architecture' of the United Nations' system as a whole. Human rights law in particular has been charged with marginalising women's concerns to the 'ghetto'.[38] In the 1990s, for instance, UN women-specific structures were accused of having weaker implementation obligations and procedures, and of being under-resourced.[39] The Committee on the Elimination of Discrimination against Women (the Women's Committee) was considered the 'poor cousin' of its counterparts.[40] Since this view was asserted, however, an Optional Protocol[41] to the CEDAW has come into

---

[38] L. Reanda, 'Human Rights and Women's Rights: The United Nations Approach' (1981) 3 *HRQ* 11; O'Hare, 'Realizing Human Rights for Women'. Cf. A. Byrnes, 'Women, Feminism and International Human Rights Law – Methodological Myopia, Fundamental Flaws or Meaningful Marginalisation?: Some Current Issues' (1992) 12 *Aust. YB Int'l L.* 205, at 218, who argues that the 'ghettoisation' of women's human rights is perhaps too harsh a critique.

[39] See, e.g., Byrnes, 'Women, Feminism and International Human Rights Law', 216–223; N. Burrows, 'International Law and Human Rights: The Case of Women's Rights', in T. Campbell, D. Goldberg, S. McLean and T. Muller (eds.), *Human Rights: From Rhetoric to Reality* (New York: Basil Blackwell, 1986) 8, at 93–95; T. Meron, 'Enhancing the Effectiveness of the Prohibition of Discrimination Against Women' (1990) 84 *Amer. J. Int'l L.* 213; L. Reanda, 'The Commission on the Status of Women', in P. Alston (ed.), *The United Nations and Human Rights: A Critical Appraisal* (Oxford University Press, 1992) 274; A. Byrnes, 'The "Other" Human Rights Treaty Body: The Work of the Committee on the Elimination of Discrimination Against Women' (1989) 14 *Yale J. Int'l L.* 1, at 56–62; J. A. Minor, 'An Analysis of Structural Weaknesses in the Convention on the Elimination of All Forms of Discrimination against Women' (1994–95) 24 *Ga. J. Int'l and Comp. L.* 137, at 148.

[40] Byrnes, 'The "Other" Human Rights Treaty Body', 46.

[41] Optional Protocol to the United Nations Convention on the Elimination of All Forms of Discrimination against Women 2000, GA res. 54/5, UN Doc. A/54/49 (Vol. I) (2000); entered into force 22 December 2000 (OP-CEDAW).

force, allowing women to bring individual complaints to the Women's Committee as well as giving the power to the Committee to carry out fact-finding missions, albeit with the consent of the state party concerned. Despite the recent advent of these new mechanisms, they largely mirror conventional methods attached to many of the mainstream treaties, and the impact of admissibility criteria on women has been little studied. These mechanisms are outlined in more detail in Chapter 3.

It must be acknowledged that some scholars support the view long held by the UN, particularly from the 1970s to the mid-1990s, that a programme of *special* rights, such as women-specific treaties, would solve the problem of women's inequality.[42] Ann Scales, in contrast, cautions against accepting the addition of special rights to the pre-existing system, because it 'presumes we can whip the problem of social inequality by adding yet another prong to the already multi-pronged legal tests'.[43] The UN has now changed its view to the extent that a dual track is pursued that includes women *inside* mainstream institutions (that is gender mainstreaming, as outlined in Chapter 1) as well as maintaining women-specific institutions and programmes. In the 2000s, however, UN reform proposals in relation to the treaty bodies have recommended uniting all the bodies together, as discussed in Chapter 8.[44]

Another change since such critiques were first made is that the Women's Committee has relocated to Geneva and hence is no longer the only human rights treaty-monitoring body located in New York, which had been one source of feminist complaints related to the marginalisation of women's rights.[45] But not all believe moving the Women's Committee to Geneva to be a step in the right direction. Some of the members of the Women's Committee objected to their transfer to Geneva, fearing that the good working relationship they had established within the UN in New York, coupled with extended meeting times, may be lost in any relocation.[46] UN reform initiatives have reignited debate about whether women's human rights are in better hands in mainstream or 'sidestream' (or specialist) mechanisms. These are discussed further in Chapter 8.

[42] See, e.g., M. Etienne, 'Addressing Gender-Based Violence in an International Context' (1995) 18 *Harv. Women's L. J.* 139.

[43] A. C. Scales, 'The Emergence of Feminist Jurisprudence: An Essay' (1986) 95 *Yale L. J.* 1373, at 1382.

[44] UN reform of the treaty bodies is dealt with in Chapter 8.

[45] The relocation occurred in January 2008.

[46] See, H. B. Schöpp-Schilling, 'Treaty Body Reform: the Case of the Committee on the Elimination of Discrimination Against Women' (2007) 7 *Hum. Rts. L. Rev.* 201, at 218–223 (on challenges of servicing/relocating the Women's Committee to Geneva); F. J.

In spite of its early marginalisation to the 'sidestream' of human rights discourse, over time the work of the Women's Committee has filtered into and been heavily influential in the work of the mainstream treaty bodies, as shown throughout this book.

A further aspect of the marginalisation argument is that women-specific treaties have attracted large numbers of reservations that have not been made to the more mainstream instruments. This dichotomy has occurred in part because decisions to ratify the general human rights treaties do not appear to focus primarily on the implications of those treaties for the human rights of women.[47] There is no doubt that reservations to the CEDAW, for example, serve to undermine women's access to human rights protection. The lack of any effective and systematic review of CEDAW reservations reinforces ideas that women are unworthy of international legal protection. It also undermines the universal character of international human rights law. Both the UN Human Rights Committee (HRC), the treaty body that oversees the International Covenant on Civil and Political Rights 1966[48] (ICCPR), as well as the Women's Committee, have asserted their jurisdiction to test whether a reservation is legitimate under international law amid considerable controversy.[49] In addition, many of the reservations to the CEDAW are to the central provisions relating to non-discrimination on the basis of sex, obligations to which many states parties are already bound by virtue of their ratification of other human rights treaties, or under customary international law (discussed further in Chapter 3).

Hampson, 'An Overview of the Reform of the United Nations Human Rights Machinery' (2007) 7 *Hum. Rts. L. Rev.* 7. See, further, Chapter 8.

[47] For more on reservations, see, e.g., S. Mullally, *Gender, Culture and Human Rights: Reclaiming Universalism* (Oxford: Hart Publishing, 2006), Chapter 6; Minor, 'An Analysis of Structural Weaknesses'; R. Cook, 'Reservations to the Convention on the Elimination of All Forms of Discrimination Against Women' (1990) 3 *Va. J. Int'l L.* 642; B. Clark, 'The Vienna Convention Reservations Regime and the Convention on Discrimination Against Women' (1991) 85 *Amer. J. Int'l L.* 281.

[48] International Covenant on Civil and Political Rights 1966, GA res. 2200A (XXI), 16 December 1966, 999 UNTS 171; entered into force 23 March 1976 (ICCPR).

[49] See, HRC, General Comment No. 24: General Comment on Issues relating to Reservations made upon Accession to the Covenant or the Optional Protocols thereto, or in relation to Declarations under Article 41 of the Covenant (1994), UN Doc. CCPR/C/21/Rev.1/Add.6, 2 November 1994. Following the HRC's adoption of this General Comment, the United States expressed its concern in a written communication to the Chairperson of the Committee, letter dated 28 March 1995, UN Doc. A/50/40. The United Kingdom also objected, letter dated 21 July 1995, UN Doc. A/50/40. See, also, CEDAW, General Recommendation No. 4: Reservations to the Convention (1987); CEDAW, General Recommendation No 20: Reservations to the Convention (1992), 20 September 1992.

The very fact of a women-specific instrument has, therefore, allowed states to register backdoor reservations that they have not otherwise made (or been permitted to make) to mainstream treaties. While this does not affect the obligations of states parties under these other treaties, and therefore many of the reservations to the CEDAW are effectively meaningless in law, they nonetheless serve to undermine the political significance of the CEDAW as an instrument for the advancement of women's rights. Siobhán Mullally argues, for example, that reservations seek to limit the transformative potential of international human rights law.[50] She also remarks that the reservations dialogue is highly gendered in so far as the divisions between the public and the private that the CEDAW seeks to overcome are reasserted.[51] In particular, states confer priority on religious or cultural traditions over gender equality, indicating that states define individuals first and foremost as group members.[52] The latter concern sits at the juncture of the universalism/cultural relativism debate, which is discussed below in section 4 of this chapter, 'Essentialised women'.

2 Human rights as 'men's rights'

2.1 Privileging patriarchy

A second general critique of international human rights law is that it privileges the realities of men's lives while it ignores or marginalises those of women. Feminist scholars have argued that international human rights norms were initially articulated[53] and continue to be interpreted and applied to reflect men's experiences while overlooking harms that most commonly or disproportionately affect women.[54] This results from structural rather than mere formal inequality. When I refer to 'structural inequality' within this book, I mean the underlying causes of women's exclusion or marginalisation from human rights mechanisms and the denial of the enjoyment of their rights. These underlying causes include, inter alia, patriarchy, exclusion, and oppression, combined with poverty, harmful or discriminatory cultural and religious practices, and political disenfranchisement.

---

[50] Mullally, *Gender, Culture and Human Rights*, 100.
[51] *Ibid.*, 102.   [52] *Ibid.*, 105.
[53] On the history of women's involvement in the development of international human rights law, see A. S. Fraser, 'Becoming Human: The Origins and Development of Women's Human Rights' (1999) 21 *HRQ* 853.
[54] See, Gallagher, 'Ending the Marginalization'.

As noted above, the liberal or numerical inclusion of women within mainstream institutions is considered an insufficient strategy for the demolition of patriarchy, yet it remains an important target. In many ways, this second critique is a direct attack on the alleged short-sightedness of the liberal feminists of the first critique as regards their failure to deal with the structural causes of women's exclusion. These two critiques are, however, interconnected to the extent that equal and fair representation of women within mainstream human rights mechanisms can, and has been shown to, affect the interpretation and application of laws to women and, in this way, to deal with one of the causes of structural inequality.

Broadly speaking, feminist scholars argue that international human rights law is conceived as a set of 'male' rights.[55] By 'male' rights, feminists mean that rights are 'defined by the criterion of what men fear will happen to them';[56] that the content of the rules of international law privilege men and fail to acknowledge, or otherwise marginalise or silence, women's interests;[57] and that the very choice and categorisation of subject matter deemed appropriate for international regulation reflects male priorities.[58] In this way, the system of international law is said to be a 'thoroughly gendered [or sexist] system'.[59] As an example of this gendered discourse, feminist scholars routinely refer to the definition of 'torture' in the Convention against Torture and Other Cruel, Inhuman or Degrading Treatment or Punishment 1984[60] (UNCAT). This is because the definition

---

[55] See, e.g., R. Eisler, 'Human Rights: Toward an Integrated Theory for Action' (1987) 9 *HRQ* 287; C. Bunch, 'Women's Rights as Human Rights: Toward a Re-Vision of Human Rights' (1990) 12 *HRQ* 486; Charlesworth, Chinkin and Wright, 'Feminist Approaches to International Law'; R. J. Cook, 'Women's International Human Rights Law: The Way Forward' (1993) 15 *HRQ* 230; H. Charlesworth and C. Chinkin, 'The Gender of *Jus Cogens*' (1993) 15 *HRQ* 63; H. Charlesworth, 'Human Rights as Men's Rights', in Peters and Wolper (eds.), *Women's Rights, Human Rights: International Feminist Perspectives*, 103; G. Binion, 'Human Rights: A Feminist Perspective' (1995) 17 *HRQ* 509, at 514.

[56] Charlesworth, Chinkin and Wright, 'Feminist Approaches to International Law', 628–630; Charlesworth and Chinkin, 'The Gender of *Jus Cogens*'; C. Bunch, 'Transforming Human Rights from a Feminist Perspective', in Peters and Wolper (eds.), *Women's Rights, Human Rights: International Feminist Perspectives*, 11, at 13.

[57] Charlesworth, Chinkin and Wright, 'Feminist Approaches to International Law', 614–615.

[58] Charlesworth and Chinkin, *The Boundaries of International Law*, 18.

[59] *Ibid.*

[60] Article 1, United Nations Convention against Torture and Other Cruel, Inhumane or Degrading Treatment or Punishment 1984, GA res. 39/46, 10 December 1984, 1465 UNTS 85; entered into force 26 June 1987 (UNCAT).

under this instrument prioritises violence perpetrated within the context of state custody, a form of harm more typically meted out against men than women.[61] Whether this is still a valid critique in relation to torture is explored in Chapter 5. MacKinnon sums up this view as follows: 'Human rights have not been women's rights – not in theory or in reality, not legally or socially, not domestically or internationally.'[62]

2.2   Standardising 'men' under international law

Furthermore, feminist theory criticises international human rights law for adopting the 'male' sex as the standard against which all individuals are judged. Women, in turn, become the deviation from this standard.[63] Meanwhile, governments accept and promote this perspective as the rule of law.[64] It is clear that many apparently non-gender-specific (or so-called gender neutral) principles of human rights law are in fact quite specific in their relevance and application to men's lives.[65] Kathleen Mahoney asserts that male hegemony over public life and institutions meant that rights came to be defined by men.[66] These arguments, while valid in many contexts, nevertheless rest on dichotomous gendered understandings of the roles of men and women respectively, overlook women who do not conform to those roles, and accept that it is possible to speak for and about women collectively, discussed further below under 4 'Essentialised women'.

2.3   Trouble defining 'women's human rights'

These views provoke a series of questions, such as: What are women's rights? What are women's experiences, concerns, and interests? What do feminists mean when they refer to them?

---

[61]   Charlesworth, Chinkin and Wright, 'Feminist Approaches to International Law', 628.

[62]   MacKinnon, 'Rape, Genocide, and Women's Human Rights', 5.

[63]   See, e.g., C. A. Littleton, 'Equality and Feminist Legal Theory' (1987) 48 *U. Pitt. L. Rev.* 1043, 1050–1052; N. Naffine, 'Sexing the Subject (of Law)', in M. Thornton (ed.), *Public and Private: Feminist Legal Debates* (Melbourne: Oxford University Press, 1995) 18, at 24–25; S. L. Bem, *The Lenses of Gender* (New Haven, CT: Yale University Press, 1993), 2; C. Gould, 'The Woman Question: Philosophy of Liberation and the Liberation of Philosophy', in C. Gould and M. W. Wartofsky (eds.), *Women and Philosophy: Toward A Theory of Liberation* (New York: Putnam, 1976) 1, at 5–6.

[64]   Hernández-Truyol, 'Women's Rights as Human Rights', 651.

[65]   H. Charlesworth, 'General Introduction', in Askin and Koenig (eds.), *Women and International Human Rights Law*, Vol. 1, xix, xx. See, also, Byrnes, 'Women, Feminism and International Human Rights Law'.

[66]   Mahoney, 'Theoretical Perspectives on Women's Human Rights'.

Many feminists fail to respond to these basic questions or simply fail to identify concerns that are specific to women. In arguing that the 'male' conception of human rights law has led to the omission from mainstream human rights instruments of a number of fundamental rights relevant to women, Anne Gallagher refers to underdevelopment, extreme poverty, illiteracy, gender segregation, and lack of reproductive choice as being among the missing issues.[67] Other writers, too, have argued that international human rights law has ignored or belittled such violations as forced childbirth, sexual slavery, rape, genital mutilation, female infanticide, domestic violence, sexual harassment,[68] gender-based violence, reproductive freedom, education, the right to vote, economic policies, and structural adjustment programmes.[69] Apparently neutral principles of international law, such as the principle of self-determination, have also been held to exacerbate the inferior position of women,[70] which in turn puts women at risk of violence. Even though many of these issues, such as underdevelopment, poverty, economic policies, education, and illiteracy, affect men as well as women, they remain of particular relevance to women in many societies worldwide as women experience these deprivations of rights in different ways, for different reasons, or to different degrees.

Since the introduction of the UN's policy on gender mainstreaming, there has been a shift away from merely producing lists of women's concerns, to applying so-called gendered techniques to evaluate the impact of particular policies and programmes on women and men respectively. This approach means that, if implemented, one should be able to determine the particular effect of all human rights laws, policies, and programmes on women and their communities, and to guard against the negative or unintended consequences of them. In some ways, it represents a shift away from formal to substantive equality, or from a paradigm focused on equality of opportunity to one of equality of result.

The inability to conceptualise women's rights in the mainstream is also levelled against women-specific instruments. According to Noreen Burrows, 'women's rights [as articulated in international human rights law] are not ... rights which are specific to women, but are rather

---

[67] Gallagher, 'Ending the Marginalization', 290–291.
[68] E. Broadbent, 'Getting Rid of Male Bias', in J. Kerr (ed.), *Ours By Right: Women's Rights as Human Rights* (London: North-South Institute, 1993), 10.
[69] Hernández-Truyol, 'Women's Rights as Human Rights', 610.
[70] See, e.g., K. Knop, *Diversity and Self-Determination in International Law* (Cambridge University Press, 2002).

universally recognised rights held by all people by virtue of their common humanity and regardless of their sex'.[71] She states that it is misleading to speak of women's rights, because there has been no attempt to define the exact sphere of women's rights or to enumerate those rights that might be said to be peculiar to women.[72] Andrew Byrnes finds that it is not always possible to distinguish between women's rights and general human rights anyway,[73] although he argues that the main model applied by the UN to define human rights has been 'a largely androcentric one'.[74] Even the CEDAW has faced criticism for not recognising or protecting rights that are specific to women's 'gendered experience and corporeality'.[75] Nonetheless, apart from rights relating to pregnancy, reproduction, and the consequences of childbirth, which are included to some degree in mainstream as well as women-specific treaties,[76] all other rights are relevant to both women and men, albeit to different degrees in different contexts. The real difficulty of defining the corpus of women's rights is that issues of concern to women can broadly be linked to manifestations of unequal power relations or patriarchy, and to gender inequality, which can vary between societies, cultures, and over time. Thus, any attempt to list women's rights is fraught with difficulties, including the real possibility of overlooking areas of disadvantage that have yet to be considered.

Feminist scholars have not only pointed to a number of omissions to argue that human rights law has failed women,[77] but they argue further that existing provisions have neither been recognised as relevant to women nor interpreted to reflect women's experiences. That is, they argue that the operation of human rights law, in structure, process, and substantive

---

[71] Burrows, 'International Law and Human Rights', 82.

[72] *Ibid.*, 80.

[73] Byrnes, 'Using International Human Rights Law', 82.

[74] Byrnes, 'Women, Feminism and International Human Rights Law', 224.

[75] D. Otto, 'A Post-Beijing Reflection on the Limitations and Potential of Human Rights Discourse for Women', in Askin and Koenig (eds.), *Women and International Human Rights Law*, Vol. 1, 115, at 120.

[76] E.g. Article 10(2), International Covenant on Economic, Social and Cultural Rights 1966, GA res. 2200A (XXI), 16 December 1966, 993 UNTS 3; entered into force 3 January 1976 (ICESCR) (provides for special protection for mothers during and after childbirth); Article 12, CEDAW (non-discrimination in relation to health care, including access to family planning, etc.).

[77] E.g., a right to nationality was included in the UDHR but it was not transferred to the ICCPR except in relation to a right to a nationality for children and this has caused many problems for women: see, C. Chinkin and K. Knop, *Final Report on Women's Equality and Nationality in International Law* (International Law Association, Committee on Feminism and International Law, 2000). Similarly, explicit mention of reproductive health is missing from the ICESCR.

content, excludes women's concerns and experiences. One way this occurs is through a balancing of 'competing' rights by decision-making bodies, which reduces women's power.[78] At the level of international law, this is played out in the balancing between, for example, rights to equality before the law and freedom of religion, which is ultimately decided by men for women. Another example would include the competing rights to liberty versus privacy in the context of marital rape and domestic violence. Some regional human rights instruments, for example, assert the inviolability of the right to privacy, thus trumping privacy over women's safety.[79] Charlesworth, Chinkin, and Wright have argued that particular rights, such as the right to freedom of religion or to the protection of the family, can in fact justify the oppression of women.[80] The proliferation of rights, which has occurred markedly at the level of international law, may further lead to increased competition, political divisiveness, and weaker rights claims.[81]

Despite statements to the contrary by UN governing bodies,[82] the human rights system is legally hierarchical in the sense that not all rights are of equal legal value. There are many layers of rights, from those that are non-derogable to those that are absolute, limited, accessory, or qualified.[83] Charlesworth and Chinkin argue that in this hierarchy, women's rights have not achieved the same level of protection or symbolic labelling as other rights.[84] They have highlighted the very abstract and formal

---

[78] C. Smart, *Feminism and the Power of Law* (London: Routledge, 1989), 138.

[79] See, F. Banda, *Women, Law and Human Rights: An African Perspective* (Oxford: Hart Publishing, 2005) (e.g., for discussion on human rights instruments adopted by the League of Arab States).

[80] Charlesworth, Chinkin and Wright, 'Feminist Approaches to International Law', 635–638. See, also, D. Arzt, 'The Application of International Human Rights Law in Islamic States' (1990) 12 *HRQ* 202, at 204.

[81] Ronald Dworkin refers to this as 'rights as trumps' in R. M. Dworkin, *Taking Rights Seriously* (Cambridge, MA: Harvard University Press, 1977); R. M. Dworkin, *A Matter of Principle* (Cambridge, MA: Harvard University Press, 1981), referred to in Lacey, 'Feminist Legal Theory and the Rights of Women', 39.

[82] See, particularly, Vienna Declaration and Programme of Action, 5: 'All human rights are universal, indivisible and interdependent and interrelated. The international community must treat human rights globally in a fair and equal manner, on the same footing, and with the same emphasis. While the significance of national and regional particularities and various historical, cultural and religious backgrounds must be borne in mind, it is the duty of States, regardless of their political, economic and cultural systems, to promote and protect all human rights and fundamental freedoms.'

[83] See, further, T. Meron, *Human Rights in Internal Strife: Their International Protection* (Cambridge: Grotius, 1987), 43–70.

[84] Charlesworth and Chinkin, 'The Gender of *Jus Cogens*', 75.

development of *jus cogens* as reflecting the prized 'masculine' form of reasoning. *Jus cogens* is seen as giving privileged status to specific norms, which in themselves largely reflect a male perspective.[85] Ranking rights according to their importance is also at play in the concepts of derogability in times of public emergency,[86] the failure to recognise the justiciability of specific types of rights,[87] and ideas of immediate versus progressive implementation.[88] Equality and non-discrimination provisions, although considered central tenets of international human rights law, have been especially criticised by feminist scholars (see Chapter 4).

2.4   Double standards

International human rights law is further criticised as imposing double standards. Rachael Johnstone asserts that, in practice, sex discrimination is tolerated by the international community in ways that simply would not be accepted if the distinctions were made on grounds of race.[89] Race relations in many countries have been historically fought on male terms, and rights achieved by black men, for example, have not always been extended to women – whether white or black. Racial factors were a prominent, if not a defining element in the slavery context,[90] while the gender dimensions of the practice were largely absent. In fact, some defenders of slavery, in seeking to justify it, analogised slaves to the position of women and children.[91] In critiquing the development of equality guarantees under

---

[85] *Ibid.*, 67.

[86] These issues are further discussed in relation to specific rights in later chapters of this book.

[87] The initial failure to agree an Optional Protocol to the ICESCR, for example, was based on the belief that economic, social, and cultural rights are non-justiciable. For more, see Chapter 3.

[88] For example, early views of states parties and the treaty bodies that ICCPR rights are 'immediately enforceable' and ICESCR rights are 'to be realised progressively'. It is now clear that some rights of the ICESCR are immediately enforceable (e.g. non-discrimination): see, CESCR, General Comment No. 16: The Equal Right of Men and Women to the Enjoyment of All Economic, Social and Cultural Rights (Article 3) (2004), UN Doc. E/C.12/2005/3, para. 3.

[89] Johnstone, 'Feminist Influences on the United Nations Human Rights Treaty Bodies', 151.

[90] T. Obokata, *Trafficking of Human Beings from a Human Rights Perspective: Towards a Holistic Approach* (Leiden: Martinus Nijhoff Publishers, 2006), 11.

[91] In 1850 George Fitzhugh, one of the foremost defenders of slavery in the United States, analogised slavery to the position of women and children: G. Fitzhugh, 'Slavery Justified by a Southerner', in E. McKitrick, *Slavery Defended* (1963), 37–38, as referred to in P. Murray, 'The Negro Woman's Stake in the Equal Rights Amendment' (1970–1971) 6 *Harv. C.R. – C. L. L. Rev.* 253, at 257. Cf., in 1944 a North Carolina Supreme Court judge

international law, Charlesworth, too, argues that international law has developed a hierarchy of forms of discrimination in which race discrimination is considered more serious than other forms.[92]

2.5   Universality versus cultural relativity

Likewise, cultural relativity arguments that justify cultural practices in conflict with universal human rights standards are frequently made by governments in relation to women's rights, when these same arguments would not be tolerated against non-gender-specific rights. This is partly explained by the view that women's rights (and women) are seen as the preserve of patriarchal cultures. 'Women are the bearers of culture not just in the clichéd senses that they socialize children or (some believe) embody the gentler aspirations of each civilization, but in the more fundamental sense that groups of people define their identities – what makes them different – in large part through the statuses and roles that they ascribe to women.'[93] The question of culture has come to dominate feminist discourse in the late 1990s to the 2000s, with one effect being a number of direct challenges to many foundational feminist principles, such as shared oppression and patriarchy (discussed further at 4 'Essentialised women').[94]

2.6   'Mere' formal equality versus structural equality

International human rights law is further criticised for largely being unable to give due weight to structural explanations for the universal subordination of women, owing to its focus on individual rights.[95] Elizabeth Gross argues that 'rights discourse overly simplifies complex power

---

noted 'the barbarous view of the inferiority of women which manifested itself in civil and political oppression so akin to slavery that we can find no adequate word to describe her present status with men except emancipation'. See, *State* v. *Emery*, 224 N.C. 581, 31 S.E. 2d. 858, 868 (1944) (Seawell, J. dissenting), cited in Murray, 'The Negro Woman's Stake in the Equal Rights Amendment', 253, at 257.

[92] H. Charlesworth, 'Concepts of Equality in International Law', in G. Huscroft and P. Rishworth (eds.), *Litigating Rights: Perspectives from Domestic and International Law* (Oxford: Hart Publishing, 2002) 137, at 143–147.

[93] A. J. Nathan, 'Universalism: A Particularistic Account', in L. S. Bell, A. J. Nathan and I. Peleg (eds.), *Negotiating Culture and Human Rights* (New York: Columbia University Press, 2001) 249, at 356. See, also, Y. Ertück, 'The Due Diligence Standard: What Does It Entail for Women's Human Rights?', in C. Benninger-Budel (ed.), *Due Diligence and its Application to Protect Women from Violence* (Leiden and Boston: Martinus Nijhoff Publishers, 2008) 27, at 34.

[94] For an overview of 'The Culture Question,' see Engle, 'International Human Rights and Feminisms', 57–58.

[95] Bunch, 'Women's Rights as Human Rights', 491.

relations and their promise is constantly thwarted by structural inequalities in power'.[96] Along these same lines, Anne Orford argues that human rights institutions have refused to acknowledge the links, for example, between women's human rights and militarism, economic liberalisation, and globalisation;[97] while Chinkin identifies economic restructuring and poverty as related, yet forgotten, links to women's rights.[98] In favour of the collective over the individual, some feminist scholars theorise that 'in one sense rape [and other forms of violence against women] is never truly individual but is an integral part of the system of ensuring the maintenance of the subordination of women'.[99] Nonetheless, although power inequality may account for a climate in which rape is perpetrated and for impunity for it in law, victims still feel individually aggrieved and are entitled to individual redress.[100] Pursuing collective forms of redress overlooks gendered power relations within those collective systems, as well as questions of who is making the decisions and on whose behalf.

2.7   Prioritisation of civil and political rights over economic, social, and cultural rights

Part of this wider critique of the irrelevance of human rights norms to women is the primacy that the international community bestows on civil and political rights over economic, social, and cultural rights. Feminist scholars argue that this operates to the disadvantage of women. In part this is because the dominance of civil and political rights has entailed a preoccupation with constraints on the power of the state rather than an emphasis on its affirmative duties to ensure rights.[101] This division, with its origins rooted in historical power struggles between the East

---

[96] E. Gross, 'What is Feminist Theory?', in C. Pateman and E. Gross (eds.), *Feminist Challenges: Social and Political Theory* (Sydney: Allen & Unwin, 1986) 190, at 192.

[97] A. Orford, 'Contesting Globalization: A Feminist Perspective on the Future of Human Rights', in B. H. Weston and S. P. Marks (eds.), *The Future of International Human Rights* (Ardsley, NY: Transnational Publishers, 1999) 157, at 179.

[98] C. Chinkin, 'Feminist Interventions into International Law' (1997) 19 *Adel. L. R.* 13.

[99] J. G. Gardam, 'The Law of Armed Conflict: A Gendered Regime?', in D. G. Dallmeyer (ed.), *Reconceiving Reality: Women and International Law* (American Society of International Law, 1993) 171, at 174.

[100] See, various authors in R. Rubio-Marín (ed.), *What Happened to the Women? Gender and Reparations for Human Rights Violations* (New York: Social Science Research Council, 2006). See, also, A. Saris and K. Lofts, 'Reparation Programmes: A Gendered Perspective', in C. Ferstman, M. Goetz and A. Stephens (eds.), *Reparations for Victims of Genocide, War Crimes and Crimes against Humanity: Systems in Place and Systems in the Making* (The Hague: Martinus Nijhoff Press, 2009) 79.

[101] Sullivan, 'The Public/Private Distinction in International Human Rights Law', 127.

and the West[102] rather than in gender divisions,[103] is nonetheless said to reinforce a gendered discourse on human rights.[104] While feminist writers generally acknowledge that the civil and political rights of women should be fully protected, they argue that these are not the harms from which women most need protection.[105] In other words, many of the violations perpetrated against women are bound up with the disadvantages they suffer in the economic and social fields.[106] A more hardline stance is that of Charlesworth, Chinkin, and Wright, who wrote in their 1991 article that civil and political rights 'may have very little to offer women generally' as the 'major forms of oppression of women operate within the economic, social and cultural realms'.[107]

Furthermore, some feminists argue that the extent to which the debate on violence against women is located within the civil and political rights paradigm and outside the economic, social, and cultural rights framework limits possibilities for transformation.[108] In fact, the distinction between these two categories or 'generations' of rights makes it difficult to develop comprehensive solutions. If violence against women, for example, is viewed in isolation of its underlying causes, such as women's economic

---

[102] See, e.g., K. Vasak, 'Pour une Troisième Génération des Droits de l'Homme', in C. Swinarski (ed.), *Etudes et Essais sur le Droit International Humanitaire et sur les Principes de la Croix-Rouge* (The Hague: Martinus Nijhoff, 1984) 837, at 837; D. J. Harris, *Cases and Materials on International Law* (5th edn, London: Sweet & Maxwell, 1998), 625; D. H. Ott, *Public International Law in the Modern World* (London: Pitman Publishing, 1987), 239; Y. Yokota, 'Reflections on the Future of Economic, Social and Cultural Rights', in B. H. Weston and S. P. Marks (eds.), *The Future of International Human Rights* (New York: Transnational Publishers, 1999), 201.

[103] In fact, the early work of the UN Commission on the Status of Women (CSW) focused on the political rights of women, see UN CSW, *Short History on the Commission on the Status of Women*, 5, available at: www.un.org/womenwatch/daw/CSW60YRS/ CSWbriefhistory.pdf (last accessed 25 October 2008).

[104] Charlesworth, Chinkin and Wright, 'Feminist Approaches to International Law'. Other critiques focus on the emphasis given to civil and political rights over economic, social, and cultural rights: see, B. Stark, 'The International Covenant on Economic, Social and Cultural Rights as a Resource for Women', in Askin and Koenig (eds.), *Women and International Human Rights Law*, Vol. 2, 209.

[105] See, e.g. C. Chinkin, 'Strategies to Combat Discrimination against Women', in M. O'Flaherty and G. Gisvold (eds.), *Post-War Protection of Human Rights in Bosnia and Herzegovina* (The Hague: Kluwer Law International, 1988) 173; Gallagher, 'Ending the Marginalization'; C. Romany, 'Women as Aliens: A Feminist Critique of the Public/Private Distinction in International Human Rights Law' (1993) 6 *Harv. Hum. Rts. J.* 87.

[106] Byrnes, 'Women, Feminism and International Human Rights Law', 222.

[107] Charlesworth, Chinkin and Wright, 'Feminist Approaches to International Law', 635.

[108] Chinkin, 'Feminist Interventions into International Law'.

or educational disadvantage, then a rights-based approach will have limited effect. On the other hand, broad policy solutions do not remove the need or desire of individual victims of violence to be able to assert their rights within an international judicial system that outlaws individual crimes and offers individual means of redress. It may be clichéd, yet it is no less true, that women need civil and political empowerment in order to articulate their economic, social, or cultural grievances. Similarly, economic independence can enhance opportunities to assert legal rights, noting in particular the financial cost of justice. As Amartya Sen has argued – political rights are important because they can fulfil needs as well as the formulation of what those needs are.[109]

Furthermore, for the purposes of individual litigation, it is a far more difficult proposition to trace the cause of violence against women to economic inequality, rather than asserting that the violence caused physical, sexual, or psychological harm to the woman (what would typically fall within the civil rights field). In fact, as this book attests in later chapters, requiring female litigants to link the harm they suffer to structural causes of inequality adds an additional layer to their claims, one that is not applied to men, and thus it amounts to the unequal treatment of women under international law. This is not to suggest in any way that root causes are not critical to strategies to eradicate violence against women, nor economic empowerment; rather it is to note that both the collective and the individual routes to change ought to be pursued.

2.8   Dominance of masculine language, individualism, and abstract justice

An additional factor that excludes women from mainstream human rights is the choice of language within international instruments and discourse. Feminists commonly see language as supporting the exclusion of women from the scope of protection offered by human rights law. The constant use of masculine vocabulary, it is argued, operates at both a direct and subtle level to exclude women.[110] In addition, such language is said to 'reinforce hierarchies based on sex and gender, even if it is intended to be generic'.[111] Dale Spender argues that both language and material resources have been used by the dominant group to structure women's

---

[109] A. Sen, 'Freedom and Needs' (1994) 10 and 17 *New Republic* 31.
[110] H. Charlesworth, 'What are "Women's International Human Rights"?', in Cook (ed.), *Human Rights of Women: National and International Perspectives*, 58, at 68.
[111] Charlesworth, Chinkin and Wright, 'Feminist Approaches to International Law', 628.

oppression.[112] In particular, feminists point to the use of the masculine pronoun throughout international human rights instruments as creating a situation in which '[a] man is sure that he is included; a woman is uncertain'.[113] Of the eight core human rights treaties in force, only four utilise the feminine pronoun (including the CEDAW).[114] However, while acknowledging the deep-seated problems of masculine terminology in mainstream human rights treaties and the way it can play into the exclusionary culture of human rights institutions, it should not be overstated. Such language is surrounded by provisions on non-discrimination on the basis of sex and equality of rights between women and men (notably with their own set of challenges as outlined in Chapter 4).

More problematic than the prevalence of the masculine pronoun in human rights treaties is the meaning given to substantive norms, such as torture and the right to life, which are discussed in Chapters 5 and 6.

More conservative feminists have asserted that rights language is 'fundamentally adversarial and negative', whereas they claim that '[f]eminists seek a framework that emphasizes positive values such as helping, cooperating and acting out of love, friendship or relatedness, as well as fairness'.[115] These views very much conform to the work of Carol Gilligan who, writing from a psychosocial perspective, asserted that the search for universal, abstract, hierarchical standards is more a masculine than feminine mode of thinking.[116] Her work was heavily influential in getting feminism to celebrate differences between women and men. Feminists then asserted that women's so-called 'ethic of care' identified by Gilligan should be added to men's 'ethic of justice' in order to bring about substantial reforms of justice. It led to arguments that legal institutions are

---

[112] See, D. Spender, *Man Made Language* (2nd edn, London: Pandora, 2001).

[113] H. Bequaert Holmes, 'A Feminist Analysis of the Universal Declaration of Human Rights', in C. Gould (ed.), *Beyond Domination: New Perspectives on Women and Philosophy* (Totowa, NJ: Rowman & Allanheld, 1983) 250, at 259.

[114] See, the CEDAW; United Nations Convention on the Rights of the Child 1989, GA res. 44/25, 20 November 1989, 1577 UNTS 3; entered into force 2 September 1990 (CRC); International Convention on the Protection of the Rights of All Migrant Workers and Members of Their Families 1990, GA res. 45/148, 18 December 1990, 2220 UNTS 93; entered into force 1 July 2003 (IMWC); and the United Nations Convention on the Rights of Persons with Disabilities 2006, GA res. 61/106, 13 December 2006; entered into force 3 May 2008 (ICRPD).

[115] H. Bequaert Holmes and S. R. Petersen, 'Rights Over One's Own Body: A Woman-Affirming Health Care Policy' (1981) 3 *HRQ* 71, at 73. See, also, as the starting point of such discourse: C. Gilligan, *In a Different Voice: Psychological Theory and Women's Development* (Cambridge, MA: Harvard University Press, 1982), 25–51.

[116] Gilligan, *In a Different Voice*, 25–51.

hierarchical, adversarial, and exclusionary.[117] MacKinnon, for example, asserts that '[a] key mechanism for the institutionalisation of this male power is the law's claim to gender-neutrality and objectivity, epitomised in the appeal to abstract rights'.[118] Scales, too, cautions that '[w]e should be especially wary when we hear lawyers, addicted to cognitive objectivity as they are, assert that women's voices have a place in the existing system'.[119]

Such views, however, overgeneralise the differences between women and men, and ignore entirely differences *between* women; and suggest, too, that law (one of the primary pillars of society and the pursuit of justice) is irrelevant to them anyway. Such arguments must be resisted. A variation on this theme is that of Rachel West who criticises the individual as the subject of international human rights law as alienating to women whose experiences and concerns are 'not easily translated into the narrow, individualistic, language of rights'.[120] Again, there are counterpositions to these views as well, not least that women were among the first users of the human rights treaty body complaints system, indicating the usefulness of the individual rights approach.[121]

At the national level, legal actors are viewed as abstract and socially detached entities, and the legal system is seen as decontextualised, generalised, and conflict-driven.[122] As a second-tier legal system, international law becomes an even more abstract and remote form of justice, with access being granted only after the exhaustion of domestic remedies and fulfilment of the panoply of other criteria.[123] Nonetheless, the international human rights system, with its range of legal, quasi-legal, and non-legal mechanisms, holds out greater promise of being able to take account of particularity, cooperation, and context than many domestic legal systems that are very much centred on litigious processes. At the international level there have been many attempts at new and innovative approaches to questions of justice, especially in the aftermath of armed conflict, in which truth and reconciliation commissions have replaced in some contexts, or

[117] See, Scales, 'The Emergence of Feminist Jurisprudence'; Smart, *Feminism and the Power of Law*.
[118] MacKinnon, 'Feminism, Marxism, Method and the State', 658.
[119] Scales, 'The Emergence of Feminist Jurisprudence', 1382.
[120] R. West, 'Feminism, Critical Social Theory and Law' (1989) *Uni. Chicago Legal F.* 59, at 59.
[121] See, Chapter 3.
[122] See, I. M. Young, *Justice and the Politics of Difference* (Princeton University Press, 1990), 101; Munro, *Law and Politics at the Perimeter*, 46–47.
[123] For an overview of these criteria see, Chapter 3.

operated alongside in others, liberal legal redress mechanisms.[124] It is not clear, though, that such mechanisms have satisfied victims' calls for justice in all contexts, including those of women.[125] Moreover, the abstraction of rights is not simply a woman question but affects all disempowered persons. A further component of this criticism is that rights have historically been represented by residual liberties protected by negative freedom rather than the positive definition of rights and interests.[126]

While acknowledging that there has been some broader use of women-inclusive language in international instruments more recently, in particular through 'gender mainstreaming' efforts, the language has been seen as untransformative, resulting in little change on the ground. Chinkin argues that '[a]ll this activity has not really challenged the gendered assumptions about the structures of global political and economic power, nor [sic] of the construction of knowledge in the rapidly changing environment of international law'.[127] The best that has been achieved is an 'add women and stir' approach that does not demand any radical rethinking of programmes or gender awareness.[128] In a similar way, Charlesworth is sceptical of the UN's efforts at gender mainstreaming.[129] Nonetheless, in spite of these and other reservations, both Charlesworth and Chinkin concede that rights discourse offers a 'recognised vocabulary to frame political and social wrongs', 'an empowering function' to women, and a 'focus for international feminism that can translate into action'.[130] Despite criticisms of human rights, most feminists agree that rights language ought not to be abandoned entirely.[131]

3   The public/private dichotomy

A third major feminist critique of the international system is the distinction drawn between the public and private spheres of everyday life for the

---

[124] See, Rubio-Marín (eds.), *What Happened to the Women?*

[125] *Ibid.*

[126] Lacey, 'Feminist Legal Theory and the Rights of Women', 38.

[127] Chinkin, 'Feminist Interventions into International Law', 26.

[128] *Ibid.*, 26.

[129] See, H. Charlesworth, 'Not Waving but Drowning: Gender Mainstreaming and Human Rights in the United Nations' (2005) 18 *Harv. Hum. Rts. J.* 1.

[130] Charlesworth and Chinkin, *The Boundaries of International Law*, 210–211. See, also, M. Minow, 'Interpreting Rights: An Essay for Robert Cover' (1987) 96 *Yale L. J.* 1860, 1910.

[131] Charlesworth, 'What are "Women's International Human Rights"?', 61; Minow, 'Interpreting Rights, 1910; P. J. Williams, 'Alchemical Notes: Reconstructing Ideals from Deconstructed Rights' (1987) 22 *Harv. C.R-C.L. Rev.* 401, at 431; P. J. Williams, *The Alchemy of Race and Rights* (Cambridge, MA: Harvard University Press, 1991), 159.

purposes of international legal rules. The argument is that international law privileges the public sphere of life and thereby refuses to recognise the 'specificity of the female life in the private sphere'.[132] The public sphere has been consistently represented as the sphere of 'rationality, culture and intellectual endeavour', as compared with the domestic sphere being one of 'nature, nurture, and non-rationality'.[133] Margaret Thornton puts it this way: 'The public sphere, mediated through law, has enabled bench-mark men to construct normativity, like God, in their own image.'[134] This so-called public/private dichotomy is said to be the source of women's exclusion from international law, in particular because it is manifest in the theory of state responsibility for human rights abuses.[135] The boundaries between the 'public' and the 'private' and the allocation of men and women thereto, are 'deeply political and inherently constructed'.[136] Ursula O'Hare refers to this poignantly as the 'gendered fault-line'.[137]

Given the historical state-based nature of international law, the primary subject of international law remains the state.[138] International human rights law, in contrast, is an exception to the horizontal application of international law as governing relations between states, and introduced a quasi-vertical system of state responsibility for individual rights. Nonetheless, the system has focused almost exclusively on state action directed against individuals, rather than on so-called 'private' attacks against women in their homes or in other private settings. In fact, some argue that the framework of civil and political rights is structured so as to safeguard activities in the private sphere (for example through the right to privacy)[139] or that accepting statehood and sovereignty as fundamental

---

[132] Naffine, 'Sexing the Subject (of Law)', 20 and 32.

[133] M. Thornton, 'The Cartography of Public and Private', in M. Thornton (ed.), *Public and Private: Feminist Legal Debates* (Melbourne: Oxford University Press, 1995), 2, at 11–12.

[134] *Ibid.*, 13.

[135] O'Hare, 'Realizing Human Rights for Women', 368.

[136] Munro, *Law and Politics at the Perimeter*, 13. See, also, Sullivan, 'The Public/Private Distinction in International Human Rights Law', 126, 134 ('an inherently political process').

[137] O'Hare, 'Realizing Human Rights for Women', 368.

[138] Of course non-state actors often play a role under various components of international law, not least in relation to non-state armed groups and international humanitarian law. For more on non-state actors and international law, see, A. Clapham, *Human Rights Obligations of Non-State Actors* (Oxford University Press, 2006).

[139] See, e.g., C. A. MacKinnon, *Feminism Unmodified: Discourses on Life and Law* (Cambridge, MA: Harvard University Press, 1987); Charlesworth, Chinkin and Wright, 'Feminist Approaches to International Law', 625–628.

components of the international legal order 'narrows our imaginative universe and the possibilities for reconstruction'.[140] Furthermore, the male-gendered conception of the public world as 'superior' to the private creates a 'hierarchy of oppressions' in which men fear oppression from the state whereas women fear oppression by men in the private world.[141] According to Rhonda Copelon, this dichotomy explains the 'persistent trivialisation of violations against women'.[142]

On a practical level, the effect of distinguishing between the public and the private has 'rendered invisible', or at least less important, the many violations that women suffer in private.[143] Excluding issues of violence against women from the international human rights agenda arose from a failure to see the oppression of women as political.[144] In this way, it leaves the private or family realm, where the majority of women spend the bulk of their lives, unregulated, unprotected, and susceptible to abuse.[145] Many violent acts committed against women at the hands of men occur prior to or without direct state involvement.[146] At the domestic level, for example, women have trouble convincing law enforcement officials that violent acts within the home are criminal.[147] At the international level this is translated into difficulties women face in convincing the international community that domestic violence is of international, in addition to national, concern.[148] Kenneth Roth associates such difficulties with an early view of human rights guarantees, especially those under the ICCPR, that they applied to victims only of politically motivated abuse, and even then only

---

[140] H. Charlesworth, 'Alienating Oscar? Feminist Analysis of International Law', in D. G. Dallmeyer (ed.), *Reconceiving Reality: Women and International Law* (American Society of International Law, 1993) 1.

[141] F. E. Olsen, 'The Family and the Market: A Study of Ideology and Legal Reform' (1983) 96 *Harv. L. Rev.* 1497.

[142] R. Copelon, 'Recognizing the Egregious in the Everyday: Domestic Violence as Torture' (1994) 25 *Colum. Hum. Rts. L. Rev.* 291, at 295–296.

[143] Gallagher, 'Ending the Marginalization', 290; Binion, 'Human Rights: A Feminist Perspective', 515–516; Romany, 'State Responsibility Goes Private', 85; Romany, 'Women as Aliens', 87.

[144] Bunch, 'Transforming Human Rights from a Feminist Perspective', 14.

[145] Bunch, 'Women's Rights as Human Rights'; H. Charlesworth, 'The Mid-Life Crisis of the Universal Declaration of Human Rights' (1998) 55 *Wash. & Lee L. Rev.* 781.

[146] C. A. MacKinnon, 'On Torture: A Feminist Perspective on Human Rights', in K. E. Mahoney and P. Mahoney (eds.), *Human Rights in the Twenty-First Century: A Global Challenge* (Dordrecht: Martinus Nijhoff Publishers, 1993) 21, at 25.

[147] D. Russell and N. Van de Ven (eds.), *Crimes against Women: Proceedings of the International Tribunal* (East Palo Alto, CA: Frog in the Well, 1984), 58–67 and 110–175.

[148] For an overview of domestic violence and international law, see B. Meyersfeld, *Domestic Violence and International Law* (Oxford and Portland, OR: Hart Publishing, 2010).

if the abuse was at the hands of government agents.[149] Bunch has stated that '[f]emale subordination runs so deep that it is still viewed as inevitable or natural rather than as a politically constructed reality maintained by patriarchal interests, ideology, and institutions'.[150] She identifies the physical territory of this political struggle as being women's bodies.[151]

Likewise, MacKinnon finds that the legal concept of privacy has preserved male supremacy over women by 'shield[ing] the place of battery, marital rape, and women's exploited labour'.[152] Economic rights include remuneration for production outside the home, but not for reproduction or housework.[153] The interpretation of torture has been, for the most part, strictly confined to state-sanctioned violence in custody, whereas women are much more likely to suffer violations by so-called 'private' actors in so-called 'private' settings.[154] In fact, the public/private divide is said to be nowhere as pronounced as in relation to the issue of violence against women.[155]

There are several feminist theories that attempt to explain why the public/private dichotomy is maintained in international law. Gayle Binion asserts three main reasons. First, she argues it is in the interests of the state to retain its pre-eminent position in international law. In this way, states are able to shield various institutions from external investigation. Second, allowing a deconstruction of the patriarchal nature of family (or private) life may lead to improved understanding of the patriarchal and hierarchical structures of the society by citizens, who may then attempt to reconstruct them. Other actors may also benefit from the current division of power, such as religious institutions, corporate organisations, international agencies, non-governmental organisations, rebel groups, mercenaries, terrorist cells, and men in general as husbands, fathers, and brothers. The third explanation for the maintenance of the public/private divide in international law is that many fear a dilution of human rights

---

[149] K. Roth, 'Domestic Violence as an International Human Rights Issue', in Cook (ed.), *Human Rights of Women: National and International Perspectives*, 326, at 327.

[150] Bunch, 'Transforming Human Rights from a Feminist Perspective', 14–15.

[151] *Ibid.*, 15.

[152] MacKinnon, *Feminism Unmodified*, 101. See, also, Romany, 'Women as Aliens', 103.

[153] Charlesworth and Chinkin, 'The Gender of *Jus Cogens*', 72–73.

[154] Charlesworth, Chinkin and Wright, 'Feminist Approaches to International Law', 627–628; O'Hare, 'Realizing Human Rights for Women', 369.

[155] Binion, 'Human Rights: A Feminist Perspective', 515, n. 25; O'Hare, 'Realizing Human Rights for Women', 368. See, also, P. Goldberg and N. Kelly, 'International Human Rights and Violence Against Women' (1993) 6 *Harv. Hum. Rts. J.* 195.

principles if they are expanded beyond their traditional canons.[156] This view is even held by some human rights theorists[157] and activist groups,[158] and some feminist theorists argue for only a very limited reconceptualisation of human rights.[159]

Not all feminists, however, conceptualise the public/private dichotomy in the same way. A few feminists have questioned whether the public/private divide might not be a 'false dichotomy'[160] to the extent that the 'private' *is* subject to 'legal regulation and outside scrutiny'.[161] For example, the 'family', as the ultimate symbol of the 'private' sphere, is subject to international legal supervision, at least in relation to rights regarding marriage, consent to marriage, and child-rearing.[162] Express provisions in the CEDAW incorporate discrimination against women in both public as well as private areas of life.[163] Paradoxically, many feminist scholars have criticised human rights instruments as over-emphasising the family.[164]

Riane Eisler argues that, even though human rights law has attempted to regulate the private sphere, it has simply failed to do so in respect of issues that particularly touch women's lives.[165] Despite theorising the public/private dichotomy, Karen Engle in contrast cautions against over-emphasising it, arguing that doing so may exclude important parts of women's experiences, that is, those within the 'public' sphere. She also argues that speaking in such dichotomies assumes that the 'private' is bad for women, whereas it has some benefits for women.[166] Engle analyses the public/private distinction as taking one of two forms: either the 'private' – a sphere in which women operate – is excluded from the scope of international law, so the law cannot be said to be universal; or,

---

[156] Binion, 'Human Rights: A Feminist Perspective', 516–517.

[157] See, e.g., P. Alston, 'Conjuring Up New Human Rights: A Proposal for Equality Control' (1984) 78 *Amer. J. Int'l L.* 607.

[158] See, e.g., Amnesty International, 'Women in the Front Line', AI Publications, 1991. See, further, Roth, 'Domestic Violence as an International Human Rights Issue', 332–333.

[159] See, e.g., Thomas and Beasley, 'Domestic Violence as a Human Rights Issue', 43 (arguing that a link to the state is still needed).

[160] Binion, 'Human Rights: A Feminist Perspective', 518.

[161] Eisler, 'Human Rights: Toward an Integrated Theory for Action', 293; Hernández-Truyol, 'Human Rights through a Gendered Lens'; Binion, 'Human Rights: A Feminist Perspective'.

[162] See, Article 23, ICCPR and Article 10, ICESCR.

[163] Article 2(e), CEDAW. See, further, Chapter 4.

[164] See, Charlesworth, Chinkin and Wright, 'Feminist Approaches to International Law', 636.

[165] Eisler, 'Human Rights: Toward an Integrated Theory for Action'.

[166] K. Engle, 'After the Collapse of the Public/Private Distinction: Strategizing Women's Rights', in D. G. Dallmeyer (ed.), *Reconceiving Reality: Women and International Law* (American Society of International Law, 1993), 143.

alternatively, international law does not really exclude the private, but rather uses the public/private divide as a 'convenient screen' to avoid addressing women's issues.[167] My own view is that reality is closer to the latter. Liberal feminists such as Martha Nussbaum, too, challenge dimensions of the public/private divide, arguing that the liberal tradition of equality must be extended to relations between women and men within the family.[168] Jacqueline Greatbatch, writing in relation to international refugee law, similarly reveals that the public/private dichotomy 'roots women's oppression in sexuality and private life, thereby disregarding oppression experienced in non-domestic circumstances [such as the labour force], and the inter-connections of the public and private spheres'.[169]

In a similar way, other feminists object to the way in which the labels 'public' and 'private' have been applied. Johnstone argues that the dichotomy is itself questionable, 'because all activities have both public and private natures'.[170] She asserts that 'political decisions to allocate certain activities to the private sphere have been used to justify states' abdication of responsibility for that activity'.[171] Michael Heyman, writing in relation to domestic violence as a ground for claiming asylum under international refugee law, argues that 'it is senseless to view domestic violence as purely private conduct'.[172] He argues that perceiving the perpetrator of domestic violence as a private actor is 'ambiguous, even incoherent' as it either means that the non-state actor operates in a private domain (that is, 'in a virtual vacuum', which he argues is not the case)[173] or that he acts remote from public view.[174] In other words, the decision to leave issues to the private sphere is itself an exercise of political choice.[175]

In relation to violence against women specifically, Charlesworth and Chinkin argue for a reconceptualisation of how such violence is viewed. If it is understood not just as aberrant behaviour but as part of

---

[167] Ibid.

[168] See, e.g., M. Nussbaum, Sex and Social Justice (Oxford University Press, 1999), 55–80.

[169] J. Greatbatch, 'The Gender Difference: Feminist Critiques of Refugee Discourse' (1989) 1 Int'l J. Ref. L. 518, at 520.

[170] Johnstone, 'Feminist Influences on the United Nations Human Rights Treaty Bodies', 152, referring to Charlesworth, Chinkin and Wright, 'Feminist Approaches to International Law', 625–630.

[171] Ibid.

[172] M. G. Heyman, 'Domestic Violence and Asylum: Toward a Working Model of Affirmative State Obligations' (2005) 17 Int'l J. Ref. L. 729, at 740.

[173] Ibid., 739.   [174] Ibid., 740.

[175] Romany, 'State Responsibility Goes Private', 115.

the structure of the universal subordination of women, it cannot be considered a purely 'private' act.[176] Bunch has stated that such violence is caused by the structural relationships of power, domination, and privilege between men and women in society. Violence against women, she asserts, is central to maintaining those relations at home, at work, and in all public spaces.[177]

Resistance to linking violence against women to human rights law has partly arisen due to the view of some states and scholars that it would devalue traditional (read: male) canons of human rights.[178] Others have heralded the use of a discrimination framework to make what would otherwise be perceived as 'private' or beyond the law a political matter.[179] Engle criticises feminist scholars for using the language of 'private' as a 'proxy' for women. She asserts that, when feminist scholars complain that international law has excluded the private sphere, they actually mean that it has excluded women.[180] The two are not the same; and we should be clearer about what we mean.

Despite the many valid criticisms of the public/private dichotomy – not least that it is a rather blunt instrument of analysis – it has been a useful feminist lens through which to highlight the bias in international law in favour of state rather than non-state actions or omissions. The effect of this dichotomy has been to draw attention to the fact that particular concerns of women, such as violence within the home, have not generally been considered issues either for domestic or international regulation. The public/private dichotomy is thus a helpful starting point for discovering the gender gaps in international law and, as such, is applied as a means of analysis throughout this book. It is, however, only the first step in any grounded analysis of international law and its relationship to violence against women.

Arguments around the public/private dichotomy are, for example, value-laden and based on stereotypes and assumptions concerning women's lives. They overlook the fact that while men dominate the public sphere

---

176 Charlesworth and Chinkin, *The Boundaries of International Law*, 235.
177 C. Bunch, *Passionate Politics Essays 1968–1986: Feminist Theory in Action* (New York: St. Martin's Press, 1987), 491.
178 H. Charlesworth and C. Chinkin, 'Violence against Women: A Global Issue', in J. Stubbs (ed.), *Women, Male Violence and the Law* (Sydney: Institute of Criminology Series No. 6, 1994) 13, 25; Charlesworth, 'Alienating Oscar?', 144.
179 See, K. Bower, 'Recognizing Violence against Women as Persecution on the Basis of Membership in a Particular Social Group' (1993) 7 *Geo. Immigr. L. J.* 173, at 184.
180 Engle, 'After the Collapse of the Public/Private Distinction: Strategizing Women's Rights', 146.

of the state, they also dominate the private. Most so-called 'private' issues do have public dimensions, either because they are subject to regulation under law (the problem is often *how* they have been regulated rather than a lack of regulation) or because they are grounded in public systems of oppression, patriarchy, or gendered international relations. Additionally, the reliance of international feminist theory on the public/private dichotomy as a means of explaining the exclusion of women from mainstream human rights mechanisms carries its own gendered entrenchment – it keeps women in the 'private' and ignores or downplays their roles and participation in public spaces. Moreover, the private has been shown to be sometimes useful for women, such as in the context of women's rights to sexual freedom, reproductive health, and abortion; and therefore a total collapsing of the public/private dichotomy may not be always in the best interests of women.

4   Essentialised women

The fourth feminist critique of the international human rights system outlined in this book is that the system relies on and reinforces a collective female identity. That is, 'gendered' interpretations of human rights norms assume that women share a common experience and identity. This is played out by the human rights treaty bodies and other international courts in their treatment of issues such as violence against women, as shown in later chapters of this book. The desire to include equal representation of women on law-making bodies, for example, assumes that women speak with one voice, a voice that differs from that of the male. The feminist classification that human rights are 'men's rights' relies, too, on a central dichotomy between the lives of men and women. Meanwhile, women are collectively located in the private sphere in feminist literature, with limited, if any, regard to women operating in the public realm. As women's rights activists and human rights non-governmental organisations have sought to put 'women's rights' on the international human rights agenda, they too have engaged in and encouraged an 'essentialist' discourse. This same critique is levelled against feminism itself. In addition, essentialising women results in the essentialising of men, who are perceived as the binary opposite of women, and thus it has negative consequences for the deconstruction of gender.

Dianne Otto, for example, sees the text of the ICCPR as constructing 'woman' in 'procreative and heterosexual terms as mother and wife and as inevitably subject to and dependent on "men" in their various forms: individually as fathers and husbands and collectively as the State, the military, and the emergent United Nations'.[181] She points out that some of this emphasis is due to the endorsement of 'protective' or paternalistic instruments by the women's movement, such as early instruments on women's employment,[182] international trafficking of white women for the purpose of prostitution,[183] and the regulation of armed conflict.[184] Early anti-trafficking instruments have been particularly criticised by some feminist scholars who argue that narratives of 'white slavery' or 'trafficking in women' function as 'cultural myths', 'grounded in the perceived need to regulate female sexuality under the guise of protecting women'.[185] Alain Corbin states, for example:

> [It was] the martyrdom of virginity ... not the fact of women being sold but the idea of the virgin being ravished that aroused its rather salacious disapproval.[186]

Similarly, Ngaire Naffine argues that essentialism is a problem with law generally (and, by extension, international law) as women cannot be both

[181] Otto, 'A Post-Beijing Reflection', 118. See, further, D. Otto, 'Disconcerting "Masculinities": Reinventing the Gendered Subject(s) of International Human Rights Law', in D. Buss and A. Manji (eds.), *International Law: Modern Feminist Approaches* (Oxford: Hart Publishing, 2005), 105.

[182] See, e.g., International Labour Organization (ILO), Maternity Protection Convention 1919 (ILO Convention No. 3); ILO, Convention Concerning Night Work for Women Employed in Industry 1919 (ILO Convention No. 4); and ILO, Convention Concerning the Employment of Women on Underground Work in Mines of All Kinds 1935 (ILO Convention No. 45).

[183] International Agreement for the Suppression of the White Slave Traffic 1904, 18 May 1904, 35 Stat. 426, 1 LNTS 83; entered into force 18 July 1905; International Convention on the Suppression of the Traffic in Women and Children 1921, 30 September 1921, 9 LNTS 415; entered into force 15 June 1922; International Convention for the Suppression of the Traffic in Women of Full Age 1933, 11 October 1933, 53 UNTS 13; entered into force 24 August 1934.

[184] Early instruments made no mention of women even though there was already a long history of sexual abuse committed against women during armed conflict. Otto points out that later instruments referred to women indirectly, in the context of requiring an occupying power to respect 'family honour and rights.' See, Article 46, Convention Respecting the Laws and Customs of War on Land (Hague Convention II), 29 July 1899; and Article 46, Convention Respecting the Laws and Customs of War on Land (Hague Convention IV), 18 October 1907, 36 Stat 2277, 1 Bevans 631: Otto, 'Disconcerting "Masculinities"', 108.

[185] J. Doezema, 'Loose Women or Lost Women? The Re-emergence of the Myth of White Slavery in Contemporary Discourses of Trafficking in Women' (2000) 18 *Gender Issues* 23, at 24.

[186] A. Corbin, *Women for Hire: Prostitution and Sexuality in France after 1850* (translated by Alan Sheridan, Cambridge, MA: Harvard University Press, 1990), 277, as referred to in *ibid.*

women and legal subjects, since law offers only 'the old story of sex differentiation: the strong man, the weak woman; the male subject, the female
object'.[187]

A further feminist critique is that the family-related provisions in
international human rights law have overemphasised the woman as
'homemaker',[188] mentioned briefly in 3 above. Such discourse fails to recognise woman as an autonomous human being and relegates her into a
single figure of mother and wife located in the 'private' sphere. However,
not all feminist scholars agree that the balance struck between the competing, or at least the myriad, identities that women possess is fair or
useful.

Rebecca Hillock has criticised, for example, the approach of the Women's
Committee as 'continually degrad[ing] the status of motherhood'.[189]
Similarly, Radhika Coomaraswamy has queried the assumption within
rights discourse of 'a free, independent, individual woman', whereas this
image, she asserts, may be less powerful in protecting women's rights than
other ideologies such as 'women as mothers'.[190] While adopting strategies
that characterise women as 'weak' or 'helpless' may play into stereotypical male instincts as 'protector' and 'liberator' and thereby achieve some
short-term gains, little will change in respect of an accurate portrayal of
the realities of women's lives, or where they would like to see their future.
Motherhood has been identified as one of several areas of disagreement
between Western and Third World Feminisms.[191]

From a Third World Feminist perspective, the criticism is not only
that women individually and as a group are generally excluded from the

---

[187] Naffine, 'Sexing the Subject (of Law)', 35.
[188] See, e.g., Charlesworth, Chinkin and Wright, 'Feminist Approaches to International
       Law', 636; Otto, 'A Post-Beijing Reflection', 121 (criticising the raft of provisions in the
       CEDAW which privilege the homemaker as the primary female subject of international
       law).
[189] See, e.g., R. L. Hillock, 'Establishing the Rights of Women Globally: Has the United
       Nations Convention on the Elimination of All Forms of Discrimination against Women
       made a Difference?' (2004–2005) 12 *Tulsa J. Comp. and Int'l L.* 481, at 504 (referring to
       observations on state party reports on Armenia, UN Doc. A/52/38/Rev.1 (Part II), paras.
       35–68 (1997) and Czech Republic, UN Doc. A/53/38, paras. 167–207 (1998)).
[190] R. Coomaraswamy, 'To Bellow Like a Cow: Women, Ethnicity and the Discourse
       of Rights', in R. J. Cook (ed.), *Human Rights of Women: National and International
       Perspectives* (Philadelphia: University of Pennsylvania Press, 1994), 43, at 55.
[191] See, Banda, *Women, Law and Human Rights: An African Perspective*, 8. Other areas of
       disagreement identified include 'radical feminism, … language, sexuality, priorities,
       (gender) separatism.'

protection of human rights law, but also that *non*-Western women and *non*-Western values and experiences are largely absent from the whole debate.[192] Berta Hernández-Truyol anatomises the norm of human rights law as 'white, Western/Northern European, Judeo-Christian, heterosexual, propertied, educated, male'.[193] Third World Feminists likewise criticise Western feminists for 'essentialising' women in their own image[194] as white, Western/Northern European, Judeo-Christian, heterosexual, propertied, educated, *women* – in a similar way that feminists in general criticise the foundations of international law as 'normalising' maleness. A primary critique levelled against Western feminism is that the world is seen through white middle-class glasses.[195] The construction of a category of 'women' without regard to other identity-based characteristics that shape and influence their lives – whether in law, policy, or feminist discourse itself – has now been widely criticised by feminist scholars,[196] as have the difficulties of claiming a common experience of all women in all cultural contexts.[197]

---

[192] See, e.g., C. Harries, 'Daughters of Our Peoples: International Feminism Meets Ugandan Law and Custom' (1984) 25 *Colum. Hum. Rts. L. Rev.* 493; V. Amos and P. Parmar, 'Challenging Imperial Feminism' (1984) 17 *Feminist Rev.* 3; J. A. M. Cobbah, 'African Values and the Human Rights Debate: An African Perspective' (1987) 9 *HRQ* 309; A. P. Harris, 'Race and Essentialism in Feminist Legal Theory' (1990) 42 *Stan. L. Rev.* 581; N. Kim, 'Toward a Feminist Theory of Human Rights: Straddling the Fence Between Western Imperialism and Uncritical Absolutism' (1993) 25 *Colum. Hum. Rts. L. Rev.* 49; J. Oloka-Onyango and S. Tamale, '"The Personal is Political" or Why Women's Human Rights are Indeed Human Rights: An African Perspective on International Feminism' (1995) 17 *HRQ* 691; T. E. Higgins, 'Anti-Essentialism, Relativism, and Human Rights' (1996) 19 *Harv. Women's L. J.* 89; E. Brems, 'Enemies or Allies? Feminism and Cultural Relativism as Dissident Voices in Human Rights Discourse' (1997) 19 *HRQ* 136; K. Engle, 'Culture and Human Rights: The Asian Values Debate in Context' (2000) 32 *NYU J. Int'l L. & Pol.* 291.

[193] Hernández-Truyol, 'Women's Rights as Human Rights', 651.

[194] Higgins, 'Anti-Essentialism, Relativism, and Human Rights', 89.

[195] See, Banda, *Women, Law and Human Rights: An African Perspective*, 7; K. Bhavanani, *Feminism and Race* (Oxford University Press, 2001); M. Mohanty, A. Russo and L. Torres (eds.), *Third World Women and the Politics of Feminism* (Bloomington, IN: Indiana University Press, 1991); E. Spelman, *Inessential Women: Problems of Exclusion in Feminist Thought* (London: The Women's Press, 1988).

[196] See, e.g., C. Mohanty, 'Under Western Eyes: Feminist Scholarship and Colonial Discourses', in Mohanty, Russo and Torres (eds.), *Third World Women and the Politics of Feminism*, (Bloomington, IN: Indiana University Press, 1991), 51; Spelman, *Inessential Women*.

[197] See, e.g., I. Gunning, 'Arrogant Perception, World Travelling and Multicultural Feminism: The Case of Female Genital Surgeries' (1991/1992) 23 *Colum. Hum. Rts. L. Rev.* 189; K. Engle, 'Female Subjects of Public International Law: Human Rights and the Exotic

Where women from the developing world do feature in international law or feminist theory, Ratna Kapur has criticised the reliance on what she calls the 'authentic victim subject', namely that 'the image that is produced is that of a truncated Third World woman who is sexually constrained, tradition-bound, incarcerated in the home, illiterate, and poor'.[198] This same critique can be asserted against international human rights legal exchanges that have largely ignored women as agents of change; instead women have been portrayed as victims of culturally depraved or 'primitive' or 'backward' harms. There is much evidence to show, however, that the image of women from the developing world as victims and not agents is a creation of a lack of awareness and limited documentation of activism in these regions.[199] Women's groups in parts of Africa, for example, have grown in numbers and sophistication since the Nairobi Conference and have been active participants at, inter alia, UN world conferences on women and at local levels.[200] Nonetheless, these images remain common in international discourse.

The heavy focus on rape and sexual violence in international jurisprudence also plays into this essentialist discourse.[201] The focus by feminists and later by international courts on widespread rape during and after the conflicts in the former Yugoslavia in the 1990s has come under scrutiny. Engle argues that all this attention to sexual violence classed or identified all women as victims of rape, even when women denied that this had occurred to them.[202] Although it is imperative that such violence is brought to international attention and condemned, it is equally important that the manner in which women are portrayed does not downplay the many other roles they play in wartime, or the actual extent of other forms of violence that women suffer during conflict or

---

Other Female' (1992) 26 New England L. Rev. 1509; J. G. Gardam and M. J. Jarvis, Women, Armed Conflict and International Law (The Hague: Kluwer Law International, 2001), 12.

[198] R. Kapur, 'The Tragedy of Victimization Rhetoric: Resurrecting the "Native" Subject in International/Post-Colonial Feminist Legal Politics' (2002) 15 Harvard Hum. Rts. J. 1, at 18.

[199] See, generally, R. Ray and A. C. Korteweg, 'Women's Movements in the Third World: Identity, Mobilization, and Autonomy' (1999) 25 Annual Rev. of Sociology 37.

[200] Oloka-Onyango and Tamale, '"The Personal is Political"', 703.

[201] Kapur, 'The Tragedy of Victimization Rhetoric', 2. See, also, M. R. Mahoney, 'Victimization Or Oppression? Women's Lives, Violence, and Agency', in M. A. Fineman and R. Mykitiuk (eds.), The Public Nature of Private Violence: The Discovery of Domestic Abuse (New York: Routledge, 1994) 59.

[202] K. Engle, 'Feminism and Its (Dis)Contents: Criminalizing Wartime Rape in Bosnia and Herzegovina' (2005) 99 Am. J. Int'l L. 779, at 794: 'At some level, all Bosnian Muslim women were imagined to have been raped.'

in peacetime,[203] or does not render them into stereotyped categories of 'helpless victims'.

Western feminists and international human rights institutions have been accused of oversensationalising practices such as female genital mutilation, veiling, and dowry murders.[204] As this book shows, the majority of references to violence against women within the jurisprudence of the treaty bodies targets particular forms of violence that are primarily found in developing countries, especially those linked to cultural practices or religious norms. Concern has been raised that the international human rights regime articulates a particular cultural system, one rooted in 'a secular transnational modernity'[205], in which cultural difference, whatever its form, is condemned. Culture is seen as a problem rather than a resource.[206] However, it is not every form of cultural difference that is at issue under the universal human rights system. Rather for women's rights, it is those practices directed at reinforcing a woman's inferior position,[207] that hinder her ability to engage in all areas of life, and those acts which are harmful. International human rights law does not dismiss culture or religion (it in fact protects them within certain limits[208]), but it rejects those practices that are harmful to equal relations or to the physical, psychological, and sexual security of women. At the same time, however, the treaty bodies tend to downplay or overlook old and new forms of violence perpetrated against women in countries from the global 'north', which are also built on stereotypes and cultural norms that reflect the inferiority of women to men (discussed later).

Relying on a single 'essence' of women is further said to fail to recognise the intersection of sex/gender and other identity-based characteristics such as race, ethnicity, class, poverty, colonial oppression, religion, or sexuality.[209] The interrelationship between sexual and racial prejudice

---

[203] See, A. Edwards, 'Everyday Rape: International Human Rights Law and Violence against Women in Peacetime', in C. McGlynn and V. Munro (eds.), *Rethinking Rape Law: International and Comparative Perspectives* (London: Routledge-Cavendish, 2010) 92.

[204] See, e.g., Engle, 'Female Subjects of Public International Law'; Kapur, 'The Tragedy of Victimization Rhetoric'.

[205] S. Engle Merry, 'Constructing a Global Law – Violence against Women and the Human Rights System' (2003) *L. & Soc. Inquiry* 941, at 945.

[206] *Ibid.*, 947.

[207] See, Article 5(a), CEDAW.

[208] See, e.g., Article 27, ICCPR; Article 15, ICESCR. See, CESCR, General Comment No. 21: Right of Everyone to Take Part in Cultural Life (Article 15, para. 1(a) of the International Covenant on Economic, Social and Cultural Rights), UN Doc. E/C.12/GC/21, 20 November 2009.

[209] J. E. Bond, 'International Intersectionality: A Theoretical and Pragmatic Exploration of Women's International Human Rights Violations' (2003) 52 *Emory L.J.* 71, at 76;

has been widely studied and confirmed, but far less has been explored in relation to the other indicators. Elizabeth Spelman argues that one cannot correct the problem of 'white solipsism'[210] merely by adding an analysis of the race issue to the gender issue, because race changes how women experience gender.[211] Spelman argues that race is a *different* basis for oppression that involves different forms of subordination and requires different forms of liberation.[212] Similarly, Chandra Mohanty has pointed out that '[w]omen are constituted as women through the complex inter-action between class, culture, religion and other ideological institutions and frameworks. They are not "women" – a coherent group – solely on the basis of a particular economic system or policy.'[213] Munro perhaps sums up the dilemma of efforts to speak with a single voice. She argues that it 'obscure[s] the question of whether all women are subordinate to all men in the same way or to the same degree. Thus, it risk[s] purchasing power-ful rhetoric and conceptual neatness at the cost of recognising intersec-tionality between gender and other axes of social stratification.'[214]

MacKinnon has argued, for instance, that genocidal rape is not just about women's identity as women, but it is equally about women's identity in a particular racial group.[215] As Jasminka Kalajdzic states:

> The overemphasis on gender to the exclusion of all other possible motiv-ating factors can obscure other characteristics of a woman's identity that determine *which* women are raped. ... Sexism and racism, therefore, operate in conjunction to determine which women are raped. Indeed, rape survivors are women *and* members of a given national, political, or religious group. Their identities as women cannot be separated from their membership in a particular race or religion.[216]

S. Tamale, *When Hens Being to Crow: Gender and Parliamentary Politics in Uganda* (Kampala: Fountain Publishers, 1999) (on interlinkages between women's position in parliamentary politics in Uganda and the role of colonial history); A. Edwards, 'Age and Gender Dimensions in International Refugee Law', in E. Feller, V. Türk and F. Nicholson (eds.), *Refugee Protection in International Law: UNHCR's Global Consultations on International Protection* (Cambridge University Press, 2003) 46. In this article I refer to the 'personalised' inquiry of refugee status determination and I identify compounding factors of persecution, such as age, gender, race, ethnicity, etc.

[210] A. Rich, 'Disloyal to Civilization: Feminism, Racism, Gynephobia [sic]', in *On Lies, Secrets, and Silences* (1979) 299, as referred to in K. T. Bartlett, 'Feminist Legal Methods' (1990) 103 *Harv. L. Rev.* 829, at 847.

[211] Spelman, *Inessential Women*, 114–115.   [212] *Ibid.*, 125.

[213] Mohanty, 'Under Western Eyes', 74.

[214] See, Munro, *Law and Politics at the Perimeter*, 111.

[215] MacKinnon, 'Rape, Genocide, and Women's Human Rights'.

[216] J. Kalajdzic, 'Rape, Representation, and Rights: Permeating International Law with the Voices of Women' (1996) 21 *Queen's L. J.* 457, at 477–478.

The human rights treaty bodies have rarely analysed in detail the inter-relationship of sex/gender and other identity-based characteristics, as evidenced in later chapters of this book, even if they regularly use such language as 'double' or 'multiple discrimination'.[217]

A further consequence of essentialism in UN strategies of prioritising women-specific or gender-related violence is that other, equally serious, harms perpetrated against women that do not conform to these stereotypes are not widely acknowledged or publicised, either by the UN, international law, or feminist scholars themselves. MacKinnon sums this up as follows:

> When what happens to women also happens to men, like being beaten and disappearing and being tortured to death, the fact that those it happened to are *women* is not registered in the record of human atrocity.[218]

Although a few feminist writers acknowledge that women also suffer harm that falls within the traditional constructs of human rights norms, such as torture within state custody, they argue that even in these circumstances the international provisions do not fully reflect the nature and extent of violations faced by women in the public sphere.[219] Chapter 5 of this book reveals, as an example, that women were the first users of the human rights individual communications system of the UNCAT, contrary to feminist scholars' assertions that torture as understood in that instrument does not apply to women. Tracy Higgins concludes that this is what makes 'woman' a 'troublesome term' in feminism and in law.[220]

In fact, essentialism affects all women. It also affects men. As MacKinnon rightly points out, it is unknown what traits women would exhibit if they were not constrained by patriarchal society.[221] According to Rebecca Cook and Simone Cusack, 'Stereotypes degrade women when they assign them to subservient roles in society, and devalue their attributes and characteristics ... [and can] exacerbate a climate of impunity with respect

---

[217] The Women's Committee has regularly made mention of double or multiple discrimination: see, e.g., CEDAW, Annual Report 2008, UN Doc. A/63/38 (2008). See, Chapters 4, 5 and 6.

[218] MacKinnon, 'Rape, Genocide, and Women's Human Rights', 5.

[219] See, e.g., A. Byrnes, 'The Convention against Torture', in Askin and Koenig (eds.), *Women and International Human Rights Law*, Vol. 1, 183, at 184. See, further, Chapter 5.

[220] T. Higgins, 'By Reason Of Their Sex: Feminist Theory, Postmodernism and Justice' (1995) 80 *Cornell L. Rev.* 1536, at 1537.

[221] C. A. MacKinnon, 'From Practice to Theory, or What is a White Woman Anyway?' (1991) 4 *Yale J. L. and Feminism* 13, at 13.

to violations of women's rights.'[222] The issue, then, is not whether women are all the same or that they all experience violence in the same way. The issue for international human rights law is whether it is able to accommodate the diversity of women and women's lives without compromising its strength that lies in its appeal to universality and the promotion of gender equality.

While noting differences in women's experiences on account of, inter alia, class, race, or nationality, and accepting that these factors can give rise to differing power relations *between* women (and between women and men), Charlesworth believes that 'patriarchy and the devaluing of women, although manifested differently within different societies, are almost universal'.[223] She argues that 'we can speak "as women" in an international context. It *is* possible to describe women as having "a collective social history of disempowerment, exploitation and subordination extending to the present."'[224] Adopting a controversial position to many anti-essentialist theorists, African scholar Sylvia Tamale recounts that '[t]he issues for women [in Africa] are in fact issues that concern all world citizens'.[225] She further asserts that cultural, religious, and economic fundamentalisms 'threaten to roll back feminist achievement and to silence [women] into total patriarchal submission'.[226]

Many of the gains achieved by women in international human rights law have been secured by such strategies of speaking with one voice.[227] The increasingly dominant approach of international treaty bodies to violence against women, for example, is to perceive of it as 'widely pervasive and structural'.[228] How that violence is played out may vary between cultures, but it is seen as having shared underlying roots in oppression, patriarchy, exclusion, and inequality. Solidarity in numbers has been powerful

---

[222] R. Cook and S. Cusack, *Gender Stereotyping: Transnational Legal Perspectives* (Philadelphia: University of Pennsylvania Press, 2010), 1.

[223] H. Charlesworth, 'Human Rights as Men's Rights', 103.

[224] Charlesworth, 'Alienating Oscar?', 5, referring to MacKinnon, 'From Practice to Theory', 15.

[225] S. Tamale, 'African Feminism: How Should We Change?' (2006) 49 *Dev't* 38, at 39.

[226] *Ibid.*, 40.

[227] Higgins, 'By Reason Of Their Sex', 1537. See, e.g., Amnesty International's Stop Violence against Women campaign, various documents available at: www.amnesty.org.

[228] See, e.g., R. Holtmaat, 'Preventing Violence against Women: The Due Diligence Standard with Respect to the Obligation to Banish Gender Stereotypes on the Grounds of Article 5(a) of the CEDAW Convention', in Benninger-Budel (ed.), *Due Diligence and its Application to Protect Women from Violence* 63, at 63 referring to CEDAW, General Recommendation No. 25: Temporary Special Measures (2008).

in raising awareness of issues that transcend national borders. As a pragmatic strategy, therefore, speaking with one voice has allowed women's rights activists as well as international lawyers to search for the sources of international and national power and to attempt to gain access to that power. For these reasons, rejecting common 'essences' causes consternation among feminism and women's rights activism and, in turn, poses uncertainties for international human rights institutions in dealing with 'women's rights' and 'women's issues'.

The ultimate cost for women, feminism, and the women's movement of rejecting a collective identity, or at least some fundamental commonalities shared by women, is potentially the end of feminism as a theory or method with an identifiable subject matter.[229] For international human rights institutions, it risks diluting the dominant rhetoric of absolutism or universality, and it reopens cultural relativity debates in favour of recalcitrant governments that overstate *difference* in order to evade human rights obligations. Why is it that culture is always paraded out in relation to women's issues, but not those affecting men?[230]

The failure of international law to intervene in instances of violence against women before the 1990s can be attributed to the fact that such violence was perceived as 'a matter of unwanted behaviour of some men and/or a matter of some backward or primitive cultures'.[231] Resolution of the culture–gender equality clash has in many ways moved on from this imperially driven myth. The CEDAW, for example, expressly recognises the 'culture clash'[232] and contains provisions to safeguard against any prejudice regarding women's equality.[233] Frances Raday points to several important international decisions that either expressly or indirectly reject cultural or religious practices as legitimate justifications for discrimination against women.[234] Thus, in any 'clash between cultural practices or

---

[229] N. Naffine, 'In Praise of Legal Feminism' (2002) 22 *Legal Stud.* 71, at 72.

[230] Tamale, *When Hens Being to Crow*, Conclusion.

[231] Holtmaat, 'Preventing Violence against Women', 63.

[232] Amartya Sen warns against oversensationalising the language of 'clash of civilizations': A. Sen, *Identity & Violence: The Illusion of Destiny* (London: Penguin Books, 2006).

[233] See, Article 5(a) and 2(f), CEDAW. See, further, F. Raday, 'Culture, Religion, and CEDAW's Article 5(a)', in H. B. Schöpp-Schilling and C. Flinterman (eds.), *Circle of Empowerment: Twenty-Five Years of the UN Committee on the Elimination of Discrimination against Women* (New York: Feminist Press, 2007) 68, at 69.

[234] Raday refers to, for example, *Lovelace* v. *Canada*, HRC 24/1977 (30 July 1981); *Aumeeruddy-Cziffra et al.* v. *Mauritius (the Mauritian Women's* case), HRC 35/1978 (9 April 1981); *Leyla Sahin* v. *Turkey*, (2005) 41 EHRR 8; *Refah Partisi [Welfare Party] and Others* v. *Turkey*, (2003) 37 EHRR 1, as referred to in Raday, 'Culture, Religion, and CEDAW's Article 5(a)'.

religious norms and the right to gender equality, it is the right to gender equality that must have normative hegemony'.[235] This confirms the position adopted by the HRC that:

> Inequality in the enjoyment of rights by women throughout the world is deeply embedded in tradition, history and culture, including religious attitudes. ... States parties should ensure that traditional, historical or cultural attitudes are not used to justify violations of women's right to equality before the law and to equal enjoyment of all Covenant rights ...
>
> The rights which persons belonging to minorities enjoy under Article 27 of the Covenant in respect of their language, culture and religion do not authorize any State, group or person to violate the right to equal enjoyment of any Covenant rights, including the right to equal protection of the law.[236]

Likewise, the CESCR has stated that 'no one may invoke cultural diversity to infringe upon human rights guaranteed by international law, nor to limit their scope'[237] and, specifically in relation to women, that the equal enjoyment of culture in Article 15 of the International Covenant on Economic, Social and Cultural Rights 1966 (ICESCR) involves 'eliminat[ing] institutional and legal obstacles, as well as those based on negative practices, including those attributed to customs and traditions, that prevent women from fully participating in cultural life, science education and scientific research'.[238]

Nonetheless, there has been as yet no clear elaboration of the extent of a state's obligations to alter cultural and traditional practices in order to secure women's rights.[239]

For women's rights activists, rejecting an essential image of womanhood would mean the end to powerful and effective campaigns that benefit from speaking on behalf of 50 per cent of the world's population, even with its attendant negatives. Nancy Hartsock argues that anti-essentialism sits uncomfortably with feminist politics that has relied on a

Some of these cases are dealt with further in Chapter 4. See, further, Cook and Cusack, *Gender Stereotyping: Transnational Legal Perspectives* (who identify a wide number of international and national cases that have addressed negative gender stereotypes).

[235] Raday. 'Culture, Religion, and CEDAW's Article 5(a)', 81.

[236] HRC, General Comment No. 28: Equality of Rights Between Men and Women (Article 3) (2000), UN Doc. CCPR/C/21/Rev.1/Add.10, paras. 5 and 32.

[237] CESCR, General Comment No. 21: Right of Everyone to Take Part in Cultural Life (Article 15, para. 1 (a) of the International Covenant on Economic, Social and Cultural Rights), UN Doc. E/C.12/GC/21, 20 November 2009, para. 18.

[238] *Ibid.*, para. 25.

[239] See, further, Holtmaat, 'Preventing Violence against Women'; Cook and Cusack, *Gender Stereotyping Transnational Legal Perspecties*.

united female front,[240] while Munro notes that multiple voices 'threaten feminist political paralysis'.[241] Very effective feminist techniques, such as 'asking the woman question' or 'consciousness-raising', rely, for instance, on foundations of commonality.[242]

According to MacKinnon, anti-essentialism, as a wholly abstract theory, is incapable of grasping the realities of the social world and is fundamentally incompatible with a meaningful practice of women's rights let alone a women's movement.[243] Offering a compromise, Gayatari Spivak has proposed what she calls 'strategic essentialism'. In recognising that there is no shared or essential reality, feminism (and, by analogy, human rights institutions) should not reject the rhetoric and ideology of women altogether.[244] While recognising that claims about 'women' and 'women's situations' are generalisations, they are made with the intention to attain specific political outcomes rather than to be statements about 'apolitical depictions of reality'.[245] I would add to Spivak's strategy the need to develop the identity of women's roles and status beyond those prescribed by this feminist agenda.

There is also a sense that the implementation of such legal obligations as Article 5(a) of the CEDAW, which calls upon states to alter negative cultural and traditional stereotypes concerning women and men, requires a different implementation strategy that limits the charges of cultural hegemony or imperialism. Calls have been made for a non-abolitionist strategy, one of 'internal discourse and cross-cultural dialogue'.[246] In other words, reforms may need to be rooted in existing practices and religious systems if they are to be accepted.[247]

---

[240] N. Hartsock, 'Foucault on Power – A Theory for Women', in L. Nicholson (ed.), *Feminism/Postmodernism* (New York: Routledge, 1990) 157.

[241] Munro, *Law and Politics at the Perimeter*, 114.

[242] *Ibid.*, referring to the techniques of Bartlett, in Bartlett, 'Feminist Legal Methods', as also outlined in the Introduction.

[243] C. MacKinnon, 'Symposium on Unfinished Feminist Business: Some Points against Postmodernism' (2000) 75 *Chicago-Kent L. Rev.* 687 at 698–99.

[244] G. C. Spivak, 'Subaltern Studies: Deconstructing Historiography', in R. Guha and G. Spivak (eds.), *Selected Subaltern Studies* (New York: Oxford University Press, 1988), 25.

[245] L. Nicholson, 'Gender', in A. M. Jaggar and I. M. Young (eds.), *A Companion to Feminist Philosophy* (London: Blackwell, 1998) 289, at 295.

[246] See, e.g., C. I. Nyamu, 'How Should Human Rights and Development Respond to Cultural Legitimization of Gender Hierarchy in Developing Countries?' (2000) 41 *Harv. Int'l L. J.* 381, 393, referred to in Holtmaat, 'Preventing Violence against Women', 87.

[247] See, also, Merry, *Human Rights and Gender Violence*, 90–92, referring to A. A. An-Na'im, 'Toward a Cross-Cultural Approach to Defining International Standards of Human Rights: The Meaning of Cruel, Inhuman or Degrading Treatment or Punishment', in A. A. An-Na'im (ed.), *Human Rights in Cross-Cultural Perspectives: A Quest for Consensus*

In my view, shared oppression is still the underlying uniting force of feminism and the women's rights movement, as is the exclusion of women from any meaningful participation or doctrinal purchase in respect of municipal and international human rights systems. Women may experience oppression differently or be subjected to different types of violence in different societies, communities, or cultures, but nowhere have women attained gender equality with men on equal terms (or on women's terms), and nowhere are women free from violence, including in 'northern' locations. If one studies the manifestations of violence across communities, the experiences are marked by their similarities rather than their differences. Kapur concedes that '[t]he perception that women are victims and objects in need of rescue continues to inform contemporary feminist politics both "here" and "there"'.[248] Even as oppression subsides and patriarchy is dismantled in some societies, women share a historical experience of oppression,[249] and violence against women appears to be without end.

Like Charlesworth, I believe that we are able to speak with one voice (and at times we need to), that we are capable of finding united commonalities while, at the same time, respecting our differences within feminism and within international human rights law.[250] For international human rights institutions, it is critical that they continue to identify and embrace a core corpus of women's rights and that gender equality trumps other competing rights, such as those based on culture or religion, which serve to negate women's full membership in society. Without this core, international human rights law risks being rendered irrelevant and undermined by state-driven cultural relativity agendas. Like Sally Engle Merry, I believe it is possible to embrace the international human rights system (despite its shortcomings) 'precisely because it differs from many prevailing practices and it is internationally legitimate'.[251] It can offer oppressed women and others a language in which to base and frame their grievances and arguments for change. At the same time, one must recognise that in a given situation, local knowledge, local religions, and local customs may themselves offer the better hopes of change. At a minimum, they need

---

(Philadelphia: University of Pennsylvania, 1992) 19 and A. A. An-Na'im (ed.), *Cultural Transformation and Human Rights in Africa* (London: Zed Books, 2002).

[248] R. Kapur, 'Human Rights in the 21st Century: Take a Walk on the Dark Side' (2006) 28 *Sydney L. Rev.* 665, at 679.

[249] Otto similarly talks about shared resistance, see Otto, 'Disconcerting "Masculinities"', 107.

[250] Charlesworth, 'Human Rights as Men's Rights'.

[251] Engle Merry, *Human Rights and Gender Violence*, 90.

to be engaged. However, it is also important to acknowledge that appeal to existing religions and cultures may not always be fruitful as they may be unable to accommodate women's rights as envisaged by the human rights system and that some beliefs about the role and value of women are intractably entrenched in those systems.[252]

Moreover, this approach does not reject the truth that women are multidimensional human beings who experience different forms of violence in different ways, often in very personal ways. Rather, it is to recognise their shared experiences of gender inequality, which may manifest differently in different societies. I have yet to meet a woman, whatever her background, who has rejected a desire for the right to participate in decision-making that regulates her life, to be free from violence, or to attain economic security. Any differences that exist between women tend to be overstated and tend to focus on the violation (for example genital mutilation) rather than the goal (for example gender equality).[253] This equates with the view that the rejection of rights is the 'luxury' of the privileged few.[254] Writing in relation to the liberation movement of African Americans in the United States, Patricia Williams argues instead that 'politically effective action has occurred mainly in connection with asserting or extending rights'.[255] She points out that '[the United States'] worst historical moments have not been attributable to rights-*assertion*, but to a failure of rights-*commitment*'.[256]

For the purposes of individual human rights litigation (as opposed to strategic feminist activism, discussed above), concepts such as intersectionality and multiple discrimination can be useful analytical tools and must be utilised more effectively. These concepts contribute to a better-informed individualised assessment of the facts of a case and, therefore, lead to a more accurate account. Part of any assessment would include gender factors. These concepts further serve to reject standard gendered assumptions about how women should behave or respond to harm.[257] At the same time, in endorsing intersectionality, advocates and decision-

---

[252] See, also, Raday, 'Culture, Religion, and CEDAW's Article 5(a)'.

[253] See, e.g., Gunning, 'Arrogant Perception, World Travelling and Multicultural Feminism', (the focus of the debates surrounding female genital mutilation tended to focus on the act itself, rather than what women hoped for their lives).

[254] P. J. Williams, 'Alchemical Notes', 57. See, also, A. H. Villmoare, 'Women, Differences and Rights as Practices: An Interpretative Essay and Proposal' (1991) 25 *Law & Soc. Rev.* 392.

[255] Williams, 'Alchemical Notes', 57.   [256] *Ibid.*, 61.

[257] See, further, Kaufman and Lindquist, 'Critiquing Gender-Neutral Treaty Language', 117.

makers must nonetheless stay attuned to the potential for old gender-based stereotypes to be simply replaced by new victim categories such as those based on sex/race, sex/class, or sex/sexuality.[258]

Despite the difficulties that this fourth critique presents for both feminist theory and advocacy as well as the international human rights system, we should not reject feminist discourse or its techniques, especially in the nascent human rights system that is only just beginning to develop jurisprudence on women's equality and issues such as violence against women.[259] At a minimum, it is necessary to be conscious of how human rights discourse plays into the ways in which women are presented as victims, rendered only as mothers, or as the 'Exotic Other Female'.[260] This does not, however, mean a rejection of human rights law or feminist views of oppression, but instead it calls for a rebalancing of the emphasis of international human rights law on all facets of women's lives from all geographic, socio-economic, racial, and political backgrounds.

Feminist methods such as those outlined in Chapter 1 of this book, too, need a degree of updating, such as a more socially constructed understanding of gender,[261] a heightened focus on women and women's lives rather than becoming bogged down in distinctions between sex and gender,[262] as well as a shift from asking the woman question to a contextualised woman question that positions her within her own social, cultural, political, religious, economic, and family contexts.[263]

Rarely is feminist theory or human rights law, for example, concerned with women as human rights defenders or political activists, as humanitarian workers, as child soldiers,[264] as peacekeepers or international police officers, as presidents, as politicians, and as policymakers. The current image of women – whether from developed or developing countries – is a distorted one. Once there is more balance in the images of women within human rights law, including by the treaty bodies, it is possible that the

---

[258] A. Edwards, 'The "Feminizing" of Torture under International Human Rights Law' (2006) 19 *Leiden J. Int'l L.* 349.

[259] Cf. Halley, *Split Decisions* (who suggests we take a break from feminism to explore other theories, but she does not, however, suggest a rejection of feminism altogether). Discussed further in Chapter 7.

[260] See, Engle, 'Female Subjects of Public International Law'.

[261] Otto, 'Disconcerting "Masculinities"'.

[262] This is not to suggest that the rights of men and boys, and the violence perpetrated against them, should not also form part of international human rights dialogues.

[263] See, Chapters 1 and 7.

[264] See, as an exception, R. Brett, *Girl Soldiers: Challenging the Assumptions* (Quaker United Nations Office, 5 November 2002), available at: www.quno.org/geneva/pdf/Girl_Soldiers.pdf (last accessed 10 September 2008).

system can be transformed to take account of and to understand the very different lives of women within and across communities in many parts of the world, including the intersectionality of gender with a range of other identity-based characteristics,[265] as well as personal experiences that transcend these categories.[266]

Underlying all of these efforts must be a renewed focus on women as legal subjects or rights claimants under international law, and an acceptance that women do share common attributes and experiences with other women as well as differences. Just because an individual does not fit within the same socio-economic, political, or racial group does not mean she cannot empathise with other women, or that she does not share experiences. Do you have to be raped to fear it, to feel oppressed by the possibility, or to want to fight to rid other women's lives of it? To accept otherwise would be to reject the basic human rights foundations of humanity, universality, and shared dignity, and to give way to ideas of cultural relativity, dominance, and perpetual oppression.

D   Conclusion

This chapter has outlined four principal feminist critiques (or themes) of the international human rights system, and various sub-themes therein. It has shown the complexity as well as the depth of feminist engagement with international law. It has confirmed that the lack of women in positions of authority within the UN system remains a major stumbling block to reform and women's inclusion within that system. Many examples have been given as to how the system of international human rights law operates to privilege men and to exclude, marginalise, or silence women. Nonetheless, the way forward is not to reject international human rights law altogether but to work with it to ensure that women's experiences are recognised. The conundrum is that the international human rights system may never fully accommodate the range of experiences of women, and thus it is crucial to keep checks on how women are included within it. It is essential that the dominant strategy of inclusion is continually

---

[265] N. Lacey, 'Feminist Legal Theory and the Rights of Women', 51. Lacey, for example, believes that this is possible under the CEDAW as a framework embracing both universalism and particularism, and she argues that it is 'probably the best and perhaps the only available legal strategy for escaping this kind of rights-based essentialism'.

[266] See, Edwards, 'Age and Gender Dimensions in International Refugee Law' (in which I argue that some of the experiences of refugee women are entirely personal and do not equate with any externally presumed characteristics or identities).

evaluated. This book is part of that process. As the later chapters in this book reveal, there has been some real progress in terms of incorporating women's experiences of violence within existing provisions, although how the process reached this stage is rather arbitrary and unpredictable, reliant more on creative interpretations than on universal consensus. At the same time, the process of interpretative inclusion has had the negative effect of doubling the burdens on women by requiring them to meet additional legal criteria. The inequality this reproduces is explained in later chapters.

In my exploration in the next few chapters of how women have fared within the international human rights jurisprudence, especially in the context of violence against women, these four themes will be revisited and reflected upon as to their continuing relevance and applicability to the existing international legal order. The following chapters will discuss the extent to which women's lives and women's voices are now reflected within the jurisprudence of the international human rights treaty bodies; the extent to which the 'public' remains prioritised over the 'private' in the international human rights system to the disadvantage of women; and the extent to which human rights bodies engage with the multiple identities and the intersectionality of women's lives. A range of questions guides the analysis in the following chapters: Are international human rights institutions still dominated by men? What has been the impact of this domination on human rights norms? How are women's rights affected by the state-based nature of international law? How have human rights norms been initially drafted and later interpreted and applied? Do human rights norms apply to women, and if they do, is it on an equal basis with men?

3

The international human rights treaty system: practice and procedure

A Introduction

As the primary focus of this book is on the jurisprudence of the UN human rights treaty bodies with respect to violence against women, this chapter outlines the mandates, procedural rules, and composition of these bodies. I summarise the main functions of the treaty bodies and recite a number of general problems with the treaty body system, before analysing the particular consequences of this system of human rights protection for women. The UN system of human rights protection is flawed in many respects, which can in turn affect women's access to and participation within it. This chapter addresses the first feminist critique outlined in Chapter 2 – that the institutions, structures, and processes established to implement international human rights norms exclude or sideline women from equal or meaningful participation and power-sharing.[1] Do the rules of the treaty bodies governing membership, working methods, and admissibility criteria prioritise men and the male experience? Do women have equal access to these mechanisms and their benefits? Where are the women?

The chapter is divided into three main parts. Immediately following this brief introduction, Part B outlines the general mandates of the treaty bodies; Part C then reviews the membership and expertise of these bodies; while Parts D–H set out and analyse the primary functions of the treaty bodies, summarised below.

B Mandates

International supervision of the implementation by states parties of most of their international human rights treaty obligations is carried out by

---

[1] This book deals with only one part of the general human rights protection system and does not, for instance, deal with Charter-based bodies or special procedures: see, e.g., N. Rodley, 'United Nations Human Rights Treaty Bodies and Special Procedures of the Commission on Human Rights – Complementarity or Competition?' (2003) 25 *HRQ* 882.

independent committees or treaty bodies. The UN human rights treaty body system consists of eight international treaty bodies overseeing the implementation of eight human rights treaties.[2] These are:

- the Human Rights Committee (HRC), monitoring the International Covenant on Civil and Political Rights 1966 (ICCPR);[3]
- the Committee on Economic, Social and Cultural Rights (CESCR), monitoring the International Covenant on Economic, Social and Cultural Rights 1966 (ICESCR);[4]
- the Committee on the Elimination of Racial Discrimination (CERD), monitoring the International Convention on the Elimination of All Forms of Racial Discrimination 1965 (ICERD);[5]
- the Committee on the Elimination of Discrimination against Women (the Women's Committee), monitoring the Convention on the Elimination of All Forms of Discrimination against Women 1979 (CEDAW);[6]
- the Committee against Torture (CAT), monitoring the UN Convention against Torture and Other Cruel, Inhuman or Degrading Treatment or Punishment 1984 (UNCAT);[7]
- the Committee on the Rights of the Child (the Children's Committee), monitoring the Convention on the Rights of the Child 1989 (CRC);[8]

---

[2] Office of the High Commissioner for Human Rights (OHCHR), *The United Nations Human Rights Treaty System: An Introduction to the Core Human Rights Treaties and the Treaty Bodies*, Fact Sheet No. 30, undated, available at: www.unhchr.org/. There are a range of other human rights treaties, such as the Convention on the Prevention and Punishment of the Crime of Genocide 1948, GA res. 260 A (III), 9 December 1948, 78 UNTS 277; entered into force 12 January 1951; and the Convention for the Suppression of the Traffic in Persons and of the Exploitation of the Prostitution of Others 1949, GA res. 317 (IV), 2 December 1949, 96 UNTS 271; entered into force 25 July 1951, however, these treaties do not establish monitoring mechanisms in the same way as those listed in the text.

[3] International Covenant on Civil and Political Rights 1966, GA res. 2200A (XXI), 16 December 1966, 999 UNTS 171; entered into force 23 March 1976 (ICCPR).

[4] International Covenant on Economic, Social and Cultural Rights 1966, GA res. 2200A (XXI), 16 December 1966, 993 UNTS 3; entered into force 3 January 1976 (ICESCR).

[5] International Convention on the Elimination of All Forms of Racial Discrimination 1965, GA res. 2106 (XX), 21 December 1965, 660 UNTS 195; entered into force 4 January 1969 (ICERD).

[6] Convention on the Elimination of All Forms of Discrimination against Women 1979, GA res. 34/180, 18 December 1979, 1249 UNTS 13; entered into force 3 September 1981 (CEDAW).

[7] Convention against Torture and Other Cruel, Inhumane or Degrading Treatment or Punishment 1984, GA res. 39/46, 10 December 1984, 1465 UNTS 85; entered into force 26 June 1987 (UNCAT).

[8] Convention on the Rights of the Child 1989, GA res. 44/25, 20 November 1989, 1577 UNTS 3; entered into force 2 September 1990 (CRC).

- the Committee on the Rights of Migrant Workers (MWC), monitoring the International Convention on the Protection of the Rights of All Migrant Workers and Members of their Families 1990 (IMWC);[9]
- the Committee on the Rights of Persons with Disabilities (CRPD), monitoring the Convention on the Rights of Persons with Disabilities 2006 (ICRPD).[10]

Each treaty body was established pursuant to the treaty they monitor or by UN resolution.[11] The committees sit on a part-time basis and meet two or three times per year for periods of two to three weeks per session, with some committees also meeting in pre-sessional working groups.[12] Their combined meeting time is around 60 weeks per year.[13]

A further committee, the Committee on Enforced Disappearances, overseeing the International Convention for the Protection of All Persons from Enforced Disappearances 2006 (ICED),[14] is due to commence work as soon as twenty ratifications have been received.[15] In addition to these committees, a Sub-Committee on the Prevention of Torture (SPT) was established in 2006 under the Optional Protocol to the Convention

---

[9] International Convention on the Protection of the Rights of All Migrant Workers and Members of Their Families 1990, GA res. 45/48, 18 December 1990, 2220 UNTS 93; entered into force 1 July 2003 (IMWC).

[10] Convention on the Rights of Persons with Disabilities 2006, GA res. 61/106, 13 December 2006; entered into force 3 May 2008 (ICRPD).

[11] HRC (Article 8, ICCPR); CESCR (ECOSOC res. 1985/17, 28 May 1985); CERD (Part III, ICERD); Women's Committee (Part V, CEDAW); CAT (Part II, UNCAT); Children's Committee (Part II, CRC); MWC (Part VII, IMWC); CRPD (Article 34, ICRPD).

[12] HRC (normally three sessions per year of three weeks' duration, with Working Group on Communications meeting prior to that); CERD (two sessions per year for three weeks and one week pre-sessional working group); CERD (two sessions per year of three weeks); Women's Committee (Article 20, CEDAW originally envisaged 'not more than 2 weeks annually', but now meets for three sessions per year of three weeks); CAT (two sessions per year, one of two weeks, one of three weeks, plus one week pre-sessional working group); Children's Committee (Article 43, CRC provides 'normally annually' but the Children's Committee actually meets for three sessions per year of three weeks plus one week pre-sessional working group. In 2006 the Children's Committee sat in two separate chambers of nine members in order to clear the backlog, as an exceptional and temporary measure); MWC (Article 75, IMWC provides that the MWC should 'normally' meet annually and as at October 2008, the Committee meets annually).

[13] OHCHR, 'Report of the Fourth Inter-Committee Meeting of Human Rights Treaty Bodies,' UN Doc. A/60/100, 10 August 2005, para. 59, which noted that the combined meeting time was 57 weeks, but this figure did not include the CRPD.

[14] International Convention for the Protection of All Persons from Enforced Disappearances 2006, GA res. 61/177, 20 December 2006, opened for signature 6 February 2007 (not yet in force at August 2010) (ICED).

[15] Article 39, ICED.

against Torture and Other Cruel, Inhuman or Degrading Treatment or Punishment 2002 (OP-CAT)[16] to carry out inspection visits to places of detention.

The functions of the treaty bodies are fourfold. First, the treaty bodies receive and examine reports submitted by states parties on a periodic basis.[17] Second, the treaty bodies issue authoritative statements or guidance to states parties on the meaning of substantive rights, the obligations of states parties, and other common issues (known as either General Comments or General Recommendations).[18] Third, some of the treaty bodies have jurisdiction to receive and consider interstate communications relating to a dispute between two states parties,[19] although not a single communication has ever been lodged. Fourth, half of the committees receive and consider petitions by individuals alleging violation of one or more of their human rights by a state party (known as 'individual communications').[20] In addition, some of the committees have

---

[16] Optional Protocol to the Convention against Torture and Other Cruel, Inhuman or Degrading Treatment or Punishment 2002, GA res. A/RES/57/199, 18 December 2002, 42 ILM 26 (2003); entered into force 22 June 2006 (OP-CAT).

[17] HRC (Article 40, ICCPR); CESCR (Article 17, ICESCR); CERD (Article 9, ICERD); Women's Committee (Article 18, CEDAW); CAT (Article 19, UNCAT); Children's Committee (Article 44, CRC); MWC (Article 73, IMWC).

[18] General Comments or General Recommendations are not explicitly provided for in the treaties themselves, but have developed from practice drawing on vague language in some of the treaties relating to state party reporting: see, e.g., Article 41, ICCPR: 'may transmit its reports, and such general comments as it may consider appropriate ...'.

[19] HRC (Article 41, ICCPR – on an optional basis – subject to declaration accepting the jurisdiction of the HRC); CERD (Article 11, ICERD – automatic jurisdiction upon ratification of the ICERD); CAT (Article 21, UNCAT – on an optional basis – subject to declaration accepting jurisdiction of the CAT); MWC (Article 76, IMWC – on an optional basis – subject to declaration accepting jurisdiction of the MWC, but it has yet to enter into force). On 18 June 2008 a resolution agreeing the draft Optional Protocol to the ICESCR was adopted by the UN Human Rights Council (UNHRC), in which individual and interstate communications are catered for: UNHRC res. 8/2, 18 June 2008, and confirmed by the General Assembly unanimously, GA res. A/RES/63/117, 10 December 2008 (OP-ICESCR). It has not yet entered into force as of 1 August 2010.

[20] HRC (Optional Protocol to the ICCPR, GA res. 2200A (XXI), 16 December 1966, 999 UNTS 302; entered into force 23 March 1976); CERD (Article 14, ICERD); Women's Committee (Optional Protocol to the CEDAW, GA res. 54/5, 15 October 1999; entered into force 22 December 2000 (OP-CEDAW)); CAT (Article 22, UNCAT); MWC (Article 77, IMWC) (note that the individual communications mechanism has yet to receive the appropriate number of ratifications to enter into force); Optional Protocol to the ICRPD, GA res. 61/106, 13 December 2006, UN Doc. A/61/49 (2006); entered into force 3 May 2008. The Optional Protocol to the ICESCR includes an individual communications procedure: Optional Protocol to the ICESCR 2008, GA res. A/RES/63/117, 10 December 2008 (OP-ICESCR).

mechanisms to conduct fact-finding inquiries[21] or have developed early warning procedures.[22] Almost all of the committees report annually to the General Assembly.[23] The functions are outlined in more detail below under their respective headings. First, however, I turn to the composition and expertise of the various committees.

C   Membership and expertise of the treaty bodies

1   Treaty provisions on membership and expertise

The size of each committee varies from ten to twenty-three members.[24] With the exception of the members of the CESCR, who are elected by the UN Economic and Social Council (ECOSOC),[25] members are nominated

---

[21] OP-CEDAW provides an optional procedure to allow the Women's Committee to respond when it receives reliable information indicating grave or systematic violations of human rights, which may include carrying out country visits (Article 8–10, OP-CEDAW). The CAT operates a confidential inquiry and urgent reporting procedure when it receives reliable information about well-founded indications of torture that is being systematically practised, which may include visits to the territory in cooperation with the state party (Article 20, UNCAT). In addition, the OP-CAT establishes an international inspection body with the capacity to make unannounced visits to places of detention in order to reduce the occurrence of torture or cruel, inhuman, or degrading treatment or punishment. On the OP-CAT, see M. D. Evans, 'Getting to Grips with Torture' (2002) 51 *ICLQ* 365; M. Evans and C. Haenni-Dale, 'Preventing Torture? The Development of the Optional Protocol to the UN Convention Against Torture' (2004) 4 *Hum. Rts. L. Rev.* 19; M. Nowak and E. McArthur, *The United Nations Convention against Torture: A Commentary* (Oxford University Press, 2008), 879–1191.

[22] The CERD has developed an ad hoc early warning or urgent procedure in order to prevent the escalation of situations into conflict or to prevent resumption of hostilities, based on a working paper: UN Doc. A/48/18, paras. 15–19 and Annex 3.

[23] HRC (Article 40, ICCPR – may also transmit reports to ECOSOC); CERD (Article 9, ICERD); Women's Committee (Article 21, CEDAW – Secretary-General to transmit reports also to Commission on the Status of Women); CAT (Article 24, UNCAT); Children's Committee (Article 45, CRC, provides for biannual reporting); MWC (Article 74, IMWC). The exception is the CESCR, which was established by ECOSOC, and it is elected by and reports to ECOSOC, per para. (f), ECOSOC res. 1985/17, 28 May 1985.

[24] HRC (18 members) (Article 28, ICCPR); CESCR (18 members) (para. (b), ECOSOC res. 1985/17, 28 May 1985); CERD (18 members) (Article 8, ICERD); Women's Committee (23 members) (Article 17, CEDAW); CAT (10 members) (Article 17, UNCAT); Children's Committee (18 members) (Article 43, CRC); MWC (10 members) (Article 72, IMWC). Note that the IMWC provides for an additional four members after the forty-fifth ratification.

[25] CESCR (para. (c), ECOSOC res. 1985/17, 28 May 1985 and Articles 16–17, ICESCR). ECOSOC is a UN body established under the UN Charter (Articles 61–71) to deal with international economic, social, cultural, educational, health and related matters. It consists of fifty-four members who are elected by the General Assembly.

by their own governments and elected by states parties to the treaty in question.[26] They are elected by secret ballot from a list of persons possessing the requisite qualifications. In theory, members sit in their personal capacity and not as government representatives.[27] They are expected to be of 'high moral character and recognized competence in the field of human rights', and consideration is given to those with legal experience, though this is not a prerequisite to nomination and/or election.[28]

Members are elected for four-year terms and may be re-elected if renominated.[29] The newer conventions limit the possibility of re-election to two terms.[30] Elections are organised so that half of the members of each committee are elected at intervals.[31] States parties may not normally nominate more than one national of the same state for a committee position.[32]

The UNCAT refers to the 'usefulness' of HRC members serving simultaneously on the CAT,[33] although this has not occurred in practice. The ICCPR, the ICERD, and the IMWC, meanwhile, refer expressly to 'impartiality'.[34] The expenses and subsistence allowances of sitting members are allocated in the UN budget, but the positions are otherwise unpaid.[35]

---

[26] HRC (Article 29, ICCPR); CERD (Article 8, ICERD); Women's Committee (Article 17, CEDAW); CAT (Article 17, UNCAT); Children's Committee (Article 43, CRC); MWC (Article 72, IMWC).

[27] HRC (Article 28 and 38, ICCPR); CESCR (para. (b), ECOSOC res. 1985/17, 28 May 1985); CERD (Article 8, ICERD); Women's Committee (Article 17, CEDAW); CAT (Article 17, UNCAT); Children's Committee (Article 43, CRC); MWC (Article 72, IMWC).

[28] HRC (Article 28, ICCPR); CESCR (para. (b), ECOSOC res. 1985/17, 28 May 1985); CERD (Article 8, ICERD); Women's Committee (Article 17, CEDAW); CAT (Article 17, UNCAT); Children's Committee (Article 43, CRC); MWC (Article 72, IMWC).

[29] HRC (Article 32, ICCPR); CESCR (para. (c), ECOSOC res. 1985/17, 28 May 1985); CERD (Article 8, ICERD); Women's Committee (Article 17, CEDAW); CAT (Article 17, UNCAT); Children's Committee (Article 43, CRC); MWC (Article 72, IMWC).

[30] E.g., Article 9, OP-CAT; Article 34(7), ICRPD (available for re-election once).

[31] HRC (Article 32, ICCPR); CESCR (para. (c), ECOSOC res. 1985/17, 28 May 1985); CERD (Article 8, ICERD); Women's Committee (Article 17, CEDAW); CAT (Article 17, UNCAT); Children's Committee (Article 43, CRC); MWC (Article 72, IMWC).

[32] Article 8(1), ICERD; Article 17, CEDAW; Article 17, UNCAT; Article 43, CRC; Article 72, IMWC. The exception is the nomination process for the HRC that allows no more than two nominations per state party (Article 29, ICCPR). No mention is made in the ECOSOC res. 1985/17 in relation to the CESCR.

[33] Article 17, UNCAT.

[34] Article 38, ICCPR (to serve on the Committee 'impartially and conscientiously'); Article 8, ICERD; Article 72(1)(b), IMWC.

[35] A token US$1 is paid to each of the treaty body members per annum. HRC (Article 35, ICCPR); CESCR (para. (e), ECOSOC res. 1985/17, 28 May 1985); CERD (the original Article 8(6), ICERD, provided for expenses to be the responsibility of the states parties, but was later amended by GA res. 47/111, 16 December 1992 in which finances are to

The various treaties and resolutions provide that consideration shall be given to 'equitable geographical distribution' and, variously, to representation of 'the different forms of civilization' and of the 'principal legal systems'.[36] No formal system is, however, in place to ensure that such a balanced geographical or other distribution is attained, and in fact, the modern workability of the UN's geographic blocs has been questioned.[37] Informally, however, it appears that the geographical representation requirement is internalised within the trading of positions between states parties, leading to a relatively balanced representation across the treaty bodies.[38]

2   General problems

As membership of the treaty bodies is secured via nomination and election processes, these processes are inherently politicised, resulting in turn in a lack of genuine interest in the qualifications and expertise of those nominated and elected.[39] In fact, it has been asserted by one senior official of the Office of the High Commissioner for Human Rights (OHCHR) that expertise is simply irrelevant to election.[40] Additionally, although members of all of the committees are expected to act in a personal capacity

come from the regular UN budget); Women's Committee (Article 17(8), CEDAW); CAT (the original Articles 17 and 18, UNCAT, provided for expenses to be the responsibility of the states parties but, like the ICERD, this was amended by GA res. 47/111, 16 December 1992 in which finances are to come from the regular UN budget); Children's Committee (Article 43, CRC); MWC (Article 72, IMWC).

[36] HRC (Article 28, ICCPR); CESCR (para. (b), ECOSOC res. 1985/17, 28 May 1985); CERD (Article 8, ICERD); Women's Committee (Article 17, CEDAW); CAT (Article 17, UNCAT); Children's Committee (Article 43, CRC); MWC (Article 72, IMWC).

[37] See, e.g., R. Thakur (ed.), *What is Equitable Geographic Representation in the Twenty-First Century?* (Tokyo: United Nations University, 1999). It has led to the establishment of a UN General Assembly Open-Ended Working Group on the Question of Equitable Representation on and Increase in the Membership of the Security Council and Other Matters Related to the Security Council; for further information, see www.un.org/ga/president/61/follow-up/securitycouncilreform.shtml.

[38] See, UN, *Report of the Chairpersons of the Human Rights Treaty Bodies on their Twenty-First Meeting*, UN Doc. A/64/280, 6 August 2009, Part V Discussion of Equitable Geographic Representation, in which it was noted the absence of African and Asian members on the SPT and under-representation of Eastern Europe on some of the other committees, but otherwise did not observe widespread geographic discrepancies.

[39] J. Crawford, 'The UN Human Rights Treaty System: A System in Crisis?', in P. Alston and J. Crawford (eds.), *The Future of the UN Human Rights Treaty Monitoring* (Cambridge University Press, 2000) 1, at 9.

[40] Interview with senior official of the OHCHR, 16 June 2008. This does not suggest, however, that there are no qualified candidates or members as that is not the case.

and do not therefore sit as government representatives, it is unlikely that states will nominate persons who are outwardly opposed to their policies.[41] Furthermore, because of the part-time nature of the committees and the lack of remuneration, a minority continue to hold government posts. These two factors also limit those available for nomination to persons who are individually wealthy, hold academic positions, or who are former or current public or government servants, the latter frequently being rewarded with a UN post for former service to the state and to the government. Anne Bayefsky found in her 2000 study that an average of 50 per cent of all those persons elected to the treaty bodies were employed in some capacity by their governments.[42] Little has changed in the make-up of today's committees.

The nomination and election processes were created as a compromise to give states a sense of influence over the direction of the committees.[43] No guidance is offered to states parties on who should be nominated as committee members (apart from general character and qualifications criteria, listed above) or how to do so.[44] In fact, the procedures in most countries are not transparent and are far from democratic (even in democratic states), and rarely subject to public scrutiny. Other governments show interest in simply ensuring that a national of their own country wins international office.[45] It is predictable, then, that when domestic political and judicial institutions are dominated by men, this translates into a repeated pattern of male dominance at the international level. For example, in Sweden, where female participation in government is 45 per cent in lower or single

---

[41] See, e.g., S. Joseph, J. Schultz and M. Castan, *The International Covenant on Civil and Political Rights: Cases, Materials, and Commentary* (2nd edn, Oxford University Press, 2004), n. 56, referring to the failure in 1994 of the Federal Republic of Yugoslavia (now Serbia-Montenegro) to renominate Mr Vojin Dimitrijevic as an HRC member. Mr Dimitrijevic was originally nominated by the government of the former Yugoslavia in 1982.

[42] A. F. Bayefsky, *The UN Human Rights Treaty System: Universality at the Crossroads* (April 2001), 108.

[43] A. Boulesbaa, *The UN Convention on Torture and the Prospects for Enforcement* (The Hague: Martinus Nijhoff Publishers, 1999), 240.

[44] Article 28(1), ICCPR; para. (b), UN Doc. ECOSOC res. 1985/17, 28 May 1985; Article 17(1), UNCAT; Article 8(1), CERD: Article 17(1), CEDAW; Article 43(2), CRC; Article 72(1)(b), IMWC.

[45] E.g. in 2005 the then Australian Liberal Government supported the nomination of Gareth Evans, former Minister for Foreign Affairs of the former opposition Labor Government, to the position of UN High Commissioner for Refugees. He was ultimately unsuccessful. See, 'Former Portuguese Premier Chosen to Lead UN Refugee Agency', *New York Times*, 25 May 2005.

chambers of parliament,[46] the highest in the industrialised world, it has consistently nominated women to international office. James Crawford has found that '[v]ote trading between unrelated UN bodies is so common [as] to be unremarked'.[47] Similarly, Andrew Clapham has criticised the treaty body election process for failing to ensure genuine expertise.[48] Deals are done between states, which ultimately affects the ability of women to attain office.[49]

3   Where are the women?

The UN Charter specifically provides that there shall be 'no restrictions on the eligibility of men and women to participate in any capacity and under conditions of equality in its principal and subsidiary organs'.[50] No system of appointments of women to positions of power has yet been comprehensively included in the UN system.[51] The Women's Committee has, in addition, twice issued General Recommendations calling on governments to ensure that women, 'on equal terms with men and without any discrimination', enjoy the opportunities to represent their countries at the international level and to participate in the work of international organisations.[52] None of the first seven treaties listed above included provisions calling for equal representation on the basis of sex, unlike a call for balanced geographic representation, as already explained. Of the treaties adopted since 2006, however, each now calls for 'balanced gender [read: sex] representation' in the make-up of the bodies they establish.[53] Despite this, early data on the Sub-Committee on the Prevention of Torture (SPT), which contains such a provision and yet was able to elect

---

[46] UN Statistics Division, Table 6 Women in Parliament, at http://unstats.un.org/unsd/demographic/products/indwm/ww2005/tab6.htm (accessed 5 March 2006).

[47] Crawford, 'The UN Human Rights Treaty System: A System in Crisis?', 9.

[48] A. Clapham, 'UN Human Rights Reporting Procedures: An NGO Perspective', in Alston and Crawford (eds.), *The Future of the UN Human Rights Treaty Monitoring*, 175, at 188.

[49] On vote-trading in international institutions, see O. Eldar, 'Vote-Trading in International Institutions' (2008) 19 *Eur. J. Int'l L.* 3.

[50] Article 8, UN Charter.

[51] J. Ulrich, 'Confronting Gender-Based Violence with International Instruments: Is a Solution to the Pandemic Within Reach?' (1999–2000) 7 *Ind. J. Global Legal Stud.* 629, 635.

[52] CEDAW General Recommendation No. 8 (1988); CEDAW General Recommendation No. 10 (1989), para. 3.

[53] Article 34(4), ICRPD; Article 5(4), OP-CAT. See, also, Article 26, ICED.

only two female members out of ten, indicates that explicit provisions on gender balance make little difference to the composition of these bodies. As the provisions are couched in discretionary language only, there is limited imperative to institute systems to improve the participation rates of women. Women have not (yet) become the bargaining ground for states in the same way as equitable geographic representation has.

As a consequence, women make up less than 50 per cent of the membership of the treaty bodies and are still concentrated in specialist committees dealing with the rights of women and children. A major study on the work of four of the treaty bodies in 2000 found that less than 20 per cent of the membership was female.[54] As at December 2009, women made up exactly 40 per cent of the membership of the eight treaty bodies (see Table 3.1). Excluding the Women's Committee and the Children's Committee, however, this figure drops to around 20 per cent (see Table 3.1). The Children's Committee is the only committee that has achieved equal numbers of men and women.[55] In its twenty-five-year history, the Women's Committee has only ever had three male members.[56] In 1991 Charlesworth, Chinkin, and Wright complained rightly when the Women's Committee faced pressure to increase male representation, whereas no 'male dominated' committees at that time faced criticism for having too few women.[57] Alarmingly, there has been no systematic change in the number of women occupying committee positions. Any progress in women's representation appears to be haphazard rather than deliberate. There is no evidence of increased incremental participation of women over the history of the treaty bodies. Instead, there is periodic minor increased participation of women on some committees (and decreased participation on others) (see Table 3.1).

---

[54] The four committees studied were the CERD, the CESCR, the HRC, and the CAT. See, Bayefsky, *The UN Human Rights Treaty System*, 110.

[55] For up-to-date information on membership of the committees, see: www.ohchr.org/english/bodies/crc/members.htm.

[56] For up-to-date information on the membership of the Women's Committee, see: www.un.org/womenwatch/daw/cedaw/members.pdf.

[57] H. Charlesworth, C. Chinkin and S. Wright, 'Feminist Approaches to International Law' (1991) 85 *Amer. J. Int'l L.* 613, at 624; H. Charlesworth and C. Chinkin, *The Boundaries of International Law: A Feminist Analysis* (Manchester University Press, 2000), 174–187; A. Gallagher, 'Ending the Marginalization: Strategies for Incorporating Women into the United Nations Human Rights System' (1997) 19 *HRQ* 283, at 294–309.

Table 3.1 Progression of membership of the treaty bodies – by sex

Committee (first session unless specified otherwise)	Total Membership	First Election		December 2009		% change in women's representation
		Men (%)	Women (%)	Men (%)	Women (%)	
HRC (1985)	18	17 (94%)	1 (6%)	13 (72%)	5 (28%)	Increase
CESCR (1992*)	18	15 (83%)	3 (17%)	15 (83%)	3 (17%)	No change
CERD (1986*)	18	17 (94%)	1 (6%)	17 (94%)	1 (6%)	No change
Women's Committee (1986*)	23	0 (0%)	23 (100%)	2 (7%)	21 (91%)	Decrease
CAT (1988)	10	8 (80%)	2 (20%)	6 (60%)	4 (40%)	Increase
Children's Committee (1992)*	18 (10 originally)	5 (50%)	5 (50%)	9 (50%)	9 (50%)	No change
MWC (2005)	10	8 (80%)	2 (20%)	7 (70%)	3 (30%)	Increase
CRPD (2008)	12	7 (58%)	5 (42%)	7 (58%)	5 (42%)	No change
SPT (2009)	10			9 (90%)	1 (10%)	–
Totals**	119–127	77/119 (65%)	42/119 (35%)	76/127 (60%)	51/127 (40%)	Increase
Totals excluding Women's and Children's Committees	86	72 (84%)	14 (16%)	65 (76%)	21 (24%)	Increase

* Note that these figures represent the composition of the treaty body for the earliest publicly available records rather than the first session (CERD, 35th Session, UN Doc. A/42/18 (1987); CEDAW, 5th Session, UN Doc. A/41/45 (1986); CESCR, 7th Session, UN Doc. E/C.12/1992/2 (1992); CRC, 2nd Session, UN Doc. CRC/C/10 (1992))

** The figures for SPT are not included as there is no comparable data.

4 Where is the expertise in women's rights and gender?

It has been asserted that expertise and qualifications are irrelevant to treaty body membership. It seems the same can be said for expertise in women's rights and/or gender. In a review of the curricula vitae of sitting experts on the HRC, for example, only four out of eighteen members explicitly identified any expertise on women's human rights or gender; and only one female member out of the four sitting members is included in this total, the remaining being male members.[58] Likewise, only two out of the ten members of the CAT explicitly indicate expertise on women's rights in their publicly available curricula vitae. Unlike the HRC, however, the two who did are two of the three female members on that committee.[59] This is to be contrasted with the Women's Committee members, most of whom have particular experience and expertise in women's rights.[60] The concentration of such expertise in a specialist committee on women's rights, and away from the other treaty bodies, is concerning, not least because it raises the question of how gender issues can be mainstreamed in the absence of appropriate expertise.

5 Why argue for more women? What are the consequences of more women for decision-making?

Calls for greater parity of women in politics and, by analogy, in decision-making positions, have been framed in four main ways. First, women's equal representation is a question of justice and fits alongside feminist challenges to sexual exclusion or segregation wherever it occurs.[61] A second argument is that women would bring to politics (and, in this case, to decision-making) a different set of values, experiences, and expertise.[62] Third, any system that consistently excludes the voices of women

---

[58] Based on membership as at 31 December 2009.

[59] Based on membership as at 31 December 2009.

[60] Based on membership as at 31 December 2009.

[61] H. M. Hernes, *Welfare State and Woman Power: Essays in State Feminism* (Norwegian University Press, 1987), as summarised in A. Phillips, *Engendering Democracy* (London: Polity Press, 1991, 1993, and 1997), 62–63. See, also, A. Phillips, 'Democracy and Representation: Or, Why Should it Matter Who our Elected Representatives Are?', in A. Phillips (ed.), *Feminism and Politics: Oxford Readings in Feminism* (Oxford University Press, 1998) 224 (referring to four arguments in favour of gender parity in politics: (1) women politicians act as role models for other women; (2) justice; (3) women's interests are better served by women; and (4) questions of democracy and representation).

[62] Phillips, *Engendering Democracy*.

is not just unfair; 'it does not begin to count as representation'.[63] And a fourth argument is that female judges or decision-makers act as role models for other women and girls. Each of these perspectives is relevant to the participation of women within the human rights treaty body system, and international institutions more broadly, and they are discussed in turn below.

5.1   Equal representation as a human rights issue

The under-representation of women on the treaty bodies is a matter of basic principles of justice and human rights, in particular that of equality. The 'distorted distribution' in decision-making bodies (political, diplomatic, and judicial) is evidence of either or both intentional and structural discrimination.[64] In other words, the under-representation of women on international bodies constitutes a violation of women's right to equality.[65] Equality is normally used in this context to refer to formal (or liberal) equality or the parity in numbers of men and women in positions of power. It can likewise be seen as a form of substantive equality by tackling underlying oppression or patriarchy by putting women in positions with real power. To achieve this balancing at the level of international law, however, equality of access to the nomination and election process is needed; which in turn requires strategies to overcome structural inequality and causes of women's exclusion from such processes.[66]

As the international legal system is reliant on municipal participation and systems, changes at the municipal level would also need to occur. As long as disproportionately more men are nominated to committee positions, they will continue to be elected in disproportionate numbers. The Women's Committee stated in 1988 that it is not within its remit to tell states parties how and who to nominate to international office.[67] However,

---

[63] *Ibid.*   [64] *Ibid.,* 225.

[65] H. Charlesworth, 'The Gender of International Institutions' (1995) 89 *ASIL Proceedings* 84.

[66] For more on the meaning of equality and non-discrimination on the basis of sex, see Chapter 4.

[67] See, A. Byrnes, 'The "Other" Human Rights Treaty Body: The Work of the Committee on the Elimination of Discrimination Against Women' (1989) 14 *Yale J. Int'l L.* 1, at 9, n. 27, in which he refers to a rejected proposal in 1988 for a General Recommendation to states parties that they nominate men for election to the Women's Committee. It was rejected for two reasons: that the Women's Committee should not presume to tell states parties how to exercise the prerogative to nominate persons to the Women's Committee; and it could lead to the loss of the only human rights treaty body in which a clear majority of the members were women.

as noted above, the same Committee has on at least two prior occasions called on states parties to ensure women have the same opportunities as men to represent their countries and to work for international organisations.[68] It seems to me to be entirely legitimate for the treaty bodies to inquire into all areas of inequality, including those within their own bodies. At a minimum, nomination processes at the municipal level should be open and transparent. In addition, one might need to consider a gender-based rotating nomination process such that if a state party nominates and has elected a male member to a particular committee, a woman would be put forward for any other bodies to which the state party is considering nominating, and also be put forward once the male member's two terms have expired. It follows suit that after the female member's two terms expire, it would then return to a male nominee.[69] An alternative model might be one in which a state must nominate candidates from among the under-represented sex, as attempted before the European Court of Human Rights (ECtHR) (discussed further in Chapter 8 on treaty body reform). If all states parties adopted a similar pattern of nomination, it would numerically increase the number of women nominated and (in turn) ultimately elected. Recruitment drives may also need to be conducted at the municipal level to encourage women to put themselves forward for nomination. The treaty bodies also ought to operate internal procedural rules that ensure balanced gender representation in key committee functions, such as rotating chairpersons and rapporteurships.[70] Non-governmental organisations also have an important role to play in publicising nomination processes and identifying appropriate candidates for nomination.

[68] CEDAW General Recommendation No. 8 (1988); CEDAW General Recommendation No. 10 (1989), para. 3.
[69] The suggestion of gender rotation was put forward by Kim Rubenstein in her address on Australian constitutional arrangements and the position of Governor-General which had not been filled by a woman in its 107-year history: see, K. K. Rubenstein, 'From Suffrage to Citizenship: A Republic of Equality', 2008 Dymphna Clark Lecture, Canberra, March 2008. Note that in 2008 Australia appointed its first female Governor-General: Quentin Bryce, *Australia Gets First Female Governor General*, Reuters, 13 April 2008, available at: www.reuters.com/article/idUSSYD18779220080413.
[70] It is noted that rotating the chairperson and rapporteur positions may cause difficulties in committees with few women and this could result in the few women becoming overburdened with responsibilities. However, for those committees in which over 30 per cent of the membership are women, any burden could be shared between them. Moreover, rotating positions may encourage states to nominate more women to committee positions if they know that their male nominees are only half as likely to attain important positions in the committees than women members.

5.2   Impact of female members on decision-making

The second argument in favour of more women on decision-making bodies is a belief that they bring to the task different modes of thinking, rationalising, and reasoning. That is, equal participation requires both quantitative and qualitative equality.[71] Andrew Byrnes notes that, where novel claims or arguments that draw heavily on women's experiences are presented, the male domination of a body may reduce the chances of the acceptance and ultimate success of such arguments.[72] While I accept that this is often the case, his analysis does not, however, take account of other research that shows that women, in politics at least, are wary of speaking for women, or that there is a numerical threshold at which women will feel comfortable raising issues of sex.[73] According to British constitutional lawyer J. A. G. Griffith, social attributes such as class, religion, place, and nature of education, and ethnicity, have considerable effects on the nature and content of judgments.[74] Relying on the work of Carol Gilligan in particular,[75] some feminist scholars assert that it follows that sex/gender could be one of these characteristics.[76]

In terms of judging, the argument is made that as women have such different characteristics, more women judges will lead to a radically different law and legal system, as women use their skills and perspectives to interpret the law in a different manner to men. Thus, some have argued that: women lawyers are more likely to seek to mediate disputes than litigate them; women lawyers are more concerned with public service; women judges are more likely to emphasise context and de-emphasise general principles; and, women judges are more compassionate.[77]

Despite the methodological difficulties in proving or disproving such assertions, some research is available to suggest that women judges may

---

[71] See, e.g., in the context of the Supreme Court of Canada, M. Eberts, 'Feminist Perspectives on the Canadian Charter of Rights and Freedoms', in P. Alston (ed.), *Promoting Human Rights Through Bills of Rights: Comparative Perspectives* (New York: Oxford University Press, 1999, reprinted 2003) 241; A. Byrnes, 'Toward More Effective Enforcement of Women's Human Rights Through the Use of International Human Rights Law and Procedures', in R. J. Cook (ed.), *Human Rights of Women: National and International Perspectives* (Philadelphia: University Pennsylvania Press, 1994) 189, at 200.

[72] Byrnes, 'Toward More Effective Enforcement of Women's Human Rights', 200.

[73] See, Chapter 2.

[74] J. A. G. Griffith, *The Politics of the Judiciary* (5th edn, London: Fontana, 1997), as referred to in C. McGlynn, 'Will Women Judges Make a Difference?' (1998) 148 *New Law J.* 813.

[75] See, Chapter 2.

[76] McGlynn, 'Will Women Judges Make a Difference?'.

[77] *Ibid.*

adopt more so-called 'feminine' modes of decision-making.[78] Women judges themselves have argued that women tend to make more liberal decisions to uphold individual rights.[79] At the same time, however, arguments that women bring feminist reasoning to the judiciary have been used to keep women out of the 'male', 'rational', and 'objective' world of the bench. This was played out in the 2009 US Senate Judiciary Committee's confirmation hearings into the appointment of Sonia Sotomayer to the US Supreme Court, in which Sotomayer recanted, to the nearly all-white male committee of senators, any previous statements to the contrary that judicial decision-making is anything other than a 'neutral' or 'objective' practice.[80] It begs the question of 'whose objectivity' is being prioritised.

Margaret Thornton writes, for example, that the selection criterion of 'merit' is a pseudonym for power reinforced by the abstractness of the term and the lack of transparency in judicial appointment processes.[81] At the international level, the UN has noted that women tend to support peace initiatives, protection of the environment, and the creation and maintenance of social services to a greater extent than men.[82] It further found that women tend to favour more inclusive and less polarising forms of decision-making.[83] Equivalent studies in the context of the decision-making of the treaty bodies have not been undertaken, perhaps owing to the difficulty in distinguishing the views of female and male members under a largely consensual decision-making approach (see the discussion below). Some insights can, however, be gleaned from the working practices of the treaty bodies.

Almost all of the treaty bodies have adopted informal divisions of labour, in which members put forward their interest in a particular subject matter or article of the relevant treaty. This division of labour appears to divide along gender lines. On the Women's Committee, for instance, the only three male members in the history of the Committee indicated interest in

---

[78] See, e.g., S. Sherry, 'Civil Virtue and the Feminine Voice of Constitutional Adjudication' (1986) 72 *Vanderbilt L. Rev.* 543, at 593; Cf. J. Aliotta, 'Justice O'Connor and the Equal Protection Clause: A Feminine Voice?' (1995) 78 *Judicature* 232.

[79] Justice Atkinson of the Supreme Court of Queensland, Australia, quoted in N. Rose, 'International Bar Association Conference: Top Judge Calls for More Women on the Bench to Uphold Individual Rights' (2005) 8 *Law Society Gazette* (no page).

[80] See, http://judiciary.senate.gov/nominations/SupremeCourt/Sotomayor/. Two out of sixteen of the senators on the Judiciary Committee were women at the date of nomination.

[81] M. Thornton, '"Otherness" on the Bench: How Merit is Gendered' (2007) 29 *Sydney L. Rev.* 391, at 408.

[82] UN, *Women in Decision-Making* (1992), 107, referred to in Charlesworth, 'The Gender of International Institutions'.

[83] *Ibid.*

issues such as reservations rather than in any substantive rights.[84] On the CRC, the informal division of labour, even though aligned with professional expertise, interestingly still tends to see women members take up the issues of education, health, and disability, while male members typically focus on juvenile justice.[85] On the CESCR, the debate over the appropriate venue in which to discuss women's issues has stalled progress, with some members reluctant to deal with women's issues because they feel that such issues should be raised in the specialist treaties.[86]

Notably, some NGOs have observed that the presence of a single female member on the CAT, for example, led to the frequent raising of women's interests.[87] Meanwhile, they worry that such issues may disappear entirely without female members.[88] The system in place presents a 'fragile' protection for women's rights to the extent that, if a treaty body loses a member dedicated to women's issues, that expertise is lost.[89] For this reason, the 'mere' presence of the Women's Committee may balance out such concerns and it can be seen that the work of the Women's Committee has influenced the work of the other treaty bodies to take up issues of gender inequality.[90] Likewise, it has been argued that the increased participation of women in the European Parliament in 1979 coincided with an increased attention to issues of sexual equality.[91] Nonetheless, where there is only one female member or she is one of very few women, it takes some time to convince the other members of the committee (read: the male members) of her worthiness to be on the committee at all, especially if she chooses to take up a gender agenda.[92]

There is some evidence at the international level to support claims that women add a new dimension to decision-making, or are at least more open to new interpretations. For example, the first historic, and so far only,[93] international decision that found rape to be an act of genocide,

---

[84]   Interview with member of the Women's Committee, 19 June 2008.

[85]   Interview with former member of the CRC, 19 June 2008.

[86]   Interview with member of the CESCR, 18 June 2008.

[87]   Interviews conducted with officials of five international non-governmental organisations between 2006 and 2008.

[88]   *Ibid.*

[89]   Interview with senior official of the OHCHR, 16 June 2008.

[90]   Interview with former members of the Women's Committee and the HRC, 10 June 2006.

[91]   V. Randall, *Women and Politics: An International Persepctive* (2nd edn, University of Chicago Press, 1987), 155–156, referred to in Charlesworth, 'The Gender of International Institutions'.

[92]   Interview with senior official of the OHCHR, 16 June 2008.

[93]   While rape has been raised as a crime in a number of decisions before the International Criminal Tribunal for the former Yugoslavia (ICTY), it has not (yet) been tried as

which was delivered by the International Criminal Tribunal for Rwanda (ICTR),[94] emerged only after serious lobbying by women's groups that the indictment be amended to include rape. Akayesu, a town mayor, was not initially charged with any crimes against women, but as the trial developed, evidence emerged through testimony of the large number of such crimes. An amendment to the charges and permission to admit such evidence was allowed by the only female judge on the case, Justice Pillay.[95] The Chief Prosecutor at the time, however, was also female and had not prioritised cases of gender or sexual violence;[96] and according to NGOs lobbying on such issues, required much convincing to pursue such cases.[97] This has been argued in a similar way in other jurisdictions, such as the ECtHR, in which a feminist dissent has not been apparent despite the increase in female judges.[98]

Although there are some examples in which the presence of women on treaty bodies contributed to an improved reflection of gender or women's concerns within the interpretation of existing provisions, many groundbreaking human rights decisions that carry positive ramifications for women developed in cases that involved men and/or no apparent gender dimensions. The 'due diligence' concept, which allows the actions of non-state or 'private' actors to be brought within the purview of international

genocide: see, e.g., *Prosecutor v. Delalic, Mucic, Delic and Landzo (Celebici)*, ICTY, Case No. IT-96-21-I (21 March 1996) (the ICTY found rape and sexual assault of camp detainees constituted grave breaches of the Geneva Conventions and violations of the laws and customs of war); *Prosecutor v. Anto Furundzija*, ICTY, Case No. IT-95-17/1-T (10 December 1998) (convicted of two counts of violating the laws or customs of war, as a co-perpetrator of torture and as an aider and abettor of outrages upon personal dignity, including rape); *Prosecutor v. Kunarac, Kovac and Vukovic*, ICTY Case No. IT-96-23-T and IT-96-23/1-T (22 February 2001); upheld on appeal, Case No. IT-96-23 and IT-96-23/1 (12 June 2002) (rape held to constitute torture).

[94] *Prosecutor v. Jean-Paul Akayesu*, ICTR, Case No. ICTR-96-4-A (2 September 1998); *Prosecutor v. Jean-Paul Akayesu* (Appeal), ICTR, Case No. ICTR-96-4-A (1 June 2001).

[95] K. D. Askin, 'Prosecuting Wartime Rape and Other Gender-Related Crimes under International Law: Extraordinary Advances, Enduring Obstacles' (2003) 21 *Berkeley J. Int'l L.* 288, at 318. This case is discussed further in Chapter 5.

[96] The Chief Prosecutor at the time was Ms Louise Arbour, who then went on to become the UN High Commissioner for Human Rights from 1 July 2004 to September 2008. She was appointed to the position of Chief Prosecutor of the International Criminal Tribunals for the former Yugoslavia and Rwanda in 1996 and served until 1999, when she was replaced by Ms Carla Del Ponte. Interestingly, Justice Pillay has now gone on to take up the position of UN High Commissioner for Human Rights from September 2008.

[97] Discussions with NGOs and others involved in the campaign to change the indictment in *Akayesu*, 2008.

[98] M-B. Dembour, *Who Believes in Human Rights? Reflections on the European Convention* (Cambridge University Press, 2006), 192, n. 24.

law by attributing that 'private' harm to the state through its failures to prevent it, for example, developed initially before the Inter-American Court of Human Rights, involved no analysis of gender.[99] Similarly, the first decisions in the context of international refugee law that held that gender-related persecution is a ground for asylum did not involve women,[100] although the courts did acknowledge that their analysis would be of benefit to women's claims. These two examples support the view that there is no guarantee that female members will be more attuned to issues affecting women than their male counterparts or that men are incapable of reaching such decisions. As stated in Chapter 2, arguments that suggest that women are 'naturally' inclined to adopt different techniques to men 'recall the old myths [women] have struggled to put behind [them].'[101] These old myths must be rejected as wedding women to biology and reinforcing social stereotypes. They also play into assumptions that women and women's decision-making are exceptions to the norm.[102]

Furthermore, to accept the argument that women are needed on judicial or quasi-judicial bodies to ensure that decision-making reflects and takes account of gender (rather than simply their right to participate equally with men) often leads to the situation in which one of the female committee members (or the only female member) becomes informally identified as responsible for bringing attention to women's concerns.[103] Rather, it must be the responsibility of each and every member of the committee. In addition, there are theorists who point out that women may not always be willing to advocate for women's rights.[104] Overall, therefore, it is possible for women as well as men to adopt feminist methods of analysis, but it may be that, at least initially, women have a greater stake in doing so.

---

[99] *Velásquez Rodríguez* v. *Honduras*, I-ACtHR, Ser. C, No. 4 (29 July 1988). See, also, *Godina-Cruz* v. *Honduras*, I-ACtHR, Ser. C, No. 5 (20 January 1989). These cases are discussed further in Chapter 5.

[100] See, A. Edwards, 'Age and Gender Dimensions in International Refugee Law', in E. Feller, V. Türk and F. Nicholson, *Refugee Protection in International Law: UNHCR's Global Consultations on International Protection* (Cambridge University Press, 2003) 46. See, e.g., *Acosta* v. *Immigration and Naturalization Service*, US, BIA LEXIS 2, 19 I & N Dec. 211 (1985) and *Canada (Attorney-General)* v. *Ward*, SCC, Can. S.C.R. LEXIS 35, 2 Can. S.C.R. 689 (1983).

[101] S. Day O'Connor, 'Portia's Progress' (1991) 66 *NYU Law Rev.* 1546 at 1553.

[102] R. Graycar, 'The Gender of Judgments: An Introduction', in M. Thornton (ed.), *Public and Private: Feminist Legal Debates* (Melbourne: Oxford University Press, 1995) 262.

[103] Interviews conducted with officials of five international non-governmental organisations between 2006 and 2008.

[104] See, Chapter 2.

5.3   Arguments based on democracy and universality

The third argument posited in favour of women's equal representation in politics in particular is that democracy requires it. This argument is also relevant to the UN system, based as it is inter alia on the principle of universality. Just as geographic representation is valued in the UN system, so too must sexual equality be valued when women make up 50 per cent of the world's population. Closely tied to equality arguments, the framing of arguments for women's participation within the broader concept of universality can lead to 'a more ambitious programme of dispersing power'.[105] As Karen Knop argues, women should be able to decide international cases, not because they will make better or even different decisions, but 'because they as a group ... should be able to make decisions that affect their lives'.[106] Similarly, Justice Sandra Day O'Connor, the first woman appointed to the US Supreme Court in 1981, has stated in response to questions about whether women bring different modes of reasoning to the Court by virtue of being women:

> There is simply no empirical evidence that gender differences lead to discernible differences in rendering decisions.[107]

I wonder, however, whether it is simply that the empirical evidence has not yet been collected.

5.4   Female decision-makers as role models

The fourth argument in favour of the inclusion of women in decision-making positions is that it can 'help[-] to shatter stereotypes about the role of women in society that are held by male judges and lawyers, as well as by litigants, jurors and, witnesses'.[108] In a similar vein it has been asserted that the male-dominated composition of some of the treaty bodies is a reason for women's reluctance to utilise the individual complaints procedures.[109] In other words, there is a correlation between women as judges and women as litigants. Justice O'Connor has also acknowledged that having women on the bench and in positions of prominence is significant,

---

[105] Phillips, 'Democracy and Representation', 238.

[106] K. Knop, 'Re/Statements: Feminism and State Sovereignty in International Law' (1993) 3 *Transnat. L. & Contemp. Prob.* 293, at 306–307.

[107] S. Day O'Connor, *The Majesty of the Law: Reflections of a Supreme Court Justice* (London: Random House, 2004), 191

[108] S. Sherry, 'The Gender of Judges' (1986) 4 *Law & Inequality* 159, 160.

[109] Byrnes, 'Toward More Effective Enforcement of Women's Human Rights'.

in part because of the role-model function it serves for young women that women are not cast in fixed roles.[110] The impact, therefore, of women as decision-makers is part of the process of breaking down structural barriers to women's equality.

5.5 Summary

In my view, the strongest arguments for women's equal representation and participation in the work of the treaty bodies are those based on the right to equality in all fields and the principle of universality upon which the UN system is based, which are in turn related to the role-model function of girls being able to see women in positions of power and the overall hope that future representation will be more equal. It is also acknowledged that there is some evidence to suggest that women bring to the table or bench different life experiences, which may filter into their decision-making. At the same time, however, there is also evidence to suggest that positive decision-making for women's rights can be made in their absence, raising hope that equal numerical participation of women is not the precursor to positive decision-making in favour of women, especially as only one of the eight treaty bodies (the CRC) has ever achieved parity in numbers.

D   State party reports

1   General overview

The receipt and consideration of periodic state party reports, common to all the committees, is the primary means of monitoring the implementation of human rights treaty obligations under the treaty body system.[111] Treaty body reporting is aimed at establishing a dialogue between the state party and the committee in the hope of assisting governments to implement better their human rights treaty obligations. Initial reports are due one or two years after ratification, with follow-up reports due between two, four, or five years after the initial report, or whenever the treaty body

---

[110] Day O'Connor, *The Majesty of the Law*, 187.

[111] See, A. F. Bayefsky, 'Making the Human Rights Treaties Work', in L. Henkin and J. L. Hargrove (eds.), *Human Rights: An Agenda for the Next Century* (American Society of International Law, Studies in Transnational Legal Studies No. 26, 1994) 229; A. F. Bayefsky, 'Conclusions and Recommendations', in A. F. Bayefsky (ed.), *The UN Human Rights System in the 21st Century* (The Hague: Kluwer Law International, 2000); H. Niemi and M. Scheinin, 'Reform of the United Nations Human Rights Treaty Body System Seen from the Developing Country Perspective', Institute for Human Rights, Abo Akademi University, June 2002, at www.abo.fi/instut/imr/norfa/heli-martin.pdf.

so requests.[112] The state party is expected to report on the steps taken to implement its obligations, including legislative, judicial, administrative, and other measures that have been adopted, and any difficulties that have been experienced in meeting treaty obligations.[113] In order to ensure that reports supply adequate information for the treaty bodies to do their work, each body issues guidelines on the form and content of state reports,[114] although there is considerable variation in the form in which reports are presented.[115] In 2005 the states parties agreed on harmonised reporting guidelines, as part of moves towards reform (discussed in Chapter 8).

According to the UN High Commissioner for Human Rights, the reporting process should 'encourage and facilitate, at the national level, popular participation, public scrutiny of government policies and programmes, and constructive engagement with civil society'.[116] Some states incorporate comments and criticism from NGOs in their reports; others submit their reports to parliamentary scrutiny before submission.[117] Some other states, of course, do neither. Still others have opted to hire consultants to draft and prepare their reports, ultimately defeating the purpose of self-evaluation, review, and 'constructive dialogue'. The OHCHR stresses that this process is not adversarial or judicial but dialogic, with the aim being to assist governments in their efforts to implement the treaty in question.[118]

Once submitted, the report is scheduled for consideration by the committee at one of its regular sessions. Reports are then examined in a public session by the relevant treaty body in the presence of representatives of the state party. In advance of that face-to-face meeting, the committee draws up a List of Issues and questions, which it submits to the state party. This allows the committee to request additional information that may have

---

[112] Article 40, ICCPR (initial report one year after ratification and then 'usually every 4 years'); Part IV, ICESCR (initial report two years after ratification and then every five years); Article 9, ICERD (initial report one year after ratification and then every two years or whenever requested); Article 18, CEDAW (initial report after one year and then every four years or whenever requested); Article 19, UNCAT (initial report after one year and then every four years or whenever requested); Article 44, CRC (initial report after two years and then every five years, no spontaneous requests); Article 73(1)(a), IMWC (one year after ratification, then every five years or upon request).

[113] Article 40, ICCPR; Article 17, ICESCR; Article 9, ICERD; Article 18, CEDAW; Article 19, UNCAT; Article 44, CRC; Article 73, IMWC.

[114] See, e.g., UN, *Compilation of Guidelines on the Form and Content of Reports to be Submitted by States Parties to the International Human Rights Treaties*, UN Doc. HRI/GEN/2/Rev.2/Add.1, 6 May 2005.

[115] OHCHR, Fact Sheet No. 30, 28.   [116] *Ibid.*, 27.   [117] *Ibid.*, 27.

[118] *Ibid.*, 31.

been omitted or which members consider necessary to be able to assess the degree of implementation of the treaty in the country under review. This is especially necessary where there has been a time delay between the submission of the report and the hearing.[119] Sometimes the state party may submit written responses to the List of Issues, which form a supplement to the report. At least in the case of the CAT, the List of Issues and the state party's responses have been adopted as the state party report, without the state party needing to furnish a separate report.[120] The CAT has seen this as a shift towards 'customised' reporting.

In addition to the information furnished by the state party, the treaty bodies may receive information on a country's human rights situation from other sources, including UN agencies, other intergovernmental organisations, NGOs, academic institutions, and the press.[121] Most committees allocate specific plenary time to hearing submissions from UN agencies and NGOs. Depending upon when the information is received, related questions may be added to the List of Issues submitted to the state party in advance of the session. Increasingly, UN country teams prepare confidential reports submitted to the relevant committee. Some UN agencies also become involved in the drafting process, but this can undermine the process of states preparing their own reports.[122]

At the conclusion of the examination, the committees adopt 'concluding observations' (or 'concluding comments') which are transmitted to the state party and summaries of which are presented in the annual report to the UN General Assembly.

2 General problems

There are a number of general problems with state party reporting; some of these are outlined here. First of all, each treaty body suffers from a large number of overdue reports,[123] and at the same time there are substantial delays, owing to human and financial constraints, in dealing with those

---

[119] *Ibid.*, 29.
[120] Annual Report of the CAT to the General Assembly, UN Doc. A/62/44 (6–24 November 2006 and 30 April–18 May 2007), paras. 23–25.
[121] OHCHR, Fact Sheet No. 30, 30. Some treaties provide explicitly for the receipt of such information; see Article 18 and 19, ICESCR; Article 22, CEDAW; Article 45, CRC; Article 74, IMWC.
[122] Interview with senior official of the OHCHR, 16 June 2008.
[123] At the end May 2007 the number of overdue reports was: ICCPR (90); ICESCR (213); CEDAW (247); UNCAT (170); CERD (483); CRC (103); CRC Optional Protocol on the Sale of Children, Child Pornography and Child Prostitution (72); CRC Optional

reports that are submitted on time.[124] According to the OHCHR, states that have ratified all seven treaties (now eight) and their optional protocols place themselves under a legal obligation to produce, over a ten-year period, twenty-two reports to the various treaty bodies, an average of one every five and a half months.[125] As ratifications increase, the pressure on the treaty bodies also increases, and this has led to several discussion papers on reform of the treaty body system, discussed in Chapter 8. Meeting times are inadequate to deal with the large volume of reports, resulting in minimal time spent considering each report.[126] Some of the committees have introduced a system of amalgamating reports into a 'combined report' when a particular state party has not met the deadlines for submission or where the committee has not scheduled a session before a subsequent report has fallen due.[127] Reports vary in quality and substance.[128]

A second problem with state reports is that they are 'quintessentially government reports'.[129] As they are prepared and compiled by state officials, they reflect a degree of government propaganda, and governments commonly avoid controversial areas of policy or practice, which can include women's rights.[130] Otherwise, some of the most culpable states parties claim that all their treaty obligations are satisfied.[131]

A third problem with the treaty body system is its distance from the everyday lives of its main beneficiaries: human beings. Very few governments accept the input of NGOs. The effectiveness of the reporting process relies on transparency and public reporting; however, owing to a lack of understanding among the general population, limited information

Protocol on Children in Armed Conflict (65); IMWC (29): P. Parker, *The State of the UN Human Rights Treaty Body System 2007: An NGO Perspective* (Minnesota Advocates for Human Rights, 20 June 2007), 4.

[124] OHCHR, *Monitoring Implementation of the International Human Rights Instruments: An Overview of the Current Treaty Body System*, Background Conference Document for the Fifth Session of the Ad Hoc Committee on a Comprehensive and Integral International Convention on Protection and Promotion of the Rights and Dignity of Persons with Disabilities, UN Doc. A/AC.265/2005/CRP.2, January 2005, para. 31.

[125] *Ibid.*, para. 23.

[126] Bayefsky, 'Making the Human Rights Treaties Work', 234.

[127] E.g. the Women's Committee and the CAT: Bayefsky, 'Making the Human Rights Treaties Work', 235.

[128] J. Morijn, *UN Human Rights Treaty Body Reform: Toward a Permanent Unified Treaty Body* (Civitatis International, April 2006), 4.

[129] Independent Expert, *Interim Report on Updated Study by Mr Philip Alston*, UN Doc. A/CONF.157/PC/62/Add.11/Rev.1, 22 April 1993, 43, para. 99.

[130] Byrnes, 'The "Other" Human Rights Treaty Body', 13.

[131] Bayefsky, 'Making the Human Rights Treaties Work', 233.

provided to citizens in many countries, and the proliferation of treaties and reporting requirements,[132] meaningful participation in the process is increasingly elusive. Some studies have argued that the process is 'essentially catalytic'[133] and that the benefits of state reporting lie more in the process of report preparation than in the actual output.[134] Others, in contrast, have noted that the state party reporting process, and especially the concluding observations of the committees, has had 'significant influence' in giving meaning to human rights standards, including their use as interpretative guidance in domestic courts.[135]

However, in many countries reports are not translated into local languages, and high levels of illiteracy, especially among women, mean that access to such information or participation in its collection is limited. Bayefsky argues that the preparation of these reports is mostly seen as 'a bureaucratic exercise or diplomatic chore and not as an opportunity for self-analysis and the amendment of national laws or practices'.[136] She finds that the 'so-called "constructive dialogue" with such states is a hoax' and, furthermore, that the system of state reporting should be dismantled and replaced with country rapporteurs or treaty-monitoring bodies with fact-finding mandates.[137] James Crawford explains that such problems are inherent in a system based on self-criticism and good faith.[138] My own views on preferred reforms are outlined in Chapter 8.

A fourth criticism of the current system is the overlap in mandates over specific norms. This has been criticised as duplicating efforts[139]

---

[132] On the issue of UN reform of the treaty bodies and the proliferation of treaties, see M. O'Flaherty and C. O'Brien, 'Reform of the UN Human Rights Treaty Monitoring Bodies: A Critique of the Concept Paper on the High Commissioner's Proposal for a Unified Standing Treaty Body' (2007) 7 *Hum. Rts. L. Rev.* 141. See, also, UN Report of the Secretary-General, *Strengthening the United Nations: An Agenda for Further Change*, UN Doc. A/57/387, 9 September 2002.

[133] Independent Expert, *Interim Report of Update Study by Mr Philip Alston*, UN Doc. A/CONF.157/PC/62/Add.11/Rev.1, 22 March 1997 para. 12.

[134] OHCHR, *Report of the Chairpersons of the Human Rights Treaty Bodies on their Sixteenth Meeting*, UN Doc. A/60/2000, 10 August 2005, para. 45.

[135] C. Heyns and F. Viljoen, 'The Impact of the United Nations Human Rights Treaties on the Domestic Level' (2001) 23 *HRQ* 483, 487 and 488.

[136] Bayefsky, 'Making the Human Rights Treaties Work', 233.

[137] *Ibid.*, 264.

[138] J. Crawford, 'The UN Human Rights Treaty System', 7.

[139] E. Tistounet, 'The Problem of Overlapping among Different Treaty Bodies', in P. Alston and J. Crawford (eds.), *The Future of UN Human Rights Treaty Monitoring* (Cambridge University Press, 2000) 383, at 393. This duplication is under review as to how to minimise the burden on state parties.

and is exacerbated by limited knowledge of or cross-referencing to each committee's outputs.[140]

3 What about women and women's issues?

The above general problems hinder the effective monitoring of human rights obligations, whether they apply to women and/or men. However, the system also has a particular impact on women. The lack or absence of women in relevant government positions in most countries can influence the extent to which women's issues are taken up during the preparation of state party reports. For example, experts in women's affairs are not necessarily experts in human rights reporting, and experts in human rights reporting may lack knowledge of women's affairs.[141] Although the treaty bodies have developed mechanisms to deal with these gaps, such as Lists of Issues (outlined above), they can also lead to a state party confining references to women to the context of the particular question rather than integrating women's issues throughout the report as a whole. In practice, responses by states parties can amount to little more than form over substance, or state reporting may simply 'add women and stir'.[142] At a minimum, the treaty bodies seek sex-disaggregated statistics, but their practices vary beyond this.

The fact that few countries involve civil society in the preparation of their reports, including the exclusion of women's organisations, can skew results in favour of 'official' records rather than reality. Even in countries that admit NGO comments on draft state party reports or the participation of NGOs in their delegations,[143] the resource-intensive nature of research and report-writing means that 'shadow' or 'alternative' reporting is an ad hoc process. The ability to prepare shadow reports is reliant on previously collated research, which can be hindered by a denial of an entry visa to visit the country in question.[144] Another issue is that even large international NGOs in periods of funding or

---

[140] See, W. Vandenhole, *The Procedures Before the UN Human Rights Treaty Bodies: Divergence or Convergence?* (Antwerp: Intersentia, 2004), xix; Morijn, *UN Human Rights Treaty Body Reform*, 5.

[141] Byrnes, 'The "Other" Human Rights Treaty Body', 13.

[142] See, Chapter 2.

[143] UN Report of the Secretary-General, *Strengthening the United Nations: An Agenda for Further Change*, UN Doc. A/57/387, 9 September 2002, para. 136 (also noting that some delegations include NGO representatives).

[144] It is well known that organisations such as Amnesty International have been denied visas to enter particular countries to carry out their work.

staff shortages tend to deprioritise women's issues.[145] Women's groups operating at national and local levels are often more affected by lack of resources, limited access to reliable information, political influence, or poor organisation to be able to engage fully. Nonetheless, if they are able to supply information to the committees, this can open up 'democratic space' or dialogue with the government that may not otherwise be available at home.[146]

In 2005, as part of initiatives on treaty body reform, Draft Harmonized Guidelines were prepared to provide uniform guidance to states on the form and content of periodic reports.[147] A single report to span across treaties was rejected at a consultation meeting, but an expanded 'common core document' was accepted, which is to be produced alongside specialist treaty reports to each committee. The expanded common core document is to include statistical data (disaggregated by sex and other population groups[148]), an overview of the general framework for the protection and promotion of human rights in the country, and information on the implementation of congruent provisions (that is, substantive provisions that are shared across treaties). Non-discrimination on the basis of sex and equality between women and men were identified, inter alia, as 'congruent' provisions.[149] For women, there are both positive and negative possible consequences of this initiative.

On the positive side, requiring states parties to supply information on non-discrimination and equality in an expanded core document is likely to highlight the crosscutting nature of these issues. It confirms that sex

---

[145] Interviews conducted with officials of five international non-governmental organisations between 2006 and 2008. As one example, an international NGO informed its staff that monitoring the Women's Committee would not be carried out until further notice due to staff and resource shortages, whereas the HRC and the CAT would continue to be monitored as usual. For a positive example of NGO input into state party reports, see: C. Benninger-Budel and L. O'Hanlon, *Violence against Women: 10 Reports/Year 2003* (World Organization against Torture (OMCT), 2004).

[146] Interview with senior official at the OHCHR, 16 June 2008.

[147] Fourth Inter-Committee Meeting, *Revised Draft Harmonized Guidelines for Reporting under the International Human Rights Treaties including Guidelines for a Common Core Document and Treaty-Specific Targeted Documents*, UN Doc. HRI/MC/2005/3, 1 June 2005.

[148] Fourth Inter-Committee Meeting, *Revised Draft Harmonized Guidelines*, paras. 37–38.

[149] *Ibid.*, para. 19. The other crosscutting provisions included effective remedies, procedural guarantees, and participation in public life. See further on non-discrimination, paras. 58–66 (non-discrimination), 67–68 (equality before the law), and 69–70 (special measures).

discrimination is relevant to all treaty bodies, not just reporting under the CEDAW. In addition, the core document will place sex discrimination and equality within the ambit of deliberations of even those treaties that do not contain express non-discrimination provisions.[150] The new harmonised guidelines also ask states parties to describe the process of reporting and to provide information about constituent groups that participated in the process, such as women.[151]

However, a foreseeable problem with an expanded core document is that states parties may treat it as a static document and only superficially update it while they concentrate on the treaty-specific report at hand. After all, the idea behind the consolidated core report was to reduce the workload on states parties, not to increase it by requiring a larger core document to be reviewed regularly.[152] With non-discrimination on the basis of sex and equality identified as congruent provisions and thereby falling into the core report, issues of equality could be downplayed or even sidelined, rather than highlighted, elsewhere in the report. Moreover, the intersectional nature of non-discrimination and equality guarantees may be lost if they are isolated in a core document and not interwoven into the treaty-specific reports.

E General Comments and women

Each of the committees has adopted the practice of issuing General Comments or General Recommendations.[153] These documents began as guidance to states parties on how to prepare and formulate their periodic reports[154] and have developed over time into authoritative statements as

---

[150] E.g. UNCAT and ICERD.

[151] Fourth Inter-Committee Meeting, *Revised Draft Harmonized Guidelines*, para. 50(d).

[152] The *Revised Draft Harmonized Guidelines* note that the core document will need to be updated for each submission: Fourth Inter-Committee Meeting, *Revised Draft Harmonized Guidelines*, para. 23.

[153] The HRC, the CESCR, the CAT, and the Children's Committee use the term 'General Comments', while the CERD and the Women's Committee use the term 'General Recommendations'. There are some efforts underway to harmonise language to General Comment.

[154] See, e.g., HRC, General Comment No. 1: Reporting Obligation (1981) and General Comment No. 2: Reporting Guidelines (1981); CESCR, General Comment No. 1: Reporting by States Parties (1989), UN Doc. E/1989/22, in which it listed seven main purposes of state party reporting; CEDAW, General Recommendation No. 1 (1986) (dates for submission of reports); CEDAW, General Recommendation No. 2 (1987) (form, content, and date of reports).

to the interpretation of particular provisions. They thus perform a hybrid function. They vary in quality and length (from a single paragraph to ten or so pages). Not all the treaty bodies have embraced this way of communicating to states parties to the same extent.[155]

Deciding the subject matter for a General Comment is largely ad hoc. It is reliant more on the interests of the committee members than any long-term strategy. The General Comment is normally the brainchild of a particular committee member, with drafts prepared by that member or by the Secretariat, but they are increasingly being drafted by academics or other independent consultants. Feedback from NGOs is increasingly being sought. The OHCHR now has a policy of putting up draft General Comments on their website, but not all committees do this. Although they have improved in terms of quality – from brief statements to more detailed exposés – many remain general statements as to the meaning of particular terms or rights without explaining fully the background to, or reasons for, such an interpretation.

In terms of the representation of women's concerns within General Comments, women are largely missing from specific mention in the early documents. Since the UN's gender mainstreaming policy was adopted in 1997, however, there have been various efforts to issue women-specific General Comments. For example, both the HRC and the CESCR have issued specific General Comments on the equal rights of men and women to enjoyment of human rights.[156] Like other UN practices, women's issues tend to be located in women-specific documents and have yet to be fully 'mainstreamed'. Only the Children's Committee has adopted a holistic approach to General Comments, which they find has been possible because of the thematic rather than article-by-article approach they adopt.[157] Further analysis of some of these General Comments is undertaken in relation to the three rights studied in this book (see Chapters 4–6).

---

[155] E.g. the CAT has only issued two General Comments (General Comment No. 1: Implementation of Article 3 (1996), UN Doc. A/53/44 and General Comment No. 2: Implementation of Article 2 by States Parties (2008), UN Doc. CAT/C/GC/2, 24 January 2008), whereas the Women's Committee has issued 26 General Recommendations and the HRC has issued 33.

[156] HRC, General Comment No. 28: Equality of Rights between Men and Women (Article 3) (2000), UN Doc. CCPR/C/21/Rev.1/Add.10; CESCR, General Comment No. 16: The Equal Rights of Men and Women to the Enjoyment of All Economic, Social and Cultural Rights (Article 3) (2005), UN Doc. E/C.12/2005/4.

[157] Interview with former member of the Children's Committee, 18 June 2008.

F   Interstate communications and women

Exactly half of the core human rights treaties contain interstate dispute mechanisms, in which one state may lodge a written communication regarding the non-compliance of another state with their treaty obligations.[158] In most cases the dispute procedure requires states parties to make separate declarations recognising the competence of the treaty body to hear any such complaints.[159] Only the ICERD does not require an additional jurisdictional declaration,[160] although reservations may be entered against the relevant provision.[161]

Although the interstate dispute mechanism has never been activated under any of the treaties,[162] it is mentioned here because of the symbolic significance of this procedure in allowing one state party to bring a complaint against another state party for alleged violations of human rights.[163] It is further worth noting that this procedure, although never having been formally activated, has been used strategically in diplomatic disputes. The threat of another state bringing a public action before one or more of the human rights treaty bodies can act as a stick to resolving a dispute.[164]

The omission of an interstate communications procedure from the CEDAW,[165] and later from the Optional Protocol to the CEDAW

---

[158] There are no interstate complaints mechanisms under the OP-CEDAW and the CRC.

[159] See, e.g., Article 41, ICCPR; Article 21, UNCAT; Article 76, IMWC.

[160] Article 11, ICERD.   [161] Article 20, ICERD.

[162] F. G. Isa, 'The Optional Protocol for the Convention on the Elimination of All Forms of Discrimination Against Women: Strengthening the Protection Mechanisms of Women's Human Rights' (2003) 20 *Ariz. J. Int'l & Comp. L.* 291, at 309 claiming that the interstate procedure has 'hardly ever been used', but in fact it has never been activated: see, OHCHR, *Concept Paper on High Commissioner's Proposal for a Unified Standing Treaty Body*, UN Doc. HRI/MC/2006/2, 22 March 2006, para. 21.

[163] T. Meron, 'Enhancing the Effectiveness of the Prohibition of Discrimination Against Women' (1990) 84 *Amer. J. Int'l L.* 213, at 217.

[164] Communication with former Australian senior government/diplomatic official who was aware of at least two occasions in which the threat of interstate communications was used to resolve a dispute: confidential email dated 14 August 2008 (on file with the author). It is not clear though how often this takes place because it occurs without or with virtually no publicity.

[165] A number of states during the drafting process called for interstate and individual communications mechanisms, including as a result of the precedent set by the ICERD, see L. A. Rehof, *Guide to the* Travaux Préparatoires *of the United Nations Convention on the Elimination of All Forms of Discrimination against Women* (Dordrecht: Martinus Nijhoff Publishers, 1993), 238–239.

(OP-CEDAW),[166] is therefore equally symbolic. One of the primary aims of the OP-CEDAW was finally to treat women's rights as being of equal worth to other human rights.[167] As shown in Chapter 2, until the introduction of the OP-CEDAW, the CEDAW had been criticised for its weaker implementation mechanisms. But the failure to include an inter-state complaints mechanism in the OP-CEDAW reinforces the different and unequal treatment of women's rights compared with other rights. The fact that subsequent optional protocols, for example to the ICESCR, have included provision for it – also reveals bias. Above all, its omission from the OP-CEDAW sends a sombre message to women that states parties could not imagine even a single situation in which one state party would bring an action against another state party, no matter how egregious or widespread the violations against women.[168] Neither, therefore, can a recalcitrant state party be threatened, even in private diplomatic discussions, with such action in the context of women's rights under the CEDAW.

G   Individual communications and women

1   General procedures

Over half of the treaty bodies receive and consider communications from individuals (also known as complaints or petitions) alleging the violation of their rights by a state party.[169] Not unlike the interstate communica-tions procedure (see above), the individual communications procedure was initially attached to the more mainstream treaties (the ICCPR, the ICERD, and the UNCAT). With the increasing acceptance that these procedures can be effective enforcement mechanisms, most of the treat-ies have now been amended or are in the process of being amended to include such a procedure (the CEDAW, the IMWC, the ICESCR, and the

---

[166] The OP-CEDAW was negotiated in informal meetings so there are no travaux prépara-toires for the OP-CEDAW. It is therefore difficult to determine why it was excluded. There seems to be no explanation for its omission except that the draft under discussion did not contain such a procedure and the meeting decided it was not worthwhile: per confidential email from senior official at OHCHR who attended the drafting meetings, 15 September 2008 (on file with the author).

[167] Isa, 'The Optional Protocol for the Convention on the Elimination of All Forms of Discrimination Against Women', 306 (see also for an overview of the history to the development of the Optional Protocol).

[168] Interpretative or application disputes, however, may be resolved by recourse to the International Court of Justice: Article 29(1), CEDAW. There are a large number of reser-vations to this article.

[169] See, under B in this chapter.

ICRPD). The CRC appears the most resistant to change.[170] According to the OHCHR, '[i]t is through individual complaints that human rights are given concrete meaning. In the adjudication of individual cases, international norms that may otherwise seem general and abstract are put into practical effect. When applied to a person's real-life situation, the standards contained in international human rights treaties find their most direct application.'[171] The committees may hear complaints relating only to a state party that has accepted the jurisdiction of the committee to do so, either by a declaration under the relevant treaty provision[172] or by accepting the relevant optional protocol.[173] The procedure is in other words optional for states parties, and the decisions they render are non-binding.[174] Most of the treaties allow communications from individuals, but not all allow groups of individuals to lodge communications (that is, collective or group actions).[175]

There are several procedural steps before consideration of the merits, which are generally shared across the treaty bodies. First, a communication will be registered by the Secretariat of the OHCHR if it provides minimal information, such as the complainant's name, nationality, and date of birth; the state party against which the complaint is made; and a statement of the facts, in chronological order, on which the claim is based.[176] A complainant does not need a lawyer or to be familiar with legal and technical language; nor does the complainant need to articulate which treaty provision has been violated. However, the OHCHR encourages both, and the records show that decisions tend to be more favourably decided when legal representation on behalf of the complainant is engaged,[177] as well as when the relevant provisions have been specifically identified. No legal aid funded by the UN is available, and very few, if any, governments provide it. Claims may be brought on one's own behalf, or on behalf of another person as long as proof of their consent is supplied or, if unavailable, reasons are given for the failure to supply that consent. The communication needs to be submitted in one of the six working languages

---

[170] This is largely owing to concerns about how children would exercise their rights to petition.

[171] OHCHR, *Complaints Procedures*, Fact Sheet No. 7/Rev.1, 2.

[172] Article 22, UNCAT; Article 14, ICERD; Article 76, IMWC.

[173] OP-ICCPR; OP-CEDAW.

[174] Article 5(3), OP-ICCPR: Article 14(7)(b), ICERD; Article 22(7), UNCAT; Article 7, OP-CEDAW.

[175] E.g., Article 14, ICERD and Article 2, OP-CEDAW provide for group complaints.

[176] OHCHR, *Complaints Procedures*, Fact Sheet No. 7/Rev.1, 3–4.

[177] *Ibid.*, 4.

of the UN, and the OHCHR advises that the processing of claims will be accelerated if any documents in another language are already translated upon submission.[178]

After registration, the communication is transmitted to the state party. Within three to six months of receipt, the state party must submit written explanations or statements addressing the complaint, including admissibility issues and the remedy, if any, that has been taken.[179] After the state party replies, the complainant is given another opportunity to comment, usually within six weeks. If the state party does not reply, reminders are sent. If there is still no response, the committee will consider the case on the basis of the original complaint.

In order to examine the communication, the committee holds closed meetings and examines the written record.[180] Although some of the treaty bodies can hold oral hearings as per their rules of procedure, this is rarely, if ever, done. The communication is generally considered in two stages: the admissibility stage and the substance/merits stage. For the purposes of this chapter, I focus on the admissibility criteria. Later chapters deal with the substantive provisions.

In order for a complaint to be considered on the merits, an individual must first satisfy all of the admissibility criteria, which are largely identical across the treaties.[181] In summary, the admissibility criteria are as follows:

1. Is the complainant an individual (or group of individuals in the case of the ICERD and the CEDAW) subject to the jurisdiction of a state party?
2. Is the complainant a victim of a violation(s) of any of the rights in the treaty?
3. Has the complainant exhausted domestic remedies?
4. Is the communication anonymous, or an abuse of the right of submission, or incompatible with the provisions of the treaty?

---

[178] *Ibid.*, 4.
[179] Article 4, OP ICCPR (6 months); Article 14(6), ICERD (3 months): Article 6, OP-CEDAW (6 months); Article 22(3), UNCAT (6 months); Article 77(4), IMWC (6 months).
[180] Article 5(3), OP ICCPR; Article 14, ICERD (no mention of closed meetings, but the assessment of the claims is confidential); Article 7, OP-CEDAW; Article 22(6), UNCAT; Article 77(6), IMWC.
[181] See, e.g., Article 14, ICERD; OP-ICCPR; entered into force 23 March 1976; Article 22, UNCAT; Articles 2, 3, and 4, OP-CEDAW; Article 77, IMWC.

5. Has the communication been heard, or is it being heard, by another international dispute or settlement procedure?[182]
6. Does the communication relate to an event that occurred after the relevant state party ratified the treaty?

Each committee has the facility to take urgent action (or interim measures) to avoid irreparable harm being done to the complainant if the communication was heard in the usual course.[183] This power is derived either from the express wording of the treaty or by implication. At the conclusion of the review, the committee issues non-binding 'views'. These 'views' usually indicate an appropriate remedy, such as payment of compensation, release from detention, or a stay of execution or deportation. The Women's Committee has adopted the practice of issuing not only findings in relation to the individual communication in question, but also outlining more general recommendations to improve the state apparatus – legislative, administrative, judicial, or any other area – in order to avoid the repetition of such violations.[184]

Although decisions are non-binding and none of the treaty bodies have enforcement powers, the committees do follow up with the state party by requesting updates on steps taken to remedy the situation, normally within three to six months of transmitting the decision.[185] A summary of activities are included in each committee's annual reports, and decisions are accessible via the website of the OHCHR.

2   General weaknesses

The individual communications system suffers from a number of general weaknesses. First, it has been argued that the procedure can do little to

[182] E.g., the HRC has concluded that studies into the same or similar facts by international organisations, such as Inter-American Human Rights Commission, or UN Special Rapporteurs do not count for the purposes of this admissibility criterion: *Baboeram et al.* v. *Suriname*, HRC Nos. 146, 148–154/1983, decided 4 April 1985.

[183] See, e.g., Rule 86, HRC Rules of Procedure; Rule 91(3), CERD Rules of Procedure; Rule 108(1), CAT Rules of Procedure; Article 5, OP-CEDAW and Rule 63, CEDAW Rules of Procedure.

[184] See, e.g., *A. T.* v. *Hungary*, CEDAW 2/2003 (26 January 2005), in which a number of general recommendations are listed in the context of a domestic violence complaint, such as to take all necessary measures to ensure that the national strategy for prevention and effective treatment of violence within the family is promptly implemented and evaluated.

[185] Some of the committees then have additional follow-up measures, such as by referral to a committee member tasked with following up with the state party: see, OHCHR, *Complaints Procedures*, Fact Sheet No.7/Rev.1.

protect individual rights because '[i]t starts too late, takes too much time, does not lead to binding results and lacks any effective enforcement'.[186] The procedures have faced criticism for being of a voluntary character, of last resort, and without effective remedies.[187] Like state party reporting, the procedure has been criticised for its slowness, especially as domestic remedies must first be exhausted before access is granted.[188] Best estimates suggest that it may take several years to achieve a legal remedy.[189] Unsuccessful claims can also function as a 'ceiling for human rights protection' at the national level, impeding political and legal change.[190] One technique adopted by some regional human rights bodies that has filtered into the human rights treaty system is deference to decisions of national authorities under the doctrine of a margin of appreciation,[191] which can have the effect of watering down the universal character of human rights.

The nature of the decision-making process of the treaty bodies is, in most cases, consensual, although it has provision for individual opinions to be expressed. The advantage of this general approach is that it can avoid the 'factional battles' that dominate the other human rights bodies.[192] Nonetheless, its main disadvantage is that it can easily lead to a compromise to the lowest common denominator or a decision with little or no supporting reasoning.[193] Since 2000 it is possible to see a marked increase in the number of minority or dissenting opinions, although it is not clear what has led to this change.

---

[186] B. Graefrath, 'Reporting and Complaint Systems in Universal Human Rights Treaties', in A. Rosas and J. Helgesen (eds.), *Human Rights in a Changing East/West Perspective* (London and New York: Pinter, 1990), referred to in Byrnes, 'Toward More Effective Enforcement of Women's Human Rights', 198.

[187] Byrnes, 'Toward More Effective Enforcement of Women's Human Rights', 198–190.

[188] Exceptions have emerged in relation to this criterion where the domestic remedy is ineffective (see below).

[189] Byrnes, 'Toward More Effective Enforcement of Women's Human Rights', 199.

[190] See, e.g., A. Clapham, 'The European Convention on Human Rights in the British Courts: Problems Associated with the Incorporation of International Human Rights', in P. Alston (ed.), *International Human Rights Law: A Comparative Perspective* (Oxford: Clarendon Press, 1994), as referred to in Byrnes, 'Toward More Effective Enforcement of Women's Human Rights', 200.

[191] Although developed in the jurisprudence of the European Court of Human Rights, it has been adopted by the HRC in at least one decision: *Hertzberg* v. *Finland*, HRC 61/1979 (2 April 1982), as referred to in Byrnes, 'Toward More Effective Enforcement of Women's Human Rights', 201.

[192] H. J. Steiner, P. Alston and R Goodman, *International Human Rights in Context: Law, Politics, Morals* (2nd edn, Oxford University Press, 2000), 708.

[193] Byrnes, 'Toward More Effective Enforcement of Women's Human Rights', 201.

Often decisions do not resolve all the alleged violations listed by the claimant but settle instead upon the least difficult (or alternatively the right upon which consensus can be reached). If the original complaint does not identify the articles at issue, the Secretariat tends to opt for the most obvious rather than all possibilities. Decisions are typically short, around ten pages. Prepared by the Secretariat, they read as templates rather than judicial decisions and are not binding on states parties.[194] On a positive note, their length makes them more accessible to the general public. However, as they rarely contain little more than blanket statements on whether a particular provision has or has not been violated, it is not always clear why a particular decision has been reached, or what factors counted in making the final determination.

3   Where are the female complainants? What about women?

So what about women? Women continue to be under-represented in bringing complaints before the treaty bodies. Of petitions lodged by women, their cases tend to revolve around rights relating to equality and non-discrimination, marriage and family, or privacy. In terms of substance, Byrnes acknowledges that the committees have had some success in dealing with straightforward claims of differential treatment on the basis of sex, but they experience considerably more difficulty in responding to claims that challenge the distinction between public and private and that seek to attribute responsibility to a state for violations committed by private individuals.[195] To some extent, this has improved because of the development of the concepts of due diligence.[196] These mechanisms are also not well geared towards complaints arising from two or more states, such as trafficking of women and children across national boundaries or sex tourism.[197] They also do not address systematic patterns or trends of human rights violations, although there are other international mechanisms available to do so, albeit these are generally political rather than judicial in nature.[198]

---

[194] Cf. some former members of the committees who argue that the 'views' are judicial, or at least authoritative: F. Pocar, 'Legal Value of the Human Rights Committee's Views' (1991–1992) *Canadian Hum. Rts. YB* 119; C. Tomuschat, 'Evolving Procedural Rules: The United Nations Human Rights Committee's First Two Years Dealing with Individual Communications' (1980) 1 *Hum. Rts. L. J.* 249.

[195] Byrnes, 'Toward More Effective Enforcement of Women's Human Rights', 203.

[196] See, Chapters 4–6.

[197] Byrnes, 'Toward More Effective Enforcement of Women's Human Rights', 204.

[198] See, e.g., 1503 procedure of the UN Human Rights Council.

In the context of violence against women, the number of petitions from women is even lower. Of the twenty-two cases decided before the CAT between January 2007 and May 2009, for example, women featured as the principal complainant in only two of them. Furthermore, there have been no individual cases brought before the HRC, for example, relating to slavery, servitude, or trafficking; or decided under the right-to-life provision in the context of violence against women.[199] Additionally, there have been more communications brought by women under the torture prohibition claiming non-gender-specific torture rather than gender-related harms. As mentioned in Chapter 2, women were in fact among the first applicants before the HRC relating to Article 7 of the ICCPR, either on behalf of themselves or other persons, including other women.[200] These cases tended to involve so-called traditional (read: 'male') claims of physical abuse, poor prison conditions, or disappearances,[201] and they dispute feminist claims that human rights law, as initially conceived, does not apply to women.[202] This is taken up further in Chapter 5. Regrettably, none of the treaty bodies compiles any sex-disaggregated statistics on communications received,[203] even though the committees, without exception, call upon states to disaggregate statistics within the context of the reporting process, as discussed above.[204] Feminist scholars have theorised at length why women are excluded or under-represented in judicial or quasi-judicial processes. Some of this material is also relevant in relation to the UN system of individual complaints as the quasi-litigious arm of the treaty bodies.

First of all, as already noted, not all of the treaty bodies permit the bringing of individual communications.[205] The initial failure of both

---

[199] Cf. *Rantsev* v. *Cyprus and Russia*, ECtHR, Applic. No. 25965/04 (7 January 2010).

[200] See, e.g., *Massera et al. (including Moriana Hernandez Valentini de Bazzano)* v. *Uruguay*, HRC 5/1977 (15 August 1979); *Weissmann and Perdomo (including Ann Maria Garcia Lanza de Netto)* v. *Uruguay*, HRC 8/1977 (3 April 1980); *de Bouton* v. *Uruguay*, HRC 37/1978 (27 March 1981); *Burgos (submitted by Delia Saldias de Lopez)* v. *Uruguay*, HRC 52/1979 (29 July 1981).

[201] See, e.g., *Laureano* v. *Peru*, HRC 540/1993 (25 March 1996); *Arredondo* v. *Peru*, HRC 688/1996 (27 July 2000).

[202] See, Chapter 2.

[203] Information supplied by the OHCHR, 25 September 2008.

[204] See, e.g., UN, *Compilation of Guidelines on the Form and Contents of Reports to be submitted by States Parties to the International Human Rights Treaties*, UN Doc. HRI/GEN/2/Rev.1 (2001), Ch. VII. See, also, CEDAW, General Comment No. 9: Statistical Data concerning the Situation of Women (1989).

[205] The CRC and the ICESCR do not provide for individual communications, although an Optional Protocol to the ICESR has now been agreed, ns. 20 and 208.

the ICESCR and the CEDAW to include provision for individual communications supports feminist critiques about the 'gendered' nature of international law and the exclusion of women's concerns, especially in the economic, social, and cultural rights fields, as outlined in Chapter 2. In respect of the CEDAW, this has now been rectified by the agreement in 2000 of an optional individual petitions system. Although no reservations are allowed to the individual communications component of the OP-CEDAW,[206] because any individual communications must relate to rights contained in the CEDAW, reservations to the parent treaty will still have effect.[207] For the ICESCR, a draft optional protocol has been agreed but has yet to enter into force.[208] In lieu of a separate complaints system attached to the ICESCR, the HRC has exercised jurisdiction over rights of equal access to economic, social, and cultural rights via Article 26 of the ICCPR.[209]

Second, feminist theorists speculate that litigation-style processes do not serve women. Drawing on the psycho-social research of Gilligan already mentioned in Chapter 2, some feminist scholars argue that the assertion of rights is a very male trait.[210] Writing on international law, Chinkin questions whether adjudicative or quasi-adjudicative processes that emphasise individual behaviour or misbehaviour can be effective where there is a systematic power imbalance and disadvantage to

---

[206] Article 17, OP-CEDAW.

[207] See, Chapter 2. On problems of the Optional Protocol, see K. L. Ritz, 'Soft Enforcement: Inadequacies of the Optional Protocol as a Remedy for the Convention on the Elimination of All Forms of Discrimination against Women' (2001–2002) 25 *Suffolk Transnat. L. Rev.* 191.

[208] Initial supervision arrangements under the ICESCR were weak, requiring only that states submit reports to the UN Security-General who shall transmit them to the ECOSOC. In 1985, by virtue of an ECOSOC resolution, a committee was established to carry out the monitoring roles previously held by ECOSOC (UN Doc. ECOSOC res. 1985/17, 28 May 1985). The ICESCR did not initially contain an individual petition system, largely due to a sense that economic, social, and cultural rights are non-justiciable. A draft Optional Protocol to the ICESCR was adopted by the UN Human Rights Council (UNHRC): UNHRC res. 8/2, 18 June 2008, and confirmed unanimously by the UN General Assembly, GA res. A/RES/63/117, 10 December 2008, and is open for ratification. For background see: *Report of the Open-Ended Working Group to Consider Options regarding the Elaboration of an Optional Protocol to the International Covenant on Economic, Social, and Cultural Rights*, Ms. Catarina de Albuquerque, UN Doc. E/CN.4/2004/44, 15 March 2004.

[209] See, Chapter 4.

[210] C. Gilligan, *In a Different Voice: Psychological Theory and Women's Development* (Cambridge, MA: Harvard University Press, 1982), 54. See, also, C. Smart, *Feminism and the Power of Law* (London: Routledge, 1989); J. A. Freyer, 'Women Litigators in Search of a Care-Oriented Judicial System' (1995–1996) 4 *Am. U. J. Gender & L.* 199.

women.[211] A similar point is made by Smart in arguing that adversarial processes that position the rights holder against the infringer may not be appropriate where they are set against the reality of women's economic and social dependence on men.[212] Although the power imbalance between an individual and the state is without question an inhibiting factor to bringing forward claims, the procedure is mostly carried out through written correspondence, which can minimise the adversarial or confrontational nature of the proceedings. It does not, however, reduce the power of the state to intimidate or harass the complainant beyond the view of the treaty bodies. Nonetheless, the early usage of the treaty bodies by women questions the foundations of these alienation theories.

Third, other scholars argue that litigation is not an effective guarantor of human rights in any event, whether for men or for women.[213] This point is borne out by Bayefsky's study mentioned above, in which she found that individuals have generally made little use of the petition system in the UN context.[214] She calculates that annually there are 3,000 pieces of correspondence, fewer than 100 registered cases, fewer than 100 decisions taken, and approximately thirty final decisions.[215] Beyond a certain point, both mainstream and women-specific human rights mechanisms may not be effective, and recourse to 'other sources of moral, political, or other normative authority' may be necessary.[216] For example, litigation has been seen as problematic when the system requires revolutionary change in a conservative community that is ready for, at most, evolutionary

---

[211] C. Chinkin, 'Feminist Interventions into International Law' (1997) 19 *Adel. L. Rev.* 13, at 20.

[212] Smart, *Feminism and the Power of Law*, 139.

[213] For more, see R. J. Cook, 'International Human Rights Law Concerning Women: Case Notes and Comments' (1990) 23 *Vand. J. Transnat'l L.* 779

[214] A. F. Bayefsky, 'Direct Petition in the UN Human Rights Treaty System' (2001) 95 *ASIL Proceedings* 71, at 71.

[215] Notably, the number of potential claimants has increased since Bayefsky's study with the constant accession to the core human rights treaties. Bayefsky identified a number of issues discouraging the submission of communications to the treaty bodies, including (a) the practice of streaming complaints to other UN mechanisms; (b) lack of media interest; (c) failure to produce remedies; (d) lack of follow-up; (e) link of committee members to governments; (f) overlap and lack of coordination; (g) language problems; or (h) personnel and infrastructure problems: Bayefsky, 'Direct Petition in the UN Human Rights Treaty System', *ibid.*

[216] A. Byrnes, 'Using International Human Rights Law and Procedures to Advance Women's Rights', in K. D. Askin and D. M. Koenig (eds.), *Women and International Human Rights Law* (Ardsley, NY: Transnational Publishers, 2000), Vol. 1, 79, at 84.

change.[217] Moreover, litigation can be short-sighted, as 'sexism is not a mere legal error'.[218]

A fourth concern with the treaty body system of individual communications is the admissibility criteria. The admissibility criteria outlined above act as the first line of rejection of women's claims. It is arguable that these criteria reflect 'male' standards of access and do not take account of the particular situation of many women. One concern with the admissibility criteria is that most of the treaty bodies, with the exception of the CERD and the Women's Committee, do not allow groups of individuals to lodge collective complaints for violations of their human rights.[219] The mechanism for group or collective complaints allows women who may hold shared experiences, such as widespread rape or sexual violence during armed conflict, to benefit from collective representation. In addition, collective complaints by women may be better placed to address structural causes of violence and inequality.[220] States' concern with the wider scope of such actions has meant that such provisions have attracted a large number of interpretative statements.[221]

Related to the desire for collective representation to be permitted, the individual nature of the procedures presupposes that women are in a position to bring communications on their own behalf. In the words of Coomaraswamy, human rights mechanisms assume that women are 'free, independent and individual'.[222] While many women *are* in a position to

---

[217] R. J. Cook, 'Women's International Human Rights: The Way Forward' (1993) 15 *HRQ* 230, at 232.

[218] A. C. Scales, 'The Emergence of Feminist Jurisprudence: An Essay' (1986) 95 *Yale L. J.* 1373, 1382. See, also, C. A. MacKinnon, *Sexual Harassment of Working Women: A Case of Sex Discrimination* (New Haven, CT: Yale University Press, 1979), 102.

[219] Article 14(2), ICERD and Article 2, OP-CEDAW. The OP-CEDAW specifically allows communications to be submitted on behalf of individuals or groups of individuals with their consent, or where it can be explained why consent has not been obtained: Article 2, OP-CEDAW. In a similar way, the African Court of Human and Peoples' Rights operates to permit NGOs with observer status to appear before the African Commission on Human and Peoples' Rights or individuals to institute cases directly with the Court, although this is at the discretion of the Court: Article 5(3), Protocol to the African Charter on Human and Peoples' Rights for the Establishment of an African Court on Human and Peoples' Rights 1998, adopted on 9 June 1998, OAU Doc. OAU/LEG/EXP/AFCHPR/PROT (III); entered into force 1 January 2004.

[220] Chinkin, 'Feminist Interventions into International Law', 20.

[221] Isa, 'The Optional Protocol for the Convention on the Elimination of All Forms of Discrimination Against Women', 312.

[222] See, Chapter 2. See, also, R. Coomaraswamy, 'To Bellow Like a Cow: Women, Ethnicity and the Discourse of Rights', in R. J. Cook (ed.), *Human Rights of Women: National and International Perspectives* (Philadelphia: University of Pennsylvania Press, 1994) 43, at 55.

bring individual communications, and frequently do so, including on behalf of other persons, it does not address the myriad factors preventing more women from accessing these mechanisms. Such factors might include the debilitating effect of trauma arising from violence, the shame they may feel, which perpetuates their silence, or a fear of reprisals if they were to take such action.[223] At least in relation to the last point, the committees now include safeguards (interim measures) against ill-treatment or intimidation against complainants, as discussed above, and all the committees allow names to be removed from the public written records. However, the latter does not keep the identity of the victim secret from the state party, not least because admissibility criteria disallow anonymous submissions,[224] but also because to do so would prevent the state party responding to the particular facts at hand. The lack of a binding decision or effective or suitable remedies at the end of the process may further discourage women applicants, who may be unwilling to take the risk of adjudication to achieve only an unenforceable statement of wrongdoing.[225]

A lack of resources, high levels of female illiteracy in many countries,[226] and a lack of access to legal aid or to information on the procedures generally or in a language they can read and understand are all factors that contribute to the difficulties that women face in using these mechanisms. Legal systems often discriminate against persons living in poverty who are unable to afford legal advice, are illiterate, and are powerless to change legislative processes.[227] In its experience, Amnesty International

---

[223] E. Evatt, 'The Right to Individual Petition: Assessing its Operation before the Human Rights Committee and its Future Application to the Women's Convention on Discrimination' (1995) 89 *ASIL Proceedings*. 227, at 228.

[224] See admissibility criteria outlined in the text above.

[225] There is much literature, for example, on women/gender and transitional justice and questions of reparations: see, e.g., K. M. Franke, 'Gendered Subjects of Transitional Justice' (2006) 15 *Colum. J. Gender & L.* 813; R. Rubio-Marín (eds.), *What Happened to the Women? Gender and Reparations for Human Rights Violations* (New York: Social Science Research Council, 2006); A. Saris and K. Lofts, 'Reparation Programmes: A Gendered Perspective', in C. Ferstman, M. Goetz and A. Stephens (eds.), *Reparations for Victims of Genocide, War Crimes and Crimes against Humanity: Systems in Place and Systems in the Making* (The Hague: Martinus Nijhoff Press, 2009) 79.

[226] Amnesty International, *The Optional Protocol to the Women's Convention*, AI Index: IOR 51/04/97, December 1997, 10. See, further, UN Statistics Division, Table 4c, Illiteracy, at http://unstats.un.org/unsd/demographic/products/indwm/ww2005/tab4c.htm. Even in areas of high illiteracy generally, women's levels are generally higher: see, e.g., Benin where 41.8% of men are illiterate between the ages of 15–24, 67.5% of women of the same age are illiterate; Burkina Faso: 74.5% men, 86% women; Bangladesh: 42.2% men, 58.9% women.

[227] M. Anderson, 'Access to Justice and Legal Process: Making Legal Institutions Responsive to Poor People in LDCs', SOAS Institute of Development Studies Working Paper No. 178, 2003, available at: www.ids.ac.uk/ids/bookshop/wp/wp178.pdf.

has found that those most in need of redress are often the least able to come forward.[228]

Furthermore, the gendered nature of the rights contained in the human rights treaties and their interpretation as 'men's rights' can prevent women recognising their experiences within the language of human rights terms. Women may not, for instance, equate the domestic violence they have suffered with the terminology of 'torture'.[229] Moreover, as the remainder of this book shows, the committee members may also regard the abuses in question as falling outside the terms of the treaties. Recourse to international law is also remote from view and outside everyday experience. In this way, it is rightly charged with being abstract.[230]

A further inhibiting factor is that the admissibility criteria address *past* abuses, practices, or events, rather than preventive action, which may have limited utility for some women. In other words, the petition system deals with the *symptoms* of human rights violations, not the *underlying causes*.[231] The admissibility requirement to be a 'victim of a violation'[232] prohibits actions being brought challenging a particular law, policy, or practice, even where domestic remedies have failed to take account of any compatibility with international human rights legal obligations. Women who face threats to their life from domestic violence or who face irreversible genital mutilation may have little use for the individual petitions system, as it is geared towards post-abuse reparation rather than preventative action.

The 'victim' criterion is also linked to the need to first exhaust domestic remedies before seeking international assistance. Although this was

---

[228] Amnesty International, *The Optional Protocol to the Women's Convention*, 10.

[229] Similar arguments are made in relation to international refugee law; see Edwards, 'Age and Gender Dimensions in International Refugee Law'.

[230] See, Chapter 2.

[231] A. Byrnes, 'Women, Feminism and International Human Rights Law – Methodological Myopia, Fundamental Flaws or Meaningful Marginalisation?: Some Current Issues' (1992) 12 *Aust. YB Int'l L.* 205, at 222–223.

[232] The HRC explained in *Aumeeruddy-Cziffra et al.* v. *Mauritius (the Mauritian Women case)* what it means by 'victim' within the sense of Article 1 of the Optional Protocol to the ICCPR: 'A person can only claim to be a victim in the sense of article 1 of the Optional Protocol if he or she is actually affected. It is a matter of degree how concretely this requirement should be taken. However, no individual can in the abstract, by way of an *actio popularis*, challenge a law or practice claimed to be contrary to the Covenant. If the law or practice has not already been concretely applied to the detriment of that individual, it must in any event be applicable in such a way that the alleged victim's risk of being affected is more than a theoretical possibility.' *Aumeeruddy-Cziffra* v. *Mauritius*, HRC 35/1978 (9 April 1981), para. 9.2. In this case, women whose husbands were at risk of deportation because their residence permits might be withdrawn at any time were considered 'victims', but unmarried women were not.

initially a high hurdle for many women and others who lack general access to domestic legal systems, the committees have now adopted reasonably broad interpretations of this provision. The HRC, for example, allows cases where the domestic remedies available offer no reasonable prospect of redress[233] or where they are considered inadequate or ineffective, such as by reason of indigence and lack of legal aid.[234] The OP-CEDAW expressly provides that the criterion of exhaustion of domestic remedies is waived where such remedies are 'unreasonably prolonged or unlikely to bring effective relief'.[235] Nonetheless, the Women's Committee has shown unwillingness to render communications admissible where sex discrimination has not been raised explicitly as an issue in domestic proceedings, even where it was implicit.[236] It has, however, ruled sympathetically on women's claims that a constitutional challenge 'could not be regarded as a remedy ... which was likely to bring effective relief to a woman whose life was under a criminal dangerous threat'.[237] Similarly, the HRC has found that where 'there is no administrative remedy which would enable a pregnancy to be terminated on therapeutic grounds, nor any judicial remedy functioning with the speed and efficiency required to enable a woman to require the authorities to guarantee her right to a lawful abortion within the limited period', the remedies are taken to have been exhausted.[238]

A further fundamental criterion that raises concern for women complainants is that they must establish a violation of a treaty right by *a state*

---

[233] See, e.g., *Colamarco* v. *Panama*, HRC 437/1990 (21 October 1994), para. 5.2.

[234] See, e.g., *Vincente et al.* v. *Colombia*, HRC 612/1995 (14 March 1996), para. 5.2; *Barbato* v. *Uruguay*, HRC 84/1981 (12 October 1982); *Henry* v. *Jamaica*, HRC 230/1988 (1 November 1991); *Douglas, Gentles and Kerr* v. *Jamaica*, HRC 352/1989 (19 October 1993). The latter two cases stated that failure to access domestic remedies as a result of indigence and correlative lack of legal aid was sufficient to establish exhaustion of domestic remedies. In a similar manner, the American Court on Human Rights has advised that this admissibility requirement is fulfilled if a complainant is 'unable' to access a remedy, such as by reasons of poverty or generalised fear such that lawyers refuse to represent him or her: *Exceptions to Exhaustion of Domestic Remedies* (Advisory Opinion), I-ACtHR, Ser. A, No. 11 (10 August 1990).

[235] Article 4(1), OP-CEDAW.

[236] See, e.g., *Kayhan* v. *Turkey*, CEDAW 8/2005 (27 January 2006) (in all the complainant's domestic proceedings in relation to her dismissal for wearing the headscarf, she had not argued that it was sex discrimination, so the Women's Committee held that she had not exhausted domestic remedies); *N. S. F.* v. *United Kingdom*, CEDAW 10/2005 (30 May 2007) (in which sex discrimination had not been raised directly in appeals against a negative asylum determination and other decisions that did not recognise the complainant's right to remain in the UK).

[237] See, *Goecke* v. *Austria*, CEDAW 5/2005 (6 August 2007), para. 7.5.

[238] *K. L.* v. *Peru*, HRC 1153/2003 (24 October 2005), para. 5.2.

party. That is, the human rights petition system is not supplementary to failing national criminal laws or civil proceedings that allow victims to face, or bring actions directly against, their perpetrators.[239] The individual petitions system does not operate as a court of law in which the actual perpetrator is on trial. Rather, the system is positioned within the public/private divide between international and national laws, and between official and private violations.[240] It recognises only vertical applications of human rights (state–individual), not horizontal (individual–individual). This is so even under the CEDAW, which specifically prohibits discrimination by 'any person, group or enterprise'.[241]

In order to introduce 'private', or horizontal, violations, a woman must establish that the state has failed to act to prevent the harm or to properly investigate, prosecute, or punish alleged offenders under national laws. As will be shown in later chapters of this book, women must mount two hurdles before gaining redress under international law for 'private' violations. They need to establish, first, that they have been subjected to or threatened with violent conduct by a non-state actor, and second, that the state is responsible under international law for that act by reason of its failure to act with due diligence to prevent or prosecute it. How this second tier plays out to the disadvantage of women is explored in more detail in later chapters.

Despite these many problems relating to women's access to the treaty body petition system, their use of it must be strengthened, not abandoned. This is because the individual petitions system is one of few effective ways to develop principles and rules under international law. The alternative routes, through the UN Security Council or General Assembly or other diplomatic/political bodies, such as the Human Rights Council, which are even more cumbersome and based on issues such as security and state interests, are arguably more biased in favour of the reflection of 'male' views. These latter mechanisms do not seek to be independent and impartial (the principles that govern the work of the treaty bodies) but are firmly entrenched in state/political interests. Furthermore, the individual petitions system must be further strengthened because 'a claim of right can be an assertion of one's self-worth and an affirmation of one's moral value and entitlement'.[242] At the same time, rights claims represent a collective

---

[239] Although the criminal justice system must also be subject to scrutiny as it is the state that brings a prosecution on behalf of the victim/public against the alleged perpetrators.

[240] See, Chapter 2.   [241] Article 2(e), CEDAW.

[242] E. M. Schneider, *Battered Women and Feminist Lawmaking* (New Haven, CT: Yale University Press, 2000), 39.

selfhood, giving women a sense of group identity and pride.[243] Many studies now confirm that, in seeking justice for violence perpetrated against them, women seek to have their day in court and to be heard.[244] Judicial processes are no longer only about developing winners and losers; they are also about recovery, reconciliation, and reparation.[245]

Successful rights claims also give women's rights activists and NGOs a sense of progress being made that would otherwise be difficult to measure. Case law can represent a stepping stone towards the ultimate destination of women's equality. As Patricia Williams has stated: 'For the historically disempowered, the conferring of rights is symbolic of all the denied aspects of their humanity ...'.[246] Likewise, Rebecca Cook argues that cases can indicate trends and show that human rights abuses represent government policies rather than merely individual aberrations. She argues further that an individual case 'raised to popular consciousness through the victim's name, illuminates transcending oppression and injustice'.[247] At the same time as endorsing the value in individual litigation, it must be part of a wider process of reform. Although claiming legal rights holds out 'the promise of greater power on members of the subordinate group', it (paradoxically) simultaneously reaffirms basic elements of the existing legal order, including legal constructs that oppress such groups.[248] There is no denying that, by utilising a system of male privilege and male rights, the system itself can be strengthened, legitimised, or even emboldened to reinforce those privileges and rights.

---

[243] *Ibid.*, 40.

[244] See, studies on reparations and transitional justice mentioned at n. 226 above of this chapter.

[245] See, studies on reparations and transitional justice mentioned at n. 226 above of this chapter.

[246] P. J. Williams, *The Alchemy of Race and Rights* (Cambridge, MA: Harvard University Press, 1991), 53.

[247] R. J. Cook, 'State Responsibility for Violations of Women's Human Rights' (1994) 7 *Harv. Hum. Rts. J.* 125, at 135. As examples, she refers to the powerful names of Anne Frank, Steven Biko, and Guatemalan Nobel Laureate Rigobertu Menchu. One might add the more recent cases of *Prosecutor* v. *Jean-Paul Akayesu*, ICTR, Case No. ICTR-96–4-T (2 September 1998) before the International Criminal Tribunal for Rwanda, or *Aydin* v. *Turkey* (1997) 25 EHRR 251 before the European Court of Human Rights, to illustrate successful steps towards condemning violence against women. See, further, A. Edwards, '*Aydin v Turkey, Akayesu* and Abu Ghraib: Re-conceptualising "Torture" under International Law from a Feminist Perspective', Australian and New Zealand Society of International Law Annual Conference, Canberra, June 2005.

[248] S. F. Goldfarb, 'Applying the Discrimination Model to Violence against Women: Some Reflections on Theory and Practice' (2002–2003) 11 *Am. U. J. Gender Soc. Pol'y & L.* 251, at 258.

In the absence of an alternative system, however, women are left with very few practical choices. Either they engage with the existing international legal system and try to reform the system from within, or they sit on the sidelines and hope someone is listening. In fact, there have been several innovative approaches adopted by the treaty bodies that encourage women to utilise more frequently the complaints mechanisms. For example, the HRC and the Women's Committee have held that, if the effects of past abuse are felt beyond the date at which a state party ratified the relevant treaty, then they can still be admitted, as they constitute 'continuing violations'. This opens up possibilities for women to bring claims relating to ongoing psychological trauma or permanent physical disfigurement from past violent and other events.[249] Women (and others) also benefit from the position of the HRC in stating that the onus of proof does not rest solely on the complainant but must be shared with the state party,

---

[249] See, e.g., *Lovelace v Canada*, HRC 24/1977 (30 July 1981); *J. L. v. Australia*, HRC 491/1992 (28 July 1992); *A. T. v. Hungary*, CEDAW 2/2003 (26 January 2005) (serious physical domestic violence was considered to be part of a 'clear continuum of regular domestic violence' and because of lack of action by the state, the complainant's life was considered to still be in danger from her husband); *Szijarto v. Hungary*, CEDAW 4/2004 (14 August 2006) (coerced sterilisation carried out against a Hungarian woman of Roma ethnicity prior to the entry into force of the CEDAW for Hungary was held to be admissible as it was considered to be permanent and irreversible and, therefore, of a continuous nature extending after the date of entry into force); *Kayhan v. Turkey*, CEDAW 8/2005 (27 January 2006) (although this case was ultimately ruled to be inadmissible on other grounds, the Committee noted that the decision to dismiss the complainant from her teaching position due to her wearing a headscarf was taken prior to the entry into force of the CEDAW for Turkey; nonetheless the consequence was the loss of status as a civil servant. The effects of this loss were considered to continue after the date of entry into force. Such effects included her means of subsistence to a great extent, the deductions that would go towards her pension entitlement, interest on her salary and income, her education grant, and her health insurance.) A similar view has been taken in the context of international refugee status determination. The US Court of Appeals has held that female genital mutilation is a 'continuing violation' because it 'permanently disfigures a woman, causes long term health problems, and deprives her of a normal and fulfilling sexual life'. See, *Khadija Mohammed v. Attorney-General*, US, 400 F.3d 785 (10 March 2005). The Women's Committee has been criticised, however, for being inconsistent in its treatment of 'continuing' versus 'completed' violations: see, A. Byrnes and E. Bath, 'Violence against Women, the Obligation of Due Diligence, and the Optional Protocol to the Convention on the Elimination of All Forms of Discrimination against Women – Recent Developments' (2008) 8 *Hum. Rts. L. Rev.* 517, 532, in which they argue that the finalisation of a divorce on what was claimed to be a discriminatory basis and the continuing economic loss resulting from this in the case of *B. J. v. Germany*, CEDAW 1/2003 (14 July 2004) (a communication that was declared inadmissible) could be analysed in the same way as the above cases, but it was not.

given their access to particular information, thereby balancing the power between the two parties.[250]

Despite its flaws, the individual communications system is an important component of the wider international human rights system, and it is particularly relevant to rights assertion within the context of violence against women and the interpretation and application of norms in that context. These procedures are not, however, the only tools available for women and women's rights activists to address human rights violations, and strategic choices must be made. Other mechanisms that are available but not dealt with in this book include monitoring, fact-finding, periodic reporting, negotiating, and discourse.[251]

H   Inquiry or fact-finding procedures and women

The final human rights mechanism of relevance to this chapter is that of inquiry or fact-finding procedures. Several of the treaty bodies have some kind of inquiry or fact-finding procedure.[252] The CAT operates a confidential inquiry and urgent reporting procedure when it receives reliable information about well-founded indications that torture is being systematically practised, which may include visits to the territory in cooperation with the state party.[253] The OP-CAT establishes an international inspection body, complementing national prevention mechanisms, with the capacity to make unannounced visits to places of detention in order to reduce the occurrence of torture or cruel, inhuman, or degrading treatment or punishment. In addition, the ICERD, the OP-CEDAW, the IMWC, the ICRPD, and the Optional Protocol to the ICESCR (OP-ICESCR) contain similar procedures, although not all have yet taken effect.[254] Of these I am particularly interested in the new procedure under the OP-CEDAW.

The OP-CEDAW includes a provision allowing the Women's Committee to undertake confidential inquiries when it receives reliable information of grave *or* systematic violations.[255] Upon receipt of such information, the state party in question will be asked to cooperate in the examination of the material. One or more members of the Committee are then designated

---

[250] *Bleier* v. *Uruguay*, HRC 30/1978, decided 29 March 1982, para. 13.3.

[251] For an overview of human rights mechanisms, see M. O'Flaherty, *Human Rights and the UN Practice before the Treaty Bodies* (2nd edn, The Hague: Martinus Nijhoff Publishers, 2002).

[252] See, above under B in this chapter.   [253] Article 20, UNCAT.

[254] See, above under B in this chapter.   [255] Article 8, OP-CEDAW.

to conduct an inquiry and to report urgently to the Committee as a whole. Where warranted, the inquiry may include a visit to the territory of the state party, subject to the latter's consent.[256] The OP-CEDAW allows states parties to opt out of these procedures.[257] Proposals to require states to 'opt in' rather than 'opt out' were rejected.[258] Given the effect of the large number of reservations to the parent treaty,[259] states agreed that no reservations be allowed to the Optional Protocol.[260]

For the inquiry procedure to be activated, the information must relate to multiple violations by virtue of the use of the plural form in the relevant provision. Such violations do not, however, necessarily need to be systematic (in the sense of being entrenched or widespread) provided they are 'grave'. The language of 'serious', which was in the initial draft, was replaced by the arguably higher standard of 'grave' during the drafting process.[261] The information may derive from any source, provided it is reliable. The procedure has been widely welcomed, in spite of its reliance on state cooperation and its confidential nature.[262] However, to date it has been underutilised. As at August 2010, the Women's Committee had conducted only one inquiry in nearly a decade.[263] Likewise, the CAT had conducted only seven fact-finding missions since 1987.[264]

These fact-finding or confidential inquiries also offer an alternative form of monitoring, allowing the committees to gather and assess the human rights situation first-hand rather than relying on secondary materials from state party reports and from UN agencies and NGOs. Nonetheless, the process is not fast and has been underutilised. According to the OHCHR, it takes approximately eight months between an initial proposal for a visit and the Secretariat arranging it, with follow-up

---

[256] Article 8, OP-CEDAW.   [257] Article 10, OP-CEDAW.

[258] Isa, 'The Optional Protocol for the Convention on the Elimination of All Forms of Discrimination Against Women', 317 (on the negotiations to the Optional Protocol).

[259] See, R. J. Cook, 'Reservations to the Convention on the Elimination of All Forms of Discrimination Against Women' (1990) 30 *Va. J. Int'l L.* 643.

[260] Article 17, OP-CEDAW.

[261] CEDAW, *Report of the Committee on the Elimination of Discrimination against Women*, UN Doc. A/50/38 (1996), para. 17.

[262] Article 8(5), OP-CEDAW.

[263] CEDAW, *Report on Mexico produced by the Committee on the Elimination of Discrimination against Women, and Reply from the Government of Mexico*, UN Doc. CEDAW/C/2005/OP.8/MEXICO, 27 January 2005.

[264] As at mid-2008, inquiries had been completed for Brazil, Egypt, Mexico, Peru, Sri Lanka, Turkey, and Yugoslavia (Serbia and Montengro). There was some discussion in 2006 for additional inquiries to be conducted, but they were not held: Colombia, Guatemala, Nepal, Togo, and Uzbekistan; see UN Doc. CAT/C/37/2 (2006).

taking several more months.[265] Delays may undermine the purpose of any visit, particularly in the context of grave violations. Moreover, any benefit gained from the threat of carrying out a fact-finding visit does not hold up to the same extent as the interstate dispute mechanism, because the fact-finding mission is entirely dependent on the consent of the state party.[266]

I   Conclusion

This chapter has shown that the lack of women in positions of power within the UN system is not simply part of the historical record; it continues to inhibit and influence the work of the international treaty bodies. As Charlesworth argues:

> Unless the experiences of women contribute directly to the mainstream international legal order, beginning with women's equal representation in law-making forums, international human rights law loses its claim to universal applicability.[267]

System-wide, women are still under-represented in all of the treaty bodies except those on women and children, and gender expertise is not readily apparent in the make-up of any of the committees apart from the Women's Committee.[268] Experience shows that legal guarantees of balanced sex representation are inadequate without constant lobbying and monitoring by women's groups. Women are under-represented for various reasons, including the low levels of female nominees, arising from sexist municipal systems, and the political nature of the election process, which is less concerned with equal representation or qualifications and more concerned with political trading and bargaining. Early evidence drawn from the membership of the SPT, which as noted above contains a provision calling for 'balanced gender representation', confirms that legal provisions are insufficient on their own to guarantee equal participation of women.

---

[265] Interview with senior official of the OHCHR, 16 June 2008.

[266] As noted earlier in this chapter, the SPT established under the OP-CAT has the capacity to visit places of detention without the consent of the state party.

[267] H. Charlesworth, 'Human Rights as Men's Rights', in J. Peters and A. Wolper (eds.), *Women's Rights, Human Rights: International Feminist Perspectives* (New York: Routledge, 1995) 103, at 105.

[268] This is not to suggest that the committee members are all unqualified. There are many well-qualified members on various committees. Rather it is to state that there is a certain level of expertise lacking, in particular in respect of women's rights.

Apart from the Women's Committee and the Children's Committee, the only international institution that has attained near parity in membership in decision-making positions is the International Criminal Court (ICC).[269] Although it is a court rather than a treaty body, it is a useful comparator in terms of processes for ensuring equal representation.[270] Heavy lobbying by NGOs, including women's organisations,[271] succeeded in securing language in the Rome Statute of the ICC that required 'fair representation of female and male judges' on the bench and stipulated that judges with legal expertise in certain areas, including violence against women, be considered favourably.[272] This type of lobbying was missing from the drafting of the first seven human rights treaties.

Together with state commitment and continued pressure by international women's groups, the result was an initial bench composed of an unprecedented number of women members: seven women judges elected out of a total of eighteen (or 38 per cent). The second election of six judges in January 2006 saw an even split, with three female and three male judges elected, although more men had been nominated (six to four).[273] The membership in 2009 saw for the first time the number of female judges outnumber their male counterparts (ten out of eighteen judges, or 56 per cent). Globally, however, women make up only 23 per cent of the total number of judges sitting on international and regional international courts (72 out of 316).[274]

Nonetheless, the success with respect to the ICC is limited to the composition of the bench. The same gender-balance criterion applies in relation to filling staffing requirements of the ICC Office of the Prosecutor, and

---

[269] Rome Statute of the International Criminal Court, UN Doc. A/CONF.183/9, 17 July 1998, 2187 UNTS 90; entered into force 1 July 2002.

[270] For more information on the ICC, see O. Bekou and R. Cryer, *The International Criminal Court* (Aldershot and London: Ashgate Publishing, 2004).

[271] Particular mention here is due to the Women's Caucus for Gender Justice (now Women's Initiatives for Gender Justice), which was set up with its primary purpose to ensure women were given a voice in the creation of the ICC. See, www.iccwomen.org/

[272] Article 36(8), ICC Statute. D. M. Koenig and K. D. Askin, 'International Criminal Law and the International Criminal Court Statute: Crimes against Women', in K. D. Askin and D. M. Koenig (eds.), *Women and International Human Rights Law* (Ardsley, NY: Transnational Publishers, 2000), Vol. 2, 3, at 12. See, also, *Women's Caucus for Gender Justice in the International Criminal Court* (June 1998).

[273] See, www.icc-cpi.int/library/asp/E_judgeselected_finalresults_26jan1615.pdf.

[274] Women's Initiative for Gender Justice, *Profile of Judicial Candidates for January 2009 Election: Six Judges Elected*, available at: www.iccwomen.org/news/docs/Election_of_Judges_January_2009_Information_Sheet.pdf.

the Registry.[275] The Chief Prosecutor is additionally required to appoint advisors with expertise on specific issues, including, but not limited to, sexual and gender violence,[276] while the Victims and Witnesses Unit is expected to include staff with expertise in trauma, including trauma relating to crimes of sexual violence.[277] Despite the success in the election of judges, the Women's Initiatives for Gender Justice (WIGJ) identified in 2006 that only 17 of 109 appointees to the Court as legal counsel were women (equivalent to 9 per cent), and 70 per cent of these women were from the Western Europe and Other States Group (WEOG).[278] Having now turned its attention to the overall staffing of the ICC, the WIGJ's 2009 *Gender Report Card* indicates a much-improved composition of the professional ranks of the court and registry with near parity at many levels, and in some instances higher levels of women than men.[279]

Left to their own devices, however, international institutions, dominated by men and backed up by domestic systems dominated by men, revert to gender inequality. The feminist claims outlined in Chapter 2 continue to ring true with women's participation generally marginalised into the treaties on women and children. Any reform of the existing treaty system, which is dealt with in Chapter 8, would need to ensure that women's representation is secured, including in terms of substantive expertise.

This chapter has also shown that, while there has been an improvement in the inclusion of women's concerns within state party reports, including the attention paid by the treaty bodies to such issues, it remains a haphazard process driven by local and national priorities. It has further been demonstrated that women are under-represented as complainants in the individual petitions system, where they face a range of legal, procedural, and practical challenges to the admission of their cases. It follows that the less accessible the human rights system is to women, the more abstract it becomes, and the more it supports feminist views that it is irrelevant to women's lives. To date, the treaty bodies have spent little time reflecting upon the effect of their procedural rules on women, and very few initiatives have been instituted to improve women's access, such as the provision of legal aid, other funding opportunities to support claims, or educational campaigns. To make the treaty bodies relevant to

---

[275]   Article 36(8)(a)(iii) and (b), ICC Statute.
[276]   Article 42(9), ICC Statute.   [277]   Article 43(6), ICC Statute.
[278]   Women's Initiatives for Gender Justice, *Gender Report Card 2005*, available at: www.iccwomen.org/news/2005_11_29.php.
[279]   WIGJ, *Gender Report Card 2009*, available at: www.iccwomen.org/news/docs/GRC09_web-version.pdf.

women's lives, much more needs to be done at international, national, and grass-roots levels to ensure that ostensible 'gender-neutral' procedures do not hide the exclusion of women and that women are able to access all components of the treaty body system. In particular, for women to utilise the individual petitions system, they need to be able to rely on consistent interpretations and applications of traditional norms to their everyday experiences. I now turn to the issue of interpretation and application in the three chapters that follow.

4

Equality and non-discrimination on
the basis of sex

A   Introduction

This chapter explores how the international human rights treaty bodies, and other international institutions, have responded to violence against women via the principles of equality between men and women and non-discrimination on the basis of sex. In the absence of an explicit prohibition on violence against women within any international instrument at the time, the Women's Committee in 1989, and again in 1992, declared that violence against women is a form of sex discrimination (VAW=SD). Other treaty bodies and international human rights courts and tribunals also adopt similar approaches. In this chapter I am particularly interested in how sex discrimination and inequality are understood under international law; what these understandings mean for the inclusion of women and their lives within these prohibitions; and whether the 'gender mainstreaming' strategy of incorporating violence against women as a form of sex discrimination has produced any real results for women, or whether it has in fact bolstered the myriad feminist critiques of the international system outlined in Chapter 2.

This chapter is divided into two main parts. The first part analyses how these principles have been understood generally under international law, followed by their application to cover violence against women in particular. I explore five issues relating to equality/non-discrimination: formal versus substantive equality; discrimination versus equality; public and private discrimination; structural inequality; and multiple discrimination. Within this exploration, relevant feminist critiques are highlighted, as well as three feminist proposals for reconceptualising how we understand equality under international law. The second part then evaluates the VAW=SD strategy.

In relation to the latter, I argue that as a pragmatic solution to the absence of an explicit prohibition, it is clear that guarantees of equality have been used to plug a worrying gap in the law. At the same time, however, I find the approach to be inherently problematic. First, it equates violence against women to sex discrimination and is, therefore, subject to understandings of the latter term, which have proven to be complex and unsettled. Second, this strategy covers only *gender-related* forms of violence against women, rather than all forms of violence, and creates, therefore, a two-tiered system of protection, or a hierarchy of oppressions. Third, I find the rhetoric of equality to be weaker than the language of violence and this plays into treating violence against women as a 'women's only' issue, rather than a serious human rights violation per se. And finally, this strategy reinforces an international legal system that disadvantages women by their subjection to additional, different, or unequal criteria. That is, women are only protected against violence indirectly. By requiring women to characterise the violence they suffer as sex discrimination, rather than as violence per se, they are treated unequally under law.

B   Equality and non-discrimination: general concepts and feminist critiques

Equality has been recognised as one of the fundamental principles of liberal democracies and government by the rule of law, and it has been absorbed into many legal systems,[1] including the system of international law. '[E]quality before the law is in a substantial sense the most fundamental of the rights of man [sic]. It occupies the first place in most written constitutions. It is the starting point of all other liberties.'[2] '[I]t is philosophically related to the concepts of freedom and justice.'[3] Nonetheless, some have considered 'equality' so vague and so wide a term as to be almost meaningless.[4] Douglas Rae in his 1981 study stated that '[e]quality is the simplest and most abstract of notions ...'.[5] In fact, he identified more than 108 'structurally distinct interpretations' of

[1] Daniel Moeckli reports that 111 states guarantee some form of equality in written constitutions: D. Moeckli, *Human Rights and Non-Discrimination in the 'War on Terror'* (Oxford University Press, 2008).

[2] Sir H. Lauterpacht, *An International Bill of the Rights of Man* (New York: Columbia University Press, 1945), 115.

[3] *South West Africa Cases (Liberia v. South Africa; Ethiopia v. South Africa)* 1962 ICJ Rep. 319; 1966 ICJ Rep. 4, 303 (per Justice Tanaka (dissent)).

[4] J. F. Stephen, *Liberty, Equality, Fraternity* (Cambridge University Press, 1873), 201, as referred to in W. McKean, *Equality and Discrimination under International Law* (Oxford: Clarendon Press, 1983), 2.

[5] D. Rae, *Equalities* (Cambridge, MA: Harvard University Press, 1981), 3.

equality.[6] So what do the concepts of equality and non-discrimination on the basis of sex mean?

The principles of equality and non-discrimination in law are deeply contested. As ideals of justice, they are well-accepted principles,[7] but their content is less obvious. At one end of the spectrum of views on equality is the liberal democratic tradition of equality as the comparison of similar situations.[8] This is also referred to as the Aristotelian view of equality as 'treating like alike'[9], or that persons in similar positions should not be treated unequally.[10] The problem with this view is that it does not address what differences are relevant to determining whether individuals are equals or unequals.[11] In terms of equality between men and women, it is problematic on two levels. First, it assumes that the point of comparison is male; and second, it cannot be applied where a comparable male is missing.[12] This view of equality has largely been translated into national modern laws as equality of opportunity (or formal equality) and has faced much feminist and other criticism.[13] In other words, any distinction, exclusion, or restriction is permissible provided it is not 'arbitrary'. It will not be 'arbitrary' if it can be justified on the basis of 'objective' and 'reasonable' criteria. However, what these criteria are has varied widely within the case law at national, regional, and international levels.[14] As Aileen McColgan states, '[L]ikeness is whatever the legislation declares

---

[6] *Ibid.*, 133.

[7] This was not always the case, and remains a challenge in some countries. Early formulations of equality and non-discrimination were directed at equality between *men* of different religious, nationality, or linguistic minorities, or even limited to different classes: see, Moeckli, *Human Rights and Non-Discrimination in the 'War on Terror'* for an excellent summary of the origins of the principles of equality and non-discrimination generally.

[8] B. Gaze, 'Some Aspects of Equality Rights: Theory and Practice', in B. Galligan and C. Sampford (eds.), *Rethinking Human Rights* (Annandale, NSW: Federation Press, 1997) 189, at 190.

[9] C. A. MacKinnon, 'Equality Remade: Violence Against Women', in C. A MacKinnon, *Are Women Human? And Other International Dialogues* (Cambridge, MA: Harvard University Press, 2006) 105.

[10] McKean, *Equality and Discrimination under International Law*, 3.

[11] *Ibid.*

[12] K. Frostell, 'Gender Difference and the Non-Discrimination Principle in the CCPR and the CEDAW', in L. Hannikainen and E Nykänen (eds.), *New Trends in Discrimination Law – International Perspectives* (Turku Law School, 1999) 29, at 29.

[13] See, e.g., P. Weston, 'The Empty Idea of Equality' (1982) 95 *Harv. L. Rev.* 537; M. Gold, 'The Canadian Concept of Equality' (1986) 46 *Uni. Toronto L. J.* 349; A. McColgan, 'Cracking the Comparator Problem: Discrimination, "Equal" Treatment and the Role of Comparisons' (2006) 6 *Eur. Hum. Rts L. Rev.* 649.

[14] See, for a good overview, McColgan, 'Cracking the Comparator Problem'.

it to be.'[15] A further gap in the analysis has been identified as the fact that there is no moral judgment about whether persons who are alike or similarly situated should be treated alike.[16]

Formal equality – such as equality before the law and equal rights – are at the centre of liberal feminist goals of equal participation in employment, the economy, and education.[17] Yet these liberal feminist goals have been criticised by other feminist scholars for ignoring difference. '[T]he prohibition of discrimination is not a prohibition of differentiation ... [D]istinctions are prohibited only to the extent that they are unfavourable. Equality could easily be transformed into injustice if it were to be applied to situations which are inherently unequal.'[18] For writers such as Margareth Etienne, the paradigm of 'equality as parity' employed under national and international laws fails to recognise that 'equality is not freedom to be treated without regard to sex but freedom from systematic subordination because of sex.'[19] Because of this, she argues, women do not receive special protection against harms specific to their experiences as women. It has also been asserted that the orientation of the Convention on the Elimination of All Forms of Discrimination against Women (CEDAW)[20] around non-discrimination will not compel 'a broader, nonrights-based examination of female subordination' because Article 1 defines discrimination in terms of unequal rights.[21]

An alternative approach to equality of access is in terms of outcome (or substantive equality). This formulation may envisage social justice as the end objective, albeit with a particular standard of social justice in mind. It permits deviations from strict equality, such as 'special measures' or differences in treatment designed to elevate persons to that standard.[22]

---

[15] Ibid., 662.

[16] Weston, 'The Empty Idea of Equality'; Gold, 'The Canadian Concept of Equality'.

[17] N. Lacey, 'Legislation Against Sex Discrimination: Questions from a Feminist Perspective' (1987) 14 J. L. and Soc'y 411, at 413. See, further, Chapter 2.

[18] F. Krill, 'The Protection of Women in International Humanitarian Law' (1985) 249 Int'l Rev. Red Cross 337, at 339.

[19] M. Etienne, 'Addressing Gender-Based Violence in an International Context' (1995) 18 Harv. Women's L. J. 139, at 148, referring to H. Charlesworth, C. Chinkin and S. Wright, 'Feminist Approaches to International Law' (1991) 85 Amer. J. Int'l L. 613, at 630.

[20] Convention on the Elimination of All Forms of Discrimination against Women 1979, GA res. 34/180, 18 December 1979, 1249 UNTS 195; entered into force 3 September 1981 (CEDAW).

[21] J. Ulrich, 'Confronting Gender-Based Violence with International Instruments: Is a Solution to the Pandemic Within Reach?' (1999–2000) 7 Ind. J. Global Legal Stud. 629, 643.

[22] McKean, Equality and Discrimination under International Law, 3.

Substantive equality can be achieved, for example, through positive or affirmative action, protective or corrective measures, a recharacterisation of human rights, or a gender-conscious discrimination principle.[23] Recognising that the goal of formal equality does not take full account of women's *structural* disadvantage, especially in the so-called 'private' sphere, many legal jurisdictions have replaced it with ideas of *substantive* equality. Substantive equality is geared towards bringing about not just formal but 'effective and genuine' equality.[24] Although there have been some shifts away from traditional constructions of equality as sameness/difference under international law, the traditional equality paradigm remains the dominant framework, even after the Beijing World Conference.[25]

Defining equality prompts further debate on issues such as: what distinctions can be justified as compatible with equality principles and upon what criteria should those distinctions be judged; determining whether or not intention is a requirement for discrimination; deciding on the relevance of purpose and effect;[26] and articulating whether there is any real difference between discrimination and inequality. Because of the concerns with existing understandings of equality and non-discrimination and the many questions that remain unanswered, many feminist scholars have sought to theorise new ways of conceptualising these concepts. The work of three scholars is outlined here.[27]

Drawing on the jurisprudence of the Canadian Supreme Court, Kathleen Mahoney has recommended a new vision of equality in terms of 'socially created advantage and disadvantage' instead of sameness and difference.[28] She claims that the sameness/difference model does not permit any examination of how the legal system maintains and constructs the

---

[23] Frostell, 'Gender Difference and the Non-Discrimination Principle in the CCPR and the CEDAW', 30.

[24] *Minority Schools in Albania, Greece v. Albania* (Advisory Opinion), PCIJ, Ser. A/B, No. 64 (6 April 1935) 21.

[25] R. J. Cook, 'Advancing International Law Regarding Women' (1997) 91 *ASIL Proceedings* 308, at 316.

[26] K. E. Mahoney, 'Canadian Approaches to Equality Rights and Gender Equity in the Courts', in R. J. Cook (ed.), *Human Rights of Women: National and International Perspectives* (Philadelphia: University of Pennsylvania Press, 1994) 437, at 442.

[27] There are of course many other ideas of how equality should be reframed, but it is beyond the scope of the book to deal with each of them here. For example, Sandra Fredman identifies specific values that can be used to develop a conception of equality, namely distributive justice, remedial aims, participation, and dignity: S. Fredman, *Introduction to Discrimination Law* (Oxford University Press, 2002). Dignity is dealt with further below.

[28] Mahoney, 'Canadian Approaches to Equality Rights and Gender Equity in the Courts', 441.

disadvantage of women, or how the law is 'male-defined and built on male conceptions of problems and of harms'.[29] The problem with the sameness/ difference model is that it serves women only in 'a derivative way', that is, when they suffer violations in the same way as men. This in turn reinforces the 'male world-view and supports male dominance in the international order'.[30] It cannot cope with or take account of female-specific circumstances. Moreover, under the Aristotelian model, systemic and persistent disadvantage is not contemplated. Instead, the model assumes that social institutions should continue to exist as they are. To be equal, women need only the same chance as men to participate in those institutions.[31] Mahoney writes: 'This universalistic, gender-neutral approach does not recognize that institutional structures may impinge differently on men and women.'[32] Mahoney supports the replacement of the Aristotelian test for one that focuses on the impact of laws and on the context of the claimant. What is at issue is the disadvantage suffered. Under this view, no male comparator is needed:

> If a person is a member of a persistently disadvantaged group and can show that a distinction based on personal characteristics of the individual or group not imposed on others continues or worsens that disadvantage, the distinction is discriminatory whether intentional or not.[33]

This test requires decision- and policy-makers to look at women or other claimants 'in their place in the real world' and 'to confront the reality that the systemic abuse and deprivation of power [that] women experience is because of their place in the sexual hierarchy'.[34]

Iris Marion Young has proposed an analysis of inequality in terms of oppression and domination rather than distributive justice. Existing models of sameness/difference equality fail to consider issues of institutional organisation and decision-making power.[35] She argues that reliance on discrimination as the benchmark is problematic because, as Robert Fullinwider observes: '[I]f we do not do preferential hiring, we permit discrimination to exist. But preferential hiring is also discrimination. Thus, if we use preferential hiring, we also permit discrimination to exist. The

---

[29] Ibid., 442.   [30] Ibid., 438.   [31] Ibid., 442–443.   [32] Ibid., 443.

[33] Ibid., 444, referring to Andres v. Law Society of British Columbia, 1 S.C.R. 143 (1989), and subsequent decisions in Reference Re Workers' Compensation Act 1983 (Nfld), 1 S.C.R. 992 (1989) and R. v. Turpin 1 S.C.R. 1296 (1989).

[34] Ibid., 445.

[35] I. M. Young, Justice and the Politics of Difference (Princeton University Press, 1990), 193.

dilemma is that whatever we do, we permit discrimination.'[36] Admitting that affirmative action policies discriminate, Young suggests that the focus of the debate has been skewed. She claims that we must acknowledge that discrimination is not the only or primary wrong that certain groups suffer. Instead, '[o]ppression, not discrimination, is the primary concept for naming group-related injustice.' She notes:

> While discriminatory policies sometimes cause or reinforce oppression, oppression involves many actions, practices, and structures that have little to do with preferring or excluding members of groups in the awarding of benefits.[37]

Under her analysis, special measures would not be framed as exceptions to the principle of non-discrimination, but rather as one strategy to deal with structures of oppression and domination.[38] Supporting the view of Young, Hilary Charlesworth has suggested that less emphasis be given to non-discrimination. Instead, she recommends that a broader idea of equality ought to be developed and has argued that the elision between the two concepts has constrained their ability to deal with women's realities.[39]

Catharine MacKinnon is the third feminist scholar I wish to mention who has recommended a reorientation in our understanding of equality. Because women are below men in social, economic, and political indicators, she argues that the movement for equality should not be oriented to being the same as men but on 'ending violation and abuse and second-class citizenship' of women because of their sex.[40] The mainstream equality model of sameness/difference relies on a male standard and thereby relegates women to a status of inferiority indefinitely. That model has been unable to cope with real differences such as pregnancy, or systematic social disadvantages such as sex segregation in the workforce resulting in lack of equal pay for work of comparable worth, or violence against women that is systematically tolerated worldwide.[41] It offers only two alternative

---

[36] R. Fullinwider, *The Reverse Discrimination Controversy* (Totowa, NJ: Rowman & Allanheld, 1980), 156, as cited in Young, *Justice and the Politics of Difference*, 194.

[37] *Ibid.*, 195.

[38] H. Charlesworth, 'Concepts of Equality in International Law', in G. Huscroft and P. Rishworth (eds.), *Litigating Rights: Perspectives from Domestic and International Law* (Oxford: Hart Publishing, 2002) 137, at 147.

[39] *Ibid.*

[40] MacKinnon, 'Equality Remade: Violence against Women', 108.

[41] C. A. MacKinnon, 'Making Sex Equality Real', in C. A MacKinnon, *Are Women Human? And Other International Dialogues* (Cambridge, MA: Harvard University Press, 2006) 71, at 73.

routes: to be the same as men or to recognise women's differences and to grant 'special benefits' or 'double standards'.[42] According to MacKinnon, the problem with this is that '[t]he sameness standard gets women, when they are like men, access to what men already have; the differences rule seeks to cushion the impact of women's distinctiveness or value women as they are under existing conditions'.[43] For the most part, the mainstream equality model has granted men the benefit of those few things women have historically had.[44] 'If systematic relegation to inferiority is what is wrong with inequality, the task of equality law is to end that status, not to focus on conditions under which it can be justified.'[45]

In MacKinnon's reorientation, the concept that has emerged, and which she suggests has already taken place in many different jurisdictions, is:

> equality as lack of hierarchy, rather than sameness or difference, in a relative universality that embraces rather than eliminates or levels particularity. A refusal to settle for anything less than a single standard of human dignity and entitlement combines here with a demand that the single standards themselves are equalized. All this leaves Aristotle in the dust ... Its principles include: if men do not do it to each other, they cannot do it to us ...[46]

Inequality is about dominance and subordination, not sameness/difference. 'The fundamental issue of equality is not whether one is the same or different; it is not the gender difference; it is the difference gender makes.'[47] MacKinnon argues that, as soon as all forms of violence against women in society, and impunity for it in law, are recognised as sex-inequality violations as reimagined by her, 'law will be made new in women's hands'.[48]

Within MacKinnon's reconceptualisation is reference to the language of human dignity, although she does not give it full attention. There is now a sizeable volume of literature on the issue of dignity and equality, as well as a number of decisions in which it has been relied on.[49] Despite suffering from accusations that the language is vague, non-justiciable, or of limited

---

[42] Ibid., 72.   [43] Ibid., 72.   [44] Ibid., 73.   [45] Ibid., 74.

[46] MacKinnon, 'Equality Remade: Violence against Women', 108–109.

[47] MacKinnon, 'Making Sex Equality Real', 74.

[48] MacKinnon, 'Equality Remade: Violence against Women', 111.

[49] For case law that has applied the concept of dignity in equality cases, especially in Canada and South Africa, but also in Germany, Hungary, and Israel, see: R. O'Connell, 'The Role of Dignity in Equality Law: Lessons from Canada and South Africa' (2008) 6 Int'l J. Const. L. 267.

utility,[50] it nonetheless has a contribution to make, albeit it should not be the central or only form of analysis. Appearing centrally within human rights instruments, starting with the UN Charter and the Universal Declaration of Human Rights 1948 (UDHR),[51] it can inform the way in which equality is framed under international law. In particular, it brings to the fore ideas of fairness, justice, social respect, integrity, disadvantage, prejudice, stereotyping, and autonomy; and if nothing else, like the other reconceptualisations above, it moves away from the 'treat like alike' ideology associated with discrimination laws in many jurisdictions, which have had limited effect on achieving equality on the basis of sex.

Although each of these scholars has articulated their reconceptualisation of equality/non-discrimination in a slightly different way, and it has not been possible to deal with the related critiques in any detail, it is possible to draw out three common factors. First, they agree that the sameness/difference equality model is inadequate to tackle the underlying social disadvantage or sexual hierarchy that exists. This is because it seeks to put women in the same position as men without deconstructing institutional systems that reinforce that inequality. At a minimum, it does not take account of female-specific differences. This view of equality is also reinforced by a focus on narrow ideas of discrimination as distinction instead of broader conceptions of equality as the end of oppression or disadvantage. Second, the sameness/difference model posits men's experiences as the norm and by doing so, the reality of women's lives or the context in which women live and work is ignored. Third, they each argue that the answer to these shortcomings of existing equality laws is to adopt a broad view of inequality as social injustice or social disadvantage/oppression/hierarchy in order to identify what is really happening in women's lives, and to construct policies and programmes around that reality.

The merits of these reformulations of equality will be evaluated alongside the sameness/difference ideology in this chapter. First, though, how have the principles of equality and non-discrimination been translated into international law?

---

[50] For a range of concerns with the term and its application in the equality context, see: G. Moon and R. Allen, 'Dignity Discourse in Discrimination Law: A Better Route to Equality?' (2006) 6 *Eur. Hum. Rts L. Rev.* 610.

[51] First preambular para. in the Charter of the United Nations, 26 June 1945, 1 UNTS XVI; entered into force 24 October 1945: 'to reaffirm faith in fundamental human rights, in the dignity and worth of the human person, in the equal rights of men and women and of nations large and small'; Article 1, UDHR, GA res. 217 A (III), 10 December 1948: 'All human beings are born free and equal in dignity and rights. They are endowed with reason.'

C   Equality and non-discrimination on the basis of sex in international law

1   The UN Charter and the Universal Declaration of Human Rights

The notions of equality and non-discrimination are foundational principles of the UN system of international law. The UN Charter 1945 endorsed equality between men and women as a fundamental human right.[52] Of the UN Charter, the UN has stated that 'no previous legal document had so forcefully affirmed the equality of all human beings, or specifically outlawed sex as a basis for discrimination'.[53] These principles were elaborated in the UDHR. Article 1 of the UDHR provides: 'All human beings are born free and equal in dignity and rights. They are endowed with reason and conscience and should act towards one another in a spirit of brotherhood.'[54] It is claimed by some scholars that the 'spirit of brotherhood' was extended to women only with the adoption of the CEDAW.[55] Article 2 of the UDHR provides: 'Everyone is entitled to all the rights and freedoms set forth in this Declaration, without distinction of any kind, such as race, colour, sex, language, religion, political or other opinion, national or social origin, property, birth or other status.' Article 7 of the UDHR further guarantees equality before the law, stating:

> All are equal before the law and are entitled without any discrimination to equal protection of the law. All are entitled to equal protection against any discrimination in violation of this Declaration and against any incitement to such discrimination.

The UDHR also calls for equal rights in respect of courts and tribunals,[56] within marriage,[57] to public service and political participation,[58] and in

---

[52] Articles 1(3), 8 and 55(c), UN Charter. See, also, Preambular para. 2, UN Charter: 'reaffirm ... faith in fundamental human rights, in the dignity and worth of the human person, in the equal rights of men and women.'

[53] United Nations, *The United Nations and the Advancement of Women 1945–1996* (New York: Dept of Public Information, 1995 and 1996), para. 33.

[54] Article 1, UDHR.

[55] R. L. Hillock, 'Establishing the Rights of Women Globally: Has the United Nations Convention on the Elimination of All Forms of Discrimination against Women made a Difference?' (2004–2005) 12 *Tulsa J. Comp. & Int'l L.* 481, at 482.

[56] Article 10, UDHR.   [57] Article 16, UDHR.

[58] Article 21, UDHR. This provision is, though, limited to citizens (and permanent residents) in its references to political participation in the government of 'his country.'

the workplace.[59] All other rights apply to 'everyone', with the exception of measures of special protection during motherhood and childhood.[60] 'Everyone' in this sense includes men as well as women.[61]

As pointed out in Chapter 2, the inclusion of guarantees of equality in the UN Charter and the UDHR resulted from heavy lobbying from women delegates and NGOs.[62] Although sex was always listed alongside other identity-based attributes such as race, religion, and political opinion in early UN documentation, it has been argued that the concept of equality that was initially conceived in international law related to the principle of equality of states[63] rather than equality between persons. Early equality rights also focused heavily on racial discrimination rather than sex discrimination.[64]

2   International and regional human rights instruments

These general principles in the UDHR were transferred, with little change, in binding form to the two general human rights covenants: the International Covenant on Civil and Political Rights (ICCPR)[65] and the International Covenant on Economic, Social and Cultural Rights

---

[59] Article 23, UDHR.   [60] Article 25, UDHR.

[61] At one stage during the drafting process of the UDHR, specific reference to 'equality between men and women' had been removed. The language was reinserted due to arguments by some delegates that the additional non-discrimination phraseology was essential because 'everyone' did not necessarily mean every individual, regardless of sex, in some countries. Similarly, an early version of Article 1 that started with 'all men' was corrected, albeit amid considerable resistance. Even Eleanor Roosevelt stated that it had become customary to refer to 'mankind' when also referring to women, or that translation problems made it unadvisable to use 'human beings' instead of 'men': UN Doc. AC.2/SR.2/p.4. In fact, the Commission on Human Rights (CHR) had voted upon and accepted the phrase 'all people, men and women ...', but it is not clear how the final version reverted to 'all human beings'. See, J. Morsink, *The Universal Declaration of Human Rights: Origins, Drafting, and Intent* (Philadelphia: University of Pennsylvania Press, 1999), 118.

[62] United Nations, *The United Nations and the Advancement of Women 1945–1996*, para. 32; Morsink, *The Universal Declaration of Human Rights*, 117–118.

[63] I. Brownlie, *Principles of Public International Law* (5th edn, Oxford University Press, 1998), 289–90, as referred to in Charlesworth, 'Concepts of Equality in International Law', 137.

[64] See, e.g., Convention on the Prevention and Punishment of the Crime of Genocide 1949, GA res. 260 A (III), 9 December 1948, 78 UNTS 277; entered into force 12 January 1951; ICERD; and the International Convention on the Suppression and Punishment of the Crime of Apartheid 1973, GA res. 3068 (XXVIII), 30 November 1973, 1015 UNTS 243; entered into force 18 July 1976.

[65] Article 2, 3, and 26, International Covenant on Civil and Political Rights 1966, GA res. 2200A (XXI), 16 December 1966, 999 UNTS 171; entered into force 23 March 1976.

(ICESCR).[66] Each treaty contains an overarching accessory prohibition on non-discrimination, in which the provisions of the treaty are to be applied to all individuals within the territory and subject to the jurisdiction of the state party 'without distinction of any kind', including on the basis of sex.[67] Each document includes an additional provision that spells out that states parties to each covenant 'undertake to ensure the equal right of men and women to the enjoyment of all [the] rights' contained therein.[68] Regardless of overlap, the Third Committee of the General Assembly at the time of drafting the ICESCR stated that the purpose of Article 3 in addition to Article 2(3) was for emphasis.[69] This same argument can be extended to the drafting model in the ICCPR, and it has been accepted by a number of commentators who recall the positive nature of Article 3 of the ICCPR.[70]

These non-discrimination guarantees are non-derogable and cannot be removed or weakened by states even during states of emergency.[71] Similar accessory non-discrimination provisions are found in most of the major human rights instruments, including the Convention on the Rights of the Child (CRC),[72] the International Convention on the

---

[66] Articles 2 and 3, International Covenant on Economic, Social and Cultural Rights 1966, GA res. 2200A (XXI), 16 December 1966, 993 UNTS 3; entered into force 3 January 1976.

[67] Article 2(1), ICCPR; Article 2(1), ICESCR.

[68] Article 3, ICCPR; Article 3, ICESCR.

[69] The Third Committee stated that 'the same rights should be expressly recognized for men and women on an equal footing and suitable measures should be taken to ensure that women ha[ve] the opportunity to exercise their rights ... Moreover, even if article 3 overlapped with article 2, paragraph 2, it was still necessary to reaffirm the equality rights between men and women. That fundamental principle, which was enshrined in the Charter of the United Nations, must be constantly emphasized, especially as there were still many prejudices preventing its full application.' Draft International Covenants on Human Rights Report of the Third Committee, UN Doc. A/53/65, 17 December 1962, para. 85, as restated in CESCR, General Comment No. 16: The Equal Right of Men and Women to the Enjoyment of All Economic, Social and Cultural Rights (Article 3) (2004), UN Doc. E/C.12/2005/3, para. 2.

[70] E.g., M. Nowak, U.N. Covenant on Civil and Political Rights: CCPR Commentary (2nd edn, Kehl: Engel, 2005), 77, who argues that Article 3 was inserted merely for emphasis, although with a 'positive goal in mind'. See, also, Lord Lester of Herne Hill QC and S. Joseph, 'Obligations of Non-Discrimination', in D. Harris and S. Joseph (ed.), The International Covenant on Civil and Political Rights and United Kingdom Law (Oxford: Clarendon Press, 1995) 565, who state that Article 2 relates to non-discrimination (a negative obligation), whereas Article 3 guarantees equality (a positive obligation).

[71] Article 4, ICCPR; Article 2(1), ICESCR, as interpreted by CESCR, General Comment No. 3: The Nature of States Parties Obligations (Article 2(1)) (1990), UN Doc. E/1991/23, para. 1.

[72] Convention on the Rights of the Child 1989, GA res. 44/25, 20 November 1989, 1577 UNTS 3; entered into force 2 September 1990 (CRC). Article 2(1), (CRC): 'States Parties

Protection of the Rights of All Migrant Workers and Members of their Families (IMWC),[73] and the Convention on the Rights of Persons with Disabilities (ICRPD).[74] However, there are no provisions outlawing sex discrimination or inequality between men and women in, inter alia, the UN Convention against Torture and Other Cruel, Inhuman or Degrading Treatment or Punishment (UNCAT)[75] or the International Convention on the Elimination of All Forms of Racial Discrimination (ICERD).[76]

The ICCPR also guarantees: equal rights to marriage, during marriage, and at its dissolution (Article 23); equality before courts and tribunals (Article 14(1)); and the right to vote for citizens and to be elected based on universal and equal suffrage, and equal access to public service (Article 25). Under the ICCPR, children are entitled to measures of protection

---

shall respect and ensure the rights set forth in the present Convention to each child within their jurisdiction without discrimination of any kind, irrespective of the child's or his or her parents' or legal guardian's race, colour, sex, language, religion, political or other opinion, national, ethnic or social origin, property, disability, birth or other status.' Article 2(2), CRC imposes positive obligations to protect against discrimination in particular circumstances: 'States Parties shall take all appropriate measures to ensure that the child is protected against all forms of discrimination or punishment on the basis of the status, activities, expressed opinions, or beliefs of the child's parents, legal guardians, or family members.'

[73] International Convention on the Protection of the Rights of All Migrant Workers and Members of Their Families 1990, GA res. 45/148, 18 December 1990, 2220 UNTS 93; entered into force 1 July 2003 (IMWC). Article 7, (IMWC): 'States Parties undertake, in accordance with the international instruments concerning human rights, to respect and to ensure to all migrant workers and members of their families within their territory or subject to their jurisdiction the rights provided for in the present Convention without distinction of any kind such as to sex, race, colour, language, religion or conviction, political or other opinion, national, ethnic or social origin, nationality, age, economic position, property, marital status, birth or other status.'

[74] Convention on the Rights of Persons with Disabilities 2006, GA res. 61/106, 13 December 2006; entered into force 3 May 2008. Article 4, (ICRPD). The ICRPD also contains a stand-alone non-discrimination provision: Article 5, ICRPD.

[75] Convention against Torture and Other Cruel, Inhumane or Degrading Treatment or Punishment 1984, GA res. 39/46, 10 December 1984, 1465 UNTS 85; entered into force 26 June 1987 (UNCAT).

[76] International Convention on the Elimination of All Forms of Racial Discrimination 1965, GA res. 2106 (XX), 21 December 1965, 660 UNTS 195; entered into force 4 January 1969 (ICERD). Clearly the ICERD is a non-discrimination instrument, but it is specifically focused on racial discrimination. The CERD has, though, recognised the intersectionality of race and sex: CERD, General Recommendation No. XXV: Gender-Related Dimensions of Racial Discrimination (2000), UN Doc. HRI/GEN/1/Rev.7. Other human rights instruments that omitted provisions outlawing discrimination on the basis of sex include, for example, the Convention relating to the Status of Refugees 1951, GA res. 429 (V), 14 December 1950, 189 UNTS 150; entered into force 22 April 1954 (Article 3).

in line with their status as a minor on the basis of non-discrimination, including sex (Article 24). The ICESCR guarantees equality in the context of fair wages, equal remuneration for work of equal value, and access to promotion without discrimination (Article 7). It further provides for primary education to be provided to all, secondary education to be generally available, and higher education to be equally accessible based on capacity (Article 13).

In addition to these rights, the ICCPR includes a stand-alone or autonomous right to equality in Article 26, which guarantees equality before the law and equal protection of the law.[77] Although there is no equivalent in the ICESCR, Article 26 of the ICCPR has been interpreted broadly so as to protect against unequal treatment in any area of law, including economic, social, and cultural rights (see below).

The first UN treaty devoted entirely to equality and non-discrimination was the ICERD. The ICERD builds on the UN Charter references to dignity and equality and translates them into the context of race discrimination,[78] which is defined as:

> any distinction, exclusion, restriction or preference based on race, colour, descent, or national or ethnic origin which has the purpose or effect of nullifying or impairing the recognition, enjoyment or exercise, on an equal footing, of human rights and fundamental freedoms in the political, economic, social, cultural or any other field of public life.[79]

The second treaty in which rights to equality and non-discrimination have been developed is in the specific context of sex. In 1979 the UN General Assembly adopted the CEDAW. In many respects, its provisions parallel those of the ICERD. In particular, the definition of sex discrimination in the CEDAW is very similar to that of race discrimination in the ICERD:

> any distinction, exclusion or restriction made on the basis of sex which has the effect or purpose of impairing or nullifying the recognition, enjoyment or exercise by women, irrespective of their marital status, on the basis of

---

[77] Article 26, ICCPR provides: 'All persons are equal before the law and are entitled without any discrimination to the equal protection of the law. In this respect, the law shall prohibit any discrimination and guarantee to all persons equal and effective protection against discrimination on any ground such as race, colour, sex, language, religion, political or other opinion, national or social origin, property, birth or other status.'

[78] Charlesworth, 'Concepts of Equality in International Law', 138.

[79] Article 1(1), ICERD.

equality of men and women, of human rights and fundamental freedoms in the political, economic, social, cultural, civil or any other field.[80]

Among the main discussions held during the drafting process to the CEDAW before the Commission on the Status of Women (CSW) was whether the treaty ought to be limited in its scope to sex discrimination against women specifically or on grounds of gender/sex more generally.[81] The final version was a synthesis of these two views, with both discrimination 'against women' and 'distinction, exclusion or restriction on the basis of sex' included,[82] although the treaty clearly covers sex discrimination only as it applies to women.

Coupled with Article 2 of the CEDAW, which condemns discrimination against women in all its forms and calls on governments to take all appropriate measures to eliminate such discrimination 'by any person, organization or enterprise', the CEDAW prohibits discrimination in the public and in the private sphere. Further, Articles 2(f) and 5(a) impose obligations upon states to address cultural and traditional practices that constitute discrimination against women and, in effect, they seek to redress structural causes of inequality.

The CEDAW also permits the introduction of temporary special measures (or time-limited measures of affirmative action), providing:

1. Adoption by States Parties of temporary special measures aimed at accelerating de facto equality between men and women shall not be considered discrimination as defined in the present Convention, but shall in no way entail as a consequence the maintenance of unequal or separate standards; these measures shall be discontinued when the objectives of equality of opportunity and treatment have been achieved.

2. Adoption by States Parties of special measures, including those measures contained in the present Convention, aimed at protecting maternity shall not be considered discriminatory.[83]

The third discrimination-based treaty at the UN level is the ICRPD. It borrows the definition employed in the two earlier treaties, with

---

[80] Article 1, CEDAW.

[81] See, L. A. Rehof, *Guide to the* Travaux Préparatoires *of the United Nations Convention on the Elimination of All Forms of Discrimination against Women* (Dordrecht: Martinus Nijhoff Publishers, 1993), 44. See, also, McKean, *Equality and Discrimination under International Law* on the background to the drafting of the CEDAW and other instruments on equality between women and men.

[82] Rehof, *Guide to the* Travaux Préparatoires *of the CEDAW*, 44.

[83] Article 4, CEDAW.

an important addition in relation to 'reasonable accommodation' of difference:

> any distinction, exclusion or restriction on the basis of disability which has the purpose or effect of impairing or nullifying the recognition, enjoyment or exercise, on an equal basis with others, of all human rights and fundamental freedoms in the political, economic, social, cultural, civil or any other field. It includes all forms of discrimination, including denial of reasonable accommodation;
>
> 'Reasonable accommodation' means necessary and appropriate modification and adjustments not imposing a disproportionate or undue burden, where needed in a particular case, to ensure to persons with disabilities the enjoyment or exercise on an equal basis with others of all human rights and fundamental freedoms.[84]

Unlike the ICERD, the ICRPD contains two further provisions that acknowledge the multiple forms of discrimination suffered by women with disabilities.[85] The ICRPD recognises that 'women and girls with disabilities are subject to multiple discrimination and in this regard [states parties] shall take measures to ensure the full and equal enjoyment by them of all human rights and fundamental freedoms'.[86] It further calls upon states parties '[t]o combat stereotypes, prejudices and harmful practices relating to persons with disabilities, including those based on sex and age, in all areas of life'.[87]

Some other forms of discrimination have been dealt with in non-binding international instruments.[88] Major regional instruments also contain either stand-alone or accessory prohibitions on sex discrimination as well as guarantees of equal protection before the law.[89] Meanwhile, in the African Union context, a special treaty on the rights of women, premised

---

[84] Article 2, ICRPD. See, also, Article 5, which provides further explanations for what constitutes equality and non-discrimination.

[85] See, Articles 3(a) and 6, ICRPD.   [86] Article 6(a), ICRPD.

[87] Article 8(b), ICRPD.

[88] See, e.g., UN Declaration on the Elimination of All Forms of Intolerance and of Discrimination Based on Religion or Belief 1981, GA res. 36/55, 25 November 1981, 21 ILM 205.

[89] See, e.g., Article 2, American Declaration of the Rights and Duties of Man 1948, OAS res. XXX, adopted by the Ninth International Conference of American States (1948), OEA/Ser.L.V/II.82 doc.6 rev.1 at 17 (1992); Article 14, European Convention on the Protection of Human Rights and Fundamental Freedoms 1950, 4 November 1950, 213 UNTS 222; entered into force 3 September 1953, as amended; Articles 1 and 24, American Convention on Human Rights 1969, 22 November 1969, OAS Treaty Series No. 36, 1144 UNTS 123; entered into force 18 July 1978 (ACHR); Articles 2, 3, 19, 22 (peoples' equality), 28 (duties), African Charter on Human and Peoples' Rights 1981, 27 June 1981, OAU Doc. CAB/LEG/67/3 rev. 5, 21 ILM 58; entered into force 21 October 1986 (ACHPR).

on equality principles, has been adopted.[90] Apart from the omission of equality guarantees in a few human rights instruments,[91] the principles of equality and non-discrimination are now well established in international and regional legal instruments. The problem with the international legal framework is not that rights to equality and non-discrimination on the basis of sex are missing. Rather, the issue is how these concepts have been interpreted and applied. Some of the difficulties arise from the explicit definitions outlined above that focus on distinctions, exclusions, and restrictions; that is, they focus on the negative face of discrimination rather than on the positive face of equality. How have these concepts been interpreted and applied in practice?

3   International human rights jurisprudence

3.1   Formal versus substantive equality and the use of comparators

Cases raising equality and non-discrimination date to the period between the First and Second World Wars. The Permanent Court of International Justice (PCIJ) considered a number of cases dealing with the treatment of minorities in Europe. In *Minority Schools in Albania*, the PCIJ noted:

> Equality in law precludes discrimination of any kind; whereas equality in fact may involve the necessity of different treatment in order to attain a result which establishes equilibrium between different situations.[92]

The PCIJ's successor, the International Court of Justice (ICJ), has also dealt with non-discrimination in a number of cases.[93] Of particular note is the dissenting opinion of Judge Tanaka in the *South West Africa Cases*. In rejecting South Africa's claim that differential treatment on the basis of race (apartheid) was consistent with international law, he held that '[t]he fundamental point in the equality principle is that all persons have

---

[90] Protocol to the ACHPR on the Human Rights of Women 2000, adopted by the 2nd Ordinary Session of the Assembly of the African Union, AU Doc. CAB/LEG/66.6, 13 September 2000; entered into force 25 November 2005 (PRWA).

[91] E.g. sex discrimination is not explicitly prohibited in the UNCAT.

[92] *Minority Schools in Albania, Greece v. Albania* (Advisory Opinion), PCIJ, Ser. A/B, No. 64 (6 April 1935).

[93] See, e.g., *Rights of Nationals of the USA in Morocco (France v. USA)*, ICJ, 1952 ICJ Rep. 176 (27 August 1952) (in this case, France was exempted from import controls in Morocco whereas the USA was subjected to them. The ICJ held unanimously that this was discrimination in favour of France and that the USA could claim for its unfavourable treatment).

an equal value in themselves'.[94] In endorsing the Aristotelian view that treating different matters equally would be as unjust as treating equal matters differently, Judge Tanaka nonetheless offered some parameters on how to determine acceptable differentiation. He referred specifically to justice and reasonableness. He also rejected the idea that motive or purpose was relevant to determining whether a distinction is arbitrary or unlawful.[95]

In 1981 the Human Rights Committee (HRC), in its General Comment on Article 3, stated that the provision applies to equality both in law and in fact.[96] In 1989 the HRC adopted a subsequent General Comment on equality and non-discrimination in relation to Article 26. This General Comment provides that '[n]on-discrimination, together with equality before the law and equal protection of the law without any discrimination, constitutes a basic and general principle relating to the protection of human rights'.[97] Referring to the definitions of discrimination contained in the ICERD and the CEDAW, the HRC stated:

> the Committee believes the term 'discrimination' as used in the Covenant should be understood to imply any distinction, exclusion, restriction or preference which is based on any ground such as race, colour, sex, language, religion, political or other opinion, national or social origin, property, birth or other status, and which has the purpose or effect of nullifying or impairing the recognition, enjoyment or exercise by all persons, on an equal footing, of all rights and freedoms.[98]

This definition of discrimination is 'relatively broad' in two main respects: it does not require proof of discriminatory intent, and it encompasses both direct and indirect discrimination.[99] In addition, the HRC noted that treatment on an 'equal footing' does not mean identical treatment in every instance. However, it observed that any exceptions are explicitly referred to in the ICCPR itself.[100] In spite of its suggestion that

---

[94] *South West Africa Cases (Liberia v. South Africa; Ethiopia v. South Africa)* 1962 ICJ Rep. 319; 1966 ICJ Rep. 4, 288 and 303 (per Justice Tanaka (in dissent)).

[95] *Ibid.*, 304 (per Justice Tanaka (in dissent)).

[96] HRC, General Comment No. 4: Equality Between the Sexes (Article 3) (1981), UN Doc. HRI/GEN/1/Rev.1, para. 2.

[97] HRC, General Comment No. 18: Non-Discrimination (1989), UN Doc. HRC/GEN/1/Rev.5, para. 1. See, also, CERD, General Recommendation XIV: Definition of Discrimination (Article 1(1)) (1993), UN Doc. A/48/18, para. 1.

[98] HRC, General Comment No. 18: Non-Discrimination (1989), para. 7.

[99] Charlesworth, 'Concepts of Equality in International Law', 140.

[100] HRC, General Comment No. 18 (1989): Non-Discrimination, para. 8. The HRC gives the examples of Articles 6(5) (exception to the death penalty for pregnant women or

any exceptions to identical treatment are self-contained in the ICCPR, the HRC has added that 'not every differentiation of treatment will constitute discrimination, if the criteria for such differentiation are reasonable and objective and if the aim is to achieve a purpose which is legitimate under the Covenant'.[101] The HRC further accepts that affirmative action may be required to satisfy equality guarantees and that the former does not contravene the latter.[102]

Like the HRC, the Committee on Economic, Social and Cultural Rights (CESCR) and the Committee on the Elimination of Racial Discrimination (CERD) have each accepted that equality includes both formal and substantive equality.[103] According to the CESCR, formal equality is achieved if a law or policy treats men and women in a 'neutral manner' (that is, regardless of their sex), whereas substantive equality requires the effect of those laws, policies, and practices to alleviate any 'inherent disadvantage' of either sex.[104] Here we see echoes of the work of Mahoney, Young, and MacKinnon. In regard to the latter, the CESCR has acknowledged that temporary special measures may be needed to bring disadvantaged groups 'to the same substantive level as others'.[105] Its 2009 General Comment explains that, in exceptional circumstances, such measures may be of a permanent nature, referring to 'interpretation services for linguistic minorities and reasonable accommodation of persons with sensory impairments in accessing health care facilities'.[106] Deferring to the definition of discrimination in the ICERD and the CEDAW, the CESCR has stated that direct discrimination occurs when differential treatment is based exclusively on sex and characteristics of women that cannot be objectively justified.[107] Indirect discrimination, in contrast, occurs when a law, policy, or practice does not appear on the face of it

---

individuals under eighteen years of age), 10(3) (segregation of minors from adults in prisons), and 25 (guarantee of political rights, exception of non-citizens).

[101] *Ibid.*, para. 13.   [102] *Ibid.*, para. 10.

[103] CESCR, General Comment No. 16: The Equal Right of Men and Women to the Enjoyment of All Economic, Social and Cultural Rights, paras. 6–15; CERD, General Recommendation XIV: Definition of Discrimination.

[104] CESCR, General Comment No. 16: The Equal Right of Men and Women to the Enjoyment of All Economic, Social and Cultural Rights, paras. 7 and 8.

[105] *Ibid.*, para. 15.

[106] CESCR, General Comment No. 20: Non-Discrimination in Economic, Social and Cultural Rights (Article 2, para. 2) (2009), UN Doc. E/C.12/GC/20, para. 9.

[107] CESCR, General Comment No. 16: The Equal Right of Men and Women to the Enjoyment of All Economic, Social and Cultural Rights, para. 12. See, also, CESCR, General Comment No. 20: Non-Discrimination in Economic, Social and Cultural Rights, para. 7.

to be discriminatory but is discriminatory in its effect.[108] Discriminatory purpose or intent is considered irrelevant.

Generally, the HRC has held that laws that discriminate on the face of them between men and women breach Article 26. It has done so in the fields of, inter alia, immigration regulations, unemployment benefits, widow pensions, and access to courts in relation to matrimonial property.[109] However, the HRC has rejected other cases of ostensibly discriminatory law. In *Vos* v. *The Netherlands*, for example, the HRC accepted ostensibly discriminatory legislation on the basis that there was no discriminatory intent,[110] contrary to the general position of international law since Judge Tanaka's judgment in the *South West Africa Cases*. In fact, the intent of the legislation was to streamline pensions and to afford subsistence-level income to all persons who qualified. The law allowed Dutch men with a disability to retain the right to a disability allowance when their wives died; but on the death of their husbands, disabled women were eligible only for a widow's pension, which in Ms Vos's case was less than the disability pension. Charlesworth has criticised this decision for being based on 'outmoded historical assumptions about the working habits of women and [for] privileg[ing] administrative convenience over the guarantees in Article 26'.[111] In fact, the *Vos* judgment conflicts with other,

---

[108] CESCR, General Comment No. 16: The Equal Right of Men and Women to the Enjoyment of All Economic, Social and Cultural Rights, para. 13.

[109] See, e.g., *Aumeeruddy-Cziffra* v. *Mauritius*, HRC 35/1978 (9 April 1981) (Mauritian legislation that required foreign husbands of Mauritian nationals to apply for residence permits, but did not make the same requirement of foreign wives of Mauritian nationals, was found to violate a number of ICCPR provisions, including Article 26); *Avellanal* v. *Peru*, HRC 172/1984 (28 October 1988) (a Peruvian law that prevented married women from taking legal action with respect to matrimonial property was held to breach Article 26); *Broeks* v. *The Netherlands*, HRC 172/1984 (9 April 1987) (Mrs Broeks was successful in her challenge of unemployment legislation that excluded her from continued unemployment benefits because she was married at the time in question, which would not have been the case if she were a man, married or unmarried); *Pauger* v. *Austria*, HRC 716/1996 (9 July 1997) (a widower successfully invoked Article 26 to challenge Austrian law that distinguished between widowers, who were entitled to two-thirds of the full pension entitlement compared with widows, who were entitled to the full pension); *Zwaan de Vries* v. *The Netherlands*, HRC 182/1984 (9 April 1987) (the municipality rejected the application for continued support under unemployment benefits legislation as she was not married, although the legislation applied to married men. The HRC found discrimination on grounds of sex and marital status).

[110] *Vos* v. *The Netherlands*, HRC 786/1997 (29 March 1989).

[111] Charlesworth, 'Concepts of Equality in International Law', 141. Note that the dissenting opinion submitted by Urbina and Wennergren rejected the analysis of the majority, claiming that some degree of flexibility was required in the application of the two conflicting pension schemes so that an individual was not discriminated against on

earlier decisions of the HRC that disregarded questions of intent, as well as with its 1989 General Comment outlined above. Dissenting opinions in other decisions have made allowances for socio-economic developments to permit a margin of discretion to states in relation to discriminatory legislation.[112] This leniency contrasts with the view of the CESCR that, while economic and social rights are to be 'progressively realised', equality guarantees are of immediate effect.[113]

The CERD has similarly endorsed the view that '[a] distinction is contrary to the [ICERD] if it has either the purpose or effect of impairing particular rights and freedoms'.[114] The CERD derives its view from the language of Article 2(1)(c), which imposes an obligation on states parties to nullify any law or practice that has the effect of creating or perpetuating racial discrimination.[115] The CERD also indicates that any differentiation of treatment is to be judged against 'the objectives and purposes of the Convention'[116] and that '[i]n seeking to determine whether an action has an effect contrary to the Convention, it will look to see whether that action has an *unjustifiable disparate impact* upon a group distinguished by race, colour, descent, or national or ethnic origin' [my emphasis].[117]

grounds of sex or marital status. Other problematic cases include *Ballantyne, Davidson and McIntyre* v. *Canada*, HRC 359/1989 and 385/1989 (31 March 1993) (a law that prohibited Canadian citizens from displaying commercial signs outside a business premises in English was held not to breach Article 26 on the grounds that 'the prohibition [of using English] applies to French speakers as well as English speakers'. The HRC did accept other breaches, such as that of Article 19).

[112] *Sprenger* v. *The Netherlands*, HRC 395/1990 (22 March 1991), per Messrs Ando, Herndl, and N'diaye, who argued that it was necessary to take into account 'the reality that the socio-economic and cultural needs of society are constantly evolving ...' in suggesting that discrimination in socio-economic rights may lag behind developments in other fields. See, also, *Oulajin and Kaiss* v. *The Netherlands*, HRC 406 and 426/1990 (23 October 1992), per Messrs Herndl, Müllerson, N'diaye, and Sadi.

[113] CESCR, General Comment No. 16: The Equal Right of Men and Women to the Enjoyment of All Economic, Social and Cultural Rights, para. 16. The only allowable exception for the non-discriminatory application of economic rights by states parties to the ICESCR is for non-citizens located in developing countries: Article 4(3), ICESCR.

[114] W. Vandenhole, *Non-Discrmination and Equality in the View of the UN Human Rights Treaty Bodies* (Antwerp: Intersentia, 2005), 37.

[115] Article 2(1)(c) provides: 'States Parties condemn racial discrimination and undertake to pursue by all appropriate means and without delay a policy of eliminating racial discrimination in all its forms and promoting understanding among all races, and, to this end: (c) Each State Party shall take effective measures to review governmental, national and local policies, and to amend, rescind or nullify any laws and regulations which have the effect of creating or perpetuating racial discrimination wherever it exists.'

[116] CERD, General Recommendation XIV: Definition of Discrimination, para. 2.

[117] *Ibid.*

The position taken by CERD appears to be broader than that adopted by the HRC and the CESCR in two main respects. First, it requires any justifications for differential treatment to be in line with the principles and purposes of the Convention, compared with the position taken by the HRC and the CESCR, which accept 'reasonable and objective justifications' uncoupled from the treaty scope. Second, the CERD suggests that the assessment standard should be 'unjustified disparate impact upon a group'. It thus considers racial discrimination within the context of collective disadvantage rather than as an individual aberration.

In the specific context of discrimination against non-citizens, in which some minor distinctions are permitted within the text of various treaties (such as the right to political participation or to hold public office), the CERD has stated that 'differential treatment based on citizenship or immigration status will constitute discrimination if the criteria for such differentiation, judged in the light of the objectives and purposes of the Convention, are not applied pursuant to a legitimate aim, and are not proportional to the achievement of this aim'.[118]

Like the HRC and the CESCR, the Women's Committee has endorsed a broad reading of discrimination. It has held that 'discrimination against women is a multifaceted phenomenon that entails indirect and unintentional as well as direct and intentional discrimination'.[119] The Women's Committee has argued against maintaining a sole focus on formal or *de jure* equality, because doing so 'tends to impede a proper understanding of the complex issue of discrimination, such as structural and indirect discrimination'.[120] Both qualitative and quantitative equality are considered to be at the heart of the CEDAW.[121] Despite these general statements, its case law has been mixed. In *Nguyen v. The Netherlands* the Women's Committee rejected a case based on *direct* discrimination in relation to financial compensation for maternity leave that differed between salaried and self-employed women, owing to a restriction of a so-called anti-accumulation clause.[122] The complainant was a part-time salaried employee as well as a co-working spouse in her husband's business. Only

---

[118] CERD, General Recommendation No. 30: Discrimination against Non-Citizens (2004), UN Doc. HRI/GEN/Rev.7/Add.1, para. 4.

[119] CEDAW, Concluding observations on Ukraine, UN Doc. A/57/38 (Part II), para. 279 (2002); Kyrgyzstan, UN Doc. A/54/38/Rev.1 (Part I), para. 113 (1999).

[120] CEDAW, Concluding observations on Bulgaria, UN Doc. A/53/38/Rev.1 (Part I), para. 232 (1998).

[121] CEDAW, General Recommendation No. 25: Temporary Special Measures (Article 4(1)) (2004), UN Doc. HRI/GEN/1/Rev.7, para. 9.

[122] *Nguyen v. The Netherlands*, CEDAW 3/2004 (14 August 2006).

the joint dissenting opinion stated that the so-called anti-accumulation clause may constitute a form of *indirect* discrimination:

> This view is based on the assumption that an employment situation, in which salaried part-time and self-employment is combined, as described by the complainant, is one which mainly women experience in the Netherlands, since, in general, it is mainly women who work part-time as salaried workers in addition to working as family helpers in their husbands' enterprises.[123]

Unlike the HRC and the CESCR (and most other international bodies),[124] however, the Women's Committee is to be praised for not accepting what is considered the 'widely used pragmatic' definition of discrimination, that is, differential treatment in a comparable situation without a reasonable and objective justification.[125] The Women's Committee has indicated that 'any objective and reasonable justification' be used only as a basis for the implementation of temporary special measures,[126] not otherwise.

The general approach at the level of international human rights law has been to treat or attempt to treat men and women identically by adopting a sameness/difference methodology. Although there is an emphasis in the definitions employed to ensure women have equal enjoyment of their rights and freedoms, the end goal still appears to be identical treatment unless any differences in treatment can be justified according to 'reasonable and objective' criteria. These approaches bear out the need for a comparison to be made with the dominant or benefiting group, with the second step analysing only whether the distinction in treatment could be justified based on the above criteria. Little has thus changed since the *Belgian Linguistics* case before the European Court of Human Rights (ECtHR) in 1968.[127] Although formal and substantive equality are

---

[123] *Ibid.*

[124] *Ibid.*, per Gabr, Schöpp-Schilling and Shin, para. 10.5.

[125] Vandenhole, *Non-Discrmination and Equality*, 71.

[126] CEDAW, Concluding observations on Peru, UN Doc. A/53/38/Rev.1 (Part II) (1998), paras. 319–320.

[127] *Belgian Linguistics Cases*, ECtHR, Applic. Nos. 1474/62; 1677/62; 1691/62; 1769/63; 1994/63; 2126/64 (23 July 1968). This case involved allegations that Belgian law violated the rights of over 800 French-speaking children, in particular their rights under Article 8 (family life) in conjunction with Article 14 (non-discrimination) and Article 2 of Protocol 1 (the right to education) ECHR. The legislation in question basically stated that the language of education shall be Dutch in the Dutch-speaking region, French in the French-speaking region and German in the German-speaking region. The applicants asserted, inter alia, that the law of the Dutch speaking regions where they lived did not include adequate provisions for French-language education. They also complained that the Belgian state withheld grants from institutions in these regions that did not comply with

now accepted goals, they continue to be pursued via the ideology of identical treatment between men and women or, at least, to treat women in a similar manner to men, rather than on the ending of oppression, domination, or second-class citizenship of women. In other words, a comparator is still the first stage in the process and, as explained earlier, this can be particularly problematic.

Some of the difficulties associated with the comparator approach is exemplified in the jurisprudence of the European Court of Justice (ECJ). In the case of *Grant* v. *Southwest Trains* the ECJ held there was no illegal discrimination on the grounds of sex because a company decision to deny family benefits to a woman employee's female partner would have been equally denied to a male homosexual employee's male partner.[128] The selection of comparator here is crucial to the final outcome of the case. As the International Centre for the Legal Protection of Human Rights has stated, 'Comparing the employee against a heterosexual employee of either sex would have led to a different result.'[129] There are many other cases decided at national and regional levels that have adopted a similarly flawed strategy.[130] As noted above, there may in fact be no equivalent comparator, such as in the case of pregnancy, and this undermines the ability of the comparator approach to work in many settings of inequality.[131]

I find this general approach of the treaty bodies and other international and regional human rights courts problematic on three grounds,

---

the linguistic provisions set out in the legislation for schools and refused to homologate certificates issued by these institutions. Further, the state did not allow the applicant's children to attend French classes in certain places, forcing applicants to enroll their children in local schools, contrary to their aspirations, or send them further afield, which entailed risks and hardships. The Court found by a majority of 8 to 7 that only one of the Acts violated Article 14, but also found unanimously that there had been no breach of Articles 8 and 14 of the Convention, and Article 2 of of the Protocol. The Court opined that the right to education implied the right to be educated in the national language, and did not include the provision that the parent's linguistic preferences be respected.

[128] *Grant* v. *Southwest Trains*, ECJ, Case C-249/96, [1998] ECR 1–621.

[129] INTERIGHTS, *Non-Discrimination in International Law: A Handbook for Practitioners* (Interights, January 2005, edited by K. Kitching), 117.

[130] For further case law, see McColgan, 'Cracking the Comparator Problem'.

[131] See, e.g., *Webb* v. *EMO Cargo (UK) Ltd*, ECJ, Case C-32/93, [1994] ECH 1–3567, in which a woman hired to cover another woman employee during her maternity leave fell pregnant herself shortly after the conclusion of the employment contract. The ECJ held that dismissal of a woman for being pregnant constitutes direct discrimination and furthermore, that a woman in the situation of pregnancy who is incapable of fulfilling the role for which she was hired cannot be compared to a man similarly incapable because of medical or other reasons, since pregnancy is not in any way comparable to a pathological condition, and even less so with incapability to work for non-medical reasons.

summarised here but repeated throughout this chapter. First, the approach continues to advance a 'male' standard of achievement (for women to be the treated the same as men), whether they are dealing with formal or substantive equality. This has the effect of relegating women to a position of inferiority indefinitely. This in turn reinforces the need to identify a comparator, which is problematic in various situations including where making a comparison makes no sense, or where no real comparator is available. Second, it disregards the gendered application of criteria such as 'reasonableness and objectivity' and assumes that these are gender-neutral terms. This is dealt with further below. Finally, it confines ideas of equality to distinctions and differences rather than, for example, to ideas of the liberation of women from patriarchy, the right to be treated as human beings with dignity instead of as subhuman, or questions of fairness. There are glimpses of a broader approach being applied by some of the treaty bodies, such as in the use of language of 'inherent disadvantage' by the CESCR, although the use of 'inherent' too is not without potential faults, suggesting a 'natural' problem rather than a socially constructed one.

3.2   Discrimination versus inequality

What, then, is discrimination? And how does it relate to equality? The principles of non-discrimination and equality are often used interchangeably, but they are also accorded subtly different meanings. According to the Inter-American Court of Human Rights (I-ACtHR), 'the concepts of equality and non-discrimination are reciprocal, like the two faces of one same institution. Equality is the positive face of non-discrimination. Discrimination is the negative face of equality.'[132] The CESCR has stated that they are 'integrally related and mutually reinforcing'.[133] Similarly, the Women's Committee has noted that the elimination of discrimination and the promotion of equality are 'two different but equally important

---

[132] *Proposed Amendments to the Naturalization Provisions of the Constitution of Costa Rica* (Advisory Opinion), I-ACtHR, Ser. A, No. 4 (19 January 1984), Separate Opinion of Judge Rodolfo E. Piza, para. 10. See, also, *Minority Schools in Albania* (Advisory Opinion), PCIJ, Ser. A/B, No. 64 (6 April 1935) ('Equality in law precludes discrimination of any kind.'); Protocol No. 12 to the ECHR, Explanatory Report, E.T.S. No. 177, para. 15; A. F. Bayefsky, 'The Principle of Equality or Non-Discrimination in International Law' (1990) 11 *Hum. Rts. L. J.* 1, at 1; B. G. Ramcharan, 'Equality and Nondiscrimination', in L. Henkin (ed.), *The International Bill of Rights: The Covenant on Civil and Political Rights* (New York: Columbia University Press, 1981) 246, at 252.

[133] CESCR, General Comment No. 16, The Equal Right of Men and Women to the Enjoyment of All Economic, Social and Cultural Rights, para. 3.

goals in the quest for women's empowerment'.[134] A 2005 study was inconclusive on whether there is any real difference between the two terms as they are applied under international law.[135] It is generally accepted that, at a minimum, non-discrimination is a negative right as it prohibits the making of distinctions between individuals or giving preferences on the basis of irrelevant criteria or without reasonable and objective justification. Equality, by comparison, ought to be viewed as the goal, centred around social justice, freedom, and dignity. Equality may also require additional and positive measures (formal and substantive) to reach that goal, rather than 'mere' non-discrimination.

I would argue that, within the equality/non-discrimination discourse, non-discrimination should be conceived as a subset of equality. That is, it can be a tool to guide us on the path to equality in particular situations where women seek identical treatment to men. Nonetheless, it is not as far-reaching as equality (in fact, it can be rather narrow as illustrated above) and cannot achieve equality on its own. Sole reliance on non-discrimination principles is unlikely to bring about transformative, liberating, or empowering outcomes for women, as it deals largely with apparent distinctions rather than more complex issues of oppression, disadvantage, or patriarchy. Its use by men to challenge laws that exclude them reveals that it can operate quite separately from issues of oppression, disadvantage, or patriarchy.

For those scholars who argue that equality should be recast as oppression/domination, advantage/disadvantage, or the end of hierarchy, non-discrimination tends to hold back progress as far as it is fixed to the sameness/difference ideology. That is, non-discrimination is based on the idea that there are justified and unjustified distinctions and that 'men' are the standard against which progress is to be determined. I agree with those who assert that the focus of international law on discrimination has been to the detriment of higher goals of equality.[136] Although a sameness/difference ideology worked, for example, in the context of racial discrimination and the ending of apartheid in South Africa, it has struggled to be useful beyond legal equality. The same ideology has not kept pace with the problems of social inequality that continue to exist long after unequal laws have been regulated, nor does it adequately respond to the specific

---

[134] CEDAW, Concluding observations on Belgium, UN Doc. A/57/38 (Part II) (2002), para. 146.

[135] Vandenhole, *Non-Discrimination and Equality*, 34.

[136] See, e.g., Charlesworth, 'Concepts of Equality in International Law'.

needs of women, some of which are based on sexual differences, such as in the area of reproductive rights. Rather than comparing women against the male standard, which reinforces women's inferior position in society, equality law should instead be asking how to deconstruct domination, disadvantage, or hierarchy.

3.3   Public and private discrimination

In 2000 the HRC issued a second General Comment related to equality of rights between women and men.[137] Building on its earlier statements, the HRC asserted that 'Articles 2 and 3 [of the ICCPR] mandate States parties to take all steps necessary, including the prohibition of discrimination on the ground of sex, to put an end to discriminatory actions both in the public and the private sector[s] which impair the equal enjoyment of rights.'[138] According to the HRC, therefore, both public and private forms of inequality are accepted as falling within the scope of the ICCPR. In clarifying its general position on public and private violations of human rights, the HRC stated:

> the positive obligations on States Parties to ensure Covenant rights will only be fully discharged if individuals are protected by the State, not just against violations of Covenant rights by its agents, but also against acts committed by private persons or entities that would impair the enjoyment of Covenant rights in so far as they are amenable to application between private persons or entities. There may be circumstances in which a failure to ensure Covenant rights as required by article 2 would give rise to violations by States Parties of those rights, as a result of States Parties' permitting or failing to take appropriate measures or to exercise due diligence to prevent, punish, investigate or redress the harm caused by such acts by private persons or entities.[139]

Unlike the ICCPR, the CEDAW has the advantage of an express provision that covers discrimination in both public and private spheres of life.[140] As a core provision,[141] the Women's Committee has asserted that any reservation to it is contrary to the object and purpose of the treaty and, therefore,

---

[137] HRC, General Comment No. 28: Equality of Rights Between Men and Women (Article 3) (2000), UN Doc. CCPR/C/21/Rev.1/Add.10.

[138] *Ibid.*, para. 4.

[139] HRC, General Comment No. 31: The Nature of the General Legal Obligation Imposed on States Parties to the Covenant (Article 2) (2004), UN Doc. CCPR/C/21/Rev.1/Add.13, para. 8.

[140] Article 2(e), CEDAW.

[141] CEDAW, General Recommendation No. 19: Violence against Women (1992), UN Doc. HRI/GEN/1/Rev.7, para. 10.

incompatible with international law.[142] Under what has become known as the concept or test of 'due diligence', the Women's Committee holds states parties responsible for 'private acts' if they fail 'to act with due diligence to prevent violations of rights, or to investigate and punish acts of violence, and to provide compensation'.[143] This paradigm has become the accepted test for incorporating the acts of non-state actors in international law and in regional human rights courts,[144] yet it remains vague in many respects, including the failure so far of the courts and supervisory bodies to articulate the extent of a state's positive obligations in this and other contexts, as discussed later in this book.

In *Goekce v. Austria*, the Women's Committee held Austria liable for the failure on the part of the Austrian police to respond to an emergency call, which led to the death by shooting of the complainant at the hands of her husband.[145] It stated:

> The Committee considers that given this combination of factors [which included increasing frequency of violent incidents by the husband over a three-year period], the police knew or should have known that Şahide Goekce was in serious danger; they should have treated the last call from her as an emergency, in particular because [her husband] had shown that he had the potential to be a very dangerous and violent criminal. The Committee considers that in light of the long record of earlier disturbances and battering, by not responding to the call immediately, the police are accountable for failing to exercise due diligence to protect Şahide Goekce.[146]

The Women's Committee has also held that a perpetrator's right to liberty cannot supersede a woman's human rights to life and to physical and mental integrity.[147] Yet despite its explicit mandate over 'private' actors in

---

[142] CEDAW, Concluding observations on Morocco, UN Doc. A/52/38/Rev.1, para. 59. Cf. CEDAW, General Recommendation No. 4: Reservations (1987) (no UN Doc.), does not identify specific articles.

[143] CEDAW, General Recommendation No. 19: Violence against Women, para. 9.

[144] The due diligence standard first emerged in the Inter-American Court of Human Rights in *Velásquez Rodriguez v. Honduras*, I-ACtHR, Ser. C, No. 4 (29 July 1988), in which the state was held liable for failing to take reasonable steps to prevent, prosecute, punish, and provide remedies to the victim. It has also been accepted by the European Court of Human Rights (e.g. *M. C. v. Bulgaria* (2003) 40 EHRR 20). See, further, Chapter 5.

[145] *Goekce v. Austria*, CEDAW 5/2005 (6 August 2007).

[146] *Ibid.*, para. 12.1.4. See, also, *Yildirim v. Austria*, CEDAW 6/2005 (6 August 2007) (the case concerned a Turkish woman subjected to physical abuse who was eventually stabbed to death by her husband. The Women's Committee considered that the failure to detain the husband breached the state party's due diligence obligation to protect the complainant).

[147] See, *A. T. v. Hungary*, CEDAW 2/2003 (26 January 2005); *Goekce v. Austria*, CEDAW 5/2005 (6 August 2007); *Yildirim v. Austria*, CEDAW 6/2005 (6 August 2007).

Article 2(e), the Women's Committee has extended its mandate no further than the other treaty bodies. International human rights law has not yet recognised, for example, the right of individuals to bring actions directly against their perpetrators, whether government officials or private individuals, before an international court.[148] That is, international human rights law does not have direct horizontal effect.[149] This is arguably one of the real barriers to dismantling the public/private dichotomy. Although private acts can now be brought within the purview of international human rights law, a close linkage with the state is still required. Moreover, international human rights law has not kept pace with developments in international criminal law, which involves direct prosecution of some perpetrators of violence. It raises fundamental questions about how we characterise violence against women in peacetime and in armed conflict.[150] Chapter 5, on torture, further discusses the problems this poses for women's claims.

3.4   Culture, custom, and structural inequality

Several of the treaty bodies have examined structural causes of discrimination. The Women's Committee, for example, has made statements that discrimination is rooted in 'traditional attitudes by which women are regarded as subordinate to men or as having stereotyped roles'.[151] The CEDAW contains a number of provisions that impose obligations upon states parties to address cultural and traditional practices that constitute discrimination against women. Article 2(f), for example, calls on states parties '[t]o take all appropriate measures, including legislation, to modify or abolish existing laws, regulations, customs and practices

---

[148] One could argue that the international criminal tribunals and the International Criminal Court serve this purpose, but they are generally confined to criminal prosecution in the context of crimes committed during war or on a widespread or systematic scale, and limited to crimes in the 1949 Geneva Conventions.

[149] The HRC stated that 'article 2, paragraph 1, obligations are binding on States [Parties] and do not, as such, have direct horizontal effect as a matter of international law'. HRC, General Comment No. 31: The Nature of the General Legal Obligation Imposed on States Parties to the Covenant, para. 8. Although not permitted by the individual communications system, there have been proposals for an international human rights court that would permit horizontal complaints as discussed in Chapter 8: see, M. Nowak, 'The Need for a World Court of Human Rights' (2007) 7 *Hum. Rts. L. Rev.* 251.

[150] See, further, A. Edwards, 'Everyday Rape: International Human Rights Law and Violence against Women in Peacetime', in C. McGlynn and V. Munro (eds.), *Rethinking Rape Law: International and Comparative Perspectives* (London: Routledge-Cavendish, 2010) 92.

[151] CEDAW, General Recommendation No. 19: Violence against Women, para. 10.

which constitute discrimination against women'.[152] Article 5(a) further provides:

> States Parties shall take all appropriate measures: (a) To modify the social and cultural patterns of conduct of men and women, with a view to achieving the elimination of prejudices and customary and all other practices which are based on the idea of the inferiority or the superiority of either of the sexes or on stereotyped roles for men and women.

The inclusion of civil, cultural, economic, political, and social rights in a single treaty places the Women's Committee in a better position than the HRC to tackle, in a holistic manner, structural aspects of violence against women, such as poverty and socio-economic disadvantage. Both the International Covenants have, however, referred to tradition, history, religion, and culture as being at the basis of inequality.[153] In *Lovelace* v. *Canada*, for instance, the HRC impliedly stated that the protection of culture cannot discriminate against women on the basis of their sex. In this case, Canadian law had removed the applicant's Native Indian status because she had married a non-Native Indian man. Under the relevant legislation, a man would not have lost his status by marrying a non-Native Indian woman. The HRC held that there was no reasonable justification for the domestic legislation applying to the complainant's particular situation, as she had divorced her non-Native Indian husband.[154] The HRC held that the ongoing denial of her Indian status and her rights to return to the reserve following her divorce violated her right as a person belonging to a minority read in the context of her right to equality and non-discrimination on the basis of sex. As mentioned in Chapter 2, issues of culture and religion have not been without controversy, including within feminism.

Lovelace v. *Canada*, for instance, could easily have been differently decided – as one of the arguments for the legislation in the first place was

---

[152] Article 2(f), CEDAW. Article 10(c) also provides: 'States Parties shall take all appropriate measures to eliminate discrimination against women in order to ensure to them equal rights with men in the field of education and in particular to ensure, on a basis of equality of men and women: ... (c) The elimination of any stereotyped concept of the roles of men and women at all levels and in all forms of education by encouraging coeducation and other types of education which will help to achieve this aim and, in particular, by the revision of textbooks and school programmes and the adaptation of teaching methods.'

[153] HRC, General Comment No. 28: Equality of Rights Between Men and Women, para. 5; CESCR, Concluding observations on Zambia, UN Doc. E/C.12/1/Add.106 (2005), para. 14; Chile, UN Doc. E/C.12/1/Add.105 (2004), para. 15; Malta, UN Doc. E/C.12/1/Add.101 (2004), para. 11; Benin, UN Doc. E/C.12/1/Add.78 (2002), para. 8.

[154] *Lovelace* v. *Canada*, HRC 24/1977 (30 July 1981).

the preservation of culture protected by Article 27 of the ICCPR. In fact, the Canadian Supreme Court had rejected Lovelace's claim, stating that her exclusion from the community was reasonable in light of the aim of the legislation and it did not, therefore, amount to discrimination.[155] This reveals the difficulty of applying the sameness/difference model that permits *reasonable* excuses for differential treatment; and confirms that it is not every distinction that is unlawful. Rather the emphasis is on what could be described as 'arbitrary' discrimination, or discrimination that cannot be justified. In many respects, it is the patriarchal context in which decisions on discrimination are made that determines what falls within or outside the discrimination framework.

The Women's Committee has also had difficulties identifying structural causes of inequality. In the case of *Muñoz-Vargas y Sainz de Vicuña* v. *Spain*, in which the complainant argued that as the first-born daughter of Enrique Muñoz-Vargas y Herreros de Tejada, who held the nobility title of 'Count of Bulnes', she should succeed to that title.[156] Instead, Spanish law maintained that first-born daughters would succeed only if they had no younger brothers. Upon the death of her father, the complainant's younger brother succeeded to the title. She alleged that male primacy in the order of succession to titles of nobility constituted a violation of the CEDAW. The application was declared inadmissible on two grounds, one of which is of relevance here.[157] Eight members of the Women's Committee adopted a concurring opinion in which they stated:

> It is undisputed in the present case that the title of nobility in question is of a purely symbolic and honorific nature, devoid of any legal or material effect. Consequently, we consider that claims of succession to such titles of nobility are not compatible with the provisions of the Convention [and are therefore inadmissible], which are aimed at protecting women from discrimination which has the effect or purpose of impairing or nullifying the recognition, enjoyment or exercise of women on a basis of equality of men and women, of human rights and fundamental freedoms in all fields.[158]

---

[155] *Attorney-General of Canada* v. *Lavell, Isaac* v. *Bedard*, SCC, SCR 1349 (1973).

[156] *Muñoz-Vargas y Sainz de Vicuña* v. *Spain*, CEDAW 7/2005 (9 August 2007).

[157] The other ground of inadmissibility was that it involved an issue that had been resolved prior to the entry into force of the CEDAW on the state party, which was also disputed by the single dissenting judge (Dairiam).

[158] *Muñoz-Vargas y Sainz de Vicuña* v. *Spain*, CEDAW 7/2005 (9 August 2007), para. 12.2 per Dominquez, Flinterman, Patten, Pimentel, Saiga, Simms, Tan, and Zou.

The same view was expressed by the HRC in two similar cases which were dismissed.[159] While recognising that titles of nobility are generally incompatible with ideals of equality, human rights, or democratic governance, the case was still one that implicated issues of equality on the basis of gender. In dissent, Shanthi Dairiam invoked Article 5(a) of the CEDAW and reoriented the issue in the communication around 'the negative effects of conduct [or laws] based on culture, custom, tradition and the ascription of stereotypical roles that entrench the inferiority of women'.[160] She noted:

> when Spanish law, enforced by Spanish courts, provides for exceptions to the constitutional guarantee for equality on the basis of history or the perceived immaterial consequence of a differential treatment, it is a violation, in principle, of women's right to equality. Such exceptions serve to subvert social progress towards the elimination of discrimination against women using the very legal processes meant to bring about this progress, reinforce male superiority and maintain the status quo. This should neither be tolerated nor condoned on the basis of culture and history. Such attempts do not recognize the inalienable right to non-discrimination on the basis of sex which is a stand-alone right. If this is not recognized in principle regardless of its material consequences, it serves to maintain an ideology and a norm entrenching the inferiority of women that could lead to the denial of other rights that are much more substantive and material.[161]

I agree with Dairiam that inequality should not be tolerated in any situation, and the very fact that inequality exists should characterise it as a human rights issue. Titles of nobility and other titular awards, however antithetical to human rights and fundamental freedoms, and regardless of the conferral of material benefit, must be granted on the basis of equality until they are fully dismantled. As part of the very fabric and foundations of many societies, their retention in unequal forms reinforces a society built on inequality. At a minimum, the right to equal treatment before the law should have been at issue as Spanish law endorsed the passage of lineage through the male line. The Committee members clearly failed to engage in 'feminist contextual reasoning' in this case. Had they done so, they would have realised that such titles are not 'devoid of any legal or material effect' but in fact reinforce a social system that posits

---

[159] See, *Hoyos v. Spain*, HRC 1008/2001 (30 March 2004) and *Barcaiztequi v. Spain*, 1019/2001 (30 March 2004).

[160] *Muñoz-Vargas y Sainz de Vicuña v. Spain*, CEDAW 7/2005 (9 August 2007), para. 13.9 per Dairiam.

[161] *Ibid.*

men as superior to women. Conceptualising inequality as an issue of social justice or around the concepts of oppression/domination, advantage/disadvantage, or hierarchy may have helped the majority of the Women's Committee to arrive at a different result, as social titles, transferred through sex, are based on a social and power-based hierarchy that posits men above women. Under this hierarchy, men are the beneficiaries of privilege, while women are seen as benefiting only secondarily.

In 2009 the CESCR explained its use of 'systematic discrimination', albeit briefly, as 'legal rules, policies, practices or predominant cultural attitudes in either the public or private sector which create relative disadvantages for some groups, and privileges for other groups'.[162]

3.5   Multiple discrimination

The intersection of sex and other identity-based attributes has been recognised by several of the treaty bodies, and by many regional human rights courts. The committees have recognised the intersection of sex and other forms of discrimination on the grounds of colour, language, religion, political and other opinion, national or social origin, property, birth, or other status, such as age, disability, marital status, a refugee or immigration status.[163] Of all the treaty bodies, the CERD has dealt with this issue most holistically. In 2000 the CERD issued a General Recommendation on the gender-related dimensions of racial discrimination. It noted that racial discrimination does not always affect women and men equally or in the same way.[164] It recognised, for example, that certain forms of racial discrimination may be directed towards women specifically because of their sex, such as sexual violence committed against female members of

---

[162] CESCR, General Comment No. 20: Non-Discrimination in Economic, Social and Cultural Rights, para. 12.

[163] See, e.g., CESCR, General Comment No. 3: The Nature of States Parties Obligations, para. 5; CESCR, General Comment No. 5: Persons with Disabilities (1994), UN Doc. HRI/GEN/1/Rev.6, paras. 19 and 31; CEDAW, General Recommendation No. 18: Disabled Women (1991), UN Doc. HRI/GEN/1/Rev.7; CEDAW, Concluding observations on Sweden, UN Doc. A/56/38 (Part II), para. 334 (the Women's Committee has called on governments to adopt legislation for residence permits for individuals who have a well-founded fear of being persecuted on the basis of gender/sex, particularly in cases of discrimination against women); CRC, General Comment No. 7: Implementing Child Rights in Early Childhood (2006), UN Doc. CRC/C/GC/7/Rev.1, 20 September 2006, para. 11(b)(v); CRC, General Comment No. 9: The Rights of Children with Disabilities (2007), UN Doc. CRC/C/GC/9, 27 February 2007, para. 10. See, further, Vandenhole, *Non-Discrmination and Equality*, ns. 443, 444, 445, and 446.

[164] CERD, General Recommendation No. XXV: Gender-Related Dimensions of Racial Discrimination, para. 1.

particular racial or ethnic groups in detention or during armed conflict; the coerced sterilisation of indigenous women; or the abuse of women workers by their employers in the informal or domestic sectors.[165] It further acknowledged that the consequences of racially motivated violence may be different between women and men, such as social ostracism for victims of rape, or the pregnancy and birth of children resulting from rape. Furthermore, women may have greater difficulties accessing remedies and complaints mechanisms relating to racial discrimination because of gender-related impediments such as gender bias in the legal system and discrimination against women in private spheres of life.[166] The CERD called upon states parties to describe, as far as possible in quantitative and qualitative terms, the factors affecting and difficulties experienced in ensuring the equal enjoyment by women, free from racial discrimination, of rights under the ICERD.[167]

Again in 2000, the CERD issued a General Recommendation relating to discrimination against Roma, noting that Roma women are often victims of double discrimination.[168] Unfortunately the CERD has no recent case law that deals with the intersection of gender and race discrimination. Its only case on the issue is *Yilmaz-Dogan* v. *The Netherlands*, in which the CERD failed to address the question of discrimination based on gender stereotypes when an employer sought to terminate the employment of a Turkish woman who was pregnant. The state party summed up the issue from its perspective, as:

> When a Netherlands girl marries and has a baby, she stops working. Our foreign women workers, on the other hand, take the child to neighbours or family and at the slightest setback disappear on sick leave under the terms of the Sickness Act. They repeat that endlessly … [W]e cannot afford such goings-on.[169]

Other cases that have peripherally raised issues of gender or gender stereotyping have been dealt with as cases of race discrimination.[170]

---

[165] *Ibid.*, para. 2.

[166] *Ibid.*   [167] *Ibid.*, para. 7.

[168] CERD, General Recommendation XXVII: Discrimination against Roma (2000), UN Doc. A/55/18, Annex V, para. 6.

[169] *Yilmaz-Dogan* v. *The Netherlands*, CERD 1/1994 (10 August 1988).

[170] See, e.g. *P. O. E. M and F. A. S. M.* v. *Denmark*, CERD 22/2002 (19 March 2003) and *Quereshi* v. *Denmark*, CERD 33/2003 (10 March 2004) (both cases involving racially inciteful comments against Muslims as a group, including allegations about mass rapes committed by Muslims against Danish women); *Mohammed Hassan Gelle* v. *Denmark*, CERD 34/2004 (15 March 2006) (similar case in which statements were made in public

Likewise, in a decision in a 2006 case involving the coerced sterilisation of a Hungarian woman of Roma ethnicity during an emergency operation to remove her dead foetus, the Women's Committee did not comment upon the impact the woman's ethnicity may have had on her treatment by the state.[171] This was in spite of well-documented reports at the time that discrimination against Roma was (and remains) one of the main human rights concerns in Hungary.[172] It was also in spite of the state party raising irrelevant considerations in its defence, such as the complainant's inability to pay for health care. Issues such as the language (Latin) and manner of explanation of the sterilisation procedure and on the consent form, the speed with which the decision to sterilise her was taken (within seventeen minutes from admission to termination of the surgery), and the assumptions made about her former knowledge about family planning were taken for granted by the state party. In a supplementary submission, the complainant recalled 'her extremely vulnerable situation when she sought medical attention ... as a woman who would lose her child and as a member of a marginalized group of society – the Roma'.[173] No comment was made in relation to this aspect of her argument by the state party, nor by the Committee in its final 'views'. Again, this case reveals a lack of attention to the potential interplay between gender and ethnicity. As aptly summarised by the Canadian Supreme Court (SCC):

> We will never address the problem of discrimination completely, or ferret it out in all its forms, if we continue to focus on abstract categories and generalizations rather than specific effects. By looking at the grounds of discrimination instead of at the impact of the distinction ... we risk undertaking an analysis that is distanced and desensitised from real people's real experiences. To make matters worse, in defining the appropriate categories upon which findings of discrimination may be based,

criticising the government for seeking the input of the Somali community into new laws banning female genital mutilation. The statement compared the involvement of the Somali community in this way to asking 'paedophiles or rapists' to comment on laws outlawing paedophilia or rape. The CERD found in this case that the comments were generally offensive, as they 'generalise negatively on an entire group of people based solely on their ethnic or national origin and without regard to their views, opinions or actions regarding the subject of female genital mutilation (FGM)'. The CERD also stated that they strongly condemned the practice of FGM.)

[171] *Szijarto* v. *Hungary*, CEDAW 4/2004 (14 August 2006).

[172] See, e.g., CERD, Concluding observations on Hungary, UN Doc. A/57/18 (2002); HRC, Concluding observations on Hungary, UN Doc. A/57/40, vol. I (2002); CEDAW, Concluding observations on Hungary, UN Docs. A/51/38 (1996) and A/57/38 (2002).

[173] *Szijarto* v. *Hungary*, CEDAW 4/2004 (14 August 2006), para. 9.4.

we risk relying on conventions and stereotypes about individuals within these categories that, themselves, further entrench a discriminatory *status quo*. More often than not, disadvantage arises from the way in which society treats particular individuals, rather than from any characteristic inherent in those individuals.[174]

4   Equality law and the UN treaty bodies: some interim findings

International instruments and jurisprudence on equality have faced considerable scrutiny by feminist scholarship, as outlined in this chapter and in Chapter 2. Many of these criticisms are still relevant today. The dominant paradigm of equality employed by the human rights treaty bodies remains centred around sameness and difference. This is driven by an emphasis on non-discrimination rather than equality. The standard for achievement of equality is the 'male' sex, or his life experiences. Put another way, it calls for a female-to-male progression, that is, men are the standard against which all individuals are judged under international law. It reinforces a hierarchy in which men are above women. Inequality under this paradigm is when women are not treated the same as men; special treatment is allowed only as far as it will lead to their eventual identical position as men. The majority of the case law on equality at the level of international law brought by women alleges apparently unequal treatment compared with men in a similar or the same situation (or at least a comparable situation). Occasionally, men have brought complaints along the same lines.[175] Cases raising structural inequality arguments have not been readily apparent nor have the issues always been addressed by the treaty bodies, although this is slowly changing. On the positive side of the ledger, discriminatory intent seems to have been set aside permanently as an irrelevancy, with the focus instead on the effect or impact of any measure, law, or action on women. However, the impact of such laws or actions has not always been

---

[174]   *Egan* v. *Canada*, SCC, [1995] 2 S.C.R. 513, at para. 53 (the case involved a long-term homosexual partner who was denied a spousal pension to which he would have been entitled had he been married or in a long-term cohabitating heterosexual relationship. Although 'sexuality' was not listed as a prohibited ground for discrimination in Article 15 of the Canadian Charter of Rights and Freedoms, the Supreme Court of Canada ruled that it was nonetheless analogous to the other terms in Article 15 and therefore within the ambit of the provision).

[175]   See, e.g., *Vos* v. *The Netherlands*, HRC 786/1997 (26 July 1999), which found discrimination on the basis of sex in a situation where married men were required to reach a greater age than married women to be entitled to a pension.

fully comprehended, and at times has been dismissed, as shown in *Vos v. The Netherlands* and *Muñoz-Vargas y Sainz de Vicuña v. Spain.*

According to most of the treaty bodies, any distinctions between the treatment of men and women under the sameness/difference paradigm should be justified according to criteria of 'reasonableness' and 'objectivity'. Reasonableness is also used in international law in the context of assessing whether a state has fulfilled its obligations under due diligence, which is studied later in this book. As already briefly outlined, under this standard of care, a state is required to take only *reasonable* steps to prevent acts of violence. Reliance on standards such as reasonableness has proven problematic as they are regularly tied to masculinity and thereby risk a biased interpretation. Feminist scholars have argued that there is no such thing as an objective or reasonable standard, as it gives rise to questions such as 'Who decides?' and 'By whose standard of reasonableness and objectivity is one being judged?' In the area of tort law, for example, the 'reasonable person' standard has been criticised for being premised on the behaviour of the 'reasonable *man*' rather than the 'reasonable *person*',[176] with some suggesting that the shift in language from 'man' to 'person' is 'no more than cosmetic'.[177] Drucilla Cornell, for example, has asserted that '[r]easonableness is not natural and objective but rather socially and politically constructed through the identification of this supposedly neutral concept with masculinity'.[178] It is not clear why a standard linked to a 'reasonable *state*' would fare any better.

Only the Women's Committee has rejected what could be labelled the 'reasonable excuse' approach, while the CERD has offered a more nuanced version. In other words, what is prohibited is 'arbitrary' discrimination rather than discrimination per se. This was in fact the intention of the drafters of some of the instruments.[179] The focus on discrimination,

---

[176] M. Moran, *Rethinking the Reasonable Person: An Egalitarian Reconstruction of the Objective Standard* (Oxford University Press, 2003), 199.

[177] See, e.g., L. Bender, 'A Laywer's Primer on Feminist Theory and Tort' (1988) 38 *J. Legal Educ.* 3; L. M. Finley, 'A Break in the Silence: Including Women's Issues in a Torts Course' (1989) 1 *Yale J. L. & Feminism* 41; N. R. Cahn, 'The Looseness of Legal Language: The Reasonable Woman Standard in Theory and in Practice' (1991–1992) 77 *Cornell L. Rev.* 1398; R. Martin, 'A Feminist View of the Reasonable Man: An Alternative Approach to Liability in Negligence for Personal Injury' (1994) 23 *Anglo-Amer. L. Rev.* 334.

[178] D. Cornell, 'Living Together: Psychic Spaces and the Demand for Sexual Equality', in A. J. Cahill and J. Hansen (eds.), *Continental Feminism Reader* (London: Rowman & Littlefield, 2003) 196, at 206.

[179] McKean, *Equality and Discrimination under International Law*, 186 (pointing out that the United Nations Declaration on the Elimination of Violence against Women, GA res. A/RES/48/104, 23 February 1994, the predecessor to the CEDAW, was based on this premise).

nonetheless, overemphasises differences between men and women, and it gives space to biological arguments to justify oppressive practices. It is time for the committees to indicate that there are limited biological differences between women and men that are relevant to justifying any difference in treatment; the rest remain socially, politically, and economically constructed. These differences include reproductive health, childbirth, pregnancy, and pre- and post-natal issues, which may require special measures. In addition, gendered social and cultural patterns of the roles and responsibilities assigned to women and the economic and political inequalities between men and women may also justify the introduction of special measures in order to bring about equality *writ large*. This is at the heart of the sex/gender distinction and the difficulties therein.

At this juncture in this chapter it is possible to observe that the principles of equality and non-discrimination on the basis of sex remain contested, as reflected in the rather mixed case law. There is also inconsistency within committees and between committees, although some of the procedural harmonisation measures outlined in Chapter 3 have begun to reduce these discrepancies. While the committees tend to speak the rhetoric of 'multiple discrimination', they have proven largely unable to identify the range of identity-based factors at issue or to assess their impact in their case law, although admittedly very little case law is available. Distinctions still seem to be made between race and sex discrimination, reinforcing a hierarchical system that posits race above sex. Any distinctions between sex discrimination and inequality also remain unclear. Whether the terms are considered by the treaty bodies and other international and regional courts as synonyms or qualitatively different is 'inconclusive'.[180] The underlying structural disparities between women and men of a social, economic, or political nature tend to be minimised under discrimination law as it prioritises individuals or individual issues rather than equality, which bears a broader ambit. Of course, it must be conceded to some degree that the nature of individual communications, as mechanisms of individual redress, naturally distorts this view in that direction.

By and large, the treaty bodies have accepted few of the state party excuses for unfair distinctions in law or practice between women and men, although there have been serious slippages when irrelevant considerations such as administrative convenience have been taken into account. There has also been a rhetorical acceptance of direct and indirect forms of discrimination, although the committees have not always addressed both

---

[180] Vandenhole, *Non-Discrimination and Equality*, 34.

aspects in individual cases. The committees have, furthermore, tended to disregard structural causes of inequality in their case law, which can mean they are assessing a particular case in isolation of its social and cultural context. Positively, the practice of the Women's Committee in particular of indicating at the end of an individual communication a number of general recommendations, in addition to the individual decision (see Chapter 3), has highlighted that inequality requires structurally based solutions. The CERD has tended to perform better in its assessments of what constitutes discrimination by looking at the *differential impact* it will bear on *the group* as a whole; meanwhile, the CESCR has used language of *inherent disadvantage*, albeit still confined within a sameness/difference model, not to mention problems using language such as 'inherent' and links with biological determinism. Overall, international human rights law continues to struggle in its handling of these fundamental concepts, although much progress has been made, even within the confines of a sameness/difference paradigm.

The first half of this chapter has highlighted the hazards inherent in an equality law framed around sameness and difference. So, what if an alternative vision of equality was adopted by the treaty bodies? What if one of the reconceptualisations of equality of Mahoney, Young, or MacKinnon were adopted? A broader analysis that locates the individual woman within her lived context of group disadvantage, hierarchy, under-representation, and limited or lack of political or economic power, would call upon the treaty bodies to ask deeper questions about the role that gender plays in her life. It would require questions to be framed around what needs to be done to ensure that, in the words of Judge Tanaka of the PCIJ, she is recognised as having 'an equal value in [herself]'.[181] It would go further than simply permitting her to participate in the institutions or processes from which she has been excluded or to gain access to benefits that have been denied her, unless reasonable excuses for such denials could satisfy the decision-maker. If nothing else, a reconceptualisation would untie women from the need to compare themselves to the norm of men.

I now turn to the second main portion of this chapter and the main focus of the book and outline and evaluate the approach developed by the Women's Committee and adopted by several of the other treaty bodies of treating violence against women as a form of sex discrimination. I first outline what the approach entails before exploring what it means for

---

[181]   *South West Africa Cases (Liberia v. South Africa; Ethiopia v. South Africa)*, 288 and 202.

female victims of violence. In particular, I ask: is it a satisfactory approach to the protection of women from violence under international law?

D   Violence against women as sex discrimination (VAW = SD): evaluating a feminist strategy

1   General overview

In 1989 the Women's Committee issued its first General Recommendation on violence against women. It cited only Articles 2, 5, 11, 12, and 16 of the CEDAW as imposing obligations upon states to protect women against violence of any kind occurring within the family, at the workplace, or in any other area of social life.[182] Elaborating upon its earlier position, the Women's Committee adopted a more comprehensive Recommendation in 1992 in which it dealt with individual treaty provisions and links between sex discrimination and violence against women.[183] The Women's Committee was particularly concerned that, despite its 1989 General Recommendation, not all state party reports adequately reflected the close connection between discrimination against women, gender-based violence, and violations of human rights and fundamental freedoms.[184] The 1992 General Recommendation emerged at a time when heightened focus was placed on violence against women within the UN system.

As outlined in the Introduction to this book, the 1985 Nairobi Forward-looking Strategies for the Advancement of Women articulated a set of measures to combat violence against women,[185] but their implementation proved problematic. In 1991 the Economic and Social Council (ECOSOC) recommended that a framework for an international instrument be developed that would explicitly address this issue.[186] Debate ensued at that time as to whether a new instrument was the way forward. Among the

---

[182] CEDAW, General Recommendation No. 12: Violence against Women (1989), UN Doc. HRC/GEN/1/Rev.7, Preamble. Articles 2 (policy obligations of states parties); 5 (sex role stereotyping and prejudice), 11 (employment), 12 (health), and 16 (marriage and family life).

[183] CEDAW, General Recommendation No. 19: Violence against Women.

[184] *Ibid.*, Background para. 4.

[185] United Nations, Report of the World Conference to Review and Appraise the Achievements of the United Nations Decade for Women: Equality, Development and Peace, Nairobi, 15–26 July 1985 (New York: Dept of Public Information, Sales No. E.85.IV.10, 1985), Chapter 1. See, also, UN Report of the UN Secretary-General, Efforts to Eradicate Violence against Women within Society and the Family, UN Doc. E/CN.6/1988/6 (1987).

[186] ECOSOC res. 1991/18, 30 May 1991.

arguments against any new instrument was that an entirely new instrument could create confusion over the relevance of existing human rights instruments, that it risked limited ratification, and there was concern over the cost of implementation.[187] Furthermore, any new instrument, it was argued, would open up controversial debate on how to define such violence. Alternative approaches, including the drafting of a Declaration, the appointment of a Special Rapporteur on the subject, and the issuing of a General Recommendation by the Women's Committee, were preferred, although the possibility of a new treaty if these other approaches proved unsuccessful was noted as still being available.[188]

The 1992 General Recommendation that ensued declared that '[g]ender-based violence is a form of discrimination that seriously inhibits women's ability to enjoy rights and freedoms on a basis of equality with men'.[189] In other words, the Women's Committee developed a formula equating violence against women (VAW) with sex discrimination (SD), namely VAW = SD. It stated that the definition of 'discrimination' in Article 1 of the CEDAW:

> includes gender-based violence, that is, violence that is directed against a woman because she is a woman or that affects women disproportionately. It includes acts that inflict physical, mental or sexual harm or suffering, threats of such acts, coercion and other deprivations of liberty.[190]

Clarifying its approach, the Committee stated:

> Gender-based violence, which impairs or nullifies the enjoyment by women of human rights and fundamental freedoms under general international law or under human rights conventions, is discrimination within the meaning of article 1 of the Convention.[191]

In particular, the Committee held that '[g]ender-based violence may breach specific provisions of the Convention, regardless of whether those provisions expressly mention violence'.[192] Concerns over the wording of these definitions are dealt with in Chapter 1 of this book.

In many ways, the development of the VAW = SD formula transformed the CEDAW from an anti-discrimination treaty into a gender-based

---

[187] J. Fitzpatrick, 'The Use of International Human Rights Norms to Combat Violence Against Women', in R. J. Cook (ed.), *Human Rights of Women: National and International Perspectives* (Philadelphia: University Pennsylvania Press, 1994), 538.

[188] UN Doc. E/CN.6/1992/4, paras. 25–27 (1991), as referred to in *ibid.*, n. 41.

[189] CEDAW, General Recommendation No. 19: Violence against Women, Background para. 1.

[190] *Ibid.*, para. 6.   [191] *Ibid.*, para. 7.   [192] *Ibid.*, para. 6.

violence treaty. Not only is equality seen as a foundational principle of the CEDAW, the Women's Committee argued that so, too, is gender-related violence. The two issues are seen as inseparable, as they both limit and restrict women's enjoyment of all other human rights.

In its 1992 General Recommendation, the Women's Committee, furthermore, drew a link between custom and tradition, and violence. The General Recommendation provided that '[t]raditional attitudes by which women are regarded as subordinate to men or as having stereotyped roles perpetuate widespread practices involving violence or coercion, such as family violence and abuse, forced marriage, dowry deaths, acid attacks and female circumcision'.[193] The Committee further stated that '[s]uch prejudices and practices may justify gender-based violence as a form of protection or control of women' as well as contribute to the maintenance of women in subordinate roles, their low level of political participation, and low levels of education, skills, and work opportunities.[194] In other words, '[t]he effect of such violence on the physical and mental integrity of women is to deprive them of the equal enjoyment, exercise, and knowledge of human rights and fundamental freedoms'.[195] Moreover, the Committee asserted that '[t]hese attitudes also contribute to the propagation of pornography and the depiction and other commercial exploitation of women as sexual objects, rather than as individuals. This in turn contributes to gender-based violence.'[196] I have no arguments here with this line of argument: violence carried out against women can indeed interfere with a range of their other human rights.

Adopting a near-identical approach to the Women's Committee, the CESCR stated over a decade later in 2004:

> Gender based violence is a form of discrimination that inhibits the ability to enjoy rights and freedoms, including economic, social and cultural rights, on a basis of equality. States parties must take appropriate measures to eliminate violence *against men and women* and act with due diligence to prevent, investigate, mediate, punish and redress acts of violence against them by private actors.[197]

Here, however, the CESCR considers that gender-related violence can affect both men and women. Although their approach is compatible with the UN's 'gender mainstreaming' policy, which explains 'gender' as informing the relations between men and women and therefore it is not

[193] *Ibid.*, para. 11.   [194] *Ibid.*   [195] *Ibid.*   [196] *Ibid.*, para. 12.
[197] CESCR, General Comment No. 16: The Equal Right of Men and Women to the Enjoyment of All Economic, Social and Cultural Rights, para. 27 (my emphasis).

owned by either sex nor rooted in inequality specifically, it is problematic (see Chapter 1 for general criticisms of gender mainstreaming). In particular this approach creates a gender-neutral understanding of inequality and discrimination, incorporating both positive and negative aspects of gender relations, and therefore it renders it almost meaningless and certainly powerless for the subordinated group. Under this view, rape and sexual violence against women would constitute gender-related violence against women; meanwhile forced military recruitment of young men and boys would constitute gender-related violence against these men and boys. While the latter is a serious matter of international law, it is detached from any suggestion that men and boys in the communities in question are selected for recruitment owing to their inferior position on the basis of their sex. Rather, they are selected for a range of other reasons, such as poverty, age, size, and agility.[198]

What the CESCR's approach does is to neutralise the power that an equality lens may have provided to particular situations of sexual inequality. It actually makes gender-related violence simply violence against either men or women, regardless of the social, political or economic context in which that violence occurs. It is thus based on the biology (or sex) of the affected group, rather than on account of any position of inferiority, subordination, or inequality. It is therefore detached from any discriminatory basis.

The approach of the HRC has been similar but less direct in its linkages between sex discrimination and violence against women. In 2000 the HRC stated that Article 3 of the ICCPR, which provides that all human beings should enjoy the rights provided for in the Covenant on 'an equal basis' and 'in their totality', is impaired whenever any person is denied the full and equal enjoyment of any right.[199] From the catalogue of forms of violence outlined in the General Comment as being of relevance to Article 3 (and other provisions; see below), it is clear that the HRC considered violence against women as one issue that impairs women's entitlement to enjoy ICCPR rights in equality and in totality. It is not evident that

---

[198] Moreoever, the protection of underage children (both boys and girls) from forced military recruitment is expressly covered by international human rights law (Article 38, CRC) as well as under international humanitarian law and within the Rome Statute of the ICC. In addition, while military recruitment is usually required of men only, any complaints on this practice should be covered by discrimination laws to the extent that it is an unfair burden on men without objective and justifiable reasons why women cannot also perform it.

[199] HRC, General Comment No. 28: Equality of Rights Between Men and Women, para. 2.

the HRC considers violence against women to be a *form* of sex discrimination per se, in the same manner as the Women's Committee, without additional considerations.

In contrast to the CEDAW, the ICERD contains an explicit prohibition against racially motivated violence.[200] Here, again, the hierarchy of forms of discrimination is evident with a similar provision missing from the CEDAW. As noted above, the CERD has recognised that certain forms of racial discrimination may be directed towards women specifically because of their sex.[201]

So what are the advantages and disadvantages of the VAW = SD strategy of the treaty bodies for women and women's claims for protection from violence?

2   VAW = SD: an assessment of the strategy

At the outset, it must be acknowledged that characterising violence against women as sex discrimination has importantly filled a gap in international human rights law, namely the absence of an explicit binding prohibition on violence against women. This book in no way suggests that the interpretative inclusion approach should be rejected, or that it is not a workable form of analysis when properly applied. Rather this book seeks to delve deeper into the approach, and to question what it means as a feminist strategy. It finds overall that it carries its own set of problems for women. Most significantly, it reinforces inequality under international law by subjecting women to additional legal burdens. This in turn highlights the ultimate paradox of international law, discussed in Chapters 2 and 7, that the more that women work within existing norms, the more the unequal structures of that system are reinforced. This makes the VAW = SD strategy at best a stopgap measure to the eventual enactment of a specific treaty or provision on this issue.

2.1   Advantages

The first, and most obvious, advantage of the VAW = SD formula is that, had it not been developed, the UN treaty bodies would be constrained in their treatment of violence against women. In much the same way

---

[200] Article 4, ICERD.
[201] CERD, General Recommendation No. XXV: Gender-Related Dimensions of Racial Discrimination, para. 2.

as MacKinnon's work on sexual harassment in the USA, in which she argued that sexual harassment is sex discrimination in order to locate a legal cause of action before US courts, the approach of the Women's Committee is a pragmatic response to a gap in the law.[202] Prior to the 1992 General Recommendation, violence against women as a specific issue was not given official attention by the UN treaty bodies as it fell outside their terms of reference.

Under the strategy, the Women's Committee has addressed a wide range of issues of violence against women, such as sexual violence, including gang rape and marital rape, domestic violence, physical violence, sexual harassment, and pornography.[203] The Committee has identified measures to eliminate violence against women, including criminalisation, awareness-raising and education, the training of police, judicial, and other personnel, national action plans, and assistance to victims in the form of crisis centres, hotlines, legal, medical, psychological, and emotional support, socio-economic integration measures, and effective remedies.[204] Sexual harassment in the workplace has also been identified as an issue of equality by the Women's Committee, which notes that '[e]quality in employment can be seriously impaired when women are subjected to gender-specific violence, such as sexual harassment in the workplace'.[205]

This strategy has also given arguments to the other committees to take up the issue of violence against women within an equality paradigm. For example, the CESCR has made references to the lack, in many states, of

---

[202] See, C. A. MacKinnon, *Sexual Harassment of Working Women: A Case of Sex Discrimination* (New Haven, CT: Yale University Press, 1979), taken up in *Meritor Savings Bank* v. *Vinson*, 477 US 57 (1986).

[203] See, e.g., CEDAW, Concluding observations on The Netherlands, UN Doc. A/49/38 (1994), para. 274 (the Netherlands' delegate disputed that the legality of pornography had led to the increase in sexual violence); Japan, UN Doc. A/49/38 (1994), para. 577; South Africa, UN Doc. A/53/38/Rev.1, para. 104 (1998); Algeria, UN Doc. A/54/38/Rev.1 (1999), para. 79; Kyrgyzstan, UN Doc. A/54/38/Rev.1 (1999), para. 122; India, UN Doc. A/55/38 (2000), para. 68; Democratic Republic of Congo, UN Doc. A/55/38 (2000), para. 202; Burkina Faso, UN Doc. A/55/38 (2000), para. 270; Finland, UN Doc. A/56/38 (2001), para. 301; Nicaragua, UN Doc. A/56/38 (2001), para. 292; Trinidad and Tobago, UN Doc. A/57/38 (2002), para. 145; Iceland, UN Doc. A/56/38 (2002), para. 225; Brazil, UN Doc. A/58/38 (2003), para. 112; Kuwait, UN Doc. A/59/38 (2004), para. 78; Samoa, UN Doc. A/60/38 (2005), para. 29; Cambodia, UN Doc. A/61/38 (2006), para. 33; Eritrea, UN Doc. A/61/38 (2006), para. 77.

[204] Vandenhole, *Non-Discrmination and Equality*, 152–153, referring to a range of concluding observations on state party reports.

[205] CEDAW, General Recommendation No. 19: Violence against Women, paras. 17 and 18.

legislation outlawing sexual harassment,[206] and it has linked the right to family life and inequality in the context of domestic violence, forced marriage, and gender-based violence generally.[207] The CESCR has, furthermore, raised concern regarding family laws that provide an obligation upon a wife to obey her husband[208] and for polygamy,[209] unilateral divorce by husbands,[210] more severe punishment for adultery imposed upon women,[211] and 'honour' crimes.[212] The HRC has similarly linked inequality between women and men and violence with a range of ICCPR rights, including in relation to female genital mutilation,[213] the pledging of girls for economic gain,[214] the detention of women rejected by their families,[215] domestic violence,[216] a lack of rape prosecutions[217] or exemption from prosecution if marriage follows rape,[218] the sexual exploitation of foreign

---

[206] CESCR, Concluding observations on Chile, UN Doc. E/C.12/1/Add.105 (2004), para. 21.

[207] CESCR, General Comment No. 16: The Equal Right of Men and Women to the Enjoyment of All Economic, Social and Cultural Rights, para. 27.

[208] CESCR, Concluding observations on Algeria, UN Doc. E/C.12/1/Add.71 (2001), para. 14.

[209] *Ibid.*   [210] *Ibid.*

[211] CESCR, Concluding observations on Syrian Arab Republic, UN Doc. E/C.12/1/Add.63 (2001), para. 31.

[212] *Ibid.*

[213] See, e.g., HRC, Concluding observations on Kenya, UN Doc. CCPR/CO/83/KEN (2005) (Articles 3 and 7), para. 12; Benin, UN Doc. CCPR/CO/82/BEN (Articles 3 and 23), para. 11; Mali, UN Doc. CCPR/CO/77/MLI (2003) (Articles 3 and 7), para. 11; Yemen, UN Doc. CCPR/CO/75/YEM (2002) (Articles 3, 6 and 7), para. 6; Zimbabwe, UN Doc. CCPR/C/79/Add.89 (1998) (Articles 3, 7, 23, 24 and others), para. 12; Nigeria, UN Doc. CCPR/C/79/Add.65 (1996), para. 29.

[214] HRC, Concluding observations on Zimbabwe, UN Doc. CCPR/C/79/Add.89 (1998) (Articles 3, 7, 23, 24 and others), para. 12.

[215] See, e.g., HRC, Concluding observations on Yemen, UN Doc. CCPR/CO/75/YEM (2002) (Articles 3, 9 and 26), para. 12.

[216] See, e.g., HRC, Concluding observations on Mauritius, UN Doc. CCPR/CO/83/MUS (2005) (Articles 3 and 7), para. 10; Uzbekistan, UN Doc. CCPR/CO/83/UZB (2005) (Articles 3, 7 and 26), para. 23; Yemen, UN Doc. CCPR/CO/75/YEM (2002) (Articles 3 and 7), para. 6; Iceland, UN Doc. CCPR/CO/83/ISL (2005) (Articles 3, 7 and 26), para. 12; Albania, UN Doc. CCPR/CO/82/ALB (2004) (Articles 2, 3 and 26), para. 10; Poland, UN Doc. CCPR/CO/82/POL (2004) (Articles 3 and 7), para. 11; Morocco, UN Doc. CCPR/CO/82/MAR (2004) (Articles 3 and 7), para. 28; Benin, UN Doc. CCPR/CO/82/BEN (2005) (Articles 3 and 7), para. 9.

[217] See, e.g., HRC, Concluding observations on Iceland, UN Doc. CCPR/CO/83/ISL (2005) (Articles 3, 7 and 26), para. 11.

[218] See, e.g., HRC, Concluding observations on Egypt, UN Doc. CCPR/CO/76/EGY (2002) (Articles 3 and 26), para. 9; Venezuela, UN Doc. CCPR/CO/70/VEN, para. 20; Mongolia, UN Doc. CCPR/C/79/Add.120 (2000) (Articles 3 and 26), para. 8; Morocco, UN Doc. CCPR/C/79/Add.97, paras. 11 and 15; Lebanon, UN Doc. CCPR/C/79/Add.78 (1997) (Articles 3 and 23), paras. 18–19.

women,[219] and trafficking in women.[220] For the HRC, however, a discrimination lens has not always been centre stage. With a wider range of provisions from which to choose, the HRC has, for example, preferred to characterise forms of violence against women as torture, which is examined in Chapter 5 of this study, while the CESCR has tended to consider violence as an issue related to women's health.[221] There are advantages and disadvantages to these approaches too, but it is beyond the scope of this book to deal with them here. The analysis of the Women's Committee, however, has undoubtedly been a catalyst to an acceptance that violence against women is a human rights concern across the treaty bodies, and beyond.

The second advantage of the strategy is not only that the Women's Committee is now able to address violence against women per se, but that it can do so in a broad way that encompasses structural causes of inequality and violence. That is, there has been a conceptual breakthrough. Violence against women is recognised as a 'group-based harm, a practice of social inequality carried out on an individual level'.[222] Violence against women is no longer perceived as an individual criminal act but part of a systemic and political problem, requiring a systemic, political solution.[223] Without VAW=SD, the treaty bodies would have been able to deal only with specific incidences of violence that were otherwise linked to other treaty rights. For the Women's Committee, this may have been limited to the specific context of trafficking, which is expressly included in Article

---

[219] See, e.g., HRC, Concluding observations on the Netherlands, UN Doc. CCPR/CO/72/NET, para. 10.

[220] See, e.g., HRC, Concluding observations on Greece, UN Doc. CCPR/CO/83/GRC, para. 10; Albania, UN Doc. CCPR/CO/82/ALB (2004) (Articles 8, 24 and 26), para. 15; Serbia and Montenegro, UN Doc. CCPR/CO/81/SEMO (2004) (Articles 3, 8 and 24), para. 16; Lithuania, UN Doc. CCPR/CO/80/LTU (2004) (Articles 3 and 8), para. 14; Suriname, UN Doc. CCPR/CO/80/SUR (2004) (Articles 3 and 8), para. 13; Czech Republic, UN Doc. CCPR/CO/72/CZE (2001) (Articles 3 and 8), para. 13.

[221] CESCR, General Comment No. 16: The Equal Right of Men and Women to the Enjoyment of All Economic, Social and Cultural Rights para. 29 (unequal access to water and sanitation resources that bear on a women's health); CESCR, General Comment No. 14: The Right to the Highest Attainable Standard of Health (2000), UN Doc. HRI/GEN/1/Add.6, para. 8 (the right to health includes control over one's body and sexual and reproductive freedom) and para. 10 (a wider definition of the right to health takes into account violence and armed conflict).

[222] S. F. Goldfarb, 'Applying the Discrimination Model to Violence against Women: Some Reflections on Theory and Practice' (2002–2003) 11 *Am. U. J. Gender Soc. Pol'y & L.* 251, at 254. Sally Goldfarb makes similar comments in relation to the US' Violence against Women Act that provided a federal civil remedy for violence against women.

[223] *Ibid.*, 255.

6 of the CEDAW. Likewise, the HRC would have had only the option of dealing with violence against women as a violation of other provisions such as those on torture, slavery, security of person, or life.[224]

Instead, the Women's Committee has directly criticised a range of traditional practices that are considered discriminatory (and violent) to women, such as dowry, sati, and devadasi systems,[225] and female genital mutilation,[226] gathering together the links between custom/tradition and violence against women that the Committee identified in its 1992 General Recommendation. The Women's Committee has also referred to the non-consensual genital examinations of women,[227] unequal marriage practices between men and women, including low legal ages of marriage, dowry practices, early and forced marriage, levirate,[228] and the inheriting of women.[229]

In the Women Committee's fact-finding mission to Mexico, sex discrimination was seen as a contributing factor to the abduction, rape, and murder of poor and young women, including adolescents, in the Ciudad Juárez area of Chihuahua, Mexico, alongside social and cultural breakdown, a lack of social services, poverty, class, and other social and economic factors. The disjuncture between evolving gender roles of women and traditional 'patriarchal attitudes and mentalities' fostered an environment that was said to have developed 'specific characteristics marked by hatred and misogyny. There have been widespread

---

[224] In fact, the approach of the HRC has been to utilise the other provisions in spite of obvious sex discrimination issues: see, Chapter 5.

[225] CEDAW, Concluding observations on India, UN Doc. A/55/38 (2000), para. 68. Dowry (or bride price) is the payment of money, gifts, or estate by a woman's family to her husband in marriage. It is a practice in many societies. Sati (or widow-burning) is a funeral practice among some Hindu communities in which a recently widowed woman would immolate herself on her husband's funeral pyre. Devadasi is a Hindu practice in which girls are 'married' to a deity. Although largely derived from Hindu practices, similar practices are found elsewhere: see, A. Small Bilyeu, 'Trokosi – The Practice of Sexual Slavery in Ghana: Religious and Cultural Freedom vs. Human Rights' (1999) 9 *Ind. Int'l & Comp. L. Rev.* 457.

[226] See, e.g., CEDAW, Concluding observations on Ethiopia, UN Doc. A/51/38 (Part I) (1996), para. 155; Nigeria, UN Doc. A/59/38 (2004), para. 276; Benin, UN Doc. A/69/38 (2005), para. 132.

[227] CEDAW, Concluding observations on Turkey, UN Doc. CEDAW/C/TUR/CC/4–5, para. 25.

[228] Levirate marriage is a type of marriage in which a woman marries one of her husband's brothers after her husband's death, if there are no children, in order to continue family succession of the deceased husband. It has also been described as the wife being 'inherited' by her husband's family.

[229] Vandenhole, *Non-Discrmination and Equality*, 150.

kidnappings, disappearances, rapes, mutilations and murders.'[230] The Committee stated:

> Along with combating crime, resolving the individual cases of murders and disappearances, finding and punishing those who are guilty, and providing support to the victims' families, *the root causes of gender violence in its structural dimension and in all its forms* – whether domestic and intra-family violence or sexual violence and abuse, murders, kidnappings, and disappearances must be combated, specific policies on gender equality adopted and a gender perspective integrated into all public policies [my emphasis].[231]

Other traditional practices harmful to or discriminatory against women and girls that have been identified by the Women's Committee include dietary restrictions for pregnant women and a preference for male children.[232] It is clear that equality strategies are a necessary component of any attempt to reduce or prevent violence against women.

Practically speaking, equality rights offer equal protection of women before the law, especially in the context of criminal law, and this improves women's access to justice, and in turn, limits impunity. This might include the removal of exceptions or distinctions in criminal laws for particular forms of gender-related violence, or its selective prosecution.[233] The failure of a legal system to treat domestic violence as seriously as violence by strangers would be discriminatory against women.[234] Rape inside as well as outside of marriage would need to be classified as a criminal offence to satisfy the principle of non-discrimination on the basis of sex. The selective failure to prosecute rapists of prostitutes or members of vulnerable groups such as disabled women would also be disallowed under an equality paradigm.[235] For example, an equality paradigm could prove useful when a state investigates murder cases against men but fails to do the same or is less vigilant in respect of 'honour' killings against women.[236]

---

[230] CEDAW, Report on Mexico, UN doc. CEDAW/C/2005/OP.8/MEXICO, para. 24.

[231] *Ibid.*, para. 34.

[232] CEDAW, General Recommendation No. 19: Violence against Women, para. 20.

[233] Fitzpatrick, 'The Use of International Human Rights Norms to Combat Violence Against Women', 538.

[234] *Ibid.*

[235] *Ibid.* See, e.g., ECtHR decision, *X and Y v. The Netherlands* (1985) 8 EHRR 235, in which the rape of an institutionalised girl with mental disability was considered under the right to privacy in Article 8 ECHR, but the ECtHR did not consider it necessary to deal with the question of discrimination.

[236] A. P. Ewing, 'Establishing State Responsibility for Private Acts of Violence against Women under the American Convention on Human Rights' (1995) 26 *Colum. Hum. Rts. L. Rev.* 751, at 780.

Additionally, defences available to men that are not available to women, such as formal or customary rules that permit men to invoke unilateral divorce, or where the state maintains Hudood Ordinances that are not applied equally, would be made unlawful.[237]

Furthermore, the VAW = SD formula contextualises violence as a social justice issue rather than treating it as an individual anomaly or crime. It approves the understanding of violence against women in a wider socio-political context, characterised variously by patriarchy, traditional and cultural stereotypes of women, rigid gender roles, poverty, and a lack of economic and political autonomy and empowerment for women. Violence against women seen in this way is a symptom of a much wider social problem. As Julie Goldscheid, for example, argues:

> [T]he daily experience of domestic and sexual violence survivors reflects the ongoing legacy of sex discrimination, both in the persistent gender-based differences in who generally commits and is harmed by the abuse, and in the responses victims encounter from legal, criminal justice, and social service systems.[238]

Treating violence against women as rooted in unequal relations between women and men allows the committees to delve deeper into the causes of it. In fact, the VAW = SD formula may respond to some of the feminist critiques of international human rights law outlined in Chapter 2 regarding the law's failure to respond to women's particularised experiences, its oversimplification of complex power relations, or its disallowance of transformative outcomes.

The final value of constructing violence against women as sex discrimination is that it turns what may otherwise be characterised as a 'private indiscretion' or merely criminal activity into political violence. Inequality as a social phenomenon rather than as an individual experience (although it is played out against individual women) requires social and political responses. It deconstructs the public/private dichotomy in

---

[237] A Hudood Ordinance is a law intended to implement Shari'a law by enforcing punishments against extramarital sex, false accusation of extramarital sex, theft, or alcohol consumption. It is particularly criticised for deterring women from making complaints of rape, because if unproved, they are open to prosecution under the Hudood Ordinance for adultery, which can carry penalties of death in some countries. For more on Hudood Ordinances, see: R. Coomaraswamy, 'To Bellow Like a Cow: Women, Ethnicity and the Discourse of Rights', in R. J. Cook (ed.), *Human Rights of Women: National and International Perspectives* (Philadelphia: University of Pennsylvania Press, 1994) 43.

[238] J. Goldscheid, 'Domestic and Sexual Violence as Sex Discrimination: Comparing American and International Approaches' (2006) 28 *T. Jefferson L. Rev.* 355, at 356.

so far as so-called private violence is turned into a public issue because it is set against the structural or public context of sexual inequality.

In its first admissible decision in *A. T.* v. *Hungary*, the Women's Committee, for example, consistently pointed out the links between domestic violence and sex discrimination, recalling in several places its 1992 General Recommendation. The Committee found that the state party had failed in its due diligence responsibilities to protect A. T. who had suffered sustained domestic violence and threats of such violence at the hands of her common-law husband in breach of Article 2(a), (b), and (e) of the CEDAW. In particular the recognition by the state administrative apparatus of the unrestrictive property rights of the husband to the family home was condemned. The Committee reiterated that 'traditional attitudes by which women are regarded as subordinate to men contribute to violence against women'[239] and that these attitudes plagued the state's dealings with the complainant. Similar discussions have occurred in the above-mentioned cases of *Goekce* and *Yildirim*.[240] Notably, in those aforementioned cases, none of the General Recommendations made to the state party targeted socio-economic inequality outside the specific context of domestic violence.[241]

2.2   Concerns

Despite the many advances made by the VAW = SD strategy, it is not a panacea for the absence of an explicit prohibition on violence against women. First, the attachment of violence against women to the concepts of sex discrimination and inequality is subject to understandings of these latter terms, which, as shown in this chapter, are complex, contested, and difficult to pin down. Moreover, the exact content and meaning of these terms is far from agreed among the treaty bodies, and their implementation record varies. As noted in the first half of this chapter, these concepts are still principally tied to a sameness/difference ideology that is not as flexible a mode of analysis as the paradigms of oppression/domination, advantage/disadvantage, or lack of hierarchy.

Second, although the prohibition on discrimination is a non-derogable right, it is a limited one. Apart from the Women's Committee, all the

---

[239] *A. T.* v. *Hungary*, CEDAW 2/2003 (26 January 2005), para. 9.4.

[240] *Goekce* v. *Austria*, CEDAW 5/2005 (6 August 2007) and *Yildirim* v. *Austria*, CEDAW 6/2005 (6 August 2007).

[241] The General Recommendations, for example, called for strengthening of implementation and monitoring of the relevant legislation for the protection against violence in the family; vigilant and speedy prosecution; and enhanced coordination between law enforcement and judicial officers etc.

approaches of the treaty bodies to discrimination give room to justify-ing discriminatory practices on the basis of 'reasonable and objective' cri-teria. The CESCR has additionally added the human rights criterion of proportionality.[242] As noted above as well as in Chapter 2, such criteria are often treated as neutral terms by decision-makers, but in reality they are applied within a socio-political–cultural context and are influenced by the socio-political–cultural background and arguably the sex/gender of those decision-makers. That is, such exceptions are open to exclude or disregard the particular circumstances facing women, and they have been criticised for doing so.[243] The concern is that these same excuses are avail-able to be argued and applied to failures to protect women from certain forms of violence, to prosecute or punish alleged offenders, or to provide appropriate redress. Suggesting that there may be 'reasonable and object-ive justifications' that could excuse a state for failing to respond to an act or threat of violence against women sounds very much like tolerance of such violence, whereas it should never be acceptable.

Third, difficulties in articulating the concepts of equality and non-discrimination on the basis of sex lead to problems of implementation. Goldscheid notes that the connection between sex discrimination and sexual and domestic violence is 'not easily, nor precisely, described'.[244] The experience of the International Criminal Tribunal for the former Yugoslavia (ICTY) shows that recognising rape, for example, as discrim-inatory can be problematic. In the *Kunarac, Kovač and Vuković* case, the defendants admitted rape but argued that the rape was a personal indis-cretion rather than a political one. Although the ICTY rejected these arguments, the record notes that the defence provided that 'even if it were proved that he raped a woman, the accused would have done so out of a sexual urge, not out of hatred'.[245] Furthermore, the discrimination con-sidered relevant to this case was that of ethnicity, not sex.[246]

Similar arguments to those above are also frequently made by govern-ments under international refugee law. It is not uncommon for govern-ment lawyers to argue that acts of gender-based violence do not amount

[242] CESCR, General Comment No. 20: Non-Discrimination in Economic, Social and Cultural Rights, para. 13.

[243] N. H. Kaufman and S. A. Lindquist, 'Critiquing Gender-Neutral Treaty Language: The Convention on the Elimination of All Forms of Discrimination Against Women', in J. Peters and A. Wolper (eds.), *Women's Rights, Human Rights: International Feminist Perspectives* (New York: Routledge, 1995) 114, at 116.

[244] Goldscheid, 'Domestic and Sexual Violence as Sex Discrimination', 360.

[245] E.g., *Prosecutor v. Kunarac, Kovac and Vukovic*, ICTY, Case No. IT-96–23-T and IT-96–23/1-T (22 February 2001), para. 816. The Court did not accept this argument, however.

[246] *Ibid.*

to political persecution on the grounds that they are simply personal. In the United Kingdom House of Lords' asylum decision in the *Shah and Islam* case, Lord Hoffman acknowledged that there was a threat of violence to the claimants from their husbands, but he stated: 'This is a personal affair, directed against them as individuals.'[247] Only in recognising the inability or unwillingness of the state to do anything to protect them because they were women did state responsibility become invoked (and the political nature of the violence become acknowledged). Lord Hoffman stated that it was '[t]he combination of these two elements' that made the otherwise private violence fall within the meaning of the 1951 Convention relating to the Status of Refugees 1951, as amended by its Protocol of 1967.[248] The violence or threat of violence itself was insufficient, even though it was perpetuated within a social and legal context that endorsed discriminatory treatment between women and men, in which women were seen as second-class citizens.[249]

A fourth concern with the VAW = SD legal formula is that it encompasses only *gender-related* forms of violence, that is, violence that is *based upon or linked to* sex discrimination. It does not, for instance, cover violence perpetrated against women outside this context, such as the torture of women by physical assault or verbal abuse in state custody. Such violence remains to be dealt with under other provisions and other treaties. It thus sets up a two-tier system of protection: those acts motivated by gender and those that are not; those that are protected by one set of human rights standards and those that are protected by another. Requiring a link to be established between the act of violence at issue and discriminatory intent in order to recognise that violence is an issue of human rights law narrows considerably the scope of application of human rights law and the protection available. Gender inequality alone may not be a significant

---

[247] *R. v. Immigration Appeal Tribunal and another, ex parte Shah; Islam and others v. Secretary of the State for the Home Department*, UK House of Lords [1999] 2 AC 629, [1999] 2 All ER 545, per Lord Hoffman (no paragraph number).

[248] *Ibid.* Article 1A(2), Convention relating to the Status of Refugees 1951, GA res. 429 (V), 14 December 1950, 189 UNTS 150; entered into force 22 April 1954 and Protocol relating to the Status of Refugees 1967, GA res. 2198(XXI), 16 December 1966, 606 UNTS 267; entered into force 4 October 1967.

[249] See, also, the experience in the US domestic courts under the Violence against Women Act, which required the courts to find a link between the violent conduct and discriminatory intent, in which results were mixed. Some of the lower courts had no problem making out the link by, for example, the defendant's use of sexist epithets, the fact that the crime involved unwanted sexual conduct, the presence of multiple female victims, and the use of violence to force women into a stereotypical submissive role: see, Goldfarb, 'Applying the Discrimination Model to Violence against Women', 262, n. 58 (for cases).

or relevant factor in each act of domestic or sexual violence, or at least, advocates may have trouble establishing that it is. In other words, describing such violence as 'gender violence' may be 'underinclusive because individual acts may be informed by other socio-political factors as well as [or instead of] gender'.[250] It also speaks to some feminist scholars who have resisted the priority or exclusiveness of gender over other identity-based factors, as discussed in Chapter 2.

It has been claimed that the rhetoric of an inequality paradigm can be a powerful one. However, in domestic jurisdictions where it has been applied, commentators have noted that many if not most of the reforms or responses to sexual and domestic violence target neither sex discrimination nor other socio-political factors.[251] In contrast, at the international level, there is some evidence to suggest that broader recommendations for social or cultural change are within the responses of the treaty bodies, whether in relation to individual cases or concluding observations on state party reports.

More problematic still is that the rhetoric of inequality is arguably weaker than the language of violence. The symbolism of language cannot be underestimated. Language has both legal and moral implications. It can serve to construct and reinforce patriarchal systems. Therefore, it is important to label an act appropriately in order to ensure an appropriate response. The language of inequality or sex discrimination has tended to be applied in the context of discrimination in relation to unequal access to work or unequal pay for work of equal or comparable value. At the level of national law, sex discrimination has therefore tended to be reserved for law suits of a civil or administrative nature, and it is possible under the discrimination paradigm for the discriminatory treatment to be inadvertent. This is to be compared with violence, which carries purposeful and usually criminal behaviour and sanction. Language can also dictate the remedies available: anti-discrimination laws usually impose financial penalties or compensation, whereas violence carries harsher criminal penalties of jail or, in some jurisdictions still, execution. These in turn reflect social values and attract societal disapproval. Generally, violence is condemned in society to an extent that discriminatory treatment against women is not, albeit violence against women is tolerated in ways that violence against others is not. This reality opens up three possibilities for advocacy. Either the use of the more powerful language (violence) should be encouraged, or a reinvigoration of the weaker language to apply it with

[250] Goldscheid, 'Domestic and Sexual Violence as Sex Discrimination', 360.
[251] Ibid., 362.

greater force (sex discrimination) should be advanced. Alternatively, an interim stage might also be suggested to utilise the language of discrimination until the language of violence is legally entrenched.

In other words, using sex discrimination in the context of violence requires one to travel across disparate legal (and moral) regimes. Although inequality and discrimination may be the root cause of some forms of violence (for example, in criminal law it may be seen as an aggravating factor, such as crimes of incitement to racial hatred or genocide), a violent act has nonetheless been committed. Utilising sex discrimination law merely because it is the only available remedy almost covers up the violence that has occurred or diminishes the extent of the conduct. Similar questions in relation to framing violence as torture are raised in Chapter 5. There is something counter-intuitive about calling violent conduct discrimination rather than violence itself. Because there is a broad spectrum of discriminatory conduct – from unequal pay to unfair dismissal to denial of financial loans or access to pensions on an equal basis – labelling rape as a form of discrimination, for example, may diminish the harm or the rights violation at issue, in the eyes of the victim as well as in respect of the state's responsibility for it. Discrimination against women has been long tolerated in many societies, even when laws have been enacted to outlaw it. The language of violence conjures up, rightly or wrongly, a different calibre of violation. The problem of language and perception also raises the question of whether the prohibition against sex discrimination is being asked to do too much. As it has not yet been able to deliver in a few fundamental areas so far, it seems ambitious to be asking it to also rid the world of systemic violence against women, without additional guarantees.

Finally, and most alarmingly, the VAW = SD strategy results in the unequal treatment of men and women under international law. This is the central thesis of this book. The formula does not class violence against women as prohibited conduct per se. In particular this is to be contrasted to the ICERD, which contains an express prohibition on racially motivated violence.[252] Female victims of violence, whatever its form or manifestation, are protected by international human rights law only to the extent that they can establish that the violence is discriminatory or otherwise fits within another provision.[253] That is, they are protected indirectly, not directly; even worse still if the violence occurs in private. In the case of so-called 'private' violence, women face double indirect protection (or discrimination) because a woman will have to establish first that she has suffered discriminatory violence (rather than violence per se) and second,

---

[252] Article 5(b), ICERD.   [253] See, Chapters 5 and 6.

she will have to show that the state is responsible for that violence owing to its failures in due diligence, which may or may not be due to discrimination. Although there is no jurisprudence on this issue under international human rights law, at least one link to discrimination ought to be sufficient.[254]

In contrast, violence that disproportionately affects men is not burdened with an additional link to sex discrimination or any other additional factors. While it has been argued in feminist academic circles that rape of women, for example, is always discriminatory (because women are at risk of rape owing to gendered assumptions and stereotypes concerning the value and worth of women and because of women's oppression in society at large),[255] this view is far more difficult to prove through empirical evidence in individual cases in courts of law, as cases under international criminal law and international refugee law outlined above demonstrate. At times, it is the failure of prosecutions that can be attributed to discriminatory social attitudes to women, rather than necessarily the violence at issue in those cases. Moreover, no other area of international human rights law defines the act in question by its cause. Sex discrimination and inequality between men and women may be a root cause of violence against women, but they are not violence per se.

Of course, all this may turn on the meaning given to inequality. If one of the approaches of Mahoney, Young, or MacKinnon were adopted – discrimination as disadvantage, oppression, or hierarchy – then it may be easier to cast rape per se, for example, as discriminatory treatment. Rape, for example, is after all about the exertion of power over a victim; it is not about sexual intercourse; and thus rape could be conceived as simply playing out the unequal relations of power between women and men in society at large. Nonetheless, whatever legal arguments are employed

---

[254] This is the approach advocated under international refugee law by the United Nations High Commissioner for Refugees in so far as linking the persecution at issue to a form of gender-related discrimination: either the violent act was perpetrated for discriminatory purposes, or failing that, the state failed to protect the woman against such violence on a discriminatory basis (i.e. indirect discrimination). On either basis, the nexus or link to discrimination and therefore to a prohibited ground of persecution is established for the purposes of granting refugee status: see, UNHCR, *Guidelines on International Protection No. 1: Gender-Related Persecution within the Context of Article 1A(2) of the 1951 Convention and/or 1967 Protocol relating to the Status of Refugees*, UN Doc. HCR/GIP/02/01, 7 May 2001, para. 21.

[255] Judith Gardam has stated in the context of armed conflict that 'in one sense rape is never truly individual but is an integral part of the system of ensuring the maintenance of the subordination of women': J. G. Gardam, 'The Law of Armed Conflict: A Gendered Regime?', in D. G. Dallmeyer (ed.), *Reconceiving Reality: Women and International Law* (American Society of International Law, 1993) 171, at 174.

(many of them entirely legally workable), it does not get around the fact that women are required to engage in additional legal reasoning for acts of violence to be considered worthy of international legal attention, and this perpetuates the unequal treatment of women before the law.

E   Conclusion

Settling the meaning and content of the fundamental principles of equality and non-discrimination on the basis of sex remains one of the greatest challenges for international human rights law. This chapter has shown that the approach of international law to equality has shifted from a strict liberal (and literal) interpretation of non-discrimination that was envisaged under the UN Charter, to the inclusion of ideas of substantive equality, which are now generally accepted components of equality law. Moreover, women's equality is a far more prominent feature on the international human rights agenda than it has ever been. These advances are, however, still undermined by the usage of gender-charged criteria of exception, such as reasonableness and objectivity, and these in turn reinforce sexual hierarchies. Add to this the continuing emphasis on identifying an appropriate comparator, which may be artificial or non-existent in reality. The first half of this chapter points to a system that continues to struggle with interpreting and applying these concepts, in particular because they remain tied to a sameness/difference ideology, and this has knock-on effects for attempting to protect women from violence under a sex discrimination framework.

The meaning of discrimination is also problematic as early definitions that had intent as an element in characterising a policy or practice as discriminatory have generally been discarded. Generally this is a positive advancement, except that a sexist intent of an individual perpetrator might, for instance, be easier to establish in a given case than trying to claim that the entire social or cultural system of a particular society is discriminatory (whether because women are treated differently to men or because it is a sexually oppressive regime); and it will become increasingly difficult to do so as societies improve their performance on the human rights of women, leaving many individual women arguably without redress – their violations may in time become reduced once again to individual aberrations rather than real grievances. It will also arguably lead to a situation in which women may be treated differently by the treaty bodies depending on which society they live in. It is acknowledged that the Women's Committee has at least adopted an individual assessment in its cases of domestic violence, asking whether the police in the case at hand should have responded to the request for assistance. The Women's Committee has avoided the larger question about whether the system in question is discriminatory as a whole (unlike the European Court in *M. C. v. Bulgaria*, discussed next chapter), yet this is arguably what is required by the VAW=SD approach as the Women's Committee has no mandate over violence per se. Furthermore, the need to connect any act of violence to the state under international law requires that a discriminatory system exists, not just individual discriminatory acts. Herein lies the public/private dilemma of international law and women's human rights.

What if the meaning of equality was framed within any of the three reconceptualisations outlined in this chapter? Would it make any real difference in the context of violence against women? All three proposals – oppression/domination, advantage/disadvantage, or lack of hierarchy – are strides ahead of the current approaches of the treaty bodies to discrimination and inequality generally, as they move away from comparisons between men and women to freedoms from gender straitjackets. They do not, however, seem to overcome the difficulties of applying them in practice in the context of violence against women. Ideas of oppression/domination, advantage/disadvantage, and lack of hierarchy are also complex concepts. In addition, they too add an additional layer of proof for individual complainants. Not only does a woman need to establish that she has been raped, she also needs to prove that the rape was discriminatory, however that discrimination is conceived. Such an additional layer of analysis is not applied to men in relation to violence that disproportionately affects them, and thus contributes to the unequal protection of women before the law.

Each three of the approaches also relegates women to positions of disadvantage in perpetuity in so far as oppression, disadvantage, and hierarchy are framed as static or permanent features of society. What do we do when widespread discrimination in society cannot be easily identified, yet women continue to be beaten in their homes and harassed in their workplaces? Finally, the link between discrimination and violence, however discrimination is recast, does not get away from the fact that there is a separation between the act (the violence) and the cause (discrimination or disadvantage). In no other area of international human rights law is the cause built into the prohibition, and in doing so, the violence suffered by women is 'exceptionalised'.

In the next chapter, I explore the second case example of this book by examining whether characterising violence against women as torture or another form of cruel, inhuman, or degrading treatment or punishment is an effective feminist strategy.

Torture and other cruel, inhuman, or degrading treatment or punishment

A   Introduction

The prohibition against torture and other cruel, inhuman, or degrading treatment or punishment has attracted considerable feminist attention. This chapter is concerned with the interpretation and application of the prohibition against torture under international law to apply to women's experiences of violence (or VAW = T). I begin with an overview of how torture and other forms of cruel, inhuman, or degrading treatment or punishment have been understood generally under international law, before moving on to consider interpretations championed by some feminist scholars and women's rights activists and taken up by the treaty bodies to incorporate violence against women into the torture prohibition.

This chapter finds that the interpretation and application of the torture prohibition to women's concerns has been mixed. As a feminist strategy that benefits from the symbolism of a peremptory norm of international law, it has its advantages. In particular, it puts rape, sexual violence, and other forms of violence against women onto the international agenda. However, it also feeds into and reinforces existing structures and dialogue. Absent an international prohibition against violence against women, women and their advocates have attempted to use the torture prohibition to protect them from various forms of violence. One way this has been achieved is by equating their experiences of violence to that of torture – whether in nature, seriousness, or the identity of the perpetrator. In reality, there may be no exact equivalent. Furthermore, fitting violence against women within the criteria of the torture prohibition subjects women and their advocates to an additional layer of analysis: they must first substantiate that they have been raped *and then* that that rape amounts to torture, or alternatively that any distinctions in their treatment compared to the norm (read: male) justifies the creation of an exception to the rule. Under the VAW = T approach, rape and other forms of violence against women are not prohibited conduct per se. The consequence of this approach is that women are treated unequally under international law.

B   Torture and other cruel, inhuman, or degrading treatment or punishment under international law

1   International instruments

Ranked among the most important human rights provisions and as a *jus cogens* norm of customary international law, the first modern prohibition against torture is found in Article 5 of the Universal Declaration of Human Rights 1948 (UDHR).[1] Article 5 provides:

> No one shall be subjected to torture or to cruel, inhuman or degrading treatment or punishment.

This prohibition is replicated in Article 7 of the International Covenant on Civil and Political Rights 1966 (ICCPR),[2] with an additional phrase prohibiting non-consensual medical and scientific experimentation. Article 7 of the ICCPR provides:

> No one shall be subjected to torture or to cruel, inhuman or degrading treatment or punishment. In particular, no one shall be subjected without his [or her] free consent to medical or scientific experimentation.

Article 7 is an absolute right; no restrictions are permitted.[3] Its status as a fundamental right or *jus cogens* norm of international law is widely accepted, even though the exact meaning given to its terms has yet to be fully resolved and is constantly evolving.

Amid concern that the incidence of torture was increasing as a tool of repression against political opponents in many autocratic regimes throughout the world,[4] the UN General Assembly issued a Declaration on the Protection of All Persons from Being Subjected to Torture and Other Cruel, Inhuman or Degrading Treatment or Punishment

---

[1] Universal Declaration of Human Rights 1948, GA res. 217 A (III), 10 December 1948 (UDHR).

[2] International Covenant on Civil and Political Rights 1966, GA res. 2200A (XXI), 16 December 1966, 999 UNTS 171; entered into force 23 March 1976 (ICCPR).

[3] Article 4(2), ICCPR.

[4] For a summary of the lead-up to the creation of the United Nations Convention against Torture and Other Cruel, Inhuman or Degrading Treatment or Punishment 1984 (UNCAT), *infra* see: J. H. Burgers and H. Danelius, *The United Nations Convention against Torture: A Handbook on the Convention against Torture and Other Cruel, Inhuman or*

in 1975[5] (1975 Declaration on Torture). The 1975 Declaration on Torture asserted that 'every act of torture is a grave offence against human dignity'.[6] Shortly afterwards, in 1977, the General Assembly formally requested the Commission on Human Rights to draft the text of a binding treaty based on the 1975 Declaration on Torture. The drafting of an explicit treaty soon took shape, with its unanimous acceptance by the General Assembly in March 1984.[7] The UN Convention against Torture and Other Cruel, Inhuman or Degrading Treatment or Punishment 1984 (UNCAT)[8] hoped to 'achiev[e] a more effective implementation of the existing prohibition under international and national law ...'[9] Article 7 of the ICCPR had been unable on its own to halt the alarming practices of some governments.

Following the 1975 Declaration on Torture definition, Article 1 of the UNCAT defines 'torture' as:

1. For the purposes of this Convention, the term 'torture' means any act by which severe pain or suffering, whether physical or mental, is intentionally inflicted on a person for such purposes as obtaining from him [or her] or a third person information or a confession, punishing him [or her] for an act he [or she] or a third person has committed or is suspected of having committed, or intimidating or coercing him [or her] or a third person, or for any reason based on discrimination of any kind, when such pain or suffering is inflicted by or at the instigation of or with the consent or acquiescence of a public official or other person acting in an official capacity. It does not include pain or suffering arising only from, inherent in or incidental to lawful sanctions.

2. This article is without prejudice to any international instrument or national legislation which does or may contain provisions of a wider application.

It is one of few international human rights instruments that provide a definition of 'torture'.[10] Article 16 of the UNCAT contains a

---

Degrading Treatment or Punishment (The Hague: Martinus Nijhoff Publishers, 1988), 13–15.

[5] United Nations Declaration on the Protection of All Persons from Being Subjected to Torture and Other Cruel, Inhuman or Degrading Treatment or Punishment 1975, GA res. 3452 (XXX), 9 December 1975 (UN Declaration on Torture).

[6] Article 2, UN Declaration on Torture 1975.

[7] M. Nowak and E. McArthur, *The United Nations Convention against Torture: A Commentary* (Oxford University Press, 2008), 3.

[8] United Nations Convention against Torture and Other Cruel, Inhumane or Degrading Treatment or Punishment 1984, GA res. 39/46, 10 December 1984, 1465 UNTS 85; entered into force 26 June 1987 (UNCAT).

[9] Preambular para. 5, UNCAT.

[10] Other instruments that include a specific definition of 'torture' include the 1975 Declaration on Torture; Article 2 of the Inter-American Convention to Prevent and to Punish Torture

separate definition of 'cruel, inhuman or degrading treatment or punishment' as:

1. Each State Party shall undertake to prevent in any territory under its jurisdiction other acts of cruel, inhuman or degrading treatment or punishment which do not amount to torture as defined in article 1, when such acts are committed by or at the instigation of or with the consent or acquiescence of a public official or other person acting in an official capacity. In particular, the obligations in articles 10, 11, 12 and 13 shall apply with the substitution for references to torture of references to other forms of cruel, inhuman or degrading treatment or punishment.

2. The provisions of this Convention are without prejudice to the provisions of any other international instrument or national law which prohibits cruel, inhuman or degrading treatment or punishment or which relates to extradition or expulsion.

Apart from a lower severity threshold, the main distinction between the two definitions in the UNCAT is that the purpose requirement is missing from the definition of cruel, inhuman, or degrading treatment or punishment.[11] The removal of the purpose element has the effect of broadening the types of scenarios that may fall under the heading of cruel, inhuman, or degrading treatment or punishment rather than torture; yet they share the state custody component.

In addition to offering definitions of relevant terms, the UNCAT outlines a range of obligations imposed upon states parties; it clarifies some that were already associated with the prohibition under international law,

1985 (adopted at the Fifteenth Regular Session of the OAS General Assembly at Cartagena De Indias, Colombia, 9 December 1985, OAS Treaty Series No. 67, entered into force 28 February 1987, reprinted in Basic Documents Pertaining to Human Rights in the Inter-American System, OEA/Ser.L.V/II.82 doc.6 rev.1 at 83 (1992)); and Article7(2)(e) of the Statute of the International Criminal Court (UN Doc. A/CONF.183/9, 17 July 1998, 2187 UNTS 90; entered into force 1 July 2002) (Rome Statute of the ICC). The Inter-American Convention defines 'torture' as: 'For the purposes of this Convention, torture shall be understood to be any act intentionally performed whereby physical or mental pain or suffering is inflicted on a person for purposes of criminal investigation, as a means of intimidation, as personal punishment, as a preventive measure, as a penalty, or for any other purpose. Torture shall also be understood to be the use of methods upon a person intended to obliterate the personality of the victim or to diminish his physical or mental capacities, even if they do not cause physical pain or mental anguish. The concept of torture shall not include physical or mental pain or suffering that is inherent in or solely the consequence of lawful measures, provided that they do not include the performance of the acts or use of the methods referred to in this article.' The Statute of the ICC defines 'torture' in Article 7(1)(e) as 'the intentional infliction of severe pain or suffering, whether physical or mental, upon a person in the custody or under the control of the accused; except that torture shall not include pain or suffering arising only from, inherent in or incidental to, lawful sanctions.'

[11] CAT, General Comment No. 2: Implementation of Article 2 by States Parties (2004), UN Doc. CAT/C/GC/2, 24 January 2008, para. 10.

while it codifies others. The overarching obligation upon states parties is to 'take effective legislative, administrative, judicial or other measures to prevent acts of torture in any territory under its jurisdiction'.[12] Specifically, this includes:

- the creation and prosecution of offences of torture under domestic criminal law and the extradition of alleged offenders where necessary;[13]
- the inclusion of education and information on torture in the training of law-enforcement personnel, civil or military personnel, medical personnel, public officials, or other persons who may be involved in the custody, interrogation, or treatment of any arrested, detained, or imprisoned individuals;[14]
- the conduct of systematic reviews of interrogation rules, instructions, methods, and practices;[15]
- prompt and impartial investigations;[16]
- the establishment of complaints procedures for alleged victims, and prompt and impartial examinations of such complaints by competent authorities;[17]
- provision of redress mechanisms within the legal system and an enforceable right to fair and adequate compensation, including full rehabilitation for victims or, where death results from torture, the entitlement of dependants to compensation;[18]
- safeguards against the admission of any statements made as a result of torture as evidence in any proceedings.[19]

One of the fundamental guarantees of the UNCAT is its inclusion of an explicit protection against expulsion, refoulement, or extradition where there are substantial grounds for believing that a person would be in danger of being subjected to torture.[20] The majority of decisions before the Committee against Torture (CAT) has involved Article 3 of the UNCAT.[21]

Although most of the above-listed obligations are drafted as to apply to torture, Article 16 of the UNCAT specifically notes that obligations

---

[12] Article 2(1), UNCAT.   [13] Articles 4–9, UNCAT.   [14] Article 10, UNCAT.
[15] Article 11, UNCAT.   [16] Article 12, UNCAT.   [17] Article 13, UNCAT.
[18] Article 14, UNCAT.   [19] Article 15, UNCAT.   [20] Article 3, UNCAT.
[21] Office of the High Commissioner for Human Rights (OHCHR), *Combating Torture*, Fact Sheet No. 4/Rev.1 (undated), 14.

arising under Articles 10, 11, 12, and 13 also apply to acts short of torture. This does not mean, however, that other obligations do not also arise with respect to cruel, inhuman, or degrading treatment or punishment. The use of the term 'in particular' in Article 16 indicates that the list of provisions was not intended to be exhaustive. No agreement could be reached during the drafting, however, on whether Articles 3 (non-refoulement), 14 (right to compensation), and 15 (prohibition against the use of statements in evidence) should also apply to Article 16 abuses.[22] In a 2008 General Comment the CAT clarified that the other provisions should also apply as a general principle to lesser forms of ill-treatment,[23] although its jurisprudence indicates that the Article 3 non-refoulement guarantee applies only to torture as defined in Article 1.[24] This is contrary to the view taken by the Human Rights Committee (HRC) in respect of Article 7[25] as well as those of several regional human rights institutions.[26]

Like Article 7 of the ICCPR, torture under the UNCAT is a non-derogable right. The strong language of Article 2(2) of the UNCAT reads: 'No exceptional circumstances whatsoever, whether a state of war or a threat of war, internal political instability or any other public emergency, may be invoked as justification of torture.' The non-derogable status is not expressly applied to cruel, inhuman, or degrading treatment or punishment. Article 2(3) further clarifies that superior orders may not be invoked as a justification for acts of torture.

Versions of the prohibition against torture are also found in the UN Convention on the Rights of the Child 1989 (CRC),[27] the Convention

---

[22] UN Doc. HRXXXVI/WG.10/Wp.5/Rev.1. See, also, Burgers and Danelius, *The United Nations Convention against Torture*, 70–71.

[23] CAT, General Comment No. 2: Implementation of Article 2 by States Parties, para. 3.

[24] CAT, General Comment No.1: Implementation of Article 3 of the Convention in the Context of Article 22 (1997), UN Doc. A/53/44, Annex IX, 21 November 1997.

[25] HRC, General Comment No. 31: The Nature of the General Legal Obligation Imposed on States Parties to the Covenant (Article 2) (2004), para. 12, which clarifies that an obligation not to extradite, deport, expel, or otherwise remove a person from their territory exists under Article 7 of the ICCPR where there are substantial grounds for believing that there is a real risk of irreparable harm in either the country of removal or any other country to which the person may be subsequently removed.

[26] See, e.g., *Bulus* v. *Sweden*, ECmHR, Applic. No. 9330/81 (8 December 1984); *X* v. *Belgium*, ECmHR, Applic. No. 984/61 (29 May 1961); *X* v. *Switzerland*, ECmHR, Applic. No. 9012/80 (1980); *Soering* v. *United Kingdom* (1989) 11 EHRR 439, para. 91. For more details, see, D. J. Harris, M. O'Boyle and C. Warbrick, *Law of the European Convention on Human Rights* (London: Butterworths, 1995), 74–78.

[27] Articles 37 and 39, Convention on the Rights of the Child 1989, GA res. 44/25, 20 November 1989, 1577 UNTS 3; entered into force 2 September 1990 (CRC).

on the Rights of Persons with Disabilities 2006 (ICRPD),[28] all the major regional human rights treaties,[29] the 1949 Geneva Conventions,[30] the treaties establishing the various international criminal tribunals,[31] and the Statute of the International Criminal Court 1998.[32] To further strengthen the anti-torture regime, an Optional Protocol to the Convention against Torture (OP-CAT) was agreed in 2002.[33] Its aim is preventive in nature, through the establishment of an international Sub-Committee on the Prevention of Torture, which has a mandate to make unannounced visits to places of detention. It also requires states parties to form or designate complementary national preventive mechanisms.[34] There are also a large number of soft law instruments that regulate the torture prohibition.[35]

---

[28] Article 15, Convention on the Rights of Persons with Disabilities 2006, GA res. 61/106, 13 December 2006; entered into force 3 May 2008 (ICRPD).

[29] Article 3, European Convention on the Protection of Human Rights and Fundamental Freedoms 1950, 4 November 1950, 213 UNTS 222; entered into force 3 September 1953, as amended (ECHR); Article 5(2), American Convention on Human Rights 1969, 22 November 1969, OAS Treaty Series No. 36, 1144 UNTS 123; entered into force 18 July 1978 (ACHR); Article 5, African Charter on Human and Peoples' Rights 1981, 27 June 1981, OAU Doc. CAB/LEG/67/3 rev. 5, 21 ILM 58; entered into force 21 October 1986 (ACHPR).

[30] Articles 3(1)(a) and (c), 27, 29, 31, and 147, Geneva Convention (IV) relative to the Protection of Civilian Persons in Time of War, adopted 12 August 1949, 75 UNTS 287; entered into force 21 October 1950.

[31] E.g., Articles 2(b) and (c), 5(f) and (i), Statute of the International Tribunal for the Prosecution of Persons Responsible for Serious Violations of International Humanitarian Law Committed in the Territory of the Former Yugoslavia since 1991, SC res. S/RES/827, 25 May 1993; Articles 3(f) and (i), 4(a) and (e), Statute of the International Criminal Tribunal for the Prosecution of Persons Responsible for Genocide and Other Serious Violations of International Humanitarian Law Committed in the Territory of Rwanda and Rwandan Citizens Responsible for Genocide and Other Such Violations Committed in the Territory of Neighbouring States, between 1 January 1994 and 31 December 1994, SC res. S/RES/955, 8 November 1994, 33 ILM 1598, 1600 (1994).

[32] Articles 7(1)(f) and 8(2)(a)(ii), (b)(xxi) and (c), Rome Statute of the International Criminal Court, UN Doc. A/CONF.183/9, 17 July 1998, 2187 UNTS 90; entered into force 1 July 2002.

[33] Optional Protocol to the Convention against Torture and Other Cruel, Inhuman or Degrading Treatment or Punishment, GA res. A/RES/57/199, 18 December 2002, 42 ILM 26 (2003) (OP-CAT).

[34] For more on the OP-CAT, see M. D. Evans, 'Getting to Grips with Torture' (2002) 51 *ICLQ* 365; M. Evans and C. Haenni-Dale, 'Preventing Torture? The Development of the Optional Protocol to the UN Convention Against Torture' (2004) 4 *Hum. Rts. L. Rev.* 19; Nowak and McArthur, *The United Nations Convention against Torture: A Commentary*, 879–1191.

[35] See, e.g., Standard Minimum Rules for the Treatment of Prisoners 1955, adopted by the first UN Congress on the Prevention of Crime and the Treatment of Offenders and approved by ECOSOC res. 663 C (XXIV), 31 July 1957 and res. 2076 (LXII), 13

The definition of torture as applied by the UN treaty bodies has been influenced by developments in these other fields.

A torture prohibition is not included in the International Covenant on Economic, Social and Cultural Rights 1966 (ICESCR),[36] the Convention on the Elimination of All Forms of Discrimination against Women 1979 (CEDAW),[37] the International Convention on the Elimination of All Forms of Racial Discrimination 1965 (ICERD),[38] or the International Convention on the Protection of the Rights of All Migrant Workers and Members of their Families 1990 (IMWC)[39]

2   International jurisprudence: traditional constructs of torture

Articulating the meaning of 'torture' and other forms of inhuman treatment under international law continues to be one of the greatest juridical challenges for the UN treaty bodies, and other international courts and tribunals. Although it is agreed that torture is inherently undesirable, the UN treaty bodies have had difficulty defining it and, where a definition

May 1977; Code of Conduct for Law Enforcement Officials 1979, GA res. 34/169, 17 December 1979; Principles of Medical Ethics relevant to the Role of Health Personnel, particularly Physicians, in the Protection of Prisoners and Detainees against Torture and Other Cruel, Inhuman or Degrading Treatment or Punishment 1982, GA res. 37/194, 18 December 1982. Other instruments have followed the general scope of the UNCAT, namely the Body of Principles for the Protection of All Persons under Any Form of Detention or Imprisonment 1988, GA res. 43/173, 9 December 1988; Basic Principles on the Use of Force and Firearms by Law Enforcement Officials 1990, adopted by the eighth UN Congress on the Prevention of Crime and the Treatment of Offenders, Havana, Cuba, 7 September 1990; Basic Principles for the Treatment of Prisoners 1990, GA res. 45/111, 14 December 1990; Manual and Principles on the Effective Investigation and Documentation of Torture and Other Cruel, Inhuman or Degrading Treatment or Punishment 1999 ('the Istanbul Protocol'), produced by a coalition of forty organisations and institutions. The Principles are annexed to GA res. 55/89, encouraging states to 'reflect on the Principles as a useful tool in efforts to combat torture' (para. 3).

[36] International Covenant on Economic, Social and Cultural Rights 1966, GA res. 2200A (XXI), 16 December 1966, 993 UNTS 3; entered into force 3 January 1976 (ICESCR).

[37] Convention on the Elimination of All Forms of Discrimination against Women 1979, GA res. 34/180, 18 December 1979, 1249 UNTS 13; entered into force 3 September 1981 (CEDAW).

[38] International Convention on the Elimination of All Forms of Racial Discrimination 1965, GA res. 2106 (XX), 21 December 1965, 660 UNTS 195; entered into force 4 January 1969 (ICERD). The ICERD does, however, contain a prohibition on violence generally, see Articles 4(a) (legislation) and 5(b).

[39] International Convention on the Protection of the Rights of All Migrant Workers and Members of Their Families 1990, GA res. 45/148, 18 December 1990, 2220 UNTS 93; entered into force 1 July 2003 (IMWC).

exists, applying it in practice. Despite the substantial convergence in meaning between the views of the CAT and the HRC, they are autonomous bodies, governed by separate treaties, and being free to adopt their own variations on the term, they have done so. This section of the study sets out early constructions of torture, and the subsequent section outlines the main feminist critiques of these constructions.

Four elements of the torture prohibition can be distilled from the early jurisprudence concerning Article 7 of the ICCPR and Article 1 of the UNCAT. These elements are that the harm must be of a serious nature, whether physical or mental; intentionally inflicted; for a purpose related to interrogation, confession, or arrest; and committed by an official or another person acting in an official capacity, or with his/her consent or acquiescence. First and foremost, the torture prohibition under international law was initially taken as applying to serious pain or suffering inflicted by government or public officials within the context of state custody for the purposes of interrogation, arrest, or related reasons. The 1973 draft resolution that called on the General Assembly to examine the question of torture was framed 'in relation to detention and imprisonment'.[40] This resolution, and the political environment in which it was promoted, set the scene for the scope of the discussions on the UNCAT, limiting the meaning of 'torture' to harmful conduct perpetrated within the context of detention and imprisonment.[41] This was the most commonly accepted understanding of torture at that time (and arguably continues today), including under Article 7 of the ICCPR. The application of the torture prohibition has, however, been extended to harmful acts carried out in teaching or medical institutions[42] and, as shown below, in some instances to violence outside the context of state custody.

The main challenge for jurists and decision-makers has been to determine what types of treatment would qualify as torture. The HRC's first

---

[40] GA res. 3059 (XXVIII), 2 November 1973.

[41] For commentary on the GA discussions and lead-up to the CAT, see N. S. Rodley, *The Treatment of Prisoners Under International Law* (2nd edn, Oxford: Clarendon Press, 1999), Chapter 1.

[42] HRC, General Comment No. 7: Torture or Cruel, Inhuman or Degrading Treatment or Punishment (Article 7) (1982), para. 2 (referred to corporal punishment, including excessive chastisement as an educational or disciplinary measure); HRC, General Comment No. 20: Torture and Cruel, Inhuman or Degrading Treatment or Punishment (Article 7) (1992), paras. 5, 10, and 11 (accepted that torture or ill-treatment or punishment may occur within teaching or medical institutions). See, further, *Higgins* v. *Jamaica*, HRC No. 792/1998 (28 March 2002) (imposition or execution of a sentence of whipping with a tamarind switch violated Article 7).

General Comment on Article 7 of the ICCPR stated that the purpose of Article 7 is to protect the 'integrity and dignity' of the individual.[43] The HRC has stated that the addition of 'cruel, inhuman or degrading treatment or punishment' extends the term 'torture' far beyond its normal meaning.[44] While frequently repeated verbatim by academic scholars to support or encourage a broad interpretation of the provision,[45] the HRC's statement is not entirely clear. Negotiating states to the ICCPR generally agreed that the word 'treatment' was broader in scope than the word 'punishment',[46] the latter referring specifically to disciplinary action. However, some states observed that the word 'treatment' should not be completely unlimited and, to that end, it should not apply to degrading situations that might be due to general economic and social factors.[47] Compared with other forms of ill-treatment, torture was accepted as being reserved for the most abhorrent acts.

The word 'torture' is generally understood as including both physical and mental harm.[48] What degree of severity would determine whether a particular act or omission would be included within the term was left aside during the drafting conference. Article 1 of the UNCAT makes clear that torture is to be reserved for the most severe forms of ill-treatment, and the general discussions at the time of drafting supported this view.[49] Nigel Rodley, former UN Special Rapporteur on Torture, has stated that it is 'virtually impossible' to sum up the issue of how severe or aggravated specific treatment has to be for it to amount to torture.[50] In its 2008 General Comment, the CAT acknowledged the overlap between the terms, noting

[43] HRC, General Comment No. 7: Torture or Cruel, Inhuman or Degrading Treatment or Punishment, para. 1.

[44] *Ibid.*, para. 2.

[45] See, e.g., A. Conte, 'Security of the Person', in A. Conte, S. Davidson and R. Burchill, *Defining Civil and Political Rights: The Jurisprudence of the United Nations Human Rights Committee* (Aldershot: Ashgate Publishing, 2004) 85, at 94.

[46] UN Doc. E/CN.4/SR.141, paras. 33 and 38 (Egypt), para. 37 (the Philippines), para. 39 Chairman), para. 41 (Lebanon). See, also, M. J. Bossuyt, *Guide to the 'Travaux Préparatoires' f the International Covenant on Civil and Political Rights* (Dordrecht: Martinus Nijhoff Publications, 1987), 150.

[47] UN Doc. E/CN.4/365 (the Philippines). See, also, Bossuyt, *Guide to the 'Travaux Préparatoires' of the ICCPR*, 150.

[48] UN Doc. E/CN.4/SR.149, paras. 33 and 38 (Egypt), para. 37 (the Philippines), para. 39 (Chairman), para. 41 (Lebanon). See, also, Bossuyt, *Guide to the 'Travaux Préparatoires' of the ICCPR*, 150. See, later, HRC, General Comment No. 20: Torture and Cruel, Inhuman or Degrading Treatment or Punishment, paras. 2 and 5.

[49] See, Burgers and Danelius, *The United Nations Convention against Torture.*

[50] Rodley, *The Treatment of Prisoners Under International Law*, 98.

that the 'definitional threshold between ill-treatment and torture is often not clear'.[51] Similarly, the HRC has not found it necessary to define or distinguish between the terms, although it has noted that any distinctions would depend on the 'nature, purpose and severity' of the particular act in question.[52] Navigating the boundaries between torture on the one hand and other forms of ill-treatment on the other has proven difficult for the treaty bodies, as it has for other human rights courts.

In order to avoid the boundaries between the terms, the HRC has simply discussed ill-treatment in a broad sense or declared that there has been a violation of Article 7 of the ICCPR without specifying which of its components are involved. Owing to the structure of the UNCAT, the CAT, in contrast, has been unable to get away with the same level of generality. With two separate provisions that impose slightly differing obligations on states parties (as noted above), the CAT has had to be more specific in its findings, especially under its communications procedure in relation to Article 3 obligations,[53] which has arguably narrowed its imaginative potential.

The traditional mainstay of the CAT's jurisprudence has included beatings, mock executions, solitary confinement, electric shocks, kicking, and threats of reprisals to family members.[54] Torture has been established

---

[51] CAT, General Comment No. 2: Implementation of Article 2 by States Parties, para. 3.

[52] HRC, General Comment No. 7: Torture or Cruel, Inhuman or Degrading Treatment or Punishment, para. 2. This is to be contrasted with the position of the European Commission and Court on Human Rights which have taken the view that the inclusion of three separate terms in Article 3 of the ECHR shows a clear intention to distinguish between them. See, *Ireland* v. *United Kingdom* (1978) 2 EHRR 25, para. 167. Article 3 of the ECHR provides: 'No one shall be subjected to torture or to inhuman or degrading treatment or punishment.'

[53] See, e.g., exacerbation of mental or physical health has been specifically rejected by the CAT as grounds to prevent deportation (*G. R. B.* v. *Sweden*, CAT 83/1997 (15 May 1998), para. 6.7); considerable hardship for an applicant caused by deportation to an area outside their region of origin and the 'mere fact that he may not be able to return to his family and his home village' was not held to amount to risk of torture protected by Article 3 (*B. S. S.* v. *Canada*, CAT 183/2001 (12 May 2004), para. 11.5); family separation did not amount to protection from refoulement under Article 3 (*M. V.* v. *The Netherlands*, CAT 201/2002 (2 May 2003); *Attia* v. *Sweden*, CAT 199/2002 (17 November 2003). This follows the position of the ECtHR in *Berrehab* v. *The Netherlands* (1988) 11 EHRR 322; *Moustaquim* v. *Belgium* (1991) 13 EHRR 802; *Beldjoudi* v. *France* (1992) 14 EHRR 801. However, the ECtHR has also permitted stays on deportation in situations of persons in the last stages of HIV/AIDS with limited medical facilities and family members in the country of origin: see, *N* v. *United Kingdom*, ECtHR, Applic. No. 26565/05 (27 May 2008).

[54] See, e.g., *A. R.* v. *The Netherlands*, CAT 203/2002 (14 November 2003); *M. O.* v. *Denmark*, CAT 209/2002 (12 November 2003); *A. D.* v. *The Netherlands*, CAT 96/1997 (12 November 1999).

before the HRC, either individually or cumulatively, in the form of systematic beatings, electric shocks, burns, repeated immersion in a mixture of water, blood, vomit, or excrement (referred to as 'submarino'), prolonged hanging from the hands (referred to as 'Palestinian hanging') and/or leg chains, standing for extended periods (referred to as 'planton'), simulated executions, and amputations.[55] The public official requirement has meant that such action has been perpetrated by government or public officials or other persons acting with official sanction, or with their consent or their acquiescence. Extended understandings of the terms are examined further below.

Thus, the intentions of the drafters of Article 7 of the ICCPR and Articles 1 and 16 of the UNCAT were to ban and take action against state-sponsored terror against political dissidents, and secondarily to the same types of harm perpetrated against non-political prisoners. The jurisprudence of the treaty bodies has largely kept this focus as the core meaning of the torture prohibition. The majority of individual communications under Article 7 of the ICCPR and under the UNCAT, for example, concern these traditional constructions of torture. In addition, the concurrent raising of Articles 7 and 10(1) (on humane treatment in detention) of the ICCPR reinforces this understanding. Article 10(1) of the ICCPR has been accepted as applying to less serious forms of treatment within detention.[56] The question at this juncture in the book is what these traditional or early applications of torture mean for women.

3 Feminist critiques of traditional constructs of torture

The main feminist critique of the original construction of the torture prohibition is that it has all the hallmarks of a 'gendered' prohibition. That is, the torture prohibition reflects and responds to the experiences of men rather than women. Traditionally conceived as a prohibition on physical assault perpetrated by public officials against political dissidents or

---

[55] See, e.g., *Motta* v. *Uruguay*, HRC 11/1977 (29 July 1980); *Burgos (submitted by Delia Saldias de Lopez)* v. *Uruguay*, HRC 52/1979 (29 July 1981); *Sendic* v. *Uruguay*, HRC 63/1979 (28 October 1981); *Estrella* v. *Uruguay*, HRC 74/1980 (29 March 1983); *Cariboni* v. *Uruguay*, HRC 159/1983 (27 October 1987); *Acosta* v. *Uruguay*, HRC 162/1983 (25 October 1988); *Rubio* v. *Colombia*, HRC 161/1983 (2 November 1987); *Peñarrieta* v. *Bolivia*, HRC 176/1984 (2 November 1987). See, also, S. Joseph, J. Schultz and M. Castan, *The International Covenant on Civil and Political Rights: Cases, Materials, and Commentary* (2nd edn, Oxford University Press, 2004), 213–214.

[56] Article 10(1), ICCPR provides: 'All persons deprived of their liberty shall be treated with humanity and with respect for the inherent dignity of the human person.'

common criminals, it fits within the 'male' paradigm of international law. The UNCAT, in particular, is cited as a prime example of the 'gendered' nature of international law precisely because, under its definition of torture, 'the severe pain or suffering' must be inflicted 'by a public official or other person acting in an official capacity' [my emphasis].[57] According to feminist scholars, women are more likely to suffer abuse at the hands of private citizens than by public officials, and thus such violations fall outside the protection of international law.[58] Put another way, the form of torture traditionally accepted as prohibited under international law involves a perpetrator – who is an official of the state, such as the police, the security forces, or the military – and a male victim – who is a political dissident or a prisoner of a common crime. If women are represented in the discourse at all, it is as the wives, mothers, or daughters of these victims. They are thus recognised under international law by virtue of their familial relationship with the victim rather than as autonomous actors. That is, women have historically gained access to the protective scope of the torture prohibition on male-defined and male-determined terms.

In the 1990s feminist scholars and women's rights activists began challenging the traditional view of torture in the context of the ethnically based conflict in the former Yugoslavia, and later in Rwanda. During the Balkans conflict, widespread and systematic rape and sexual violence against women were used deliberately as part of the military and political strategy intended to terrorise the other ethnic group. Calls were made to prosecute and punish those responsible for these crimes and to recognise rape and other forms of violence against women as torture (VAW = T). It is now widely documented that similar strategies have been pursued in many modern armed conflicts.[59]

According to Rhonda Copelon, there are two obstacles to the recognition of gender-based violence as torture under international law. The first is the role of the public/private dichotomy in international law, explained

---

[57] See, e.g., H. Charlesworth, C. Chinkin and S. Wright, 'Feminist Approaches to International Law' (1991) 85 *Amer. J. Int'l L.* 613, at 628–630; H. Charlesworth and C. Chinkin, 'The Gender of *Jus Cogens*' (1993) 15 *HRQ* 63; A. Byrnes, 'The Convention Against Torture', in K. D. Askin and D. M. Koenig (eds.), *Women and International Human Rights Law* (Ardsley, NY: Transnational Publishers Inc., 1999), Vol. 2, 183; C. A. MacKinnon, 'On Torture: A Feminist Perspective on Human Rights', in K. E. Mahoney and P. Mahoney (eds.), *Human Rights in the Twenty-First Century: A Global Challenge* (Dordrecht: Martinus Nijhoff, 1993) 21; R. Copelon, 'Recognizing the Egregious in the Everyday: Domestic Violence as Torture' (1994) 25 *Colum. Hum. Rts L. Rev.* 291.

[58] See, Chapter 2.

[59] See, e.g., the conflicts in Sierra Leone, Liberia, and the Democratic Republic of Congo in the 1990s and 2000s.

in Chapter 2; that is, the initial criterion that the state be the direct perpet-rator of the harm, for example, reinforces the public/private dichotomy to the extent that women are more likely to suffer violence at the hands of non-state actors in 'private' than from public officials in state custody. The purposive requirement in the UNCAT that the harm be inflicted for the purposes of extracting information or a confession reinforces this view. The second barrier to viewing rape as torture, according to Copelon, is the persistent trivialisation of violence against women, even to the point of not seeing or recognising domestic (or other forms of) violence against women as a form of violence.[60] In calling for the torture prohibition to apply to domestic and other forms of violence against women, Copelon asserts: '[W]hen stripped of privatization, sexism and sentimentality, pri-vate gender-based violence is no less grave than other forms of inhumane and subordinating official violence.'[61]

MacKinnon puts forward similar arguments. She argues that what distinguishes torture from domestic or sexual violence against women is that 'torture is done to men as well as to women'.[62] She refers to this as a 'double standard' – that is, torture is regarded as sufficiently serious to warrant international attention because it is done to men (as well as women), whereas there is less international attention paid to domestic or sexual violence because it is only or primarily a woman's problem.[63] Copelon agrees when she notes that 'history teaches us that there is an almost inevitable tendency for crimes that are seen simply or primar-ily as crimes against women to be treated as of secondary importance'.[64] This is evidenced, for example, in the near total lack of international prosecutions for rape or other forms of sexual violence after the First and Second World Wars.[65] In peacetime, this is reflected, for example, in the continuation of marriage as a defence against rape in many national statutes.[66]

Identifying control, intimidation, or elimination as the 'generally recognized' purposes of torture, MacKinnon argues that there is little

---

[60] Copelon, 'Recognizing the Egregious in the Everyday', 295–296.
[61] Ibid., 296. [62] MacKinnon, 'On Torture', 21. [63] Ibid.
[64] R. Copelon, 'Gender Crimes as War Crimes: Integrating Crimes against Women into International Criminal Law' (2000–2001) 46 McGill L. J. 217, at 234.
[65] One of the cited exceptions to this was the Dutch prosecution of Japanese soldiers in Indonesia for the crime of 'enforced prostitution' of Dutch (but not Indonesian) women: see, U. Dolgopol and S. Paranjape, Comfort Women, An Unfinished Ordeal: Report of a Mission (International Commission of Jurists, 1994), 135–137.
[66] See, e.g., CAT, Concluding observations on Cameroon, UN Doc. CAT/C/CR/31/6, 5 February 2004, para. 7.

difference between torture and rape or other forms of sexual violence.[67] Moreover, she does not reject the state nexus criterion required to establish torture. Rather, she argues that the state is not absent from the crimes committed against women: rape and other sexual violence are 'neither random nor individual' but 'defined by the distribution of power in society'.[68] She argues that the state is 'typically deeply and actively complicit in the abuses under discussion, collaborating in and condoning them'.[69] She claims that '[t]he abuse is systematic and known, the disregard is official and organized, and the effective governmental tolerance is a matter of law and policy'.[70]

Feminist activists and writers have harnessed the VAW = T school of thought owing to the status attached to torture under international law. Viewing rape as a form of torture, for instance, is thought to equate the severity of the assault with one of the most serious human rights violations. Hannah Pearce argues that doing so 'give[s] the crime specific symbolic significance that recognises it as an affront to personal integrity, rather than as a crime against honour or custom'.[71] MacKinnon similarly recommends relying on the 'recognized profile' of torture, partly because it carries with it effective legal sanctions and penalties.[72] Similar arguments have been framed in the context of rape and sexual violence as genocide. Katharine Franke, for example, has praised the Prosecutor and the International Criminal Tribunal for Rwanda (ICTR) for finding that rape in the Rwandan conflict constituted a form of genocide. She states:

> Rather than rely upon special laws that isolate rape and/or sexual assault as a privileged kind of injury … [the Tribunal] has chosen to tailor the construction of these crimes to the way in which sex-related violence figures in the physical or mental destruction of a people or person.[73]

In other words, some feminist scholars acknowledge the benefit of 'the rhetorical connection of rape to genocide' because it has brought attention to the pervasive extent of rape in war.[74] The same arguments are used in relation to rape as torture. In addition, it has been considered necessary to prevent the high-profile attention to rape (and other violence against

---

[67] MacKinnon, 'On Torture', 21.   [68] Ibid., 22.   [69] Ibid., 23.   [70] Ibid., 25.

[71] H. Pearce, 'An Examination of the International Understanding of Political Rape and the Significance of Labeling it Torture' (2002) 14 Int'l J. Ref. L. 534, at 540.

[72] MacKinnon, 'On Torture', 25.

[73] K. M. Franke, 'Putting Sex to Work' (1998) 75 Denver U. L. Rev. 1139, at 1177.

[74] For an overview of these views, see K. Engle, 'Feminism and Its (Dis) Contents: Criminalizing Wartime Rape in Bosnia and Herzegovina' (2005) 99 Am. J. Int'l L. 778, at 787.

women) from becoming a short-lived or 'fashionable' episode,[75] as rape as torture should always be treated as a 'violation of the highest order'.[76]

This inclusive approach has been challenged by other feminist scholars. Karen Engle, for instance, criticises the debates that emerged among feminist international legal scholars during and after the Yugoslav conflict in relation to rape and genocide. She argues that this discourse served to 'reify ethnic difference, diminish women's capacity to engage in sexual activity with the "enemy" during the war, and downplay the extent to which any but extraordinary women could be perpetrators in war'.[77] It might also be argued that focusing so heavily on rape and sexual violence results in debate that ignores the fact that women are subject to other forms of 'non-gendered' torture under its traditional construction. Women were, for example, among the first users of the individual communications procedures, alleging torture either on their own behalf or on behalf of other persons, including other women.[78] Nevertheless, Byrnes argues that, even under these traditional circumstances, the international provisions do not fully reflect the nature and extent of violations faced by women in the public sphere.[79] The VAW = T approach is further open to criticism for playing into the male-gendered international system by seeking to raise the profile of violence against women through equating the seriousness of the harm with male conceptions of torture rather than as grave human rights violations in their own right.

Clare McGlynn has questioned the merit of pursuing the feminist strategy of 'rape as torture' on two fronts. First, she argues that state complicity cannot extend to every rape. The difficulty of linking the state to any act of rape in question appears more punctuated in peacetime than in wartime, where in the latter, deliberate strategies targeting particular

---

[75] Pearce, 'An Examination of the International Understanding of Political Rape', 547.

[76] L. Kois, 'Dance, Sister, Dance!', in B. Duner (ed.), *An End to Torture: Strategies for its Eradication* (London: Zed Books, 1998) 90. It is worth noting that this push to use existing instruments to the advantage of women has arisen alongside calls for the creation of separate instruments addressing violence against women, but has so far only culminated in a General Assembly Declaration on the Elimination of Violence against Women, GA res. A/RES/48/104, 20 December 1993 (DEVAW).

[77] Engle, 'Feminism and Its (Dis)Contents', 784.

[78] See, e.g., *Massera et al. (including Moriana Hernandez Valentini de Bazzano) v. Uruguay*, HRC 5/1977 (15 August 1979); *Weissmann and Perdomo (including Ann Maria Garcia Lanza de Netto) v. Uruguay*, HRC 8/1977 (3 April 1980); *de Bouton v. Uruguay*, HRC 37/1978 (27 March 1981); *Burgos (submitted by Delia Saldias de Lopez) v. Uruguay*, HRC 52/1979 (29 July 1981); *Laureano v. Peru*, HRC 540/1993 (25 March 1996); *Arredondo v. Peru*, HRC 688/1996 (27 July 2000).

[79] Byrnes, 'The Convention Against Torture', 184.

women for sexual violence or a disregard that it is taking place may be identified. In peacetime, on the other hand, governments may pursue a range of policies and programmes to combat violence against women that may be entirely ineffective. While acknowledging that 'rape does happen because of gender inequalities', McGlynn additionally asserts that viewing rape as torture will have no effect on reducing the prevalence of the crime or on ensuring that more perpetrators are brought to justice.[80]

Second, McGlynn considers that the rhetoric of 'rape' is perhaps as powerful, if not more powerful, than that of 'torture'.[81] Likewise, in Chapter 4, I have argued that the language of 'violence' is perhaps more obvious and, therefore, may be more effective as a feminist strategy to combat violence against women than the 'weaker' language of sex discrimination. Many feminists agree that violence against women is a human rights violation, but where they disagree is in relation to the choice of provision and terminology. Contrary to McGlynn's approach of retaining the language of 'rape', I question whether 'rape' as a crime has gained the same status of abhorrence at a domestic level in any society as that attributed to torture at either a domestic or an international level. The symbolism of labelling an act as 'rape' is socially and culturally contingent. Precisely because it is a crime generally considered to be perpetrated against women, it has not attained the same status under domestic or international laws. Perversely, the same could be said of the language and practice of torture. Not every society objects to torture or comprehends its boundaries in the same way. Nonetheless, at the level of international law, torture has attained a particular peremptory status. Rape, on the other hand, is not an identifiable international crime or human rights violation in its own right. Other scholars have argued that strategies that include the language of both rape and torture ought to be pursued: 'There is a need to recognize the general – rape as torture – as well as the particular – rape as rape. An accurate classification of abuse is important not just to give victims a voice, not only to break down stereotypes and not merely to accurately record the picture.'[82]

Clearly, any effective feminist strategy must rely on terminology that invokes the most disapproval, and in the absence of an explicit prohibition on violence against women, women's rights activists are justified in

---

[80] C. McGlynn, 'Rape as "Torture"? Catharine MacKinnon and Questions of Feminist Strategy' (2008) 17 *Fem. Legal Stud.* 71, at 84.

[81] *Ibid.*, 78.

[82] S. Sivakumaran, 'Sexual Violence Against Men in Armed Conflict' (2007) 18 *Eur. J. Int'l L.* 253, at 257.

using the means at their disposal. However, the VAW = T approach is not without its problems in the context of violence against women.

One of the weaknesses of the VAW = T formula is that it is subject to the political environment in which it is posited. The VAW = T school of thought gained acceptance in the 1990s during a period in which the international community had moved its attention away from the auto-cratic regimes of the 1970s and 1980s to the wars in the former Yugoslavia and Rwanda, which were believed to be fought 'on and through women's bodies'.[83] Following the terrorist attacks carried out against the United States on 11 September 2001 and the 'war on terror' that followed, inter-national human rights law has been subject to a number of attempts at boundary redrawing in the counter-terrorism aftermath.[84] Within this dialogue, national and international discussions on what constitutes tor-ture have retreated to the traditional canon of acts perpetrated by gov-ernment (and in particular military) agents within custodial settings. Meanwhile, advances made by women's rights groups in attempting to get violence against women on the international radar by advocating rape as torture, whether perpetrated by state or non-state actors, have lost some momentum.[85] This reveals that tying the hopes of women's rights to trad-itional rights that were initially conceived to apply to a specific, 'male' set of circumstances is a strategy vulnerable to the peaks and troughs of the system of international relations as a whole.

Conversely, rejecting the VAW = T approach is risky, as doing so plays into the hands of those sceptics or so-called legal purists who argue that torture has a specific legal meaning and that it should not be 'watered

[83] See, C. Bunch, 'Transforming Human Rights from a Feminist Perspective', in J. Peters and A. Wolper (eds.), *Women's Rights, Human Rights: International Feminist Perspectives* (New York: Routledge, 1995) 11, at 15.

[84] One example is the challenge to the precedent in *Chahal* v. *United Kingdom* (1996) 23 EHRR 413 (15 November 1996), in which the Grand Chamber of the ECtHR held that there was an absolute prohibition against return to substantial risk of torture. This deci-sion was challenged unsuccessfully in the case of *Saadi* v. *Italy*, ECtHR, Applic. No. 37201/06 (28 February 2008), with the United Kingdom intervening to argue that there should be exceptions to the general position. Another challenge is still pending: *Ramzy* v. *The Netherlands*, ECtHR, Applic. No. 25424/05 (Admissibility decision 27 May 2008), with the UK intervening. See, also, D. Moeckli, '*Saadi v Italy*: The Rules of the Game Have *Not* Changed' (2008) 8 *Hum. Rts. L. Rev.* 534.

[85] See, e.g., H. Charlesworth, 'The Hidden Gender of International Law' (2002) 16 *Temple Int'l & Comp. L. J.* 93; H. Charlesworth and C. Chinkin, 'Editorial Comment: Sex, Gender, and September 11th' (2002) 96 *Amer. J. Int'l L.* 600; C. A. MacKinnon, 'Women's September 11th: Rethinking the International Law of Conflict', in C. A. MacKinnon, *Are Women Human? And Other International Dialogues* (Cambridge, MA: Harvard University Press, 2006) 259.

down' by reference to violence against women. Rejecting the inclusion of women's concerns within existing provisions leaves women outside the protection of the law.[86] For feminist strategists, this is a fine line to walk, and it highlights further obstacles that must be overcome in equating violence against women with torture.

Responding to feminist literature, women's activism, and international criminal jurisprudence,[87] the UN human rights treaty bodies have in principle adopted the pragmatic approach of equating violence against women with torture (VAW = T). Their practice has, however, been inconsistent and reveals some additional practical problems of this approach, which are discussed below.

C   Violence against women as torture: emerging interpretations

1   Typologies of violence against women as torture

Although slow to incorporate women's experiences of violence within the prohibition against torture and other cruel, inhuman, or degrading treatment or punishment, the HRC, and to a lesser extent the CAT, now do so as a matter of routine. Under Article 7 of the ICCPR, the HRC has condemned domestic violence,[88] rape and sexual violence, female genital mutilation,[89] clandestine abortions,[90] unequal treatment in relation to punishment for adultery, the failure to outlaw marital rape[91]

---

[86] See, also, H. Charlesworth, 'Alienating Oscar? Feminist Analysis of International Law', in D. G. Dallmeyer (ed.), *Reconceiving Reality: Women and International Law* (American Society of International Law, 1993) 1.

[87] For developments under international criminal law, see, R. C. Carpenter, *'Innocent Women and Children': Gender, Norms and the Protection of Civilians* (London: Ashgate, 2006); N. N. R. Quénivet, *Sexual Offenses in Armed Conflict & International Law* (Ardsley, NY: Transnational Publishers, 2005); J. G. Gardam and M. J. Jarvis, *Women, Armed Conflict and International Law* (The Hague: Kluwer Law International, 2001).

[88] See, e.g., HRC, Concluding observations on Sri Lanka (para. 20); Colombia (para. 14); Germany (para. 12); Lithuania (para. 9); Liechtenstein (para. 8); and Gambia (para. 16(c)): Report of the Human Rights Committee, UN Doc. A/59/40 (Vol. I) (2004).

[89] See, e.g., HRC Concluding observations on Uganda (para. 10): Report of the Human Rights Committee, UN Doc. A/59/40 (Vol. I) (2004); Mali (para. 11): Report of the Human Rights Committee, UN Doc. A/58/40 (Vol. I) (2003); Sweden (para. 8); Yemen (para. 6): Report of the Human Rights Committee, UN Doc. A/57/40 (Vol. I) (2002). In the 2003 report on Mali, the HRC called for the practice to be prohibited and criminalised.

[90] See, e.g., HRC, Concluding observations on Sri Lanka (para. 12); Colombia: Report of the Human Rights Committee, UN Doc. A/59/40 (Vol. I) (2004). Unsafe abortion has also been referred to in a number of states parties' reports under Article 6.

[91] See, e.g., HRC, Concluding observations on Sri Lanka (para. 20): Report of the Human Rights Committee, UN Doc. A/59/40 (Vol. I) (2004).

or levirate,[92] 'honour' crimes,[93] and early marriage.[94] The HRC has called upon states parties to ensure: that their justice systems incorporate restraining orders to protect women from violent family members; that shelters and other support are provided to victims; that measures are established to encourage women to report domestic violence to the authorities;[95] and that 'material and psychological relief to victims' is available.[96] The HRC has also referred to the particular issues facing women within state custody, including sexual violence against female prisoners.[97]

Similarly, the CAT has referred to many specific experiences of torture faced by women. It regularly 'expresses its concern' for sexual violence and assault against female detainees and prisoners by law-enforcement personnel,[98] which includes its use to extract information on the whereabouts of their husbands or other relatives.[99] It has raised the issue of inter-prisoner sexual assaults.[100] It has recommended to the USA, for example, that it take action to investigate, prosecute, and punish those who violate the torture prohibition, 'especially those who are motivated by discriminatory purposes or sexual gratification'.[101] The CAT has also expressed

[92] The HRC referred to Articles 3, 16 and 23 in relation to the practice of levirate in Mali: Report of the Human Rights Committee, UN Doc. A/58/40 (Vol. I) (2003). See, Chapter 4 for a definition of levirate.

[93] The HRC referred to so-called 'honour' crimes committed mostly against girls and women of foreign extraction in Sweden (para. 8) without identifying a particular ICCPR article: Report of the Human Rights Committee, UN Doc. A/57/40 (Vol. I) (2002).

[94] The HRC referred to Articles 3 and 26 in Sweden's report (para. 8): Report of the Human Rights Committee, UN Doc. A/57/40 (Vol. I) (2002).

[95] See, e.g., HRC, Concluding observations on Hungary (para. 10): Report of the Human Rights Committee, UN Doc. A/57/40 (Vol. I) (2002); Lithuania (para. 9): Report of the Human Rights Committee, UN Doc. A/59/40 (Vol. I) (2004).

[96] See, e.g., HRC, Concluding observations on Liechtenstein (para. 8): Report of the Human Rights Committee, UN Doc. A/59/40 (Vol. I) (2004).

[97] See, e.g., HRC, Concluding observations on the Philippines (para. 11): Report of the Human Rights Committee, UN Doc. A/59/40 (Vol. I) (2004), in which the HRC expressed concern for 'harassment, intimidation and abuse, including of detainees, many of whom are women and children, that have neither been investigated nor prosecuted'. See, also, concern over sexual abuse of female prisoners, Tanzania (para. 404): Report of the Human Rights Committee, UN Doc. A/53/40 (Vol. I) (1998).

[98] E.g. CAT, Concluding observations on the USA, contained in Report of Committee against Torture, UN Doc. A/55/44 (2000), para. 179.

[99] E.g. CAT, Concluding observations on Egypt, contained in Report of Committee against Torture, UN Doc. A/55/44 (2000), para. 209; Concluding observations on Tunisia, UN Doc. A/54/44 (1999), para. 99. The Special Rapporteur on Torture has recognised sexual violence as a method of physical torture, UN Doc. E/CN.4/1986/15, para. 119.

[100] E.g. CAT, Concluding observations on the Netherlands, UN Doc. A/55/44 (2000), para. 187.

[101] E.g., CAT, Concluding observations on the USA, contained in Report of Committee against Torture, UN Doc. A/55/44 (2000), para. 180.

concern over issues of female genital mutilation,[102] domestic violence,[103] and the sexual harassment of girls.[104] The CAT has focused on criminal laws, raising concern, for example, that the Cameroonian Criminal Code permits an exemption from punishment of a rapist if he subsequently marries the victim.[105] The CAT has congratulated the People's Republic of China and Hong Kong Special Administrative Region for 'increas[ing] sentences for certain sexual crimes, such as incest'.[106] The Committee has further praised moves by Georgia to prosecute and punish violence against women, thus suggesting that it falls generally within the remit of the UNCAT.[107]

In enumerating the above range of forms of violence against women, the committees acknowledge that these acts satisfy the severity threshold for findings of torture. That is, the committees accept in principle that these acts are as serious as traditional acts of torture or other forms of cruel, inhuman, or degrading treatment or punishment. Very little attention has been paid by the committees to differences in the severity of these violent acts, and how this may impact on whether a particular rape, for example, meets the torture threshold or a lesser form of ill-treatment. This issue is discussed further below. Additionally, in spite of the rhetoric, the committees have not always stayed attuned to gender factors in their decision-making (see below). There is very limited guidance offered by either committee to determine on what legal basis these forms of violence against women may be said to be relevant to the torture prohibition, or why they specifically meet the torture threshold. Providing reasoned arguments is an important step to legitimising the approach taken. Without it, accusations that the committees have gone beyond

---

[102] E.g., CAT, Concluding observations on Cameroon, UN Doc. CAT/C/CR/31/6, 5 February 2004, para. 7.

[103] E.g., CAT, Concluding Observations on Greece, UN Doc. CAT/C/CR/33/2, 10 December 2004, para. 5(k); Zambia, UN Doc. A/57/44, 25 August 2002, para. 7(c).

[104] E.g., CAT, Concluding observations on Greece, UN Doc. CAT/C/CR/33/2, 10 December 2004, para. 5(h); Egypt, UN Doc. CAT/C/CR/29/4, 23 December 2003, paras. 5(d) and (e).

[105] CAT, Concluding observations on Cameroon, UN Doc. CAT/C/CR/31/6, 5 February 2004, para. 7.

[106] CAT, Concluding observations on Peoples' Republic of China and Hong Kong Special Administrative Region, Report of the Committee against Torture, UN Doc. A/55/44 (2000), para. 136. On this, see further C. Lambert, 'Partial Sites and Partial Sightings: Women and the UN Human Rights Treaty System', in S. Pickering and C. Lambert (eds.), *Global Issues, Women and Justice* (Sydney: Sydney Institute of Criminology Series No. 19, 2004) 136.

[107] CAT, Concluding observations on Georgia, UN Doc. A/56/44, 7 May 2001, para. 2(j).

their respective mandates are more easily supported by those who object to the approach, including by states.

1.1 Rape and sexual violence

Of all the forms of violence against women, the issue of rape and sexual violence as torture has been given the most attention by international treaty bodies, courts, and tribunals. As noted above, this arose out of calls for the prosecution of persons responsible for the widespread and systematic rapes in the former Yugoslavia and Rwanda in the 1990s. A landmark decision, or at least the first decision of its kind, in terms of recognising women's claims of having been subjected to torture (and genocide) during wartime is that of *Prosecutor* v. *Jean-Paul Akayesu*.[108] The Trial Chamber of the ICTR ruled that, in certain circumstances, rape may constitute a form of torture for the purposes of criminal liability. The Trial Chamber stated:

> Like torture, rape is used for such purposes as intimidation, degradation, humiliation, discrimination, punishment, control or destruction of the person. Like torture, rape is a violation of personal dignity.[109]

Similar findings have been made by the International Criminal Tribunal for the former Yugoslavia (ICTY).[110] Although decided under the *lex specialis* of international criminal law and international criminal responsibility, the analogy between rape and torture is clear. A similar statement that equates rape with torture under human rights law is the case of *Raquel Martí de Mejía* v. *Peru*.[111] The Inter-American Commission on Human Rights (I-ACmHR) referred to both the physical as well as the mental suffering caused by the act of rape upon the applicant.[112] Additionally, the

---

[108] *Prosecutor* v. *Jean-Paul Akayesu*, ICTR, Case No. ICTR-96-4-T (2 September 1998); (Appeal), ICTR, Case No. ICTR-96-4-A (1 June 2001).

[109] *Ibid.*, para. 687.

[110] See, e.g., *Prosecutor* v. *Kunarac, Kovac and Vukovic*, ICTY, Case No. IT-96-23-T and IT-96-23/1-T, 22 February 2001; upheld on appeal, Case No. IT-96-23 and IT-96-23/1, 12 June 2002, paras. 482 and 496. The Trial Chamber found the three defendants guilty of torture, rape, and enslavement as both crimes against humanity and war crimes, pertaining to a 'rape camp' near Foca, a small Bosnian town southeast of Sarajevo, where they held women for many months and who were subjected to multiple rapes, including being 'sold' or 'rented out'.

[111] *Raquel Martí de Mejía* v. *Peru*, I-ACmHR, Case No. 10.970, Res. No. 5/96 (1 March 1996).

[112] Note, also, the case of *Loayza-Tamayo* v. *Peru*, in which the I-ACmHR accepted that the applicant had been raped and that this constituted inhumane treatment (*Loayza-Tamayo* v. *Peru*, I-ACmHR, Applic. No. 11154 (6 May 1993)), while the Court ruled that

I-ACmHR mentioned expressly the fact that rape can cause a woman to suffer 'public ostracism', stating:

> The fact of being made the subject of abuse of this nature [that is, rape] also causes a psychological trauma that results, on the one hand, from having been humiliated and victimized, and on the other, from suffering the condemnation of the members of their community if they report what has been done to them.[113]

In 1995 the I-ACmHR report on the human rights situation in Haiti specified that rape not only represents inhumane treatment that infringes upon physical and moral integrity, but that it is also a form of torture in the sense of Article 5(2) of the American Convention on Human Rights (ACHR).[114] Likewise, the Inter-American Court of Human Rights (I-ACtHR) in its judgment in the Castro-Castro Prison case accepted that a range of gender-related crimes committed against women amounted to inhumane treatment.[115] Relying in part on the Inter-American Convention on the Prevention, Punishment and Eradication of Violence against Women (IA-VAW),[116] the I-ACtHR stated, in particular, that digital penetration of female prisoners by male guards amounted to vaginal rape, and further that it was 'an especially gross and reprehensible act, taking into account the victim's vulnerability and the abuse of power displayed by the agent'.[117] Surprisingly, in the 2009 decision of *González et al*

---

the accusation of rape could not be substantiated given the evidence (*Loayza-Tamayo v. Peru*, I-ACtHR, Ser. C, No. 33 (17 September 1997)). This case is interesting as the I-ACtHR was prepared to accept other evidence relating to incommunicado detention, solitary confinement, intimidation with threats of further violence, etc. but not in relation to the rape (para. 58). It is thus arguable that a different level of proof was expected for an accusation of rape.

[113] *Mejia v. Peru*, I-ACmHR, Case No. 10.970, Res. No. 5/96 (1 March 1996), 157.

[114] I-ACmHR, *Report of the Situation of the Human Rights in Haiti*, OEA/Ser.L/V/II.88, Doc. 10 rev. (1995), para. 134. See, American Convention on Human Rights 1969, 22 November 1969, OAS Treaty Series No. 36, 1144 UNTS 123; entered into force 18 July 1978 (ACHR).

[115] *Miguel Castro-Castro Prison v. Peru* (Merits, Reparations and Costs), I-ACtHR, Ser. C, No. 160 (25 November 2006). The acts that amounted to inhumane treatment in contravention of Article 5 of the ACHR included: the suffering of pregnant women during the attack on the prison holding alleged terrorists; the forced nudity of women in front of male armed guards at the hospital; the failure to supply the women with hygiene supplements; vaginal 'inspections'; confinement; and the lack of pre- and post-partum attention to the pregnant women.

[116] Inter-American Convention on the Prevention, Punishment and Eradication of Violence against Women, 33 ILM 1534, 6 September 1994; entered into force 3 May 1995 (IA-VAW).

[117] *Castro-Castro Prison* case, para. 311.

('*Cotton Field*') v. *Mexico*, in which the I-ACtHR found that the failure to investigate the sexually related disappearances and murders of several women violated their rights to life, to humane treatment, and to personal liberty under the ACHR, the majority did not classify the acts in question as 'torture'.[118] In a separate concurring opinion, Medina Quiroga noted that: 'From a practical and juridical perspective, whether or not a conduct is classified as torture does not make much difference.'[119] Nonetheless, she indicated it was important to call the acts torture because of 'the scale of the treatment inflicted on [the women]'.[120]

The European Court of Human Rights (ECtHR) has similarly held rape to be a form of torture in a number of decisions, discussed below.

Despite the above general statements on the broad scope of Article 7 of the ICCPR by the HRC, there have been very few female applicants who have brought proceedings alleging a breach of Article 7 as a result of sexual or other violence outside the traditional construction of torture within state custody.[121] Moreover, in cases that raise specific forms of harm suffered by women, their concerns are either almost entirely absent from deliberations, or it appears that higher standards of proof may be required for crimes of a sexual nature than other forms of harm. These two issues are dealt with in turn below.

(a) Blindness to women's experiences of torture In relation to the neglect of the specific forms of harm suffered by women, the case *Gedumbe* v. *Democratic Republic of Congo* (DRC) is a case in point. In this case a male teacher from the DRC brought a claim under Article 7 of the ICCPR,

---

[118] *González et al ('Cotton Field') v. Mexico*, I-ACtHR, Preliminary Objection, Merits, Reparations and Costs, Ser. C No. 205 (16 November 2009).

[119] *Ibid.*, para. 2 (per concurring opinion of Cecilia Medina Quiroga).

[120] *Ibid.*, para. 8 (per concurring opinion of Cecilia Medina Quiroga).

[121] Sexual violence, for example, has been asserted in a number of cases, but not by women: see, e.g., *Motta* v. *Uruguay*, HRC 11/1997 (29 July 1980), in which the HRC found evidence of torture and inhuman treatment, in which the perpetrators, together with other forms of maltreatment, inserted bottles or barrels of automatic rifles into the male author's anus; *Ajaz and Jamil* v. *Republic of Korea*, HRC 644/1995 (19 March 1997), in which the authors asserted that electric shocks had been applied to their genitals in order to force a confession, but on the evidence before it, the HRC found no violation; *Rodriguez* v. *Uruguay*, HRC 322/1988 (19 July 1994), in which one of the alleged violations was of electric currents being applied to his eyelids, nose, and genitalia. See, also, *K. L. B-W.* v. *Australia*, HRC 499/1992 (30 March 1993), in which a woman claimed to have been sexually assaulted as a hospital patient. Her case failed at the admissibility stage because the alleged assault occurred prior to the entry into force of the Optional Protocol on the state party concerned.

alleging injury to himself. He taught at a consular school in Bujumbura, Burundi.[122] His accusation was that a former ambassador had embezzled his salary 'in order to force him to yield his wife [to the ambassador]'.[123] The complainant argued that the arbitrary deprivation of his employment, the embezzlement of his salary, and the destabilisation of his family caused by the alleged 'adultery' (language taken from the complaint itself) constituted torture and cruel and inhuman treatment.[124] He also claimed, inter alia, breaches of Articles 17 and 23(1) of the ICCPR.[125] Although finding that the author's claims were unsubstantiated, and therefore declaring certain aspects of the case to be inadmissible, the HRC did not state that such allegations would have fallen outside the parameters of Article 7 should they have been otherwise substantiated. Of significance for present purposes is that the HRC did not comment upon the fact that the complainant's wife was also an aggrieved party and arguably the proper complainant for such a communication, especially in relation to her 'forced' affair (potentially a case of sexual slavery under Article 8 of the ICCPR or, at a minimum, degrading and inhuman treatment in terms of being treated as chattel to be bargained over). In fact, the author argued that being forced to 'yield' his wife to the ambassador constituted ill-treatment to him, but not against his wife. Her circumstances were completely absent from the communication.

Other cases, too, show oversight of the circumstances of women. A case raising a similar issue involved a male complainant who alleged that his exclusion from military service owing to a finding of guilt by a military tribunal was unlawful as he had not been given the possibility of mounting a defence. He claimed that his discharge was because he 'tolerated the dishonourable lifestyle of his wife' (no details were provided as to what this entailed) and that it constituted 'an attack on *his* honour' [my emphasis] and degrading treatment *to him*.[126] Again, there was no mention of his wife, nor was she a complainant.

---

[122] *Gedumbe* v. *Democratic Republic of Congo*, HRC 641/1995 (10 July 1997).

[123] *Ibid.*, para. 2.1.   [124] *Ibid.*, paras. 3.1 and 3.2.

[125] Article 17 provides: '1. No one shall be subjected to arbitrary or unlawful interference with his privacy, family, home or correspondence, nor to unlawful attacks on his honour and reputation. 2. Everyone has the right to the protection of the law against such interference or attacks.' Article 23(1) provides: 'The family is the natural and fundamental group unit of society and is entitled to protection by society and the State.'

[126] *V. E. M.* v. *Spain*, HRC 467/1991 (16 July 1991). The HRC declared the claim inadmissible, in accordance with Spain's reservation to Article 5(2)(a) of the Optional Protocol, as the same matter had been examined and declared inadmissible by the European Commission on Human Rights. This decision was made notwithstanding the European

Another case further illustrates a similar pattern of gender blindness. Information was provided in the complainant's statements that government forces had visited his house where his pregnant wife lived. The house was ransacked, and she was beaten to the point of causing her to suffer a miscarriage. Although it is beyond dispute that the husband was also a victim of egregious violations of Article 7, his wife was not added as a party to the communication, nor did the HRC comment upon this omission or the vicious attack upon her.[127] As shown in Chapter 3, there is nothing in the procedural rules of the treaty bodies that would prevent any complaint from being amended to include the injuries to the complainant's wife or to otherwise comment on gendered aspects of such cases, yet the HRC has struggled to do so.

Like the HRC, there have been few individual communications before the CAT raising rape or sexual violence as a form of torture. In its early case law the CAT did not confront the issue head on, but its approach has improved. In *Kisoki* v. *Sweden*, for example, the CAT shied away from explicitly finding rape as a form of torture. In fact, the CAT simply did not refer to the written testimony from the complainant that as a political activist of an opposition party in what was at the time Zaire she was raped on more than ten occasions during her one year in detention.[128] Caroline Lambert has argued that 'the sexualised nature of the torture, particularly the rape[s], was erased from the committee's consideration of the issue'.[129] Instead, the CAT stated that 'her political affiliation and activities, her history of detention and torture, should be taken into account when determining whether she would be in danger of being subjected to torture upon return'.[130] Although it can be implied from this decision that rape in detention *is* a form of torture, it was not explicitly articulated, even in such an obvious case.

In a later case, that of *A. S.* v. *Sweden*, the CAT held that Sweden would be in breach of Article 3 of the UNCAT (the non-refoulement obligation) if it were to return an Iranian woman to Iran. As a widow of a 'martyr',

Commission's summary dismissal of the case and that it had not been considered on its merits. No details were available on what the alleged 'dishonourable lifestyle' entailed.

[127] *Blanco v Nicaragua*, HRC 328/1988 (20 July 1994), para. 6.7. Blanco was an engineer and university professor who was sentenced to thirty years' imprisonment for outspoken criticism of the 'Marxist orientation of the Sadinistas' (para. 2.1). He served ten years of the sentence and was subjected to serious forms of abuse.

[128] *Kisoki* v. *Sweden*, CAT 41/1996 (8 May 1996). See, also, *Abad* v. *Spain*, CAT 59/1996 (14 May 1998).

[129] Lambert, 'Partial Sites and Partial Sightings', 152–153.

[130] *Kisoki* v. *Sweden*, CAT 41/1996 (8 May 1996), para. 9.3.

she had been forced into a sighe or mutah marriage after the death of her husband. During this so-called 'marriage' she had had an affair with a Christian man, resulting in her being sentenced to death by stoning for having committed adultery.[131] Although being far from clear in its findings, the decision in favour of her implies that either alone or in concert both these acts (the forced marriage and the punishment for adultery) amounted to a form of torture for the purposes of applying Article 3 pertaining to non-refoulement protection.[132] Despite its overall positive finding, the CAT did not deal adequately with the gender aspects of the case. The CAT did not, for example, elaborate upon or mention in its final statements the sexual slavery attributed to the sighe or mutah marriage. Further, the CAT did not comment upon A. S.'s harsh questioning by the Zeinab Sisters – the female equivalents of the Pásdárán or the Iranian Revolutionary Guards – who investigate women suspected of 'un-Islamic behaviour', nor did they refer to the domestic violence she suffered at the hands of her sighe or mutah 'husband' after being delivered to him by the police following that investigation.[133]

The performance of the CAT has improved, however, since the above decisions were made. The CAT has, for example, expressly stated in at least two cases that multiple rapes constitute an act of torture. In *C. T. and K. M.* v. *Sweden*, a Rwandan citizen and her son sought to stay a deportation order. C. T. claimed that her forced deportation to Rwanda would amount to a breach of Article 3 of the UNCAT because she feared that she would be immediately detained and tortured by the Rwandan Directorate of Military Intelligence and subjected to rape and interrogation. She claimed that she had been detained in Rwanda in 2002 as

---

[131] *A. S.* v. *Sweden*, CAT 149/1999 (24 November 2000). A *sighe* or *mutah* marriage is a short-term or fixed-term contract of marriage, usually accompanied by dowry payments, which is believed to have its origins in Islam. Its apparent aim is to avoid the repercussions of adultery or sexual intercourse outside marriage. The marriage ends without divorce upon the expiration of the contractual period. In the case of A. S., the period was one and a half years. If the marriage is consummated, then the woman is not allowed to remarry until a certain period of time has elapsed. The practice is widely criticised by women's rights groups as denying a woman her internationally recognised rights associated with equality and marriage, such as consent, mutual divorce, and joint responsibility for children. Frequently, these marriages are not consensual.

[132] *Ibid.*, para. 8.4.

[133] *Ibid.*, para. 2.5. On the issue of punishment for adultery, see *Jabari* v. *Turkey*, ECtHR, Applic. No. 40035/98 (11 July 2000), in which it was held to be contrary to Article 3 ECHR to return an Iranian woman to Iran who faced stoning to death for adultery. The ECtHR stated that the punishment itself constituted a breach of Article 3, regardless of any extenuating or subjective circumstances of the case.

a member of the PDR-Ubuyanja political party and that she had been repeatedly raped under threat of execution during her detention. As a result of the rapes, she became pregnant with her son K. M. Finding in her favour, the CAT held:

> The first named complainant was *repeatedly raped* in detention and *as such was subjected to torture* in the past. On examining the dates of her detention and the date of the birth of her son, the Committee considers it without doubt that he was the product of rape by public officials, and is thus a constant reminder to the first named complainant of her rape [my emphasis].[134]

The second case, that of *V.L. v. Switzerland*, involved a woman who claimed that her return to Belarus would violate Article 3 of the UNCAT.[135] Prior to her initial departure from Belarus, she claimed that she had been inter-rogated and raped by three police officers seeking information on the whereabouts of her husband, who had been politically active and critical of the president of Belarus. Her husband had fled Belarus, seeking asylum abroad. During the interrogations she was beaten and penetrated with objects. After complaining to the officer-in-charge about the sexual abuse, she was subjected to a campaign of harassment, until one day the same officers who had previously raped her then kidnapped her and drove her to an isolated spot and raped her again. In relation to whether the rapes constituted acts of torture, the CAT set about linking the components of her situation to the definition in Article 1:

> The acts concerned, constituting among others multiple rapes, surely con-stitute infliction of severe pain and suffering perpetrated for a number of impermissible purposes, including interrogation, punishment, retaliation and discrimination based on gender. Therefore, the Committee believes that the sexual abuse by the police in this case constitutes torture.[136]

In relation to any suggestion that torture has to occur within an official place of detention, the CAT clarified:

> In assessing the risk of torture in the present case, the Committee con-siders that the complainant was clearly under the physical control of the police even though the acts concerned were perpetrated outside formal detention facilities … Therefore, the Committee believes that the sexual abuse by the police in this case constitutes torture even though it was per-petrated outside formal detention facilities.[137]

---

[134] *C. T. and K. M. v. Sweden*, CAT 279/2005 (17 November 2006), para. 7.5.
[135] *V. L. v. Switzerland*, CAT 262/2005 (20 November 2006).
[136] *Ibid.*, para. 8.10.   [137] *Ibid.*, para. 8.10.

These two cases, therefore, set aside any lingering doubts that rape by public officials can constitute torture under Article 1 of the UNCAT. The CAT has been clear that rape is considered to be both sufficiently painful and serious to meet the severity threshold, plus it can be committed for a range of proscribed purposes, including gender discrimination. Although these cases represent an important conceptual breakthrough for the CAT, they remain within the paradigm of state-perpetrated or state-sponsored terror against political opponents or their family members. At the same time, they serve to remind us of the political affiliations and activities of women and their risk of torture by reasons of association.

(b) Potentially higher standards of proof for cases of a sexual nature   A second emerging negative trend in human rights jurisprudence is what could be conceived of as the requirement for a higher standard of proof in cases of sexual violence. Although these cases are drawn from other jurisdictions, it highlights an emerging concern. In the case of *Loayza-Tamayo v. Peru*, a female professor accused of terrorism-related offences alleged that she had been subjected to forms of torture by officers of the Peruvian National Police Force, including, inter alia, rape, fondling, threats of drowning, beating, and solitary confinement, in order to force a confession. Cumulatively these acts, with the exception of the rape, were held by the I-ACmHR to infringe her dignity and to amount to inhuman treatment. However, when the case reached the I-ACtHR, despite the assertion by the I-ACmHR that she had been raped, the Court stated 'upon an examination of the file and, given the nature of this fact', it could not be substantiated. The I-ACtHR does not elaborate what it meant by taking into account the 'nature of this fact', nor what would be required to substantiate the allegation, but given that the I-ACtHR accepted a number of other forms of physical violence, including 'blows and maltreatment', the decision raises speculation that a different standard of proof was being expected to establish rape.[138] This case is to be compared with that of *Dianne Ortíz v. Guatemala*, in which the I-ACtHR held that the kidnapping, physical assault, and repeated rape by state agents of a United States' citizen and Catholic nun constituted torture. The I-ACtHR found that, although she could not substantiate the rape (she could substantiate the other violence she suffered through medical evidence), any sexual violence would have formed part of the torture to which she was

---

[138] *Loayza-Tamayo* v. *Peru*, I-ACtHR, Ser. C, No. 33 (17 September 1997), para. 58.

subjected.[139] Again, queries about substantiation of rape compared with other forms of ill-treatment begs the question about general mistrust relating to such allegations, ignorance of the difficulty of establishing such crimes through physical evidence, and potentially higher standards of proof being imposed unfairly on the complainants. Likewise, in *Aydin* v. *Turkey*, the minority judgment rendered by the ECtHR engaged in what could only be described as inappropriate questioning of the post-rape action of the complainant, thus disputing her credibility on the question of the alleged rape, which is discussed further below.[140]

As shown above, the case law in relation to rape and sexual violence as a form of torture or other cruel, inhuman, or degrading treatment is mixed. There has been an important shift from complete gender blindness to a general willingness to recognise such cases as torture, albeit in the case of the CAT still confined to the 'public' parameters of Article 1 of the UNCAT. This progress is partly a reflection of growing expertise and analysis within the treaty bodies, with NGOs and women's rights groups contributing to the evolution in legal reasoning. At a minimum, rape is recognised as a form of torture in a specific set of circumstances. Nonetheless, there continue to be a number of practical and conceptual problems with the VAW = T approach, not least due to the mixed jurisprudential record. Taking into account the many reasons why women hesitate to raise claims of rape or sexual violence before national or international bodies,[141] the fact that there have been only a handful of such cases brought before the treaty bodies, and before other international bodies, arguably suggests a lack of confidence in these bodies and their gender expertise. The mixed record questions whether women are yet able to rely on the international law to deliver consistent case outcomes. Moreover, the experiences of violence of many women fall outside these 'public' contexts of Article 1 of the CAT; and even though the HRC has a broader mandate, it does not (yet) appear to be the theatre of choice for such claims.

1.2   Psychological forms of torture

Sexual violence, of course, is not the only harm from which women seek protection and/or redress, although the focus on sexual violence within feminist literature could suggest otherwise. Since the initial discussions

---

[139] *Dianne Ortíz v. Guatemala*, Case, I-ACmHR, Case No. 10.526, Res. No. 31/96, (16 October 1996).
[140] *Aydin* v. *Turkey* (1997) 25 EHRR 251.   [141] See, Chapter 3.

over the terminology to be incorporated into Article 7 of the ICCPR and Articles 1 and 16 of the UNCAT, there has been no question that torture can include psychological forms of intimidation or threats of violence in addition to physical or sexual ones. The travaux préparatoires show an acceptance that Article 7 of the ICCPR, for example, embraces both physical and mental torture.[142] This has been confirmed in the HRC's 1992 General Comment on torture[143] and is endorsed in the views of both committees.

Specifically relevant to women's experiences is the HRC's acceptance that Article 7 applies to 'indirect' torture or, in other words, the suffering and torment endured by third persons, such as close relatives of detained or 'disappeared' persons. The HRC stated in *Quinteros v. Uruguay*:

> [T]he Committee ... understands the anguish and stress caused to the mother by the disappearance of her daughter and by the continuing uncertainty concerning her fate and whereabouts. The author has the right to know what has happened to her daughter. In these respects, she too is a victim of the violations of the Covenant suffered by her daughter in particular, of article 7.[144]

This particular decision has given voice to the many claims of women as wives, mothers, sisters, and daughters of politically active persons or of relatives in prison, and can be regarded as a positive expansion of the torture prohibition for women (as well as for other family members). It is notable, too, that this case bucks the trend of decisions involving the traditional fodder of the torture prohibition that tend to centre around

---

[142] UN Doc. E/CN.4/SR.149, paras. 33 and 38 (Egypt), para. 37 (the Philippines), para. 39 (Chairman), para. 41 (Lebanon).

[143] HRC, General Comment No. 20: Torture and Cruel, Inhuman or Degrading Treatment or Punishment, para. 5.

[144] *Quinteros v. Uruguay*, HRC 107/1981 (23 July 1983), para. 14. The HRC found that anguish and stress caused to the mother by the abduction and disappearance of her daughter by security forces and by the continuing uncertainty concerning her fate and whereabouts breached Article 7. Similarly, in *Banderenko (submitted by Natalia Schedkov) v. Belarus*, HRC 886/1999 (3 April 2003), a breach was found where a mother was not informed of the date, nor the hour, nor the place of her son's execution, nor the exact place of her son's subsequent burial. The latter was found to amount to inhuman treatment. See, also, *Lyashkevich v. Belarus*, HRC 887/1999 (3 April 2003); *Jensen v. Australia*, HRC 762/1997 (22 March 2001); *C v. Australia*, HRC 900/1999 (28 October 2002); *Sarma v. Sri Lanka*, HRC 950/2000 (16 July 2003). The HRC has not always taken into account the psychological harm to the family members of victims: see, *Tshishimbi v. Zaire*, HRC 542/1993 (25 March 1996), in which the main victim had been abducted and was missing. No mention was made of the suffering of the wife, the person submitting the application on her husband's behalf.

male prisoners, in so far as the principal complainant was a 'disappeared' daughter, and it was her mother who brought the case. The decision serves to highlight and to remind us that women are not monodimensional characters but participate in both the public and the private spheres of everyday life: a factor often overlooked by international institutions as well as women's rights advocates.

1.3 Forced sterilisation

In respect of the second sentence of Article 7 (prohibition against non-consensual medical or scientific experimentation), the Working Group of the Third Committee of the UN General Assembly commented during the drafting debate that '[c]ertain kinds of treatment became cruel, inhuman or degrading only because they were administered without the subject's free consent'.[145] Similarly, the HRC has stated in its 1992 General Comment:

> The Committee ... observes that special protection in regard to such experiments is necessary in the case of persons not capable of giving valid consent, and in particular those under any form of detention or imprisonment. Such persons should not be subjected to any medical or scientific experimentation that may be detrimental to their health.[146]

An absence of consent can thus be a contributing factor to the characterisation of a particular act as torture or ill-treatment, whether or not it is within the context of medical or scientific experimentation. It can be implied from the language of the HRC's 1992 General Comment that experimentation within detention or imprisonment is but one example of such prohibited acts. In support of this, the HRC has referred to the sterilisation of women without their consent as a breach of Article 7, both in a number of concluding observations on states parties' reports[147] and in a General Comment issued in 2000.[148]

In its concluding observations on Slovakia in 2003, for example, the HRC raised concern about the 'forced or coerced sterilisation' of Roma

---

[145] E/CN.4/56 (Working Party); Third Committee, 13th Session in 1958; Bossuyt, *Guide to the 'Travaux Préparatoires' of the ICCPR*, 147 and 158 respectively.

[146] HRC, General Comment No. 20: Torture and Cruel, Inhuman or Degrading Treatment or Punishment, para. 7.

[147] See, also, HRC, Concluding observations on Japan (1998) UN Doc. CCPR/C/79/Add.102, para. 31; Peru (2000) UN Doc. CCPR/CO/70/PER, para. 21; Slovakia (2003) UN Doc. CCPR/CO/78/SCK, para. 12.

[148] HRC, General Comment No. 28: Equality of Rights Between Men and Women (Article 3) (2000), para. 11.

women 'without [their] free and informed consent'.[149] Forced sterilisation has also been noted as being of particular concern for disabled women and girls.[150] Despite these statements by the HRC, however, very few individual communications have raised issues of non-consensual experimentation, and these cases have fallen into the category of traditional forms of ill-treatment, such as the use of hallucinogenic drugs or electroconvulsions to force confessions.[151]

1.4   Discrimination as torture or degrading treatment

The interlinkages between discrimination and torture also feature in the committees' jurisprudence and are of particular relevance to female claimants. In many of its concluding observations, for example, the HRC discusses Article 7 concerns in conjunction with Article 3 (equality between men and women), but there has been no consistency in its approach. Initially, the HRC did not point out the need (and requirement) for states to interpret and apply Article 7 of the ICCPR without discrimination. General Comment No. 20 (1992) concerning the prohibition against torture noted two provisions that impact on the interpretation and application of Article 7, naming Articles 10 and 2(3) explicitly.[152] No reference, however, was made to Article

---

[149] HRC, Concluding observations on Slovakia (2003), UN Doc. A/58/40 (Vol. I) (2003), para. 12

[150] See, CRC, General Comment No. 9: The Rights of Children with Disabilities (2007), UN Doc. CRC/C/GC/9, 27 February 2007, para. 60 (noting that disabled girls are subjected to forced sterilisation, which the Children's Committee considers to violate their rights to physical integrity).

[151] See, e.g., *Weisz* v. *Uruguay*, HRC 28/1978 (29 October 1980) (forced use of hallucinogenic drugs); *Estrella* v. *Uruguay*, HRC 74/1980 (29 March 1983) (forced use of hallucinogenic drugs); *Viana* v. *Uruguay*, HRC 110/1981 (29 March 1984) (claimed subjection to psychiatric experiments for three years by the forced injection of tranquilisers every two weeks); *K. L. B.-W.* v. *Australia*, HRC 499/1992 (30 March 1993) (subjected involuntarily to a regime of electro-convulsion therapy, being maintained in deep sleep without food, and on drug dosages that exceeded forensic limits and without muscle relaxants).

[152] Article 2(3) of the ICCPR provides: 'Each State Party to the present Covenant undertakes:
  (a) To ensure that any person whose rights or freedoms as herein recognized are violated shall have an effective remedy, notwithstanding that the violation has been committed by persons acting in an official capacity;
  (b) To ensure that any person claiming such a remedy shall have his [sic] right thereto determined by competent judicial, administrative or legislative authorities, or by any other competent authority provided for by the legal system of the State, and to develop the possibilities of judicial remedy;
  (c) To ensure that the competent authorities shall enforce such remedies when granted.'

2(1) (the non-discrimination clause) of the ICCPR.[153] Such an omission was later 'corrected' by a subsequent General Comment on the equality of rights between women and men, in which the HRC pointed out the issues at stake for women under each of the Covenant provisions.[154] In relation to torture, the HRC referred to domestic or other types of violence against women, including rape, the denial of access to safe abortion when pregnancy has resulted from rape, forced abortion or forced sterilisation, and the practice of genital mutilation.[155] Although acknowledging the listing of these acts of violence as relevant to Article 7, the HRC failed to explain why or how they satisfy the scope of the torture prohibition. As stated earlier in this chapter, the failure to explain its reasoning provides scope for questions to be raised about the legitimacy of these views by opponents of the VAW = T strategy, especially states parties.

In addition, the listing of these acts within a separate General Comment on the issue of equality between women and men, rather than within a General Comment on torture, follows what has become a familiar isolationist method of UN treaty bodies in which women's concerns are dealt with separately from mainstream human rights.[156] In other words, gender mainstreaming, which was outlined in the Introduction in Chapter 1 to this book, remains an 'add women and stir' process.

Discrimination as a form of 'degrading treatment', rather than as torture, has been recognised in other jurisdictions, albeit with mixed success (see below). The HRC has not yet received a communication that would establish its views on the relevance of discrimination to a finding of torture. However, the HRC has confronted allegations that biased tribunals (or discrimination more generally) could give rise to claims under Article 7 generally. Two cases are relevant here. The first concerned allegations that proceedings for determining refugee status by a biased tribunal amounted to cruel, inhuman, and degrading treatment. In this case, the applicant, a Ghanaian citizen seeking asylum in Canada, alleged that one of the commissioners, also of Ghanaian origin but of a different ethnicity to the applicant, was biased. His communication was declared

---

[153] Cf. HRC, General Comment No. 9: Humane Treatment of Persons Deprived of Liberty (Article 10) (1982), para. 1(3) (Article 10, ICCPR to be applied without discrimination).
[154] HRC, General Comment No. 28: Equality of Rights Between Men and Women.
[155] HRC, General Comment No. 28: Equality of Rights Between Men and Women, para. 11. See, also, para. 15 which refers to separation of men and women in prisons.
[156] See, H. Charlesworth, 'Not Waving but Drowning: Gender Mainstreaming and Human Rights in the United Nations' (2005) 18 *Harv. Hum. Rts. J.* 1; H. Charlesworth, 'The Mid-Life Crisis of the Universal Declaration of Human Rights' (1998) 55 *Wash. & Lee L. Rev.* 781.

inadmissible by the HRC on a number of grounds, including that he had not complained about the bias during the proceedings for refugee status.[157] A second case raised sexist and racist bias in alleging that the Australian court system was corrupt and that it was biased against women and immigrants. On the facts before it, the HRC ruled that the applicant had not substantiated her claims, stating that they remained 'sweeping allegations'.[158] Although neither of these cases proceeded past the admissibility stage, they remain relevant in so far as neither the HRC nor the states parties concerned sought to argue that claims raising bias (or, for that matter, discrimination) are beyond the parameters of Article 7. This may suggest that, should similar cases be raised in the future, properly substantiated, they would be considered by the HRC to be within Article 7.

The question of whether sex discrimination constitutes a form of inhuman or degrading treatment is complex, not least because it is tied to problems inherent in the discrimination hierarchy that has developed under international law. This hierarchy, as described in Chapter 4, posits race discrimination as being of a more serious character than sex discrimination. For example, a 1973 European Commission decision held that racially discriminatory legislation that prevented Asian residents in Kenya and Uganda who had retained their United Kingdom citizenship from entering the UK for the purpose of settlement constituted, inter alia, 'degrading treatment' within the meaning of Article 3 of the ECHR.[159] In this case the European Commission stated that 'a special importance should be attached to discrimination based on race' and that such discrimination 'could, in certain circumstances, of itself amount to degrading treatment ...'[160] In contrast, the European Court of Human Rights (ECtHR) has arguably taken a different approach to immigration laws that differentiate rights on the basis of sex. In *Abdulaziz, Cabales and Balkandali* v. *United Kingdom*,[161] the ECtHR accepted the arguments of three female applicants lawfully and permanently settled in the UK that laws which refused permission for their husbands to join them in the UK were discriminatory on the basis of sex, race, and, in the case of Mrs Balkandali, birth. However, the ECtHR was not satisfied that such discrimination constituted 'inhuman or degrading treatment' under Article 3. In its ruling, the ECtHR stated that 'the difference of treatment

---

[157] *Abu* v. *Canada*, HRC 654/1995 (18 July 1997).
[158] *B. L.* v. *Australia*, HRC 659/1995 (8 November 1996).
[159] *East African Asians* v. *United Kingdom* (1973) 3 EHRR 76.
[160] *Ibid.*, paras. 196 and 207.
[161] *Abdulaziz, Cabales and Balkandali* v. *United Kingdom* (1985) 7 EHRR 471.

complained of did not denote any contempt or lack of respect for the personality of the applicants and it was not designed to, and did not, humiliate or debase but was intended solely to achieve the aims ...' of limiting immigration and protecting the domestic labour market in times of high unemployment.[162] There has, therefore, been no blanket statement that sex discrimination, whatever its form or effect, is degrading (or inhumane), unlike the intimations in the *East African Asians* case in which 'mere' race discrimination was sufficient to a finding of degrading treatment.

For the CAT, the question of discrimination has emerged within the context of the purpose element of the definition in Article 1 of the UNCAT. The list of proscribed 'purposes' in the final version of Article 1 is broader than the 1975 UN Declaration on Torture on which the UNCAT is based. Of particular relevance here is that the UNCAT definition includes 'discriminatory purposes'.[163] However, the 'discriminatory purposes' ground was not without its sceptics at the time of drafting. The UK delegate to the drafting conference stated:

> The United Kingdom shares the concern to eliminate all forms of torture, including any motivated by discrimination. The United Kingdom is doubtful of the need to isolate this particular motivation and in practical terms the United Kingdom thinks that there will in any case be difficulties in doing so with the necessary degree of precision for a criminal offence.[164]

The 'discriminatory purpose' ground has been raised by at least one applicant before the CAT, arguing that his Romani ethnicity should be taken into account. He asserted that his membership in a 'historically disadvantaged minority group' rendered him particularly vulnerable to 'degrading treatment' – in this case in the form of physical and verbal abuse. He was kicked and beaten while the police insulted his ethnic origins and cursed his 'gypsy mother'. He argued: 'All else being equal, a given level of physical abuse is more likely to constitute "degrading or inhuman treatment or punishment" when motivated by racial animus and/or coupled with racial epithets than when racial considerations are absent.'[165] Unfortunately the CAT did not comment on this aspect of the claim, finding in any event that the alleged abuses amounted to torture within the meaning of Article 1.

---

[162] *Ibid.*, para. 91.

[163] Article 1 of the UNCAT also includes 'coercive' purposes, which was not contained in the UN Declaration on Torture 1975.

[164] UN Doc. E/CN.4/L.1470, para. 27.

[165] *Dimitrijevic* v. *Serbia and Montenegro*, CAT 207/2002 (24 November 2004), para. 3.1.

In 2008 the CAT issued its second General Comment, in which the issue of discrimination featured as an indicator of torture. The General Comment provides: 'The Committee [against Torture] emphasizes that the discriminatory use of mental or physical violence or abuse is an important factor in determining whether an act constitutes torture.'[166] In adopting the 'historic' language of non-discrimination rather than equality,[167] the CAT stated:

> The protection of certain minority or marginalized individuals or populations especially at risk of torture is a part of the obligation to prevent torture or ill-treatment. States parties must ensure that, insofar as the obligations arising under the Convention are concerned, their laws are in practice applied to all persons, *regardless of* race, colour, ethnicity, age, religious belief or affiliation, political or other opinion, national or social origin, gender, sexual orientation, transgender identity, mental or other disability, health status, economic or indigenous status, reason for which the person is detained, including persons accused of political offences or terrorist acts, asylum-seekers, refugees or others under international protection, or any other status or adverse distinction. States parties should, therefore, ensure the protection of members of groups especially at risk of being tortured, by fully prosecuting and punishing all acts of violence and abuse against these individuals and ensuring implementation of other positive measures of prevention and protection, including but not limited to those outlined above [my emphasis].[168]

The CAT followed up this general non-discrimination statement by requesting specific information from states parties in their periodic reports in relation to women:

> State reports frequently lack specific and sufficient information on the implementation of the Convention with respect to women. The Committee emphasizes that gender is a key factor. Being female intersects with other identifying characteristics or status of the person such as race, nationality, religion, sexual orientation, age, immigrant status etc. to determine the ways that women and girls are subject to or at risk of torture or ill-treatment and the consequences thereof. The contexts in which females are at risk include deprivation of liberty, medical treatment, particularly involving reproductive decisions, and violence by private actors in communities and homes. Men are also subject to certain gendered violations of the Convention such as rape or sexual violence and abuse. Both men and women and boys and girls may be subject to violations of the

---

[166] CAT, General Comment No. 2: Implementation of Article 2 by States Parties, para. 20.
[167] See, Chapter 4.
[168] CAT, General Comment No. 2: Implementation of Article 2 by States Parties, para. 21.

Convention on the basis of their actual or perceived non-conformity with socially determined gender roles. States parties are requested to identify these situations and the measures taken to punish and prevent them in their reports.[169]

Eliminating employment discrimination and conducting ongoing sensitization training in contexts where torture or ill-treatment is likely to be committed is also key to preventing such violations and building a culture of respect for women and minorities. States are encouraged to promote the hiring of persons belonging to minority groups and women, particularly in the medical, educational, prison/detention, law enforcement, judicial and legal fields, within State institutions as well as the private sector. States parties should include in their reports information on their progress in these matters, disaggregated by gender, race, national origin, and other relevant status.[170]

2   Meeting the severity threshold

According to international law, for an act to be characterised as a form of torture, it must 'attain a minimum level of severity'.[171] This is to be judged according to all the circumstances of the case, as discussed below under 4 Contextual analysis. The general approach of the HRC has been to identify the types of acts as meeting the threshold of Article 7 of the ICCPR, without engaging in analysis of whether they are torture or cruel, inhuman, or degrading treatment or punishment. Very little has been stated expressly by the HRC about how serious the violence must be to differentiate it from a lesser form of ill-treatment. The best that one can do is to try to identify some trends in its jurisprudence which, as outlined above, is far from straightforward. This follows its general approach to Article 7 of the ICCPR, which has been not to spend too long distinguishing between the various forms. The CAT does not have this same luxury, as it has separate heads of harms with slightly different criteria. It is nonetheless generally the view of the committees that violence against women in the form of rape, for example, meets the threshold level of severity for torture. For other forms of harm, it is far less clear.

At least in the context of rape, there has been some serious academic engagement with this question.[172] Writing on the approach of the ECtHR to rape, McGlynn congratulates the ECtHR for accepting that rape per se

---

[169]   *Ibid.*, para. 22.   [170]   *Ibid.*, para. 24.

[171]   *Ireland* v. *United Kingdom* (1978) 2 EHRR 25, para. 162.

[172]   See, in particular, C. McGlynn, 'Rape, Torture and the European Convention on Human Rights' (2009) 58 *Int'l & Comp. L. Qty* 565.

satisfies the threshold level of severity for Article 3 of the ECHR, regardless of the type of rape at issue. She recounts that all rapes, and not just violent, stranger rapes, can result in serious, adverse, and long-term consequences for the victims. This is because the seriousness of rape lies in its violation of sexual autonomy, which, she recalls, is a fundamental value protected by human rights norms and instruments.[173] It does not, in other words, rest on the degree of any associated threats, coercion, force, or other violent or aggravated circumstances. As noted by the ICTY in *Delalic*: 'The Trial Chamber considers that rape of any person to be a despicable act which strikes at the very core of human dignity and physical integrity.'[174] In *Kunarac* the ICTY likewise noted that 'some acts establish per se the suffering of those upon whom they are inflicted. Rape is obviously such an act.'[175] As noted by McGlynn, the advantages of this approach are several:

> Such an approach has the benefit of simplicity: it always being clear that once rape has been established, the harm threshold for torture has been satisfied. It may obviate intrusive questioning of victims regarding the impact of the rape and its adverse effects. It may also ensure that the egregious nature of the rape is better recognized, being assimilated with torture. For these reasons and more, it is an approach widely recommended by feminist scholars.[176]

There are, however, those who disagree with this approach, to the extent that it 'reinforce[s] the understanding that women are not capable of not being victimized by rapes'.[177] Moreover, as McGlynn points out, most legal systems differentiate between different forms of rape – aggravated rape, statutory or child rape, and so forth.[178] From my perspective, there are already enough criteria built into the torture prohibition that differentiate it from lesser forms of ill-treatment (in particular the purposive requirement). Furthermore, if the accepted definition of rape under international law turns on the question of an absence of consent, rather than coercion

---

[173] *Ibid.*, 572.
[174] *Prosecutor* v. *Delalic, Mucic, Delic and Landzo (Celebici)*, ICTY, Case No. IT-96–21-I (21 March 1996), para. 495, as referred to by McGlynn, 'Rape, Torture and the European Convention on Human Rights', 572.
[175] *Prosecutor* v. *Kunarac, Kovac and Vukovic*, ICTY, Case No. IT-96–23 and IT-96–23/1 (12 June 2002), para. 150, as referred to by McGlynn, 'Rape, Torture and the European Convention on Human Rights', 573.
[176] McGlynn, 'Rape, Torture and the European Convention on Human Rights', 573. Here she refers to the views of C. A. MacKinnon, *Are Women Human? And Other International Dialogues* (Cambridge, MA: Harvard University Press, 2006), 17, reproduced from her essay 'On Torture', 21.
[177] Engle, 'Feminism and its (Dis)Contents', 813.
[178] McGlynn, 'Rape, Torture and the European Convention on Human Rights', 574.

or force, then reinvoking the latter criteria in order to meet the threshold level of torture seems to downplay the sexual autonomy basis for rape; and further downplays the question of sexual autonomy to women's human rights. While in my mind rape should be seen in all cases as a form of torture, the above discussion highlights further questions about the difficulties of protecting women from violence, and offering remedies, within the framework of the torture prohibition. I do not believe that the R = T (rape as torture) approach need surrender women to being victimised by rape in every case; rather it grants women a right to a remedy of the highest order for violations of their sexual autonomy. Having said this, there is nothing stopping the treaty bodies and international courts from engaging in discussions on severity thresholds about particular types of rapes. By doing so, however, they reinforce the argument of this book that the VAW = T strategy is less than perfect in addressing women's experiences of violence, partly because it was designed with a different set of circumstances in mind. In addition, it raises, arguably unnecessarily, questions around why certain forms of violence against women are seen as particularly abhorrent compared with other forms. There is also a serious gap in the literature in relation to these other forms of violence against women and questions of the severity threshold, which needs to be filled.

3 Public/private dichotomy

As noted in Chapter 2, the demarcation between public and private spheres of everyday life for the purposes of international rules is at the source of women's exclusion from international human rights law. The torture prohibition is no exception. Traditionally, international law was concerned only with state-perpetrated torture. As shown above, there has been a shift to incorporate acts of equivalent seriousness committed by non-state actors within the torture prohibition; however, to do so has required a link to be established between the act in question and the state. Under the ICCPR and most international human rights treaties, this requirement is known as the concept or test of 'due diligence'. First elaborated in *Velásquez Rodríguez* v. *Honduras* by the Inter-American Court of Human Rights (I-ACtHR), a state will be held accountable for the harm in question if the state has failed to prevent the harm by taking all reasonable steps or if it has failed to protect the victim, to investigate and prosecute those responsible, and to provide redress:

> An illegal act which violates human rights and which is initially not directly imputable to a State (for example, because it is the act of a private

person or because the person responsible has not been identified) can lead to international responsibility of the State, *not because of the act itself* but because of the lack of due diligence to prevent the violation or to respond to it as required by the Convention [my emphasis].[179]

The I-ACtHR in *Velásquez Rodríguez* v. *Honduras* characterised the duty on states to exercise 'due diligence' as including obligations to prevent, investigate, and punish violations of human rights and to ensure that victims have access to adequate compensation.[180] The duty to prevent, according to the I-ACtHR, 'includes all those measures of a legal, political, administrative and cultural nature that promote the protection of human rights and ensure that any violations are considered and treated as illegal acts, which, as such, may lead to the punishment of those responsible and the obligation to indemnify the victims for damages'.[181] The broadly framed concept of 'due diligence' has substantially extended the reach of international human rights law and the obligations of states, but it also has its limitations.[182]

Although heralded as a triumph for women's claims in so far as the standard permits the inclusion of non-state violence within international law,[183] the case of *Velásquez Rodríguez* was decided in the absence of any gender analysis. In this case, the 'disappeared' person fitted within the traditional rights-bearer scenario as a man accused of political crimes and subjected to torture who was then 'disappeared', yet the Court still found it necessary to comment on non-state forms of harm. The realisation that violence committed by non-state or private actors is a universal, rather than an exclusively female, issue is a fact that is often missing from feminist analyses of the law. It is not only women's claims that benefit from a collapsing of the division between the public and the private for the purposes of international law. Similarly, as noted in Chapter 3, the first cases that successfully accepted that the 'refugee' definition in the 1951 Convention relating to the Status of Refugees applied to persecution at the hands of non-state actors in circumstances where the state is 'unable or unwilling'

[179] *Velásquez Rodriguez* v. *Honduras*, I-ACtHR, Ser. C, No. 4 (29 July 1988), para. 291. See, also, *Godina-Cruz* v. *Honduras*, I-ACtHR, Ser. C, No. 5 (20 January 1989).
[180] *Velásquez Rodriguez* v. *Honduras*, paras. 173–174.
[181] *Ibid.*, para. 175.
[182] For further discussion on due diligence, see A. Byrnes and E. Bath, 'Violence against Women, the Obligation of Due Diligence, and the Optional Protocol to the Convention on the Elimination of All Forms of Discrimination against Women – Recent Developments' (2008) 8 *Hum. Rts. L. Rev.* 517.
[183] See, e.g., Amnesty International, *The Duty of States to Address Violence against Women*, AI Index: ACT 77/049/2004, 2004.

to protect the individual against such abuse did not involve a gender component or women,[184] although there was acknowledgement that women's gendered claims would benefit from such an analysis, recognising 'sex' as an innate and immutable characteristic satisfying the 'social group' category in Article 1A(2) of that Convention.[185] Of course, the emergence of the due diligence test in men's rather than women's cases, even though 'private' abuse disproportionately affects women, reminds us that, until an issue is of relevance to men, it is not an issue worth pursuing at the level of international law, and it will remain marginalised.

A different standard appears to have developed in the early jurisprudence of the CAT. According to the wording in Article 1 of the UNCAT, a state is responsible for the torture perpetrated 'by or at the instigation or with the *consent or acquiescence* of a public official or other person acting in an official capacity' [my emphasis]. This provision accepts that non-state torture occurs, but it ties responsibility to the state only in circumstances where a state official or other person acting in an official capacity instigated, consented, or acquiesced in that harm. Whether there is any real difference between the two approaches will be examined in turn below.

In its first General Comment on Article 7 in 1982, the HRC stated that Article 7 prohibits ill-treatment 'even when committed by persons acting *outside or without* any official authority' [my emphasis].[186] Almost from the outset, therefore, the HRC included within Article 7 the *ultra vires* actions of public or government officials, although it had yet to include purely (if there is such a thing) 'private' harm. Rape and other violent acts that were not part of a deliberate government policy could not, therefore, be excused as being mere criminal activities of a few rogue officers, as had been past practice under national and international laws. Under this analysis, the state has responsibility for its officials even if they act beyond their prescribed roles and orders.

The HRC's subsequent General Comment issued in 1992 goes a step further by providing that Article 7 prohibits acts 'whether inflicted by

---

[184] See, A. Edwards, 'Age and Gender Dimensions in International Refugee Law', in E. Feller, V. Türk and F. Nicholson, *Refugee Protection in International Law: UNHCR's Global Consultations on International Protection* (Cambridge University Press, 2003) 46, at 60, n.78.

[185] See, *Acosta v. Immigration and Naturalization Service*, 1985 BIA LEXIS 2, 19 I & N Dec 211 (1985); *Canada (Attorney-General) v. Ward*, SCC, Can. S.C.R. LEXIS 35, 2 Can. S.C.R. 689 (1983).

[186] HRC, General Comment No. 7: Torture or Cruel, Inhuman or Degrading Treatment or Punishment, para. 2.

people acting in their official capacity, outside their official capacity *or in a private capacity*' [my emphasis].[187] This General Comment seems to expand the definition of torture to embrace the actions of non-state actors who are not linked to any official position. Similarly, General Comment No. 31 (2004) on the nature of general legal obligations under the ICCPR clarifies that the obligations of states parties will be fully discharged only if individuals are protected by the state, not just against violations of Covenant rights by its agents, but also against acts committed by private persons or entities that would impair the enjoyment of those rights. The 2004 General Comment provides that a state would be in violation of its obligations as a result of permitting or failing to take appropriate measures or to exercise due diligence to prevent, punish, investigate, or redress the harm caused by 'private' acts. This duty to take positive measures to protect persons against 'private' harm is, therefore, 'implicit' within Article 7.[188] These statements square with the decision of the I-ACtHR in *Velásquez Rodríguez* v. *Honduras*, outlined above.

Despite the willingness expressed by the HRC to integrate 'private' harm perpetrated against women within Article 7, the exploitation of 'due diligence' to do so remains embryonic in jurisprudential practice. There have been only a handful of individual cases before the treaty bodies that directly discuss the question of persons acting outside their official capacity (in many cases, it is assumed that their actions were officially condoned), and even fewer invoke liability as a result of failing to act to counter 'private' acts of harm.

In *Wilson* v. *The Philippines*,[189] for example, the HRC utilised language that appears to be more usually associated with the UNCAT (see below) than with the ICCPR. In this case, the HRC decided that a breach of Article 7 arose in circumstances where other inmates beat the complainant, either on the guards' direct orders, or 'with their acquiescence'. The HRC did not explain precisely what it meant by 'acquiescence', but there was some indication that prisoner-on-prisoner violence was known to occur, if not encouraged, in specific circumstances and that the guards did not intervene to stop it.[190] Concluding observations of the HRC on periodic reports by states parties have mentioned positive obligations

---

[187] HRC, General Comment No. 20: Torture and Cruel, Inhuman or Degrading Treatment or Punishment, paras. 2 and 13.
[188] HRC, General Comment No. 31: The Nature of the General Legal Obligation Imposed on States Parties to the Covenant, para. 8.
[189] *Wilson* v. *The Philippines*, HRC 868/1999 (30 October 2003).
[190] *Ibid.*, para. 7.3.

of Article 7 such as enacting legislation outlawing torture and training state officials: efforts aimed at *protecting* individuals from and *preventing future* situations of abuse. So far, however, the HRC's jurisprudence tends to refer exclusively to positive *post*-abuse measures such as duties to investigate claims, to prosecute and to punish offenders, and to pay compensation to victims; and has yet to articulate prevention obligations in the context of non-state abuse.

Because of the paucity of jurisprudence before the HRC invoking the due diligence standard in respect of women's claims, the decisions of other human rights bodies may provide some guidance on how the standard is to be applied, and these are therefore highlighted here. In *M. C. v. Bulgaria*,[191] the applicant (a fourteen-year-old girl who alleged she was raped by two men) claimed that Bulgarian law and practice did not provide 'effective protection' against rape and sexual abuse, as only those cases where the victim physically resisted were prosecuted. In line with decisions of other international and regional bodies, the ECtHR held that Bulgaria had a positive obligation both to enact criminal legislation to punish rape effectively and to apply this legislation through effective investigation and prosecution. In particular, the ECtHR criticised the Bulgarian law for emphasising force rather than consent in defining the crime of rape. The ECtHR noted in particular that victims of sexual abuse, particularly girls below the age of majority, often fail to resist for a variety of psychological reasons or through fear of further violence from the perpetrator. The ECtHR held that rape laws must reflect changing social attitudes requiring respect for the individual's sexual autonomy and for equality. Not only is this a landmark decision in terms of the ECtHR's emphasis on consent rather than force in relation to definitions of rape, it also effectively applied concepts such as sexual autonomy and equality to support its findings.[192] It was held that the state had failed in its due diligence obligations under Article 3 (the torture prohibition) of the ECHR.

---

[191] *M. C. v. Bulgaria* (2003) 40 EHRR 20. This case involved a fourteen-year-old girl who claimed that she was raped by two men, aged twenty and twenty-one years old. Criminal investigations in Bulgaria found insufficient evidence that M. C. had been compelled to have sex with the two men. The district prosecutor terminated the proceedings on the grounds that the use of force or threats had not been established beyond reasonable doubt and that no resistance on her part had been established.

[192] See, also, *X and Y v. The Netherlands* (1985) 8 EHRR 235, in which the ECtHR found that failing to have a law allowing for criminal proceedings against perpetrators of sexual assault against a mentally handicapped girl violates the ECHR.

In a later decision of *Osman* v. *United Kingdom*, the ECtHR further articulated the scope of due diligence, arguably adopting a more conservative stance, stating:

> For the Court, and bearing in mind the difficulties involved in policing modern societies, the unpredictability of human conduct and the operational choices which must be made in terms of priorities and resources, such an obligation must be interpreted in a way which does not impose an impossible or disproportionate burden on the authorities. [...] In the opinion of the Court where there is an allegation that the authorities have violated their positive obligation to protect the right to life [...] it must be established to its satisfaction that the authorities knew or ought to have known at the time of the existence of a real and immediate risk to the life of an identified individual or individuals from the criminal acts of a third party and that they failed to take measures within the scope of their powers which, judged reasonably, might have been expected to avoid that risk.[193]

In the 2009 judgment of *Opuz* v. *Turkey*, which found violations of Articles 2, 3, and 14 of the ECHR (see further Chapter 6), the ECtHR found that the state had failed in its due diligence duties by, inter alia, not deterring the applicant's husband and by failing to provide shelter to the applicant. The case involved physical and psychological abuse against Mrs Opuz and her children over a twelve-year period, in which the applicant had reported her fears to the police on numerous occasions, which were followed by a litany of failings by the authorities. In making its decision, the ECtHR stated that the state's failure to protect the applicant must have left Mrs Opuz feeling 'as though the violence had been inflicted under state supervision.'[194]

Case law in the Inter-American system has also served to delineate the boundaries of the due diligence standard. In the *Pueblo Bello* case, drawing on earlier case law, the I-ACtHR established that:

> the Court acknowledges that a State cannot be responsible for all the human rights violations committed between individuals within its jurisdiction. Indeed, the nature *erga omnes* of the treaty-based guarantee obligations of the States does not imply their unlimited responsibility for all acts or deeds of individuals, because its obligations to adopt prevention and protection measures for individuals in their relationships with each

---

[193] *Osman* v. *The United Kingdom*, Applic. No. 87/1997/871/1083 (28 October 1998), para. 116. This analysis was later repeated in *Kilic* v. *Turkey*, ECtHR, Applic. No. 22492/93 (28 March 2000), para. 63, and *Opuz* v. *Turkey*, ECtHR, Applic. No. 33401/02 (9 June 2009). para. 129 (discussed below and in Chapter 6).

[194] *Opuz* v. *Turkey*, ECtHR, Applic. No. 33401/02 (9 June 2009), para. 155.

other are conditioned by the awareness of a situation of real and imminent danger for a specific individual or group of individuals and to the
reasonable possibilities of preventing or avoiding that danger. In other
words, even though an act, omission or deed of an individual has the legal
consequence of violating the specific human rights of another individual,
this is not automatically attributable to the State, because the specific circumstances of the case and the execution of these guarantee obligations
must be considered.[195]

Drawing on the above decision, *González et al ('Cotton Field')* v. *Mexico*
confirmed that failure to adopt a 'general policy' in relation to the known
widespread rapes, disappearances, and murders committed against
women in the Ciudad Juárez region amounted to a breach of the obligation to prevent.[196] The case did not find a violation in relation to the
specific disappearances of the three victims in question on the basis that
the state had not become aware that they were in 'real and imminent
danger'.[197] The I-ACtHR did find, however, a violation of their rights after
they had gone missing, because the state at this stage 'was aware of the real
and imminent risk that the victims would be sexually abused, subjected
to ill-treatment and killed.'[198]

Although not dealt with as a torture issue, the UN Committee on the
Elimination of Discrimination against Women (the Women's Committee)
likewise held Hungary to be in violation of the CEDAW in having failed
in its duty of due diligence to provide a female victim of domestic violence
with effective protection from the serious risk to her physical integrity,
her physical and mental health, and her life – such risks being posed by
her common-law husband.[199] The Women's Committee concluded in *A. T.*
v. *Hungary* that the state had failed in its obligations under the CEDAW
because it had not enacted specific legislation to combat domestic violence and sexual harassment, because no shelters existed for the immediate protection of a woman in the victim's circumstances with a disabled
child, and because there was no injunctive relief, such as a restraining
order, available to her.[200] Although the Women's Committee did not

---

[195] *Case of Pueblo Bello Massacre v. Colombia*, I-ACtHR, Merits, Reparations and Costs, Ser.
C No. 140 (31 January 2006), para. 123, drawing on decisions in *Case of Sawhoyamaxa
Indigenous Community v. Paraguay*, I-ACtHR, Merits, Reparations and Costs, Ser. C No.
146 (29 March 2006), para. 155 and *Valle Jaramillo et al.* v. *Colombia*, I-ACtHR, Merits,
Reparations and Costs, Ser. C. No. 192, para. 78.
[196] *González et al ('Cotton Field')* v. *Mexico*, I-ACtHR, Preliminary Objection, Merits,
Reparations and Costs, Ser. C No. 205 (16 November 2009), para. 282.
[197] *Ibid.*   [198] *Ibid.*, para. 823.
[199] *A. T.* v. *Hungary*, CEDAW 2/2003 (26 January 2005).
[200] *Ibid.*, para. 9.3.

analyse this case in light of international torture provisions, its findings, specifically the itemising of actions that ought to be taken by a state in order to fulfil its obligations of 'prevention and protection',[201] may have ramifications for the test of due diligence applied by the HRC and other courts and bodies.

It is worth noting that most of the violence against women cases have been extreme situations of abuse, in which it could hardly be argued that the litany of procedural and substantive errors would give rise to findings of human rights violations. It is not yet clear, however, where exactly the limits of the test lie. I now turn to the approach of the CAT to non-state actor violence.

As described above, the most criticised aspect of Article 1 of the UNCAT is the nexus requirement that the severe pain or suffering must be inflicted or instigated by or have the consent or acquiescence of a public official or other person acting in an official capacity. At the time of its drafting, there was some discussion as to whether or not the definition of torture should be limited to acts of public officials.[202] It was generally agreed that the UNCAT should apply both to acts committed by public

[201] Hungary had indicated that the Hungarian Parliament had adopted a resolution on a national strategy for the prevention and effective treatment of violence within the family, including the following: 'introducing a restraining order into legislation; ensuring that proceedings before the Courts or other authorities in domestic violence cases are given priority; reinforcing existing witness protection rules and introducing new rules aimed at ensuring adequate legal protection for personal security of victims of violence within the family; elaborating clear protocols for the police, child care organs and social and medical institutions; extending and modernizing the network of shelters and setting up victim protection crisis centres; providing free legal aid in certain circumstances; working out a complex nationwide action programme to eliminate violence within the family that applies sanctions and protective measures; training of professionals; ensuring data collection on violence within the family; requesting the judiciary to organize training for judges and to find a way to ensure that cases relating to violence within the family are given priority; and launching a nationwide campaign to address indifference to violence within the family and the perception of domestic violence as a private matter and to raise awareness of State, municipal and social organs and journalists' (para. 5.7). It also recommended 'prompt and effective intervention by the police and other investigating authorities; medical treatment of pathologically aggressive persons and application of protective measures for those who live in their environment; operation of 24-hour "SOS" lines; organization of rehabilitation programmes; organization of sport and leisure activities for youths and children from violence-prone families; integration of non-violent conflict resolution techniques and family-life education into the public educational system; establishment and operation of crisis intervention houses as well as mother and child care centres and support for the accreditation of civil organizations by municipalities; and launching of a media campaign against violence in the family.' (A. T. v. Hungary, CEDAW 2/2003 (26 January 2005), para. 5.8).

[202] Burgers and Danelius, The United Nations Convention against Torture, 45.

officials as well as to acts for which public officials could be considered to bear some responsibility. France was alone in arguing that an act of torture relates to the 'intrinsic nature of the act of torture itself, irrespective of the status of the perpetrator'.[203] Because of the inclusion of this phrase in Article 1, it has been criticised by feminist writers as impliedly excluding private acts. The case law on this point has been mixed, with progression towards adopting the HRC's due diligence standard.

In *G. R. B.* v. *Sweden*,[204] in which the complainant said she objected to being returned to Peru because members of Shining Path had raped her and she feared the group's reprisals, the CAT found that her claim failed on two grounds. First, the CAT held that a state party does not have an obligation to refrain from expelling a person who might risk pain or suffering inflicted by a non-governmental entity without the consent or acquiescence of the government. Such cases, it held, fall outside the scope of Article 3 of the UNCAT.[205] Second, the complainant failed to show that she would be personally at risk.[206]

McCorquodale and La Forgia rightly criticise this decision as the CAT did not deal with the issue of state acquiescence, as required by the definition in Article 1. They argue that the CAT ought to have decided whether the government of Peru had properly investigated the rape, how many reported rapes had not been investigated, and whether non-state actors were able to rape because of the lack of state action.[207] That is, the CAT should have analysed whether the state had acquiesced in her rape owing to failures to respond, or to take her complaints seriously. The complainant submitted that her parents had reported the events to the police, 'but they did not show any interest in the matter'. This decision is particularly troublesome in light of the well-documented evidence of rape and other violence perpetrated against women by Shining Path, including the assassination of twelve leading feminists.[208] Human Rights Watch reported in 1992 that the Peruvian military engages in widespread rape and that such abuse has been considered only 'an occasional, regrettable excess'.[209] This decision is indicative of a number of factors. First, it shows that members

---

[203] *Ibid.*   [204] *G. R. B.* v. *Sweden*, CAT 83/1997 (15 May 1998).

[205] *Ibid.*, para. 6.5.

[206] See, also, *M. P. S.* v. *Australia*, CAT 138/1999 (30 April 2002).

[207] R. McCorquodale and R. La Forgia, 'Taking Off the Blindfolds: Torture by Non-State Actors' (2001) 1 *Hum. Rts L. Rev.* 189, at 209–210.

[208] G. Robertson Q.C., *Crimes against Humanity: The Struggle for Global Justice* (2nd edn, London: Penguin Books, 2002), 364.

[209] Americas Watch and Women's Rights Project, *Untold Terror: Violence against Women in Peru's Armed Conflict* (New York: Human Rights Watch, 1992), 65.

of the CAT do not always grasp how the issue of 'acquiescence' should be applied and second that, while the definition of 'torture' has scope to include abuse by non-state actors where the state is taken as 'acquiescing' in that abuse, the CAT is not always attuned to it. The public/private dichotomy can, therefore, be overcome only when the CAT pays closer attention to it. However, the third observation drawn from this case is the difficulty of applying international human rights law in the contexts of internal armed conflict, fragile states, or states confronting armed opposition. There appears to be an underlying reluctance on the part of the treaty bodies (and other international courts) to attribute violence committed by non-state groups to the state in these circumstances, especially where the state is openly opposed to such violence.

Another case, *S. V. et al. v. Canada*,[210] in which the author feared return to Sri Lanka owing to the actions of the Liberation Tigers of Tamil Eelam (LTTE), represents part of this pattern of decision-making. Like *G. R. B. v. Sweden*, this ruling seems to centre on the fact that the government of Sri Lanka did not support the actions of the LTTE or any other insurgent group, that is, it did not consent or acquiesce in LTTE's actions. Rather, they simply did not have control of the territory in which the LTTE were operating. These cases may suggest that in order to satisfy the 'consent or acquiescence' requirement something more than an 'inability' to act is needed: arguably a higher thershold than that under due diligence as applied by the HRC. As understood by the CAT, the consent or acquiescence requirement implies some knowledge of the activities of the non-state actors, general agreement with those actions, or a purposive refusal to act. However, the CAT, in *S. V. et al. v. Canada*, did not consider the issue of whether LTTE members had attained a certain level of quasi-government status, at least as far as their control over a particular territorial area was concerned, or whether the second limb of Article 1 applied ('other person acting in an official capacity'). Here, again, the emphasis of the CAT seems to be placed on the 'goodwill' of the state, rather than on the right of an individual to obtain a remedy for such harms, which is also a right recognised under international law.[211] It is envisaged that similar obstacles would be placed in the way of complaints relating to domestic violence or human trafficking. It has already been argued, for example, that human trafficking is a question of criminal law, rather than human rights law, especially in circumstances where the state is not

---

[210] *S. V. et al. v. Canada*, CAT 49/1996 (15 May 2001).
[211] See, e.g., Article 2(3), ICCPR.

directly involved in the trafficking but has taken steps to guard against it.[212] Questions abound as to the required standard of prevention and protection to implicate state complicity, as yet undefined.

The extent to which complainants are required to inform or complain to the local authorities in order to meet the 'consent or acquiescence' standard is another issue begging further analysis, of which no guidance is available in committees' jurisprudence.

The case of S. V. can be contrasted with a subsequent decision in Elmi v. Australia,[213] in which the CAT was prepared to characterise Somali warring factions as 'other persons acting in an official capacity' for the purposes of Article 1 of the UNCAT. The clans in question prescribed their own laws, had their own law-enforcement mechanisms, and provided their own education, health, and taxation systems.[214] The CAT distinguished the Elmi case from G. R. B. v. Sweden because in Elmi there was a situation in which the non-state actors were in 'effective' control and there was an absence of a central government from which Mr Elmi could have sought protection.[215] Strikingly, the 'lack of a central government' criterion is likely to exclude almost all claims in which non-state groups acting in an official capacity directly perpetrate the harmful conduct, as very few states, if any, lack a central government. Rather the situations that are likely to arise concern states that have lost control of parts of their territory.

In fact, a subsequent, near identical, case of H. M. H. I. v. Australia,[216] involving a rejected Somali asylum-seeker's claim that his return to Somalia would breach Australia's obligations under Article 3, distinguished the case of Elmi. The CAT did so by stating that the 'exceptional' situation of a country wholly lacking state authority (that existed at the time of the Elmi decision) no longer existed in Somalia, owing to the existence of the Transitional National Government (TNG). The TNG was considered by the CAT to be a state authority, partly because of its relations with the international community. Because H. M. H. I. feared torture at the hands of non-state actors, and not from the new state authorities, his claim was considered to fall outside the scope of Article 3 of the UNCAT.

---

[212] See, R. Piotrowicz, 'The Legal Nature of Trafficking in Human Beings' (2009) 4 Intercultural Hum. Rts L. Rev., 175.

[213] Elmi v. Australia, CAT 120/1998 (14 May 1999). For further analysis on Elmi v. Australia, see McCorquodale and La Forgia, 'Taking Off the Blindfolds'.

[214] Elmi v. Australia, para. 5.5.

[215] Ibid., para. 5.2. McCorquodale and La Forgia, 'Taking Off the Blindfolds', 197.

[216] H. M. H. I. v Australia, CAT 177/2000 (1 May 2002).

However, the CAT did not deliberate on whether the state authority would 'acquiesce' in the feared acts of other clans or other 'private' citizens, either through inaction (which seems to be insufficient), by not having put in place measures to protect such persons against this type of fear, or because of impunity.

In contrast to the above decisions, the CAT has held in a communication with a different set of facts that actions of non-state or private actors can fall within the UNCAT by virtue of the terms 'consent or acquiescence', albeit in more limited circumstances than under the ICCPR. In the case of *Dzemajl et al.* v. *Yugoslavia*,[217] the CAT was satisfied that Roma residents subjected to violent attacks by non-Roma neighbours had a claim under the UNCAT. The CAT accepted that the police had been informed of the immediate risk facing the complainants by a 'mob' of several hundred non-Roma residents armed with stones, Molotov cocktails, and other objects and who had broken car and house windows and then set them on fire. At the end of the rage, the whole settlement had been levelled, and all properties belonging to the Roma residents were either burnt or completely destroyed.[218] In finding that the police had not taken any appropriate measures to protect the complainants, the police were found to have 'acquiesced' in the actions in the sense of Article 16 (and *ipso facto* in the sense of Article 1, although the latter was not found to have been breached).[219] If the reasoning in this ruling is followed, it could prove pivotal to holding the state responsible in specific domestic or family violence or other non-state actor cases.

These cases demonstrate that, for the most part, the UNCAT definition of 'torture' has been interpreted more restrictively than its ICCPR equivalent by the HRC and by most other international bodies. The specific wording in Article 1 of the UNCAT has given scope to the CAT (or confined the CAT) to limit the types of cases that would otherwise satisfy the torture threshold. This is not to say that the actions of non-state or private actors do not fall within the remit of Articles 1 or 16 of the UNCAT. The CAT itself has raised concern, for example, in its concluding observations on state reports about the perpetration of torture, arbitrary detention, or ill-treatment at the hands of non-state actors, such

---

[217] *Dzemajl et al.* v. *Yugoslavia*, CAT 161/2000 (21 November 2002).

[218] *Ibid.*, paras. 2.7–2.9.

[219] The CAT has reiterated its concern regarding alleged failures of the state to prevent and to fully and promptly investigate violent attacks by non-state actors against ethnic and other minorities: see, Concluding observations on Croatia, UN Doc. CAT/C/CR/32/3, 11 June 2004, para. 8(f).

as 'traditional chiefs, sometimes with the support of the forces of law and order'.[220]

However, not every act of a non-state actor will fall within the definition, as it will depend on the role played by the state itself or another person acting in an official capacity, the latter being, so far, limited by the CAT to quasi-governmental structures that exercise effective control over a territory and where there is no central government.[221] This latter interpretation limits its application to very few, if any, situations worldwide. The current jurisprudence of the CAT does not protect women against brutal rapes or mass killings by rebel soldiers, for example, except where it can be said that the soldiers were in effective control of the territory and there was no central government. Of course, they may be protected by international humanitarian law, although it too suffers from a limited application in the context of internal armed conflict and does not apply to anything short of an 'armed conflict'. Similarly, this interpretation of the UNCAT does not protect women from harm if the state has no knowledge of it and cannot be said, therefore, to have consented or acquiesced in it, even if they may have failed in a more global sense in their responsibilities of due diligence. A mere inability to act or lack of knowledge would not meet the CAT's early understandings of 'consent or acquiescence'.

In contrast to the above analysis, and contrary to its case law thus far, the CAT in 2008 stated emphatically that the 'due diligence' test guided its work in relation to non-state actors. General Comment No. 2 states:

> The Committee has made clear that where State authorities or others acting in official capacity or under colour of law, know or have reasonable grounds to believe that acts of torture or ill-treatment are being committed by non-State officials or private actors and they fail to exercise due diligence to prevent, investigate, prosecute and punish such non-State officials or private actors consistently with the Convention, the State bears responsibility and its officials should be considered as authors, complicit or otherwise responsible under the Convention for consenting to or acquiescing in such impermissible acts. Since the failure of the State to exercise due diligence to intervene to stop, sanction and provide remedies to victims of torture facilitates and enables non-State actors to commit

---

[220] CAT, Concluding observations on Cameroon, UN Doc. CAT/C/CR/31/6, 5 February 2004, para. 4(c).

[221] It has been argued that under the law of state responsibility, this is the only interpretation that the CAT could have adopted: see, K. Fortin, *Rape as Torture: A Triumph or a Straight Jacket?*, LL.M Dissertation, Utrecht University, The Netherlands, 2008 (published by Faculty of Law, Utrecht University, Science Shop of Law, Economics and Governance, 2008).

acts impermissible under the Convention with impunity, the State's indifference or inaction provides a form of encouragement and/or de facto permission. The Committee has applied this principle to States parties' failure to prevent and protect victims from gender-based violence, such as rape, domestic violence, female genital mutilation, and trafficking.[222]

This is a significant shift in relation to how the CAT has applied the interpretation of Articles 1 and 16. Perhaps the tide is turning on how the CAT handles non-state torture? The above General Comment appears to suggest that failures to fulfil due diligence obligations would also satisfy the consent or acquiescence wording of Articles 1 and 16 as a matter of course. In fact, the case of *Velásquez Rodríguez* used the language of acquiescence in framing the due diligence duty:

> What is decisive is whether a violation of the rights recognised by the Convention has occurred with the support of, or *the acquiescence* of the government, or whether the State has allowed the act to take place without taking measures to prevent it or to punish those responsible [my emphasis].[223]

That is, consent or acquiescence requires no more than a failure to fulfil due diligence obligations of prevention, investigation, prosecution, punishment, and redress. So far, however, the CAT's general practice has been to apply a stricter interpretation of its mandate. What, then, is the difference between the duty of 'due diligence' applied in other human rights areas and the 'consent or acquiescence' standard of the UNCAT as applied in the above case law?

As far as can be determined from the approaches of the two treaty bodies, the duty of due diligence requires states to take both pre- and post-abuse measures. For example, states are required to take steps to *prevent* domestic violence generally, including through legislation and other measures. If they fail to act to the level of due diligence required, they could be held responsible for an actual occurrence of domestic violence on their territory. Thus, a state would be responsible for domestic violence if it were lawful for a man to beat or rape his wife under the law or if the police were instructed not to prevent such violations or not to offer assistance, whether or not they knew or acquiesced in a particular incident. The state is also obligated to investigate, prosecute, and punish those responsible and to offer compensation to those aggrieved. This is a positive outcome for female claimants.

[222] CAT, General Comment No. 2: Implementation of Article 2 by States Parties, para. 18.
[223] *Velásquez Rodriguez* v. *Honduras*, I-ACtHR, Ser. C, No. 4 (29 July 1988), para. 173.

In contrast, the jurisprudence outlined in this book shows that the 'consent or acquiescence' element of the UNCAT has been approached by the CAT as requiring *actual* knowledge of a particular incident and *actual* refusal to act: a higher standard of proof than due diligence, which can be implicated by mere failures to act. The CAT's approach in these decisions does not appear to create any pre-abuse preventative obligations on a state, although a state may be held to breach other individual provisions of the UNCAT.[224] Nonetheless, it is possible for female victims of domestic violence who have suffered 'severe pain or suffering' and who have reported such incidents to the police to no avail to mount successful claims before the CAT if the police or other government officials fail in their duties to offer assistance, or to investigate, prosecute, or punish alleged offenders. Nonetheless, as long as some form of recognised state structure exists, this rationale will not protect women from the actions of non-state armed groups who control parts of the territory, even if that structure is not wholly effective. There are myriad examples of women (and men) who are therefore not protected by the UNCAT under this construction. Apart from the 2008 General Comment, 'acquiescence' has not been read by the CAT as including an inability to act, nor does it include failing to have the appropriate mechanisms in place to prevent such actions or to protect persons against such harm.

Feminist scholars are, therefore, right to criticise the definition of torture under the UNCAT, but not only on the basis that a link must be established between a particular harm and a 'public official' or the state (a prerequisite for any human rights violation under international law). Rather, the terms 'consent or acquiescence' and 'other person acting in an official capacity' have not been interpreted in the way the drafters of the treaty intended, nor do the interpretations available reflect evolving realities. The Chairman-Rapporteur for two years of the drafting process stated: 'All such situations where responsibility of the authorities is somehow engaged are supposed to be covered by [this] rather wide phrase appearing in Article 1.'[225] This has not been the accepted interpretation of the UNCAT to date, with the exception of the 2008 General Comment, which hints that the CAT is attempting to conform to the generally

---

[224] E.g. by failing to enact legislative, administrative, judicial, or other measures to prevent acts of torture (Article 2), to criminalise torture (Articles 4 and 5), to educate and train law enforcement personnel, civil or military, medical personnel, public officials or other persons involved in custody, interrogation (Article 10), to investigate (Article 12), etc.

[225] Burgers and Danelius, *The United Nations Convention against Torture*, 120. See, also, McCorquodale and La Forgia, 'Taking Off the Blindfolds'.

accepted position at international law of due diligence and to break with its own precedent. The public/private dichotomy has thus been fractured under the UNCAT, albeit partially. Moreover, there remain gaps, too, with the due diligence standard, particularly in relation to the content of the obligation to prevent.

4   Contextual analysis

A final issue that merits attention is the way in which the treaty bodies have adopted a contextual analysis to torture cases. To what extent are the individual's subjective characteristics relevant to a determination of whether an act meets the severity threshold for torture? Almost repeating the language used by the ECHR in *Ireland* v. *United Kingdom*,[226] the HRC stated in *Vuolanne* v. *Finland*:

> [T]he assessment of what constitutes inhuman or degrading treatment falling within the meaning of Article 7 depends on all the circumstances of the case, such as the duration and manner of the treatment, its physical or mental effects as well as *the sex, age and state of health of the victim* [my emphasis].[227]

Similarly, in the case of *Kindler* v. *Canada*, the HRC referred to 'personal factors' in determining whether the imposition of capital punishment would constitute a violation of Article 7.[228] These statements indicate that subjective factors are relevant to whether the nature of a particular act constitutes torture or another form of ill-treatment or punishment. It is not, therefore, a purely objective test. Obviously, there are some forms of harm that would constitute a breach of Article 7 regardless of the particular characteristics of the victim. Nonetheless, there may be other forms of harm that would not reach the requisite level of seriousness of torture or a lesser form of ill-treatment or punishment if only so-called objective or (gender-) neutral standards were applied. According to feminist scholars, applying only objective or neutral standards would be disadvantageous, if not discriminatory, for women because the standard applied would most likely be 'male'.[229]

---

[226] *Ireland* v. *United Kingdom* (1978) 2 EHRR 25.
[227] *Vuolanne* v. *Finland*, HRC 265/1987 (7 April 1989), para. 9.2.
[228] *Kindler* v. *Canada*, HRC 470/1991 (30 July 1991). The HRC also referred to the specific conditions of detention on death row, and whether the proposed method of execution is particularly abhorrent.
[229] See discussion in Chapter 2.

In its list of issues for state party reports, the CAT, too, has referred to gender, age, and geographical location as relevant to a determination of torture, as well as asking that states parties legislate with 'specific provisions regarding gender based breaches of the Convention, such as sexual violence'.[230] However, more specifically, in the case of V. L. v. Switzerland the CAT proved sympathetic to gendered reasons why a woman would not be forthcoming regarding alleged sexual assaults. The Swiss authorities raised doubt about her story because she had failed to mention the sexual abuse in the early stages of her asylum procedure. The CAT responded:

> It is well known that the loss of privacy and prospect of both humiliation based on revelation alone of the acts concerned may cause both women and men to withhold the fact that they have been subject to rape and/or other forms of sexual abuse until it appears absolutely necessary. Particularly for women, there is the additional fear of shaming and rejection by their partner or family members.[231]

Giving weight to subjective factors in the recognition of particular acts as torture or other ill-treatment, including questions of gender, can be determinative. Intimidating language that may fall short of Article 7 ICCPR abuse when applied against an adult may reach the threshold if inflicted upon a child, for example. Assaulting a known haemophiliac would be more serious than the same conduct perpetrated against a non-haemophiliac. Solitary confinement or psychological forms of intimidation might be additionally severe for an individual with mental illness.[232] Sexual intimidation of male Arab Muslims at the hands of female Western soldiers may take on a different tone than the same conduct perpetrated against non-religious Western men, although still unlawful.[233] This approach could be equated to the 'thin skull' rule in the tort law of negligence, or to take your victim as you find her.[234] Alternatively,

---

[230] See, e.g., CAT, List of Issues to be Considered During the Examination of the Periodic Report of Denmark, UN Doc. CAT/C/DNK/Q/5/Rev.1, 19 February 2007, Item 20; Italy, UN Doc. CAT/C/ITA/Q/4/Rev.1, 6 February 2007, Item 20; Mexico, UN Doc. CAT/C/MEX/Q/4, 19 October 2005, Item 42.

[231] V. L. v. Switzerland, CAT 262/2005 (20 November 2006), para. 8.8.

[232] See similar arguments raised in relation to refugee law: Edwards, 'Age and Gender Dimensions in International Refugee Law'.

[233] See, A. Edwards, 'Aydin v Turkey, Akayesu and Abu Ghraib: Re-Conceptualising "Torture" Under International Law from a Feminist Perspective', Australian and New Zealand Society of International Law Annual Conference, Canberra, June 2005.

[234] This rule, also called the 'eggshell skull' rule, holds one liable for all consequences resulting from tortious (usually negligent) activities leading to injury to another person, even if the victim suffers an unusually high level of damage arising from a pre-existing illness

it could be considered simply good legal reasoning, or even a form of 'contextual analysis' and part of feminist methods of legal reasoning, outlined in Chapter 1. There may, however, be exceptions where, for example, the act in question is about loss of sexual autonomy, in the case of rape, rather than questions of coercion or force, as discussed above, with the former meeting the threshold of severity without need to consider additional factors.

The capacity of the treaty bodies to take into account subjective factors in its deliberations, including the victim's sex and gender, is an essential part of 'gender mainstreaming'. Even though the HRC has stated that subjective factors are relevant (and the CAT has accepted the same approach, albeit less directly), one can detect an absence of such references in its jurisprudence. Apart from the cases mentioned above, in *Darwinia R. Mónaco (Ximena Vicario) v. Argentina*, the HRC made reference to special protections owed to children under Article 24 of the ICCPR. However, in this decision the HRC did not go on to use the child's age or maturity to help it apply Article 7 in an age-friendly manner, but instead opted to make a finding under Article 24.[235] In establishing torture, the CAT requires the individual to be 'personally at risk'. Nonetheless, the CAT has not interpreted this requirement as inferring subjective factors rather than causal ones. So far, this requirement has not been interpreted in such a way for subjective factors to have the effect of lowering the 'objectively' determined severity threshold.

The ECtHR in *Aydin v. Turkey*[236] illustrates how such an approach would work in practice, subject to some limitations. The Grand Chamber

or condition. It is also applied in some criminal law systems and is referred to as 'take your victim as you find them' (or *talem qualem*).

[235] *Darwinia R. Mónaco (Ximena Vicario) v. Argentina*, HRC 400/1990 (3 April 1995). The author's granddaughter (Ximena Vicario) was taken to the headquarters of the federal police with her mother in February 1977. Her father was apprehended the following day. Both parents and the child subsequently disappeared. An investigation was launched but the parents were never located. X. V. was subsequently found in the home of a nurse who claimed to have taken care of the child. The nurse was preventatively detained by the state on grounds of having committed a crime of concealing the whereabouts of a minor and forgery of documents. In 1989 the author was given provisional guardianship of X. V., but the nurse was also granted visiting rights. Although the grandmother objected to this in court, she was told she had no standing as she was neither the child's parents nor her legal guardian. Various other appeals were made against the visits on the basis that they were psychologically damaging to the child. The author claimed, inter alia, that the visits and the delayed proceedings constituted a breach of various rights, including Article 7. The HRC did not rule on whether the visits amounted to psychological torture.

[236] *Aydin v. Turkey* (1997) 25 EHRR 251.

of the European Court of Human Rights in this case ruled (fourteen to seven):

> Rape of a detainee by an official of the State must be considered to be an especially grave and abhorrent form of ill-treatment given the ease with which the offender can exploit the vulnerability and weakened resistance of his victim. Furthermore, rape leaves deep psychological scars on the victim which do not respond to the passage of time as quickly as other forms of physical and mental violence. The applicant also experienced the acute physical pain of forced penetration, which must have left her feeling debased and violated both physically and emotionally. [237]

The Grand Chamber referred to both the sex and youth of the applicant (a seventeen-year-old girl) in making its decision, as well as to associated conditions of her treatment.[238] The ECtHR accepted that the 'accumulation of acts of physical and mental violence' and 'especially the cruel act of rape' amounted to torture in breach of Article 3, adding that the Court would have reached the same conclusion 'on either of these grounds taken separately'.[239] This case not only represents the first case before the ECtHR to recognise rape as a form of torture, but it is also one of the first findings of 'torture', rather than a lesser form of ill-treatment, issued by the Court.

Despite the positive outcome of the case, the minority's analysis can only be described as factually deficient, and at worst based on unfounded gender-based stereotypes of the 'proper' response of women to rape. First, they engaged in mathematical reasoning as to the alleged date of sexual assault and the birth of the applicant's first child. Second, without providing any information or evidence to support their statements, they suggested that the complainant's subsequent marriage to her cousin only a few days after the alleged rape was 'surprising in the cultural context of the region'. Nor did the minority request the applicant to furnish it with further information as to the reasons for her 'quick' marriage.[240] There was no discussion about whether this unfounded information was in fact relevant to the case at hand. As noted above in respect of jurisprudence before the I-ACtHR, there are intimations of a higher standard of proof being required for cases of sexual violence than for other forms of harm; and further, that in cases of rape at least, with the focus on deprivation of sexual autonomy, such issues should arguably be irrelevant. Despite

[237] Ibid., para. 83.   [238] Ibid., para. 84.   [239] Ibid., para. 86.
[240] See, Joint Dissenting Opinion of Gölcüklü, Matscher, Pettiti, De Meyer, Lopes Rocha, Makarczyk and Gotchev, 42–45.

the minority dissenting opinion, this decision represents a reversal of the 1976 European Commission Report in *Cyprus* v. *Turkey*,[241] in which it was concluded (twelve to one) that incidents of rape carried out by Turkish soldiers against Cypriot nationals constituted only 'inhuman treatment', not torture, within the meaning of Article 3 of the ECHR.

The above shows both how contextual reasoning and alertness to subjective factors can work to allow a more accurate picture of what actually happened, and the effect of those events, to be painted that better reflects the circumstances and experiences of individual victims. At the same time, however, it evidences that contextual analysis is itself subject to pre-existing gender prejudice. Gender is an important, albeit only one of the, factors that may be relevant to any particular case.

5   The Women's Committee and torture

As previously noted, the CEDAW does not contain a specific prohibition against 'torture' or other associated forms of ill-treatment. It would seem that the drafters of the CEDAW failed to recognise that women are victims of torture and in need of such protection. This omission occurred during the 1970s and 1980s, a period of increasing heavy-handedness of autocratic regimes in many parts of the world, including against women, either as activists themselves or by being implicated by membership in the family of politically active relatives. This reverse gender blindness may explain the Women's Committee's own treatment of torture in its jurisprudence.

In its first fact-finding inquiry carried out in the Ciudad Juárez area of Chihuahua, Mexico, referred to in Chapters 4 and 6 of this book, the Women's Committee appears to adopt the traditional interpretation of 'torture' derived from Article 1 of the UNCAT. Its statement at paragraph 67 illustrates its approach:

> As far as [the Committee] know[s], the method of these sexual crimes begins with the victims' abduction through deception or by force. [The women] are held captive and subjected to sexual abuse, including rape *and, in some cases, torture*, until they are murdered. Their bodies are then abandoned in some deserted spot [my emphasis].[242]

This approach to torture is more conservative than that of some other international and regional bodies. The term 'torture' in this report seems

---

[241] *Cyprus* v. *Turkey* (1976) 4 EHRR 482.
[242] CEDAW, Report on Mexico, UN doc. CEDAW/C/2005/OP.8/MEXICO, paras. 232, 241, 273, 274.

to be used in a very traditional sense to refer to physical or psychological pain or suffering committed by public officials or others acting in an official capacity to extract confessions or information from detainees. Torture here is distinguished as something distinct from rape or other forms of sexual assault carried out by private citizens. This distinction highlights one of the problems of characterising rape as a form of torture in that using two terms to apply to the same act can become confusing when trying to describe exactly what occurred. Was it rape, was it torture, or was it rape as torture? In conflating old and new interpretations of the same term, the VAW = T school of thought is problematic in so far as it may obscure the reality and complexity of the issue.

D   The feminist record on VAW = T

So how far have the UN human rights treaty bodies come in terms of incorporating the realities of women's lives within the torture provisions? From the above review it can be seen that significant rhetorical progress has been made since the 1990s to accept non-traditional understandings of torture as rightly within the mandates of various committees. Recognising rape and other forms of sexual violence as meeting the severity threshold of torture or cruel, inhuman, or degrading treatment or punishment must be heralded as a great leap forward, albeit long delayed. It is in many ways a feminist triumph that should not be underestimated. At a minimum, it brings violence against women within the fold of international human rights law, rather than being the concern of national authorities alone. This position is now accepted by all the major human rights courts as well as by the range of international criminal law tribunals and courts. The jurisprudence indicates a departure from the view of rape and, by analogy, other forms of violence against women 'as sexual, not political, a permissible "private" indiscretion, rather than as a tool of political domination'.[243]

Specifically in relation to rape, it is now accepted by every international and regional human rights body with a mandate over torture that rape is a sufficiently serious form of harm as to constitute torture under international law.[244] This consensus position must now be said to crystallise

---

[243] Copelon, 'Recognising the Egregious in the Everyday', n. 100, citing various US decisions. See, also, C. Bunch, 'Women's Rights as Human Rights: Toward a Re-Vision of Human Rights' (1990) 12 *HRQ* 486; D. Blatt, 'Recognizing Rape as a Method of Torture' (1992) 19 *NYU Rev. L. & Soc. Change* 821.

[244] The African Commission on Human and Peoples' Rights (ACmHPR) has similarly found that forced nudity, electricity burns, and sexual assaults 'constitute, together and

rape at least into a prohibited form of torture under customary international law. What has yet to be sufficiently analysed by the committees is whether rape per se should be found to satisfy the severity threshold for torture rather than a lesser form of treatment or punishment. The crime of rape appears to have attained a special position among the various forms of violence committed against women, but there has been limited clarification of whether this approach is justified, or on what basis it can be explained.[245]

In addition to rape, the HRC has found, inter alia, female genital mutilation, domestic violence, and forced abortion or forced sterilisation to fall within Article 7 protections, while the CAT has referred to domestic violence, forced marriage, incest, and stoning for adultery as relevant to its mandate. There has also been some recognition that discriminatory laws or conduct may breach the ill-treatment provisions, although such laws or conduct would probably not be of sufficient severity to reach the threshold reserved for findings of 'torture' itself. In the absence of an international treaty outlawing violence against women, it could be argued that the torture provisions are fast becoming the primary human rights protection in this area.[246] Accepting this, the real question for this study is whether it is an effective feminist strategy.

Although the record of the treaty bodies has not been consistent, with many decisions still continuing to omit references to or to exclude an analysis of relevant gender factors, the overall picture presented indicates an acceptance at the level of international law that the torture provisions can be interpreted and applied to reflect the *nature and type* of harm predominantly affecting women. As noted, the torture provisions have always been available to detained female political dissidents and activists, even if this has not been widely acknowledged. As the HRC stated in its first General Comment on Article 7 of the ICCPR: 'As appears from the terms of this article, the scope of protection required goes far beyond torture as normally understood.'[247] These interpretations have updated the torture prohibitions, and they also reflect a better understanding of the importance of the non-discrimination and equality foundations of international

---

separately, violations of Article 5.' See, *Commission Nationale des Droits de l'Homme et des Libertés* v. *Chad* (Merits), ACmHPR, Comm. No. 74/92 (October 1995).

[245] See, discussion above, and McGlynn, 'Rape, Torture and the European Convention on Human Rights' for a provocative article on this very question.

[246] Cf. Chapters 4 and 6. Note, too, that Articles 8 (slavery; servitude) and 9 (security of person) of the ICCPR have not been used to the same degree.

[247] HRC, General Comment No. 7: Torture or Cruel, Inhuman or Degrading Treatment or Punishment, para. 2.

human rights law. The real linguistic difficulties appear to lie less in the appearance of the masculine pronoun, as some feminists suggest,[248] than in the specific meanings acquired over time for the term 'torture'. It remains without doubt that torture has come to be accepted as representing particular forms of prohibited conduct of state-sponsored terror, which continues to cloud the imagination of the treaty bodies in applying the definition of torture outside this context.

Positive findings of torture, for example, in each of the cases mentioned in this chapter still need to prove a connection between the act of abuse *and* the state; not to mention that the number of positive decisions can still be counted in single digits. For some feminist scholars, therefore, attempts at dismantling the public/private divide remain unsatisfactory and continue to exclude women from the full protection of the law. Under the UNCAT torture must be perpetrated by either a public official, another person acting in an official capacity, or with an official's consent or acquiescence (or at their instigation). In order to invoke state responsibility for 'private' harm, the CAT has, until its 2008 General Comment, strictly construed the 'consent or acquiescence' element as requiring actual knowledge (it is still unclear whether constructive knowledge would suffice) of the events in question, as well as a purposive refusal to act on the part of the public official or other person acting in an official capacity. Provided a government official is aware of, for example, a domestic dispute and refuses to act or does not take appropriate steps to protect the applicant, there is a human rights violation by 'acquiescence'.[249] The CAT has not, however, been challenged greatly to secure this position, owing to the limited number of cases raising 'private' violations.

A further problem remains in relation to who qualifies as an 'other person acting in an official capacity' in Article 1. The CAT has required that the 'other person acting in an official position' exercise effective control of the territory in a state that does not have a central government. That is, the person must form part of a de facto government, and even better if they form part of the *de jure* government. By this reasoning, the CAT has ruled out a whole range of situations in which women (and men) seek protection from torture at the hands of non-state actors. Women subjected to abduction, rape, or beating by rebel soldiers, for example, would not be protected by the torture provisions following this reasoning unless it could be proved that the rebel group had 'effective control of territory'

[248] See, Chapter 2.
[249] See, *Dzemajl et al.* v. *Yugoslavia*, CAT 161/2000 (21 November 2002).

and there was no central government. It limits this aspect of the UNCAT provisions to only a few countries and situations worldwide, and therefore renders it virtually worthless in this regard. It also pushes victims to rely on international humanitarian law rather than international human rights law and thereby to settle for a narrower set of protections. The public/private dichotomy remains a major stumbling block to women's equal benefit of the protection of the torture prohibition, as does the state-based nature of international law. The extent to which the public/private–state/ non-state division remains supports feminist critiques that statehood and sovereignty interfere with creative or reconstructionist interpretations of these provisions.[250]

Non-state or private abuses are recognised under the ICCPR (and under other regional human rights instruments) where the state fails to satisfy the evolving international law notion/duty of 'due diligence'. The CAT's 2008 General Comment also indicates that it is likely to expand its above-outlined approach along similar lines, but it is not yet clear how 'consent and acquiescence' matches 'due diligence'. Although the articulation of the duty of 'due diligence' is still relatively elusive, it has allowed women's previously 'private' claims to become the responsibility of the state where it is either unable or unwilling to offer protection against such harm. At the level of international criminal responsibility, the ICTY and ICTR have both ruled that the 'public' official requirement of the UNCAT is not part of customary international law for the purposes of individual criminal responsibility.[251] The Statute of the ICC has adopted the same position. International refugee law also accepts that, subject to the other elements of the definition of a 'refugee' in the Convention relating to the Status of Refugees 1951,[252] as amended by its Protocol 1967,[253] where a claim to refugee status is based on the actions of a non-state actor as the source of the persecutory conduct, status will be granted if the state is

---

[250] Charlesworth, 'Alienating Oscar?'.

[251] See, e.g., *Prosecutor* v. *Jean-Paul Akayesu* (Appeal), ICTR, Case No. ICTR-96-4-A (1 June 2001), in which the Appeal Court stated: 'outside the framework of the Convention Against Torture, the "public official" requirement is not a requirement under customary international law in relation to individual criminal responsibility for torture as a crime against humanity.' See, also, *Prosecutor* v. *Kunarac, Kovac and Vukovic*, ICTY, Case No. IT-96-23-T and IT-96-23/1-T (22 February 2001); Case No. IT-96–23 and IT-96–23/1 (12 June 2002); *Prosecutor* v. *Krnojelac*, ICTY, Case No. IT-97–25-T (15 March 2002).

[252] Convention relating to the Status of Refugees 1951, GA res. 429 (V), 14 December 1950, 189 UNTS 137; entered into force 22 April 1954.

[253] Protocol relating to the Status of Refugees 1967, GA res. 2198(XXI), 16 December 1966, 606 UNTS 267; entered into force 4 October 1967.

'unable or unwilling' to provide protection against that harm.[254] What is still unclear, though, is how vigilant the state must be in taking steps to prevent these types of abuses, and it appears that only 'reasonable' steps must be taken.

Certainly, the ECtHR has recognised that inadequate legislation and ineffective investigation would bring a state into violation of Article 3 of the ECHR for so-called 'date rape'.[255] In addition, the first decision of the Women's Committee, although framed as a case of discrimination rather than as torture, itemised a whole plethora of state responsibilities to protect women against domestic violence, including legislative, administrative, and social welfare changes.[256] Such decisions are likely to be useful to other treaty bodies in giving content and meaning to the notion/duty of 'due diligence', at least as far as cases of domestic violence are concerned. The Special Rapporteur on Violence against Women, Its Causes and Consequences has also attempted to set benchmarks or indicators to assess progress at the international level on violence against women,[257] and the OHCHR is in the process of refining these for external release. The specific obligations imposed upon states parties in Articles 2–15 of the UNCAT may also offer minimum standards and be useful guidance to other international and regional mechanisms.

E   Conclusion

From the perspective of proponents of gender mainstreaming, doctrinal inclusion, or the 'rape as torture' schools of thought, this chapter points towards much progress and, for some, a feminist triumph. There is, at a minimum, rhetorical acceptance that various forms of violence against women are human rights violations when they are as serious as torture

---

[254] UNHCR, *Handbook on Procedures and Criteria for Determining Refugee Status under the 1951 Convention and the 1967 Protocol relating to the Status of Refugees* (Geneva, 1979, re-edited 1992), para. 65; UNHCR, 'Guidelines on International Protection: Gender-Related Persecution within the Context of Article 1A(2) of the 1951 Convention and/or 1967 Protocol relating to the Status of Refugees', UN Doc. HCR/GIP/02/01, 7 May 2002, para. 19. For a list of relevant cases, see Edwards, 'Age and Gender Dimensions in International Refugee Law'.

[255] See, *M. C. v. Bulgaria* (2003) 40 EHRR 20.

[256] *A. T. v. Hungary*, CEDAW 2/2003 (26 January 2005), Conclusions on the Merits, II. para. 9.6, II. General, (a)–(h).

[257] Report of the Special Rapporteur on Violence against Women, Its Causes and Consequence, *Indicators on Violence against Women and State Response*, UN Doc. A/HRC/7/6, 29 January 2008, para. 21.

in nature, impact, and effect. In particular, rape per se appears to reach the required severity threshold. One limitation to this approach has been a lack of competence on the part of the members of the treaty bodies, who collectively continue to display difficulty in identifying and taking account of gender dimensions in case law, or who otherwise cannot agree by consensus on its relevance. This is played out in case law that suggests a higher standard of proof in relation to allegations of crimes of a sexual nature. This leaves female complainants vulnerable to the competence limitations of the treaty bodies and other international courts and tribunals. The committees generally show a willingness to recognise violence against women as torture, but they ultimately do not make it convincing, in particular because they fail to articulate their legal reasoning in sufficient detail. As noted in Chapter 3, the committees' working methods and style of decision-making do not assist outsiders in understanding fully the meaning and impact of their decisions, which in turn affects the legitimacy of their decisions and their acceptance by states parties and by victims.

On the other hand, the VAW = T strategy feeds into a system that distinguishes between the public and private spheres of everyday life, albeit with more ways available to satisfy the nexus requirement between the state and the harm in question. Like the VAW = SD formula outlined in Chapter 4, the VAW = T strategy fails to acknowledge that violence against women is a serious violation worthy in its own right of separate international legal regulation and condemnation. Instead, in order to be heard, women have to fit their experiences into provisions with entrenched meanings, and these meanings generally describe and cover the harm that men fear rather than the fears of women. Instead, for women to be heard, they must establish either that what they have suffered is equivalent to these traditional understandings or that such treatment warrants the creation of an exception to the rule: the former approach reinforces sexual hierarchies manifest in the 'male' standard of international law, while the latter exceptionalises the experiences of women and in turn 'essentialises' her into the stereotyped role of a victim of 'sexual non-political violence' or of culturally depraved acts. This system places a double and, therefore, unequal burden on women who are disproportionately subjected to forms of harm that do not fit within the traditional construct of torture. Women are thus yet to be treated equally under international law.

I now turn to the last of the three rights studied in this book: the right to life.

6

The right to life

A Introduction

The right to life is fundamental to the UN human rights system. Without it, all other rights would be 'devoid of meaning'.[1] In this chapter I examine how this right has been interpreted and applied by the UN treaty bodies in particular to respond to the context of violence against women. Like the other chapters, it draws upon jurisprudence from other international and regional courts where relevant. Of the three rights studied in this book, it has attracted the least attention and analysis by international feminist legal scholars, even though it is specifically relevant to women's lives. In many national jurisdictions, in contrast, the right to life has been and remains a site of feminist struggle.[2]

This chapter begins with an overview of how the right to life is conceived under international law generally, with a specific focus on Article 6 of the International Covenant on Civil and Political Rights (ICCPR).[3] I then consider how it has been extended to apply to particular issues of violence against women. Like the other rights studied in this book, I ask whether it has been an effective guarantor of protection for women against violence. I find that the traditional structure of the international prohibition of Article 6 of the ICCPR favours men's experiences to the extent that they are more likely than women to be subjected to the death penalty, military

---

[1] M. Nowak, *U.N. Covenant on Civil and Political Rights: CCPR Commentary* (2nd edn, Kehl: Engel, 2005), 121.

[2] See, e.g., debates over the issue of abortion: A. McColgan, *Women under the Law: The False Promise of Human Rights* (Harlow: Longman, 2000), Chapter 4; D. McBride Stetson, *Abortion Politics, Women's Movements, and the Democratic State* (Oxford University Press, 2001); R. M. Baird and S. E. Rosenbaum, *The Ethics of Abortion: Pro-Life vs. Pro-Choice* (3rd edn, New York: Prometheus Books, 2001); J. McMahan, *The Ethics of Killing: Problems at the Margins of Life* (Oxford University Press, 2002), Chapter 4; R. Solinger, *Pregnancy and Power: A Short History of Reproductive Politics in America* (New York University Press, 2005).

[3] International Covenant on Civil and Political Rights 1966, GA res. 2200A (XXI), 16 December 1966, 999 UNTS 171; entered into force 23 March 1976 (ICCPR).

conscription, or arbitrary deprivation of their lives by the state: the traditional subject matter of the prohibition. Women enter the picture as an
exception to capital punishment as far as they represent the reproductive guardians of unborn children. At the same time, however, women
are portrayed as being of a calibre of criminals who may be put to death
by the state, rather than as being only *victims* of crime. This dichotomy
challenges feminist arguments that women are portrayed only as victims
under international law rather than as autonomous actors.[4]

I also note that since the mid-1980s the interpretation of the right to
life has progressed from a narrow view of traditional legal protection
against arbitrary state killing to a broader view that requires states to protect individuals against the acts of non-state actors and to satisfy the basic
'survival' requirements of its citizens. This chapter finds that the modern
elaboration of the right to encompass 'quality of life' (or dignity) issues has
transformed it from a right that primarily pertained to men's fears to one
that also includes a host of concerns affecting women, including economic
and social disadvantage. In terms of feminist strategies to combat violence against women, campaigning on the right to life in international law
presents many of the same challenges as similar campaigns at the national
level, such as debates around competing rights relating to reproductive
freedom, privacy, and equality. The right to life is thus contested ground.
Not all of these issues have yet been dealt with fully by the treaty bodies,
or by international law. For these reasons, the right to life, centred around
Article 6 of the ICCPR, is a complex tool for feminists; however, it is also a
potentially powerful right in the fight against violence against women. At
a minimum, it ought to form part of any campaigns or legal strategies to
combat violence against women.

B   The right to life under international law

1   International instruments

The right to life is found in Article 3 of the Universal Declaration of
Human Rights 1948 (UDHR),[5] which was later transposed to Article 6 of
the ICCPR, albeit in longer form. Article 6 of the ICCPR provides:

---

[4] See, Chapter 2.
[5] Universal Declaration of Human Rights 1948, GA res. 217 A (III), 10 December 1948
(UDHR). Article 3 provides: 'Everyone has the right to life, liberty and security of
person.'

1. Every human being has the inherent right to life. This right shall be protected by law. No one shall be arbitrarily deprived of his [or her] life.

2. In countries which have not abolished the death penalty, sentence of death may be imposed only for the most serious crimes in accordance with the law in force at the time of the commission of the crime and not contrary to the provisions of the present Covenant and to the Convention on the Prevention and Punishment of the Crime of Genocide. This penalty can only be carried out pursuant to a final judgement rendered by a competent court.

3. When deprivation of life constitutes the crime of genocide, it is understood that nothing in this article shall authorize any State Party to the present Covenant to derogate in any way from any obligation assumed under the provisions of the Convention on the Prevention and Punishment of the Crime of Genocide.

4. Anyone sentenced to death shall have the right to seek pardon or commutation of the sentence. Amnesty, pardon or commutation of the sentence of death may be granted in all cases.

5. Sentence of death shall not be imposed for crimes committed by persons below eighteen years of age and shall not be carried out on pregnant women.

6. Nothing in this article shall be invoked to delay or to prevent the abolition of capital punishment by any State Party to the present Covenant.

Article 6 is a non-derogable right that has been characterised as a *jus cogens* norm of international law;[6] but it is not unlimited. As discussed below, it is not an absolute guarantee but is subject to several limitations. The death penalty, for example, is one of the contested permissible exceptions to the right to life under international law. In 1991 a Second Optional Protocol to the ICCPR entered into force with the aim of abolishing the death penalty altogether.[7]

In addition to Article 6 of the ICCPR, the Convention on the Prevention and Punishment of the Crime of Genocide 1948 prohibits a specific form of arbitrary deprivation of life aimed at destroying, in whole or in part,

---

[6] Article 4(2), ICCPR explicitly prescribes Article 6 as a non-derogable right. See, further, HRC, General Comment No. 29: States of Emergency (Article 4) (2001), UN Doc. CCPR/C/21/Rev.1/Add.1, 31 August 2001, paras. 7 and 11. See, also, Nowak, *CCPR Commentary* (2005), 121.

[7] Second Optional Protocol to the International Covenant on Civil and Political Rights, aiming at the abolition of the death penalty 1989, GA res. 44/128, 15 December 1989; entered into force 11 July 1991.

a national, ethnic, racial, or religious group.[8] The prohibition on genocide is also a peremptory norm of international law.[9] Article 6(3) of the
ICCPR reiterates the non-derogable status of genocide as specifically proscribed under international law. Genocide is also located as a crime under
international humanitarian law[10] and in the Statute of the International
Criminal Court (ICC).[11] Having taken on a specific legal meaning and
being *lex specialis* within the context of international criminal law/inter-
national humanitarian law, and having been well studied by feminist
scholars, genocide does not form part of this book.[12]

---

[8]   Convention on the Prevention and Punishment of the Crime of Genocide 1948, GA res. 260
      A (III), 9 December 1948, 78 UNTS 277; entered into force 12 January 1951. The crime of
      genocide is defined in Article II as: 'any of the following acts committed with intent to des-
      troy, in whole or in part, a national, ethnical, racial or religious group, as such: (a) Killing
      members of the group; (b) Causing serious bodily or mental harm to members of the group;
      (c) Deliberately inflicting on the group conditions of life calculated to bring about its phys-
      ical destruction in whole or in part; (d) Imposing measures intended to prevent births
      within the group; (e) Forcibly transferring children of the group to another group.'
[9]   I. Brownlie, *Principles of International Law* (5th edn, Oxford University Press, 1998), 517.
      See, especially, *Prosecutor* v. *Rutaganda* (Judgment and Sentence), ICTR, Case No. ICTR-
      96-3-T (6 December 1999), 451; *Prosecutor* v. *Servashago* (Sentence), ICTR, Case No. ICTR-
      98-39-5 (2 February 1999), 15, where genocide is described as 'the crime of crimes'.
[10] See, Article 27, Geneva Convention (IV) relative to the Protection of Civilian Persons
      in Time of War 1948, adopted 12 August 1949, 75 UNTS 287, entered into force 21
      October 1950 (Fourth Geneva Convention); Articles 49 and 75, Protocol I Additional
      to the Geneva Conventions of 12 August 1949 relating to the Protection of Civilians of
      International Armed Conflict 1977, adopted 8 June 1977, 1125 UNTS 3, entered into force
      7 December 1978 (Protocol I Additional to the Geneva Conventions 1977); and Article
      14, Protocol II Additional to the Geneva Conventions of 12 August 1949 relating to the
      Protection of the Victims of Non-International Armed Conflicts 1977, adopted 8 June
      1977, 1125 UNTS 609, entered into force 7 December 1978 (Protocol II Additional to the
      Geneva Conventions 1977).
[11] Article 6, Statute of the International Criminal Court, UN Doc. A/CONF.183/9, 17 July
      1998, 2187 UNTS 90; entered into force 1 July 2002. See, also, Article 4, Statute of the
      International Tribunal for the Prosecution of Persons Responsible for Serious Violations
      of International Humanitarian Law Committed in the Territory of the Former Yugoslavia
      since 1991, SC res. S/RES/827, 25 May 1993; Article 2, Statute of the International Criminal
      Tribunal for the Prosecution of Persons Responsible for Genocide and Other Serious
      Violations of International Humanitarian Law Committed in the Territory of Rwanda
      and Rwandan Citizens Responsible for Genocide and Other Such Violations Committed
      in the Territory of Neighbouring States, between 1 January 1994 and 31 December 1994,
      SC res. S/RES/955, 8 November 1994, 33 ILM 1598, 1600 (1994).
[12] For more on feminist analyses of the crime of genocide, see, e.g., J. G. Gardam and
      M. J. Jarvis, *Women, Armed Conflict and International Law* (The Hague: Kluwer
      Law International, 2001); N. N. R. Quénivet, *Sexual Offenses in Armed Conflict and
      International Law* (Ardsley, NY: Transnational Publishers, 2005); R. C. Carpenter,
      'Innocent Women and Children': Gender, Norms and the Protection of Civilians
      (London: Ashgate, 2006).

The International Covenant on Economic, Social and Cultural Rights (ICESCR)[13] does not contain a separate right to life equivalent to Article 6 of the ICCPR. However, 'life' is mentioned in various places, including in the right to an 'adequate standard of living'[14] and the right 'to take part in cultural life'.[15] Additionally, in respect of the special care and protection required for children, the ICESCR provides that they must be protected against economic exploitation or work that is dangerous to their health or life, or economic and social development.[16]

The Convention on the Rights of the Child (CRC)[17] has arguably adopted the most progressive approach to the right to life, linking it to issues of survival as well as development.[18] Article 6 of the CRC provides:

1. States Parties recognize that every child has the inherent right to life.
2. States Parties shall ensure to the maximum extent possible the survival and development of the child.

Article 6 is considered to be one of the four general principles of the CRC, alongside the principles of non-discrimination (Article 2), the best interests of the child as a primary consideration (Article 3), and the right to have a child's views respected (Article 12).[19] Article 37 of the same treaty prohibits the imposition of capital punishment and life imprisonment without the possibility of release for offences committed by persons below eighteen years of age, matching the protection in Article 6(5) of the ICCPR. The right to education in the CRC is also aimed at preparing children 'for responsible life in a free society, in the spirit of understanding, peace, tolerance, equality of sexes, and friendship among all peoples, ethnic, national and religious groups and persons of indigenous origin'.[20] The CRC further contains a special protection for children with mental or physical disabilities that they

---

[13] International Covenant on Economic, Social and Cultural Rights 1966, GA res. 2200A (XXI), 16 December 1966, 993 UNTS 3; entered into force 3 January 1976 (ICESCR).

[14] Article 11, ICESCR.

[15] Article 15(1)(a), ICESCR.

[16] Article 10(3), ICESCR.

[17] Convention on the Rights of the Child 1989, GA res. 44/25, 20 November 1989, 1577 UNTS 3; entered into force 2 September 1990 (CRC).

[18] For an overview of the right to life, survival, and development in the CRC, see M. Nowak, *The Right to Life, Survival and Development* (The Hague: Martinus Nijhoff Publishers, 2005).

[19] See, e.g., CRC, General Comment No. 3: HIV/AIDS and the Rights of the Child (2003), UN Doc. CRC/GC/2003/3, 17 March 2003, para. 5.

[20] Article 29(d), CRC.

'should enjoy a full and decent life, in conditions which ensure dignity, promote self-reliance and facilitate the child's active participation in the community'.[21] Article 10 of the Convention on the Rights of Persons with Disabilities 2006 (ICRPD)[22] equally affirms that 'every human being has the inherent right to life and shall take all necessary measures to ensure its effective enjoyment by persons with disabilities on an equal basis with others'.[23]

A specific right to life is also guaranteed to migrant workers and members of their families.[24] In different variations, the right to life is also found in all the regional human rights treaties.[25] A text for an International Convention on the Protection of All Persons from Enforced Disappearances has been

---

[21] Article 23, CRC.

[22] Convention on the Rights of Persons with Disabilities 2006, GA res. 61/106, 13 December 2006; entered into force 3 May 2008 (ICRPD).

[23] Many other provisions of the ICRPD refer to the participation of persons with disabilities in 'all aspects of life': see, e.g., Articles 8(1) (combating stereotypes and prejudice in all aspects of life); 26 (habilitation and rehabilitation); 29 (participation in political and public life); and 30 (participation in cultural life).

[24] Article 9, IMWC: 'The right to life of migrant workers and members of their families shall be protected by law.'

[25] E.g., Article 2, European Convention on the Protection of Human Rights and Fundamental Freedoms 1950, 4 November 1950, 213 UNTS 222; entered into force 3 September 1953, as amended (ECHR), provides: '1. Everyone's right to life shall be protected by law. No one shall be deprived of his [or her] life intentionally save in the execution of a sentence of a court following his [or her] conviction of a crime for which this penalty is provided by law. 2. Deprivation of life shall not be regarded as inflicted in contravention of this article when it results from the use of force which is no more than absolutely necessary: (a) in defence of any person from unlawful violence; (b) in order to effect a lawful arrest or to prevent escape of a person lawfully detained; (c) in action lawfully taken for the purpose of quelling a riot or insurrection.' Protocol No. 6 to the ECHR concerning the Abolition of the Death Penalty, ETS No. 155, 1 November 1998. Article 4, African Charter on Human and Peoples' Rights 1981, adopted 27 June 1981, OAU Doc. CAB/LEG/67/3 rev. 5, 21 ILM 58 (1982); entered into force 21 October 1986 (ACHPR), provides: 'Human beings are inviolable. Every human being shall be entitled to respect for his [or her] life and the integrity of his [or her] person. No one may be arbitrarily deprived of this right.' Its equivalent in Article 4(1), Protocol on the Human Rights of Women to the ACHPR, adopted by the 2nd Ordinary Session of the Assembly of the African Union, Maputo, OAU Doc. CAB/LEG/66.6, 13 September 2000; entered into force 25 November 2005, provides: 'Every woman shall be entitled to respect for her life and the integrity and security of her person. All forms of exploitation, cruel, inhuman or degrading punishment and treatment shall be prohibited'. Article 4(1), American Convention on Human Rights 1969, 22 November 1969, OAS Treaty Series No. 36, 1144 UNTS 123; entered into force 18 July 1978 (ACHR), provides: 'Every person has the right to have his [or her] life respected. This right shall be protected by law and, in general, from the moment of conception. No one shall be arbitrarily deprived of his [or her] life.'

agreed, but it has yet to enter into force.[26] The right to life also takes shape in non-binding form in the UN Declaration on the Rights of Indigenous Peoples 2007, in which the right to life is framed as:

1. Indigenous individuals have the rights to life, physical and mental integrity, liberty and security of person.
2. Indigenous peoples have the collective right to live in freedom, peace and security as distinct peoples and shall not be subjected to any act of genocide or any other act of violence, including forcibly removing children of the group to another group.[27]

Specific right-to-life provisions equivalent to Article 6 of the ICCPR are not, however, found in the Convention on the Elimination of All Forms of Discrimination against Women 1979 (CEDAW),[28] the International Convention on the Elimination of All Forms of Racial Discrimination 1965 (ICERD),[29] or the UN Convention against Torture and Other Cruel, Inhuman or Degrading Treatment or Punishment 1984 (UNCAT).[30] Despite the myriad provisions, the discourse in international human rights law on the right to life has tended to centre on Article 6 of the ICCPR. I will focus on how Article 6 of the ICCPR has been interpreted and applied as the first pronouncement of a general right to life, though influenced by these other provisions.

2   International jurisprudence: the scope and meaning of the right to life

The right to life in Article 6 of the ICCPR is not drafted as an absolute prohibition on the taking of life. There are three purported limitations to the right. The first is that states are obligated to protect an individual's right to

---

[26] International Convention for the Protection of All Persons from Enforced Disappearances 2006, GA res. 61/177, 20 December 2006, opened for signature 6 February 2007 (not yet in force at August 2010) (ICED).

[27] Article 7, UN Declaration on the Rights of Indigenous Peoples 2007, GA res. 61/295, 13 September 2007.

[28] Convention on the Elimination of All Forms of Discrimination against Women 1979, GA res. 34/180, 18 December 1979, 1249 UNTS 13; entered into force 3 September 1981 (CEDAW).

[29] International Convention on the Elimination of All Forms of Racial Discrimination 1965, GA res. 2106 (XX), 21 December 1965, 660 UNTS 195; entered into force 4 January 1969 (ICERD).

[30] Convention against Torture and Other Cruel, Inhumane or Degrading Treatment or Punishment 1984, GA res. 39/46, 10 December 1984, 1465 UNTS 85; entered into force 26 June 1987 (UNCAT).

life in law, but not necessarily also in fact. This is now generally considered to be a minimal rather than the only obligation of Article 6. The second limitation is that Article 6 is considered to protect an individual against the arbitrary deprivation of life by the state. This restrictive view has been challenged by calls for the right to apply to 'quality of life' issues. Finally, the third constraint is that the provision is subject to a number of specified exceptions or limitations. These three purported limitations are dealt with in turn below.

2.1 Protected by law?

The wording of Article 6 of the ICCPR raises an immediate question of whether legal protection is sufficient to discharge a state's obligations. In 1969 James Fawcett asserted that the right to life as contained in the European Convention on the Protection of Human Rights and Fundamental Freedoms 1950 (ECHR) does not protect 'life' per se; rather, it is concerned with the right to life as protected by law. He understood that the right to life would therefore not cover accidental deaths caused, in part, by a failure to impose speed limits on roads or to enact safety legislation for industrial work.[31] Manfred Nowak argued similarly in his 1993 commentary on the ICCPR that '[a] violation of the duty of protection flowing from Art[icle] 6(1) [of the ICCPR] can be assumed only when State legislation is lacking altogether or when it is manifestly insufficient as measured against the actual threat'.[32] At its heart, the duty concerns legal protection.

However, Nowak makes clear in his 2005 commentary that the right includes positive measures and 'all-around effects', including on the horizontal level.[33] Citing Articles 2(1) and (2) of the ICCPR, he claims that the right imposes 'duties to take judicial, administrative or other measures'.[34] Articles 2(1) and (2) relate to obligations of non-discrimination and for states to adopt 'legislative and other measures'. Nowak argues that the placement of the *inherent* right to life in the first sentence of Article 6(1) has led the Human Rights Committee (HRC) to conclude that it must not be interpreted restrictively:

---

[31] J. Fawcett, *The Application of the European Convention on Human Rights* (Oxford University Press, 1969), 30–31, as cited in B. G. Ramcharan, 'The Concept and Dimensions of the Right to Life', in B. G. Ramcharan (ed.), *The Right to Life in International Law* (Dordrecht: Martinus Nijhoff Publishers, 1985) 1, at 3.

[32] Nowak, *U.N. Covenant on Civil and Political Rights: CCPR Commentary* (Kehl: Engel, 1993), 106. See, also, similar position in Nowak, *CCPR Commentary* (2005), 123.

[33] Nowak, *CCPR Commentary* (2005), 122.

[34] See, also, Nowak, *CCPR Commentary* (2005), 122–124.

> The expression 'inherent right to life' cannot properly be understood in
> a restrictive manner, and the protection of this right requires that States
> adopt positive measures.[35]

It is now generally accepted by the HRC that the right to life requires more
than protection in law. Article 6 imports both negative as well as positive
obligations and the latter extend beyond the enactment of special laws.[36]
Citing a host of statements by various UN and regional human rights bodies, Bertrand Ramcharan supports the view that this putative distinction
between 'the right to life' (legal protection) and 'life' (all-encompassing)
does not stand up.[37]

2.2   The arbitrary deprivation of life?

The second limitation on Article 6 is the reference to the arbitrary deprivation of life in Article 6(1) in the third sentence, which has been stated to
protect individuals from interference by state organs, with the emphasis
not on all deprivations of life, but only those deemed 'arbitrary'.[38] Not
unlike its usage in respect of other human rights provisions, arbitrariness suggests elements of unlawfulness, injustice, capriciousness, and
unreasonableness.[39] However, its usage in Article 6 of the ICCPR was
criticised at the drafting conference owing to its ambiguity. It was clarified that the term 'arbitrary' meant both 'illegally' and 'unjustly'.[40] The
HRC's first General Comment on Article 6 placed 'paramount importance' on this aspect of Article 6(1). The focus at that time in 1982 was
entirely on the taking of life by the authorities, such as arbitrary killing
by security forces.[41] It is worth noting that several early communications

---

[35] HRC, General Comment No. 6: The Right to Life (Article 6) (1982), para. 5.
[36] According the HRC, General Comment No. 6, The Right to Life, para. 4, the right to life
imposes a duty on states parties to investigate state killings. See, also, *Baboeram et al.
v. Suriname*, HRC 146, 148–154/1983 (4 April 1985); *Rubio v. Colombia*, HRC 161/1983
(2 November 1987). See, further, S. Joseph, J. Schultz and M. Castan, *The International
Covenant on Civil and Political Rights: Cases, Materials, and Commentary* (2nd edn,
Oxford University Press, 2004), 162–164.
[37] Ramcharan, 'The Concept and Dimensions of the Right to Life', 4.
[38] Nowak, *CCPR Commentary* (1993), 110, who distinguishes it from 'intentional' deprivation of life used in the ECHR. See, too, Nowak, *CCPR Commentary* (2005), 129–131.
[39] Nowak, *CCPR Commentary* (2005), 128.
[40] UN Commission on Human Rights, *Annotations on the draft text of the International
Covenants on Human Rights*, New York, UN Doc. A/2929, 1 July 1955, as reprinted in
Ramcharan (ed.), *The Right to Life in International Law*, 43.
[41] HRC, General Comment No. 6: The Right to Life, para. 3: 'The deprivation of life by the
authorities of the State is a matter of the utmost gravity.'

involved women subjected to enforced 'disappearances' at the hands of the state.[42]

Yoram Dinstein endorses the narrow approach and has said: 'The right to life, in effect, is the right to be safeguarded against (arbitrary) killing.'[43] He states:

> To be sure, homicide may be carried out through a variety of means, including starving someone, exposing a person to extreme temperature or contamination by disease. But, for example, the mere toleration of malnutrition by a State will not be regarded as a violation of the human right to life, whereas the purposeful denial of access to food, e.g. to a prisoner, is a different matter. Failure to reduce infant mortality is not within Article 6, while practicing or tolerating infanticide would violate the article.[44]

The distinctions drawn by Dinstein appear to shift between negative and positive obligations, and between purposeful action and 'blind' omissions. However, when Dinstein applies his approach to specific examples, it breaks down: why is 'tolerating infanticide' distinct from 'failing to reduce infant mortality'? Is not failing to reduce infant mortality equivalent to tolerating it? Why is one arbitrary, but not the other? Both situations involve a state making an (arbitrary) decision not to address or to ignore/tolerate a particular social issue. Cumbersome and unworkable, the only justification for Dinstein's approach seems to rest in the divide between civil and political rights (infanticide/killing) and economic, social, and cultural rights (infant mortality arising from poverty, famine, or malnutrition, all of which a state may claim to have less control over and by virtue of such arguments absolve itself of responsibility).[45] Przetacznik is also of the view that a distinction should be made between the 'right to life' in a strict sense, correlating to Article 6 of the ICCPR, and the 'right to living', which he considers to fall within the system of economic, social, and cultural rights in the ICESCR.[46] Ramcharan, too, dismisses this distinction between these

[42] See, Chapter 5.
[43] Y. Dinstein, 'The Right to Life, Physical Integrity, and Liberty', in L. Henkin (ed.), *The International Bill of Rights: The Covenant on Civil and Political Rights* (New York: Columbia University Press, 1981) 114, at 115.
[44] *Ibid.*, 115.
[45] For further criticism of Dinstein's approach, see, also, F. Menghistu, 'The Satisfaction of Survival Requirements', in Ramcharan (ed.), *The Right to Life in International Law*, (Dordrecht: Martinus Nijhoff Publishers, 1985), 63.
[46] F. Przetacznik, 'The Right to Life as a Basic Human Right' (1976) IX *Hum. Rts. J.* 585–609, as cited in Ramcharan, 'The Concept and Dimensions of the Right to Life', 4.

two alleged rights, claiming that the 'right to living' idea has never been satisfactorily explained.[47]

While arbitrary killing by state authorities remains an important and basic component of the right to life, if not the mainstay of the individual communications under Article 6, debate in the 1980s began to question the logic of ignoring the masses dying of disease, famine, or environmental catastrophes. Menghistu has argued that there are at least two main ways of depriving people of the right to life:

(1) by execution, disappearances, torture, and various forms of cold-blooded murder [that is, by direct violation of civil and political rights];
(2) by starvation and lack of fulfilment of basic needs such as food, basic health facilities, and medical care [that is, by failure to respect economic, social, and cultural rights].[48]

And he argues further that 'it is meaningless to differentiate killing by an act of a state and by starving a person to death, because both forms of behaviour constitute the worst forms of cruelty'.[49] So what has been the approach of the HRC and other treaty bodies to the right to life?

In rejecting the long-worn distinction between these two sets of rights – civil and political rights on the one hand, and economic, social, and cultural rights on the other – many UN and regional human rights bodies have pronounced on the relevance of economic, social, and cultural rights to an understanding of the parameters of the right to life. The Commission on Human Rights stated in 1982, for example, that the 'safeguarding of this *foremost right* is an essential condition for the enjoyment of the entire range of economic, social and cultural, as well as civil and political rights'.[50] By 2005 this general position had converted into explicit statements such as: 'The right to life encompasses existence in human dignity with the minimum necessities of life.'[51]

The Inter-American Commission on Human Rights (I-ACmHR) has rationalised that the fulfilment of the right to life is dependent upon and interlinked with the physical environment.[52] Likewise, the

[47] Ramcharan does not, however, dismiss the role of economic and social indicators to the right to life: Ramcharan, 'The Concept and Dimensions of the Right to Life'.
[48] Menghistu, 'The Satisfaction of Survival Requirements', 63.
[49] *Ibid.*
[50] Commission on Human Rights (CHR) res. 1982/7, 19 February 1982. See, further, CHR res. 1983/43, 9 March 1983. (emphasis in original)
[51] CHR res. 2005/16, Human Rights and Extreme Poverty, UN Doc. E/CN.4/2005/16, 14 April 2005, para. 1(b) (adopted without a vote).
[52] See, *Yanomami v. Brazil*, I-ACmHR, Case No. 7615, Res. No. 12/85 (5 March 1985).

Inter-American Court of Human Rights (I-ACtHR) has held that the right to life:

> is a fundamental human right, and the exercise of this right is essential for the exercise of all other human rights. If it is not respected, all rights lack meaning. Owing to the fundamental nature of the right to life, restrictive approaches to it are inadmissible. In essence, the fundamental right to life includes, not only the right of every human being not to be deprived of his [or her] life arbitrarily, but also the right that he [or she] will not be prevented from having *access to the conditions that guarantee a dignified existence* [my emphasis].[53]

In an Advisory Opinion on the *Juridical Condition and the Human Rights of the Child*, the I-ACtHR reiterated that the conditions of care of children required by Article 4 (the right to life) of the American Convention on Human Rights (ACHR) involve:

> [not only] the prohibitions set forth in that provision, but also the obligation to provide the measures required for life to develop under *decent conditions*. The concept of *a decent life*, developed by this Court, relates to the norm set forth in the Convention on the Rights of the Child, Article 23(1) of which states the following, with reference to children who suffer some type of disability:
>
> 1. States Parties recognize that a mentally or physically disabled child should enjoy a full and decent life, in conditions which ensure dignity, promote self-reliance and facilitate the child's active participation in the community [my emphases].[54]

The I-ACtHR has further advised:

> [A]lthough the right to work cannot be confused with the right to life, work is a condition of a decent life, and even of life itself: it is a subsistence factor. If access to work is denied, or if a worker is prevented from receiving benefits, or if the jurisdictional and administrative channels for claiming his [or her] rights are obstructed, his [or her] life could be endangered and, in any case, he [or she] would suffer an impairment of the quality of his [or her] life, which is a basic element of both economic, social and cultural rights, and civil and political rights.[55]

---

[53] *Villagrán-Morales et al.* v. *Guatemala* (the 'Street Children' case), I-ACtHR, Ser. C., No. 63 (19 September 1999), para. 144 (case involving the execution of five street children and signs of torture, including acid burns and eyes and ears cut off).

[54] *Juridical Condition and Human Rights of the Child* (Advisory Opinion), I-ACtHR, OC-17/02 (18 August 2002), para. 80.

[55] *Ibid.*, para. 28.

Under the ECHR, the right to life has generally been considered to have three main aspects: '[T]he duty to refrain, by its agents, from unlawful killing; the duty to investigate suspicious deaths; and, in certain circumstances, a positive obligation to take steps to prevent the avoidable loss of life.'[56] In relation to the last, case law indicates that positive obligations have been found to be extensive.[57]

The right to life has also been seen as at issue in relation to environmental damage. Judge Weeramantry of the International Court of Justice (ICJ) stated in the *Danube Dam* case:

> The protection of the environment is ... a vital part of contemporary human rights doctrine, for it is [an indispensable requirement] ... for numerous human rights such as the right to health and the right to life itself.[58]

Not having articulated its position in the manner of the I-ACtHR or other judicial authorities, the HRC has nonetheless addressed under its non-restrictive interpretative approach such issues as the reduction of infant mortality and increasing life expectancy, especially by adopting measures to eliminate malnutrition and epidemics,[59] unequal access to HIV/AIDS treatment, and issues of family planning and maternal health.[60] Meanwhile, the Committee on Economic, Social and Cultural Rights (CESCR) has stated that the UDHR emphasised 'an economic and social

---

[56] C. Ovey and R. White, *Jacobs and White: The European Convention on Human Rights* (4th edn, Oxford University Press, 2006), 57.

[57] *Ibid.*, referring to case law involving obligations to inform individuals about possible health consequences of nuclear tests (*L. C. B.* v. *United Kingdom* (1998) 27 EHRR 212); the obligation to establish effective deterrence mechanisms against unlawful killing (*Öneryildiz* v. *Turkey* (2005) 41 EHRR 325); the obligation to ensure that vulnerable individuals in prison, such as patients with mental disabilities, are protected (*Keenan* v. *United Kingdom* (2001) 33 EHRR 903); and protections from dangerous but lawful activities by systems of regulation, supervision, and control (see, e.g., *Guerra* v. *Italy*, Applic. 14967/89, Judgment 19 February 1998, (1998) 26 EHRR 357).

[58] *Hungary* v. *Slovakia (Case Concerning the Gabčikovo-Nagymaros Project)* 1997 ICJ 92 (Separate Opinion of Judge Weeramantry), para. A(b).

[59] HRC, General Comment No. 6: The Right to Life, para. 5.

[60] See, variously, HRC, Concluding observations on reports of the Democratic Republic of Congo, HRC Report UN Doc. A/56/40 (Vol. I), 85th sess., 17 October–3 November 2005, 86th sess., 13–31 March 2006, 10–28 July 2006, para. 14; Kenya, HRC Report, UN Doc. A/60/40 (Vol. I), 82nd sess., 18 October–5 November 2004, 83rd sess., 14 March – 1 April 2005, 11–29 July 2005, para. 14; Mali, HRC Report, UN Doc. A/58/40 (Vol. I), 76th sess., 14 October–1 November 2002, 17 March–6 April 2003, 78th sess., 14 July–8 August 2003, para. 14; Ukraine, HRC Report, UN Doc. A/57/40 (Vol. I) (2002), paras. 11 and 16; Sweden, HRC Report, UN Doc. A/57/40 (Vol. I) (2002), para. 15.

content of the right to life, or in other words the right to live, the right to a certain quality of life'.[61] The CESCR has explicitly dealt with improving average life expectancy.[62] The Committee on the Rights of the Child (the Children's Committee) has recognised, too, that the right to health in the context of HIV/AIDS is central alongside rights to life, survival, and development in Article 6 of the CRC.[63] It further states:

> Children have the right not to have their lives arbitrarily taken, as well as to benefit from economic and social policies that will allow them to survive into adulthood and develop in the broadest sense of the word. State obligation to realize the right to life, survival and development also highlights the need to give careful attention to sexuality as well as to the behaviours and lifestyles of children, even if they do not conform with what society determines to be acceptable under prevailing cultural norms for a particular age group. In this regard, the female child is often subject to harmful traditional practices, such as early and/or forced marriage, which violate her rights and make her more vulnerable to HIV infection, including because such practices often interrupt access to education and information. Effective prevention programmes are only those that acknowledge the realities of the lives of adolescents, while addressing sexuality by ensuring equal access to appropriate information, [to] life skills, and to preventive measures.[64]

Notably, violence against girls is mentioned here.

Although questions surrounding 'quality of life' ideas and how far the right to life extends are not agreed between international and regional bodies, it is generally accepted by the UN human rights treaty bodies that the right to life carries obligations in relation to economic, social, and cultural matters. It is also agreed that the right is not confined to arbitrary state killing in a narrow sense, but involves positive obligations to protect against abuse by non-state or private actors. Ramcharan argues that the right to life protects each individual from 'all possible threats' and 'seeks each individual to: have access to the means of survival; realize full life expectancy; avoid serious environmental risks of life; and enjoy the protection by the State against unwarranted deprivations of life whether by State authorities or by other persons within society'.[65] The jurisprudence indicates a shift from the early position of the UN to one that understands

---

[61] CESCR, Concluding observations on Sri Lanka, UN Doc. E/1999/22 (1999), para. 69.
[62] CESCR, Concluding observations on Guinea, UN Doc. E/C.12/1996/6 (1997), para. 193.
[63] CRC, General Comment No. 3: HIV/AIDS and the Rights of the Child, para. 5.
[64] Ibid., para. 11.
[65] Ramcharan, 'The Concept and Dimensions of the Right to Life', 7.

the interlinkages between economic, social, and cultural rights on the one hand and civil and political rights on the other. The views of Dinstein and others of confining the scope of Article 6 of the ICCPR, and their view on the right to life more generally, is no longer the dominant one.

Despite the fact that the broader approach is gaining acceptance at international law, the right to life has been typically applied in cases involving state counter-terrorism measures,[66] subjection to the death penalty in violation of the provision,[67] nuclear weapons,[68] state killings or disappearances[69] and failure to properly investigate or prosecute such crimes,[70] deaths in custody,[71] deaths resulting from degrading treatment or excessive use of violence during the course of forcible deportation of aliens,[72] violence or deprivation of food, water, or medical treatment from prisoners or failure to prevent suicide in detention,[73] and war and mass violence.[74] What these applications mean for women is examined below.

2.3   Exceptions to the prohibition

The sub-paragraphs of Article 6 of the ICCPR constitute the third limitation on its scope of application, in addition to any other exceptions

---

[66] See e.g., HRC, Concluding observations on Sweden, UN Doc. A/57/40 Vol. I (2002) 57, para. 79(10); New Zealand, UN Doc. A/57/40 Vol. I (2002) 63, para. 81(11).

[67] HRC, Concluding observations on Viet Nam, UN Doc. A/57/40 Vol. I (2002) 67, para. 82(7); Egypt, UN Doc. A/58/40 Vol. I (2002) 31, paras. 77(12) and 77(16) (death penalty not reserved for most serious crimes).

[68] HRC, General Comment No. 14: Nuclear Weapons and the Right to Life (Article 6) (1984), refers specifically to the threat posed by the manufacture, distribution, and production of weapons of mass destruction.

[69] See, e.g., *Suárez de Guerrero*, HRC 45/1979 (31 March 1982); *Baboeram et al.* v. *Suriname* (*December Murders in Suriname* case), HRC 146, 148–154/1983 (10 April 1984). See, e.g., cases referred to in Report of the HRC (Vol. II), UN Doc. A/57/40 (2002).

[70] See, e.g., HRC, Concluding observations on United Kingdom of Great Britain and Northern Ireland, UN Doc. A/57/40 Vol. I (2002), para. 75(8); Georgia, UN Doc. A/57/40 Vol. I (2002) 53, para. 78(7).

[71] See, e.g., HRC, Concluding observations on Georgia, UN Doc. A/57/40 Vol. I (2002) 53, para. 78(7); CERD, Concluding observations on Canada, UN Doc. A/57/18 (2002) 56, para. 333 (high incidence of deaths of indigenous persons).

[72] See, e.g., HRC, Concluding observations on Switzerland, UN Doc. A/57/40 Vol. I (2002) 44, para. 76(13).

[73] See, e.g., CRC, Concluding observations on Cameroon, UN Doc. CRC/C/111 (2001) 71, para. 353.

[74] HRC, General Comment No. 6: The Right to Life, paras. 2 and 4, in which the HRC noted the obligation on states parties to prevent war, genocide, and other forms of mass violence. See, further, Concluding observations on Togo, UN Doc. A/58/40 (Vol. I) (2002), para. 9.

enacted by law and not otherwise being arbitrary. It was not accepted by the drafters that the right to life would be absolute.[75] In rejecting an absolute prohibition on the deprivation of life in any circumstances, a second view was that any exceptions should be defined within the provision itself. However, it was considered that any enumeration would be incomplete and might convey the impression that greater importance was attached to the exceptions than to the right itself.[76] This is where the 'arbitrary deprivation of life' and 'protected by law' language crept in. The death penalty became the only explicit exception to Article 6, ICCPR.[77] Of specific relevance for this book is the exclusion, contained in Article 6(5), of 'pregnant women' from capital punishment, which is dealt with in the next section.

A number of further exceptions have developed and have been read into the right to life – such as those around military conscription in wartime or compulsory military service.[78] In relation to the latter, the argument proceeds that, provided compulsory military service is regulated by law, it would not be arbitrary within the meaning of Article 6(1). It has subsequently been argued that, provided there are alternatives available to compulsory military service, it would also not interfere with religious rights for those who conscientiously object.[79]

3   Feminist critiques of traditional understandings of the right to life

The first impression of Article 6 of the ICCPR, and the early approach of the HRC, other international bodies, and commentators alike, is of a right that contemplated the lives and bodies of men: men are disproportionately affected by the arbitrary deprivation of life by the state, by capital penalties, as soldiers in armed conflict, and as the principal subjects of policies and laws on military conscription and military service. Feminist scholars argue that, for women, the 'right to life' is understood

---

[75] UN Commission on Human Rights, *Annotations on the draft text of the International Covenants on Human Rights*, New York, UN Doc. A/2929, 1 July 1955, as reprinted in Ramcharan (ed.), *The Right to Life in International Law*, 43.

[76] *Ibid.*

[77] Article 6(2), (4)-(6), ICCPR.

[78] See, e.g., UNHCR, 'Guidelines on International Protection: Religion-Based Refugee Claims under Article 1A(2) of the 1951 Convention and/or the 1967 Protocol relating to the Status of Refugees', UN Doc. HCR/GIP/04/06, 28 April 2006, paras. 25 and 26.

[79] For more on conscientious objection, see K. Musalo, 'Conscientious Objection as a Basis for Refugee Status: Protection for the Fundamental Right of Freedom of Thought, Conscience, and Religion' (2007) 26 *Ref. Surv. Qty* 69.

in an entirely different context.[80] During their lives women and girls may be subjected to a range of life-threatening behaviour, including 'honour' killings, acid violence, bride-burning, domestic violence, female infanticide, death during labour or by reproductive complications, or resulting from infections from female genital mutilation or HIV/AIDS.[81] That is to say, women are more likely to fear threats to their lives from non-state actors rather than the arbitrary deprivation of life at the hands of the state. They are also more at risk of threats to their lives brought about by negligence or neglect on the part of the state in respect, for example, of childbirth and reproductive health, poverty, famine, and economic disadvantage, rather than direct state killing. These types of threats to women's lives are largely excluded under the traditional, narrow approach of the right to life.

At first glance, therefore, women's everyday lives seem largely absent from the scope of the protection except in so far as they otherwise satisfy its narrow interpretation.[82] Article 6 of the ICCPR is, however, unique from the other rights studied in this book, as well as, arguably, those contained in other human rights treaties, in terms of its treatment and depiction of women. Most other provisions suffer from a lack of clear applicability to women's lives and, at other times, a total ignorance of their concerns. Women are not visible in the explicit language of many provisions, and this is reinforced by the exclusive use of the masculine pronoun. Instead, in relation to the right to life, women arguably benefit from a heightened protection of their right to life as there are no exceptions that target their sex. That is, men are far more likely than women to fall within one of the permitted exceptions to Article 6. As outlined above, Article 6 provides that pregnant women must not be put to death, as an exception to capital punishment.

The pregnant-woman exception should not be overstated, however, as it does not recognise the value of women *qua* women, or even as mothers.

---

[80]   See, e.g., R. J. Cook, 'International Protection of Women's Reproductive Rights' (1992) 24 *N.Y.U.L.J.* 689, in relation to capital punishment as an issue that more realistically affects men than women; D. Bogecho, 'Putting it to Good Use: The International Covenant on Civil and Political Rights and Women's Rights to Reproductive Health' (2004) 13 *S. Cal. Rev. L. & Women's Stud.* 229, arguing that women are more concerned by reproductive complications leading to death than capital punishment.

[81]   See, inter alia, UNICEF, *The State of the World's Children: Women and Children – The Double Dividend of Gender Equality* (2007). See, also, Plan International, *Because I am a Girl: The State of the World's Girls* (2007), available at http://plan-international.org/what-you-can-do/campaigns/because-i-am-a-girl-campaign.

[82]   See, e.g., *Lantsova v. Russia*, HRC 763/1997 (26 March 2002).

Rather they are protected as reproductive bodies.[83] The exception is intended primarily to protect the unborn child, whatever sex, and not the mother, who will no longer benefit from the exception once she has given birth. In this sense, the final version of Article 6(5) differs from the original Yugoslavian proposal that sought to protect the mother even after the birth of the child.[84] Without success, several other delegates during the drafting process argued in favour of an amendment similar to the Yugoslavian proposal, albeit still with the interests of the unborn child placed above those of the woman. They called for the effects of execution or the constant fear of it on the development of the unborn or newborn child to be taken into account.[85] Surprisingly, the final version of Article 6 does not extend as far as protections under international humanitarian law in which both pregnant women and mothers with dependent children are exempt from the execution of the death penalty, although as with the human rights guarantee, these too protect the mother only as far as she is of value to the unborn child or to the early nourishing or raising of that child.[86] As such, the final version of Article 6 can be interpreted as a rejection of the 'protective' model of international law, which has been

---

[83] The same arguments are put forward by Gardam and Jarvis in relation to the equivalent provisions under the 1949 Geneva Conventions, see Gardam and Jarvis, *Women, Armed Conflict and International Law*.

[84] UN Doc. E/CN.4/573, as referred to in Nowak, *CCPR Commentary* (2005), 147.

[85] Nowak, *CCPR Commentary* (2005).

[86] See, Article 76(3) of the Protocol I Additional to the Geneva Conventions 1977: 'To the extent feasible, the Parties to the conflict shall endeavour to avoid the pronouncement of death on pregnant women or mothers having dependant children, for an offence related to armed conflict. The death penalty for such offences shall not be executed on such women.' Article 6(4) of the Protocol II Additional to the Geneva Conventions 1977 similarly provides: 'The death penalty shall not be … carried out on pregnant women or mothers of young children.' The Fourth Geneva Convention contains a raft of provisions giving special protection to expectant mothers (see, e.g., Articles 14, 16, 23, 38(5), 50(5), 89(5), 132(2), 138); Geneva Convention (III) relative to the Treatment of Prisoners of War 1949, adopted 12 August 1949, 75 UNTS 135, entered into force 21 October 1950 (Third Geneva Convention) includes some special protections for pregnant mothers (see, e.g., Annex I(B)((7) (transfer of pregnant women or those with infants or small children to a neutral country)); the First and Second Geneva Conventions contain only a single provision indicating that '[w]omen shall be treated with all consideration due to their sex' (Article 12(4), Geneva Convention (I) for the Amelioration of the Condition of the Wounded and Sick in Armed Forces in the Field, adopted 12 August 1949, 75 UNTS 31, entered into force 21 October 1950; and Article 12(4), Geneva Convention (II) for the Amelioration of the Condition of Wounded, Sick and Shipwrecked Members of Armed Forces at Sea adopted 12 August 1949, 75 UNTS 85, entered into force 21 October 1950, respectively).

heavily criticised by many feminist writers as classifying all women as 'vulnerable' and in need of protection.[87]

To the extent that women are valued in Article 6 only in relation to their roles as mothers and their bodies as reproductive vessels, the view of the drafters was not that of women as perpetual victims or as weak and subservient persons in need of special protection, but rather as perpetrators of crimes sufficiently serious to warrant the imposition of the death penalty. Despite this explicit sub-paragraph, no specific mention is made to it in any of the HRC's General Comments on Article 6, and no individual communication has been heard raising this issue,[88] although the HRC has occasionally referenced it when such protections are missing from state legislation.[89]

Nonetheless, Article 6 of the ICCPR has been a focus of feminist activism. Dina Bogecho, for example, outlines two reasons why Article 6 of the ICCPR is to be preferred to rights contained in the CEDAW in fighting for women's reproductive rights. First, she argues that the CEDAW remains a controversial instrument, with many states parties entering reservations against Articles 11, 12, 14, or 16, or in other words, those rights relating to reproductive health.[90] The second reason she gives for utilising the ICCPR over the CEDAW is the greater enforcement capacity of the HRC, although she bases her argument on the fact that the HRC has more experience[91] rather than on any substantive evidence of a more sympathetic approach. And today both mechanisms each permit the possibility for individual communications so the enforcement capacity of them would appear identical, subject of course to agreement of the state party in question to accept the jurisdiction of the treaty body.[92]

In terms of interpretations of Article 6 of the ICCPR that favour the inclusion of 'quality of life' issues, feminist concerns that the international human rights system marginalises economic, social, and cultural issues to the disadvantage of women are addressed. The right to life as initially conceived to prohibit arbitrary state killing ignored the suffering of

---

[87] See, Chapter 2.
[88] See, HRC, General Comment No. 6: The Right to Life, in which the death penalty is discussed but not the 'pregnant woman' exception. See, also, Joseph, Schultz and Castan, *The International Covenant on Civil and Political Rights*, 175.
[89] HRC, Concluding observations on Kuwait, UN Doc. A/55/40 (Vol. I) (2000), para. 467.
[90] Writing in 2004, she calculates that of the 175 states parties, 24 had entered reservations to these articles: Bogecho, 'Putting it to Good Use', 239.
[91] *Ibid.*
[92] See, Chapter 3.

millions of people from poverty, famine, hunger, ill-health, and disease. Feminist scholars argue that these are among the issues of most relevance to women.[93] I do not subscribe fully to this view (believing that the full range of rights are important to women, including political rights, especially so that women can frame their economic, social, and cultural grievances); however, I recognise that women's socio-economic disadvantage perpetuates their unequal position in society and permits a system that treats them as second-class citizens. This in turn feeds into a system that tolerates or condones violence suffered by women. Under this rubric, the HRC has commented upon high infant and maternal mortality rates due to denial of access to health and family planning services and low levels of education.[94] UNICEF has documented that women aged between fifteen and twenty-four in sub-Saharan Africa are more at risk of HIV infection than men of the same age, yet have far less knowledge about it.[95] The Children's Committee has also highlighted that children, both girls and boys, orphaned by AIDS may be at risk of falling prey to sexual and economic exploitation, including prostitution and trafficking.[96] The rates for girls far outstrip those of boys. The Women's Committee has noted that the right to life is impaired or nullified by gender-based violence.[97] The Women's Committee's fact-finding mission to the Ciudad Juárez area of the Chihuahua region of Mexico stated: '[The practice of abduction, rape, and murder] discriminates against women whose conduct may not conform to the accepted "moral code", but who have an *equal right to life*' [my emphasis].[98] In a related case, the I-ACtHR held that Mexico had violated

---

[93] See, e.g., A. Gallagher, 'Ending the Marginalization: Strategies for Incorporating Women into the United Nations Human Rights System' (1997) 19 *HRQ* 283, at 290–291 and other writers outlined in Chapter 2.

[94] See, variously, HRC Concluding observations on reports of the Democratic Republic of Congo, HRC Report UN Doc. A/56/40 (Vol. I), 85th sess., 17 October–3 November 2005, 86th sess., 13–31 March 2006, 10–28 July 2006, para. 14; Kenya, HRC Report, UN Doc. A/60/40 (Vol. I), 82nd sess., 18 October–5 November 2004, 83rd sess., 14 March–1 April 2005, 11–29 July 2005, para. 14; Mali, HRC Report, UN Doc. A/58/40 (Vol. I), 76th sess., 14 October–1 November 2002, 17 March–6 April 2003, 78th sess., 14 July–8 August 2003, para. 14; Ukraine, HRC Report, UN Doc. A/57/40 (Vol. I) (2002), paras. 11 and 16; Sweden, HRC Report, UN Doc. A/57/40 (Vol. I) (2002), para. 15.

[95] UNICEF, *The State of the World's Children: Women and Children – The Double Dividend of Gender and Equality* (2007), Figure 1.3.

[96] CRC, General Comment No. 3: HIV/AIDS and the Rights of the Child, para. 36.

[97] CEDAW, General Recommendation No. 19: Violence against Women (1992), UN Doc. HRI/GEN/1/Rev.7, para. 7(a).

[98] CEDAW, Report on Mexico, UN Doc. CEDAW/C/2005/OP.8/MEXICO, 27 January 2005, para. 275.

the right to life of three women by failing to investigate properly their disappearances and murders owing to an indifferent and discriminatory attitude on the part of the authorities.[99]

The Women's Committee has also referred to maternal mortality,[100] low life expectancy in relation to indigenous women,[101] the lower life expectancy of women compared with men in some societies,[102] and the control of sexually transmitted diseases and HIV/AIDS[103] or its high prevalence among women.[104] It has also 'highlighted the urgent need to ensure that globalization, policies and plans of action that facilitate international trade and the transition to market economic policies are gender-sensitive and improve the *quality of life* of women, who constitute more than 50 per cent of the population in almost all countries' [my emphasis].[105] Of course, the Women's Committee refers to these issues within its overarching mandate over discrimination 'in all fields', rather than directly to a right to life, which is missing from the CEDAW.[106]

As Menghistu notes: 'The right to life is meaningless without access to the basic and minimum material goods and services essential to sustain life.'[107] Under this conceptualisation of the right to life, states can be held accountable for acts of gross negligence, neglect, the misuse and abuse of resources, or other failures to prevent breaches of the right to life, including in its economic and social manifestations, and whether committed directly by state or non-state actors. This has positive ramifications for all persons, but it also allows scope for the committees to deal with violent conduct that directly threatens life, as well as the intersection of violence against women and life-threatening situations related to poverty, lack of access to health and family planning services, and social disadvantage.

---

[99] *González et al ('Cotton Field') v. Mexico*, I-ACtHR, Preliminary Objection, Merits, Reparations and Costs, Ser. C No. 205 (16 November 2009). Also discussed in Chapter 5.

[100] CEDAW, Concluding observations on Cambodia, UN Doc. A/61/38 (2006), para. 47; Nepal, UN Doc. A/59/38 (2004), para. 212.

[101] CEDAW, Concluding observations on Cambodia, UN Doc. A/61/38 (2006), para. 247.

[102] CEDAW, Concluding observations on Nepal, UN Doc. A/59/38 (2004), para. 212.

[103] CEDAW, Concluding observations on Nepal, UN Doc. A/59/38 (2004), para. 213; Belarus, UN Doc. A/59/38 (2004), para. 356.

[104] CEDAW, Concluding observations on Ethiopia, UN Doc. A/59.38 (2004), para. 257.

[105] CEDAW, Annual Report of the CEDAW to the General Assembly, UN Doc. A/57/38 (Part I) (2002), para. 424.

[106] Article 3, CEDAW.

[107] Menghistu, 'The Satisfaction of Survival Requirements', 67.

The final issue to be dealt with in this section is the controversial question of the beneficiaries of the right to life. When does life begin for the purposes of Article 6 of the ICCPR? Who benefits from the provision? These questions are relevant to issues surrounding sex-selective abortions, as well as remedies for pregnant women who miscarry as a consequence of physical violence, dealt with further below.

4 Rights bearers: when does life begin for the purposes of Article 6?

4.1 International treaty bodies

Article 6 of the ICCPR is silent as to when life begins. Because of irreconcilable positional differences between countries on abortion at the time of drafting the ICCPR, 'compromise dictated silence' on the issue of the starting point for the right to life.[108] Consequently, Article 6 of the ICCPR does not address the issue of when life starts for the purposes of benefiting from international legal protection. At the time of drafting, it was submitted by Belgium, Brazil, El Salvador, Mexico, and Morocco that the protection of the life of the unborn child recognised in the pregnant-woman exception to the death penalty should be extended to all unborn children.[109] This was opposed by other states on the ground that it would be impossible for a state to determine the moment of conception and therefore to undertake to protect life from that moment. Moreover, it was argued by delegates that the proposed clause would involve the question of the rights and duties of the medical profession.[110] Nowak, however, asserts that it is clear from the travaux préparatoires that life in the making was not (or not from the moment of conception) to be protected.[111] The divide over abortion and the right to life continues, evidenced by the exclusion of any recommendations on the matter of women's reproductive freedom in the follow-up meetings to the 1995 World Conference on Women in Beijing.[112]

---

[108] W. Schabas, *The Abolition of the Death Penalty in International Law* (3rd edn, Cambridge University Press, 2002), 25.

[109] UN Doc. A/C.3/L.654, referred to in UN Doc. A/3764, paras. 84–120 summarised by B. G. Ramcharan, 'The Drafting History of Article 6 of the International Covenant on Civil and Political Rights', in Ramcharan (ed.), *The Right to Life in International Law* (Dordrecht: Martinus Nijhoff Publishers, 1985) 42, at 51.

[110] *Ibid.*

[111] Nowak, *CCPR Commentary* (2005), 154.

[112] See, UN Division for the Advancement of Women, Fact Sheet No. 5: Women and Health, *Gender Equality, Development and Peace for the 21st Century*, New York, 5–9 June 2000.

The view of the HRC has generally been that the right to life begins at the moment of birth rather than at conception. This is evidenced in the HRC's calls to states parties to provide access to safe and legal abortions for female victims of rape. Neither has the HRC developed tests of 'viability' of the foetus as some national jurisdictions have.[113] Illegal and clandestine abortions have also been identified as a major cause of maternal mortality and at issue in relation to Article 6.[114] Human Rights Watch, for example, asserts that 13 per cent of all maternal deaths worldwide are attributable to unsafe abortions – between 68,000 and 78,000 deaths annually.[115] The HRC has chastised states parties that do not provide family planning or other services that would avoid 'clandestine and therefore life-threatening abortions'.[116] In relation to Peru, for example, the HRC called for all the necessary measures to be implemented to ensure that women do not risk their lives because of the existence of restrictive legal provisions on abortion.[117] Frequently, such issues are dealt with by the HRC in the context of the torture prohibition rather than under the right to life, but they certainly implicate the latter also.[118] The HRC has not, however, delved into the details of how to regulate abortion; rather it has noted concern at the 'severity of existing laws relating to abortion … especially since illegal abortions have serious detrimental consequences for women's lives, health and well-being'.[119] The HRC and the CESCR have each called upon states parties to monitor female mortality rates closely, in particular by taking steps to reduce deaths from illegal abortion.[120] In Mexico, for example, the CESCR has noted that illegal abortion

---

[113] Nowak, *CCPR Commentary* (2005), 154, referring to US jurisprudence that protection offered by Article 6 might begin when the foetus is able to survive on its own (viability testing).

[114] See, e.g., HRC, Concluding Observations on Zanzibar, UN Doc. A/53/40 (Vol. I) (1998), para. 399; Mali, UN Doc. A/58/40 (Vol. I) (2003) 47, para. 81(14); El Salvador, UN Doc. A/58/40 (Vol. I) (2003) 61, para. 84(14).

[115] Human Rights Watch, *Q & A: Human Rights Law and Access to Abortion* (undated), available at: www.hrw.org/backgrounder/americas/argentina0605/.

[116] See, e.g., HRC, General Comment No. 28: Equality of Rights Between Men and Women (Article 3) (2000), UN Doc. CCPR/C/21/Rev.1/Add.10, paras. 5 and 10. See, further, HRC Concluding observations on Colombia, UN Doc. A/52/40 (Vol. I) (1997), para. 287.

[117] HRC, Concluding observations on Peru, UN Doc. A/52/40 (Vol. I) (1997), para. 167.

[118] See, Chapter 5.

[119] See, e.g., HRC, Concluding observations on El Salvador, UN Doc. A/58/40 (Vol. I) (2003) 61, para. 84(14).

[120] See, e.g., HRC, Concluding observations on Peru, UN Doc. A/52/40 (Vol. I) (1997), para. 167; HRC, Concluding observations on El Salvador, UN Doc. A/58/40 (Vol. I) (2003), para. 84 (14); CESCR, Concluding observations on Mexico, UN Doc. E/C.12/1999/11 (2000), para. 405.

is the fourth highest cause of death of women.[121] Likewise, the Children's Committee has referred to the issue of unsafe abortion and high rate of maternal mortality and the impact of punitive legislation on maternal mortality rates.[122]

The HRC has further relied on a range of other rights to reinforce its position. In the absence of express provisions relating to reproductive rights in the ICCPR, the HRC has addressed the dangers associated with illegal or clandestine abortions under other provisions, such as rights to equality, privacy, or family life. For example, privacy rights have been invoked by the HRC in order to protect women's reproductive functions where, for example, states impose a legal duty upon doctors and other health personnel to report women who have undergone abortions.[123] The HRC has further stated that the rights in Article 7 may also be of relevance in such situations.[124] It has argued that failure to provide access to legal abortion in particular situations results from discrimination.[125] Other treaty bodies have adopted similar approaches. The CESCR has identified the unequal status of women in society and the persistent problem in some countries of a preference for sons as manifesting itself in the high incidence of induced abortions of girl foetuses that threaten the reproductive rights of women.[126]

In *K. L.* v. *Peru*,[127] the HRC was of the view that Article 7 of the ICCPR (rather than Article 6) was breached when a seventeen-year-old Peruvian female was forced to carry an anencephalic foetus[128] to term and to breast-feed the infant in the first four days of life before it died. The complainant was subsequently diagnosed with severe depression. The HRC did not specify whether her situation amounted to torture or another form of ill-treatment. The language of the HRC's view was framed in the context of a failure to provide the complainant with 'a therapeutic abortion', not

---

[121] CESCR, Concluding observations on Mexico, UN Doc. E/C.12/1999/11 (2000), para. 405.

[122] CRC, Concluding observations on Chad, U.N. Doc. CRC/C/15/Add.107, 24 August 1999, para. 30; CRC, Concluding observations on Guatemala, U.N. Doc. CRC/C/15/Add.154, 9 July 2001, para. 40.

[123] HRC, General Comment No. 28: Equality of Rights Between Men and Women, para. 20.

[124] *Ibid.*   [125] *Ibid.*

[126] CESCR, Concluding observations on Republic of Korea, UN Doc. E/C.12/2001/17, para. 226.

[127] *K. L.* v. *Peru*, HRC 1153/2003 (24 October 2005).

[128] Anencephaly is a condition in which a foetus lacks most or all of the forebrain and such foetuses are born stillborn or die soon after birth.

necessarily a legal one.[129] That is, both the legal and practical inaccessibility of a therapeutic abortion can constitute breaches of Article 7. On this basis, the HRC decided, disappointingly, that it was unnecessary to make a ruling on Article 6, even though it had noted that the evidence pointed towards the fact that the failure to provide an abortion 'may have endangered the author's life'.[130] The decision further held that preventing her from accessing a legally entitled right to an abortion under Peruvian law in these circumstances breached her right to privacy under Article 17.[131]

Even though the human rights treaty bodies have addressed the issue of abortion and reproductive rights in the context, inter alia, of the right to life, none of the committees has expressly stated that the life of the unborn child is entirely unprotected. They have also not stated that there is a general right to abortion. Instead, they have carefully noted the interlinkages between the life and the health of the mother in calling for access to pre- and post-abortion services in particular situations.

The political divide between states on this issue is further reflected in regional laws. Like the right to life in the ICCPR, the ECHR and the African Charter on Human and Peoples' Rights 1981 (ACHPR) are silent on the starting point of the right to life (see below).

4.2   Europe

The position of the former European Commission on Human Rights (ECmHR) was that there was no absolute prohibition on abortion. Case law suggested that Article 2 of the ECHR (the right to life provision) could not be interpreted to give higher priority to the foetus than to the mother's life, partly based on the reasoning that there is no provision in the ECHR that limits the mother's life.[132] Both the ECmHR and the ECtHR have given a wide margin of appreciation to states on this question and have sought to strike a balance between the rights of the mother and the rights of the unborn child, although they note that any rights a foetus

[129] P. Kebriaei, 'The UN Human Rights Committee's Decision in *Karen Llotoy v Peru*' (2006) 15 *INTERIGHTS Bulletin* 151, 151, available at: www.interights.org/doc/Bulletin%20 15.3.pdf.

[130] *K. L.* v. *Peru*, para. 6.2.

[131] The decision further held that the failure to provide a remedy that was timely breached Article 2, ICCPR, and that there was further a breach of Article 24, ICCPR in failing to protect her health as a minor child.

[132] See, L. A. Rehof, 'Article 3', in G. Alfredsson and A. Eide (eds.), *The Universal Declaration of Human Rights: A Common Standard of Achievement* (The Hague: Martinus Nijhoff Publishers, 1999) 97, referring to the following cases: *Brüggemann and Scheuten* v. *Federal Republic of Germany*, ECtHR, Applic. No. 6959/75 (1981) 3 EHRR 244

may have are implicitly limited by the rights of the mother.[133] The ECtHR has had two occasions to address the issue of whether a foetus enjoys the protection of Article 2 as a 'person' under law, but it has skirted around the issue on both. In *Open Door and Dublin Well Women v. Ireland*, the ECtHR held that the government of Ireland was entitled to restrict access to information pertaining to the availability of abortion services outside Ireland (abortion being unlawful in Ireland). It was held not to be in violation of the right to information under Article 10 of the ECHR under the permitted exception of 'protection of morals'. The ECtHR chose not to rule, however, on whether the government was also entitled to restrict access to abortion materials on the basis of the 'rights of others' (being those of the unborn child), so the question of the rights of the foetus was not dealt with.[134]

The second case in which the issue of a right to abortion was at issue but not directly tackled is *Vo v. France*.[135] This case involved an unwanted, induced abortion that occurred when a medical doctor mistook the applicant for another patient who was having a contraceptive device removed. In its decision, the ECtHR left open the question of whether a foetus is protected by the right to life. The Grand Chamber of the ECtHR found no breach of Article 2 by the failure of French law to provide a criminal law remedy to the applicant for the unintentional destruction of a foetus. The Grand Chamber held that this was not a requirement of Article 2 in every case. In other words, the question of who is protected by the right to life in the ECHR is 'in the margins' of states' discretion.

4.3   Africa

Under the ACHPR, the Protocol on the Rights of Women specifically provides in the context of reproductive health: 'States Parties shall take all appropriate measures to: protect the reproductive rights of women by authorising medical abortion in cases of sexual assault, rape, incest, and where the continued pregnancy endangers the mental and physical health of the mother or the life of the mother or the foetus.'[136] The position under African human rights law is to impose a positive obligation upon states to provide for therapeutic abortions in the circumstances set out.

---

[133] See, A. Plomer, 'A Foetal Right to Life? The Case of *Vo v. France*' (2005) 5 *Hum. Rts. L. Rev.* 311.

[134] See, *Open Door and Dublin Well Woman v. Ireland* (1992) 15 EHRR 244.

[135] *Vo v. France* (2005) 40 EHRR 12. See, further, Plomer, 'A Foetal Right to Life?'

[136] Article 14(2)(c), Women's Protocol to the ACHPR.

Framed as a positive obligation, it is not clear whether abortions for other reasons would breach this provision for falling outside the enumerated reasons, or alternatively, whether they would breach the right-to-life provision in Article 4 of the ACHPR. Provided they are regulated by law and not otherwise arbitrary, it would seem that the right to abortion could be extended in the African context. As in the European context, there is no express statement that the foetus is unprotected per se or that all forms of abortion are permitted in all circumstances. As far as a foetus can be held to benefit from the right to life in the African context, this right is circumscribed by the listed permissible exceptions. Moreover, African states have indicated that the physical and mental health rights of women trump those of an unborn foetus.

4.4   The Americas

In contrast to the position at international law and in the regional human rights systems in the Council of Europe and under the ACHPR, states of the Americas agreed to clarify explicitly that, in their view, the right to life starts 'in general, from the moment of conception'. Reflecting the Catholic tradition of the region, the final wording of Article 4(1) of the American Convention on Human Rights (ACHR) provides:

> Every person has the right to have his [or her] life protected. This right shall be protected by law and, in general, from the moment of conception. No-one shall be arbitrarily deprived of his [or her] life.[137]

However, even in the Americas, the language of 'in general' gives scope for individual states to adopt an alternative position, or to insert exceptions to the general position. In the 'Baby Boy' case, for example, the Inter-American Commission of Human Rights (I-ACmHR) held that Article 4 of the ACHR primarily protects against the arbitrary deprivation of life and, therefore, does not protect the foetus absolutely. The fact that the drafting conference of the American Declaration of the Rights and Duties of Man 1948,[138] which was at issue in the case, chose not to include explicit language that would protect the child from the 'moment of conception' was sufficient for the I-ACmHR to conclude that there could be

---

[137] Article 4(1), American Convention on Human Rights.
[138] American Declaration of the Rights and Duties of Man 1948, OAS res. XXX, adopted by the Ninth International Conference of American States (1948), OEA/Ser.L.V/II.82 doc.6 rev.1 at 17 (1992).

no assumption as to the coverage of the right.[139] Rehof argues that this case indicates that there would be very few examples in which a 'provoked abortion' (by which he means induced termination as opposed to a miscarriage) would violate the right to life.[140]

Taken together, the international and regional jurisprudence points to a general position at international law that the right to life 'generally' starts at birth rather than at conception. However, in none of the jurisdictions has it been categorically stated that the unborn child has no rights under the right-to-life guarantees. Instead, the rights of pregnant women to undergo abortions for reasons of threats to health and life have been widely endorsed. I endorse this position owing to its advantages for women's rights and control over their lives, in particular in the context of unwanted pregnancies, including as a consequence of rape, and the correlative issues of unsafe and clandestine abortions that take the lives of thousands of women every year. However, there are two further issues that appear unresolved by this approach. The first is that the phenomenon of increasing recourse to sex-selective abortions, in which millions of girl children are removed from society prior to birth, and the second issue is that of domestic violence against pregnant women that results in miscarriage (or even in the case of *Vo* v. *France*, discussed above, in which international human rights law has nothing it seems to say where there is no criminal remedy for the loss of an unborn child by reason of negligence (including denial of motherhood)). These two issues are discussed below in the next section at 2.1 and 2.2, which deals with the effectiveness of utilising Article 6 of the ICCPR (and other right-to-life guarantees) in the context of violence against women.

C   Violence against women as a breach of the right to life

The ultimate cost of violence perpetrated against women is death. Protecting a woman's right to life is, therefore, fundamental to the enjoyment of all other rights and should form part of an integrated feminist strategy against violence. At a minimum, violence interferes with a woman's quality of life which, as discussed above, also falls within the scope of the right to life under international law. Nonetheless, the right to life as a contested concept is a complex tool for feminists and, therefore, does not

---

[139] *White and Potter* v. *United States of America* (the 'Baby Boy' Case), I-ACmHR, Case No. 2141, Res. No. 23/81 (6 March 1981).
[140] See, Rehof, 'Article 3'.

always represent an effective guarantor against all forms of violence, or always the best strategy for advocacy.

1   Benefits of the right to life

As noted in the introduction to this chapter, the right to life is a fundamental right upon which all other rights are based. Therefore, it is both symbolically and substantively important under international law. Threats to the right to life summon images of the most serious forms of violence that threaten the lives of women, and therefore such acts ought to attract powerful disapproval by the international community. This argument is not dissimilar to that mounted in respect of the torture prohibition, which has been praised by feminist scholars for its peremptory status under international law (see Chapter 5). However, unlike the torture prohibition, the right to life does not carry the same rigid ideas or prescribed definitions as to what constitutes a breach of its provisions. The right to life is a far more fluid notion than the torture prohibition, and although early discourse focused on arbitrary killing by government officials, there is some agreement that the right should not be restrictively interpreted.

In line with this non-restrictive view of Article 6 of the ICCPR, the HRC has addressed a range of forms of violence against women under it. For example, it has called on states to ensure 'that laws relating to rape, sexual abuse and violence against women provide women with effective protection'.[141] The HRC's General Comment on equality between women and men, issued in 2000, calls on states in their reporting under Article 6 to include information regarding birth rates, pregnancy and childbirth-related deaths, gender-disaggregated statistics on infant mortality rates, family planning measures to prevent unwanted pregnancies and avoid life-threatening clandestine abortions, female infanticide, widow-burning, and dowry killings.[142] It further provides that the HRC 'wishes' to have information on the particular impact on women of poverty and deprivation, although its request was not couched in obligatory terms.[143] The HRC has stated in at least one state party report that 'violence against women remains a major threat to their right to life and needs to be more effectively addressed'.[144]

---

[141] HRC, Concluding observations on Peru, UN Doc. A/52/40 (Vol. I) (1997), para. 167.

[142] HRC, General Comment No. 28: Equality of Rights Between Men and Women, para. 10.

[143] Ibid.

[144] HRC, Concluding observations on Colombia, UN Doc. A/52/40 (Vol. I) (1997), para. 287.

In addition, the HRC has noted that '[t]he subordinate role of women in some countries is illustrated by the high incidence of pre-natal sex selection and abortion of female fetuses'.[145] It has also been acknowledged that '[w]omen are particularly vulnerable in times of internal or international armed conflicts ... [to] rape, abduction and other forms of gender based violence'.[146] States parties have been called upon, variously, to adopt measures to improve accessibility to health services, including emergency obstetric care, and family planning services for women, to review abortion laws to bring them into conformity with the ICCPR, to adequately train health workers, to strengthen sex education programmes to avoid unwanted pregnancies, and to ensure that women are not forced to undergo clandestine abortions that endanger their lives.[147] The HRC has raised concern about female genital mutilation and 'honour crimes', including killings of girls and women who 'dishonour' their men, in relation to Article 6, in addition to Articles 3 and 7.[148] The World Health Organization has calculated that up to 70 per cent of female murder victims are killed by their male partners.[149]

The HRC has also addressed the issue of female infanticide, that is, the sex-selective killing of girls at or soon after birth. The HRC has held it to be an infringement of the right to life where the state fails to prevent it or to prosecute those individuals responsible. Female infanticide is now well documented as a manifestation of the unequal status attributed to girls in many societies.[150] According to the United Nations Population Fund, up to 60 million girls and women are missing from Asian populations.[151] Nobel laureate Amartya Sen has suggested that the figure is over 100 million, caused in part by low literacy, education, and lack of economic opportunities for women.[152] In its Concluding Observations on Paraguay, the HRC criticised lenient laws regarding infanticide as early as 1995.[153]

[145] HRC, General Comment No. 28: Equality of Rights Between Men and Women, para. 5.
[146] Ibid., para. 8.
[147] UNICEF, The State of the World's Children: Women and Children – The Double Dividend of Gender Equality (2007), Figure 1.3.
[148] HRC Concluding observations on Sweden, UN Doc. A/57/40 (Vol. I) (2002), para. 8. See, further, Concluding observations on Senegal, UN Doc. A/53/40 (Vol. I) (1998), para. 61 that finds that FGM is contrary to the dignity of human beings.
[149] World Health Organization, World Report on Violence and Health (2002), 118.
[150] For a general overview and statistics on female infanticide, see www.gendercide.org. It is particularly prevalent in India and China.
[151] UN Population Fund, State of the World's Population, 2005 (no page numbers).
[152] A. Sen, 'More than 100 Million Women are Missing', New York Review of Books, 20 December 1990, 61.
[153] HRC, Concluding observations on Peru, UN Doc. CCPR/C/79/Add.48 (1995), para. 16.

Female infanticide and the malnutrition of girls have been compared with forms of female genocide.[154]

Similar issues have now been raised by the Women's Committee,[155] the Children's Committee,[156] and the CESCR.[157] The jurisprudence emerging from the Women's Committee in cases of domestic violence, many mentioned in Chapter 5, have recognised the fact that such violence threatens one's physical and moral integrity as well as one's life, but absent a specific prohibition on the right to life, they have been argued and decided under different provisions.[158]

Comparable regional human rights systems have also elaborated criteria to determine a state's responsibility under the right to life in the context of domestic violence. In *Kontrova v. Slovakia*, the ECtHR stated that the right to life in Article 2 of the ECHR entails a positive obligation on states to 'take appropriate steps to safeguard the lives of those within its jurisdiction'. Although the ECtHR took into account 'the difficulties in policing modern societies, the unpredictability of human conduct and the operational choices which must be made in terms of priorities and resources',[159] there remained a primary duty to put in place effective

---

[154] C. Bunch, 'Transforming Human Rights from a Feminist Perspective', in J. Peters and A. Wolper (eds.), *Women's Rights, Human Rights: International Feminist Perspectives* (New York: Routledge, 1995) 11, at 16.

[155] See, e.g., CEDAW, Concluding observations on Yemen, UN Doc. A/57/38 (Part III) (2002), para. 390 (concern for the discriminatory nature of the Penal Code of Yemen which provides that a husband or other male relative who kills his wife in relation to adultery is not charged with murder); CEDAW, Concluding observations on Mexico, UN Doc. A/57/38 (Part III) (2002) 205, para. 439 (the disappearance and murders of women in the Cuidad Juarez region of Mexico and the apparent lack of investigations); CEDAW, Concluding observations on Brazil, UN Doc. A/58/38 (Part II) (2003) 93, para. 126; Slovenia, A/58/38 (Part II) (2003) 109, para. 214; Samoa, A/60/38 (Part I) (2005) 9, paras. 56 and 57 (high rates of maternal mortality); CEDAW, Concluding observations on Brazil, UN Doc. A/58/38 part II (2003) 93, para. 127; Paraguay, A/60/38 (Part I) (2005) 44, paras. 287 and 288 (health risks associated with clandestine or unsafe abortions); and CEDAW, Concluding observations on Turkey, UN Doc. A/60/38 part I (2005) 58, paras. 367 and 368 ('honour' killings).

[156] See, e.g., CRC, Concluding observations on India, UN Doc. CRC/C/137 (2004) 75, para. 411; Niger, UN Doc. CRC/C/118 (2002) 37, paras. 155 and 156; China, UN Doc. A/53/41 (1998), paras. 108 and 129.

[157] See, e.g., CESCR, Concluding observations on Guinea, UN Doc. E/C.12/1996/6 (1997), para. 193 (steps needed to be taken to improve life expectancy).

[158] See, e.g., *A. T. v. Hungary*, CEDAW 2/2003 (26 January 2005).

[159] *Kontrova v. Slovakia* (2007) 4 EHRR 482, para. 50. The applicant in this case had filed a criminal complaint against her husband accusing him of assaulting and beating her with an electric cable. She also stated that there was a long history of physical and psychological abuse by her husband. Some days later she went with her husband to the District Police Station and withdrew the complaint. The authorities took no further

criminal law provisions to deter the commission of offences against the person, backed up by law enforcement machinery for the prevention, suppression, and punishment of breaches of such provisions. While noting that the authorities have a positive obligation to take preventive operational measures to protect an individual whose life is at risk from the criminal acts of another individual, the ECtHR held that this must not amount to 'an impossible or disproportionate burden' on the authorities and not every claimed risk to life entails a requirement under the ECHR to take these steps. Rather, the ECtHR explained that the positive obligation arises where the 'authorities knew or ought to have known at the time of the existence of a real and immediate risk to the life of an identified individual from the criminal acts of a third party and that they failed to take measures within the scope of their powers which, judged reasonably, might have been expected to avoid that risk.'[160] Here, again, the language of 'reasonableness' creeps in to the analysis, and a woman's right to life is protected not absolutely (as in the torture prohibition) but only reasonably. In *Kontrova* v. *Slovakia* the ECtHR nonetheless determined that the police had specific obligations including accepting and registering the applicant's criminal complaint; launching a criminal investigation; commencing criminal proceedings against the applicant's husband; keeping a proper record of the emergency calls; advising the next shift of police on duty of the situation; and taking action in respect of the allegation that the applicant's husband had a shotgun and had made violent threats with it.[161]

In a 2009 decision the ECtHR likewise found a violation of both the right to life of the applicant's mother, who was killed by the applicant's ex-husband, as well as her own ill-treatment (also discussed in Chapter 5). Violations of the prohibition on torture (Article 3, ECHR)

---

action. There was a further incident some weeks later and then the husband shot and killed her two children and himself. In fact, one of the police officers assisted the complainant to alter her complaint so that it referred only to minor incidences and required no further action.

[160] *Ibid.*, 50.

[161] *Ibid.*, 53. See, also, *Tomasic* v. *Croatia*, ECtHR, Applic. No. 46598/06 (15 January 2009), which followed the same line of reasoning as *Kontrova*. In this case, the applicant alleged that her de facto husband had made repeated threats against her and her one-year-old daughter, including that he had a bomb that he would throw at her. Following complaints made by her, he was detained and criminal proceedings were instigated against him. A psychiatric assessment found that he was suffering from a profound personality disorder. He served his sentence, but shortly after his release he murdered his wife and daughter and then took his own life.

and non-discrimination on the basis of sex (Article 14, ECHR) were also made out. In relation to Article 2, the ECtHR in *Opuz* v. *Turkey*[162] held that the authorities had not pursued existing legal remedies available, that the criminal system had no deterrent effect, and there was even tolerance of this kind of behaviour. In addition to this, the ECtHR found the existence of prima facie evidence that domestic violence mainly affects women in Turkey and that the general and discriminatory judicial passivity in Turkey created a climate of impunity, amounting to a violation of Article 14 in conjunction with Articles 2 and 3:

> Research showed that, despite Law no. 4320, when victims reported domestic violence to police stations, police officers did not investigate their complaints but sought to assume the role of mediator by trying to convince the victims to return home and drop their complaint. Delays were frequent when issuing and serving injunctions under Law no. 4320, given the negative attitude of the police officers and that the courts treated the injunctions as a form of divorce action. Moreover, the perpetrators of domestic violence did not receive dissuasive punishments; courts mitigated sentences on the grounds of custom, tradition or honour.[163]

This case is a powerful reminder of the discriminatory culture and society under which women live their daily lives in many societies, and neatly deals with Articles 2, 3, and 14 of the ECHR conjointly. The ECtHR had previously found state responsibility in a domestic violence case in *Bevacqua and S.* v. *Bulgaria* (2008), although its decision was grounded in Article 8 (right to respect for family life) of the ECHR, rather than under the right to life.[164]

Apart from the implication of the right to life in circumstances involving direct threats to life arising from physical or sexual violence, the inclusion of economic and social factors as components of the right to life renders the international system of human rights even more relevant to the varied lives of women. This inclusion has breathed new life into the right to life and has expanded its relevance to millions of people living in poverty. For international lawyers, however, there is some concern that this approach has made the right to life an all-encompassing right, and it raises questions about the relevance of a number of ICESCR rights, such as the right to an adequate standard of living. In other words,

---

[162] *Opuz* v. *Turkey*, ECtHR, Applic. No. 33401/02 (9 June 2009).
[163] Press release issued by the Registrar, Chamber judgment – *Opuz* v. *Turkey*, Ref. 455 a09.
[164] *Bevacqua and S.* v. *Bulgaria*, ECtHR, Applic. No. 71127/01 (12 June 2008). This case concerned domestic violence exacerbated by excessive divorce and custody proceedings.

there is now substantial overlap between the two treaties. Legal purists might argue that this undermines the specific role of each treaty and the obligations that states parties agreed to upon ratification; meanwhile, this approach complements the UN's own indivisibility approach to human rights that human rights are 'equal, interdependent and mutually reinforcing'.[165] Because of these broad interpretations, the right to life has the capacity to include a wide range of 'quality of life' issues. It can therefore be a useful tool to deal with the interlinkages between violence and threats to life caused by poverty, lack of education, and sex discrimination.

2 Concerns with the right to life

Frequently, however, the right to life is absent in discussions on what are clearly life-threatening acts or practices. Domestic violence, for example, is regularly discussed as an issue of inequality, violence per se, or degrading treatment, but not necessarily as a threat to life. For an act to threaten one's life, it invokes ideas of seriousness that may put the threshold level out of reach for a range of violent acts committed against women that may be harmful but not life-threatening. The treaty bodies have not had to deal with this question in an individual communication. What is clear is that there has been a tendency by complainants to utilise other rights rather than the right to life. Similarly, the treaty bodies have been content to make a ruling under other provisions and to leave aside some of the difficult questions relating to the right to life.[166]

In addition, ambiguities surrounding who benefits from the protection of the right to life – for example, an unborn child? – means that it remains a contested right. The right-to-life/abortion debate that dogs national politics in the USA and elsewhere is also present at the international level, and the ambiguous position on who is a 'person' under international law highlights the difficulties of utilising this right in at least two specific circumstances of violence perpetrated against women and girls, discussed below.

---

[165] World Conference on Human Rights, Vienna Declaration and Programme of Action, UN Doc. A/CONF.157/23, 12 July 1993, para. 5.

[166] E.g., recent case of *Tysiac* v. *Poland* (2007) 45 EHRR 42, in which the denial of abortion leading to predicted blindness was discussed in relation to the right to privacy and family life in Article 8 ECHR rather than Articles 3 (which was raised but not discussed) or 2 (which was not raised, although arguably could have been argued in relation to 'quality of life' from blindness).

2.1 Sex-selective abortion – right-to-life dialogue

The increasing concern over sex-selective abortions highlights the complexity of the right-to-life/abortion dialogue. The practice of sex-selective abortions (or, for that matter, pre-implantive sex determination) is set to rise with modern diagnostic technologies becoming more widely available. Sex-selective abortion of female foetuses reinforces the perception of women as second-class citizens in many societies. Its prevalence is worse in societies that have imposed strict population control policies, such as China and India,[167] or where the social and economic value placed on boy children is higher than for girl children.[168] The payment of dowries upon marriage also feeds into the 'cost' of having girls. If this issue is left unregulated, it is also likely to rise in modern societies where couples seek to self-select their family composition.

Pre-natal sex selection is expressly included as prohibited conduct in the Cairo and Beijing Declarations.[169] Under the CEDAW, express reproductive rights are included. These rights grant a woman the right to control the number and spacing of her children.[170] It has been argued that this right does not, however, include the choice of sex of one's offspring.[171] The Children's Committee has addressed the issue of 'son preference', which it indicates is manifested by neglect, less food, and limited health care for girl children. The Children's Committee has also raised concern that a situation of inferiority for girl children favours violence and sexual abuse in the family, as well as problems associated with early pregnancy and marriage, as well as harmful traditional practices such as female genital mutilation and forced marriage.[172] While abortion may be justified under international law in specific situations as outlined above, sex-selective abortion is more complicated. As noted above, under the ICCPR, the right to life is generally accepted as beginning at birth. Therefore, an unborn

---

[167] See, e.g., CRC, Concluding observations on India, UN Doc. CRC/C/137 (2004) 75, para. 411; China, UN Doc. A/53/41 (1998), paras. 108 and 129

[168] See, e.g., CRC, Concluding observations on Niger, UN Doc. CRC/C/118 (2002) 37, paras. 155 and 156; HRC, Concluding observations on Benin, UN Doc. A/60/40 Vol. I (2004) 30, para. 83(14).

[169] UN, Programme of Action of the United Nations International Conference on Population and Development, held at Cairo, 5–13 September 1994, para. 4(16); Fourth World Conference on Women, Beijing Declaration and Platform for Action, UN Doc. A/CONF.177/20 and UN Doc. A/CONF.177/20/Add.1, 15 September 1995, para. 124.

[170] Article 16(e), CEDAW.

[171] B. Toebes, 'Sex Selection under International Human Rights Law' (2008) 9 *Medical L. Int'l* 1, at 13.

[172] CRC, Day of General Discussion on the Girl Child, UN Doc. CRC/C/38 (1995), para. 286.

child (including, therefore, unborn girl children) may not be a direct beneficiary[173] of the UN system of human rights protection.

For example, if an unborn child is not recognised as a human being for the purposes of international law, then the practice of sex-selective abortion and any harm done to the foetus is not strictly prohibited. It may amount to a criminal offence in some jurisdictions. In other jurisdictions it may be tied to a women's reproductive rights and, therefore, seen as a woman's rights issue and not criminal. As international law stands, it is generally considered that the right to life is exercisable after birth, not before. Sex-selective abortion, therefore, may fall outside the scope of international law, unless it is considered as a violation of the mother's rights (as in the contexts described above of forced abortion as a human rights violation in the form of degrading treatment, a threat to life if she is at risk because of the procedure, or where a prohibition on abortion threatens the life of the mother who is forced to bring a child to full term).[174] Behind this issue of sex-selective abortions are questions of lack of consent, force, coercion, and inequality. Issues of sex discrimination, privacy, and reproductive freedom are also implicated. Moreover, the question of sex-selective abortion sits at the junction of group versus individual rights.[175] International human rights law may have a general bias in favour of a woman's right to choose (subject to some limitations), but the right to life provision may be inadequate to deal with the systematic removal of girl children from societies by means of abortion.

Nonetheless, there has been no pronouncement that the right to life does not protect the life of the foetus in any way, shape, or form (here the protection of unborn girls is at stake), but so far, the protection of the mother's life has trumped any rights of the foetus. April Cherry questions whether the practice of sex-selective abortion to rid families and therefore society of 'the burden' of girls reveals the weaknesses in choice rhetoric.[176] She considers that the problem of sex-selective abortions should

---

[173] Cf. children who are brought to term benefit indirectly during pregnancy to the right to health under the ICESCR and other instruments.

[174] E.g. it could be regarded as degrading treatment or even torture to force a woman to undergo an abortion. Similarly, because the abortion is carried out only against women and its attendant complications – physical and emotional – are primarily experienced by women, forced abortion could be considered to be a form of discrimination on the basis of sex. As discussed in the preceding chapters, there are also difficulties with using these norms to protect women from violence.

[175] See, Toebes, 'Sex Selection under International Human Rights Law'.

[176] A. L. Cherry, 'A Feminist Understanding of Sex-Selective Abortion: Solely a Matter of Choice?' (1995) 10 *Wis. Women's L. J.* 161, at 164.

compel feminist critics to re-evaluate doctrines of choice and privacy in the area of reproductive rights. She situates the issue as a question of individual women versus women as a group. She reflects on whether these concepts of choice and non-interference 'empower women, or allow men or the state to secure their own misogynist, familial, or population control agendas'.[177] The issue also sits uncomfortably at the intersection of Western and Asian feminisms. The former have argued that any regulation of reproductive freedom, including limiting the choice of sex of offspring, infringes a woman's autonomy and her reproductive choice. Asian feminists have argued instead that account needs to be given to the cultural context in which women are generally subordinate to men and in which they do not therefore exercise 'freedom' in making such choices.[178] Others argue that sex selection permits the perpetuation of stereotyped notions of what having a child of a particular sex entails.[179]

These issues have not, however, prevented the treaty bodies from treating the issue of sex-selective abortion as a human rights issue. In fact, it would seem that silence on the question of whether a foetus enjoys the protection of the right to life enables the treaty bodies to deal with such issues as sex-selective abortion. At a minimum, terminating a pregnancy based solely on the grounds that the foetus is female would violate the prohibition on sex discrimination, which has been held to be a fundamental right.[180] Under the principle of non-discrimination, the Children's Committee has raised issue with sex discrimination in India that has led to an unequal sex ratio, and it has called upon India to ensure the effective implementation of its Pre-Conception and Pre-Natal Diagnostic Techniques (Prohibition of Sex Selection) Act 1994.[181] The CESCR has identified the unequal status of women in society and the persistent problem of 'son preference' in some countries, which manifests itself in a high incidence of induced abortions of girl foetuses and which threatens the reproductive rights of women.[182] While the committees have confronted

---

[177] *Ibid.*
[178] See, e.g., F. Moazam, 'Feminist Discourse on Sex Screening and Selective Abortion of Female Foetuses' (2004) 18 *Bioethics* 3, as referred to in Toebes, 'Sex Selection under International Human Rights Law', 5.
[179] See, e.g., J. Danis, 'Sexism and "The Superfluous Female": Arguments for Regulating Pre-Implantive Sex Selection' (1995) 18 *Harvard Women's L. J.* 219, at 241.
[180] See, Chapter 4.
[181] CRC, Concluding observations on India, UN Doc. CRC/C/137 (2004) 75, paras. 411–412.
[182] CESCR, Concluding observations on Republic of Korea, UN Doc. E/C.12/2001/17, para. 226.

these issues – largely under equality or reproductive health paradigms – they have not generally dealt with them under the right to life.

Ultimately, the right-to-life/abortion debate remains unresolved at the international level, and the ambiguity it leaves makes the effectiveness of the right to life as a protector of the missing girls contingent. This does not mean that there is no human rights protection available. It is rather to observe that the targeted removal of unborn girls from society does not neatly map onto Article 6 of the ICCPR, or equivalent provisions.

2.2 Domestic violence against pregnant women that results in miscarriage

A second issue that has yet to be dealt with by the treaty bodies in any depth under the right to life is that of domestic violence against pregnant women that results in miscarriage. In the United States, for instance, murder of pregnant women has been found to be the leading cause of death of women between 1991 and 1999.[183] As noted in Chapters 4 and 5 of this book, domestic violence has featured as a human rights issue – as torture or sex discrimination – but the issue of induced, involuntary, or forced abortion or miscarriage caused by domestic violence has not been dealt with to any great extent in the context of the right to life. As the issue of when the right to life begins has not been fully settled under international law, it presents problems in this context also.

In *Vo* v. *France*, mentioned above, the ECtHR confronted the issue of involuntary abortion caused by medical negligence and held that the state had no responsibility for failing to provide criminal remedies for the mother in this case. In an HRC case of *Blanco* v. *Nicaragua*,[184] in which the wife of the applicant was beaten by state security agents, causing a miscarriage, no reference was made to this aspect of the claim. Although domestic violence perpetrated against women is covered by international law – for example torture, discrimination, threat to life – the extent to which the right to life can deal with the loss of the child, deprivation of motherhood, or issues of reproductive choice has not been fully considered by the treaty bodies. It remains an issue that appears to fall into the gaps in international jurisprudence.

---

[183] B. Robinson, 'Why Pregnant Women are Targeted?', *ABC News*, 24 February 2005, citing a 2005 study published in the American Journal of Public Health, available at: www.abcnews.go.com.

[184] See, *Blanco v Nicaragua*, HRC 328/1988 (20 July 1994), which was discussed in Chapter 5.

D   Conclusion

Despite the contentious jurisprudence at international and national levels on the right to life, and the differing political views on when life begins and abortion in particular, the human rights treaty bodies have managed to overcome some initial feminist concerns about its inapplicability to women's lives. First, the right to life is no longer strictly concerned with the arbitrary deprivation of life by state officials, although this is still the mainstay of individual communications under Article 6 of the ICCPR.[185] Furthermore, the latest international treaty on enforced disappearances reinforces the general gender bias in the system of international law. Its definition of 'enforced disappearances' ignores the murder of women and girls by their husbands, fathers, or other relatives and the disposal of their bodies, 'honour' killings, the kidnapping of women for the purposes of sexual slavery and human trafficking, infanticide, or sex-selective abortions. Will we be arguing in years to come that these acts also rightly fall within that Convention?[186]

Threats to and deprivation of physical integrity are clearly within the protection offered by Article 6, including by non-state actors where the state fails in its duties of due diligence. In addition to issues of physical integrity, the treaty bodies have taken up a range of 'quality of life' issues under the right to life, building on the approach of the Inter-American system, such as socio-economic deprivation, maternal mortality rates, and HIV/AIDS. The public/private dichotomy appears to have been merged under the right-to-life rubric, with less distinction being made as to *who* is responsible for the harm – whether the state, the rebel group, the multinational company, the medical profession, or the individual. What are considered 'reasonable measures' to be taken by the state to protect and prevent women from threats to their lives, especially from non-state actors, has still not been fully articulated. Ultimately, the state has responsibility for regulating behaviour by law and for preventing and

---

[185] See, e.g., Joseph, Schultz and Castan, *The International Covenant on Civil and Political Rights*, Chapter 8.

[186] Article 2, ICED defines 'enforced disappearance' as: 'For the purposes of this Convention, "enforced disappearance" is considered to be the arrest, detention, abduction or any other form of deprivation of liberty by agents of the State or by persons or groups of persons acting with the authorization, support or acquiescence of the State, followed by a refusal to acknowledge the deprivation of liberty or by concealment of the fate or whereabouts of the disappeared person, which place such a person outside the protection of the law.'

protecting citizens from threats to their life. The 'dignified life' or 'quality of life' paradigm that is increasingly being accepted by international and regional bodies ought to be applied to prohibit the neglect of girls through their being deprived of the essentials of life as a result of 'son preference'. They hardly enjoy a 'quality of life' which human rights law would sanction, with their lives characterised in many countries by undernourishment, underdevelopment, lack of fulfilment, dowry and arranged/forced marriages, or sale into forced labour or sexual slavery, and early death.

Second, there is a sense under international law that a woman's health and life trumps the rights of her unborn child. The silence surrounding the starting point of the right to life gives women a right to life that cannot be limited by the life of another. Positively, this protects women's reproductive freedoms, which in turn affects both her physical life as well as her quality of life. Nonetheless, this silence also leaves other issues unresolved, such as sex-selective abortions in which the female sex as a demographic are under threat (as well as the individual girls who are removed arbitrarily from society). It also does not (yet) protect pregnant women subjected to abuse who suffer a miscarriage, who have so far not been granted a remedy for the harm (whether negligent or conscious) to themselves, the arbitrary deprivation of their motherhood, nor the rights, if any, of their offspring. At present, these types of issues are dealt with more in relation to torture and cruel, inhuman, or degrading treatment or punishment. Furthermore, the individual nature of the human rights system does not necessarily provide an adequate response to collective threats to the lives of women.[187] Arguably, the principle of inequality is directly at issue here, especially structural inequality, although, as noted in Chapter 4, the language of inequality is not always as powerful as 'unlawful killing' or 'murder'. It seems unsatisfactory to call the deliberate removal of girls from society because of the burden they put on families simply inequality which, as noted in Chapter 4, can be inadvertent.

Nevertheless, the right to life does not suffer from many of the barriers to effectiveness as do the other rights studied in this book. The right to life is not, for example, subject to rigid definitions as is the torture prohibition; and acts threatening life are considered to be particularly serious, if not fundamental to all other rights, as compared to the weaker language of sex discrimination. In addition, the fluidity and broad nature of the right to life means that women are not subjected to a double burden. Under the

---

[187] There are of course other 'collective' avenues under international human rights law, such as crimes against humanity and genocide.

right-to-life paradigm, women would need to show that any violent act was of a serious nature so as to threaten their life, or alternatively, that their life was threatened by the failure of government policies to reduce poverty or socio-economic disadvantage, the latter being more difficult to prove than the former. The threshold of seriousness also carries problems of excluding from protection a range of lesser forms of violence, but even in these circumstances the state is required to take some action per the ECtHR in *Kontrova, Tomasic and Opuz*, outlined above.

Of the three rights studied in this book, the right to life appears to be an integral one in any strategy to combat violence against women, despite the many questions that remain about its full scope and application. As noted, one of its main limitations is that it is reserved for the most serious threats of violence rather than encompassing all forms of physical, psychological, economic, or sexual violence. As the primary right upon which all other rights are based, framing violence against women under a right-to-life paradigm acknowledges that the ultimate price paid by women for direct violence against them as well as state tolerance of that violence is death. This is a vital first step towards acknowledging the human rights dimensions of women's lives. The right to life would thus need to be one of the rights included in any strategy to combat violence against women, including in any proposed treaty, but on its own it does not and cannot fill all the gaps in the human rights framework.

Conundrums, paradoxes, and continuing inequality: revisiting feminist narratives

A   Introduction

This book has examined how women's experiences of and concerns about violence are incorporated into specific provisions of international human rights treaty law. Two main feminist strategies were identified: the first was the conceptualisation of violence against women as a form of sex discrimination and the second was the creative reinterpretation of existing provisions to apply them to the experiences of women. The latter discussion focused on the rights to life and to be free from torture or other cruel, inhuman, or degrading treatment or punishment. These strategies have developed for a number of reasons, not least owing to gaps in the international legal architecture reflected in the failure of the international community to agree an explicit treaty or provision guaranteeing women protection from violence. The preference of the United Nations has been instead to opt for a non-binding declaration and a 'gender mainstreaming' strategy that requires all UN bodies to ask 'the gender question' in relation to all instruments, mechanisms, laws, policies, and programmes. This book was interested in what these two strategies have meant in reality for female victims of violence, as well as what they tell us about where feminist scholarship and the four main feminist critiques of international law outlined in Chapter 2 are today. What have these inclusion strategies meant for female victims of violence? What have they meant for the feminist critiques outlined in Chapter 2? Are these feminist critiques still relevant, or can they be set aside as finally resolved? Has there been any real progress in women's equality since the adoption of the UN Charter? This chapter revisits these central themes and questions. The final chapter will then propose a range of recommendations relevant to how to respond to the many issues considered throughout the book.

As pragmatic responses to gaps in the law and the marginalisation of women from mainstream human rights mechanisms, I have acknowledged that these inclusion or 'gender-mainstreaming' approaches have yielded some historic conceptual and substantive breakthroughs, not least the recognition of violence against women as an issue of human rights law. They have also led to the partial collapsing of the public/private dichotomy. However, they also have their shortcomings, centred on the fact that attaching violence against women to existing norms does little to dismantle existing power structures and has resulted de facto in the unequal treatment of women under international law. As Dianne Otto has explained, the real conundrum of 'feminist inclusion strategies [is the] [reproduction of] unequal relations of gender power.'[1] Reflecting on UN Security Council resolution 1325 on women in armed conflict,[2] Otto more recently observed that, despite 'the remarkable spread of feminist ideas throughout the UN system, [including] into the most unlikely places ...', resolution 1325 illustrates a number of problems with increased institutional incorporation:

> These problems include a pattern of selective engagement with feminist ideas as they are instrumentalised to serve institutional purposes; an across-the-board absence of strong accountability mechanisms, even as the outside pressure for accountability grows; and the tendency for protective stereotypes of women to normatively re-emerge following an initial flirtation with more active and autonomous representations.[3]

Otto's observations are also applicable to the 'inclusion strategies' explored in this book relating to violence against women in a broad sense. A common thread of the treatment of the three rights studied in this book is that women's experiences are seen as an exception to the main or general understandings of the particular provisions studied. That is, women are seen as a deviation from that standard and as an exception to the rule. This is the first of the unintended consequences of the inclusion or 'gender mainstreaming' strategy. Under this strategy women are still not (yet) full citizens for the purposes of benefiting from human rights protection, and thus the system perpetuates sexual hierarchies in which men and men's experiences are posited as the 'norm' of international law, and women only gain access to the system by equating their experiences to these masculine norms.

---

[1] D. Otto, 'Lost in Translation: Re-Scripting the Sexed Subjects of International Human Rights Law', in A. Orford (ed.), *International Law and Its Others* (Cambridge University Press, 2006) 318, at 351.

[2] SC res. 1325 (2000), 13 October 2000.

[3] D. Otto, "The Exile of Inclusion: Reflections on Gender Issues in International Law Over the Last Decade" (2009) 10 *Melb. J. Int'l L.* 11, at 12.

The second consequence of working within the mainstream is the reality that being held to the same standards as men *de jure* results in women's subjection to additional (and therefore unequal) legal burdens de facto. Female litigants must 'fit' their experiences of violence into male-defined criteria, which in turn reflect and reinforce a system that treats women unequally. It conjures up the old Aristotelian equality model of identical treatment, explained in Chapter 4, with the 'male' standard centre stage. Put another way, women are required to convince international decision-makers that what has been done to them is worthy of international attention, by *either* (a) equating it to harm normally perpetrated against men and incorporating their experiences into provisions designed with those of men in mind (as already noted, this reverts to applying an Aristotelian or formal model of equality); *or* (b) justifying why their experiences 'deserve' the establishment of an exception to the rule and thus treating women and their experiences as 'exceptional'. This in turn reignites the protective focus of international law (by emphasising women's victimhood) and the correlative stereotyping of 'women' as passive victims, as objects rather than subjects of law, as mothers or wives operating in the so-called 'private', or as the 'Exotic Other'.[4] Women are not treated as persons in their own right or as equal human beings under either of these approaches. Thus, the 'conundrum' of 'gender mainstreaming' is that it continues to treat women unequally under international law, supports the gender bias in the system, and prevents any deeper transformation. While the United Nations' human rights system no longer excludes women entirely from mainstream human rights, an exclusion that characterised its first fifty years, it has attained only a stage of rhetorical inclusion; equality is still to be achieved.

These strategies therefore serve to reinforce feminist criticisms of the international system outlined in Chapter 2, rather than to respond to them. This begs the question whether the myriad feminist critiques outlined in Chapter 2 can be answered within the mainstream. Have any proposals for deeper transformation been sacrificed on the altar of inclusion?

Vanessa Munro has posed further dilemmas: '[C]an one criticise rhetorically powerful strategies that have secured reformist currency (such as rights discourse) without being relegated as a perpetual outsider?; can one, as Audre Lorde puts it, dismantle the master's house with the master's tools?'[5] Zoe Pearson and Sari Kouvo describe the position that

---

[4] K. Engle, 'Female Subjects of Public International Law: Human Rights and the Exotic Other Female' (1992) 26 *New England L. Rev.* 1509.

[5] A. Lorde, 'The Master's Tools Will Never Dismantle the Master's House' in *Sister Outside: Essays and Speeches* (Berkeley: The Crossing Press, 1984), 110–114, referred to

feminist scholarship has reached in relation to international law as some-
where between 'resistance' and 'compliance'. They assert that:

> feminist scholarship aims at deconstructing international law to show
> why and how 'women' have been marginalised; at the same time femi-
> nists have been largely unwilling to challenge the core of international
> law and its institutions, remaining hopeful of international law's poten-
> tial for women.[6]

Karen Engle makes a similar point: 'No matter how hard we push on the
core, though, we never attack its essence. We are afraid that if we push
too hard, it might dissolve and become useless to us.'[7] These conundrums
cause us to reflect upon the long-term cost of working within the mainstream, which has been a central feature of this book. To me it seems that
these tensions may never be fully resolved. A further question that arises
amid these dilemmas is whether we should accept Janet Halley's invitation to 'take a break from feminism'?[8] While acknowledging the traditions and contributions of feminism, Halley compels us 'to see around the
corners of [feminism's] own construction [and its limitations]',[9] ultimately
querying whether it matters that feminist theories are largely irreconcilable. Before returning to these questions, let's first reflect on the conclusions of this study in particular.

B   Feminist narratives on international law and human rights revisited

1   The absence of women and women's voices

This first feminist critique of the human rights treaty system outlined
in Chapter 2 was the absence of women and women's voices from mainstream human rights. This was later paralleled by the 'ghettoization' of

---

in V. Munro, 'Navigating Feminisms: At the Margins, in the Mainstreams or Elsewhere?
Reflections on Charlesworth, Otomo and Pearson', in Z. Pearson and S. Kuovo (eds.),
*Between Resistance and Compliance? Feminist Perspectives on International Law in an Era
of Anxiety and Terror* (Oxford: Hart Publishing, in press 2010) (on file with the author).

[6] Z. Pearson and S. Kuovo, 'Between Resistance and Compliance? Feminist Perspectives on
International Law in an Era of Anxiety and Terror', in their edited collection of the same
name, (in press, 2010) (on file with the author).

[7] K. Engle, 'International Human Rights and Feminism: When Discourses Meet' (1992) 13
Mich. J. Int'l L. 605, at 609.

[8] J. E. Halley, *Split Decisions: How and Why to Take a Break from Feminism* (Princeton
University Press, 2005).

[9] *Ibid.,* 321.

women's concerns into separate or women-specific/sidestream forums. As shown in Chapter 3, women continue to make up less than 50 per cent of the membership of the treaty bodies collectively, and only around 20 per cent if the treaties on women and children are excluded.[10] Women are thus denied equal representation on the treaty bodies, in itself a breach of a woman's right to equal participation with men in all decision-making forums. As such, this fails to live up to the UN Charter's ambitions that women would take an equal seat in its principal and subsidiary organs.[11] Despite criticisms from other branches of feminist thought of the liberal feminist agenda of equal participation, it is still a very important unfulfilled objective for women's equality at the international level.

A second observation of this book, detailed in Chapter 3, is that women underutilise the human rights individual petitions procedures generally and in relation to violence against women in particular. This calls for more research into how admissibility criteria and the communications procedures affect female victims. Until women have equal and regular access to the treaty bodies and other international redress mechanisms, any advances made by way of interpretation will be at best theoretical. Moreover, until such interpretations become consistently applied across the treaty bodies, women will be reluctant to come forward, being unable to rely on consistent and accepted treaty body practice. The prospect of mounting a legal claim indirectly by asserting their rights on several fronts – by using the categories, for example, of torture, arbitrary killing, or sex discrimination – can be prohibitive for many women. There is no coherent and comprehensive framework available to which one can direct victims of violence. The fractured and ad hoc nature of such an endeavour means that female victims of violence are easily sidelined, and women's voices easily silenced. The following and final chapter in this book recommends some practical reforms to address these problems.

In addition, while input regarding women's concerns into state party reports has improved, feedback to states by the committees is often vacuous and rhetorical so that it fails to provide any helpful guidance to states, and women and violence against women are in many ways simply 'add-on' references. The 'template-style' comments provided by the part-time committees to states parties regularly contain inadequate explanations and directions that may otherwise bring about real and lasting change

---

[10] See, Chapter 3.
[11] Article 8, Charter of the United Nations, 26 June 1945, 1 UNTS XVI; entered into force 24 October 1945.

at municipal levels. Noting that this is a general structural problem of the treaty bodies, any improvements to this system would have positive ramifications for understanding the committees' reasoning on questions of gender also. In my opinion, the establishment of a unified standing treaty body would permit improved engagement with state party performances, as a full-time professional committee would be more likely to have the time, resources, and expertise to do so, and states parties would be pushed to take their reporting obligations more seriously. Moreover, a single treaty body would be better placed to issue consistent general comments across treaty obligations. The question of treaty body reform is dealt with in Chapter 8.

2   Human rights are 'men's rights'

The second feminist critique outlined in this book was that human rights treaties contain norms that are predominantly applicable to men's experiences and are framed around the fears of men rather than those of women. As noted above, engagement with these norms also does little to dismantle the existing power structures of the system. As we have seen, no normative amendments have been passed at the international level that alter this historical position.[12] The express language in human rights instruments has barely changed since 1945.

The torture prohibition is, for example, still predominantly applied and understood in the context of physical ill-treatment perpetrated by government or quasi-government officials against political dissidents or prisoners for the purposes of extracting information or forcing a detainee to confess. This perception of torture has been further entrenched in the context of the post-September 11th security environment, with its emphasis on terrorism and counter-terrorism measures, and the conflicts in Afghanistan and Iraq.[13] Despite the fact that various forms of violence against women have been subsumed under the torture rubric under international human rights law (as well as under international humanitarian

---

[12] As noted elsewhere in this book, there have been developments at the regional level: see, the Inter-American Convention on the Prevention, Punishment and Eradication of Violence against Women 1994, 33 ILM 1534 (1994); entered into force 3 May 1995 (IA-VAW); Protocol to the African Convention on Human and Peoples' Rights on the Human Rights of Women 2000, adopted by the 2nd Ordinary Session of the Assembly of the African Union, AU Doc. CAB/LEG/66.6, 13 September 2000; entered into force 25 November 2005 (PRWA).

[13] See, Chapter 5.

law and international criminal law), at times to great effect, this approach treats women's claims as 'exceptions to the rule' and thus props up the existing system.

Likewise, the mainstay of the right to life continues to centre on the arbitrary deprivation of life by the state, further evidenced by the recent agreement of a new treaty outlawing 'disappearances' in which the definition of an 'enforced disappearance' is again gender 'neutral', and ignores many concerns of women (except potentially as mothers of the disappeared[14]).[15] Although the meaning of the right to life has expanded to include issues of violence against women and 'quality of life' issues in some jurisdictions, with important benefits for women, it is a complex tool for feminists owing to disagreements, inter alia, over abortion.[16] Of the three rights studied in this book, however, the right to life will be a necessary part of any strategy to eradicate violence against women, reflecting as it does the ultimate cost of such violence.

Discrimination under international law has also been widely used to incorporate violence against women under human rights law but it, too, is fraught with complexities. Discrimination is most criticised on the grounds of race, rather than sex, with the former prohibition having achieved the status of *jus cogens*, but not yet the latter, although there have been some intimations that sex discrimination is also a peremptory norm of international law. These developments should be celebrated and reinforced.[17] Moreover, equality guarantees are still largely applied following a sameness/difference ideology, in which concepts of oppression, exclusion, disadvantage, and sexual hierarchies have been given limited attention. Moreover, establishing that a particular form of violence is a form of sex discrimination is complex. No other area of law builds in the cause of such violence as a component part of the definition of the act in question. All in all, women continue to be required to frame their grievances within existing masculine-centric provisions, albeit with greater success than previously.

---

[14] See, e.g., B. Meyersfeld, *Domestic Violence and International Law* (Oxford and Portland, OR: Hart Publishing, 2010), 275–29, who praises the international human rights framework for acknowledging as human rights victims the relatives of the disappeared. She does not, however, critique the omission of women as direct victims of disappearances: see, instead, *González et al ('Cotton Field)' v. Mexico*, I-ACtHR, Preliminary Objection, Merits, Reparations and Costs, Ser. C No. 205 (16 November 2009).

[15] International Convention for the Protection of All Persons from Enforced Disappearances 2006, GA res. 61/177, 20 December 2006, opened for signature 6 February 2007 (not yet in force at January 2010) (ICED).

[16] See, Chapter 6.   [17] See, Chapter 4.

In addition, as already noted, the feminine pronoun is missing from many of the major human rights treaties, reinforcing the exclusion of women from these instruments. More recently agreed instruments now apply both the masculine and feminine forms,[18] which is a welcome advance, yet little practical effect has been felt. Nonetheless, the agreement of such treaties challenges arguments that using both pronouns is overly cumbersome or legalistically otiose. Despite this, the singular use of the masculine pronoun in the earlier instruments has not blocked the relevant committees from reflecting upon and incorporating women's experiences. Such changes have not, however, been arrived at naturally, but have required strenuous lobbying by women's groups and non-governmental organisations, as well as the pressure exerted by female members within these committees. The influence of the Women's Committee on the other treaty bodies is also noteworthy.

The central concern about the inclusion of women's experiences of violent acts within traditional human rights canons (that is, under 'men's human rights') is that interpretative dialogue begins from the traditional core (that is, men's experiences of violence) and works its way outwards. As many feminist scholars have already noted, men are the standard of international law, and if women are included at all, they are seen as a deviation from that standard.[19] Because of this, women are more likely to allege traditional or non-gender-specific forms of violence against themselves or other persons when invoking the individual communications mechanisms. There have been few claims, for example, alleging rape or other forms of sexual violence brought by women, whether perpetrated directly by the state or indirectly through their omissions or negligence. One reason why this may occur is because women do not readily identify what has happened to them within the masculine terminology of human rights provisions. A woman may not, for example, identify the rape she has suffered as a form of torture (nor may her advocates). Moreover, even when women bring cases under these traditional constructs, their cases are rarely publicly acknowledged or scrutinised. This supports MacKinnon's argument that when women are subjected to the same harm as men, the

---

[18] See, e.g., Convention on the Rights of the Child 1989, GA res. 44/25, 20 November 1989, 1577 UNTS 3; entered into force 2 September 1990 (CRC); International Convention on the Protection of the Rights of All Migrant Workers and Members of Their Families 1990, GA res. 45/148, 18 December 1990, 2220 UNTS 93; entered into force 1 July 2003 (IMWC); Convention on the Rights of Persons with Disabilities 2006, GA res. 61/106, 13 December 2006; entered into force 3 May 2008 (ICRPD).

[19] See, Chapter 2.

harm that they suffer is ignored in international discourse altogether.[20] This serves in turn to reinforce gendered hierarchies of the law, as well as to entrench gender-based stereotypes of women as victims of particular forms of violence, most notably sexual violence. It does little to change perceptions of women from 'vulnerable' victims in need of protection to individuals with agency and deserving of empowerment.

A second obstacle to women's inclusion within mainstream human rights norms is that the treaty bodies have not abandoned the idea that standards of 'reasonableness' are gender-neutral and objective. In response, the Special Rapporteur on Violence against Women, Its Causes and Consequences, has attempted to develop a set of 'indicators' to direct and assess state party performance.[21] Such efforts are likely to help downplay the centrality of these 'fuzzy' and undefined concepts, to the elaboration of more specific and concrete obligations.

Related to the lack of clear guidance to states is the third identified problem with the inclusion strategies that, in the context of individual communications, decisions rarely give sufficient weight, if any, to the subjective circumstances of individual female complainants, nor do the committees always apply a contextual analysis. At most, the concepts of sex and/or gender are mentioned as somehow relevant, without a clear explanation of how or why, but mostly any discussion of them is missing. As noted in the Introduction to this book in Chapter 1, the terms of sex and gender are not well understood and are regularly used interchangeably. Shying away completely from using such language is, however, likely to distort case outcomes for women. What is needed instead is for the language of sex/gender to take its proper place in the context of the case in question, alongside other 'social stratifiers'[22] such as race, religion, culture, socio-economic status, sexuality, or education.

In addition, a woman's personalised experiences that may not conform to expected trends or stereotypes must also be given proper weight, thus recognising that not all women experience violence in the same way, or are targeted for the same reasons. Such an innovation would be a step along the road to a more nuanced dialogue that transcends gender and

---

[20] C. A. MacKinnon, 'Rape, Genocide, and Women's Human Rights' (1994) 17 *Harv. Women's L. J.* 5, at 5.

[21] Report of the Special Rapporteur on Violence against Women, Its Causes and Consequence (SR-VAW), *Indicators on Violence against Women and State Response*, UN Doc. A/HRC/7/6, 29 January 2008.

[22] CEDAW, General Recommendation No. 25: Temporary Special Measures (2008) (no UN Doc.), n. 2.

other social stratifiers, and moves closer to recognising women as persons or individuals, rather than only as members of a subordinate group. Moreover, it would make the seriousness of the harm to the victim the central feature of any inquiry, rather than whether her experience meets an outsider's expectations of women's 'proper' role in society and her 'proper' reaction to the abuse in question. Isabel Gunning's 'world travelling' could be beneficial here in educating decision-makers to recognise how their own role in decision-making and their own prejudices impact on case outcomes. This would map neatly onto Cook and Cusack's call to end gender stereotyping. They argue that '[some] transnational legal perspectives ... demonstrate [that] treating women according to their individual needs, abilities, priorities, and circumstances, and not according to stereotypical generalizations of what it means to be a woman, has contributed to their emancipation and their exercise of their human rights and fundamental freedoms.'[23] Moreover, they point to a number of legal instruments and decisions that prohibit the practice of stereotyping.[24] Failing to adopt a contextualised analysis can mean that decision-makers are likely to overlook potentially important facts relevant to a victim's situation because they are looking only for trends, stereotypes, and 'accepted/acceptable' behaviour. Nonetheless, there is also room for inserting objectively identified crimes, such as rape, as a human rights violation regardless of how women react to it.[25] More on how contextual decision-making could be improved in Chapter 8.

A fourth concern, and perhaps the greatest challenge, of these interpretative inclusion strategies is they do little to dismantle existing structural inequalities of the international human rights system. There have been no changes, for example, in the admissibility criteria of the treaty bodies or in the system of nomination and election of treaty body members. Significantly, there have been no treaty amendments under international human rights law that have addressed violence against women directly. As noted above, participating in the same system as men without fully redefining its boundaries reinforces its structural inequalities, and as identified in relation to all three rights studied in this book, the partial approach of reinterpreting existing norms adds legal burdens on women by inserting additional legal criteria that they must fulfil.

[23] R. J. Cook and S. Cusack, *Gender Stereotyping: Transnational Legal Perspectives* (Philadelphia, University of Pennsylvania Press, 2010), 174.

[24] *Ibid.*, referring in particular to Article 5(a), CEDAW as well as, e.g., *Morales de Sierra* v. *Guatemala*, I-ACtHR, Case 11.625 (2001).

[25] See, Chapter 5.

Incorporating women's rights within traditionally conceived (read: male) harms also promotes a female-to-male progression of equality. The sexual hierarchy is thus reinforced, rather than dismantled. For women's harms to be taken seriously, the international system suggests that they must be equivalent to those of men (which causes problems where no comparator is available) or so exceptional that they are accepted by men as 'deserving' of the carving-out of an exception to the rule. This in turn exceptionalises the experiences of women, even where the violence they suffer may be universal, systemic, and everyday.

3 The public/private dichotomy

While there has been acceptance that violence against women is an affront to women's physical and moral integrity and to their dignity as human beings, there is far less agreement as to a state's responsibility for that violence. None of the interpretations of the norms studied in this book appropriately dismantles the public/private divide, which I identified as the third feminist critique of the international human rights system in Chapter 2. Treaty bodies have used a range of methods to attribute so-called 'private' violence to the state, most notably by holding a state accountable for its failure to exercise due diligence to prevent such violence, to investigate, prosecute, and punish offenders, and to offer remedies to victims. The three main problems with the test of due diligence are as follows: (a) it is not yet determined with any certainty, (b) there is no clear criteria, and (c) it is not an absolute standard. It is far from an absolute prohibition against violence akin to that of, for example, torture, genocide, or slavery. It thus treats violence against women in a different manner to the most serious human rights violations, relegating it to perhaps an equivalence with the limited fundamental freedoms of expression, religion, or movement.[26] It aligns violence against women with qualified or limited rights rather than peremptory or non-derogable ones. In many ways, due diligence could also be associated with the weaker standard usually associated with the International Covenant on Economic, Social and Cultural Rights (ICESCR)[27] of 'progressive implementation', although even this requires some immediate steps to be taken.[28] Under due diligence, in

---

[26] See, Articles 19, 18, and 12, ICCPR respectively.

[27] International Covenant on Economic, Social and Cultural Rights 1966, GA res. 2200A (XXI), 16 December 1966, 993 UNTS 3; entered into force 3 January 1976 (ICESCR).

[28] CESCR, General Comment No. 3: The Nature of States Parties Obligations (Article 2(1)) (1990), UN Doc. E/1991/23, para. 2.

comparison, states are required to take only reasonable steps to eradicate violence against women in order to escape liability.[29] A starting point for such scepticism is that the due diligence test emerged in cases raising few, if any, gender questions, and not involving women. That is, there was no conscious effort to articulate new standards for women's claims. To date, the effect of the concept of due diligence has been insufficiently studied by feminist scholars.[30]

The treaty bodies have highlighted a range of preventative measures to combat violence against women, but these have yet to be couched in obligatory language. Under the obligation of due diligence, it is unclear what would constitute reasonable measures or, for that matter, what would constitute a reasonable omission or failure in respect of different forms of violence against women. As discussed in Chapters 2, 4, and 5, although reasonableness is a commonly employed legal concept, it is not interpreted and applied in a vacuum but within a social and cultural context and thus is vulnerable to sexism and prejudice. Feminist scholars in other areas of law are right to have criticised the application of similar 'reasonable person' tests as easily coopted by the male-dominated system in which they are applied, especially as they started out as 'reasonable man' standards.[31] Furthermore, successful case law that has engaged with this concept is at the extreme end of the state complicity spectrum. It is thus not yet clear where the limits of the concept lie.[32]

In essence, the concept of due diligence permits and accepts that non-state violence against women is not per se within the scope of international law. Rather, it falls within international law indirectly. That is, non-state acts of violence against women (the predominant kind) are not considered within the scope of international law unless they satisfy a threshold level of failed state behaviour in circumstances where there is no reasonable justification for that failure. On a theoretical level, therefore, the concept of due diligence based on the standard of reasonableness seems inadequate as the benchmark for the protection of women from violence, not least because it is not yet clear how to measure such failure.

---

[29] See, A. P. Ewing, 'Establishing State Responsibility for Private Acts of Violence against Women under the American Convention on Human Rights' (1995) 26 *Colum. Hum. Rts. L. Rev.* 751, at 771; D. Sullivan, 'The Public/Private Distinction in International Human Rights Law', in J. Peters and A. Wolper (eds.), *Women's Rights, Human Rights: International Feminist Perspectives* (New York: Routledge, 1995) 126, at 130.

[30] See, as an exception: C. Benninger-Budel (ed.), *Due Diligence and its Application to Protect Women from Violence* (Leiden and Boston: Martinus Nijhoff Publishers, 2008).

[31] See, Chapter 2.   [32] See, Chapters 4 and 5.

4 *Essentialised women*

Although gender factors are rarely absent from human rights discourse, the effect of all this attention on women generally and violence against women in particular is that women can become 'essentialised' in the process. Even though feminist scholars are now well aware of this paradox, the treaty bodies continue to locate women primarily within traditional perceptions of women and women's roles, and downplay their roles and responsibilities in other spheres of life. Non-governmental organisations and the media are also complicit in the elevation of particular perceptions of women.

The treaty bodies, for example, generally fail to deal with harm suffered by women prisoners, political activists, or politicians; if they do, it is in passing. Women-specific treaties that are available also concentrate on gender-related violence rather than violence against women more broadly. Regional violence against women treaties also focus solely on gender-based violence and fail to treat women as multidimensional beings who operate in both public and private worlds. Feminist scholarship and activism, too, can be criticised for feeding this essentialisation of women as victims of 'private' male violence. Feminist strategies to date have very much reflected Radhika Coomaraswamy's argument that images of woman as 'mothers' and 'victims' can be powerful lobbying tools (see Chapter 2). Herein lies a further paradox. By ignoring their long-term attachment to these 'essentialist' images of women, feminist scholarship can render women to such inferior and subservient positions indefinitely and make any analysis that takes account of the whole of a woman's experiences more remote. The focus at the level of international law on gender-related violence against women serves to reinforce stereotypes about the statuses, roles, responsibilities, and capabilities of women in law and in society at large. As already pointed out above, it posits them as 'victims' or 'the weaker sex' in need of protection rather than empowerment. All this attention on gender-specific forms of violence has the capacity to undermine women's autonomy, self-determination, and dignity as, first and foremost, human beings. The stereotyping of women under international law also results in the stereotyping of men, who are perceived as the binary opposite to women.

Such entrenched stereotyping may be attributed partly to the fact that the women-specific or sidestream instruments such as the CEDAW do not contain mainstream human rights provisions, such as rights to life, to liberty and security of person, or to torture; and some of the mainstream treaties, such as the UNCAT, do not provide sex non-discrimination guarantees. While there are legal arguments that can be made that each of these provisions fall within the relevant treaties despite their specific omission,[33] a single unified treaty body might just overcome some of these problems associated with this diffuseness, discussed further in Chapter 8.

There has also been unequal attention given to the lives of women in the global South compared with the global North, reinforcing some feminist claims that international human rights law perceives 'Southern' or 'Third World' women as 'victims' or 'others' in need of Western/Northern rights and 'saving'. At the same time, the system tends to ignore violence perpetrated against women in the global 'North'. While I do not advocate that the treaty bodies turn their attention away from violations committed against women from the global South, as they are very serious concerns for many women, or against violence against women more generally, the treaty bodies must not ignore the many violations perpetrated against women in the global North, including, for example, rape, domestic violence, spousal murder, sexual harassment, human trafficking, and prisoner violence. The treaty bodies, in their work, need to rebalance the perception of women across regions to match the varied realities of women's lives. In addition, more focus should be given to women's public roles and the violence they suffer in that domain. That is, they ought to be concerned with violence against women *wherever* it occurs. This is needed not only to reconfigure the public image of women, but also to dismantle gender-based stereotypes that are held by society at large as well as by international decision-makers whose decisions can be and often are affected by their own perceptions of the roles and status of women in particular communities and societies.

Even applying the label 'private' to harms that are more likely to affect women than men reinforces the view that women's concerns are less important than those suffered by men in the 'public' realm. The public/private distinction is in any event a false dichotomy, as the state is involved in all areas of life, whether by direct intervention, legal regulation, or policy choices not to intervene. Violence against women ought not to be seen as a personal aberration but as a public attack on equal human beings. Political motivation is an unnecessary criterion on which to establish

---

[33] E.g., Article 3, CEDAW gives the Women's Committee a mandate over inequality 'in all fields'; meanwhile, the inequality principles are arguably customary international law and thus apply in relation to the torture prohibition.

other human rights violations. For example, the political views of victims and their violators are not relevant to other harms such as arbitrary execution, torture, or inhuman treatment.[34] So why does international law cling to such requirements in recognising women as subjects of the law?

Labelling gendered violence as 'private' also sends a message to women that it is their problem, that they are to blame for it, and that they are alone in resolving it. Realising that women are united across cultures, communities, and countries in being subjected to violence in similar as well as different forms confirms the view that violence against women is not personal or private but very much a universal problem that requires universal redress. Rooted in patriarchal domination, it is clear why the international community, as represented through states that are in turn dominated by men, struggle to call violence against women an international human rights issue per se. As Charlotte Bunch has stated: 'Violence against women is a political act: its message is "stay in your place or be afraid".'[35] Taking violence against women seriously translates into taking women seriously; the latter poses, of course, a great threat to the status quo.

C Conclusion

There is no doubt that violence against women has attained a certain level of importance for the UN human rights treaty bodies and the UN system more broadly, at least rhetorically. Female genital mutilation, forced marriage, rape, sexual violence, physical violence, domestic violence, maternal mortality, incest, the neglect of girls, sex-selective abortions, female infanticide, and dowry killings, have all been recognised, rightly, as being of concern to human rights. There has been sizeable progress since Laura Reanda observed in 1981 that human rights mechanisms do not deal specifically with the human rights of women except in a marginal way or within the framework of other human rights issues.[36] Today, violence against women is of interest to most of the treaty bodies and some other international courts, but with so many other competing interests,

---

[34] K. Roth, 'Domestic Violence as an International Human Rights Issue', in R. J. Cook (ed.), *Human Rights of Women: National and International Perspectives* (Philadelphia: University of Pennsylvania Press, 1994) 326, at 329. A notable distinction may be in the context of asylum: see, G. Goodwin-Gill and J. McAdam, *The Refugee in International Law* (3rd edn, Oxford University Press, 2007), Part 1.

[35] C. Bunch, 'Women's Rights as Human Rights: Toward a Re-Vision of Human Rights' (1990) 12 *HRQ* 486, at 491.

[36] L. Reanda, 'Human Rights and Women's Rights: The United Nations Approach' (1981) 3 *HRQ* 11, at 12.

it is often sidelined. For the Women's Committee, it could be said that it has become their number one agenda priority. Today each of the treaty bodies questions states parties on their performance in relation to women's equality and violence against women. In addition, women's human rights are no longer the preserve of the Women's Committee but have filtered into the work of the other treaty bodies to a greater or lesser extent, albeit many statements made on this subject are still rather vacuous at times, conforming as they do to a template methodology, as discussed in Chapter 3. It can now be said that, at least in terms of quantity, women's rights are no longer in the 'ghetto' of international human rights law, but they do remain on the margins in terms of quality.

The second of Reanda's observations is, however, still applicable. The human rights system continues to address violence against women within a framework of 'other human rights issues'. As this is all that is required by the UN's 'mainstreaming' agenda, it highlights its fundamental weakness. Although the international community agreed a Declaration on the Elimination of Violence against Women in 1993, states have not (yet) expressed their commitment to this issue by transferring it into a binding treaty obligation, discussed further in Chapter 8.

As noted throughout this book, the real conundrum of pursuing women's equality within the existing configuration of the international human rights legal system is that the price of accommodating women's concerns and experiences within existing human rights provisions is the reinforcement of the unequal treatment of women before the law. This book has described a human rights system that only partially recognises violence against women as a human rights violation by its attachment to other human rights, or in other words, indirectly. At the same time the system reinforces sexual hierarchies in which men are the standard against which women are judged and women are, at best, a deviation from the standard. Ironically, while the goals of gender inclusion are being achieved, gender inequality is being reasserted. Within this discourse too, women can become 'essentialised' into the most extreme form of victim of sexual violence, which can distort realities on the ground and have the effect of disempowering, rather than empowering, women. Because of this, strategising next steps comes up against many theoretical and practical problems.

It is thus far from time to 'take a break'[37] from feminist theorising and activism at the level of international human rights law. Instead, we need

---

[37] See, Halley, *Split Decisions*.

to continue the engagement with the mainstream, and to further this discourse to a point where the lines between the margins and the mainstream blur. Shouting from the periphery can disintegrate into an unproductive 'us' and 'them' debate, and can relegate women to the margins in perpetuity. As Bunch stated in 1995: 'Challenging prevailing concepts of, and reinterpreting the movement for, human rights from a feminist perspective is not merely a matter of semantics. It is about the lives and deaths of individual women everywhere, every day.'[38] For this reason the debate on women's human rights needs to be moved from the periphery to the centre and focused upon the full equality, protection, and empowerment of women rather than simply their rhetorical inclusion.

At a minimum, it is hoped that this book will make policy- and decision-makers as well as feminist activists and strategists sit up and reflect on what the strategies employed to date really mean for women. Charlesworth recently bemoaned that feminist engagement with international law is more 'monologue ... than ... dialogue'.[39] She is troubled, too, by the fact that feminists keep talking to each other and have not engaged with (or been engaged by) others more broadly[40] (and, most importantly, those with more power). Although feminist theories and analysis have been catalytic in reaching this stage of rhetorical inclusion, and thus they should not be abandoned, continuous re-evaluation remains essential. Halley might be right to suggest that the various strands of feminist thought on ideas such as sex, gender, sexual equality, sexuality, power, and so forth, cannot be easily reconciled. None may have all the answers. Positively, however, her challenge to embrace rather than to attempt to reconcile the various feminist strands and tensions could thereby be a liberating influence.[41] In turning to the next stages in the development of women's human rights, we need to build on, rather than to put aside, the momentum and commitment already established in large measure thanks to feminist theorising as well as activism on international law and on human rights. Simultaneously, we also need to exercise a greater degree of self-reflection and re-evaluation.

---

[38] C. Bunch, 'Transforming Human Rights from a Feminist Perspective', in J. Peters and A. Wolper (eds.), *Women's Rights, Human Rights: International Feminist Perspectives* (New York: Routledge, 1995), 11, at 17.

[39] H. Charlesworth, 'Talking to Ourselves: Feminist Scholarship in International Law', in Z. Pearson and S. Kuovo (eds.), *Between Resistance and Compliance? Feminist Perspectives on International Law in an Era of Anxiety and Terror* (Oxford: Hart Publishing, in press 2010) (on file with the author).

[40] *Ibid.*   [41] Halley, *Split Decisions*, 9.

Strategising next steps: treaty body reform and towards humanising women

A Introduction

The issue of violence against women is gaining in prominence on the United Nations' human rights agenda, and has emerged as a policy priority. The former UN Secretary-General produced a comprehensive report on the issue in late 2006,[1] the General Assembly agreed a declaration in 2007,[2] and many NGOs and UN agencies have taken up the issue in a variety of contexts.[3] Current UN Secretary-General Ban-Ki Moon has added his commitment to ending violence against women, announcing in 2008 a multi-year campaign.[4] The Security Council issued its first resolution on women, peace, and security in 2000, with a follow-up resolution in 2008,[5] and a specific resolution on sexual violence in armed conflict in 2009.[6] Significant work has been done in particular under international humanitarian law and international criminal law, albeit still with many problems.[7] This commitment to ending violence against

---

[1] UN Secretary-General, *In-depth Study on All Forms of Violence against Women*, UN Doc. A/61/122/Add.1, 6 July 2006.

[2] Intensification of efforts to eliminate all forms of violence against women, GA res. A/RES/61/143 (19 December 2006).

[3] See, Amnesty International, Worldwide Campaign to Stop Violence against Women, launched on 4 October 2004 and ongoing, see http://web.amnesty.org/actforwomen/index-eng. See, UNIFEM's Campaign to Stop Violence against Women, www.unifem.org.

[4] See, UNiTE to end Violence against Women, www.un.org/women/endviolence/. For the campaigns and advocacy work of organisations across the world working on these issues, see Centre for Women's Global Leadership, www.cwgl.rutgers.edu/16days/biblio.html#VAW.

[5] SC res. 1325 (2000); SC res. 1820 (2008).

[6] SC res. 1888 (2009).

[7] For example, the decision by the International Criminal Tribunal for the former Yugoslavia (ICTY) to drop all sexual violence charges against Milan Lukic, allegedly committed in Višegrad, Bosnia and Herzegovina: Amnesty International, *No Justice for Rape Victims*, 22 July 2009, available at: www.bim.ba/en/176/10/21245/. Lukic was sentenced to life imprisonment for war crimes and crimes against humanity: *Prosecutor* v. *Milan Lukic*, ICTY, Case No. IT-98–31/1 (20 July 2009) (currently on appeal). Likewise,

women in armed conflict has yet to be matched, however, by commitments to international human rights law and to violations of women's
rights in peacetime, the one being a precursor to the other. That is to say
that negative views held about women do not emerge in times of armed
conflict; rather they are exploited and manipulated for instrumental
objectives during armed conflict.

The burning final question that this book addresses is how the work of
the UN human rights treaty body system can be improved. This chapter
outlines my vision for the next stages in the process of transformation,
focusing in turn on procedural, interpretative/conceptual, structural,
and substantive reforms. This chapter starts, however, with the following
three caveats. First, there is no quick fix to the issue of violence against
women, which is widespread, systematic, and everyday; second, the UN
human rights treaty bodies are only one set of actors on the international
stage, and what is more, in order to be effective, they need to be supported
at the national level;[8] and third, many of the proposals for reform I outline
in this chapter carry their own conceptual, practical, and political problems and difficulties. Specifically, they are each framed within or engaged
with the mainstream and thus, as outlined throughout this book, they
may also be complicit in reinforcing the system of human rights law as it
is, and in so doing, they may also reassert women's inequality. These recommendations are therefore unfortunately nestled within the feminist
paradox of international human rights law, discussed in Chapters 2 and 7.
Nonetheless, they are aimed at dismantling those parts of the human
rights house that reassert the unequal position of women vis-à-vis men
and they attempt to make the disparities in the system less stark.

B   Procedural reforms

1   Nomination and election of more women

The starting point for any improvement in the system is the equality and
universality arguments outlined in Chapter 3 in relation to women's participation in the treaty body system. Quite simply, states must nominate

the Prosecutor of the ICC decided in 2009 to retain charges of rape against Jean-Pierre
Bemba Gombo, President and Commander in Chief of the Mouvement de Libération du
Congo, but to drop other sexual violence crimes: *Prosecutor* v. *Jean-Pierre Bemba Gombo*,
ICC, Case No. ICC-01/05–01/08 (15 June 2009).

[8] National implementation is not addressed in this book, but it is recognised as the lynchpin
to improving the rights of women in their everyday lives.

and elect more women members to international bodies as a whole, and to the human rights treaty bodies in particular. Incorporating binding treaty language requiring states to take account of the sex balance in the composition of the treaty bodies in all new treaties is a necessary, yet insufficient, first step. As the European Court of Human Rights (ECtHR) has discovered, inserting such weak language in policy directives only (equivalent to the weak language in the treaties) is open to challenge.[9] Similarly, the newest international human rights committees, in which such language was included in the governing treaties, has not achieved gender parity in their membership.[10] For all treaties and treaty bodies, there must be improved guidance given as to how such targets can be reached.

Treaty body members should also be offered ongoing briefing (training) sessions and seminars on women's rights, gender, and feminist theory, as well as specialist areas such as reproductive rights, violence against women, the rights of displaced and stateless women, and issues of sexuality, disability, and age. In regard to the latter, the Women's Human Rights and Gender Unit within the Office of the High Commissioner for Human Rights (OHCHR) has already commenced the practice of sharing its expertise with the treaty bodies, as has the United Nations High Commissioner for Refugees, including by the production of thematic reports drawing upon gender-sensitive international and national jurisprudence.[11]

In Chapter 3 I recommended that openness and transparency in the nomination processes to international office at the municipal level was

---

[9] In an advisory opinion, the European Court of Human Rights (ECtHR) held that policy directives requiring the inclusion of the 'under-represented sex' on the composition of all nomination lists were found to be wanting as such rules were not entrenched in the European Convention on Human Rights (ECHR) itself. The ECtHR found that 'in not allowing any exception to the rule that the under-represented sex must be represented, the current practice of the Parliamentary Assembly is not compatible with the Convention.' See, *Certain Legal Questions Concerning the Lists of Candidates submitted with a View to the Election of Judges to the European Court of Human Rights* (Advisory Opinion), ECtHR (12 February 2008), para. 54, as discussed in A. Mowbray, 'The Consideration of Gender in the Process of Appointing Judges to the European Court of Human Rights' (2008) 8 *Hum. Rts. L. Rev.* 549, at 558–559.

[10] See, Chapter 3.

[11] Interview with senior official in the Women's Human Rights and Gender Unit, OHCHR, 27 October 2008. The United Nations High Commissioner for Refugees also initiated collaboration with the Women's Committee, including a joint-UNHCR-CEDAW seminar held in New York in July 2009, of which I was the principal author of the background paper: A. Edwards, *Displacement, Statelessness, and Questions of Gender Equality under the Convention on the Elimination of All Forms of Discrimination against Women*, UNHCR, Legal and Protection Policy Research Series, UN Doc. HCR/PPLAS/2009/02,

needed, and that the UN might consider a gender-based rotating nomination process in which a state party would be required to nominate a candidate of the opposite sex to its last nomination for any future nominations. This recommendation is based on the experience of national democratic election processes that have shown that without a certain percentage of candidates being female, the rate of election of women is unlikely to change.[12] If each state party adopted a similar pattern of nomination, it would lead to an increase in the number of women nominated and (in turn) elected. Recruitment drives may also need to be conducted at the municipal level to encourage women to put themselves forward for nomination. Ideally, mechanisms need to be put in place that make the nomination of women important to the political interests of states, especially if the existing system of nomination and election persists. An alternative approach might be to require states to nominate from the under-represented sex, as in the practice of the ECtHR, although this too has been resisted by some states, as discussed in Chapter 3.

Furthermore, in terms of internal procedures, the treaty bodies must start operating internal procedural rules that ensure gender balance in key committee functions, such as rotating chairpersons and rapporteurships.[13]

Apart from the above suggestions, policy guidance and pressure from the UN Security Council, the UN General Assembly, the UN Human Rights Council, and all other arms of the UN must be garnered. The adoption of a resolution by the Security Council and/or the General Assembly to increase the representation of women on mainstream treaty bodies would be welcomed, including a campaign to encourage states to

---

August 2009, Background Paper prepared for a joint-UNHCR–Women's Committee seminar to be held at the United Nations in New York, 16–17 July 2009, available at: www.unhcr.org/4a8d0f1b9.html. A. Edwards, Executive Summary of *Displacement, Statelessness, and Questions of Gender Equality under the Convention on the Elimination of All Forms of Discrimination against Women*, UN Doc. CEDAW/C/2009/II/WP.3, 1 July 2009, available at: www2.ohchr.org/English/bodies/cedaw/docs/CEDAW.C.2009.II.WP.3.pdf.

[12] See, e.g., EMILY's List, a political convention operating in the United States, the United Kingdom, and Australia, with the aim of nominating more female candidates.

[13] It is noted that rotating the chairperson and rapporteur positions may cause difficulties in committees with few women and this could result in the few women becoming overburdened with responsibilities. However, for those committees in which over 30 per cent of the membership are women, any burden could be shared between them. Moreover, rotating positions may encourage states to nominate more women to committee positions if they know that their male nominees are only half as likely to attain important positions in the committees than women members.

nominate and elect more female members. The soon-to-be established single gender entity should take up some of these issues in conjunction with the OHCHR. It is time states fulfilled their international treaty obligations, and those in the UN Charter, or at least took steps to achieve them. Like the campaign in relation to membership of the International Criminal Court (ICC), NGOs must also take up the challenge to encourage sympathetic governments to lead the way in putting forward more women for international positions, and to shame others. Making lists of qualified female candidates and challenging governments to nominate from among the list may be one way to raise the profile of the issue at national levels. As the process of nomination and election can become buried in the *real politik* of state interests, they may even consider advocating for the tying of aid to improved gender-appropriate nomination practices – at local, national, and international levels.

2   State party reporting

In terms of reviewing state party reports, the treaty bodies have made considerable progress, attributable in part to a number of initiatives. The 'Lists of Issues' that are transmitted to states parties, for example, have regularly included questions about women's rights, although form over substance remains a concern in government responses. The Harmonized Guidelines on state party reporting and the 'common core document', which identifies discrimination as a shared concern across the treaty bodies, are also positive developments. Nonetheless, it remains to be seen whether states parties will treat the core common document as static and update it only rather limitedly, thereby reducing rather than increasing the importance given to common issues, including sex discrimination. In addition, movement towards agreeing 'Indicators' for states' compliance with their human rights obligations in the context of violence against women, especially in relation to responsibility for the acts of non-state actors, must equally foreground issues of non-discrimination and equality.

3   Individual communications

This book highlighted in Chapter 3 a number of concerns with the 'litigation' arm of the UN human rights system, not least that it is underutilised by women. The underuse by women is partly explained because of inherent difficulties in the system itself, such as the problem of non-binding decisions, long waiting periods, and template-style reasoning, but equally because of obstacles to women's access to this system arising from, inter alia, high rates of illiteracy among women, poor political participation and empowerment in municipal systems, and/or a lack of legal assistance.[14] Further empirical research into the barriers to women's access is needed. These criticisms of the petition system feed into feminist claims that litigation-style processes do not suit women and that alternative dispute resolution processes are preferred.

Despite these concerns, the individual communications system is an important part of the process towards the full protection and empowerment of women, and the ending of impunity of states. Admittedly judicial or quasi-judicial processes are not the only source of remedy or redress for violence, but they are an important option. Additionally, jurisprudence developed by the treaty bodies (drawn from, inter alia, individual cases) has the potential to filter into other international courts and tribunals, and ultimately to trickle down to regional, national, local, and operational levels (and vice versa).

More consistent case outcomes generally and across the treaty bodies are also a prerequisite for women (and others) to be able to rely on the treaty bodies as one avenue to justice.

Additionally, the treaty bodies should start collating sex-disaggregated statistics on how many women are filing cases, in relation to which rights, how many pass the admissibility hurdle, and how many succeed. The statistics on how many women file claims should also be broken down into those women who file claims on their own behalf and those who file on behalf of other family members and the sex of these family members.

C   Structural reforms

1   Proposal on the table: a single unified treaty body

Since the first treaty body began work in 1969 (Committee on Elimination of Racial Discrimination (CERD)), there has been an incremental growth

---

[14] E.g. The UN Trust Fund in Support of Actions to Eliminate Violence against Women, administered by UNIFEM, prioritises funding to projects that aim to implement and strengthen national and local initiatives, policies, and action plans. Although this Fund could theoretically be a source of further support for applications to the individual communications mechanisms (framed within the context of supporting national systems) or to improve state party reporting via alternative or 'shadow' reports of national and local non-governmental organisations, it is not specifically geared towards international action. See, www.unifem.org/gender_issues/violence_against_women/trust_fund.php.

in treaties, treaty bodies, and mandates, with some likelihood that this is set to continue.[15] If one counts the existing eight treaty bodies and adds together the recently established Sub-Committee on the Prevention of Torture, as well as the Committee on Enforced Disappearances which is on the horizon, it equates to a new treaty body being established every four years. There has also been an increase in the number of ratifications. It is widely agreed that the UN must 'radically redesign' its treaty monitoring system owing to, inter alia, lack of coordination, duplication of work, and heavy reporting burdens upon states parties.[16] The former High Commissioner for Human Rights stated in 2006 that the current system had hit its limits of performance.[17] Moreover, the treaty body system is 'rarely perceived as an accessible and effective mechanism'.[18] Some of these difficulties for women were highlighted in Chapter 3. As part of wider UN reform initiatives,[19] the OHCHR proposed in 2005 the creation of a single unified standing treaty body.[20] An almost neglected question in the reform discussions, and one crucial to this book, is what a consolidated treaty body would mean for women. This section explores the debate around this issue.

Various models of a single unified treaty body were included in the OHCHR's discussion paper, including a single body with no chambers, chambers operating in parallel, chambers operating along functional lines (one for reporting, one for communications), chambers along treaty

[15] E.g., the *Yogyakarta Principles on the Application of International Human Rights Law to Sexual Orientation and Gender Identity*, agreed by a group of twenty-nine eminent international human rights experts in Yogyakarta, Indonesia, on 26 March 2007, may be a candidate for a new treaty in due course, see: www.yogyakartaprinciples.org.

[16] M. O'Flaherty and C. O'Brien, 'Reform of the UN Human Rights Treaty Monitoring Bodies: A Critique of the Concept Paper on the High Commissioner's Proposal for a Unified Standing Treaty Body' (2007) 7 *Hum. Rts. L. Rev.* 141, at 144.

[17] OHCHR, *Concept Paper on High Commissioner's Proposal for a Unified Standing Treaty Body*, UN Doc. HRI/MC/2006/2, 22 March 2006, para. 27. See, also, Note by the OHCHR, *Effective Functioning of the Human Rights Mechanisms: Treaty Bodies*, UN Doc. E/CN.4/2003/126, 26 February 2003.

[18] OHCHR, *Concept Paper on High Commissioner's Proposal for a Unified Standing Treaty Body*, para. 21.

[19] Since 1997 reform has been on the UN's agenda: see GA res. 52/12, 19 December 1997. OHCHR, *Plan of Action* submitted by the UN High Commissioner for Human Rights, Annex to Report of the Secretary-General, *In Larger Freedom: Towards Development, Security and Human Rights for All*, UN Doc. A/59/2005/Add. 3, 26 May 2005.

[20] OHCHR, *Plan of Action*, Summary, point (d). In fact, the option of a standing unified treaty body was put on the table by the Independent Expert, *Report on Enhancing the Long-Term Effectiveness of the United Nations Human Rights Treaty System*, Mr Philip Alston, UN Doc. A/44/668, 8 November 1989.

lines, chambers along thematic lines (or clustering of rights), or chambers along regional lines.[21] According to the OHCHR, a unified body would strengthen mainstreaming of the rights of particular groups in the interpretation and implementation of all human rights.[22] A single body, it is posited, would facilitate the systematic consideration of the whole range of relevant human rights concerns.[23] It may, for example, contribute to a fuller understanding of inequality, as it affects all human rights, and may allow for more attention to be given to structural causes of women's inequality. A unified body would also highlight the interdependent and indivisible nature of the obligations set out in the various treaties.[24]

The CERD has also proposed the creation of a single body to deal with communications. Its proposal was based on the belief that a single communication procedure would allow higher visibility, better accessibility to rights holders, and a more holistic interpretation of the treaties that would ensure more effective protection of rights holders.[25] A single procedure would allow a complainant to raise applicable provisions from the range of treaty bodies in a single procedure.[26] This would appear on its face to be beneficial to women, noting the choice of venue a female victim must make, including the choice of language and rhetoric (see, Chapters 4, 5, and 6).

On the other hand, there is concern that unification could reduce attention paid within the UN human rights framework to different categories of rights holders.[27] Françoise Hampson, a former member of the Sub-Commission on the Promotion and Protection of Human Rights, has rejected the single treaty body proposal as 'fundamentally flawed and irresponsible'.[28] She gives two main reasons for her view. First, she argues that it would reduce the current sitting time to fifty-two weeks per year, whereas, cumulatively, the existing bodies meet for more than this. And second, and of more relevance to this study, the particular focus and expertise developed in the specialist bodies will be lost.[29] I do not find either of her reasons for retaining the status quo particularly convincing.

---

[21] OHCHR, *Concept Paper on High Commissioner's Proposal for a Unified Standing Treaty Body*, paras. 37–45.

[22] *Ibid.*, para. 28.   [23] *Ibid.*   [24] *Ibid.*

[25] H. B. Schöpp-Schilling, 'Treaty Body Reform: the Case of the Committee on the Elimination of Discrimination Against Women' (2007) 7 *Hum. Rts. L. Rev.* 201, at 211.

[26] OHCHR, *Concept Paper on High Commissioner's Proposal for a Unified Standing Treaty Body*, para. 30.

[27] O'Flaherty and O'Brien, 'Reform of the UN Human Rights Treaty Monitoring Bodies', 166.

[28] F. J. Hampson, 'An Overview of the Reform of the United Nations Human Rights Machinery' (2007) 7 *Hum. Rts. L. Rev.* 7, at 12.

[29] *Ibid.*, 12. She suggests instead that the HRC and the CESCR be full-time, while the other treaty bodies remain part-time.

First, one of the major complaints of the current treaty body set-up is the fact that the members are part-time. The general practice is that they turn their minds to treaty body matters in the few weeks they are in session, and then return to their normal lives. As noted in Chapter 3, those persons eligible for part-time unpaid service is also limited to those with financial means, or those who work for government or academia. It thus limits the range of specialists who could take up committee positions. Hampson's complaint that a single treaty body will work for only fifty-two weeks per year is superficially correct, yet in actual hours it would also depend on how many members would be envisaged under a new system; and her criticism further fails to take account of the duplication inherent in the longer hours now spent on treaty body business by eight separate treaty bodies with a combined membership of 127 persons (137 if one includes the SPT). In response to Hampson's second complaint, the treaty bodies are meant to be staffed by qualified experts. Their time on the treaty bodies should not be seen as a 'learning ground' for non-expert members, which is somewhat envisaged by Hampson as she suggests that expertise might be lost. My own view is that a unified treaty body would bring an enhanced level of professionalism to the work of the treaty bodies that they cannot achieve at present, and cause states to take more seriously the candidates nominated and elected to these important positions.

For some members of the Women's Committee the preference has been for further harmonisation and integration rather than a unified treaty body.[30] Interestingly, this is the opposite view to their colleagues dealing with racial discrimination (see above). The Women's Committee has called for communal drafting of General Recommendations and Comments, as well as joint statements on particular issues.[31] As noted in Chapter 3 and above, the introduction of harmonised reporting procedures has gone some way toward reconciling divergent approaches, but the different and limited sitting times of the various committees and the part-time commitment of their members has made joint statements difficult to achieve.

Paradoxically, one of the arguments in favour of retaining a separate Women's Committee by Schöpp-Schilling is the lack of understanding of the causes of women's persistent inequality within the mainstream treaty

---

[30] Schöpp-Schilling, 'Treaty Body Reform', 202.

[31] CEDAW, Report of the Committee (19th session), Part II, paras. 407–408, as referred to in M. R. Bustelo, 'The Committee on the Elimination of Discrimination Against Women at the Crossroads' in P. Alston and J. Crawford (eds.), *The Future of UN Human Rights Treaty Monitoring* (Cambridge University Press, 2000) 79, at 98.

bodies.[32] While acknowledging the influence of the work of the Women's Committee on the other bodies,[33] it is an equally valid argument that the lack of coordination between the bodies has meant that the impact/influence of the Women's Committee has been circumscribed and that it could be enhanced by greater integration. The CEDAW, for example, does not add rights to those already available under other treaties; rather it clarifies how the rights ought to be guaranteed for women.[34] Early criticisms against a separate institutional framework for women claimed that it weakened the advocacy for women in general human rights forums.[35] Although mainstreaming is distinct from unification (the former being normative or substantive in nature, the latter structural or institutional),[36] improved structural frameworks have the potential to facilitate substantive advancements.

The mainstream/sidestream debate is not new to the UN system, as discussed in Chapter 2. Ironically, feminist scholars in the 1980s and 1990s criticised the fact that dealing with women's concerns in specialised, separate institutions was part of the 'ghettoisation' of women's human rights.[37] More than a decade later, it seems that the greatest fear of merging the treaty bodies appears to be that specialist expertise accumulated over the years in the 'ghetto' may be lost in 'the city'. Predicting such concerns, the OHCHR's 2006 Concept Paper emphasises that in any new model 'specificities of each treaty must be preserved and their focus on specific rights ... and the rights of particular rights holders, such as

---

[32] Schöpp-Schilling, 'Treaty Body Reform', 211. Schöpp-Schilling also states that the same lack of understanding is found in some of the staff at the OHCHR.

[33] It is widely acknowledged that the work of the Women's Committee has influenced the work of other treaty bodies: see, E. Evatt, 'Eliminating Discrimination Against Women: The Impact of the UN Convention' (1991–1992) 18 *Melb. U. L. Rev.* 435.

[34] R. L. Johnstone, 'Cynical Savings or Reasonable Reform? Reflections on a Single Unified UN Human Rights Treaty Body' (2007) 7 *Hum. Rts. L. Rev.* 173, at 181.

[35] See, D. Otto, 'Lost in Translation: Re-Scripting the Sexed Subjects of International Human Rights Law', in A. Orford (ed.), *International Law and Its Others* (Cambridge University Press, 2006) 318, at 336.

[36] O'Flaherty and O'Brien, 'Reform of the UN Human Rights Treaty Monitoring Bodies', 171.

[37] See, e.g., L. Reanda, 'Human Rights and Women's Rights: The United Nations Approach' (1981) 3 *HRQ* 11; U. A. O'Hare, 'Realizing Human Rights for Women' (1999) 21 *HRQ* 364; R. Jacobson, 'The Committee on the Elimination of Discrimination against Women', in P. Alston (ed.), *The United Nations and Human Rights: A Critical Appraisal* (Oxford University Press, 1992), 444. Cf. A. Byrnes, 'Women, Feminism and International Human Rights Law – Methodological Myopia, Fundamental Flaws or Meaningful Marginalisation?: Some Current Issues' (1992) 12 *Aust. YB Int'l L.* 205, at 218, who argues that the 'ghettoisation' of women's human rights is perhaps too harsh a critique.

children, women, and migrant workers ... should not be diminished'.[38] At the same time, the Concept Paper acknowledges that protection for particular groups could decrease owing to a single entity's potential inability 'to monitor implementation of the specificities of each treaty in sufficient depth'.[39] This is clearly the greatest challenge in any merger.

The OHCHR asserts that, at a minimum, existing obligations must be strengthened, not renegotiated.[40] The extent to which this is a likely outcome of a unified structure would also depend on measures put in place to safeguard equitable gender representation on such a unified committee and guarantees of substantive expertise in women's rights. Michael O'Flaherty and Claire O'Brien rightly call for the values of diversity, inclusion, and participation to be embodied in any new mechanism.[41] I would add the value of equality also. Based on the historical exclusion of women from mainstream forums, it is logical that there is concern from women's groups that they would again be sidelined in any merger. However, it would be a great shame for women not to benefit from improved efficiency and protection in any consolidated model. After all, the proliferation of treaty bodies and petitions systems not only burdens states parties and affects the quality, reliability, and timeliness of reports, not least those on such politically less important topics as women's rights, it also affects women and women's groups who must navigate the myriad bodies to be able to voice their grievances.

From the perspective of civil society, monitoring of a new single treaty body would be needed, modelled perhaps on the Women's Initiatives for Gender Justice, which has taken on this role in relation to the International Criminal Court.[42] For NGOs, being able to focus on one treaty body would arguably reduce the imbalance in power in which states are better able to operate across the various treaty bodies than NGOs due to financial and other resource constraints (although many states also struggle with the burden of the treaty body system and hence the call for its reform). Safeguards to ensure balanced gender representation would also be needed, discussed above in relation to procedural reforms.

Outside the treaty body system, it is worth noting the commitment shown by the international community of states to the creation of the

---

[38] OHCHR, *Concept Paper on High Commissioner's Proposal for a Unified Standing Treaty Body*, para. 7.

[39] *Ibid.*, para. 59.   [40] *Ibid.*, para. 7.

[41] O'Flaherty and O'Brien, 'Reform of the UN Human Rights Treaty Monitoring Bodies', 171.

[42] For more on Women's Initiatives for Gender Justice, see www.iccwomen.org/.

newly approved single gender entity within the UN, headed by an Under-Secretary-General. This is an example of how states can agree on the issue of gender, as well as UN reform.[43] At a minimum, it is hoped that this new entity will reduce the competition between various branches of the UN as well as the layers of bureaucracy. The single gender entity should not, however, be used as an excuse by other UN agencies and bodies to ignore gender issues. As stated above, constant monitoring will be needed. Now that this UN reform has been achieved, although yet to be implemented, it is hoped that the international community and the OHCHR can return to the issue of treaty body reform, which has unfortunately not appeared on the current High Commissioner's agenda.[44]

2   Alternative models

Some alternative models have also been proposed. Wouter Vandenhole has advocated splitting the responsibility for particular types of discrimination between the treaty bodies, but to date this has not been seriously considered.[45] Manfred Nowak recommends that it is time to consider a World Court of Human Rights, with the treaty bodies continuing to exercise their main function of examining state party reports.[46] In particular, he suggests that such a body could allow non-state actors, such as intergovernmental organisations (including the UN) and transnational corporations, to be subject to its jurisdiction.[47] He does not go as far as to suggest that victims could bring action directly against perpetrators rather than against the state or conjointly with the state, but this could

---

[43] GA res. A/RES//63/311, 2 October 2009.

[44] A recent initiative by former and current members of the treaty bodies has led to the Dublin Statement on the Process of Strengthening of the United Nations Human Rights Treaty Body System, 18–19 November 2009, available at: http://www.nottingham.ac.uk/hrlc/documents/specialevents/dublinstatement.pdf. The Dublin Convention is conservative in its conclusions, identifying reform as an ongoing process and indicating that responsibility for an improved treaty body system lies with many actors, including states parties, the treaty bodies, non-governmental organisations and civil society, and the OHCHR, etc.

[45] A. Edwards, 'Book Review: Wouter Vandenhole, *Non-Discrmination and Equality in the View of the UN Human Rights Treaty Bodies* (Antwerp: Intersentia, 2005)' (2007) 7 *Hum. Rts. L. Rev.* 267, in which I argued that such an approach would be unworkable as it ignores the universality of the principle to all rights.

[46] M. Nowak, 'The Need for a World Court of Human Rights' (2007) 7 *Hum. Rts. L. Rev.* 251.

[47] *Ibid.*, 256–257.

be a possibility. Nowak's model does not entirely reject the public/private divide in so far as not all non-state actors are envisaged as falling within its jurisdiction, but it does go further than any other proposed model. Nowak, in particular, does not refer to guerrilla or rebel groups or quasi-state entities, for example.

Similarly, Kerri Ritz has called for criminal jurisdiction over both individual and state violators of human rights.[48] A World Court could also contain binding and enforceable interim measures,[49] such as injunctive relief in cases of domestic violence.

3 My preferred model: a two-stage process towards an international human rights court

Calls for treaty body reform have somewhat stagnated as the UN turned its attention to the broader questions of reform of the UN gender architecture, which excluded the treaty body system (discussed briefly above). It is now time for renewed energy to be devoted to the treaty body reform process. My vision for reform of the treaty body system would be a two-stage process, guided by the ideas of simplification, professionalisation, and judicialisation.

Stage 1 in my reform agenda would require moving towards a single unified professional standing human rights treaty body, along the lines in the OHCHR's Concept Paper. The proliferation of treaty bodies (as opposed to treaties) is a cause of disgruntlement among states, and over the long term the treaty bodies are likely to be rendered less and less relevant the more cumbersome and ineffective they become. The treaty bodies also face growing competition from international and regional courts (with the power to issue binding decisions which the treaty bodies lack) and other forums for human rights prevention and response.[50] The proliferation of treaty bodies is also a concern for female (and other) complainants and their advocates who must navigate the myriad mechanisms and choose the most suitable one; no easy task given the overlapping mandates

---

[48] K. L. Ritz, 'Soft Enforcement: Inadequacies of the Optional Protocol as a Remedy for the Convention on the Elimination of All Forms of Discrimination against Women' (2001–2002) 25 *Suffolk Transnat. L. Rev.* 191, at 212.

[49] Nowak, 'The Need for a World Court of Human Rights', 258.

[50] E.g. the UN Human Rights Council and its Universal Periodic Review (UPR). At least as far as the UPR is concerned, states are required to respond publicly to the recommendations that they are to adopt and those that they are to reject, with reasons. This has not been the practice in relation to the treaty bodies in which all recommendations are of equal weight and therefore often little moves forward.

and various approaches of different treaty bodies to particular legal issues, especially those relevant to women. This complex system also feeds into arguments about the arbitrariness and abstractness of human rights. Fear of women being sidelined under a reformed system must be balanced against what women will gain under an integrated and (hopefully) more efficient and rights-focused system. Of course, women's full and equal participation within any reformed system will be achieved only with the support of intensive lobbying by women's groups and NGOs, adequate structural safeguards for the inclusion of balanced gender representation and gender expertise, and improved access for female victims; some of this has already been dealt with above.

My single unified treaty body would have, at a minimum, two chambers: one dealing with state party reporting, the other dealing with individual communications. The latter ought to include a specialist panel or sub-chamber that can be activated for particularly complex or serious cases raising gender or women's concerns and composed of specialists in this area.[51] An appeal chamber ought also to be established.

The longer-term view (or Stage 2) is to move towards an international human rights court, by transforming the single unified treaty body into an international court. The establishment of an international human rights court, in contrast to a treaty body, would revolutionise the human rights system from one based primarily on political compromise and negotiation to an independent and enforceable one.[52] The envisaged international human rights court would possess both vertical and horizontal jurisdiction, the latter for serious or systematic cases of human rights violations, including abuses committed by, inter alia, the state, corporate organisations, non-state armed groups, religious institutions, international organisations, or other 'private' actors, in situations where there is no national protection or at the invitation of the state party along the lines of 'complementarity' of the ICC.[53]

So what would an international human rights court add to the ICC? Although female victims can and have participated in international

---

[51] This could also occur for other special groups or for particularly difficult cases on specific provisions, although there would need to be some clear guidance to limit the abuse of the process as it could lead to the unified treaty body dissolving into a series of smaller specialist bodies in practice and thus defeating the purpose of unification.

[52] Of course, the politics would not dissipate entirely, but measures could be adopted to insulate the court from such matters.

[53] See, O. Bekou and R. Cryer, *The International Criminal Court* (Aldershot and London: Ashgate Publishing, 2004).

criminal proceedings, for example as witnesses and victims, they are passive subjects in the process (despite the many victim-friendly measures put in place[54]) – that is, they cannot exercise litigation rights in their own name but are reliant on the prosecutor or the state to act. Such a system can serve to disempower women victims by making them 'objects' rather than 'subjects' of international law; and it also operates to make international (as opposed to national) criminal law remote from their daily lives. In contrast, an international human rights court would allow women to bring actions in their own names and to be active participants as subjects of international law, and to receive the remedy they deserve in the form of a binding judgment. As the latter is already possible in an increasing number of regions, it makes the worth of women variable depending on where they live and this should be corrected by an international forum for redress.

D Contextualising interpretation: humanising women

Although institutional and procedural reforms are a necessary part of any overall improvement in women's participation and their inclusion within the UN system, they alone will not produce better decision-making that treats women equally and with dignity. Far from simply adding gender to its consideration of complaints brought by women, international decision-makers must move beyond perceiving human beings as two discrete, monolithic categories for the purposes of applying human rights rules. Instead, they must endorse a contextual analysis to any case, including broad understandings of gender, gender relations, and gender equality. As noted in Chapter 1 of this book, there are several helpful feminist techniques that expose and question the claim of international law to objectivity, impartiality, and universality. These include Bartlett's 'asking the woman question' and 'feminist practical reasoning' and Gunning's 'world travelling'. The treaty bodies need to apply these techniques more concertedly, or at least realise that different outcomes are likely should they fail to do so. As enlightening as these feminist methods are, they too could benefit from some updating.

In particular, gender and gender relations must be understood as fluid, variable, and multiple, rather than as unchangeable, static, and

---

[54] See, C. Ferstman, M. Goetz and A. Stephens (eds.), *Reparations for Victims of Genocide, War Crimes and Crimes against Humanity: Systems in Place and Systems in the Making* (Leiden and Boston: Martinus Nijhoff Publishers, 2009).

singular.[55] Ultimately, the gender *equality* goals of gender mainstreaming must take centre stage; and gender must not be watered down or obscured to the point that it means nothing at all. International 'litigation' must start from the position of *individual* women and consider their *individualised or personalised* experiences in the enjoyment, as well as the violation, of their human rights, rather than the starting point being general assumptions about women and their experiences. That is, decision-makers must take into account both objective *and* subjective factors of a particular case, including but not limited to questions of gender as recognised by the HRC in *Vuolanne* v. *Finland*[56] but rarely repeated, and successfully employed by the majority of the ECtHR in *Aydin* v. *Turkey*.[57] That is, asking 'the woman question'[58] must be adjusted to asking the woman question within her cultural-economic-political-social context.

Applying a 'contextual analysis' to law pushes decision-makers to reflect on how women experience violence on an individual basis as well as globally. This may slowly bring about a cultural shift in the decision-making of the treaty bodies, some of which has already started. A contextual analysis permits decision-makers to free themselves from the shackles of established or traditional gender-based stereotypes that hinder their ability to think contextually, and to start seeing individual women as human beings within the reality of their own variable lives. It is about seeing women within their particular lives, rather than making generalisations about women as a group.[59] Contextual analysis is not contrary to ideas of objective, impartial, or rational decision-making. Rather an objective, impartial, or rational judgement that fails to give due consideration to the cultural-economic-political-social context of the case at hand can hardly claim to be objective, impartial, or rational.

A contextual analysis ought also to take account of the intersection of gender with other identity-based characteristics such as race, caste, class, religion, sexuality, or ethnicity. Intersectionality can act as a counterbalance to 'essentialising' women.[60] However, if it is undertaken cursorily or rudimentarily, it is likely to produce and compound new stereotypes by

---

[55] See, D. Otto, 'Disconcerting "Masculinities": Reinventing the Gendered Subject(s) of International Human Rights Law', in D. Buss and A. Manji (eds.), *International Law: Modern Feminist Approaches* (Oxford: Hart Publishing, 2005) 105.

[56] See, Chapter 4.   [57] See, Chapter 4.   [58] See, Chapter 1.

[59] As noted elsewhere in this book, grand statements about the position of women may be necessary at a political level, but at the level of litigation and individual case law a much more nuanced approach is needed to reverse and to confront entrenched stereotypes about women.

[60] See, Chapter 2.

accumulating new 'victim' categories, such as those based on gender/race, gender/caste, gender/class, gender/religion, gender/sexuality, or gender/ethnicity. Decision-makers must be aware of and avoid this trap.

In order to carry out contextual intersectional reasoning, decision-makers must in particular listen to women and what they say about themselves, which would necessarily include their personal experiences of violence, even if those experiences do not map onto specific categories or, as Littleton states, what is being said about them.[61] This might entail asking questions such as: How was *she personally* affected by the act or omission in question? How did it impact upon her life? Did it put her in a worse or more disadvantaged position than before the violence vis-à-vis her position within her family, job, society, etc.? What have been the consequences of that violence for her, in terms of family relations, social relations, economic position, employment, psychological trauma, physical harm, etc.? And some deeper questions about why she was subjected to violence: What was the political and economic context in which such action was taken (or not taken)? Were there any structural factors – whether infrastructural, legal, or related to social and cultural power – that permitted violence against women to occur with impunity? What laws and policies are in place to avoid it, or to protect against it, or which permitted it or enabled it to occur? What are the prevailing attitudes and views about women in the society in question? That is, what part, if any, did inequality and discrimination play in the violence in question? Ultimately, it is hoped that international decision-making and discourse may reach a point where better-informed decisions and commentary are made that reflect the seriousness of the harm to individual women and its real impact on their lives, rather than whether or not their circumstances fit neatly within accepted gender-based and other stereotypes. Improved interpretative techniques will also benefit other disadvantaged persons, as well as men who do not conform to expected gender-based behavioural rules or who are subject to gender-related violence.

Interpretation as an inclusion strategy, as evidenced throughout this book, is restricted by the wording of particular texts and the in-built biases (including the exclusion of women) in those texts, the definitions given to particular terms, the expertise and (lack of) creativity of decision-makers, and the culture and working practices of the decision-making apparatus. Improved interpretative techniques have an essential role to play but

---

[61] C. Littleton, 'Feminist Jurisprudence: The Difference Method Makes' (Book Review) (1989) 41 *Stan. L. Rev.* 751, at 764.

are inadequate on their own. The human rights system must, therefore, be further advanced and improved. Interpretative inclusion (or gender mainstreaming) is an incomplete and somewhat fragile strategy to rely upon without additional safeguards. This is because it is rooted in what can essentially be summarised as the exclusionary structures of the treaty bodies and the treaties.

E   Substantive reforms: a proposal for a protocol on violence against women

Under the above outlined structurally reformed system, a further step towards the elimination of violence against women would be the agreement of a protocol on violence against women. A protocol on violence against women could be attached to one of the human rights instruments, logically to the CEDAW, although it could also be attached to the ICCPR. Alternatively, a stand-alone treaty might be preferred. Throughout this book it has been shown that interpretation is at best a corrective and indirect mechanism to fix the errors of the original human rights framework. In this way, protection from violence is not conceptualised as a right in and of itself, but something less than that, equivalent to an accessory or corollary right.

The failure to agree a binding treaty that expressly prohibits violence against women supports feminist critiques of the 1980s and 1990s that women are unequal subjects under the law; that human rights norms are 'defined by the criterion of what men fear will happen to them';[62] and that the content of the rules of international law privilege men to the extent that if women's interests are acknowledged at all, they are marginalised.[63] Leaving a woman's right to live free from violence to 'soft law' instruments or to interpretative discourse supports the view that '[t]he very choice and categorisation of subject matter deemed appropriate for international regulation reflects male priorities'.[64] In 1991 the ECOSOC recommended the development of an international instrument addressing

---

[62]   H. Charlesworth, C. Chinkin and S. Wright, 'Feminist Approaches to International Law' (1991) 85 *Amer. J. Int'l L.* 613; H. Charlesworth and C. Chinkin, 'The Gender of *Jus Cogens*' (1993) 15 *HRQ* 63; C. Bunch, 'Transforming Human Rights from a Feminist Perspective', in J. Peters and A. Wolper (eds.), *Women's Rights, Human Rights: International Feminist Perspectives* (New York: Routledge, 1995) 11, at 13.

[63]   Charlesworth, Chinkin and Wright, 'Feminist Approaches to International Law', 614–615.

[64]   H. Charlesworth and C. Chinkin, *The Boundaries of International Law: A Feminist Analysis* (Manchester University Press, 2000), 18.

violence against women, yet this has never been fully achieved.[65] A non-binding Declaration[66] and a General Recommendation of the Women's Committee[67] (followed by similar statements by some of the other committees), although laudable, pay only lip service to the challenges put to the international community in, for example, the Nairobi Forward-looking Strategies[68] or the Beijing Platform for Action.[69]

As previously acknowledged in this book, attempting to 'fit' violence against women within so-called masculine norms is pursued for valid, strategic purposes. As an interim strategy, interpretative inclusion must be continued, and as mentioned above, to be strengthened by broader understandings of gender, gender relations and gender equality, the application of contextual reasoning, and by taking account of other identity as well as personal characteristics of individual women. Moreover, gender-appropriate interpretation will remain a necessary component of any jurisprudential practice no matter what the legal instrument.

However, this book has been premised on the fact that the absence of an explicit treaty right against violence requires lawyers and decision-makers to engage in 'imaginative interpretation rather than a literal reading of [the] texts'.[70] It thus relies on the ability and willingness of individual decision-makers of the still male-dominated treaty bodies to apply some of the gender or contextual reasoning techniques outlined in this book. And, while there has now been some significant progress in this regard, it is still piecemeal, arbitrary at times, and far from universal.

I am cognisant of the concerns about introducing 'yet another' human rights instrument, not least arguments about proliferation of treaties. Many arguments against a protocol on violence against women have already been raised. It has been asserted for instance that viewing each

---

[65] ECOSOC res. 1991/18 of 30 May 1991.

[66] UN Declaration on the Elimination of Violence against Women 1993, UN Doc. A/RES/48/104, 20 December 1993 (DEVAW).

[67] CEDAW, General Recommendation No. 19: Violence against Women (1992), UN Doc. HRI/GEN/1/Rev.7.

[68] UN, Report of the World Conference to Review and Appraise the Achievements of the United Nations Decade for Women: Equality, Development and Peace, Nairobi, 15–26 July 1985 (United Nations publications, Sales No. E.85.IV.10).

[69] Beijing Declaration and Platform for Action, Fourth World Conference on Women, UN Doc. A/CONF.177/20 (1995) and A/CONF.177/20/Add.1 (1995), 15 September 1995.

[70] Anne Gallagher makes this point in relation to the expansion of the slavery provisions to include contemporary forms, such as trafficking for sexual slavery and prostitution: A. Gallagher, 'Contemporary Forms of Female Slavery', in K. D. Askin and D. M. Koenig (eds.), *Women and International Human Rights Law* (Ardsley, NY: Transnational Publishers, 2000), Vol. 2, 487, at 500.

act of violence against women as a human rights violation 'devalue[s] the special stigma attached to a violation of [international human rights law]'.[71] Such arguments are, however, situated within long-standing sexist frameworks that have systematically excluded women from the full protection of human rights law, as outlined in Chapter 2 of this book. How is it reasonable to argue that violence systematically perpetrated against half the world's population could devalue an international legal system aimed at the protection and advancement of the human rights of *all* persons? It is precisely the equal protection goals of international human rights law that make addressing violence against women an imperative of international law. These types of arguments are only possible under an international legal system that unequally represents the interests of particular groups within that system (read: men). Previously, these arguments had been raised more broadly to argue against international law being concerned with so-called 'private' acts of violence at all.[72]

Still other arguments suggest that singling out 'private' violence *against women* as being a human rights violation breaches the universality principle by treating such acts differently to other private acts perpetrated against other people.[73] In response, it must be seen that international human rights law can only claim universal application if it reflects and takes into account the experiences and concerns of *all* persons, not just the experiences of those privileged by the system (read: men). Identifying particular classes of persons for special attention, including, inter alia, women, children, indigenous peoples, and minority groups, who have been disadvantaged under and excluded from the existing system of patriarchal domination, is not antithetical to the principle of universality. In fact, it is the cornerstone of human rights protection. Besides, there is much precedent already in the work of international human rights law. There are already treaties on race, women, children, and persons with disabilities. At the level of international criminal law, specific provisions have been included to encompass rape, sexual slavery, and other forms of sexual abuse and exploitation. A protocol on violence against women would be likewise recognition of this specific gap in the women's rights

---

[71] See, K. Roth, 'Domestic Violence as an International Human Rights Issue', in R. J. Cook (ed.), *Human Rights of Women: National and International Perspectives* (Philadelphia: University of Pennsylvania Press, 1994) 326, at 332.

[72] See, H. Charlesworth, 'Alienating Oscar? Feminist Analysis of International Law', in D. G. Dallmeyer (ed.), *Reconceiving Reality: Women and International Law* (American Society of International Law, 1993) 1.

[73] Roth, 'Domestic Violence as an International Human Rights Issue', 332–333.

framework. To suggest that outlawing such violence would be to single out and therefore to advantage a particular group (here: women) is to adopt a narrow view of equality as assimilation, rather than equality as equal dignity and respect and the elimination of oppression/domination, disadvantage, or hierarchy, as discussed in Chapter 4. Moreover, the narrow view of equality ignores the fact that the system has been applied unequally between women and men, and that the status quo of focusing only on direct state violations ignores the experiences of half the world's people. These arguments also ignore important developments that have already taken place to encompass the effects of non-state violence within international law.

Agreeing a protocol outlawing violence against women will not, however, be free from constraints. In particular, it could serve to overemphasise the power of law and deflect attention from the many non-law-based remedies available.[74] It could marginalise the issue away from mainstream human rights norms, and into women-specific ones. Much of this debate has been canvassed in Chapter 2. In reality, any protocol will result from political negotiation and compromise, and will be reliant on good faith interpretation to set its parameters and a readiness on the part of women to rely on and to utilise the law should it come into force. That is, any new treaty will only be as strong as the political will to uphold it, and based on the actions of states parties to the CEDAW, it is likely to be faced with extensive reservations (provided these are permitted in the text itself, about which I would argue strongly that reservations should not be permitted to core provisions). Existing treaties at the regional level that cover violence against women are not, for example, without shortcomings,[75] although it is no longer possible to argue that violence against women is an extra-treaty or extra-legal issue.

There are a myriad of questions that would need to be considered to ensure that any proposed protocol is as effective as possible in the fight against violence against women. These questions are not, however, distinct to a protocol on violence against women, as many are very much

---

[74] As noted in the Introduction to this book, non-law-based measures have been outside the scope of this book, but they remain important complementary approaches to addressing violence against women.

[75] See, e.g., even the existence of the Inter-American Convention on the Prevention, Punishment and Eradication of Violence against Women 1994, 33 ILM 1534 (1996); entered into force 3 May 1995, has not resolved the fact that 'judicial responses to the problem has [sic] fallen far short of [the] severity and prevalence [of violence against women in the Americas]'. See, I-ACmHR, *Access to Justice for Women Victims of Violence in the Americas*, OAS Doc. OEA/Ser.L/V/I Doc. 68, 20 January 2007, para. 14.

part of the hurdles to agreement of any international instrument. They would nonetheless impact on the final text. These would include where in international law to locate any prohibition,[76] how to define violence (noting the difficulties outlined in Chapter 1), and the remedies to be provided. Would many states ratify such a treaty? And if there are only a few, what impact would that have on the 'inclusion' of women's injuries within the human rights corpus under existing law? What would a protocol add to the work of the treaty bodies, noting that violence against women has already been subsumed within much of their work as evidenced throughout this book?

At a minimum, any agreed protocol would need to adopt a broad reading of violence against women,[77] include a non-exhaustive listing of both traditionally conceived 'male' rights (for example, prohibition against torture, the right to life) and traditionally conceived women's injuries (for example, female genital mutilation, domestic violence, sexual violence, and so on), and set out in some detail the obligations of states parties. The latter would need to give some guidance to the concepts of 'reasonableness' and 'due diligence' as they are now applied.[78]

In my view, the advantages of a separate protocol outweigh concerns that it may remain unimplemented in some states or be subject to extensive reservations, such problems being inherent to the general human rights system rather than unique to women's rights. An international protocol also matches commitments made to this issue at regional levels.[79] Although the CEDAW already categorises violence against women as a form of sex discrimination, it does not make violence against women prohibited conduct per se. Chapter 3 highlighted a number of difficulties with this approach. Fundamentally, a protocol on violence against

---

[76] Should any amendment be a separate treaty, a protocol, or a single provision? If preference is for a protocol, should it be attached to an existing mainstream treaty or to the CEDAW? Should it have its own treaty body, or be subsumed within an existing treaty body's work? If the latter, which treaty body? These raise mainstream–sidestream and treaty proliferation questions.

[77] See, Chapter 1 of this book. Cf. views of other writers calling for treaties or Security Council resolutions to deal with specific forms of violence against women, such as domestic violence, rather than an all-encompassing treaty: see, B. Meyersfeld, *Domestic Violence and International Law* (Oxford and Portland, OR: Hart Publishing, 2010).

[78] A possible starting point might be the Report of the Special Rapporteur on Violence against Women, Its Causes and Consequence (SR-VAW), *Indicators on Violence against Women and State Response.*

[79] Note, too, that the Council of Europe has completed the first draft of a convention on preventing and combating violence against women and domestic violence: http://www. coe.int/t/DGHL/StandardSetting/Violence/.

women would state loudly that violence against women is in and of itself a violation of a woman's human rights. Furthermore, the protocol would act as a benchmark for action by states parties and replace the current ad hoc and incremental approach to defining a state's obligations in this regard, although it would need to be sufficiently broad in its general terms to ensure it can evolve and remain dynamic. Moreover, it would represent a symbolic victory to women, recognising women's equal right to human rights protection against violence within the existing system. It would complement, rather than replace, existing treaties. Arguments and strategies developed around existing norms would continue to be available. Yet it would also be more than symbolic as it would avoid some of the pitfalls of 'fitting' women within existing provisions, which this book has shown to be particularly problematic, not least the reinforcement of the unequal treatment of women under the law. For the latter reason alone, it is time to take action.

F Conclusion

As the Introduction to this chapter highlighted, there is no quick fix to the issue of violence against women. Despite the significant progress that has been made in the sixty years since the formation of the United Nations and the elaboration of the UDHR under the guidance of Eleanor Roosevelt, there remain many ongoing challenges. Women have yet to be treated as equal human beings entitled to equal protection of the law. They benefit from human rights protection only indirectly via existing norms created with the lives of men rather than women in mind. Recognition that the 'gender mainstreaming' strategies of subsuming violence and other matters of concern to women within existing norms can reinforce the structural inequalities in the system of human rights protection could act as an awakening to new ways of responding to these issues. This chapter has proposed a number of small as well as ambitious procedural, structural, interpretative/conceptual, and substantive reforms that could be pursued to equilibrate the sexual imbalances in the system, while acknowledging that much more needs to be done. It is high time that women became more than mere visitors to the human rights house and were able to make the house their own.

BIBLIOGRAPHY

Alexander, B. C., 'Convention against Torture: A Viable Alternative for Domestic Violence Victims' (2000) 15 *Am. U. Int'l L. Rev.* 895

Aliotta, J., 'Justice O'Connor and the Equal Protection Clause: A Feminine Voice?' (1995) 78 *Judicature* 232

Alston, P., 'Conjuring Up New Human Rights: A Proposal for Equality Control' (1984) 78 *Amer. J. Int'l L.* 607

Americas Watch and Women's Rights Project, *Untold Terror: Violence against Women in Peru's Armed Conflict* (New York: Human Rights Watch, 1992)

Amnesty International, *Women in the Front Line*, AI Publications, 1991

  Human Rights are Women's Rights, AI Index: 77/01/95, 1995

  The Optional Protocol to the Women's Convention, AI Index: IOR 51/04/97, December 1997

  The Duty of States to Address Violence against Women, AI Index: ACT 77/049/2004, 2004

Amos, V. and P. Parmar, 'Challenging Imperial Feminism' (1984) 17 *Feminist Rev.* 3

Anderson, M., 'Access to Justice and Legal Process: Making Legal Institutions Responsive to Poor People in LDCs', SOAS Institute of Development Studies Working Paper No. 178, 2003, available at: www.ids.ac.uk/ids/bookshop/wp/wp178.pdf

Arzt, D., 'The Application of International Human Rights Law in Islamic States' (1990) 12 *HRQ* 202

Askin, K. D., 'Prosecuting Wartime Rape and Other Gender-Related Crimes under International Law: Extraordinary Advances, Enduring Obstacles' (2003) 12 *Berkeley J. Int'l L.* 288

Aust, A., *Modern Treaty Law and Practice* (Cambridge University Press, 2000)

Baird, R. M. and S. E. Rosenbaum, *The Ethics of Abortion: Pro-Life vs. Pro-Choice* (3rd edn, New York: Prometheus Books, 2001)

Banda, F., *Women, Law and Human Rights: An African Perspective* (Oxford: Hart Publishing, 2005)

Bartlett, K. T., 'Feminist Legal Methods' (1990) 103 *Harv. L. Rev.* 829

Bayefsky, A. F., 'The Principle of Equality or Non-Discrimination in International Law' (1990) 11 *Hum. Rts. L. J.* 1

'Making the Human Rights Treaties Work', in L. Henkin and J. L. Hargrove (eds.), *Human Rights: An Agenda for the Next Century* (American Society of International Law, Studies in Transnational Legal Studies No. 26, 1994) 229

'Conclusions and Recommendations', in A. F. Bayefsky (ed.), *The UN Human Rights System in the 21st Century* (The Hague: Kluwer Law International, 2000)

'Direct Petition in the UN Human Rights Treaty System' (2001) 95 *ASIL Proceedings* 71

The UN Human Rights Treaty System: Universality at the Crossroads (April 2001)

Bekou, O. and R. Cryer, *The International Criminal Court* (Aldershot and London: Ashgate Publishing, 2004)

Bem, S. L. *The Lenses of Gender* (New Haven, CT: Yale University Press, 1993)

Bender, L., 'A Lawyer's Primer on Feminist Theory and Tort' (1988) 38 *J. Legal Educ.* 3

Benninger-Budel, C. (ed.), *Due Diligence and its Application to Protect Women from Violence* (Leiden and Boston: Martinus Nijhoff Publishers, 2008)

Benninger-Budel, C. and L. O'Hanlon, *Violence against Women: 10 Reports/Year 2003* (World Organization against Torture (OMCT), 2004)

Bequaert Holmes, H., 'A Feminist Analysis of the Universal Declaration of Human Rights', in C. Gould (ed.), *Beyond Domination: New Perspectives on Women and Philosophy* (Totowa, NJ: Rowman & Allanheld, 1983) 250

Bequaert Holmes, H. and S. R. Petersen, 'Rights Over One's Own Body: A Woman-Affirming Health Care Policy' (1981) 3 *HRQ* 71

Beveridge F. and S. Nott, 'Mainstreaming: A Case for Optimism and Cynicism' (2002) 10 *Fem. Legal Stud.* 299

Bhavanani, K., *Feminism and Race* (Oxford University Press, 2001)

Binion, G., 'Human Rights: A Feminist Perspective' (1995) 17 *HRQ* 509

Blatt, D., 'Recognizing Rape as a Method of Torture' (1992) 19 *NYU Rev. L. & Soc. Change* 821

Bogecho, D., 'Putting it to Good Use: The International Covenant on Civil and Political Rights and Women's Rights to Reproductive Health' (2004) 13 *S. Cal. Rev. L. & Women's Stud.* 229

Bond, J. E., 'International Intersectionality: A Theoretical and Pragmatic Exploration of Women's International Human Rights Violations' (2003) 52 *Emory L. J.* 71

Bossuyt, M. J., *Guide to the 'TRAVAUX PRÉPARATOIRES' of the International Covenant on Civil and Political Rights* (Dordrecht: Martinus Nijhoff Publishers, 1987)

Boulesbaa, A., *The UN Convention on Torture and Prospects for Enforcement* (The Hague: Martinus Nijhoff Publishers, 1999)

Boven, T. van, 'Distinguishing Criteria of Human Rights', in K. Vasak and P. Alston (eds.), *The International Dimensions of Human Rights* (Westport, CT: Greenwood Press, 1982) 43

Bower, K., 'Recognizing Violence against Women as Persecution on the Basis of Membership in a Particular Social Group' (1993) 7 *Geo. Immigr. L. J.* 173

Braidotti, R., 'The Exile, The Nomad, and the Migrant: Reflections on International Feminism' (1992) 15 *Women's Studies Int. Forum* 7

Brems, E., 'Enemies or Allies? Feminism and Cultural Relativism as Dissident Voices in Human Rights Discourse' (1997) 19 *HRQ* 136

Brett, R., *Girl Soldiers: Challenging the Assumptions* (Quaker United Nations Office, 5 November 2002), available at: www.quno.org/geneva/pdf/Girl_ Soldiers.pdf

Broadbent, E., 'Getting Rid of Male Bias', in J. Kerr (ed.), *Ours By Right: Women's Rights as Human Rights* (London: North-South Institute, 1993) 10

Brownlie, I., *Principles of International Law* (5th edn, Oxford University Press, 1998)

Bunch, C., *Passionate Politics Essays 1968–1986: Feminist Theory in Action* (New York: St. Martin's Press, 1987)

  'Women's Rights as Human Rights: Toward a Re-Vision of Human Rights' (1990) 12 *HRQ* 486

  'Transforming Human Rights from a Feminist Perspective', in J. Peters and A. Wolper (eds.), *Women's Rights, Human Rights: International Feminist Perspectives* (New York: Routledge, 1995) 11

Burgers, J. H. and H. Danelius, *The United Nations Convention against Torture: A Handbook on the Convention against Torture and Other Cruel, Inhuman or Degrading Treatment or Punishment* (The Hague: Martinus Nijhoff Publishers, 1988)

Burrows, N., 'International Law and Human Rights: The Case of Women's Rights', in T. Campbell, D. Goldberg, S. McLean and T. Muller (eds.), *Human Rights: From Rhetoric to Reality* (New York: Basil Blackwell, 1986) 8

Buss, D. and A. Manji (eds.), *International Law: Modern Feminist Approaches* (Oxford: Hart Publishing, 2005)

Bustelo, M. R., 'The Committee on the Elimination of Discrimination against Women at the Crossroads', in P. Alston and J. Crawford (eds.), *The Future of UN Human Rights Treaty Monitoring* (Cambridge University Press, 2000) 79

Butler, J., *Gender Trouble – Feminism and the Subversion of Identity* (London: Routledge, 1990)

Byrnes, A., 'The "Other" Human Rights Treaty Body: The Work of the Committee on the Elimination of Discrimination Against Women' (1989) 14 *Yale J. Int'l L.* 1

  'Women, Feminism and International Human Rights Law – Methodological Myopia, Fundamental Flaws or Meaningful Marginalisation?: Some Current Issues' (1992) 12 *Aust. YB Int'l L.* 205

  'Toward More Effective Enforcement of Women's Human Rights Through the Use of International Human Rights Law and Procedures', in R. J. Cook (ed.), *Human Rights of Women: National and International Perspectives* (Philadelphia: University Pennsylvania Press, 1994) 189

'The Convention against Torture', in K. D. Askin and D. M. Koenig (eds.), *Women and International Human Rights Law* (Ardsley, NY: Transnational Publishers, 2000), Vol. 1, 183

'Using International Human Rights Law and Procedures to Advance Women's Rights', in K. D. Askin and D. M. Koenig (eds.), *Women and International Human Rights Law* (Ardsley, NY: Transnational Publishers, 2000), Vol. 1, 79

Byrnes, A. and E. Bath, 'Violence against Women, the Obligation of Due Diligence, and the Optional Protocol to the Convention on the Elimination of All Forms of Discrimination against Women – Recent Developments' (2008) 8 *Hum. Rts. L. Rev.* 517

Cahn, N. R., 'The Looseness of Legal Language: The Reasonable Woman Standard in Theory and in Practice' (1991–1992) 77 *Cornell L. Rev.* 1398

Carpenter, R. C., *'Innocent Women and Children': Gender, Norms and the Protection of Civilians* (London: Ashgate, 2006)

Charlesworth, H., 'The Public/Private Distinction and the Right to Development in International Law' (1992) 12 *Aust. YB Int'l L.* 190

'Alienating Oscar? Feminist Analysis of International Law', in D. G. Dallmeyer (ed.), *Reconceiving Reality: Women and International Law* (American Society of International Law, 1993) 1

'What are "Women's International Human Rights"?', in R. J. Cook (ed.), *Human Rights of Women: National and International Perspectives* (Philadelphia: University Pennsylvania Press, 1994) 58

'The Gender of International Institutions' (1995) 89 *ASIL Proceedings* 84

'Human Rights as Men's Rights', in J. Peters and A. Wolper (eds.), *Women's Rights, Human Rights: International Feminist Perspectives* (New York: Routledge, 1995) 103

'The Mid-Life Crisis of the Universal Declaration of Human Rights' (1998) 55 *Wash. & Lee L. Rev.* 781

'Feminist Methods in International Law' (1999) 93 *Amer. J. Int'l L.* 379

'General Introduction', in K. D. Askin and D. M. Koenig (eds.), *Women and International Human Rights Law* (Ardsley, NY: Transnational Publishers, 2000), Vol. 1, xix

'Concepts of Equality in International Law', in G. Huscroft and P. Rishworth (eds.), *Litigating Rights: Perspectives from Domestic and International Law* (Oxford: Hart Publishing, 2002) 137

'The Hidden Gender of International Law' (2002) 16 *Temple Int'l & Comp. L. J.* 93

'Not Waving but Drowning: Gender Mainstreaming and Human Rights in the United Nations' (2005) 18 *Harv. Hum. Rts. J.* 1

'Talking to Ourselves: Feminist Scholarship in International Law', in Z. Pearson and S. Kuovo (eds.), *Between Resistance and Compliance?*

Feminist Perspectives on International Law in an Era of Anxiety and Terror (Oxford: Hart Publishing, in press 2010) (on file with the author)

Charlesworth, H. and C. Chinkin, 'The Gender of *Jus Cogens*' (1993) 15 *HRQ* 63

'Violence against Women: A Global Issue', in J. Stubbs (ed.), *Women, Male Violence and the Law* (Sydney: Institute of Criminology Series No. 6, 1994) 13

The Boundaries of International Law: A Feminist Analysis (Manchester University Press, 2000)

'Editorial Comment: Sex, Gender, and September 11th' (2002) 96 *Amer. J. Int'l L.* 600

Charlesworth, H., C. Chinkin and S. Wright, 'Feminist Approaches to International Law' (1991) 85 *Amer. J. Int'l L.* 613

Cherry, A. L., 'A Feminist Understanding of Sex-Selective Abortion: Solely a Matter of Choice?' (1995) 10 *Wis. Women's L. J.* 161

Chinkin, C., 'Strategies to Combat Discrimination against Women', in M. O'Flaherty and G. Gisvold (eds.), *Post-War Protection of Human Rights in Bosnia and Herzegovina* (The Hague: Kluwer Law International, 1988) Ch. 9

'Feminist Interventions into International Law' (1997) 19 *Adel. L. R.* 13

Chinkin, C. and K. Knop, *Final Report on Women's Equality and Nationality in International Law* (International Law Association, Committee on Feminism and International Law, 2000)

Chinkin, C., S. Wright, and H. Charlesworth, 'Feminist Approaches to International Law: Reflections from Another Century', in D. Buss and A. Manji (eds.), *International Law: Modern Feminist Approaches* (Oxford: Hart Publishing, 2005) 17

Clapham, A., 'UN Human Rights Reporting Procedures: An NGO Perspective', in P. Alston and J. Crawford (eds.), *The Future of the UN Human Rights Treaty Monitoring* (Cambridge University Press, 2000) 175

Human Rights Obligations of Non-State Actors (Oxford University Press, 2006)

Clark, B., 'The Vienna Convention Reservations Regime and the Convention on Discrimination Against Women' (1991) 85 *Amer. J. Int'l L.* 281

Cobbah, J. A. M., 'African Values and the Human Rights Debate: An African Perspective' (1987) 9 *HRQ* 309

Conte, A., 'Security of the Person', in A. Conte, S. Davidson and R. Burchill, *Defining Civil and Political Rights: The Jurisprudence of the United Nations Human Rights Committee* (Aldershot: Ashgate Publishing, 2004) 85

Cook, R. J., 'International Human Rights Law Concerning Women: Case Notes and Comments' (1990) 23 *Vand. J. Transnat. L.* 779

'Reservations to the Convention on the Elimination of All Forms of Discrimination Against Women' (1990) 30 *Va. J. Int'l L.* 643

'International Protection of Women's Reproductive Rights' (1992) 24 *N.Y.U.L.J.* 689

'Women's International Human Rights Law: The Way Forward' (1993) 15 *HRQ* 230

'State Responsibility for Violations of Women's Human Rights' (1994) 7 *Harv. Hum. Rts. J.* 125

'Advancing International Law Regarding Women' (1997) 91 *ASIL Proceedings* 308

Cook, R. J. and S. Cusack, *Gender Stereotyping: Transnational Legal Perspectives* (Philadelphia: University of Pennsylvania Press, 2010)

Coomaraswamy, R., 'To Bellow Like a Cow: Women, Ethnicity and the Discourse of Rights', in R. J. Cook (ed.), *Human Rights of Women: National and International Perspectives* (Philadelphia: University of Pennsylvania Press, 1994) 43

Copelon, R., 'Recognizing the Egregious in the Everyday: Domestic Violence as Torture' (1994) 25 *Colum. Hum. Rts. L. Rev.* 291

'Gendered War Crimes: Reconceptualizing Rape in Time of War', in J. Peters and A. Wolper (eds.), *Women's Rights, Human Rights: International Feminist Perspectives* (New York: Routledge, 1995) 197

'Gender Crimes as War Crimes: Integrating Crimes against Women into International Criminal Law' (2000–2001) 46 *McGill L. J.* 217

Cornell, D., 'Living Together: Psychic Spaces and the Demand for Sexual Equality', in A. J. Cahill and J. Hansen (eds.), *Continental Feminism Reader* (London: Rowman & Littlefield, 2003) 196

Crawford, J., 'The UN Human Rights Treaty System: A System in Crisis?', in P. Alston and J. Crawford (eds.), *The Future of the UN Human Rights Treaty Monitoring* (Cambridge University Press, 2000) 1

Dallmeyer, D. G. (ed.), *Reconceiving Reality: Women and International Law* (American Society of International Law, 1993)

Davidson, S., 'The Civil and Political Rights Protected in the Inter-American Human Rights System', in D. J. Harris and S. Livingstone (eds.), *The Inter-American System of Human Rights* (Oxford: Clarendon Press, 1998) 213

'Intention and Effect: The Legal Status of the Final Views of the Human Rights Committee' (2001) *NZ L. Rev.* 125

Davies, M., 'Taking the Inside Out: Sex and Gender in the Legal Subject', in N. Naffine and R. Owens (eds.), *Sexing the Subject of Law* (Sydney: Law Book Co. Ltd, 1997) 25

Day O'Connor, S., 'Portia's Progress' (1991) 66 *NYU Law Rev.* 1546

The Majesty of the Law: Reflections of a Supreme Court Justice (London: Random House, 2004)

Dembour, M.-B., *Who Believes in Human Rights? Reflections on the European Convention* (Cambridge University Press, 2006)

Dinstein, Y., 'The Right to Life, Physical Integrity, and Liberty', in L. Henkin (ed.), *The International Bill of Rights: The Covenant on Civil and Political Rights* (New York: Columbia University Press, 1981) 114

Doezema, J., 'Loose Women or Lost Women? The Re-emergence of the Myth of White Slavery in Contemporary Discourses of Trafficking in Women' (2000) 18 *Gender Issues* 23

Dolgopol, U. and S. Paranjape, *Comfort Women, An Unfinished Ordeal: Report of a Mission* (International Commission of Jurists, 1994)

Eberts, M., 'Feminist Perspectives on the Canadian Charter of Rights and Freedoms', in P. Alston (ed.), *Promoting Human Rights Through Bills of Rights: Comparative Perspectives* (New York: Oxford University Press, 1999, reprinted 2003) 241

Edwards, A., 'Age and Gender Dimensions in International Refugee Law', in E. Feller, V. Türk and F. Nicholson (eds.), *Refugee Protection in International Law: UNHCR's Global Consultations on International Protection* (Cambridge University Press, 2003) 46

'*Aydin v Turkey, Akayesu* and Abu Ghraib: Re-conceptualising "Torture" under International Law from a Feminist Perspective', Australian and New Zealand Society of International Law Annual Conference, Canberra, June 2005

'The "Feminizing" of Torture under International Human Rights Law' (2006) 19 *Leiden J. Int'l L.* 349

'Book Review: Wouter Vandenhole, Non-Discrmination and Equality in the View of the UN Human Rights Treaty Bodies (Intersentia, Antwerp, 2005)' (2007) 7 *Hum. Rts. L. Rev.* 267

'Violence against Women as Sex Discrimination: Judging the Jurisprudence of the United Nations Human Rights Treaty Bodies' (2008) 18 *Texas J. Women & L.* 1–59

Displacement, Statelessness, and Questions of Gender Equality under the Convention on the Elimination of All Forms of Discrimination against Women, UNHCR, Legal and Protection Policy Research Series, UN Doc. HCR/PPLAS/2009/02, August 2009, Background Paper prepared for a joint-UNHCR–Women's Committee seminar held at the United Nations in New York, 16–17 July 2009, available at: www.unhcr.org/4a8d0f1b9. html

Executive Summary of Displacement, Statelessness, and Questions of Gender Equality under the Convention on the Elimination of All Forms of Discrimination against Women, UN Doc. CEDAW/C/2009/II/WP.3, 1 July 2009, available at: www2.ohchr.org/English/bodies/cedaw/docs/CEDAW.C.2009.II.WP.3.pdf

'Everyday Rape: International Human Rights Law and Violence against Women in Peacetime', in C. McGlynn and V. Munro (eds.), *Rethinking Rape Law: International and Comparative Perspectives* (London: Routledge-Cavendish, 2010) 92

Eisler, R., 'Human Rights: Toward an Integrated Theory for Action' (1987) 9 *Hum. Rts. Qty* 287

Eldar, O., 'Vote-Trading in International Institutions' (2008) 19 *Eur. J. Int'l L.* 3

Emerton, R., K. Adams, A. Byrnes, and J. Connors (eds.), *International Women's Rights Cases* (London: Cavendish Publishing, 2005)

Engle, K., 'Female Subjects of Public International Law: Human Rights and the Exotic Other Female' (1992) 26 *New England L. Rev.* 1509

    'International Human Rights and Feminism: When Discourses Meet' (1992) 13 *Mich. J. Int'l L.* 605

    'After the Collapse of the Public/Private Distinction: Strategizing Women's Rights', in D. G. Dallmeyer (ed.), *Reconceiving Reality: Women and International Law* (American Society of International Law, 1993) 143

    'Culture and Human Rights: The Asian Values Debate in Context' (2000) 32 *NYU Int'l L. & Pol.* 291

    'Feminism and Its (Dis)Contents: Criminalizing Wartime Rape in Bosnia and Herzegovina' (2005) 99 *Am. J. Int'l L.* 779

    'International Human Rights and Feminisms: When Discourses Keep Meeting', in D. Buss and A. Manji (eds.), *International Law: Modern Feminist Approaches* (Oxford: Hart Publishing, 2005) 47

Engle Merry, S., 'Constructing a Global Law – Violence against Women and the Human Rights System' (2003) 28 *L. & Soc. Inquiry* 941

    Human Rights and Gender Violence: Translating International Law into Local Justice (University of Chicago Press, 2006)

Ertück, Y., 'The Due Diligence Standard: What Does It Entail for Women's Human Rights?', in C. Benninger-Budel (ed.), *Due Diligence and its Application to Protect Women from Violence* (Leiden and Boston: Martinus Nijhoff Publishers, 2008) 27

Etienne, M., 'Addressing Gender-Based Violence in an International Context' (1995) 18 *Harv. Women's L. J.* 139

Evans, M. and C. Haenni-Dale, 'Preventing Torture? The Development of the Optional Protocol to the UN Convention Against Torture' (2004) 4 *Hum. Rts. L. Rev.* 19

Evans, M. D., 'Getting to Grips with Torture' (2002) 51 *ICLQ* 365

Evans, M. D. and R. Morgan, *Preventing Torture: A Study of the European Convention for the Prevention of Torture and Inhuman or Degrading Treatment or Punishment* (Oxford University Press, 2001)

Evatt, E., 'Eliminating Discrimination Against Women: The Impact of the UN Convention' (1991–1992) 18 *Melb. U. L. Rev.* 435

    'The Right to Individual Petition: Assessing its Operation before the Human Rights Committee and its Future Application to the Women's Convention on Discrimination' (1995) 89 *ASIL Proceedings* 227

Ewing, A. P., 'Establishing State Responsibility for Private Acts of Violence against Women under the American Convention on Human Rights' (1995) 26 *Colum. Hum. Rts. L. Rev.* 751

Ferstman, C., M. Goetz and A. Stephens (eds.), *Reparations for Victims of Genocide, War Crimes and Crimes against Humanity: Systems in Place and Systems in the Making* (Leiden and Boston: Martinus Nijhoff Publishers, 2009)

Finley, L. M., 'A Break in the Silence: Including Women's Issues in a Torts Course' (1989) 1 *Yale J. L. & Feminism* 41

Fitzpatrick, J., 'The Use of International Human Rights Norms to Combat Violence Against Women', in R. J. Cook (ed.), *Human Rights of Women: National and International Perspectives* (Philadelphia: University Pennsylvania Press, 1994) 532

Fortin, K., *Rape as Torture: A Triumph or a Straight Jacket?*, LL.M Dissertation, Utrecht University, The Netherlands, 2008 (published by Faculty of Law, Utrecht University, Science Shop of Law, Economics and Governance, 2008) (on file with the author)

Franke, K. M., 'Putting Sex to Work' (1998) 75 *Denver U. L. Rev.* 1139
  'Gendered Subjects of Transitional Justice' (2006) 15 *Colum. J. Gender & L.* 813

Fraser, A. S., 'Becoming Human: The Origins and Development of Women's Human Rights' (1999) 21 *HRQ* 853

Fredman, S., *Introduction to Discrimination Law* (Oxford University Press, 2002)

Freyer, J. A., 'Women Litigators in Search of a Care-Oriented Judicial System' (1995–1996) 4 *Am. U. J. Gender & L.* 199

Friedman, E., 'Women's Human Rights: The Emergence of a Movement', in J. Peters and A. Wolper (eds.), *Women's Rights, Human Rights: International Feminist Perspectives* (New York: Routledge, 1995) 18

Frostell, K., 'Gender Difference and the Non-Discrimination Principle in the CCPR and the CEDAW', in L. Hannikainen and E. Nykänen (eds.), *New Trends in Discrimination Law – International Perspectives* (Turku, Finland: Turku Law School, 1999) 29

Gallagher, A., 'Ending the Marginalization: Strategies for Incorporating Women into the United Nations Human Rights System' (1997) 19 *HRQ* 283
  'Contemporary Forms of Female Slavery', in K. D. Askin and D. M. Koenig (eds.), *Women and International Human Rights Law* (Ardsley, NY: Transnational Publishers, 2000), Vol. 2, 487

Gardam, J. G., 'The Law of Armed Conflict: A Gendered Regime?', in D. G. Dallmeyer (ed.), *Reconceiving Reality: Women and International Law* (American Society of International Law, 1993) 171

Gardam, J. G. and M. J. Jarvis, *Women, Armed Conflict and International Law* (The Hague: Kluwer Law International, 2001)

Gaze, B., 'Some Aspects of Equality Rights: Theory and Practice', in B. Galligan and C. Sampford (eds.), *Rethinking Human Rights* (Annandale, NSW: Federation Press, 1997) 189

Gilligan, C., *In a Different Voice: Psychological Theory and Women's Development* (Cambridge, MA: Harvard University Press, 1982)

Gold, M., 'The Canadian Concept of Equality' (1986) 46 *Uni. Toronto L. J.* 349

Goldberg, P. and N. Kelly, 'International Human Rights and Violence against Women' (1993) 6 *Harv. Hum. Rts. J.* 195

Goldfarb, S. F., 'Applying the Discrimination Model to Violence against Women: Some Reflections on Theory and Practice' (2003) 11 *Am. U. J. Gender Soc. Pol'y & L.* 251

Goldscheid, J., 'Domestic and Sexual Violence as Sex Discrimination: Comparing American and International Approaches' (2006) 28 *T. Jefferson L. Rev.* 355

Goodwin-Gill, G. and J. McAdam, *The Refugee in International Law* (3rd edn, Oxford University Press, 2007)

Gould, C., 'The Woman Question: Philosophy of Liberation and the Liberation of Philosophy', in C. Gould and M. W. Wartofsky (eds.), *Women and Philosophy: Toward A Theory of Liberation* (New York: Putnam, 1976) 1

Graycar, R., 'The Gender of Judgments: An Introduction', in M. Thornton (ed.), *Public and Private: Feminist Legal Debates* (Melbourne: Oxford University Press, 1995) 262

Greatbatch, J., 'The Gender Difference: Feminist Critiques of Refugee Discourse' (1989) 1 *Int'l J. Ref. L.* 518

Gross, E., 'What is Feminist Theory?', in C. Pateman and E. Gross (eds.), *Feminist Challenges: Social and Political Theory* (Sydney: Allen & Unwin, 1986) 190

Gunning, I., 'Arrogant Perception, World Travelling and Multicultural Feminism: The Case of Female Genital Surgeries', (1991–92) 23 *Colum. Hum. Rts. L. Rev.* 189

Halley, J., *Split Decisions: How and Why to Take a Break from Feminism* (Princeton University Press, 2006)

Hampson, F. J., 'An Overview of the Reform of the United Nations Human Rights Machinery' (2007) 7 *Hum. Rts. L. Rev.* 7

Harding, S., *The Science Question in Feminism* (Ithaca, NY: Cornell University Press, 1986)

Harries, C., 'Daughters of Our Peoples: International Feminism Meets Ugandan Law and Custom' (1984) 25 *Colum. Hum. Rts. L. Rev.* 493

Harris, A. P., 'Race and Essentialism in Feminist Legal Theory' (1990) 42 *Stan. L. Rev.* 581

Harris, D. J., *Cases and Materials on International Law* (5th edn, London: Sweet & Maxwell, 1998)

Harris, D. J., M. O'Boyle and C. Warbrick, *Law of the European Convention on Human Rights* (London: Butterworths, 1995)

Hartsock, N., 'Feminist Theory and the Development of Revolutionary Strategy', in Z. R. Eisenstein (ed.), *Capitalist Patriarchy and the Case for Socialist Feminism* (New York: Monthly Review Press, 1979) 56

'Foucault on Power – A Theory for Women', in L. J. Nicholson (ed.), *Feminism/ Postmodernism* (London: Routledge, 1990) 157

Heirnaux, J., 'Biological Aspects of the Racial Question', in UNESCO, *Four Statements on the Racial Question* (UNESCO, COM.69/II.27/A, 1969) 9

Heise, L., M. Ellsberg and M. Gottemoeller, *Ending Violence against Women* (Baltimore: Johns Hopkins School of Public Health and the Center for Health and Gender Equality, 2000)

Hernández-Truyol, B. E., 'Women's Rights as Human Rights – Rules, Realities and the Role of Culture: A Formula for Reform' (1996) XXI *Brook. J. Int'l L.* 605

'Human Rights Through a Gendered Lens: Emergence, Evolution, Revolution', in K. D. Askin and D. M. Koenig (eds.), *Women and International Human Rights Law* (Ardsley, NY: Transnational Publishers, 2000), Vol. 1, 3

Heyman, M. G., 'Domestic Violence and Asylum: Toward a Working Model of Affirmative State Obligations' (2005) 17 *Int'l J. Ref. L.* 729

Heyns, C. and F. Viljoen, 'The Impact of the United Nations Human Rights Treaties on the Domestic Level' (2001) 23 *HRQ* 483

Higgins, T. E., 'By Reason Of Their Sex: Feminist Theory, Postmodernism and Justice' (1995) 80 *Cornell L. Rev.* 1536

'Anti-Essentialism, Relativism, and Human Rights' (1996) 19 *Harv. Women's L. J.* 89

Hillock, R. L., 'Establishing the Rights of Women Globally: Has the United Nations Convention on the Elimination of All Forms of Discrimination against Women Made a Difference?' (2004–2005) 12 *Tulsa J. Comp. & Int'l L.* 481

Holtmaat, R., 'Preventing Violence against Women: The Due Diligence Standard with Respect to the Obligation to Banish Gender Stereotypes on the Grounds of Article 5(a) of the CEDAW Convention', in C. Benninger-Budel (ed.), *Due Diligence and its Application to Protect Women from Violence* (Leiden and Boston: Martinus Nijhoff Publishers, 2008) 63

INTERIGHTS, *Non-Discrimination in International Law: A Handbook for Practitioners* (Interights, January 2005, edited by K. Kitching)

Isa, F. G., 'The Optional Protocol for the Convention on the Elimination of All Forms of Discrimination Against Women: Strengthening the Protection Mechanisms of Women's Human Rights' (2003) 20 *Ariz. J. Int'l & Comp. L.* 291

Jacobson, R., 'The Committee on the Elimination of Discrimination against Women', in P. Alston (ed.), *The United Nations and Human Rights: A Critical Appraisal* (Oxford University Press, 1992) 444

Jaggar, A. M. and I. M. Young (eds.), *A Companion to Feminist Philosophy* (London: Blackwell Publishers, 1998)

Joachim, J., 'Shaping the Human Rights Agenda: The Case for Violence against Women', in M. K. Meyer and E. Prügl (eds.), *Gender Politics in Global Governance* (Lanham, MD: Rowman & Littlefield Publishers, 1999) 142

Johnstone, R. L., 'Feminist Influences on the United Nations Human Rights Treaty Bodies' (2006) 26 *HRQ* 148

'Cynical Savings or Reasonable Reform? Reflections on a Single Unified UN Human Rights Treaty Body' (2007) 7 *Hum. Rts. L. Rev.* 173

Joseph, S., J. Schultz and M. Castan, *The International Covenant on Civil and Political Rights: Cases, Materials, and Commentary* (2nd edn, Oxford University Press, 2004)

Kalajdzic, J., 'Rape, Representation, and Rights: Permeating International Law with the Voices of Women' (1996) 21 *Queen's L. J.* 457

R. Kapur, 'The Tragedy of Victimization Rhetoric: Resurrecting the "Native" Subject in International/Post-Colonial Feminist Legal Politics' (2002) 15 *Harv. Hum. Rts. J.* 2

'Human Rights in the 21st Century: Take a Walk on the Dark Side' (2006) 28 *Sydney L. Rev.* 665

Kaufman, N. H. and S. A. Lindquist, 'Critiquing Gender-Neutral Treaty Language: The Convention on the Elimination of All Forms of Discrimination Against Women', in J. Peters and A. Wolper (eds.), *Women's Rights, Human Rights: International Feminist Perspectives* (New York: Routledge, 1995) 114

Kebriaei, P., 'The UN Human Rights Committee's Decision in *Karen Llotoy v Peru*' (2006) 15 *INTERIGHTS Bulletin* 151

Kim, N., 'Toward a Feminist Theory of Human Rights: Straddling the Fence Between Western Imperialism and Uncritical Absolutism' (1993) 25 *Colum. Hum. Rts. L. Rev.* 49

Knop, K., 'Re/Statements: Feminism and State Sovereignty in International Law' (1993) 3 *Transnat. L. & Contemp. Prob.* 293

Diversity and Self-Determination in International Law (Cambridge University Press, 2002),

Knop, K., (ed.), *Gender and Human Rights* (Oxford University Press, 2004)

Koenig, D. M. and K. D. Askin, 'International Criminal Law and the International Criminal Court Statute: Crimes against Women', in K. D. Askin and D. M. Koenig (eds.), *Women and International Human Rights Law* (Ardsley, NY: Transnational Publishers, 2000), Vol. 2, 3

Kois, L., 'Dance, Sister, Dance!', in B. Duner (ed.), *An End to Torture: Strategies for its Eradication* (London: Zed Books, 1998) 90

Kouvo, S., *Making Just Rights? Mainstreaming Women's Human Rights and a Gender Perspective* (Uppsala: Iustus Förlag, 2004)

Krill, F., 'The Protection of Women in International Humanitarian Law' (1985) 249 *Int'l Rev. Red Cross* 337

Lacey, N., 'Legislation against Sex Discrimination: Questions from a Feminist Perspective' (1987) 14 *J. L. & Soc'y* 411

'Feminist Legal Theory and the Rights of Women', in Karen Knop (ed.), *Gender and Human Rights* (Oxford University Press, 2004) 13

Lambert, C., 'Partial Sites and Partial Sightings: Women and the UN Human Rights Treaty System', in S. Pickering and C. Lambert (eds.), *Global Issues, Women and Justice* (Sydney: Sydney Institute of Criminology Series No. 19, 2004) 136

Lauterpacht, Sir H., *An International Bill of the Rights of Man* (New York: Columbia University Press, 1945)

Lord Lester of Herne Hill QC and S. Joseph, 'Obligations of Non-Discrimination', in D. Harris and S. Joseph (ed.), *The International Covenant on Civil and Political Rights and United Kingdom Law* (Oxford: Clarendon Press, 1995)

Levit, N. and R. R. M. Verchick, *Feminist Legal Theory: A Primer* (New York University Press, 2006)

Littleton, C. A., 'Equality and Feminist Legal Theory' (1987) 48 *U. Pitt. L. Rev.* 1043

'Feminist Jurisprudence: The Difference Method Makes' (Book Review) 41 *Stan. L. Rev.* 751

Lorber, J., *Paradoxes of Gender* (New Haven, CT: Yale University Press, 1994)

Lord, R., 'The Liability of Non-State Actors for Torture in Violation of International Humanitarian Law: An Assessment of the Jurisprudence of the International Criminal Tribunal for the Former Yugoslavia' (2003) 4 *Melb. J. Int'l L.* 112

MacKinnon, C. A., *Sexual Harassment of Working Women: A Case of Sex Discrimination* (New Haven, CT: Yale University Press, 1979)

'Feminism, Marxism, Method and the State: Toward Feminist Jurisprudence' (1983) (8) *Signs* 635

Feminism Unmodified: Discourses on Life and Law (Cambridge, MA: Harvard University Press, 1987)

'From Practice to Theory, or What is a White Woman Anyway?' (1991) 4 *Yale J. L. & Feminism* 13

'On Torture: A Feminist Perspective on Human Rights', in K. Mahoney and P. Mahoney (eds.), *Human Rights in the Twenty-First Century: A Global Perspective* (Dordrecht: Martinus Nijhoff Publishers, 1993) 21

'Rape, Genocide, and Women's Human Rights' (1994) 17 *Harv. Women's L. J.* 5

'Symposium on Unfinished Feminist Business: Some Points against Postmodernism' (2000) 75 *Chicago-Kent L. Rev.* 687

Are Women Human? And Other International Dialogues (Cambridge, MA: Harvard University Press, 2006)

'Equality Remade: Violence Against Women', in C. A. MacKinnon, *Are Women Human? And Other International Dialogues* (Cambridge, MA: Harvard University Press, 2006) 105

'Making Sex Equality Real', in C. A. MacKinnon, *Are Women Human? And Other International Dialogues* (Cambridge, MA: Harvard University Press, 2006) 71

'Sex and Violence: A Perspective', in E. Hackett and S. Haslanger (eds.), *Theorizing Feminisms: A Reader* (Oxford University Press, 2006) 266

'Women's September 11th: Rethinking the International Law of Conflict', in C. A. MacKinnon, *Are Women Human? And Other International Dialogues* (Cambridge, MA: Harvard University Press, 2006) 259

Mahoney, K., 'Theoretical Perspectives on Women's Human Rights and Strategies for their Implementation' (1996) 12 *Brook. J. Int'l L.* 799

'Canadian Approaches to Equality Rights and Gender Equity in the Courts', in R. J. Cook (ed.), *Human Rights of Women: National and International Perspectives* (Philadelphia: University of Pennsylvania Press, 1994) 437

Mahoney, M. R., 'Victimization Or Oppression? Women's Lives, Violence, and Agency', in M. A. Fineman and R. Mykitiuk (eds.), *The Public Nature of Private Violence: The Discovery of Domestic Abuse* (New York: Routledge, 1994) 59

Martin, R., 'A Feminist View of the Reasonable Man: An Alternative Approach to Liability in Negligence for Personal Injury' (1994) 23 *Anglo-Amer. L. Rev.* 334

McBride Stetson, D., *Abortion Politics, Women's Movements, and the Democratic State* (Oxford University Press, 2001)

McColgan, A., 'Cracking the Comparator Problem: Discrimination, "Equal" Treatment and the Role of Comparisons' (2006) *Eur. Hum. Rts L. Rev.* 649

Women under the Law: The False Promise of Human Rights (Harlow: Longman, 2000)

McCorquodale, R. and R. La Forgia, 'Taking Off the Blindfolds: Torture by Non-State Actors' (2001) 1 *Hum. Rts. L. Rev.* 189

McGlynn, C., 'Will Women Judges Make a Difference?' (1998) 148 *New Law J.* 813

'Rape as "Torture"? Catharine MacKinnon and Questions of Feminist Strategy' (2008) 17 *Fem. Legal Stud.* 71

'Rape, Torture and the European Convention on Human Rights' (2009) 58 *Int'l & Comp. L. Qty* 565

McGlynn, C. and V. Munro (eds.), *Rethinking Rape Law: International and Comparative Perspectives* (London: Routledge-Cavendish, in press 2010)

McKean, W., *Equality and Discrimination under International Law* (Oxford: Clarendon Press, 1983)

McMahan, J., *The Ethics of Killing: Problems at the Margins of Life* (Oxford University Press, 2002)

Menghistu, F., 'The Satisfaction of Survival Requirements', in B. G. Ramcharan (ed.), *The Right to Life in International Law* (Dordrecht: Martinus Nijhoff Publishers, 1985) 63

Meron, T., *Human Rights in Internal Strife: Their International Protection* (Cambridge: Grotius, 1987)

'Enhancing the Effectiveness of the Prohibition of Discrimination against Women' (1990) 84 *Amer. J. Int'l L.* 213

Meyersfeld, B., *Domestic Violence and International Law* (Oxford and Portland, OR: Hart Publishing, 2010)

Minor, J. A., 'An Analysis of Structural Weaknesses in the Convention on the Elimination of All Forms of Discrimination against Women' (1994–95) 24 *Ga. J. Int'l & Comp. L.* 137

Minow, M., 'Interpreting Rights: An Essay for Robert Cover' (1987) 96 *Yale L. J.* 1860

Moeckli, D., *Human Rights and Non-Discrimination in the 'War on Terror'* (Oxford University Press, 2008)
  'Saadi v Italy: The Rules of the Game Have Not Changed' (2008) 8 *Hum. Rts. L. Rev.* 534

Mohanty, C., 'Under Western Eyes: Feminist Scholarship and Colonial Discourses', in C. Mohanty, A. Russo and L. Torres (eds.), *Third World Women and the Politics of Feminism* (Bloomington, IN: Indiana University Press, 1991) 51

Mohanty, C., A. Russo and L. Torres (eds.), *Third World Women and the Politics of Feminism* (Bloomington, IN: Indiana University Press, 1991)

Moon, G. and R. Allen, 'Dignity Discourse in Discrimination Law: A Better Route to Equality?' (2006) 6 *Eur. Hum. Rts L. Rev.* 610

Moran, M., *Rethinking the Reasonable Person: An Egalitarian Reconstruction of the Objective Standard* (Oxford University Press, 2003)

Morijn, J., *UN Human Rights Treaty Body Reform: Toward a Permanent Unified Treaty Body* (Civitatis International, April 2006)

Morsink, J., *The Universal Declaration of Human Rights: Origins, Drafting, and Intent* (Philadelphia: University of Pennsylvania Press, 1999)

Mowbray, A., 'The Consideration of Gender in the Process of Appointing Judges to the European Court of Human Rights' (2008) 8 *Hum. Rts. L. Rev.* 549

Mullally, S., *Gender, Culture and Human Rights: Reclaiming Universalism* (Oxford: Hart Publishing, 2006)

Munro, V., *Law and Politics at the Perimeter: Re-Evaluating Key Feminist Debates in Feminist Theory* (Oxford: Hart Publishing, 2007)
  'Navigating Feminisms: At the Margins, in the Mainstreams or Elsewhere? Reflections on Charlesworth, Otomo and Pearson', in Z. Pearson and S. Kuovo (eds.), *Between Resistance and Compliance? Feminist Perspectives on International Law in an Era of Anxiety and Terror* (Oxford: Hart Publishing, in press 2010) (on file with the author)

Murray, P., 'The Negro Woman's Stake in the Equal Rights Amendment' (1970–1971) 6 *Harv. C.R. – C. L. L. Rev.* 253

Musalo, K., 'Conscientious Objection as a Basis for Refugee Status: Protection for the Fundamental Right of Freedom of Thought, Conscience, and Religion' (2007) 26 *Ref. Surv. Qty* 69

Naffine, N., *Law and the Sexes: Explorations in Feminist Jurisprudence* (London: Allen & Unwin, 1990)
  'Sexing the Subject (of Law)', in M. Thornton (ed.), *Public and Private: Feminist Legal Debates* (Melbourne: Oxford University Press, 1995) 18
  'In Praise of Legal Feminism' (2002) 22 *Legal Stud.* 71

Nathan, A. J., 'Universalism: A Particularistic Account', in L. S. Bell, A. J. Nathan and I. Peleg (eds.), *Negotiating Culture and Human Rights* (New York: Columbia University Press, 2001) 249

Nicholson, L., 'Gender', in A. M. Jaggar and I. M. Young (eds.), *A Companion to Feminist Philosophy* (London: Blackwell Publishers, 1998) 289

Niemi, H. and M. Scheinin, 'Reform of the United Nations Human Rights Treaty Body System Seen from the Developing Country Perspective' (Institute for Human Rights, Abo Akademi University, June 2002), available at www.abo.fi/instut/imr/norfa/heli-martin.pdf

Nowak, M., *U.N. Covenant on Civil and Political Rights: CCPR Commentary* (Kehl: Engel, 1993)

The Right to Life, Survival and Development (The Hague: Martinus Nijhoff Publishers, 2005)

U.N. Covenant on Civil and Political Rights: CCPR Commentary (2nd edn, Kehl: Engel, 2005)

'The Need for a World Court of Human Rights' (2007) 7 *Hum. Rts. L. Rev.* 251

Nowak, M. and E. McArthur, *The United Nations Convention against Torture: A Commentary* (Oxford University Press, 2008)

Nussbaum, M., 'Capabilities and Human Rights' (1997) 66 *Fordham L. Rev.* 273

Sex and Social Justice (Oxford University Press, 1999)

Women and Human Development: The Capabilities Approach (Cambridge University Press, 2000)

O'Connell, R., 'The Role of Dignity in Equality Law: Lessons from Canada and South Africa' (2008) 6 *Int'l J. Const. L.* 267

O'Flaherty, M., *Human Rights and the UN Practice before the Treaty Bodies* (2nd edn, The Hague: Martinus Nijhoff Publishers, 2002)

O'Flaherty, M. and C. O'Brien, 'Reform of the UN Human Rights Treaty Monitoring Bodies: A Critique of the Concept Paper on the High Commissioner's Proposal for a Unified Standing Treaty Body' (2007) 7 *Hum. Rts. L. Rev.* 141

O'Hare, U. A., 'Realizing Human Rights for Women' (1999) 21 *HRQ* 364

Obokata, T., *Trafficking of Human Beings from a Human Rights Perspective: Towards a Holistic Approach* (Leiden: Martinus Nijhoff Publishers, 2006)

Odinkalu, C. A., 'Africa's Regional Human Rights System: Recent Developments and Jurisprudence' (2002) 2 *Hum. Rts L. Rev*, 99

Oloka-Onyango, J. and S. Tamale, '"The Personal is Political," or Why Women's Rights Are Indeed Human Rights: An African Perspective on "International Feminism"' (1995) 17 *HRQ* 691

Olsen, F. E., 'The Family and the Market: A Study of Ideology and Legal Reform' (1983) 96 *Harv. L. Rev.* 1497

Oosterveld, V., 'The Definition of "Gender" in the Rome Statute of the International Criminal Court: A Step Forward or Back for International Criminal Justice?' (2005) 18 *Harv. Hum. Rts J.* 55

Orford, A., 'Contesting Globalization: A Feminist Perspective on the Future of Human Rights', in B. H. Weston and S. P. Marks (eds.), *The Future of International Human Rights* (Ardsley, NY: Transnational Publishers, 1999) 157

Osirim, M. J., 'Crisis in the State and the Family: Violence against Women in Zimbabwe' (2003) 7 *Afr. Studies Qtly* (no page no.).

Ott, D. H., *Public International Law in the Modern World* (London: Pitman Publishing, 1987)

Otto, D., 'Violence against Women: Something Other than a Human Rights Violation?' (1993) 1 *Aust. Fem. L. J.* 159

'A Post-Beijing Reflection on the Limitations and Potential of Human Rights Discourse for Women', in K. D. Askin and D. M. Koenig (eds.), *Women and International Human Rights Law* (Ardsley, NY: Transnational Publishers, 2000), Vol. 1, 115

'Disconcerting "Masculinities": Reinventing the Gendered Subject(s) of International Human Rights Law', in D. Buss and A. Manji (eds.), *International Law: Modern Feminist Approaches* (Oxford: Hart Publishing, 2005) 105

'Lost in Translation: Re-Scripting the Sexed Subjects of International Human Rights Law', in A. Orford (ed.), *International Law and Its Others* (Cambridge University Press, 2006) 318

'The Exile of Inclusion: Reflections on Gender Issues in International Law Over the Last Decade' (2009) 10 *Melb. J. Int'l L.* 11

Ovey, C. and R. White, *Jacobs and White: The European Convention on Human Rights* (4th edn, Oxford University Press, 2006)

Parker, P., *The State of the UN Human Rights Treaty Body System 2007: An NGO Perspective* (Minnesota Advocates for Human Rights, 20 June 2007)

Pearce, H., 'An Examination of the International Understanding of Political Rape and the Significance of Labeling it Torture' (2002) 14 *Int'l J. Ref. L.* 534

Pearson, Z. and S. Kuovo, 'Between Resistance and Compliance? Feminist Perspectives on International Law in an Era of Anxiety and Terror', in Z. Pearson and S. Kuovo (eds.) *Between Resistance and Compliance? Feminist Perspectives on International Law in an Era of Anxiety and Terror,* (Oxford: Hart Publishing, in press, 2010) (on file with the author)

Phillips, A., *Engendering Democracy* (London: Polity Press, 1991, 1993, and 1997)

'Democracy and Representation: Or, Why Should it Matter Who Our Elected Representatives Are?', in A. Phillips (ed.), *Feminism and Politics: Oxford Readings in Feminism* (Oxford University Press, 1998) 224

Phillips, A., (ed.), *Feminism and Politics: Oxford Readings in Feminism* (Oxford University Press, 1998)

Piotrowicz, R., 'The Legal Nature of Trafficking in Human Beings' (2009) 4 *Intercultural Hum. Rts L. Rev.*, 175

Plan International, *Because I am a Girl: The State of the World's Girls* (2007)

Plomer, A., 'A Foetal Right to Life? The Case of *Vo v. France*' (2005) 5 *Hum. Rts. L. Rev.* 311

Pocar, F., 'Legal Value of the Human Rights Committee's Views' (1991–1992) *Canadian Hum. Rts. YB* 119

Quénivet, N. N. R., *Sexual Offenses in Armed Conflict and International Law* (Ardsley, NY: Transnational Publishers, 2005)

Raday, F., 'Culture, Religion, and CEDAW's Article 5(a)', in H. B. Schöpp-Schilling and C. Flinterman (eds.), *Circle of Empowerment: Twenty-Five Years of the UN Committee on the Elimination of Discrimination against Women* (New York: Feminist Press, 2007) 68

Rae, D., *Equalities* (Cambridge, MA: Harvard University Press, 1981)

Ramcharan, B. G., 'Equality and Nondiscrimination', in L. Henkin (ed.), *The International Bill of Rights: The Covenant on Civil and Political Rights* (New York: Columbia University Press, 1981) 246

'The Concept and Dimensions of the Right to Life', in B. G. Ramcharan (ed.), *The Right to Life in International Law* (Dordrecht: Martinus Nijhoff Publishers, 1985) 1

'The Drafting History of Article 6 of the International Covenant on Civil and Political Rights', in B. G. Ramcharan (ed.), *The Right to Life in International Law* (Dordrecht: Martinus Nijhoff Publishers, 1985) 42

Ramcharan, B. G., (ed.), *The Right to Life in International Law* (Dordrecht: Martinus Nijhoff Publishers, 1985)

Reanda, L., 'Human Rights and Women's Rights: The United Nations Approach' (1981) 3 *HRQ* 11

'The Commission on the Status of Women', in P. Alston (ed.), *The United Nations and Human Rights: A Critical Appraisal* (Oxford University Press, 1992) 274

Rehof, L. A., *Guide to the* Travaux Préparatoires *of the United Nations Convention on the Elimination of All Forms of Discrimination against Women* (Dordrecht: Martinus Nijhoff Publishers, 1993)

'Article 3', in G. Alfredsson and A. Eide (eds.), *The Universal Declaration of Human Rights: A Common Standard of Achievement* (The Hague: Martinus Nijhoff Publishers, 1999) 97

Ritz, K. L., 'Soft Enforcement: Inadequacies of the Optional Protocol as a Remedy for the Convention on the Elimination of All Forms of Discrimination against Women' (2001–2002) 25 *Suffolk Transnat. L. Rev.* 191

Robertson, G., Q.C., *Crimes against Humanity: The Struggle for Global Justice* (2nd edn, London: Penguin Books, 2002)

Rodley, N. S., *The Treatment of Prisoners Under International Law* (2nd edn, Oxford: Clarendon Press, 1999)

Rodley, N., 'United Nations Human Rights Treaty Bodies and Special Procedures of the Commission on Human Rights – Complementarity or Competition?' (2003) 25 *HRQ* 882

Romany, C., 'Women as Aliens: A Feminist Critique of the Public/Private Distinction in International Human Rights Law' (1993) 6 *Harv. Hum. Rts. J.* 87

'State Responsibility Goes Private: A Feminist Critique of the Public/Private Distinction in International Human Rights Law', in R. J. Cook (ed.), *Human Rights of Women: National and International Perspectives* (Philadelphia: University Pennsylvania Press, 1994) 85

Roth, K., 'Domestic Violence as an International Human Rights Issue', in R. J. Cook (ed.), *Human Rights of Women: National and International Perspectives* (Philadelphia: University of Pennsylvania Press, 1994) 326

Rubenstein, K. K., 'From Suffrage to Citizenship: A Republic of Equality', 2008 Dymphna Clark Lecture, Canberra, March 2008

Rubio-Marín, R., (ed.), *What Happened to the Women? Gender and Reparations for Human Rights Violations* (New York: Social Science Research Council, 2006)

Russell, D. and N. Van de Ven (eds.), *Crimes against Women: Proceedings of the International Tribunal* (East Palo Alto, CA: Frog in the Well, 1984)

Saris A., and K. Lofts, 'Reparation Programmes: A Gendered Perspective', in C. Ferstman, M. Goetz and A. Stephens (eds.), *Reparations for Victims of Genocide, War Crimes and Crimes against Humanity: Systems in Place and Systems in the Making* (The Hague: Martinus Nijhoff Press, 2009) 79

Scales, A. C., 'The Emergence of Feminist Jurisprudence: An Essay' (1986) 95 *Yale L. J.* 1373

Schabas W., *The Abolition of the Death Penalty in International Law* (3rd edn, Cambridge University Press, 2002)

Schneider, E. M., *Battered Women and Feminist Lawmaking* (New Haven, CT: Yale University Press, 2000)

Schöpp-Schilling, H. B., 'Treaty Body Reform: the Case of the Committee on the Elimination of Discrimination Against Women' (2007) 7 *Hum. Rts. L. Rev.* 201

Sen, A., 'More than 100 Million Women are Missing', *New York Review of Books,* 20 December 1990

'Freedom and Needs' (1994) 10 and 17 *New Republic* 31

Identity & Violence: The Illusion of Destiny (London: Penguin Books, 2006)

Sherry, S., 'Civil Virtue and the Feminine Voice of Constitutional Adjudication' (1986) 72 *Vanderbilt L. Rev.* 543

'The Gender of Judges' (1986) 4 *Law & Inequality* 159

Sivakumaran, S., 'Sexual Violence against Men in Armed Conflict' (2007) 18 *Eur. J. Int'l L.* 253

Small Bilyeu, A., 'Trokosi – The Practice of Sexual Slavery in Ghana: Religious and Cultural Freedom vs. Human Rights' (1999) 9 *Ind. Int'l & Comp. L. Rev.* 457

Smart, C., *Feminism and the Power of Law* (London: Routledge, 1989)

Solinger, R., *Pregnancy and Power: A Short History of Reproductive Politics in America* (New York University Press, 2005)

Spelman, E., *Inessential Women: Problems of Exclusion in Feminist Thought* (London: The Women's Press, 1988)

Spender, D., *Man Made Language* (2nd edn, London: Pandora, 2001)

Spivak, G. C., 'Subaltern Studies: Deconstructing Historiography', in R. Guha and G. C. Spivak (eds.), *Selected Subaltern Studies* (New York: Oxford University Press, 1988) 20

Stark, B., 'The International Covenant on Economic, Social and Cultural Rights as a Resource for Women', in K. D. Askin and D. M. Koenig (eds.), *Women and International Human Rights Law* (Ardsley, NY: Transnational Publishers, 2000), Vol. 2, 209

Steiner, H. J. and P. Alston, *International Human Rights in Context: Law, Politics, Morals* (2nd edn, Oxford University Press, 2000)

Steiner, H. J., P. Alston and R. Goodman, *International Human Rights in Context: Law, Politics, Morals* (3rd edn, Oxford University Press, 2007)

Sullivan, D., 'The Public/Private Distinction in International Human Rights Law', in J. Peters and A. Wolper (eds.), *Women's Rights, Human Rights: International Feminist Perspectives* (New York: Routledge, 1995) 126

Tamale, S., *When Hens Begin to Crow: Gender and Parliamentary Politics in Uganda* (Kampala: Fountain Publishers, 1999)

'African Feminism: How Should We Change?' (2006) 49 *Dev't* 38

Thakur, R. (ed.), *What is Equitable Geographic Representation in the Twenty-First Century* (Tokyo: United Nations University, 1999)

Thomas, D. Q. and M. E. Beasley, 'Symposium on Reconceptualizing Violence against Women by Intimate Partners: Critical Issues: Domestic Violence as a Human Rights Issue' (1995) 58 *Alb. L. Rev.* 1119

Thornton, M., 'The Cartography of Public and Private', in M. Thornton (ed.), *Public and Private: Feminist Legal Debates* (Melbourne: Oxford University Press, 1995) 2

'"Otherness" on the Bench: How Merit is Gendered' (2007) 29 *Sydney L. Rev.* 391

Thornton, M. (ed.), *Public and Private: Feminist Legal Debates* (Melbourne: Oxford University Press, 1995)

Tistounet, E., 'The Problem of Overlapping among Different Treaty Bodies', in P. Alston and J. Crawford (eds.), *The Future of UN Human Rights Treaty Monitoring* (Cambridge University Press, 2000) 383

Toebes, B., 'Sex Selection under International Human Rights Law' (2008) 9 *Medical L. Int'l* 1

Tomuschat, C., 'Evolving Procedural Rules: The United Nations Human Rights Committee's First Two Years Dealing with Individual Communications' (1980) 1 *Hum. Rts. L. J.* 249

Ulrich, J., 'Confronting Gender-Based Violence with International Instruments: Is a Solution to the Pandemic Within Reach?' (1999–2000) 7 *Ind. J. Global Legal Stud.* 629

UNICEF, *The State of the World's Children: Women and Children – The Double Dividend of Gender and Equality* (2007)

Vandenhole, W., *The Procedures Before the UN Human Rights Treaty Bodies: Divergence or Convergence?* (Antwerp: Intersentia, 2004)

  Non-Discrmination and Equality in the View of the UN Human Rights Treaty Bodies (Antwerp: Intersentia, 2005)

Vasak, K., *The International Dimensions of Human Rights* (Paris: UNESCO Press, 1982)

  'Pour une Troisième Génération des Droits de l'Homme', in C. Swinarski (ed.), *Etudes et Essais sur le Droit International Humanitaire et sur les Principes de la Croix-Rouge* (The Hague: Martinus Nijhoff, 1984) 837

Villmoare, A. H., 'Women, Differences, and Rights as Practices: An Interpretative Essay and a Proposal' (2003) 25 *Law & Soc'y Rev.* 385

West, R., 'Jurisprudence and Gender' (1988) 55 *U. Chi. Law Rev.* 1

  'Feminism, Critical Social Theory and Law' (1989) *U. Chi. Legal F.* 59

Weston, P., 'The Empty Idea of Equality' (1982) 95 *Harv. L. Rev.* 537

Wilets, J. D., 'Conceptualizing Violence: Present and Future Developments in International Law: Panel III: Sex and Sexuality: Violence and Culture in the New International Order: Conceptualizing Private Violence against Sexual Minorities as Gendered Violence: An International and Comparative Law Perspective' (1997) 60 *Alb. L. Rev.* 989

Williams, P. J., 'Alchemical Notes: Reconstructing Ideals from Deconstructed Rights' (1987) 22 *Harv. C.R-C.L. Rev.* 401

  The Alchemy of Race and Rights (Cambridge, MA: Harvard University Press, 1991)

Wishik, H., 'To Question Everything: The Inquiries of Feminist Jurisprudence' (1985) 1 *Berkeley Women's L. J.* 64

Women's Initiatives for Gender Justice, *Gender Report Card 2005*, available at: www.iccwomen.org/news/2005_11_29.php

Wood, A. N., 'A Cultural Rite of Passage or a Form of Torture: Female Genital Mutilation from an International Law Perspective' (2001) 12 *Hastings Women's L. J.* 347

Yokota, Y., 'Reflections on the Future of Economic, Social and Cultural Rights', in B. H. Weston and S. P. Marks (eds.), *The Future of International Human Rights* (Ardsley, NY: Transnational Publishers, 1999) 201

Young, I. M., *Justice and the Politics of Difference* (Princeton University Press, 1990)

Zalewski, M., 'Well, What is the Feminist Perspective on Bosnia?' (1995) 71 *Int'l Aff.* 339

INDEX

A.S. v. *Sweden*, 223–224
A.T. v. *Hungary*, 190 , 243–244
Abdulaziz, Cabales and Balkandali v.
 United Kingdom, 232–233
abortions, 285–290, 291–292, 296–300,
 310
absence of women, 43–51, 307–309
abstract justice, 61–64
ACHPR *see* African Charter on
 Human and Peoples' Rights
ACHR *see* American Convention on
 Human Rights
acquiescence requirements, 245–252,
 259–261
activism in feminist theory, 43–38
add women and stir approaches, 64, 231
admissibility state party report
 criteria, 120–121, 127–129
advantage/disadvantage models,
 144–145
Africa, 24–25
 feminist theory, 75
 formal/substantive equality,
 156–157
 the right to life, 288–289
 see also Nairobi Forward-looking
 Strategies; Rwanda; South
 African cases
African Charter on Human and
 Peoples' Rights (ACHPR), 288–289
alternative reform models, 332–333
alternative state party reports, 113–114
American Convention on Human
 Rights (ACHR), 220–221, 274, 289
Americas, 289–290
Amnesty International, 128–129
anti-essentialism, 81–82

apartheid cases, 156–157
arbitrary discrimination, 170 ,
 271–277
Aristotelian models, 142–145, 156–157
armed conflict, 23–24
Asian feminism, 298–299
asking the woman question
 methodologies, 28–30
asylum, 191–192, 231–232
Aydin v. *Turkey*, 226–227, 254–256, 336

Baby Boy case, 289–290
balanced gender representation, 96
Bartlett, K., 007028–31, 335–336
Bayefsky, A.F., 112, 126–127
bearers to the right to life, 284–290
Beijing Platform for Action, 41
Beijing World Conference, 9–10
Belgian Linguistics case, 162
benefits of the right to life, 291–296
Bevacqua and S. v. *Bulgaria*, 295
Binion, G., 67–68
blindness to torture, 221–226
Bogecho, D., 281
breaches of the right to life, 290–300
Bulgaria, 241
Bunch, C., 67, 70, 318
Burrows, N., 54–55
Byrnes, A., 55, 102, 123, 213

C.T. and K.M. v. *Sweden*, 224–225
Canadian Supreme Court (SCC), 175
Castro-Castro Prison case, 220–221
CAT *see* Committee against Torture
CEDAW *see* Convention on the
 Elimination of All Forms of
 Discrimination against Women

CERD *see* Committee on the Elimination of Racial Discrimination
CESCR *see* Committee on Economic, Social and Cultural Rights
Charlesworth, H., 28, 30, 45, 56–58, 60, 64, 69–70, 79, 83–84, 97, 146, 159–160
Cherry, A., 298–299
Children's Committee *see* Convention on the Rights of a Child
Chinkin, C., 45, 56–57, 59–60, 64, 69–70, 97, 125–126
CHR *see* Commission on Human Rights
Ciudad Juárez area of Chihuahua, Mexico, 188, 256, 282
civil rights, 59–61
Clapham, A., 95–96
collective female identity, 71–86
Commission on Human Rights (CHR), 39
Commission on the Status of Women (CSW), 39, 154
Committee against Torture (CAT), 89
    individual communications, 124
    inquiry procedures, 134
    public/private dichotomy, 248–249
    treaty expertise/memberships, 93, 99
    see also torture
Committee on Economic, Social and Cultural Rights (CESCR), 10–11, 89, 275–276
    equality/non-discrimination, 158–159, 164, 172, 178 , 181–182, 184–186, 190–191
    expertise/memberships, 103–104
    feminist theories, 81
    gender/sex terminology, 14–15
    General Comments & General Recommendations, 116
    the right to life, 285–286, 299–300
Committee on Enforced Disappearances, 90
Committee on the Elimination of Discrimination against Women *see* Women's Committee

Committee on the Elimination of Racial Discrimination (CERD), 10–11, 89
    equality/non-discrimination, 158–161, 172–173, 178 , 183
    structural reforms, 328
Committee on the Rights of Migrant Workers (MWC), 90
Committee on the Rights of Persons with Disabilities (CRPD), 90
common core documentation, 114
commutations of death sentences, 265
comparators, 156–164
competing rights, 55–56
confidential inquiries *see* inquiry procedures
consent requirements, 245–252, 259, 260–261
contextual analyses, 312–313, 335–338
continuing violations, 133–134
Convention on the Elimination of All Forms of Discrimination against Women (CEDAW), 8, 39, 89
    equality/non-discrimination, 143, 153–154, 157–158, 167, 168–169, 181
    feminism, 48–51, 55, 80, 82
    individual communications, 124–125
    inquiry procedures, 134
    inter-state communications, 117–118
    structural reforms, 330
    the right to life, 281, 297
    torture, 205, 243–244, 256
Convention on the Rights of Persons with Disabilities (ICRPD), 90, 151–152, 268
    equality/non-discrimination, 154–155
    inquiry procedures, 134
    torture, 203–205
Convention on the Rights of the Child (CRC), 89, 151–152, 267–268, 276
    expertise/memberships, 103–104
    General Comments & General Recommendations, 116
    the right to life, 297, 299
    torture, 203–205

Cook, R., 132
Coomaraswamy, R., 73, 127, 316
Copelon, R., 30, 66, 210–211
Corbin, A., 72
Cornell, D., 176
Crawford, J., 95–96, 112
CRC see Convention on the Rights of the Child
CRPD see Committee on the Rights of Persons with Disabilities
cruel behaviour, 198–262
CSW see Commission on the Status of Women
culture-based violence, 22, 281–283
  cultural relativity, 58
  equality/non-discrimination, 168–172
  feminist theory, 59–61, 76, 80–84
custom-based violence, 168–172, 181
Cyprus v. Turkey, 256

Danube Dam case, 275
Darwinia R. Mónaco (Ximena Vicario) v. Argentina, 254
date rape, 265–266
death penalty, 265
decision-making processes
  expertise/memberships, 108–99
  feminist theory, 43–48
  reforms, 335–337
  treaty practice/procedure, 122–123
Declaration on the Elimination of Violence against Women (DEVAW), 9, 20–22, 25, 319, 339
deconstruction feminist theory stages, 40
defining 'women's human rights', 53–57
degrading punishment/treatment, 198–262
delegates, 47–48
democracy, 107
DEVAW see Declaration on the Elimination of Violence against Women
Dianne Ortíz v. Guatemala, 226–227

dignity, 147–148
Dinstein, Y., 272–273, 276–277
direct discrimination, 161–162
discrimination see non-discrimination
domestic violence
  equality/non-discrimination, 189–190
  feminist theory, 69
  the right to life, 300
  torture, 246–247, 250, 265–266
double standards in feminism, 57–58
Draft Harmonized Guidelines, 114
due diligence
  equality/non-discrimination, 166–167, 195
  expertise/memberships, 105–106
  feminist narratives, 314–315
  torture, 237–241, 243–245, 249–252, 260–261, 265–266
  treaty reforms, 342
Dzemajl et al. v. Yugoslavia, 248

ECHR see European Convention on the Protection of Human Rights and Fundamental Freedoms
ECJ see European Court of Justice
Economic and Social Council (ECOSOC), 179, 338–339
economic-based violence, 21, 24–25, 281–283
  feminist theory, 59–61
  the right to life, 297–300
ECOSOC (Economic and Social Council), 179, 338–339
ECtHR see European Court of Human Rights
Egan v. Canada, 174
Eisler, R., 68
election procedures, 322–325
  see also memberships to treaty bodies
Elmi v. Australia, 247
Engle, K., 68–69, 70, 75–76, 213
equality, 140–197
  expertise/memberships, 100–101
  feminist critiques/general concepts, 141–148
  feminist narratives, 304–320

equality (*cont.*)
  power, 21
  torture, 258–259
equitable geographical distribution,
  94
essentialised women, 71–86, 316–318
Etienne, M., 143
Europe, 287–288
European Convention on the
  Protection of Human Rights and
  Fundamental Freedoms
  (ECHR), 270, 275, 287–288,
  293–295
European Court of Human Rights
  (ECtHR), 220–221, 227, 232–233,
  235–236, 241, 254–256, 265–266
  procedural reforms, 323
  the right to life, 287–288, 293–295,
  300
European Court of Justice (ECJ),
  163
expanded core documentation, 114
expertise of treaty bodies, 92–108

fact-finding procedures, 134–136
family-based violence, 20, 22, 67–68,
  73
Fawcett, J., 270
female infanticide, 292–293
  see also sex-selective abortion
feminism, 2–3, 27–32, 36–87
  critiques, 43–86
  equality/non-discrimination,
    141–148
  narratives, 304–320
  practical reasoning, 31, 335–336
  principle stages, 43–38
  sex discrimination, 179–195
  the right to life, 278–284
  torture, 209–216, 257–261
forced sterilisation, 229–230
formal equality, 142–145, 156–164
  expertise/memberships,
    100
  feminist theory, 39, 58–59
Franke, K., 212
Fullinwider, R., 145–146
full-time treaty members, 329

G.R.B. v. *Sweden*, 245–246
Gallagher, A., 54
Gedumbe v. *Democratic Republic of
  Congo*, 221–222
gender mainstreaming, 3–4, 6, 42
  feminist theory, 64
  General Comments & General
    Recommendations, 116
  terminology/terms, 26–27
  torture, 231, 254–256
  treaty reforms, 335–336
gender-based rotating nomination
  processes, 100–101
gender-based violence
  blindness to torture, 221–226
  equality/non-discrimination,
    180–183, 193
  expertise/memberships, 99
  feminism, 47–48
  prohibition, 209–210
  terminology/terms, 13–19
  torture, 254–256
gendered fault-line, 65
general community-based violence,
  20–21, 22
genocide
  feminist theories, 77
  the right to life, 265–266, 292–293
  torture, 212–213
Gilligan, C., 62–63
Goekce v. *Austria*, 167, 190
Goldscheid, J., 189 , 191
González et al. ('Cotton Field') v.
  Mexico, 220–221, 243
Grant v. *Southwest Trains*, 163
grave multiple violations, 135
Greatbatch, J., 69
Griffith, J.A.G., 102
Gross, E., 58–59
Gunning, I., 31–32, 312–313, 335–336

H.M.H.I. v. *Australia*, 247–248
Hampson, F.J., 328–329
Hartsock, N., 81–82
Hernández-Truyol, B., 74
Heyman, M., 69
Higgins, T., 78
Hillock, R., 73

HIV/AIDS, 282–283
honour crimes, 292
House of Lords, 191–192
HRC *see* Human Rights Committee
human dignity, 147–148
Human Rights Committee (HRC),
    10–11, 50, 89, 272–273
  equality/non-discrimination,
    157–160, 166 , 169–171, 172
    184–186
  feminist theories, 81
  General Comments & General
    Recommendations, 116
  individual communications, 124,
    125, 130, 133–134
  the right to life, 270–272, 273, 275,
    285–287, 291–293, 300
  torture, 205–209, 216–217, 222–223,
    227–232, 235, 239–241, 252, 254,
    258–259
  treaty expertise/memberships, 93, 99
human trafficking *see* trafficking
humanising women, 342–343
Hungary, 243–244

I-ACmHR *see* Inter-American
    Commission of Human Rights
I-ACtHR *see* Inter-American Court of
    Human Rights
IA-VAW *see* Inter-American
    Convention on the Prevention,
    Punishment and Eradication of
    Violence against Women
ICC *see* International Criminal Court
ICCPR *see* International Covenant on
    Civil and Political Rights
ICED *see* International Convention for
    the Protection of All Persons from
    Enforced Disappearances
ICERD *see* International Convention
    on the Elimination of All Forms
    of Racial Discrimination
ICESCR *see* International Covenant
    on Economic, Social and Cultural
    Rights
ICJ *see* International Court of Justice
ICRPD *see* Convention on the Rights
    of Persons with Disabilities

ICTR *see* Prosecutor and the
    International Criminal Tribunal
    for Rwanda
ICTY *see* International Criminal
    Tribunal for the former Yugoslavia
IMWC *see* International Convention
    on the Protection of the Rights
    of All Migrant Workers and
    Members of their Families
inadequate gender expertise, 47–48
indigenous peoples' right to life,
    268–269
indirect discrimination, 161–162, 195,
    228
individual communications, 118–134,
    312–313, 325–326
individual petition systems, 130–132
individualism, 61–64
inequality *see* equality
infanticide, 292–293
informal divisions of labour, 103–104
inhuman behaviour, 198–262
inquiry procedures, 134–136
integrationist theory, 42–43
Inter-American Commission of
    Human Rights (I-ACmHR),
    219–221, 273–274, 289–290
Inter-American Convention on the
    Prevention, Punishment and
    Eradication of Violence against
    Women (IA-VAW), 11–12, 22–23
Inter-American Court of Human
    Rights (I-ACtHR)
  equality/non-discrimination, 164
  the right to life, 273–274
  torture, 220–221, 226–227, 237–238
International Conference on
    Population and Development, 9
International Convention for the
    Protection of All Persons from
    Enforced Disappearances (ICED),
    90
International Convention on the
    Elimination of All Forms of
    Racial Discrimination (ICERD),
    22, 89, 151–152
  equality/non-discrimination,
    153–154, 157–158, 183, 195

International Convention on the
    Elimination of All Forms of Racial
    Discrimination (ICERD) (cont.)
  inquiry procedures, 134
  inter-state communications, 117
  torture, 205
  treaty expertise/membership, 93
International Convention on the
    Protection of the Rights of All
    Migrant Workers and Members
    of their Families (IMWC), 90,
    151–152, 205
  inquiry procedures, 134
  treaty expertise/membership, 93
International Court of Justice (ICJ),
    156–157, 275
International Covenant on Civil and
    Political Rights (ICCPR), 50
  equality/non-discrimination, 150–
    151, 152–153, 157–158, 166, 183
  individual communications, 124,
    125
  the right to life, 264–266, 267–290,
    297–298, 300
  torture, 199, 206–207, 208–209,
    221–222, 227–228, 230–231, 235,
    237–238, 258–259, 260
  treaty expertise/membership, 93
International Covenant on Economic,
    Social and Cultural Rights
    (ICESCR), 89, 150–151
  equality/non-discrimination,
    152–153
  feminist theories, 81, 314–315
  individual communications,
    124–125
  inquiry procedures, 134
  the right to life, 267, 295–296
  torture, 205
International Criminal Court (ICC),
    260–261, 334–335
International Criminal Tribunal for
    Rwanda (ICTR), 104–105
International Criminal Tribunal for
    the former Yugoslavia (ICTY),
    191, 219–220, 236, 260–261
interpretative dialogue, 311–312
interpretative inclusion, 337–339

intersectionality of gender/sex, 84–85,
    172–174, 336–337
inter-state communications, 117–118

Johnstone, R., 57–58, 69
judges, 102–103
judicialisation-based reform models,
    333–335
jurisprudence, 2–3, 269–278
  equality/non-discrimination,
    144–145, 175–178
  feminist theories, 28–32
  procedural reforms, 326
  the right to life, 289–290, 293
  torture, 205–209
jus cogens, 56–57, 199, 265

Kalajdzic, J., 77
Kapur, R., 75
Karen Llontoy v. Peru, 286–287
Kaufman, N.H., 46
Kindler v. Canada, 252
Kisoki v. Sweden, 223
K. L. v. Peru, 286–287
Knop, K., 107
Kontrova v. Slovakia, 293–294, 303
Kunarac, Kovač and Vuković case, 191

La Forgia, R., 245–246
lack of central government criteria,
    247–249, 259–260
Lambert, C., 223
language
  equality/non-discrimination,
    147–148, 193–194
  feminism, 61–64, 311–312, 315
  gender mainstreaming, 26
  torture, 214, 234–235, 258–259
  treaty reforms, 337–339
law-based life rights protection,
    270–271
lawyers, 102–103
liberal equality see formal equality
Liberation Tigers of Tamil Eelam
    (LTTE), 246–247
Lindquist, S., 46
Littleton, C., 27–28
Loayza Tamayo v. Peru, 226–227

Lorber, J., 16
Lovelace v. Canada, 169–170
LTTE see Liberation Tigers of Tamil
    Eelam

M.C. v. Bulgaria, 241
MacKinnon, C., 46, 53, 63, 67, 77–79,
    82, 146–148, 184, 196, 211–212,
    311–312
Mahoney, K., 53, 144–145, 196
mainstream debates
    equality/non-discrimination,
        181–182
    feminist theory, 48–51
    structural reforms, 329–331
    see also gender mainstreaming
male feminists, 46–47
male victims, 210
mandates, 88–92
Manfred, N., 270–271
marginalisation debate, 48–53
masculine language dominance, 61–64
    see also language
McColgan, A., 142–143
McCorquodale, R., 245–246
McGlynn, C., 213–214, 235–237
memberships to treaty bodies,
    92–108
men's rights, 51–64, 309–314
Menghistu, F., 273, 283
merit selection criteria, 103
Merry, Sally Engle, 83–84
Minority Schools in Albania, 156
miscarriages, 300
Mohanty, C., 77
Mullally, S., 51
multiple discrimination, 84–85, 135,
    172–174
Muñoz-Vargas y Sainz de Vicuña v.
    Spain, 170–171
Munro, V., 46–47, 77, 81–82
mutah marriages, 223–224
MWC see Committee on the Rights of
    Migrant Workers

Naffine, N., 72–73
Nairobi Forward-looking Strategies,
    8, 179

NGOs see non-governmental
    organisations
nobility, 170–171
nomination procedures, 322–325
    see also memberships to treaty
        bodies
non-binding views, 121, 155–156
non-consensual medical/scientific
    experimentation, 229–230
non-discrimination, 140–197
    feminism, 141–148, 310, 316–317
    the right to life, 299
    torture, 230–235, 258–259
non-expert treaty members, 329
non-governmental organisations
    (NGOs), 11
    expertise/memberships, 104
    state party reports, 110, 113–114
    structural reforms, 331
non-refoulement obligations, 223–224
non-state violence, 237–252, 259–260
    see also private/public dichotomy
Nowak, M., 284, 332–333
Nussbaum, M., 69

O' Connor, J.S.D., 107–108
O'Hare, U., 65
objectivity
    equality/non-discrimination, 176,
        190–191
    feminism, 46, 312
    treaty reforms, 335–337
Office of the High Commissioner for
    Human Rights (OHCHR), 94
    General Comments & General
        Recommendations, 116
    individual communications,
        119–121
    inquiry procedures, 135–136
    procedural reforms, 323
    state party reports, 109–111
    structural reforms, 327–328,
        330–331
old myth-based discrimination, 106
Open Door and Dublin Well Women v.
    Ireland, 288
Optional Protocol CEDAW
    (OP-CEDAW), 48–49

Optional Protocol CEDAW
(OP-CEDAW) (*cont.*)
individual communications,
124–125, 130
inquiry procedures, 134–135
inter-state communications,
117–118
Optional Protocol to the Convention
against Torture (OP-CAT), 90–91,
134, 203–205
Optional Protocol-ICESCR
(OP-ICESCR), 134
Opuz v. *Turkey*, 242, 294–295, 303
Orford, A., 59
Ortiz v. *Guatemala*, see *Dianne Ortiz* v.
Guatemala
Otto, D., 17–18, 21, 71–72

pardons of death sentences, 265
part-time treaty members, 329
patriarchy, 15, 51–53
PCIJ *see* Permanent Court of
International Justice
Pearce, H., 212
periodic state party reports, 108–115
Permanent Court of International
Justice (PCIJ), 156, 178
perpetrators
right to liberty, 167–168
torture, 210
petition systems, 130–132
Pillay, J., 104–105
politics
expertise/memberships, 99
feminism, 59–61, 317–318
population control policies, 297–300
practice and procedure of rights treaty
system, 88–98
preferential hiring, 145–146
pregnant women, 279–281, 300
see also abortions
pre-implantive sex determination
see sex-selective abortion
pre-natal sex selection *see* sex-selective
abortion
private/public dichotomy
equality/non-discrimination,
166–168 , 195

feminist narratives, 314–315,
317–318
structural reforms, 332–333
torture, 237–252, 259–260
treaty reforms, 339–341
see also public/private dichotomy
privileging patriarchy, 51–53
procedural reforms, 322–326
procedure and practice of rights treaty
system, 88–98
professionalisation-based reform
models, 333–335
progressive implementation, 314–315
proliferation of treaty reforms,
333–334
proportionality criteria, 190–191
Prosecutor and the International
Criminal Tribunal for Rwanda
(ICTR), 212, 219, 260–261
Prosecutor v. *Jean-Paul Akayesu*, 219
protocol on violence against women,
342–343
Protocol to the African Charter on
Human and Peoples' Rights on
the Human Rights of Women
(PRWA), 11–12, 25
Przetacznik, F., 272–273
psychological violence, 20–22, 227–229
public/private dichotomy
equality/non-discrimination,
166–168 , 189–190
feminism, 64–71, 314–315, 317–318
rights to life, 25
structural reforms, 332–333
torture, 210–211, 237–252, 259–260
treaty reforms, 339–341
PWRA, 23–25

Quinteros v. *Uruguay*, 228

racial discrimination
equality/non-discrimination,
153–154, 160–161, 172–174
feminist theories, 57–58, 76–77
gender/sex terminology, 16–17
torture, 232–233
Raday, F., 80–81
Rae, D., 141–142

Ramcharan, B., 271, 272–273, 276–277
rape, 10–11
  equality/non-discrimination,
    187–188, 191, 196
  expertise/memberships, 104–105
  feminist theory, 40–41, 59, 75–76, 77
  terminology, 20–22
  the right to life, 285–286, 291–292
  torture, 210–214, 219–227, 235–237,
    241, 245–246, 253–258, 265–266
Raquel Martí de Mejía v. *Peru*, 219–220
reasonableness
  accommodation of difference,
    154–155
  equality/non-discrimination, 176 ,
    190–191
  feminism, 46, 312, 315
  the right to life, 293–294
  treaty reforms, 342
re-assessment feminist theory stages,
  43
reconceptualisation feminist theory
  stages, 40–43
reconstruction feminist theory stages,
  40–43
reevaluation feminist theory stages, 43
reflection feminist theory stages, 43
refugees
  procedural reforms, 323
  status acquirement, 231–232
  torture, 238–239, 260–261
regional human rights instruments,
  150–156
reinterpretation feminist theory stages,
  40–43
religion-based violence, 22, 76, 80–81,
  83–84
rights claims, 131–132
rights to life, 263–303
Ritz, K., 333
Roberto Zelaya Blanco v. *Nicaragua*,
  300
Rodley, N., 207–208
Rodriguez v. *Honduras,* see *Velasquez*
  Rodriguez v. *Honduras*
role models, 100, 107–108
Roma women, 173–174, 248
Roth, K., 66–67

Rwanda, 7, 215, 219, 224–225

S.V. et al. v. *Canada*, 246–247
sameness/difference models, 144–148,
  163, 166, 169–170, 176
Scales, A., 49, 63
SCC *see* Canadian Supreme Court
Schöpp-Schilling, 329–330
Sen, A., 61
sex discrimination
  equality/non-discrimination,
    140–179
  feminist theory, 45
  strategy assessment, 183–195
  terminology/terms, 13–19
  see also non-discrimination
sex-disaggregated statistics, 326
sex-selective abortion, 297–300
sexual enslavement, 7
sexual harassment, 184
sexual violence *see* rape
sexuality, 18–19
shadow state party reports, 113–114
Shah and Islam case, 191–192
Shanthi, D., 170–171
sidestream debates, 48–51, 329–331
sighe marriages, 223–224
Simone de Beauvoir, 18
simplification-based reform models,
  333–335
Slovakia, 229–230
Smart, C., 125–126
social rights in feminist theory, 59–61
social-based violence, 281–283,
  297–300
son preference *see* pre-natal sex
  selection
Sotomayer, S., 102–103
South West African Cases, 156–157,
  159–160
Special Rapporteurs on Violence
  against Women, 9, 11, 24–25,
  207–208, 261, 312
Spelman, E., 77
Spender, D., 61–62
Spivak, G., 82
SPT *see* Sub-Committee on the
  Prevention of Torture

standardising 'men', 53
state parties, 21, 22
    acquiescence, 245–246
    procedural reforms, 325
    treaty practice/procedure, 91–92,
        108–115
Statute of the International Criminal
    Court (ICC), 266
strategic essentialism, 82
structural equality
    equality/non-discrimination,
        168–172
    expertise/memberships, 100
    feminist theory, 51, 58–59
structural reforms, 326–335
Sub-Committee on the Prevention of
    Torture (SPT), 90–91, 96–97
subjective factors in torture, 254–256
substantive equality, 100, 143–144,
    156–164
substantive norms, 62
substantive reforms, 342–343
surfacing gender, 30
sweeping allegations, 232

Tamale, S., 79
temporary special measures, 154
The Americas, 289–290
the right to life, 263–303
    breaches of, 290–300
    concerns, 296–300
    feminism, 278–284, 310
    jurisprudence, 269–278
    rights bearers, 284
the woman question, 335–336
thin skull rule, 253–254
Third World violence, 73–75, 317
    see also Africa
Thornton, M., 65, 103
TNG see Transitional National
    Government
torture, 198–262
    contextual analyses, 252–257
    discrimination, 230–235
    emerging interpretations, 216–257
    feminism, 52–53, 67, 209–216,
        257–261, 309–310
    forced sterilisation, 229–230

    psychological forms, 227–229
    severity thresholds, 235–237
    the right to life, 291
    traditional constructs, 205–209
    Women's Committee, 256–257
tradition-based violence, 22, 168–172,
    181
trafficking, 7, 71–72, 246–247
Transitional National Government
    (TNG), 247–248
treaty bodies
    equality/non-discrimination,
        175–178
    reforms, 342–343
    the right to life, 284–287
two-stage reform models, 333–335

UDHR see Universal Declaration of
    Human Rights
UN Charter, 149–150
UN Convention against Torture
    and Other Cruel, Inhuman
    or Degrading Treatment or
    Punishment (UNCAT), 52–53, 89,
    151–152, 199–203, 206, 208–209,
    223–226, 227
    discrimination, 233
    feminism, 209–210, 259, 260–261
    psychological torture, 227–228
    public/private dichotomy, 239,
        244–245, 248–252
    torture, 207–209
    treaty expertise/membership, 93
UN Development Fund for Women
    (UNIFEM), 10
UN High Commissioner for Human
    Rights, 109
under-representation of women,
    43–47, 99–101
UNIFEM see UN Development Fund
    for Women (UNIFEM)
unified treaty body, 326–332
United Kingdom House of Lords,
    191–192
Universal Declaration of Human
    Rights (UDHR), 39, 149–150
    equality/non-discrimination,
        149–150

the right to life, 264–265
torture, 199
universality, 58, 107

V.L. v. *Switzerland*, 225, 253
Vandenhole, W., 332
Velásquez Rodríguez v. *Honduras*,
    237–239, 250
victim of a violation criteria, 129–131
Vienna Declaration on Human Rights,
    8–9
Vienna World Conference, 8, 41
Vo v. *France*, 288, 290, 300
Vos v. *The Netherlands*, 159–160
Vuolanne v. *Finland*, 252, 336

West, R., 63
Western feminism, 73–76, 298–299,
    317
Williams, P., 84, 132
Wilson v. *The Philippines*, 240–241
Women's Committee, 89
    equality/non-discrimination, 161–162,
        165, 166–171, 173–174, 178–195
    expertise/memberships, 100–101,
        103–104

feminist theory, 48–50
gender/sex terminology, 13–14
individual communications, 121,
    130, 133–134
inquiry procedures, 134–135
structural reform, 329–330
the right to life, 282–283, 293
torture, 243–244, 256–257
treaty expertise/memberships,
    96–97, 99
treaty reforms, 338–339
World Conference on Women in
    Beijing, 284
world travelling methodologies, 31–32,
    312–313, 335–336
Wright, S., 45, 56, 60, 97

Yilmaz-Dogan v. *The Netherlands*, 173
Young, I.M., 145–146, 196
youth criteria, 254–256
Yugoslavia, 7
    feminist theory, 40–41, 75–76
    the right to life, 279–281
    torture, 215, 219–220, 248

Zalewski, M., 29–30

Lightning Source UK Ltd.
Milton Keynes UK
UKOW04f1715210914

238948UK00004B/259/P